Reconstructing the Fourth Amendment

Reconstructing the Fourth Amendment

A History of Search and Seizure, 1789–1868

ANDREW E. TASLITZ

NEW YORK UNIVERSITY PRESS
New York and London

NEW YORK UNIVERSITY PRESS
New York and London
www.nyupress.org

© 2006 by New York University
All rights reserved
First published in paperback in 2009.

Library of Congress Cataloging-in-Publication Data
Taslitz, Andrew E., 1956–
Reconstructing the Fourth Amendment : a history of search and
seizure, 1789–1868 / Andrew E. Taslitz.
p. cm.
Includes bibliographical references and index.
ISBN-13: 978-0-8147-8263-7 (cloth : acid-free paper)
ISBN-10: 0-8147-8263-9 (cloth : acid-free paper)
ISBN-13: 978-0-8147-8326-9 (pbk. : acid-free paper)
ISBN-10: 0-8147-8326-0 (pbk. : acid-free paper)
1. Searches and seizures—United States—History. 2. United States.
Constitution. 4th Amendment—History. I. Title.
KF9630.T37   2006
345.73'054409034—dc22   2006010916

New York University Press books are printed on acid-free paper,
and their binding materials are chosen for strength and durability.

Manufactured in the United States of America
c 10 9 8 7 6 5 4 3 2 1
p 10 9 8 7 6 5 4 3 2 1

Contents

Preface

As a teenager and even as a preteen, I remember being appalled by the large number of black faces I saw on TV whenever there was a crime story on the news or in pulp fiction. It seemed odd to me, a white kid growing up in the Bronx, that there were so few white faces, just as a matter of sheer probabilities. I grew up in a working-class neighborhood in which many kids, white or black, were at least involved in minor crime, from drug use to graffiti to vandalism and even minor arson (torching outdoor garbage cans to see the fire trucks come). Yet I knew not a single white kid arrested for these behaviors. I am sure there must have been some, but not within my circles.

These thoughts might seem odd for a twelve- or thirteen-year-old boy, but I was a bookish kid who read widely and was always sensitive to unfairness. I was close to my dad, and he labored ten to twelve hours each day, six days a week, to feed his family, still barely making enough money to do so. It seemed to me that something was wrong with a world in which a good man who labored so hard could receive so little in return. His plight made me attentive to unfair inequalities in the world. When I found them, I tried to understand them, usually failing in that endeavor.

The need to understand never left me, and, as I aged, my quest made the world seem more, not less, complex and confusing. I promised neither to suffer my dad's fate nor to forget it. My way out was education. I studied hard, seeing the legal profession as a means for making a decent living while doing some good. I somehow never bought into the jokes about greedy lawyers or even my own granddad's pointed insistence on pronouncing the word "lawyer" like "liar." My journey paid off when I started working in my twenties at the Philadelphia, Pennsylvania, district attorney's office.

That work did not, however, bring me the clarity that I sought. On my very first day in court, I was struck, once again, with the sea of black faces. The face of almost every defendant hauled into court was black, but this was equally true for most of the victims. Offenders and accusers alike shared one primary characteristic: poverty. For all whites' fear of crime, and too many did suffer its sting, it was the African American community in that city that bore the brunt of both the problem of criminality and the criminal "justice" solution.

Later in life, I became a law professor, teaching and writing about criminal justice. In that capacity, I became involved in the innocence movement as it became clear that too many of those in our jails and prisons did not belong there. Some significant portion of those injustices stemmed from police mistakes, even perfectly well-meaning officers focusing too early on one theory of who did the crime—perhaps because of subconscious stereotyping about likely suspects—while ignoring contradicting evidence. I also heard increasingly more stories of whites suffering insults and abuse at the hands of the police, particularly during traffic stops. Meanwhile, the war on drugs was taking its toll on Hispanic communities, the war on terror on Muslim ones. The range of permissible warrantless, suspicionless searches and seizures expanded rapidly, with few political obstacles standing in the way of the crime and terror warriors.

My growing concerns did not stem from any soft-heartedness toward criminality. To the contrary, I became a prosecutor because of my sympathy for victims and my keen appreciation of the virtues of retribution. That appreciation was born of the fear of crime in the neighborhoods of my youth, my dad's having been mugged three times at gunpoint, and my own experiences of being mugged and assaulted. My zest for retribution has dimmed as time has tempered my own sense of infallibility in such matters and taught me the complexity of the human heart. But my zeal for public safety, both from street predators and governmental ones, remains strong. Yet the current system seemed to be failing on both counts, bringing neither security nor freedom.

Still worse, the current state of affairs seemed radically inconsistent with both my high school civics lessons about the nature of American democracy and my own understanding of American history. High school civics taught me that our constitutional culture was one of respect and equality for all citizens. History taught me that security and freedom were complementary, not contradictory.

My attention began to focus on the start of most criminal cases—the arrests, stops, frisks, wiretaps, and other searches and seizures that identify suspects and bring them into the criminal process. Something seemed amiss at this entry point. The Fourth Amendment to the U.S. Constitution, prohibiting "unreasonable" searches and seizures, governs that entry point. What particularly worried me was the public image of the constitutional law of search and seizure as just a way to free the guilty on a "technicality." As I recalled the history of the Fourth Amendment, it was a tale of struggle against the oppressions of the British Crown, which saw searching and seizing as a means of suppressing political dissent, weakening the opposition, and sowing discord among its members. In short, it was as much about the political rights of the "People" as of any individual suspect, and, indeed, the Fourth Amendment speaks of the "right of the People," something done in only a very few other constitutional provisions. Yet even this history seemed incomplete to me, for the original Fourth Amendment, as ratified in 1791—indeed the entire original Bill of Rights—applied only to the federal government, not to the states. It was one of the functions of the Fourteenth Amendment, ratified in 1868, to apply or "incorporate" the Bill of Rights, including the Fourth Amendment, against the states. This 1868 constitutional amendment was one of three—the Thirteenth and Fifteenth Amendments being the other two—designed to end the vestiges of slavery. The understandings of search and seizure practices during slavery and Reconstruction thus seemed particularly relevant to understanding the mutated or reconstructed Fourth Amendment of 1868. Then, as now, knowing the African American experience was central to knowing the meaning of America.

So, in a search for the complete story, I dug further into the history of both the original and the mutated Fourth Amendments. What I found did not always match my preconceptions, but it did confirm my sense that we were on the wrong path. This book looks to the past to shine light on where we once were headed in the hope that we might thereby correct our future course. The circuitous path that brought me here began with exposure to crime on the streets and, as will soon be told, it is in that same place—on the streets—that the Fourth Amendment was born and raised.

Acknowledgments

My heartfelt thanks go to Richard Delgado and Jean Stefancic for their encouragement in getting this project off the ground. Much gratitude to my editor, Deborah Gershenowitz, for her insights, suggestions, and accessibility.

I am also grateful to Robert Mosteller, Jeff Powell, George Thomas, William Cuddihy, Tracey Maclin, and Patricia V. Sun for their thoughtful comments on earlier drafts of this manuscript. My appreciation goes as well to Debbie Kim, Leah Aden, and Keri Fiore for their expert research assistance, to the Howard University School of Law for its financial support of this project, and to the entire faculty at the University of North Carolina School of Law for feedback on portions of this work at a faculty colloquium. A special thanks to Gay Lynn Kirsch, whose patience and superb secretarial skills helped this book to take shape. Endless praise to Rhea Ballard and Patricia Kidd for being law librarians who relish the search for the unusual.

To my friends Ben, Ethan, David, and Stefni Bogard; Andrew Gavil; and Nancy Schultz for being there. Most important, to the memory of my mom, Mitzi Taslitz, for always believing in me; to my dad for teaching by example; to my sister, Ellen Duncan, for teaching me persistence and hope; to my dogs, B'lanna and Odo, for comfort and inspiration; and to my wife, Patricia V. Sun, whose last name aptly captures her role in my life.

I have been pondering the ideas in this book for several years, and early versions of some of the ideas here, especially those in chapters 1, 6, and 12, were explored in portions of *Racial Auditors and the Fourth Amendment: Data with the Power to Inspire Political Action,* 66 L. & CONTEMP. PROBS. 221 (2003); *Respect and the Fourth Amendment,* 94 J. CRIM. L. & CRIMINOLOGY 15 (2003); *Stories of Fourth Amendment Disrespect: From Elian to the Internment,* 70 FORDHAM L. REV. 2257 (2002); and *Hate Crimes, Free Speech, and the Contract of Mutual Indifference,* 80 B.U. L. REV. 1283 (2000). The vast majority of this book, however, appears here for the first time in print. Thanks as well to those too numerous to name whose feedback on my earlier work helped in my efforts to make this book worthwhile.

A Stylistic Note: I hope that the text of this book will be of interest to anyone with a love of American history, specialist or not. Specialists, however, who may wish to explore a particular issue in further detail should be aware that many of the notes contain more than mere citations.

1 Plugging into the Fourth Amendment's Matrix

Entering the Matrix: State Violence as Politics

In the now-classic movie *The Matrix* the humans of the future are almost entirely enslaved by intelligent machines, which have created a "matrix," a massive, shared, interactive computer program that simultaneously runs through each human's mind. To the humans, the program in their heads *is* reality. They therefore remain complacent, divided, and blind to their condition.[1]

A small band of free humans living in the real world venture forth to do battle with the machines. Much of that battle takes place when they plug in to the matrix, searching for enslaved humans whom they can convince of the need to break their literal and mental chains. "Agents"—programs that look like the movie-stereotype of FBI law enforcement—prowl the matrix, using brutal violence on behalf of the machine "state" to locate and crush the fully sighted dissenters. The agents mean not merely to kill but to humiliate, to send the message of their invincibility and absolute rule. But the agents are afraid too, for they know that the rules that govern their world, the laws that define their society, are at stake.[2]

The agents ultimately arrest a human known as "Neo" on the pretense of suspecting him of computer crimes, but really to seek his aid in locating the renegade humans, whom they identify to Neo as "criminals." When he refuses, insisting on his rights to silence and to an attorney, the agents make Neo's lips grow together into a silencing mask. They next plant an electronic bug on him, inserting it into his abdomen, so that they can track his movements. Ultimately, however, Neo makes common cause with the renegades and discovers that he is likely "the One," the savior who will free all humanity, uniting them

1

in the consciousness that they are all indeed one. He returns to the matrix, bat-
tling the machines until he learns that he can bend their laws to his will, thus
stopping bullets, defying gravity, and even defying his death. In the two sequels that follow, Neo brings this all-pervasive violence into the real world,
crushing the machines' tyranny, replacing it with the laws of a unified mankind and human love.[3]

Perhaps only a law professor would see in *The Matrix* a metaphor for the origins and social function of the Fourth Amendment. Nevertheless, the metaphor is an apt one. The agents of the state in the matrix use violence in the
form of arrests, searches, and electronic surveillance for *political* purposes, to
silence dissent, to reinforce governing social norms, and to maintain the current distribution of power. Of course, the state's ability to use force—to govern
—is necessary to any state's existence and to the safety of its people. *The Matrix*
sequels notably reveal violence at work in the governance of the somewhat
militaristic human city of Zion—the sole haven for the few free humans. But
the humans use violence to liberate, unify, and protect. Ultimately it is the
clash of these two forms of political violence, one degrading and the other
uplifting, that are at the core of *The Matrix* films and of the everyday violence
of policing. Likewise, the Fourth Amendment is best understood as serving
to tame everyday political violence, an insight ignored by other commentators and having important implications for constitutional doctrine and police
practice.[4]

Absent a citizen's voluntary consent, all police activity involves violence or
its threat. A "search" is by definition an unwanted, thus forced, invasion of a
reasonable expectation of privacy. A "seizure" similarly is an unwanted interference with a person's freedom of movement or his possessory interest in
property. Any film or novel about the police makes the violence of their work
stark. If that violence is usually less stark in everyday policing, it is no less real.
A tremor of fear, however fleeting and mild, runs through any driver stopped
for a traffic violation, who worries that he or she may be subject to arrest or
that saying or doing the wrong thing may anger the officer. The uniform, the
holstered weapons, the command voice are all designed to make the threat of
violence clear.[5]

When that threat becomes real, it can be degrading, as both the majority
and the dissenters on the U.S. Supreme Court recently recognized in *Atwater v.
City of Lago Vista,* in which a mother unsuccessfully challenged the reasonableness of her being arrested for driving without a seatbelt, an offense punishable by a fine only. There the majority declared that "the physical incidents of
[Atwater's] arrest were merely gratuitous humiliations." The Court continued:
"Atwater's claim to live free of pointless indignity and confinement clearly out-
weighs anything the city can raise against it specific to her case."[6]

Such violence may often be legitimate, necessary to enforcing the law, to encouraging respect for it, and to catching the bad guys. But whether legitimate or not, police violence is always "political" in three related ways: first, it is committed by the state, the police's employer; second, it often affects the distribution of power resources among social groups; and third, it is essential to the coherence and survival of political society.[7]

Lockean Liberals and Virtuous Republicans

This last point is implicit in both the Lockean social contract and republican virtue theories that animated the Framers of the U.S. Constitution and form the backdrop for understanding the real meaning of the Fourth Amendment. In Lockean liberalism, a community or a People forms from the consent of individuals who, to protect themselves, transfer the personal right to execute the law of nature—to use force—to the community. The community serves as an impartial judge and as the single authoritative interpreter of nature's law. The community in turn creates a government, a set of institutions entrusted by the community to bring about the social peace and the preservation of natural rights for which the community was created. A legitimate state will pass, interpret, and execute laws for the noble purpose of preserving citizens' "property," meaning their lives, liberties, and possessions. Such a state thereby rightly acquires "political power."[8] Locke explains:

> Political power, then, I take to be a right of making laws with penalties of death, and consequently all lesser penalties, for the regulating and preserving of property, and of employing the force of the community in the execution of such laws, and in the defense of the commonwealth from injury, and all this only for the public good.[9]

The "public" or "common good" is the good of *all* the People, not of any subset or elite, preserving both the People's safety and their existence as "a People." The kind of state force involved in stops, arrests, searches, and seizures is therefore necessary to the very existence of a People and of a state. Yet Lockean liberals are simultaneously distrustful of the state, fearful that it will use its awesome force to serve factions rather than the People as a whole, imposing tyrannical rule in ways both large and small. The state's use of force must therefore be monitored and tamed by the People or by institutions legitimately acting on their behalf. The Fourth Amendment's declaration that the state use force to effect "searches and seizures" only when "reasonable" is sensibly understood as constitutionalizing the mandate that the People tame state power.[10]

Republican (as opposed to liberal) theory likewise recognized that the state must serve the common good rather than that of a faction. But the common good can be discerned only by virtuous citizens shaping a virtuous state and vice versa. Virtuous citizens' qualities include a willingness to invoke their rights in a way that makes them part of a deliberative dialogue over what kind of state and People we should be. Yet those Framers most heavily influenced by republican thinking still accepted that this political conversation could successfully be undertaken only in the context of a neo-Lockean social contract. For republicans, however, that contract was political, in the sense that it required institutions to encourage the sense of shared values necessary to an effectively functioning People. Only such a united People could tame otherwise unbridled state violence. For republicans too, therefore, the Fourth Amendment channels state force to productive purposes.[11]

For both liberals and republicans, the use of state violence to enforce the laws—modernly, the function of the police—is thus a necessary precondition to Peoplehood and to social stability. Yet neither sort of thinker trusted the state. Rules and institutions were understood to be necessary to monitor the state and to prevent its abusing its authority to use force to crush the People or to undermine the equality principles embraced by the social contract, serving the needs of a faction or elite. The Fourth Amendment is best understood, or so this book will argue, as just such an attempt to tame political violence, ensuring its service to the "security" of a free People by prohibiting unreasonable exercises of the state's use of force. Among the political dangers that constitute the state's abuse of violence are conduct sending degrading messages about human worth, insulting individuals or groups, undermining rather than reinforcing desirable republican norms, and suppressing dissenting voices. Abuse also arises when the police de-individualize justice, treating persons on the basis of stereotype or surmise rather than as "unique, a 'universe of one,'" as judged by ample and trustworthy evidence.[12]

The Original Fourth Amendment

This book's approach is historical, in part 1 recasting the history of the original Fourth Amendment of 1791 as one about the taming of expressive political violence. The origins of the amendment indeed lay in part in efforts to suppress dissent in infamous seditious-libel prosecutions. But the amendment's origins also lay in a violent dispute over what it means for the state to "represent" the People. Mob actions during the Revolutionary period were prompted to protest not simply "taxation without representation" but rather the enforcement of the tax laws by general searches, ones without adequate individualized evidence of wrongdoing. But the very authority for those searches was ostensibly granted by Parliament—the British legislature—so that mob complaints extended also to Americans' lack of voice in the decision about when and how searches may happen. The dispute over search and seizure policy was thus at the very heart of the passions and political theory motivating the Revolution.[13]

Part of the Revolutionaries' concern with oppressive general searches lay also in the insult of being subjected to actual or threatened state force. Part of that insult was class based: subordinate, uneducated, and "low-born" officers searched the homes of higher-ranked free householders. But the colonists were insulted too not simply by *who* did the searches but by *how* the suspects were chosen: arbitrarily, without adequate supporting evidence of *individual* wrong-doing and without guidelines limiting officer discretion. This arbitrary violation of principles of individualized justice was so dear to the Revolutionaries' hearts that they described it as the equivalent of slavery, the ultimate political evil. By "slavery" the colonists did not mean "chattel slavery," which they ultimately protected via specific provisions in the original Constitution of 1789. Rather, for the colonists slavery was the absence of corporate political liberty and economic independence for individuals. General searches symbolized this ultimate political degradation, marking the colonists (in their view) as outside the community of recognized political equals, silencing their voices and making them dependent on the whims of a tyrannical empire.[14]

The sense of insult stemmed not only from voiceless deindividualization but also from the related idea that the state must not use force against any citizen without strong, reliable evidence of individual wrongdoing. The American passion for this evidentiary principle—later encapsulated in the idea of "probable cause"—had its roots in fears of Continental-style inquisitions, but developed into a fairly complex and robust set of common-law concepts. The colonists were alert to the need for significant assurances of evidentiary reliability. Mere surmise or weakly supported allegations of individual wrongs would not suffice. The "probable cause" concept served to restrain state force, protecting both individuals from violence and the People from subjugation to a power other than their own. Making this point clear requires an explanation of the meaning of the "common law" and its significance in interpreting the Fourth Amendment and an explanation of the respective roles of the People, the Congress, the judiciary, and the executive in making Fourth Amendment freedoms real. Although the judiciary was assigned a special role in this process (the warrant-issuing prerogative), commentators too often de-emphasize the multi-branch responsibilities created by the amendment.[15]

Finally, part 1 of this book ends by analyzing the modern implications of understanding the original Fourth Amendment as regulating the everyday political violence of the state. These implications focus on the amendment's role in building a "monitorial," politically attentive, unified "People" from social diversity and on the expressive nature of police conduct and its consequences. More specifically, the final section of part 1 suggests a number of lessons to be drawn from the amendment's early history that require changes in current doctrine. Such changes should include the creation of incentives for other branches to create more People-inclusive search and seizure institutions, a serious commitment to individualized justice in deed and not just in words, a more careful quest for *reliable* evidence of wrongdoing, a heartfelt embrace of the close link between First and Fourth Amendment values, and a deeper appreciation for the way poorly conceived search and seizure policies can insult individuals and groups and undermine both governmental legitimacy and public safety.

The Fourth Amendment Is Not a Mere Technicality

Part 2 of this book was originally prompted by the question, Why do many minority communities experience rage at certain police search and seizure practices involving their communities' members? My apparently obvious answer: because the police act in ways that make minority communities feel disrespected. In reaching that answer, I came to recognize, however, that members of the majority also often bear the brunt of disrespectful search and seizure practices. Minorities and the majority may differ in when they believe that "respect" has been shown. History, philosophy, and social science converge in establishing that "respect" should nevertheless be at the center of all Fourth Amendment reasoning. What "respect" is, how it is conceived of by minority versus majority communities, and what psychological and social processes lead to its loss are, however, not so obvious. Nor has it yet become clear to the U.S. Supreme Court what role respect-based concerns should play in Fourth Amendment analysis. Those concerns have significant implications for every current search and seizure doctrine. Understanding the Court's current approach and its failures, and defending a respect-enhancing alternative, first requires an analysis of the dominant "mere technicality" vision of the Fourth Amendment. That vision seems at odds with the amendment's sweeping language:[16]

> The right of the people to be secure in their persons, houses, papers, and effects against unreasonable searches and seizures, shall not be violated, and no warrants shall issue, but upon probable cause, supported by oath or affirmation, and particularly describing the place to be searched and the persons or things to be seized.[17]

The right was of central importance to our nation's founders. It was included in the Bill of Rights, which the people demanded be added to the 1789 Constitution as the price for its ratification. Images of King George's troops violating "a man's castle" in search of contraband come readily to mind. The brave colonists' resistance to monarchy seems embodied in this amendment's lofty words.[18] Whatever noble ideals the amendment's ringing language might seemingly inspire, however, the amendment is in practice modernly seen by many as a pointless annoyance. Consider this scenario:

> Two police officers, Cagney and Lacey, pay off a local stool pigeon for information about a planned cocaine sale. The stoolie's information is vague, and he refuses to reveal his sources. Nevertheless, based on this tip, Cagney and Lacey guess that a cocaine sale will happen that night at a Water Street warehouse and set up a stakeout. Unable to see much, they choose to break in. Inside, they find not only a massive quantity of cocaine but also a large shipment of illegal firearms ready to hit the street. Their elation at a job well done is quickly ended when a judge suppresses the evidence. Because the search was done without a warrant or probable cause, the trial judge barred the jury from hearing or seeing anything about the drugs and weapons confiscated by the detectives. Lacking evidence, the prosecution was forced to withdraw the case, and another dangerous criminal walked free.

This image of left-wing judges allowing criminals to exploit the Fourth Amendment and other legal technicalities has long been standard fare in movies, television shows, and newspaper stories. The media feeds the impression of a massive, increasingly violent crime problem. That problem is portrayed as exacerbated by the helpless system's flooding of the streets with guilty men freed by wily lawyers. Recent reports of a declining crime problem have begun to combat the media-driven crime hysteria. That decline is portrayed by the media, however, as caused by new tough-on-crime measures to keep criminals behind bars, combined with the appointment of stricter judges. Political campaigns embrace assaults on any judges who insist on enforcing a generous constitutional vision.[19]

Amazingly, despite the media onslaught, a large majority of the public, according to at least one study, opposes the admission of illegally obtained evidence. Yet many members of the public are swayed by the reduction of a core constitutional right—namely, freedom from unreasonable searches and seizures—to a mere annoyance that obstructs justice. Perhaps more important, the decision makers and policy advisers who decide when and how searches and seizures shall be done reduce the Fourth Amendment to a mere technicality. "The criminal is to go free because the constable has blundered" is the rallying cry. Academics insist that finding the truth is what trials are all about, and the Fourth Amendment must not undermine that goal. Of course, some of these pundits pay tribute to the value of the amendment, objecting only to the remedy of suppression. They propose alternative remedies, however, that have either proven fruitless in the past or that are obviously politically dead-on-arrival. Furthermore, they pay tribute to the amendment only fleetingly, in small amounts, their tone emphasizing the social calamity caused by the amendment more than the social benefits it might bring.[20]

The police embrace this same sort of skepticism about the amendment's value. Police often perjure themselves at hearings to suppress evidence, a phenomenon so widespread that it has its own name: "testilying." They lie when they know that they have violated the amendment because they do not want to see the illegally obtained evidence suppressed. Nor do they want to see the department or themselves named in a lawsuit or to be demoted because of a pattern of Fourth Amendment suppression.[21]

And the officers know that judges usually feel the same way. Judges routinely deny suppression motions when they know that the police are lying. For example, the Fourth Amendment does not protect a defendant who has abandoned his property. Therefore, officers repeatedly testify that defendants suddenly and intentionally "drop" drugs while fleeing from the police, in the suspects' purported hope that they cannot thus be linked to the drugs. One judge explained: "[W]hen one stands back from the particular case and looks at a series of cases . . . [it] becomes apparent that policemen are committing perjury in at least some . . . [of the cases], and perhaps in nearly all of them." This judge admits that he nevertheless routinely accepts an officer's dropsy testimony as truthful in a particular case. Judges do so, he explains, because at some level they share the officers' attitude:[22]

> Policemen see themselves as fighting a two-front war—against criminals in the street and against "liberal" rules of law in court. All's fair in this war, including the use of perjury to subvert "liberal" rules of law that might free those who "ought" to be jailed. . . . It is a peculiarity of our legal system that the police have unique opportunities (and unique temptations) to give false testimony. When the Supreme Court lays down a rule to govern the conduct of the police, the rule does not enforce itself.[23]

While police "testilying" may help to subvert Supreme Court rulings, the Court too has generally accepted the view of the Fourth Amendment as a mere technicality: "After all it is the defendant, not the constable, who stands trial." Most major decisions over the past three decades increasingly stress the importance of the truth-finding function at trial. The Court subjects individual citizens' Fourth Amendment interests to a "balancing" test in which the needs of law enforcement get ever-heavier weight. Though there are important exceptions, and though the Court occasionally praises the amendment's value, the general trend is to narrow the scope of Fourth Amendment rights and, even when such rights are recognized, to narrow still further when the exclusionary remedy will be available to enforce the amendment.[24]

The burden of this narrowing vision of Fourth Amendment rights has often fallen hardest on racial and ethnic minorities. The Court purports to endorse a colorblind search and seizure jurisprudence. Ignoring race, however, is often precisely what promotes racial disparities.[25]

To use the most obvious example, an officer who stops a car going one mile over the speed limit has probable cause to believe that the law has been violated. If the officer only stops those speeders who are African American, or Hispanic American or Asian American, that seems wrong. It unsettles American notions of equal treatment. Yet if, as the Court suggests, we cannot consider the officer's racial attitudes and assumptions, or perhaps not even whether his conduct has a disparate racial impact, this "racial profiling" is tolerated by the state. The Court's position on profiling and the role of race in search and seizure decisions is a bit more complex and subtle than my claim here that they entirely ignore race. But the bottom line point would be unchanged by exploring those complexities: a colorblind search and seizure jurisprudence often results in racial injustice.[26]

Racial minorities indeed have less trust in the police than do whites. The level of trust is lowest among young African American males. Even minority-group members who may trust their local police are probably more troubled by invasive police conduct than are many whites. Many minority-group members are attentive to, and especially worried by, police violence, the stopping of young black males with little justification, or searches of homes without warrants. Correspondingly, they worry that police offer minorities inadequate and unequal protection from crime. Minority communities yearn for a police force that promotes community safety while valuing community rights. They agitate for a police force free from conduct that insults and denigrates minority communities.[27]

What is lost in the mere-technicality vision of the Fourth Amendment, therefore, is an appreciation for the ways that it affects the fate of communities of identity. The Fourth Amendment protects core interests essential to human flourishing, interests in privacy, property, and freedom of movement. Media images, police talk, and jurisprudence that address primarily the costs of the amendment and only secondarily its benefits—and that too narrowly define those benefits—miss the central point. The image of the drug hustler manipulating the justice system to his own advantage both misleads the public (drawing attention from police wrongdoing) and ignores the many benefits that the amendment bestows upon the innocent. Innocent people are stopped on the street every day, while rushing to work, walking to church, or heading for day care. Property is seized—from cars to cash to homes—from the innocent. Homes are invaded with little cause and perhaps no apology when no evidence of wrongdoing is found. These invasions are psychologically painful.[28] They send a message to their victims that they are unworthy of the government's respect:

> [S]hocking images of combat-ready officers battering their way into a private home are routine in America's cities today thanks to the war on drugs, as well as the war on illegal immigration. All across the country, the SWATification of policing has led to a proliferation of special units trained to rely on aggressive tactics, barging into homes and swooping down on citizens with impunity. . . .
>
> Unfortunately, there seems to be little public enthusiasm for this debate. That's because few voters live in neighborhoods where gang units are likely to enter their kids' names and photos into the department database merely for wearing their hats backward. Nor do most of us lose sleep worrying whether the police might batter down our doors by mistake in search of drugs.[29]

Law professor David Cole goes further, seeing discriminatory and unjustifiable police practices as encouraging distrust, anger, and even criminality among those individuals affected.[30]

But individuals' identity is often linked closely to those groups that matter most to them. When individuals are wrongly stopped because of their race, the disrespect they feel may be felt by others in their racial community. When many persons of a certain race are regularly so stopped, the impact on the broader racial community is deeper. Minority communities sense, in a way that the Court does not, that strong Fourth Amendment protections are central to fostering respect for both individuals and their communities. At the same time, as grass-roots activism and some community policing efforts have shown, respect-enhancing police actions improve law enforcement effectiveness. Citizens more actively and eagerly cooperate with a respectful police force. The result is crime reduction.[31]

"Respect" is in part about status or esteem. Each person feels respected when treated as significant and of equal worth with every other person. Groups too struggle for equal status.[32] But respect is also about inclusion, about being considered full members of the wider political community. When African Americans in Jim Crow America could not sit at white lunch counters, they felt excluded from the American community. Yet what is rarely recognized is that Jim Crow laws went to the heart of the Fourth Amendment by regulating where certain citizens could choose to work, live, eat, and play. Similarly, today, when officers employ racial profiling to stop young African American males walking down the street, the officers insult and degrade the young men and their racial group, making them feel less than full members of the American polity.[33]

Respect requires recognizing that group identity is at the core of individual identity. The state must, therefore, embrace salient groups as equal partners in creating and implementing criminal justice policy. Group voices must be heard. But individuals must also be treated as unique, judged for what they do rather than what group they belong to. There is thus a healthy tension between group and individualized justice. Moreover, each citizen and his or her group must feel that the state intrudes upon their freedoms only when there is ample and trustworthy evidence of individual wrongdoing. Furthermore, all branches of government must recognize their constitutional obligation to express respect for citizens while enforcing the law. As the testifying example illustrates, the courts cannot do the job alone. They must rely on the executive branch of police, prosecutors, state governors, and the national president, as well as the political will of state and federal legislators, to enforce constitutional mandates.[34]

Nevertheless, the courts must continue to play their role of setting "a constitutional floor protecting individuals and constraining government." That floor too often collapses under the weight of the mere-technicality vision.[35] I am not making a sharp analytical distinction here between "mere technicalities" and "rules of substance." Rather, I am describing an attitude whose strength may vary from one situation to another.[36] Judges indeed likely understand—in a way that the lay public, the police, and the media may not—that even technicalities serve purposes. Filing deadlines, for example, discourage lawyer laziness, intentional delay, and simple indifference to client needs. But if a rule is even subconsciously viewed as merely a technicality, the courts will far more easily let it bend to countervailing concerns and will defer to other legal actors' judgments about whether the rule has been met or requires an exception. To avoid that result in the area of search and seizure law, a substantive vision of the Fourth Amendment's value to our republic must replace the nearsighted view of mere technicalities. This book seeks to articulate such a vision, one rooted in the substantive value of respect.[37]

The Mutated Fourth Amendment

Part 2 of this book thus seeks to understand respect by extending the history recounted in part 1.[38] In interpreting the Fourth Amendment, courts and commentators consistently focus solely on the events surrounding the Framers' drafting, and the People's ratifying, the Bill of Rights in 1791. Although I argue in this book that other thinkers have misunderstood the significance of those events, here I take the story one step further, examining search and seizure practices during antebellum slavery, then during Reconstruction. That history matters because the original Fourth Amendment applied solely to the federal, not the state, governments. But the struggle against slavery and the Civil War led the victorious North to lead the way to the ratification of three new constitutional amendments during the period of Reconstruction: the Thirteenth Amendment, ending slavery; the Fourteenth Amendment, prohibiting any state from denying any person due process or equal protection of the laws or the privileges or immunities of U.S. citizens; and the Fifteenth Amendment, guaranteeing all male citizens the vote. One effect of the Fourteenth Amendment's Due Process Clause was that it for the first time applied most of the Bill of Rights, including the Fourth Amendment, to the states. Understanding the meaning of today's Fourth Amendment therefore requires study of the evolving meanings of search and seizure during the fight to end slavery, for it was that fight that motivated and defined the drafting and ratification of the Fourteenth Amendment. The Fourteenth Amendment thus mutated the meaning of the constitutional rules governing search and seizure. The Framers of the nineteenth century matter, therefore, as much as those of the eighteenth.

Chattel slavery was central to the nineteenth-century American experience, and that institution's violent death throes birthed the Reconstruction amendments to the Constitution. It is rarely noted, however, that slavery was sustained largely by search and seizure practices. Slave patrols, designed to prevent runaways and maintain slave discipline, consisted of state officials whose authority stemmed from an antebellum version of general warrants. State and federal fugitive-slave laws provided fairly cursory warrant procedures for the capture and return of suspected runaways, while fostering an ever-increasing federal enforcement presence that involved reluctant Northerners in enforcing the dictates of the system of bondage that many of them increasingly came to detest. State laws authorized masters' and state officials' violent punishment of "recalcitrant" or "insolent slaves," searches of slave cabins, and seizures of what slaves viewed as their property, though the law recognized no such right of slaves to "own" property. In the antebellum Southern mind, the idea of property (the slave) owning property was absurd. American slavery was thus defined by state-initiated or state-sanctioned interferences with slaves' freedom of movement, privacy, and property. Many court cases of the era concerned precisely these issues.

But Southern and federal search and seizure practices affected whites as well, particularly in an effort to suppress the speech of those who sought the abolition of human bondage. Although the abolitionists were unpopular in the North, many Northerners were nevertheless outraged by Southern and federal efforts to silence these dissenters. Abolitionist mail was seized and even burned by postal authorities, their persons banished from the Southern realm, their arrest eagerly sought to muzzle these advocates of human freedom. Southern arrests and seizures, or their threat, extended even beyond abolitionists, reaching Northern-state moderates and free Northern-state blacks, for example, arresting and selling into slavery (absent payment of the costs of arrest and deportation) black Northern seamen on ships temporarily docking in certain Southern ports. Many Northerners, despite their racism, thus came to fear that an aristocratic "Slave Power" enriched by human bondage threatened white civil liberties. The expansion of slavery into Western territories and the Supreme Court's enthusiastic endorsement of the Southern vision in such infamous cases as *Dred Scott* further fanned the flames of Northern fear and anger.

The Civil War came to seem the fulfillment of Northern anxieties. As slaves deserted plantations in massive numbers despite Southern efforts to tighten patrols and myriad other restraints on slaves' free movement, and as black troops fought bravely for Union when dire circumstances pressed the federal government into permitting escaped slaves to join the fight, Northern ideas evolved about race, the nature of "property," and the political meaning of freedom to locomote and "privacy" (though not then using that word). Northern, especially Republican Party, commitment to a "free labor" ideology, which valorized both literal and metaphorical (up the social ladder) movement and glorified private property, had always been inconsistent with slavery's spread. Now the ideology flatly rejected slavery's survival and required acceptance of some degree of recognition of slave humanity. This evolution did not come easily, however, and again grew from continuing struggles over whether fugitive-slave laws were still binding in the face of rebellion and what freedom should mean for the slaves.

After the war's end, during early Reconstruction, Southerners engaged in a counterrevolution designed to re-create slavery in fact if not in law. Under the infamous "black codes," blacks could be arrested for leaving plantations or for other "crimes" that could not be committed by whites, while facing continuing violence—sometimes overtly state-sanctioned, sometimes by "private" mobs often led by state officials—and seizures of their property. These events led in particular to the Fourteenth Amendment. Public and courtroom antebellum debates had expressly invoked the Fourth Amendment in a variety of important instances. Because the Supreme Court had clearly held, however, that the Bill of Rights did not then apply to the states, many of these debates invoked Fourth Amendment concepts but under other legal and political rubrics. The Fourteenth Amendment is best understood, however, as in important part serving to fix this problem by applying the Fourth Amendment to the states.

Search and seizure as a tool for racial domination was, of course, a major concern of the late-nineteenth-century constitutional drafters and ratifiers in a way that was not true for their eighteenth-century peers. Yet, though that concern with questions of race sparked my interest in the period, the history reveals a continuing—perhaps even further strengthened—emphasis on many of the same issues that motivated the American Revolutionaries—individualized justice, a reliance on trustworthy evidence supporting probable cause, and protection of political dissent topping the list. But many of these issues were viewed through a different lens, raising several new questions, which I will explore shortly. That exploration also reveals the continuing link among state-expressive violence in the form of searches and seizures and the political subjugation of individuals and groups, in short, with the denial of respect.

My approach to respect proceeds from the bottom up. All persons are entitled to respect. Yet certain marginalized groups in our society disproportionately bear the burden of state-imposed disrespect. Moreover, there are sometimes on-average differences in these groups' perceptions and experiences as compared to more privileged members of the polity. Understanding respect's meaning in the Fourth Amendment context therefore requires being especially attentive to whatever salient differences there may be between minority- and majority-group perspectives. Where there are differences, which group's view prevails will be a question of political morality. But it will often be the case that what benefits the oppressed benefits other people as well. Furthermore, it will always be the case that examining minority viewpoints will better inform an otherwise unduly constricted constitutional analysis.[39] Likewise, my approach to political history is to view it as a conversation between elites and ordinary men and women. Law as it is lived, including constitutional law, consists of more than the dry words of cases or statutes. Constitutional law is born and made real in the struggles of Americans on the streets of their nation—in protests, mobs, and street-corner conversations too. It is this that I mean when I speak of "law on the street." The Fourth Amendment, like all constitutional provisions, is thus a creature of the street, a text whose roots lie first in the English citizens' battle with state tyranny, then in the Americans' struggle to break free from that same mother country's smothering grip, and, finally, in that young nation's internal struggle against its own political demons.[40]

PART I

Political Violence and the Original Fourth Amendment

2 Violence as Political Expression

The political and legal world of the Fourth Amendment's Framers was in some respects radically different from our own. It was a world in which objectionable warrants were often issued by provincial governors or by legislatures— either colonial ones or by the British Parliament—rather than by judges; in which a fictionalized history of the "rights of Englishmen" played a powerful motivating role in political change, while elite and mob action simultaneously rejected as unduly cramped both the mother country's and colonial notions of "liberty"; and in which the fear of abusive searches and seizures focused on the tax man, British soldiers, and British impressment gangs "recruiting" for the Royal Navy rather than on organized police forces, which did not yet exist. British events and history (or at least the fictionalized versions of these things) thus mattered to Americans, sometimes as much as did first colonial, then state, American rhetoric and practices.

Whether the relevant events took place in England or America, search and seizure disputes were understood by the Framing generation as quintessentially tied to political violence in the long contest with England. What the prerequisites were for a valid warrant was not a mere technical legal question for the Revolutionaries. Such issues were at the core of what the Revolution and the willingness of Americans to sacrifice their "lives, . . . fortunes, and . . . sacred honor" was all about.[1] Thus, after a famously influential Revolutionary leader, James Otis, rose to protest the writs of assistance—a form of general warrant permitting certain searches and seizures without individualized suspicion or a particularized description of the persons or things to be seized—another Revolutionary leader, John Adams, said of that protest, "then and there was the Child Independence born." As Adams later wrote, the dispute over the writs marked the "Commencement of the Controversy between Great Britain and America," and virtually all modern historians agree at least that violent resistance to the writs, and Britain's equally violent response, were major causes of the American Revolution.[2]

Each violent move and countermove by British forces and the colonists thus bore symbolic power. This power was of concern not only to armies and elites but also to the everyday people, the "salt of the earth," who often coalesced as mobs to protest British abuses. The rhetoric of the street and of the intellectual converged on the same set of principles. Resistance to expressive violence by the state came to define much of the Revolution's meaning for Americans, even if they did not initially fully understand what they had done.[3]

Seditious Libel

The abusive searches and seizures that captured colonial Americans' attention frequently involved state efforts to suppress dissent. That suppression was at its starkest in seditious-libel prosecutions.[4]

Among the most striking of the early prosecutions during the colonial period was that of Sir Edward Coke, author of the *Institutes of the Laws of England,* one of the major works of the common-law tradition. Coke, along with Robert Beale, clerk of the Privy Council in 1589, and Sir William Matthew Hale, another "celebrated authority on the common law" and the influential author of the *History of the Pleas of the Crown,* "invented a rhetorical tradition against general searches" that would eventually culminate in the Fourth Amendment. Coke's writings thus had at least an indirect effect on the development of American search and seizure law, as he did on the development of the American common law generally. The Massachusetts Bay Puritans studied Coke, Jefferson praised him, and Americans admired him as "the foremost authority on English law." Coke was also one of the Crown's most influential opponents.[5]

During the reign of Charles I, general searches for documentary evidence were common. Notably, Privy Council warrants were issued "for the searching and sealing of the trunks, studies, cabinets, and other repositories of papers" of leading figures after they had given "insurrectionary speeches" in Parliament. Coke's turn came in 1634, while he was on his deathbed. In an effort to ferret out seditious papers believed to be in circulation among the Crown's opponents, the Privy Council sent a messenger to Coke's home bearing an order to search for "seditious and dangerous papers." His chambers were ransacked, his writings (including the manuscripts of his great legal works) seized, his jewelry and money carried away.[6]

Back home, one of the more infamous seditious-libel cases arose from the 1754 Massachusetts Provincial Legislature's enactment of an excise tax. The excise legislation "authorized tax collectors to interrogate any subject, under oath, on the amount of rum, wine, and other spirits he had consumed in his private premises in the past year and taxed it by the gallon." The legislation did not expressly authorize searches of private homes. But the act's opponents assumed that questioning on doorsteps inevitably meant searching inside homes.[7]

Public outrage was intense. John Lovell, a highly respected Boston schoolmaster, condemned the act as "the most pernicious attack upon *English Liberty* that was ever attempted." The minister of Brattle Church saw the act as "a revival of the Inquisition, requiring people to incriminate themselves." A flood of antitax tracts described it as violating Magna Carta, natural rights, and the castle that was each man's home. The rhetoric was apocalyptic, conveying the sense that once the excise act was established, "the progression would allegedly extirpate all constitutional liberty."[8]

Such rhetoric seemed disproportionate to the degree of danger posed, likely because the Excise Act was but the latest threat in more than a quarter century of the province's agitation over search and seizure issues. These issues particularly included searches pursuant to a local impost tax and to the work of the British customs service, the authorization of general warrants to recover the records of a failed land bank's directors, and the forced impressment of seamen into the Royal Navy. The Excise Act's interrogation clause, therefore, "was the last straw, not the first one, in public discontent with the search process."[9]

The most savage attack on the act and its authors was the pamphlet *The Monster of Monsters*. Its author "warned of the danger of the tax collector having power to break chains, doors, locks, and bolts, and invade bedchambers and wine cellars." It was a biting satirical attack on the Massachusetts House of Representatives.[10]

Daniel Fowle, suspected of being the *Monster's* author, was "dragged from his dinner one night" to answer the charge before the House. Fowle admitted only that he sold the pamphlet. He was promptly imprisoned, but public outcry won his release on his own recognizance after only six days. The House subsequently dropped the prosecution.[11]

Fowle, however, continued to agitate, recounting his version of the affair in the tract *A Total Eclipse of Liberty* and suing the Speaker of the House and the arresting messenger for illegal imprisonment. Fowle lost the suit in 1757, but, now living in New Hampshire, he refused to pay the court costs that were assessed against him in Massachusetts. Five years later, he was sued for the money. After his repeatedly petitioning the Massachusetts General Court in the mid-1760s, he was ultimately awarded both his legal costs and damages for his suffering. That result seemed a vindication of his position that his "personal freedom had been violated," a victory for the liberty of the press, and a grow-ing recognition that the voice of the legislature and of the People were not always one and the same.[12]

The seditious-libel prosecution probably most influential on colonial think-ing about search and seizure took place in England in 1763 and involved Parliamentary member John Wilkes. Wilkes anonymously published the *North Briton* series of pamphlets, including *Number 45*. *Number 45* contained unusu-ally bitter insults to a speech given by the king's ministers that defended an unpopular 1763 excise tax on cider in which the authorizing legislation granted extensive powers to search in aid of law enforcement. Lord Halifax, the secretary of state, issued a general warrant ordering four messengers "to make strict and diligent search for the authors, printers, and publishers of a seditious and treasonable paper, entitled, the North Briton, No. 45, . . . and them, or any of them, having found, to apprehend and seize, together with their papers." Under this "roving commission," the king's messengers ransacked printers' shops and houses, arresting forty-nine persons in just three days, including Wilkes and his printer, publisher, and booksellers. Some suspects were roused from their sleep, until one of them, the actual printer of *Number 45*, identified Wilkes as the author. Wilkes refused to obey the warrant, denouncing it as "a ridiculous warrant against the whole English nation." The messengers car-ried Wilkes directly to Lord Halifax's office, immediately thereafter returning to Wilkes' home, where "they had a blacksmith open the drawers of Wilkes' bureau and took away, uninventoried, all of his private papers including his will and also his pocketbook." Thousands of pages of papers and scores of books were seized from Wilkes's compatriots as well.[13]

The secretary of state committed Wilkes to the Tower of London for refusing to answer questions. Wilkes was released a few days later, however, because of his privilege as a member of Parliament. The House of Commons subsequently voted *Number 45* a seditious libel and expelled Wilkes, who was eventually con-victed and jailed for the offense.[14]

Wilkes, the printers, and all others who had suffered searches and arrests quickly filed trespass suits against all offenders, from flunky to minister. In the first of these suits, *Huckle v. Money*, Chief Justice Pratt charged the jury, "To enter a man's house by virtue of a nameless warrant, in order to procure evi-dence, is worse than the Spanish Inquisition, a law under which no English-man would wish to live an hour." The jury awarded the plaintiffs the substan-tial sum of three hundred pounds in damages. *Huckle* established the principle that Crown officers engaging in unlawful searches are liable for damages in trespass and false-imprisonment suits. Pratt also presided over the trial arising from a suit brought by Wilkes against Wood, the undersecretary who had supervised the warrant's execution. Pratt upheld the jury's award of one thousand pounds, declaring that the question of the warrant's validity "was a point of the greatest consequence that he had ever met in his whole practice."[15]

The Wilkesites' most direct victory over seditious-libel claims came, however, in *Entick v. Carrington,* later described by the Supreme Court as "one of the landmarks of English liberty." John Entick had been seized, along with his books and papers, a half year before the *North Briton* incident, pursuant to a warrant issued by Lord Halifax. Entick was the author of the *Monitor or British Freeholder.* Although the warrant specifically named Entick, the warrant was a general one concerning his papers. Entick initially tolerated the intrusion, but he later brought a trespass suit against the king's messengers after witnessing Wilkes' and the printers' successes arising from the government's *Number 45* sweep. The jury awarded Entick three hundred pounds. On appeal, former chief justice Pratt, now Lord Camden, authored an opinion in 1765 squarely challenging the use of general warrants in seditious-libel cases.[16] Said Lord Camden,

> If this point should be decided in favor of the Government, the secret cabinets and bureaus of every subject in this kingdom would be thrown open to the search and inspection of a messenger, whenever the secretary of state shall see fit to charge, or even to suspect, a person to be the author, printer, or publisher of a seditious libel.[17]

Camden considered it "cruel and unjust" for innocent and guilty alike to "incriminate" themselves by submitting to such a search, implying a link between search and seizure principles and the right against self-incrimination. Camden held that the executive lacked authority to direct arrests or issue general warrants absent legislative authorization.[18] Camden rejected the argument that the extralegal usage of these sorts of warrants since the Glorious Revolution of 1688 legitimated the flawed practice:

> There has been a submission of guilt and poverty to power and the terror of punishment. But it would be a strange doctrine to assert that all the people of this land are bound to acknowledge that to be universal law, which a few criminal book sellers have been afraid to dispute.[19]

Wilkes became a popular idol, the "personification of constitutional liberty to Englishmen on both sides of the Atlantic." "Wilkes and Liberty" became a patriot's slogan in America. Wilkes became linked to Americans' struggles for liberty when, evoking shades of Parliament's reaction to *North Briton Number 45*, the New York Assembly (the province's lower house) "stopped at nothing" to get the name of a citizen who had assailed that House for approving provisions for the king's troops in 1769. Alexander McDougall, a leader of the Sons of Liberty, was soon fingered as the offending author. As the first American indicted for seditious libel in over twenty-five years, he became America's "own Wilkes." McDougall's supporters linked him expressly to Wilkes's cause, using the number "45" (as in *North Briton Number 45*) as their symbol. Thus these supporters drank forty-five toasts to liberty—including "liberty of the press, liberty from general warrants, liberty from compulsory self-accusation, [and] liberty from seizure of private papers"—while consuming forty-five pounds of beef from a forty-five-month-old bull on the forty-fifth day of the year. On another festive day, forty-five virgins, all of whom, "according to some damned Tory," were forty-five years old, sang forty-five songs to McDougall. Editors and reporters from Boston to Charleston filled their newspapers with stories of the Wilkes cases and the theatrics of the American Wilkesites.[20]

Back in the mother country, popular pressure led to debates in the House of Commons in 1764, 1765, and 1766 over the legality of general warrants. Ultimately, the House passed three resolutions that took a narrower position than had Pratt, now Lord Camden: first, general warrants *for arrest* were condemned in all cases; second, general warrants to search *for papers* were condemned *only* if issued by the executive in seditious-libel cases; third, Secretarial or executive-issued warrants otherwise remained legal; and, fourth, the elaborate system of warrantless and general searches authorized by statute remained intact. The House of Lords rejected a fifth Commons resolution that signified a willingness to limit general warrants to cases of treason and felony. The bottom line was that "even promiscuously general searches did not violate the liberty of the subject or infringe the maxim about a man's home [being his castle] *so long as Parliament had laid down the law.*"[21]

If Wilkes's quest did not in the short run constitute an overwhelming victory over the general warrant and its role in suppressing dissent, it did provide Americans with powerful rhetorical tools, for they made highly selective and creative use of the precedent to meet their own needs. The Wilkesites offered strong fertilizer for a liberty tree branch to grow into the Fourth Amendment.[22]

A final caveat: I do not want to overstate my case. The British and American history of searches and seizures done to advance seditious-libel prosecutions is long and complex. Moreover, Americans during the Revolutionary War had used promiscuous searches and seizures to silence dissent, even harassing those who, on religious grounds, refused to take loyalty oaths. Although some historian apologists see this apparent hypocrisy as the result of war necessity, the colonies, later states, were sometimes rife with such oppression. The outlines of modern free-speech notions only started to become visible with Thomas Jefferson's election to the presidency in 1800, partly as a result of popular rejection of Federalist Party prosecutions of dissenters under the Alien and Sedition Acts. It was in the nineteenth-century contest between slavers and abolitionists that robust free-speech protections eventually came to take root.[23]

Nevertheless, the seditious-libel examples that I have chosen illustrate the close connection between search-and-seizure and free-speech principles from an early stage in the American story. Violent state invasions of privacy, property, and locomotion were used, and understood to be used, to suppress dissent, even if ideas of what dissent was *inappropriately* "licentious" were still immature. *Both* search-and-seizure *and* free-speech rights needed vigor if either were to prosper.[24]

A related principle was also at work in an area of public policy outside seditious-libel prosecutions: British silencing of American voices resisting oppressive taxation.

Taxing Voices

British search and seizure practices during the colonial period dramatically sparked widespread popular violence when done for the purpose of enforcing customs duties and other revenue-raising measures. General warrants and their close cousin, the writs of assistance, were therefore in part objectionable because they sought to further a British policy—"taxation without representation"—that symbolized Americans' exclusion from equal governance over their own affairs. Unbridled discretion in search authority designed to raise British revenue went to the heart of the Revolution's purpose.

Searching for Revenue

The offending customs duties and taxes imposed by the Empire were many. The Sugar Act of 1764 enlarged the use of writs of assistance by customs officers searching for violations of the revenue-raising laws. The list of products previously required to be exported directly to Britain, such as tobacco and sugar, was expanded to include hides, iron, and timber. New customs duties were created to enhance British revenue, raising the expense of importing foreign cloth, sugar, indigo, coffee, and wine. The British government lowered the duty imposed on imported foreign West Indian molasses, hoping that more-rigorous enforcement of a lower duty would stop smuggling and raise the demand for molasses from the British West Indies. The Empire's goal was to help to defray the enormous debts that it had incurred in the Seven Years' War, which ended in 1763.[25]

But the colonists instead saw a ministerial conspiracy to undermine liberty. The Sugar Act had expanded the juryless vice-admiralty courts' jurisdiction, courts "despised for circumventing juries, one of the traditional 'pillars' of the people's liberty." The act also increased the number of customs officials, who seemed to the colonists "to be ministerial lackeys or 'placemen.'" All this happened during hard economic times. Moreover, to keep peace with the French and Indians and regulate squatters, smugglers, and bandits, the British government decided to maintain a standing army in America during peacetime, an army double the size of the one in the colonies before the Seven Years' War. The colonists had been taught by leading figures like John Trenchard and Robert Molesworth that standing armies "were a presage of arbitrary power and therefore a threat to the people's liberty." The standing-army controversy had cooled because the troops were stationed in the newly won territories, far from population centers, but later events re-ignited that fire.[26]

In 1764, eight colonies' assemblies endorsed formal petitions sent to the royal authorities claiming that the Sugar Act was causing Americans great economic injury. The colonists worried that vigorous enforcement of the foreign molasses duty would ruin the rum industry, resulting in curtailed exports of fish, foodstuffs, and slaves to the Caribbean. Yet, in the spring of that same year, the government announced the likely passage of the Stamp Act. That act passed on March 22, 1765, to become effective that November, over loud colonial protests.[27]

The Stamp Act "levied a tax on legal documents, almanacs, newspapers, and nearly every form of paper used in the colonies." Although several colonies had resorted to stamp taxes earlier, never before had Parliament imposed such a tax in America. Stamp Act violations, like those under the Sugar Act, were to be handled by the juryless vice-admiralty courts. Equally important, the taxes cut at the "heart of the press," for "these duties, combined with the difficulty of getting stamped paper, seemed a type of censorship particularly aimed at those newspapers not governmentally supported."[28]

American reaction to the Stamp Act was fierce. Port merchants formed associations pledging not to import British goods, newspapers and pamphlets roiled with resentment at "these designing parricides" who "invited despotism to cross the ocean and fix her abode in this once happy land," and town and county meetings and assemblies spewed venomous declarations against British tyranny. Patrick Henry proposed to the Virginia House of Burgesses a series of fiery resolves, some of which were rejected by the House as too inflammatory or even treasonous, but colonial newspapers reported them all as if the assembly had adopted them in their entirety. Rhode Island's assembly declared the act unconstitutional, and by October 1765 delegates from nine colonies formed a "Stamp Act Congress," which vehemently denied by formal declaration Parliament's right to tax them.[29]

Mob violence, however, ultimately brought an end to the Stamp Act. The mobs began with an August 14, 1765, attack on the office and home of Massachusetts's stamp distributor, Andrew Oliver. Oliver backed down the next day, promising not to enforce the Stamp Act. Buoyed with this success, mob activities spread throughout the colonies.[30]

In Charleston, South Carolina, a crowd hanged in effigy figures of the devil joined with the stamp collector. "Whoever shall dare attempt to pull down these effigies," the protesters warned, "had better been born with a stone about his neck and cast into the sea." Bostonians marched with effigies past the town hall to enable colonial officials to see that it was the mob that commanded the streets. Similar demonstrations swept the continent, spreading to numerous Connecticut towns and to Newport, Rhode Island; Philadelphia, Pennsylvania; Wilmington, North Carolina; Savannah, Georgia; and numerous other places. At least sixty riots in over twenty-five different locations were sparked by the Stamp Act, creating an atmosphere in which rioting seemed permissible every day. Every mob protest sent the same message: "anyone who supported the Stamp Act had best change their mind before the crowd turned upon the real person instead of vicariously abusing his effigy." Crown officials got the point, stamp distributors in all colonies except Georgia resigning their posts by the end of 1765. Parliament repealed the Stamp Act a few months later, in February 1766.[31]

Although the Stamp Act protests were most directly aimed at the new tax itself, mob action must be placed in the context of a history of recent abusive British search and seizure activity. Perhaps most notable was the mid-1760s reissuance of the writs of assistance, on which more will be said later. The writ was a form of general warrant authorizing Crown officials to command peace officers or, if need be, any nearby subjects to assist with the warrant's execution. The writs were largely used by customs officers searching for smuggled goods and lasted for the life of the sovereign. When George II died on October 25, 1760, all writs of assistance expired soon thereafter, including one granted by the Superior Court of the Province of Massachusetts to Charles Paxton, the Surveyor of the Port of Boston.[32]

Sixty-three Boston merchants promptly petitioned for a hearing on the question of the court's granting new writs, the petitioning following quickly on the heels of a Crown decision strictly to enforce the trade laws. James Otis and his colleague Oxenbridge Thatcher argued the case for the merchants. For now, it is sufficient to note that Otis's argument included fear of abuses of unbridled discretion by customs officers. Otis worried that customhouse officers would enter private homes as they pleased, breaking all in their way, free to act even with "malice or revenge" that no man could challenge. As an example, Otis told of Mr. Justice Walley's calling before him Mr. Ware, a customs officer, "to answer for some minor offense":[33]

> As soon as he had finished, Mr. Ware asked him if he had done. He replied, "Yes." "Well then," said Mr. Ware, "I will show you a little of my power. I command you to permit me to search your house for uncustomed goods." And went on to search his house from the garret to the cellar; and then served the constable in the same manner.[34]

Otis argued that, though the writs were authorized by a 1662 statute, the statute was itself void because it was "against the Constitution" and "against natural Equity." Chief Justice Thomas Hutchinson and his colleagues on the Superior Court suspended judgment to inquire about the current practice concerning the writs in Britain's Court of Exchequer. Upon learning that general writs were commonly granted there, the Court reconvened for reargument in November 1761, and unanimously decided that the writs should be granted.[35]

Enforcement of the writs in Massachusetts "provoked increasingly violent opposition." In particular, the Stamp Act mobs vented their anger on Thomas Hutchinson, the chief justice who had granted the 1761 writs. The mobs had other reasons to dislike Hutchinson, a prominent and wealthy royalist "who justified poverty because it produced 'industry and frugality.'" Still, given the prominence of the Writs of Assistance cases, and the nature of the Stamp Act opposition, it is hard to believe that recollections of Hutchinson's decision to grant the writs did not play an important role in enraging the mob. In any event, Hutchinson's connection to the writs made him an ideal symbol of the anti–Stamp Act cause.[36] Historian Gary Nash described the destruction the mob wreaked on Hutchinson's home:

> Catching the chief justice and his family at the dinner table, the crowd smashed in the doors with axes, sent the family packing, and then systematically reduced the furniture to splinters, stripped the walls bare, chopped through inner partitions until the house was a hollow shell, destroyed the formal gardens in the rear of the mansion, drank the wine cellar dry, stole £900 sterling in coin, and carried off every moveable object of value except some of Hutchinson's books and papers, which were left to scatter in the wind.[37]

The Stamp Act Riots were not, of course, the first of the riots connected in some way to British search and seizure practices. Between 1700 and 1765, about two-thirds of colonial riots concerned customs collection, impressments, and, after 1744, civilian/military tensions. Some supporters of anti-customs-enforcement riots were smugglers facing potential economic losses if discovered. Other individuals, however, had more noble motives, but, whatever the motivation, "colonial anti-customs crowds behaved as if they were only protecting their community from intrusive outside forces." Zealous customs collectors refusing bribes were often greeted by the mob's forcible retaking of collected smuggled goods. Informers faced a similar fate, with crowds shouting threats and intimidating witnesses during proceedings or physically abusing the informers. One mob hauled an informant through the streets in a cart, while "bystanders showered him with 'filth and offal.'"[38]

Impressment riots "were a variant of a civilian/military tension that expressed local opposition to intrusion by forces outside the community." Individual workers, of course, also wanted to stay out of the navy, for "impressments for these men meant practical imprisonment, horrid conditions, and an earlier death." There were impressment disturbances in 1764 in New York, where rioters burned a naval captain's longboat; in 1742 in Boston, where a crowd destroyed a Royal Navy barge; among numerous other locations.[39] The most infamous anti-impressment action was the Knowles riot:

> In November of 1747 the people of Boston rose up with great anger. The problem started when some fifty British sailors, seeking a better life in the New World, deserted from HMS *Lark*. Commodore Charles Knowles responded by ordering a predawn sweep of the waterfront to find the deserters and, failing that, to impress other warm bodies into service on the *Lark*. Later that morning, according to an eyewitness, "a body of men arose I believe with no other motive than to rescue if possible the captivated . . . and to protest this form of like barberous abusage."[40]

Thousands of sailors and Bostonians seized naval officers as hostages, locked an under-sheriff in the town stocks, broke Council-chamber windows, threatened to burn a navy vessel, and set a longboat on fire. They occupied the bottom floor of a public building "and convinced local officials to negotiate with the navy for the suspension of the press and the release of those already taken." A frightened Governor Shirley called out the militia, but only officers heeded the call. When Commodore Knowles's threat to bombard Boston from his warships proved empty (it would likely be the rich, not the rioters, who would suffer), the mob maintained control of the city for three days until Governor Shirley relented, releasing most of the impressed seamen.[41]

Nevertheless, the Stamp Act riots were qualitatively different from these earlier mob actions. While other riots had been intermittent, the sustained, widespread nature of the Stamp Act riots and their repeated successes in bowing British power contributed to a political culture further legitimating and encouraging violent resistance to tyrannical rule. Many of the participants in the street were from the "lower ranks," mechanics, sailors, and others, "who found they wielded a new and exhilarating power." That power often reflected class antagonisms, being channeled against symbols of wealth and ostentation. Merchants, lawyers, and other colonists from the "more comfortable" classes, the "Whigs" (named after the liberal political party in Great Britain), needed the common folk but were concerned "about the rights of Englishmen, not violent social upheaval." For the Whigs, the issue was straightforward: taxation without representation. That issue was not fully real, however, for those who neither paid taxes nor voted. The Whigs thus organized "Sons of Liberty" from Newport to Charleston to help to channel the violence, direct class antagonisms toward symbols of British (rather than Whig) prosperity, and craft rhetoric with widespread appeal. The working and more prosperous classes united, at least for a time, to serve common interests. "The crisis over the Stamp Act aroused and unified Americans as no previous political event ever had." The crisis widened the circle of those who felt entitled to at least some voice in political matters, prompted bold political writings, and heightened political consciousness and participation. "This single stroke," said New York's William Smith Jr., "has lost Great Britain the affection of all her colonies."[42]

Yet the British saw only that Americans would not accept direct, "internal" taxes like the stamp tax, accordingly leading Parliament, under the leadership of Chancellor of the Exchequer Charles Townshend, to impose new import levies on glass, paint, paper, and tea. The government created three new vice-admiralty courts, a new secretaryship of state for American affairs, and, in an effort to economize, pulled back much of its army from costly remote posts, restationing them in coastal cities, where colonists would be responsible for the troops' housing and supplies.[43]

The even closer presence of a "standing army" and the continued revenue imposition without hearing the colonists' voice, both on the heels of the Stamp Act crisis, was an explosive combination. Pamphleteers geared up again, notably Philadelphia lawyer John Dickinson's widely popular *Letters from a Farmer in Pennsylvania*, excoriating all British efforts at taxing the colonies and urging revival of Stamp Act protest–style nonimportation agreements, a call that many heeded. In February 1768, the Massachusetts House of Representatives authored a "circular letter" denouncing the new Townshend duties as unconstitutional violations of the no-taxation-without-representation principle. Lord Hillsborough, the secretary of state of the new American Department, ordered the provincial House to revoke its circular letter. When the House refused, Governor Francis Bernard dissolved the assembly, with the predictable result of mob violence. Customs officials who were being attacked by Boston crowds could not do their jobs and therefore pleaded for military help. When it came in the form of a British warship arriving in Boston Harbor in June 1768, emboldened customs officials seized John Hancock's sloop *Liberty* for violating the trade laws. The seizure was done under authority of the hated writs of assistance. Given the wealthy Hancock's association with the colonial resistance, Crown officials intended the seizure to teach an "object lesson in royal authority." Instead, "Its effect . . . was to set off one of the fiercest riots in Boston's history."[44]

Customs searches of homes, seizures of sloops and of unwilling future sailors (impressment), pent-up demands for wider political participation, and mob violence thus mightily contributed to the fire that would later ignite the American Revolution. These forces eventually coalesced around resistance to "taxation without representation" as, in the view of leading modern historians, "the primary underlying cause of the American Revolution." That principle in turn came to be understood as a critical aspect of a broader commitment to the consent of the governed as legitimating the state, thus extending American complaints of flawed representation to matters beyond taxation. British search and seizure policies and practices were thus inextricably intertwined with conflicting and changing understandings of the meanings of political "representation" and associated, if implicit, notions of voice, autonomy, and inclusion.[45]

The Cracked Mirror of Representation

No Englishman denied that taxes could be imposed only on those represented in the taxing body. The dispute lay over whether representation could be "virtual" (the British position) or had to be "actual" (the American position).[46]

The eighteenth-century British electorate consisted of no more than one-sixth of the nation. Some electoral districts had few or even no voters, while others had thousands, and still others were controlled by a single landowner. Although radical reformers challenged this jumble, many Englishmen justified it by claiming that "each member of Parliament represented the whole British nation, and not just the particular locality he came from." This, then, was the theory of virtual representation: Parliament spoke for all Englishmen, even for those, like the colonists, who did not and could not vote in Parliamentary elections.[47]

The British argument was rooted in the idea of one indivisible location for the sovereignty of a nation, Parliament being that location. Parliament was the people's bulwark against the Crown's abuses and was to be trusted as the voice for all. By this logic, argued subcabinet official William Knox in 1769, if Parliament was supreme over the colonists in even one instance, then Americans are members "of the same community with the people of England." On the other hand, if Parliamentary authority over the colonists was denied in any particular, then their link to Great Britain must be dissolved, and "they are in a state of nature" with respect to their parent nation. But Parliament and colonial legislatures cannot simultaneously reign supreme.[48]

In the New World, by contrast, two out of three free eighteenth-century adult males composed the electorate. From early on, when new towns and counties were formed, they customarily elected new representatives to their provincial legislatures. "Actual representation," stressing a close connection between local voters and their representatives, characterized much of both the theory and practice of American political life. Challenges to these assumptions were not easily accepted.[49]

Virginia's experience was typical. There, the colonial assembly declared by statute in 1624 that only it had the power to tax its own inhabitants. In 1652, Virginia planters in an unrepresented county protested the imposition of a tax. Though not approved by the king, the Crown's attorney in England in 1674 endorsed, at Virginia's request, "the right of Virginians, as well other Englishmen, not to be taxed but by their consent, expressed by their representatives." In 1717, imposition of a royal postal fee produced a "great clamor" because the people of Virginia believed that no tax could be levied without the consent of their local legislature. When Virginia's governor in 1753 imposed a fee for the use of his seal on land patents, the assembly lectured him on his inability to deprive citizens "of the least of their property but by their own consent: Upon this excellent principle is our constitution founded." Each of the colonies shared similar histories. When, after the repeal of the Stamp Act, the British expressed their concept of unitary sovereignty in the Declaratory Act of 1766, which affirmed Parliament's authority to make laws governing the colonists "in all cases whatsoever," the British articulated a theory of political legitimacy that the colonists could not accept.[50]

The logic of the British position—that it is "impossible [that] there should be two independent legislatures in one and the same state"—forced Americans to choose between utter submission to Parliament or total independence. Although most Americans were reluctant to embrace true independence before the 1776 publication of Thomas Paine's hugely influential pamphlet *Common Sense*, which supported precisely that position, leading colonists nevertheless early on adopted views tending toward independence's ineluctable logic. "By 1774 the leading colonists, including Thomas Jefferson and John Adams, were arguing that only the separate American legislatures were sovereign in America." That meant that Parliament's word was not final in America, for "the colonies were connected to the empire only through the king." The colonists might accept Parliament's regulation of "external" commerce where necessary and where it served their mutual interests, but that would be a concession of prudence and choice, not sovereignty. Ultimately, with the ratification of the U.S. Constitution, Americans would craft a far more complex theory than the British one of unitary sovereignty. But the logic of that new theory, arguably vesting some aspects of sovereignty in both the individual states and in the federal government, but ultimately vesting true sovereignty in the People, further strengthened the American commitment to actual representation.[51]

The developing early American theories of actual representation required more, however, than that each significant locality have an elected representative to speak for it in the legislature. Rather, the theories focused also on the proper relationship between the electorate and its representatives, and on the whole point of having a legislature in the first place.[52]

One dominant strain in American thinking by 1776, and one still fervently espoused by the Anti-Federalist opponents to the Constitution during the ratification debates, stressed representatives' responsiveness and accountability to the local electorate. Responsiveness in turn required representatives who were both sympathetic to their constituents' feelings and versed in the local knowledge giving rise to those feelings. Sympathy and knowledge stemmed only from representatives who acted as society's "mirror." John Adams thus explained in 1776 that an assembly "should be in miniature an exact portrait of the people at large. It should think, feel, reason and act like them."[53] Theophilus Parsons echoed this sentiment in drafting the Essex County Resolutions in 1778:

> The rights of representation should be so equally and impartially distributed, that the representatives should have the same views, and interests with the people at large. They should think, feel, and act like them, and in fine, should be an exact miniature of their constituents. They should be . . . the whole body politic, with all its property, rights, and privileges, reduced to a smaller scale, with every part being diminished in just proportion.[54]

In the debate over the lower house of Congress (later to become the House of Representatives), James Wilson similarly declared that "[t]he Legislature ought to be the most exact transcript of the whole society," and George Mason agreed that representatives should reproduce their constituents' qualities "so much so, that even the diseases of the people should be represented—if not, how are they to be cured?"[55]

Mirror theory, combined with the need to mobilize an entire people for the Revolutionary War, "encouraged new constituencies and segments of the population to gain a political voice, whether by correcting existing inequities in apportionment or by inspiring calls for an enlarged suffrage." Mirror theory was also closely allied with the belief that the legislature's primary function was to restrain the exercise of arbitrary rule by the executive. A legislature reflective of the people would be a vigilant monitor of executive abuses, ever attendant to public complaint.[56]

Federalist supporters of the Constitution added a component to mirror ideology without jettisoning it: the ideal of deliberation. A representative system was required not merely as a poor but necessary substitute for popular meetings in a large polity. A republican system must promote deliberation. Via deliberation, "the public voice pronounced by the representatives of the people, will be more consonant to the public good than if pronounced by the people themselves convened for that purpose." Lawmakers must prove to be calmer and more prudent than a large gathering of citizens meeting en masse could ever be. "In all very numerous assemblies, of whatever characters composed," said James Madison in *Federalist No. 55*, "passion never fails to wrest the sceptre from reason. . . . Had every Athenian citizen been a Socrates, every Athenian assembly would still have been a mob." The small size of the House of Representatives relative to what some Anti-Federalists had proposed, the even smaller Senate with its then-indirect method for electing senators who would serve for longer terms than the members of the House, and numerous other features of the Constitution helped to promote such deliberation while balancing it with the democracy of a perhaps misty mirror.[57]

Ultimately, therefore, the use of general warrants, writs of assistance, and the like to promote collection of government levies sought to enforce an absurd system of virtual representation that came to define for the colonists the essence of tyranny. Fears of arbitrary and burdensome taxation by the proposed new federal government still burned brightly in American hearts during the debates over ratifying the Constitution and haunted the pages of Anti-Federalist literature. The Federalist strain's emphasis on deliberation, therefore, had to be defended also in terms that calmed fears of a new sort of taxation without representation, one "representative" in name but that would be ruled by an aristocratic elite in practice; the result was the uneasy fusion of mirror theory with the deliberative spirit in a complex constitutional scheme that sought to serve both goals.[58]

The Revolutionaries' assault on general warrants and writs as tools for muting the People's voice was not their only objection to unreasonable searches and seizures as antirepublican. Even if general warrants had been used for noble purposes, the process by which decisions were made in particular cases about whether and how to issue warrants was itself hopelessly corrupt, tied as it was to the degraded British parliamentary system.

Muzzling the People: The British Warrant Process

The hated writs of assistance were authorized by Parliament in 1662. The authorizing legislation empowered the Court of Exchequer to issue a writ to a customs officer, who could, with a constable or even the aid of any other nearby subject, enter "any House, shop, Cellar, Warehouse or Room or other Place and, in Case of Resistance, to break open Doors, Chests, Trunks, and other packages, there to seize" any uncustomed goods. Because the writ lasted for the life of the sovereign, it gave customs officers a "hunting license" to search for smugglers and smuggled goods.[59]

In 1696, Parliament extended 156 writs of assistance to the colonies. However, there was no Court of Exchequer in the colonies to enforce the writs. Massachusetts had purported, by statute of its provincial legislature, to have extended its own high court's jurisdiction to any matters within the jurisdiction of the Court of Exchequer, as had the copycat state of New Hampshire. Only in those two colonies, therefore, was there even the *possibility* of lawful enforcement of the writs.[60]

In 1767, Parliament corrected its oversight by passing the Townshend Acts, which imposed new or expanded customs duties or "external" taxes on the colonists in the wake of the Stamp Act's repeal. Beyond creating new taxes, the Townshend Acts also tellingly granted the highest court in each colony the power to issue writs of assistance to colonists. The Townshend Acts thus "expanded the controversy over writs of assistance from what had been a local dispute, centering mainly on Boston, to a continent-wide dispute spreading to all 13 colonies." As colonies other than Massachusetts and New Hampshire suddenly experienced the impact of the writs, mob activity roared back into life. At least twenty customs riots took place before the 1770 Boston Massacre, many in protest against the Townshend Acts. Mobs "liberated" seized goods, typically molested informants or low-level customs officials, and protected contraband items from seizure. Although Whig leaders again successfully promoted nonimportation agreements as an alternative to mob violence, broadened participation altered the nature of the movement, and mobs began operating as enforcers of the nonimportation agreements.[61]

Vocal crowds' visits to the homes of nonparticipants had "a more powerful Effect in reducing . . . such Culprits to Reason . . . than the most convincing Arguments that could be used." In Boston, nonsubscribers' signs, doors, and windows "were daub'd over in the Night time with every kind of Filth, and one of them particularly had his person treated in the same manner." In October 1769, Nathaniel Rogers grudgingly accepted nonimportation "from principles of self-preservation" after his house "had twice been 'besmeared' with dung."[62] A particularly powerful, relatively new form of humiliation now became widespread as well:

> [A]fter a tarring and feathering of a minor customs official on September 7, 1768, in Salem, Massachusetts, . . . the practice spread and became recognized as a specialty of American crowds. Within a few years, rioters employed tar and feathers throughout the colonies. Sometimes crowds varied their routine. One group of Bostonians tarred and feathered the horse of a merchant caught with imported goods in June 1770, and another coated a victim's house with excrement and a dose of feathers. Initially those tarred and feathered tended to be customs guards and others further down on the social scale. In 1775, crowds increasingly used tar and feathers, and once hostilities broke out even high born Tories became vulnerable to a fitting for a "New England Jacket."[63]

This violence had dramatic political implications. Nonimportation committees acted as investigator, judge, and jury, commandeering merchants' quarters, judging offenders, and administering punishments.[64]

Similar usurpations of state functions continued even after the Townshend duties were for the most part repealed. In 1774, Parliament's answer to the Boston Tea Party was passage of the "Coercive Acts," closing Boston's port until the destroyed tea was paid for, reorganizing Massachusetts government so that the upper house was now to be appointed by the royal governor rather than by the legislature, restricting town meetings, expanding the power to appoint sheriffs, allowing royal officials charged with capital crimes to be tried in England, giving the governor power to use private buildings for quartering troops, and appointing Thomas Gage, Commander in Chief of the British Army, as the new provincial governor. On September 5, 1774, the First Continental Congress convened, other colonists recognizing that what could happen to Massachusetts could become their fate as well. The Congress agreed to form a Continental Association to implement and enforce sweeping nonimportation and nonconsumption agreements for all the colonies. The Association would involve committees being chosen by all qualified voters to watch for violators, publish their names in gazettes, condemn them as "the enemies of American liberty," and "break off all dealings with him or her." These local committees "claimed a quasi-legitimate authority over all matters pertaining to political conduct."[65]

These committees thus strived to treat violators with "contempt." "Contempt" became understood in practice as violent ritual humiliation, again usually meaning tarring and feathering. These rituals fostered a sense of effective political involvement by common people. The pot of tar was often symbolically at the bottom end of a liberty pole. Even the many in the mob who could not vote could engage in "out-of-door politics"—"the caucuses, conventions, committees, and street mobs not officially sanctioned by law."[66] Even crude and sadistic violence had the sanction of moral authority:

> It was the Revolutionary generation that developed, intellectually, the majoritarian concept of popular sovereignty, and it was the Revolutionary generation that perfected techniques of violence to enforce popular sovereignty. . . . The idea of "the sovereignty of the people" gave an ideological and philosophical justification and an awesome dignity to the brutal physical abuse or killing of men that tarring and feathering, vigilantism, and lynching came to embody.[67]

The extension of the writs of assistance to all the colonies thus played a significant role in the forces leading up to the Revolution. It was critical, however, that the expanded jurisdiction of the writs was authorized by an unrepresentative British Parliament increasingly seen as lacking sovereign authority over America. Indeed, "Some writers revealed that their objection lay against a parliamentary empowerment [of general searches] rather than one by their own assemblies." Despite growing condemnation of general searches by intellectuals and even by the judiciary, the typical searches *actually authorized by colonial judges and legislatures* at the time were every bit as general as those under the writs of assistance.[68] The leading modern historian of the Fourth Amendment aptly summarized this state of affairs:

> Damning such searches under British auspices was one thing; renouncing them oneself was another matter.
>
> Although judicial resistance to the writs of assistance in 1769 was most intense in Connecticut, the colony's code of that year included an impost with general search warrants resembling those writs. The same conclusion applied to Pennsylvania. Had Allen, Trumbull, or any of Connecticut's newspaper essayists wished to attack general searches on principle alone, they need have looked no further than Pennsylvania and Connecticut, for local session laws and judicial search warrants had read like writs of assistance throughout the histories of those colonies.
>
> Only when promiscuous searches and seizures loomed from a foreign quarter and threatened political autonomy did local leaders proclaim the civil libertarian threat that they posed.[69]

One of the major American objections to the writs, therefore, was that their existence and content were determined by a legislative process in which the colonists had no voice. Lacking a voice in the formal machinery of the law, they found their voice through the expressive violence of mob action and the taking unto themselves of the powers usually vested in the law.

Importantly, however, the colonists did increasingly see that general searches or seizures were dangerous no matter how they were authorized. Furthermore, they ultimately drew an additional lesson from their experience under the writs: legislatures, not merely the executive, posed grave dangers to the right to be free from oppressive searches and seizures. By the time that the proposed Bill of Rights was debated in Congress, there was strong reason to believe that Americans' understanding of the common law was that it could not be a source for the power to conduct general searches. The former colonists' experience with Parliament may, however, explain their continuing zeal to condemn general warrants. The proposals ultimately leading to the Fourth Amendment would prohibit any future Congress from authorizing general searches. Customs imposts were likely to be a primary source of revenues for both the new state governments and the new national government, and customs search law was understood to be entirely a creature of statute. Furthermore, customs officers then had a unique motive to search aggressively: they were entitled to keep a significant portion of the value of any uncustomed goods that they seized. The fledgling Congress may therefore have been sorely tempted to empower customs officers with general search authority, which the officers would aggressively employ. One function of the Fourth Amendment would be to bar

Congress from giving in to that temptation. As James Madison argued in speaking to the First Congress upon the recommendation of the amendments that became the Bill of Rights, "they [the British] have gone no farther than to raise a barrier against the power of the Crown; the power of the Legislature is left altogether indefinite." After ratification of the Fourth Amendment, that would no longer be the case.[70]

Remember that neither the colonists nor the later citizens of the newly independent nation assumed that searches could never be authorized. They objected, however, not only to warrant authority's roots in an unrepresentative legislature but also to warrants that were general rather than specific in nature. One of the reasons for objection to *general* warrants but not to specific ones also involved yet a different sort of concern related to expressive political violence: the insult involved in searches and seizures by low-status officers, which contravened principles of individualized justice.

Insult

A Man's Castle, or The Liberty of the Kingdom

All searches and seizures involve an element of insult to the person being searched. Before 1760, initial colonial reaction to general searches focused on the violence and sense of "inappropriateness" imposed on those who experienced them rather than on the promiscuous nature of the warrants themselves. The insult was all that much greater when, as was so often true, the searches were of a home and violative of family life. The sanctity of the home had long been considered a central tenet of British liberty.[71] William Pitt's classic statement expresses the zeal with which the British romanticized this principle:

> The poorest man may, in his cottage, bid defiance to all the forces of the Crown. It may be frail; its roof may shake; the wind may blow through it; the storm may enter; the rain may enter; but the King of England may not enter; all his forces dare not cross the threshold of the ruined tenement.[72]

The common law, as Americans came to understand it, did not therefore authorize warrantless searches of homes. Americans came to react with outrage to Parliament's statutory authorization of home searches by general warrants and writs. The colonists worried that customs agents might "break the rights of domicil," "ransack houses," and "enter private cabinets" or "secret repositories." John Dickinson, in his *Letters from a Farmer in Pennsylvania*, a pamphlet widely circulated throughout the colonies, similarly condemned general warrants as contrary to the adage that a man's home is his castle, though Dickinson did not recommend specific warrants or warrantless searches as superior alternatives. Newspapers in the largest states reprinted the tirade of "A Son of Liberty," "who depicted federal officers dragging people off to prison after brutal confiscations that shocked 'the most delicate part of our families.' " In one of the Wilkesite cases, *Huckle v. Money,* Chief Justice Pratt declared that entering a man's house "by virtue of a nameless warrant" to procure evidence is a law "under which no Englishman would wish to live an hour." When defendants requested a new trial, arguing that a six-hour detention of a mere printer could not justify the size of the damages awarded, Pratt explained that the injury was one done to the political system itself: "The small injury done to the plaintiff, or the inconsiderableness of his station and rank in life did not appear to the jury in that striking light which the great point of the law touching the liberty of the subject appeared to them at the trial." The general warrant's issuance, Pratt continued, violated Magna Carta, "attempting to destroy the liberty of the kingdom," an affront for which the jury "have done right in giving exemplary damages." These sorts of insults could be tolerated only for a good enough reason, and the whims and suspicions of officers did not fit the bill.[73]

Offensive Discretion and Class Prejudice

Indeed, the nonspecific nature of general warrants amplified the insults done by invading homes and using violence and terror. General warrants definitionally permitted *arbitrary* invasions, ones not adequately justified by evidence of specific wrongdoing by named persons at named locations. Vesting such discretionary authority in "subordinate" executing officers was anathema to Framing-era lawyers and leading intellectuals in the mother county. Sir Edward Coke labeled unspecific arrest warrants "against reason." Sergeant William Hawkins, perhaps the eighteenth century's leading authority on criminal procedure, challenged the underlying logic of general warrants because "it would be extremely hard to leave it to the discretion of a common Officer to arrest what Persons, and search what Houses he thinks fit." Lord Mansfield in a 1765 Wilkesite case condemned general warrants because it was "not fit" for "an officer to exercise *any* judgment as to whom to arrest or where to search." Blackstone agreed, warning of the unwisdom of leaving it to officers to judge whom to arrest.[74]

But indignation at the arbitrariness of general searches was supplemented by class prejudices, which subtly melded into condescension toward the role of being a customs officer or king's messenger. Officers were generally of low social status, especially relative to the high status and wealth of magistrates. Framing-era sentiments have recently been described by legal scholar Thomas Davies as expressing "outright disdain for the character and judgment of ordinary officers." "It was disagreeable enough," says Davies, "for an elite or middle-class householder to have to open his house to a search in response to a command from a high status magistrate acting under a judicial commission." It was, however, a "gross insult to the householder's status as a 'free man' to be bossed about by an ordinary officer who was likely drawn from an inferior class."[75] The widely publicized remarks of the Boston town meeting of 1772 made the point vividly:

> Thus our houses and even our bed chambers, are exposed to be ransacked, our boxes, chests, and trunks broke open, ravaged and plundered by wretches, whom no prudent man would venture to employ even as menial servants; whenever they are pleased to say they suspect there are in the house wares . . . for which the dutys have not been paid. . . . Those Officers may under colour of law and the cloak of a general warrant . . . destroy [men's] . . . securities, carry off their property, and with little danger to themselves commit the most horred murders.[76]

Blackstone agreed that "considering what manner of men are for the most part put upon these offices, it is perhaps very well that they are generally kept in ignorance" of the full extent of their authority. Chief Justice Pratt too complained that general warrants wrongly delegated the decision to search to the king's messengers, who were of "even the lowest of the people." Derogatory descriptions of lower-class officers exercising delegated search authority pursuant to general writs of assistance were a consistent colonial theme in the war against those writs. Such officers were described as "odious harpies," "servants," "villains", "dregs," "most despicable wretches," and "ruffians." Anti-Federalists were later similarly contemptuous of those who would likely be hired as federal revenue officers under the proposed new federal Constitution. Likewise, residents of Boston, in the dispute over the Excise Act of 1754, had earlier protested that the act would permit "a petty Officer to come into a Gentleman's House, and with an Air of Authority, demand an Account upon Oath of the Liquor he has drank in his Family for the year past."[77]

Like a "Servant of Servants"

The depth of the sense of insult the colonists experienced becomes especially clear in their repeated use of slavery as a metaphor. Otis complained that general writs of assistance could be used not only by commissioned customs collectors and their deputies but also by their "menial servants," who are "allowed to lord it over us—What is this, but to have the curse of Canaan with a witness on us, to be the servant of servants, the most despicable of God's creation." The reference to "Canaan's curse" evoked a belief held by some colonists that the descendants of the biblical Canaan were cursed to live as slaves

for Canaan's sin of not averting his eyes from his father's naked, liquor-besot-
ted body. But of greater significance is that the colonists also metaphorically
described themselves, the customs officers' targets, as slaves. Thus Otis, in his
arguments against reissuing the writs of assistance, condemned them as "instruments of slavery" because based on "bare suspicion."[78] Historian William
Cuddihy summed up the colonists' sentiments this way:

> Americans began to reject the general warrant in the 1760's for the same rea-
> sons that Englishmen of earlier centuries had abnegated methods of search
> and seizure: violence, politics, and a sudden increase in the accustomed types
> of search [and] seizure. The colonists became champions of the specific war-
> rant not because it was specific but because *they associated the general warrant
> with violent British efforts to subjugate them politically.* . . . The emergence of the
> specific warrant in America was a byproduct of America's political contest
> with Britain.[79]

If the specific warrant started out as a "byproduct" of the contest with Great
Britain, specificity over time became of independent significance. The Anti-
Federalists, for example, railed against ratification of the original Constitution in part because it lacked express protection against general warrants. The
Fourth Amendment's ultimate ratification as part of the Bill of Rights reflected
this concern that even general warrants issued from our "own" institutions—
apart from the struggle with Great Britain—were condemnable. Nevertheless,
my immediate concern here is the significance of the colonists' repeated allusions to "slavery" and cognate images like "subjugation."[80]

Slavery was central to eighteenth-century political discourse as the absolute
political evil. Revolutionaries proclaimed themselves willing to die rather than
to submit to enslavement by the British; the Founding generation did not
mean *chattel* slavery, however, instead understanding "slavery" as "the absence
of political liberty for a corporate body and loss of economic independence for
the individual." Underlying these notions was a more fundamental one: "the
inability or unwillingness to be self-governing, or more specifically, the inability to control bodily lusts and passions, above all selfishness." The evil in all
three of these understandings of slavery lay in the dishonor of being subjected
to another's will rather than to the will of God or the laws of nature. "Liberty,"
the opposite of slavery, was distinguished from licentiousness, obedience to the
"passions" or the animal side of human nature. In religious terms, license was
but enslavement to Satan. True liberty required voluntarily chosen subjection
to nature's law or God's law via the faculty of human reason. It was, however,
only in a community of reciprocal obligation that each member could best
observe the collective understanding of higher law.[81]

Community and individual liberty were, therefore, inseparably linked. But liberty for the corporate body "is impossible unless all the people share in the making of the laws and give their consent freely." Otherwise, they are "the subjects of absolute government [and] are slaves." Citizens who lacked a say in how the community shaped itself and its individual members were enslaved by definition. Jonathan Mayhew, the pastor of Boston's West Church, captured this sentiment when he described the British program of taxation as threatening Americans "with perpetual bondage and slavery" because when "labor and industry may be lawfully taken" without consent, subjects are "really slaves to all intents and purposes."[82]

Economic dependence on another individual by the adult male head of a household was also feared, for, said Thomas Jefferson, it fosters "subservience and venality, suffocates the germ of virtue, and prepares fit tools for the design of ambition." The danger for the individual was being subjected "to the arbitrary will and pleasure of another." Arbitrariness meant acting according to whim or license rather than in rationally defensible ways, destroying the sovereignty that was the essence of liberty.[83]

A "tyrant" was "a self-indulgent man enslaved to his own licentious lusts and passions." Because he lacked the self-government that necessarily required obedience to the "controlling confines of community and the natural order that it was meant to reflect," the tyrant in a sense stood outside the community and thus outside its circle of reciprocal obligation. Those bowing to a tyrant's rule were also slaves because they became subject to his arbitrary power. Communities entire could become enslaved when they too abandoned a corporate life that limited arbitrary rule and behavior. For many, avoiding such subjection was a spiritual mandate, essential to avoiding deformed souls estranged from the Supreme Being or, for the rationalists, from Nature's God. The Revolutionaries would not, therefore, have seen George Washington's defense of resistance to Britain as being hyperbolic when he said that it was essential to avoid becoming "tame and abject slaves," like the Africans they ruled "over with such arbitrary sway." Another patriot warned against "the unrestrained LICENTIOUSNESS of any one Person, in any one Nation," meaning "the universal Slavery of that Nation."[84]

Most Americans of the time accepted chattel slavery, few doubting its propriety. Africans were portrayed "as natural slaves, an idea to which their putative acceptance of their bondage bore witness, and thus their enslavement was recognized as an absolute embodiment of public and private dependence, dishonor, and sinfulness." Chattel slaves were, therefore, outside the political community and thus beyond the reach of the rhetoric of political slavery and resistance to the king's arbitrary rule.[85]

References by the Founding generation to enslavement by general warrants and by writs of assistance must therefore be placed in the larger context of opposition to political slavery. General searches were a tool of arbitrary rule rather than of reason and consensual self-government. General warrants further silenced the "politically voiceless." Bowing to the authority of such warrants meant accepting treatment as strangers unworthy of membership in a political community of reason. General searches were therefore supremely insulting, for they reduced, or at least tried to reduce, free men to a status equivalent to that of the dishonored chattel slave.

Educating for Insult

Finally, general searches were implicitly seen as insulting because they violated principles of individualized justice. Arbitrary decisions by executing officers could be limited by warrants specifying when, where, how, and whom they could search and seize. Yet the growing understanding of what made a warrant specific required more. The increasingly widespread definition of a "special warrant" was one that was both particular *and* based on adequate individualized evidence that a particular person had committed a criminal act or that the evidence or fruits of that act were in a particular location. That principle would limit action by *all* branches of government, including the judiciary. Indeed, the prohibition against arbitrariness was a rejection of action without good reason. For searches and seizures, good reason generally meant evidentiary support for individualized suspicion in the form of probable cause. Probable cause gave meat to individualized justice's meaning, culminating in the goal of educating the People to view unparticularized assessments based on weak evidence as insulting to their status as individual citizens and to the People as a whole.[86]

Coke thus condemned general warrants based on "mere surmise." Hale rejected nonspecific theft warrants where the magistrate failed to examine the informant under oath to determine whether good grounds for suspicion existed. Although general searches nevertheless long pervaded colonial law and practice (including warrant manuals addressed to justices of the peace), the steady trend, particularly after the start of the American Revolution, was toward warrant specificity. The Fourth Amendment ultimately embodied therefore a repudiation rather than a celebration of colonial search and seizure precedent.[87]

The excise and impost legislation of 1756 in Massachusetts thus contained an element of probable cause, requiring informants to swear under oath what in fact happened and where and that they had "just cause" so to swear, though no independent judicial assessment of the truth or accuracy of these statements was mandated. By 1762, a Massachusetts bill required all search warrants to be as specific as those required by the 1756 excise legislation. James Otis's 1755 argument against reissuing writs of assistance had also included a ringing defense of special or specific warrants based upon the applicant's oath, and he denounced as invalid any act of Parliament authorizing warrants based on a lesser standard; Otis's argument had a powerful impact on the evolving concepts of evidentiary specificity, reflected in Massachusetts's 1762 embrace of specific warrants and in mob action protesting enforcement of the writs. Like Massachusetts, the general, if glacial, drift throughout the colonies from 1761 to 1766 was toward increasing reliance on special warrants, the start of recommendations for such warrants appearing in justice-of-the-peace manuals, and in a rhetorical commitment to specificity. Nevertheless, most local judges in practice frequently relied on general warrants. Although the Declaration of Independence did not expressly address search and seizure practices, it did spur clearer thinking about American ideals, inspiring the new state constitutions, many of which contained the first bills of rights against *all* branches of government, and showing a strong turning toward warrant specificity.[88]

The first such bill of rights, Virginia's Declaration of Rights, adopted on the eve of the Declaration of Independence, urged that general warrants ought not be granted. For arrests, warrants must be "supported by evidence" and particularly describe the suspect. For searches, probable cause was required showing that a crime had been committed, though not yet requiring a proven link to the place to be searched or specificity regarding what may be seized, nor need the warrant have been based on a sworn statement. North Carolina substantially followed Virginia, while Pennsylvania required a particularized description for *all* warrants and an oath affording sufficient supporting foundation, a model later followed by Vermont. Delaware declared general warrants illegal (thus, presumably void) rather than saying that they "ought" not be granted, and Maryland followed suit. Article XIV of the Massachusetts Declaration of Rights, written by John Adams, Otis's protégé on these matters, declared a right to be "secure" from all "unreasonable" searches and seizures and barred issuing warrants where not supported by oath listing the cause or foundation of suspicion. New Hampshire admiringly copied the Massachusetts model.[89]

During the Revolutionary War years these principles were, however, often honored in the breach, search and seizure being viewed as a legitimate means of fighting the enemy and its sympathizers. Anyone who dared not take an oath of allegiance might face baseless searches, as did Quakers who refused loyalty oaths in Pennsylvania, where forty people were arrested and ordered deported to Virginia, where they were detained until the following year. Matters improved between the war's end and the Constitution's ratification, with three states (Massachusetts, Rhode Island, and New Jersey) enacting legislation requiring specific warrants. A Connecticut court, in *Frisbie v. Butler,* voided general warrants, noting the obligation of the justice of the peace to issue particular warrants only where he "judge[s] there is reason to suspect" and limiting arrests to those persons actually found with stolen goods; that decision was to be made by an independent magistrate. Yet five states still used general warrants to enforce impost laws, with Maryland doing so to enforce excise laws and regulate bakers despite Maryland's written prohibition against general warrants.

Although a significant number of states continued using general warrants, even in those states specific warrants were becoming more common, the trend toward specificity being especially pronounced in Virginia, though belated.[90]

During the ratification debates and the hubbub about the lack of a Bill of Rights, the Anti-Federalists especially led a charge against general searches. Virginia's Richard Henry Lee, as a member of Congress, had proposed a Bill of Rights, in the hope of ruining the ratification process, that included a search and seizure provision based on the 1780 Massachusetts constitution. In his well-respected *Federal Farmer Letters,* described by some as "the best of the Anti-Federalist tracts," Lee wrote a letter listing search and seizure as a right whose absence was definitively fatal to ratification's cause. Only a search based on an informant's testimony under oath was trustworthy. Similar demands for constitutionalizing specific warrant mandates came from the Anti-Federalist Centinel, the Dissent of the Pennsylvania ratifying convention, Brutus, A Son of Liberty, Patrick Henry, and others. Virginia's convention ratified the Constitution but with recommendations to the First Congress, including passage of a guarantee that every free person be "secure from all unreasonable searches and seizures" and that warrants be based on "legal and sufficient cause." That recommendation issued from a committee that included James Madison, who would later draft the proposal that, in somewhat modified form, became the Fourth Amendment. The conventions of North Carolina, New York, and Rhode Island ratified the Constitution with similar recommendations for the addition of a search and seizure provision. The Fourth Amendment itself, of course, mandates that warrants issue only upon probable cause and a particular description of the places to be searched and the persons or things to be seized.[91]

Several weeks before Congress reported the Bill of Rights for consideration by the states, Congress enacted the 1789 Collections Act permitting general, warrantless searches of ships but mandating special warrants under oath stating the justifying cause for searches on land for suspected concealed, uncustomed goods, albeit without the magistrate's independent judgment of the adequacy of that suspicion. In March 1791, however, after the nine states needed for ratification of the Fourth Amendment had done so, Congress enacted a law explicitly empowering magistrates to make independent probable-cause decisions, issuing specific warrants only upon "reasonable cause of suspicion" made to "the satisfaction of such judge . . . and sworn under oath." Although there is some disagreement over the significance of this change, there is ample support for the view of leading historians that the 1791 congressional legislation's emphasis on independent judicial assessments of probable cause demonstrated the "swift liberalization" of search and seizure laws effected by the Fourth Amendment.[92]

Madison, in jettisoning his original opposition to a bill of rights, came to emphasize that such a bill could be more than a mere "parchment barrier" against majority tyranny. For Madison, such a bill would educate the people, thus helping to reduce their desire to oppress minorities in the first place. Virginia's Richard Henry Lee and Massachusetts's James Winthrop made similar arguments. Madison specifically feared that Congress might come to understand the Necessary and Proper Clause to authorize the use of general warrants as a means for enforcing its delegated power to raise revenue. The Fourth Amendment would stand as an obstacle to the majority of the People's representatives so abusing their delegated powers, whether on their own initiative or at the bidding of most of the People. So understood, the Fourth Amendment can be seen as serving yet a final expressive function: educating the People in the necessity for individualized justice based on adequate evidence of particular wrongdoing and on the need to restrain all three branches of government, as well as the People themselves, from exercising arbitrary power over others' lives, privacy, property, and locomotion. For the state to treat any person as less than a unique individual entitled to be free from governmental intrusions absent significant evidence of his wrongdoing violates the terms of the American social contract. Such treatment is yet another way to render the suffering individual less than an equal part of the whole, to exclude him or her from freedom's prerequisite to both living a meaningful life and participating effectively in the realm of the political.[93]

3   The Quantity and Quality of Evidence

If the Fourth Amendment embraces individualized justice, how much evidence is necessary to support a particularized showing of suspicion, and what must be the quality of that evidence? Relatedly, does the principle extend to warrantless searches and seizures, and are there any exceptions to the individualized justice principle?

Probable Cause and Warrants

Answering these questions begins with recounting the historical understanding of "probable cause."

When warrants are involved, the Fourth Amendment does purport to answer the first of these questions: probable cause is required before a warrant may issue. But probable cause is nowhere defined. The dilemma facing the criminal justice system in the development of probable cause was to "find a level of probability that was neither so low that individuals would not be damaged and resources entailed in trying the innocent would not be wasted nor so high that pretrial itself became a trial."[1]

The resolution of this dilemma began in an unlikely place: the legal tradition of Continental Europe. The ecclesiastical courts of Christendom, administering a Romano-canon inquisition process, left generally unacknowledged imprints on English evidentiary pretrial criminal procedure. That inquisition process permitted a suspect's detention, and the initiation of criminal proceedings against him, on "common fame." Common fame required a belief, by those persons who should know, that certain facts were true. That that belief might later be recognized to have been mistaken was irrelevant. Fame alone was insufficient, however, to justify either torture or a conviction. In serious criminal cases, only the testimony of "two unimpeachable witnesses" or a confession would suffice for conviction, with circumstantial evidence initially rejected as inferior. Because two good eyewitnesses were often hard to come by, as were voluntary confessions, torture to obtain the necessary incriminating statement became seen as necessary. But torture was permissible only if signs or "indicia" of guilt "were available in sufficient quality and quantity." Drawing on classical Greco-Roman rhetoricians, the inquisitors developed a learned literature of indicia justifying torture and, over time, created a role for circumstantial evidence among the relevant indicia for important classes of cases.[2]

These Romano-canon inquisitorial or "civil" law principles and procedures were taught at universities in England, and there were many civilians on the British Isles. Leading common-law thinkers like Francis Bacon and Matthew Hale studied the civil-law tradition, and by the early 1700s comparative analyses of civil law were becoming more accepted in the English tradition. Civil-law concepts like "common fame" thus apparently came to influence the developing English law of criminal procedure, particularly the closely related concepts of "reasonable" or "probable" cause and of "suspicion."[3]

As early as 1275 AD, the Act of Edward I declared that no person or community could be fined "without reasonable cause and according to the quality of his trespass." Similar holdings followed in English criminal cases, most famously the 1326 King's Bench ruling that the cause for Henry of Willingborough's arrest "seems insufficient." Forty years later, the King's Council in *Ughtred v. Musgrave,* held that a Yorkshire sheriff's arrest of reputed highway robbers was unjustifiable "by the law of the land" because it was based only on "common cry and scandal." Each of these events occurred well before the advent of warrants, much less specific warrants, thus suggesting that probable-cause-like ideas developed independently from the warrant concept. Warrants might one day require probable cause, but the probable-cause notion of individualized suspicion supported by quality evidence had roots in a warrantless world.[4]

As justices of the peace gradually acquired authority to issue preindictment arrest warrants, however, "suspicion" of committing a felony became the controlling standard. The sixteenth-century rise of printed handbooks for justices of the peace included a list of the "causes of suspicion" that is "virtually the same as the *indicia* that on the Continent served to determine if a suspect should be examined under torture."[5] A typical list

> included the age, sex, education, parentage, character, associates, and habitual behavior of the suspect, as well as his ability to commit the crime, his whereabouts at the time of the crime, the presence of witnesses and/or signs (for example, blood) that engender suspicion.[6]

The most influential seventeenth-century handbook in both England and America on this subject was Michael Dalton's *Countrey Justice*. Dalton largely adhered to traditional notions under which arrests were expected to be made by private individuals without warrants, though that role was severely contracting with the rise of the warrant-issuing authority of the justices of the peace. "There must be some just cause, or some lawful and just suspicion at the least," wrote Dalton, for a private person to make an arrest. He can do so "when he knoweth or seeth [another] to have committed a . . . felony and may deliver him to the Constable." But persons other than eyewitnesses can make felony arrests of "suspicious persons that be of evil fame," so long as the felony had actually been committed and the one making the arrest himself held the suspicion. He further had to allege "some special matter" to prove his actual suspicion. Dalton also wrote that sheriffs, bailiffs, constables, and justices of the peace who have suspicion can make arrests without warrants whenever a private person had authority to do so. But he found confusion concerning when, if at all, justices of the peace could issue preindictment arrest warrants, doing little to clarify the confusion, though the 1618 edition provided the first extant prototype for a general warrant.[7]

Handbooks often lagged behind changes in legal practice. For example, handbooks still mandated personal suspicion by the person doing the arrest long after that rule had changed. Somewhere during the sixteenth and seventeenth centuries the practice of citizen arrest became largely replaced by the estimation by justices of the peace of the validity of informants' complaints, though the handbooks often said otherwise. Coke opposed any change from tradition in this area, railing against the issuing by a justice of the peace of an arrest warrant based merely on a private citizen's suspicion.[8]

Sir Matthew Hale, however, in his eighteenth-century *History of the Pleas of the Crown*, defended the new view. Hale critiqued Coke's position: "The law is not so, and the constant practice in all places hath obtained against it, and it would be pernicious to the Kingdom if it should be as he delivers it, for malefactors would escape unexamined and undiscovered, for a man may have a probable and strong presumption of the guilt of a person, whom yet he cannot positive swear to be guilty." Said Hale, if a complainant, "A," swore that a felony had been committed and that he suspected that it was done by "B," who "shows probable cause of suspicion, the justice may grant his warrant to apprehend B" for examination. The magistrate, Hale argued, was "a competent judge of the probabilities offered to him of such suspicion."[9]

Hale's statement eventually made the probable-cause concept prominent, attaching it to the notion of suspicion, a connection that later generations deemphasized. Hale does not recite a complete list of the causes of suspicion but refers readers to Dalton's work, which did contain a by-then-familiar list that built on the rhetorical and Romano-canon approaches.[10]

Hale's probable-cause analysis was apparently unknown to his contemporaries and did not initially have a significant impact on the handbook tradition. Hawkins's 1716 *Treatise of the Pleas of the Crown* did, however, draw heavily on Hale. Hawkins's treatment differed from earlier ones also by moving his discussion of the causes of suspicion from his section on examination to the one on arrest. His treatment thereafter became "a standard part of the arrest canon of the English and the American handbook tradition." Hawkins included keeping company with known offenders, associating with those of scandalous reputation, and being a vagrant as among the causes of suspicion. Circumstantial evidence of certain types mattered too, such as behavior, like flight, that "betrays a consciousness of guilt"; being found with a "bloody sword in hand"; leaving the house of a murder victim; and possessing stolen property. Hawkins recognized that the power of the justice of the peace to issue preindictment warrants based on a complainant's report "is now become a law." Warrants may not be granted "groundlessly and maliciously, without such a probable Cause, as might induce a candid and impartial person to suspect the Party to be Guilty." Hawkins thus recognized both the concept of probable cause as one based on credible evidence of facts giving rise to suspicion and the need for evaluation of that evidence by "a candid and impartial evaluator."[11]

Richard Burns's handbook, the most influential of the eighteenth century, and the many English and American handbooks modeled on Burns's effort, followed Hawkins's approach. Blackstone followed Hawkins too by later recognizing "that both private persons and the constable might arrest on probable suspicion" and that "the justice may issue an arrest warrant, though the suspicion originated in the person who prays the warrant because the justice was competent to judge the probability of the suspicion."[12]

Although the early "common law" on which the modern justice system is based was often a diverse and conflicting set of precedents, treatises, and practices, certain American trends concerning probable cause were discernible by the 1760s. The Sugar Act of 1764 began to focus colonists' attention on concepts related to probable cause. Section 46 of that act barred shipowners' suing customs officers who seized vessels if the judge *retrospectively* found probable cause for the seizure. That rendered customs officers who met this test immune from liability even when a shipowner proved his innocence and suffered ruinous damages. Later, the movement toward specific warrants often embraced probable-cause-like ideas as definitional to the meaning of "specificity." Massachusetts notably banned unreasonable searches and seizures, offering as an example a warrant lacking "cause or foundation." Massachusetts's 1780 constitution further required warrants to comply with the "formalities of law," probably meaning specific warrants as they had been understood in Massachusetts for many years—an understanding likely including proto-probable-cause ideas.

The state constitutions did not, however, use the term "probable cause," likely reflecting a common-law insistence on an even higher standard, although the term "probable cause" was used by Americans in important search and seizure disputes with the British. By 1789, the Framers had likely come to understand the term "probable" in "probable cause" to mean "more likely than not." Moreover, the colonists by then understood probable-cause-like concepts to include important guarantees of a sufficiently trustworthy evidentiary basis.[13] These guarantees were at least threefold:

1. *Personal Knowledge*: By contrast with modern probable cause, warrants could not be issued on the basis of confidential informants. The complainant had to be identified and have personal knowledge of the circumstances establishing probable cause.[14]
2. *Oath and Accountability*: For an arrest warrant, the complainant had to swear under oath both that a crime had in fact occurred and that he had probable cause of suspicion concerning the perpetrator's identity. For a search warrant for stolen goods, he had to swear that the goods were in fact stolen and that he had probable cause of suspicion as to the location of the stolen property. If the alleged stolen property or contraband were not found, the complainant was liable for trespass. Even an officer swearing out a search warrant in an ultimately fruitless endeavor to locate untaxed goods was so liable. An officer remained immune from liability only if he performed the purely "ministerial" act of executing a specific warrant sworn by another person as the complainant.[15]
3. *Independent Assessment*: A magistrate or justice of the peace was a man of stature expected independently to assess the adequacy of the grounds for probable cause.[16]

These sorts of trustworthiness guarantees are similar in spirit to, though arguably more muscular than, those at work in the modern probable-cause concept.[17]

The Fourth Amendment as ratified, and in its form as originally proposed by Madison, loosened common-law search and seizure standards by requiring only probable cause for warrants. Proof that a felony offense had "in fact" happened or that goods to be found at a particular location were "in fact" stolen was no longer required. During ratification, Anti-Federalists complained bitterly about this watering down of common-law standards. Madison may have innovated by adopting the English customs search standard requiring only probable cause given that customs collections would be the likely primary source of the new government's revenue. What matters most, however, is that probable cause required specific, trustworthy information to make real the implicit aspiration toward individualized justice.[18]

Warrantless Searches and the Common Law

Pointedly, the text of the Fourth Amendment is silent regarding whether probable cause is required for warrantless searches. The meaning of that silence is tied up with a larger, lively, and often technical debate. On one side of the debate are those who argue that the sole specific concern in the minds of the Fourth Amendment's Framers and ratifiers was prohibiting legislative authorization of general warrants for customs searches, especially of the home. The broad requirement that all searches and seizures must be "reasonable" is thus but an emphatic way of introducing the Warrant Clause's prohibition against general warrants and has no independent significance. On the other side of the debate are those contending that the "reasonableness" clause was most sensibly understood at the Framing to mean what it means today: "contrary to sound judgment, inappropriate, excessive." I do not think it necessary to take sides in this debate (though I do find the latter view more convincing) for several reasons.[19]

First, the leading advocate for the view that the Framers understood the Fourth Amendment as being solely about general warrants of certain sorts does *not* argue that other aspects of search and seizure law were meant to be entirely unregulated. To the contrary, he argues that many relevant common-law limitations were considered relatively noncontroversial and subsumed under the concept of "due process." The Fourth Amendment was needed to address a far more controversial aspect of criminal procedure. For example, he maintains that common-law arrest standards were understood as constitutionalized by the Fifth Amendment Due Process Clause, yet these standards did require probable cause and more for warrantless arrests. The Supreme Court is highly unlikely to overturn long precedent treating nearly all search and seizure questions under the Fourth Amendment, and it is unclear, in any event, whether parceling out search and seizure regulatory responsibility between the Fourth Amendment and the Due Process Clauses would (or should) effect any real change in method or doctrine, at least in the sense that the ultimate result would still be constitutional regulation of both with-warrant and many warrantless searches and seizures.[20]

Second, this same advocate for the narrow interpretation of the Framers' original understanding acknowledges that it is hard for courts accurately to divine that understanding for many individual issues, which leaves courts relatively helpless in addressing modern concerns like technological searches, which might undermine important values in a world where policing has altered dramatically, and which "would subvert the larger purpose for which the Framers adopted the text: namely to curb the exercise of discretionary authority by officers." Framers' intentions can be understood at varying levels of generality, and although this author concedes that choosing a higher level of abstraction creates its own problems, "the fact that we now face issues the Framers never anticipated may leave us little choice but to treat the constitutional text as expressions of broad principles rather than as specific solutions to specific historical threats." The Framers' history ultimately matters most when revealing the values that originally animated adoption of the amendment and when put in the context of how and why criminal justice institutions and needs and Fourth Amendment doctrine changed. The real value of examining the Framing-era history is to "displace fictional originalist distractions and allow us to refocus attention on the critical question of what a 'right to be secure' *should* mean." That history shows that the Founding generation had an abiding concern with individualized determinations of suspicion based on significantly trustworthy evidence of wrongdoing by a particular person or at a particular location, including in important instances for which warrants were not required. Although the Fourth Amendment may not today necessarily be read as mandating probable cause for all warrantless searches and seizures, the concerns underlying the amendment caution against too easily reducing or dispensing with particularized proofs limiting arbitrary discretion.[21]

Third, probable cause was on the lips of Americans in a pair of important search and seizure cases in the contest with Great Britain; one member of that pair involved a warrantless action, and the other was treated as effectively warrantless: the seizures of the sloops *Liberty* and *Active*. Within one year of the Sugar Act's passage, customs agents and navy personnel seized ships owned by two wealthy merchants, South Carolina's Henry Laurens and Massachusetts's John Hancock. In the Laurens case, South Carolina's Admiralty Court used an after-the-fact probable-cause decree to protect customs officers from liability for a seizure that, in the colonists' view, had been "accomplished without sound reason." John Hancock's sloop *Liberty* was seized under a writ of assistance, allegedly for importing Madeira wines without paying the necessary duties. The Boston town meeting, in a report authored by James Otis, condemned the seizure for being done without probable cause. Riots resulted from the seizure, as Laurens and Hancock "Organized loud and effective political protests over the wrongful seizure of their vessels" with newspaper coverage of the incidents saturating the colonial press. After the *Liberty* was declared forfeit by the Admiralty Court, the Collector of Boston bought it for use as a coast guard. "Her existence in that capacity was short-lived. In 1769, a Newport mob, provoked by her seizures of vessels on unfounded suspicions and by the crew's insolence, scuttled and burned the ship." The disputes over the warrantless *Active* and *Liberty* seizures injected the probable-cause principle "into the American legal vocabulary as a nebulous understanding that property could not be seized without substantial reason." The point is not so much that the definition of probable cause was uncontested (it arguably was) or clear (it arguably was not), nor that the term "probable cause" necessarily meant precisely the same thing in warrantless versus with-warrant searches or that it meant the same thing to the plebeian as to the elite. Rather, what matters is the recognition that seizures that are particularized and nonarbitrary, based on sound evidence and sound reasons, were often desirable even when unsupported by a warrant.[22]

Fourth, although some common tendencies could debatably be found in the common law, it was, as James Madison would describe it in the postratification era, "not the same in any two of the Colonies" and "never was, nor by any fair construction ever can be, deemed a law for the American people as one community." For Madison, to find adoption of the common law implicit in the Constitution would further mean that "the whole code, with all its incongruities, barbarisms, and bloody maxims, would be inviolably saddled on the good people of the United States."[23]

Not everyone in the early republic agreed. The Revolutionary generation revered the common law and claimed to be defending, while simultaneously rejecting, aspects of it associated with the degenerate British political system. Justice Joseph Story, in his *Commentaries*, specifically declared the Fourth Amendment "little more than the affirmance of a great constitutional doctrine of the common law." But even if Story was right, that did not mean that the Constitution had rendered the early common law "frozen in amber." To the contrary, the Fourth Amendment at least was a provision that "broke with tradition rather than hallowing it." Many Americans shared a "legal naturalism," rejecting English common law while simultaneously invoking their own understandings of aspects of it and its leading thinkers. Massachusetts, the first state to adopt a constitutional provision barring "unreasonable searches and seizures," had notably by statute abolished the common law as a basis for search and seizure as early as 1641. Likewise during the state-level ratification debates over the proposed federal Constitution, calls were made for an amendment restraining searches "within proper bounds" or forbidding all "unreasonable searches and seizures" rather than all searches and seizures contrary to common law or current state law. This language suggested an embrace more of process and principle than rigid rules. Indeed, the colonists were influenced by Lockean liberalism and by republican virtue theory as much as by the common law. Yet rights, as Locke articulated them, were "not rooted in centuries of judicial pronouncements," appeals to "ancient wisdom" simply running "contrary to the whole thrust of the Enlightenment." The Revolutionaries' common law thus embodied a dynamism bespeaking a love for fundamental liberties more than specific rules and doctrines.[24]

Story himself described the common law as a "system of elementary principles and of general juridical truths" that were "continually expanding . . . [and] adapting" to changed circumstances and the "exigencies and usages of the country." He praised the common law's evolutionary growth relative to the "fixed" and "inflexible" statutory law.[25] Furthermore, the common law mattered to constitutional interpretation but did not control it. As political scientist James R. Stoner Jr. put it,

> Story gives the Constitution its own authority and standing as a fundamental, but positive, law. The common law provides the background out of which the Constitution emerged and establishes the general principles of jurisprudence it invokes and that aid in its interpretation, but a written constitution makes a new beginning. It is not to be submerged, like the British constitution, in the immemorial ties of common law.[26]

Story had indeed in his *Commentaries* critiqued Thomas Jefferson's defense of General Wilkinson's warrantless dragging of citizens "from their homes under military force and exposing them to the perils of a long sea voyage" as contrary to the Fourth Amendment's "plain language," yet nothing in the pre–Fourth Amendment common law mandated a warrant in that sort of case.[27]

By the Bill of Rights' ratification in 1791, judicial discretion was seen as inherent in the common law. The judge was recognized as playing a creative role in the common law's development. By 1791, "a commonly understood concept of 'common law' had become that of a process characterized by occasional flexibility and capacity for growth in order to respond to changing social pressures, rather than that of a fixed and immutable body of unchanging rules." There is little evidence that most Framers had mastered the fine points of the common law of search and seizure, and those rules of greatest interest to Americans were "widely misreported in the colonies." Most of the ratifiers were not lawyers and thus unlikely to read broad, stirring phrases like "unreasonable" search and seizure as technical legal terms of art. These observations make it even more likely that the Fourth Amendment's Framers and ratifiers viewed the common law more as a method and a set of fundamental guiding traditions and values than as a rigid compendium of search and seizure rules. The common law is not infinitely malleable. It values tradition and precedent, favors slow case-by-case evolution over rapid and abstract theoretical overhaul, and expresses a commitment to a set of values not lightly to be abandoned or forgotten. Common-law history and reasoning should offer cautionary tales that inform constitutional analysis without straightjacketing it. That is the best understanding of the common law's role in crafting search and seizure doctrine.[28]

To see the Fourth Amendment as justifiably informed by the common law is, therefore, to see the amendment as embodying a fundamental set of principles subject to evolution to fit individual fact situations and new social circumstances. The Warrant Clause's text—which unequivocally requires probable cause and particular descriptions in warrants—will not bear such a flexible reading. Only the broader, more aspirational "Reasonableness" Clause can do so.[29]

Because the amendment's text does not clearly spell out the requirements for warrantless searches, that text cannot be seen as inflexibly mandating probable cause for all such searches. Nevertheless, the evolving common law of the Revolutionary generation and the early republic reflected a favoring of probable cause, or at least an embrace of the broader principles of evidentiary quality and individualized justice underlying the probable-cause notion. Those modernly seeking to reject or modify these principles should therefore bear the burden of doing so.[30]

4 Modern Implications I

Peoplehood and Interbranch Responsibilities

The revisioning of the history of the original Fourth Amendment has numerous implications for modern search and seizure law and practice. In this chapter I briefly explore three such implications to offer the flavor of the enterprise: first, the importance of the amendment's serving to protect "the People" rather than only individuals, with particular emphasis on the need to give the People a voice in creating search and seizure policy; second, the special role of the judiciary in taming everyday political violence in a scheme of checks and balances; and, third, the use of the *political principles* derived from the relevant historical events leading up to the Fourth Amendment as guides to the evolution of modern search and seizure doctrine—a very different set of paradigms than those thus far embraced by the Court and by other scholars.

Multibranch Responsibilities: Peoplehood

Professor Thomas Davies, in arguing that the Fourth Amendment was intended *only* to prohibit general warrants for customs searches of homes, tries to explain why the amendment recognizes the right as one of "the People." Pennsylvania's state constitution was the first of two to use the peoplehood formulation, and Davies sees Madison's similar reference in the Fourth Amendment as borrowing from Pennsylvania. Davies argues that the peoplehood formulation is but a "rhetorical justification for including the ban against general warrants in the declaration."[1] "Prefacing the warrant standards with an invocation of a 'right' of 'the people,'" he continues, served to show that the warrant standards were not mere legal niceties but were sufficiently fundamental to merit inclusion in a declaration of rights. Indeed, the reference to persons, houses, papers, and possessions served to link the warrant standards to the interests that were paramount under the common law. The rhetorical explanation is especially compelling because the Pennsylvania framers were quite fond of prefacing constitutional rules with statements of rights.[2]

But Davies's argument begs the question of *why* positing a right to be one of the People rather than only of individuals would elevate the right's importance.[3] Nor does Davies explain why Madison, having numerous state constitutional models from which to choose, thought the peoplehood formulation the best, nor why he would worry about proving the worthiness of including search and seizure rights in the federal Constitution when the demand to do so had been a major theme of the Anti-Federalist opposition. Madison was steeped in Lockean and republican political theory, likely understanding as a background assumption that the right to security was a prerequisite to a people's survival. He implicitly addressed one political function of the amendment as restraining legislative excess—preventing the tyranny of a majority faction over the rest of the People, thus destroying the right to security for all. It is true that the text of Madison's original proposal is fairly read as prohibiting no more than general warrants as constituting the primary danger to the People's right to be free from unreasonable searches and seizures. But Congress altered the original unitary proposal to create a two-clause formulation, one clause declaring the people's broad right to security against unreasonable searches and seizures, another clause prohibiting general warrants. Recent evidence suggests that this alteration was neither accidental nor "merely stylistic."[4]

Davies has wrongly argued that no one has or can identify a concern of the Framing generation with anything more than general warrants. He is correct in part in that general warrants and writs of assistance for customs searches triggered many of the major protests leading to the American Revolution and were the uppermost concern in the minds of the colonists. Indeed, the state constitutions written in the immediate wake of the Revolution did reflect this primary concern. But that does not necessarily mean that Congress and the ratifiers of the Bill of Rights meant to limit the Fourth Amendment's scope only to general warrants.[5]

Moreover, Davies's view too narrowly interprets the meaning of the colonists' objections in the general-warrant controversies. Those objections, in the context of the colonies' broader history and of their understanding of the history of their mother country, were intimately linked to political concerns about the voice of the American people as a corporate body. Seditious-libel prosecutions, warrantless impressment of colonists into the Royal Navy, sei-

zures of sloops, insults based on class but also on Americans' treatment as unequal "strangers" to the British polity, and search policies stemming from legislation by a Parliament in which Americans had no say all played some role in
the social forces prompting the Fourth Amendment. The peoplehood formulation is thus best understood as one reflecting the especially critical political
role of the Fourth Amendment.[6]

Alexander Hamilton's recognition of the possibility of criminal prosecution
for breaching search and seizure rights further supports this argument that the
Fourth Amendment creates rights serving public, political functions in addition to preserving spheres of private, individual autonomy. Criminal prosecution is reserved solely for public, not private, wrongs.[7] Hamilton, writing as
Publius in *Federalist No. 83,* explained how oppressive revenue searches would
be handled under the proposed new Constitution:

> As to the conduct of the officers of the revenue, the provision in favor of trial
> by jury in criminal cases, will afford the security aimed at. Wilful abuses of a
> public authority, to the oppression of the subject, and every species of official
> extortion, are offenses against the government; for which, the persons who
> commit them, may be indicted and punished according to the circumstances
> of the case.[8]

Hamilton was, of course, writing before the Constitution's ratification and
well before that of the Bill of Rights. His statement could, therefore, reflect his
understanding of the then-current state of the common law, though no American case apparently criminalized abusive searches or seizures absent legislation.
There are, however, many good reasons why public wrongs *potentially* subject
to criminal prosecution will in practice never be criminalized. Furthermore,
Hamilton may have been speaking not of what the state of the common law
was so much as what it should be in the new federal Constitution.[9]

In any event, public wrongs not suitable for criminal prosecution can also
be addressed by the tort system's awarding punitive damages. Punitive damages
go beyond compensating a victim for injuries received, serving instead to vin-
dicate the public injury done, while furthering public ends by increasing the
law's power to deter. Such damages were readily available in British trespass
actions of the seventeenth century arising from improper search and seizure
activity. Chief Justice Pratt's articulation of this point in upholding a large
damage award in a trespass action for a wrongful search thus explained, "a jury
have it in their power to give damages for more than the injury received. Damages are designed not only as a satisfaction of the injured person, but likewise
as a punishment to the guilty, to deter from any such proceeding for the future and as a proof of the detestation of the jury to the action itself." The trespass remedy for Fourth Amendment violations thus "served a multiplicity of

ends: redress, punishment, deterrence, and morality." The amendment therefore affirmed "both private and public rights, with their corresponding modes
of redress," a reading consistent with the "natural sense" of the peoplehood
formulation "that the right is not only personal, but also collective and public." This last point has indeed been part of the burden of this entire book:
to demonstrate that the Fourth Amendment serves public, political functions
that give meaning to what it means to be a "people." The recognition that the
amendment is designed, in part, both narrowly to give the People a voice in
search and seizure policy and, more broadly, to amplify their voice in the political process more generally suggests a variety of roles for each of the three
branches of government in defending and interacting with the People.[10]

The legislature's role is a seemingly (but wisely) contradictory one. Preventing Congress from engaging in the sorts of legislative abuses done by the British Parliament in authorizing the writs of assistance was, of course, among
the primary functions of the Fourth Amendment. Simultaneously, however,
the Revolutionaries were motivated partly by the Empire's using abusive search
and seizure practices to serve the needs of an unrepresentative political system.
Nor, in particular, they complained, did they have any say in the legislative
formulation of search and seizure policy. The Fourth Amendment may, therefore, lock certain doors through which the legislature may not pass.

But the amendment also governs *all* branches of government.[11] When
placed in the context of the disputes triggering the Revolution, the legislature
must, therefore, be seen as obligated to serve as one mechanism by which the
American people have their say concerning search and seizure practices. To be
sure, that say must be expressed in dialogue with the courts to ensure no legislative lock-picking. But there are systemic things that the courts cannot do
that the legislature can, especially given its power of the purse, media access,
and large staff. Remember that the Fourth Amendment implicitly empowers
the state to use violence to protect the People, while safeguarding the People's
right to be subject to only reasonable exercises of that power. The federal legislature can, and sometimes has, sought to meet this obligation throughout
American history, with some notable successes—such as expanding protections
for the news media—and some notable failures—such as, in the short run at
least, arguably failing adequately to restrain executive overreaching in the war
on terrorism.[12]

The state legislatures have likewise at times sought to expand search and
seizure protections in important ways. Thus, in 1864, the Oregon legislature required not merely an affidavit of probable cause to support a search warrant
but also the magistrate's examination of the complainant and any witnesses
that may be provided under oath and the taking of their depositions in writing. Although the Fourth Amendment did not then apply to the states, other
state legislatures also sought on their own initiative, or in accordance with

their analogous state constitutional provisions, to make search and seizure protections real. Further state legislative actions after the Fourteenth Amendment incorporated the Fourth Amendment against the states can be seen as also reflecting federal constitutional obligations.[13]

Even one of the strongest proponents of the view that the Fourth Amendment was designed primarily to *limit* legislative power has conceded some positive role for affirmative legislative action:

> That is not to say that the state or federal Framers precisely defined the boundary of legislative power regarding criminal procedure. They certainly saw the legislature as the primary locus of law making authority, and they were not pressed to draw the exact boundary of its authority regarding criminal justice matters. Moreover, precisely because the American concept of separation of judicial from legislative and executive powers was a recent innovation, the boundary between the legislative and the judicial was clouded by the earlier English tradition of legislation that was "in affirmance of common law" and by unquestioned legislative authority to define new offenses. Indeed, I suspect that the Framers may have accepted that legislation might fill in gaps in common-law procedure.[14]

I would draw less-timid lessons from the Revolutionary generation's history. The Supreme Court has recognized that legislatures have an important role to play in crafting remedies for the violation of constitutional criminal-procedural rights, so long as those remedies are at least as effective as those designed by, and within the competence of, the courts. The courts are, however, not necessarily equipped to design comprehensive schemes for the regulation of complex matters, such as technological surveillance. Yet the high Court has not shied away from providing legislatures with roadmaps laying out the essential minima of a constitutional scheme, leaving it to the legislature to fill in the gaps. In this and other areas (at least before the start of the war on terrorism) Congress and the state legislatures have at least occasionally provided protections beyond those laid out by the Court.[15]

I would go yet one step further, imposing on the legislatures the obligation to promote the development of institutions that improve the People's ability to have a say in search and seizure policy. One recent illustration of what I have in mind is the American Bar Association Standards on Technologically-Assisted Surveillance. Those standards permit law-enforcement use of overt video surveillance of citizens on a city's streets, a tool some advocates see as necessary in the war on terrorism. However, such surveillance may be used only when a series of fairly stringent conditions are met, including the opportunity of the public likely to be affected by the surveillance to express its views on the wisdom of the effort and to propose changes in its execution, that public being heard repeatedly on these matters, both before and during the surveillance. Citizens are consulted, giving them voice and the ability to monitor governmental abuses. But no vote is taken, reducing the chance of empowering majority oppression of the minority, for example, by voting to encourage video surveillance in black but not white neighborhoods. Legislatively created mechanisms of this kind involve the People directly in the creation of search and seizure policy.[16]

The jury was and is another institution through which the People express their will. Some scholars, like Akhil Amar, have gone so far as to argue that tort remedies were specifically intended by the Framers to be the sole, or at least the primary, recourse for those aggrieved by wrongful searches. The Seventh Amendment right to a civil jury, argues Amar, ensures that juries determine what is "reasonable" under the Fourth Amendment, thus involving the People in setting search policy and in monitoring governmental abuses. Other scholars, notably Tracey Maclin, have pointed out the many procedural obstacles to Framing-era trespass suits arising from flawed searches, thereby sharply curtailing the jury's role. Nevertheless, even Maclin concedes that the civil jury is sensibly seen as *part of* the Framers' regulatory scheme. Easing the availability of tort suits and punitive damages may thus be another way to enhance the People's voice, though the short-run political obstacles make this unlikely.[17]

Perhaps the most effective and practical way to make the peoplehood ideal real is grass-roots political action. Notably, such action by a group called the Cincinnati Black United Front (BUF), eventually working in concert with the American Civil Liberties Union, recently led to a novel approach to reforming an urban police department accused of racial profiling and excessive violence. Professional mediator Dr. Jay Rothman, prodded by the filing of a lawsuit co-incident with street protests, and with the parties' agreement, surveyed eight stakeholding groups: African Americans, youths twenty-five and under, city officials and employees, religious/social-service leadership, police and their families, business/foundation leaders, whites, and other minority citizens. The responses were converted into "platforms representing consensus goals agreed upon by self-selected representatives in 12 four-hour feedback sessions." The information collected formed the basis for extensive negotiations among stakeholding groups, resulting in a "Collaborative Agreement," ratified by the BUF, the ACLU, Cincinnati's police union, and the city council. The Collaborative created, among other things, a "communications audit" to improve community awareness of police policies; an annual report; a "conciliator" to promote compliance; periodic surveys of citizen and subgroup satisfaction with the police; and regular meetings with the parties to evaluate results. In the case of the Collaborative, grass-roots political action combined with a creative judge in a pending lawsuit to produce the ultimate outcome. In other instances, such as the state-by-state movement to pass data-gathering statutes to monitor racial profiling, bottom-up political action worked in combination with sympathetic legislators. Public input and pressure can also lead to voluntary executive action, as in Chicago, where the police department introduced new procedures partly in response to an Amnesty International report documenting departmental abuses. The bottom-line lesson, of particular relevance as governmental search and seizure power grows in the war on terrorism, is this: "the struggle to define and enforce our constitutional norms is an ongoing process, and that process is aided by, and may depend upon, the actions of those who resist expansion of government power at the very time when it seems to be most needed." In short, "vocal and persistent opposition may affect the course of government [search and seizure] conduct."[18]

The Special Role of the Judiciary

The judiciary has a special role to play in regulating the state's power to search and seize. Judicial resistance to the writs of assistance had been strong, even after the Townshend Acts extended the jurisdiction of colonial courts. New York courts, for example, at first issued a deviant writ that failed to contain the language mandated by Parliament. Customs officers refused to execute the flawed writ, seeking a corrected one. But applications kept getting lost or mislaid until 1773, five years after the first application, when a New York court then held that "it did not appear to them that such writs according to the form now produced are warranted by law and they therefore could not grant the motion." In Connecticut, Chief Justice Trumbull refused to be rushed into a decision, privately telling associates that he had doubts that "the thing was in itself constitutional." Pennsylvania's chief justice, William Allen, initially declared that he had no authority to issue the writ. When customs officials filed a new application accompanied by a supporting opinion of England's attorney general, the chief justice insisted that he would grant only particular writs under oath swearing that the customs agent knew or reasonably believed that uncustomed goods would be found in a particular place. "Allen's groping toward a concept of probable cause as well as specific warrants became clearer as customs officials vainly persisted to engage his cooperation."[19]

Other provincial high courts outside Massachusetts and New Hampshire similarly stalled, compromised, or refused to grant valid applications, one court delaying for five years because the writs "trenched too severely and unnecessarily upon the safety of the subject secured by Magna Carta." The provincial courts' resistance won the colonists' respect, even though the provincial judiciary outside the area of the writs of assistance had a mixed record, too often and too long continuing issuing general warrants. Many colonists remembered too Judge Pratt's stirring words in the Wilkesite cases. The colonists therefore focused their anger more on legislative abuses than judicial ones, seeing the legislatures as boxing in the courts or crafting end runs around them. For the colonists, judges were generally seen as learned, virtuous men, who were chosen from, and should be trusted as, the best men of society.[20]

The judiciary's role in constitutional search and seizure law can also only be understood within the Revolutionaries' broader framework for the separation of powers. The mixed English Constitution of Blackstone's time was based on a balance of power between the executive and legislative branches. "From this point of view, the judiciary had an essentially executive role to play in carrying out the commands of the legislative branch." Although Blackstone understood that judges could play an important checking role in such a system, only in the era of the American Revolution was the judiciary more widely perceived by the colonists "as a functionally independent member of a governmental triad."[21]

The novelty of an independent judiciary was ably defended by Alexander Hamilton, again writing as Publius. Hamilton raised three arguments in favor of such a judiciary: (1) that it would be a "bulwark against the populist abuses likely to come from the legislative power in a republic"; (2) that it would serve as a "depository not of force or will, but legal judgment"; and (3) that its members would be "not only the guardians of the Constitution, but the schoolmasters of moderation and constitutionalism."[22]

For Hamilton, representative institutions, especially the most populous one proposed—the House of Representatives—were the seat of passion, not reason. The populist House does not necessarily act for the People entire. As Madison had earlier explained, also writing as Publius, a majority faction is a faction nevertheless. The true will of the People is embodied in the Constitution, and independent judges are best able to divine that will. Accordingly, Hamilton argues for the judiciary having the power later called "judicial review," declaring legislation inconsistent with constitutional mandate. Said Hamilton, tyranny arises when the rights of individuals are unprotected from "the effects of those ill humors, which the arts of designing men, or the influence of popular conjunctures, sometimes disseminate among the people themselves." Such review does not render unelected judges rulers over the polity, as the Anti-Federalists charged. Rather, Hamilton countered, it is "far more rational to suppose that the courts were designed to be an intermediary body between the people and the legislature, in order, among other things, to keep the latter within the limits assigned to their authority." Judicial review affirms neither judicial nor legislative supremacy, instead ensuring that "the power of the people is superior to both."[23]

Hamilton's argument is consistent with the Revolutionary era's distinction between "liberty" and "license." True liberty, remember, stems from obedience to God's will or nature's law. A man who gives in to his animal desires is licentious, a "slave to the passions" rather than self-governed. Each individual standing alone is incapable of best understanding natural law. It is in the wisdom of a community of reciprocal obligation that the law by which we should best run our lives can be found.[24]

Analogously for Hamilton, the common law, which fuses both positive manmade laws and their undergirding natural-rights principles, embodies community wisdom over time.[25] Furthermore,

> since America is a republic, Hamilton emphasizes the common-law grounding of such a judicial power in the active and tacit consent of the people to long-standing precedents that secure their liberty and happiness. Such arguments define the common-law tradition. . . . In the same vein, the common-law constitutionalism of [*Federalist*] no. 78 . . . [emphasizes] the people's consent in a fundamental document of written law. Both the people who ratify the Constitution and the judges authorized to interpret it would be bound by a written law, yet would understand that written law as itself informed, and justified, by unwritten principles of nature, reason, truth, and propriety.[26]

Accordingly, Hamilton suggests, "a sovereign republican people will realize that justice and interest are best secured by ordaining and then subordinating themselves to a fundamental law that establishes good government." Independent judges are not subject (at least not to the same degree) to the self-interested passions that may hold sway in populist institutions. Simultaneously, emphasizes Hamilton, the common-law training of judges promotes the prudence, moderation, and judgment that raise the likelihood that they will find the law unbefogged by unreason. Professional training promotes the habits of mind necessary to understanding the growing and "voluminous code of laws [that] is one of the inconveniences necessarily connected with the advantages of a free government." Precedent limits judges' "arbitrary discretion," while "the records of those precedents must unavoidably swell to a very considerable bulk," demanding "long and laborious study to acquire a competent knowledge of them." "But few men," says Hamilton, will have sufficient skill to join the judiciary, and fewer still will "unite the requisite integrity with the requisite knowledge." Such "fit characters" can be lured from lucrative private practice only by lifetime job security, a price well worth paying to create a judiciary with "an uncommon portion of fortitude . . . to do their duty as faithful guardians of the Constitution."[27]

The judiciary would also play a more gentle role as "republican schoolmasters." The legislature, aware of the challenge that might be posed to its work by the "scruples of the courts," will moderate its mischief. Indeed, the mere awareness of robed teachers looking over legislative shoulders will lead elected representatives to be cautious about passing legislation that, while not "contrary to the manifest tenor of the Constitution" (Hamilton's standard for judicial review), walks a troubling line. Similarly, legislators will be aware of a subtler judicial power to check any "spirit of injustice" by "mitigating the severity and confining the operation of unjust laws." Judicial judgment can thus oppose abusive legislative power "quietly and incrementally when a common-law judicial prudence discerns that laws, even if constitutional, are unjust, partial, or violate private rights." Judicial rulings, reasoning, and remedies can thus teach the legislature not only about constitutionality but about justice. Hamilton himself therefore saw such structural features of the Constitution like the separation of powers as more important than any bill of rights in safeguarding liberty. Yet James Madison, Hamilton's most famous partner in the trio writing as Publius, eventually came to believe that a Bill of Rights would educate the People in a way that would reduce the chances of majority tyranny in the first place. Modernly, the widespread presence of *Miranda* rights in popular entertainment may be one particularly powerful illustration that the Court may instruct not only legislatures but also lay citizens.[28]

The political functions of the Fourth Amendment shine a new light on the judiciary's role in the separation-of-powers scheme. The Fourth Amendment unequivocally places the warrant-issuing power in the hands of the judiciary, divesting it from the legislative and executive tyrants who so plagued the colonists. The colonial judiciary had its faults too, issuing general warrants well past the time when common-law reasoning and colonial political understanding condemned them. Nevertheless, the old judiciary fared better than did the other governmental branches in the colonists', later new Americans', eyes. Moreover, this was a *new* judiciary of independent, life-tenured judges. This was a judiciary empowered and obliged to check populist-branch excesses, value reason over passion, and teach principles of republican liberty.[29]

It is true that the Fourth Amendment's text does not require all searches and seizures to be authorized by a warrant, nor does it even say that warrants are ever required. Very few people, however, are willing to read that silence as meaning warrants are in fact an entirely optional policy choice. Nor does it seem right to say that they are always mandated, for there are surely instances when obtaining a warrant is impracticable. Furthermore, the colonists feared arbitrary executive discretion and legislative excess more than they did an imperial judiciary. This observation has led some scholars to recommend a warrant-preference rule with varying degrees of vigor. Under the strongest version of this rule, the police must obtain warrants unless they face a situation fitting within a narrow set of judicially recognized exceptions. The meaning of the weaker version of this rule is unclear, seeming to be a working presumption that warrants are a good idea, but there may be myriad case-specific circumstances justifying warrantless action. In an increasingly complex, technological world facing threats of terrorism, organized crime, and gang domination of poor neighborhoods, a warrant preference might arguably be objectionable not because getting warrants quickly and conveniently is hard but because the probable-cause requirement asks too much. This view, however, has a tendency over time to outgrow in practice any sort of warrant preference at all. That tendency has grown in much U.S. Supreme Court case law over the past few decades. Moreover, a politics of fear may make it hard to revive the near-moribund warrant preference.[30]

The impending (or perhaps actual) demise of that preference should not mean, however, the end of the judiciary's role in checking and balancing the other branches. The political dangers posed by warrantless searches are as great or greater than those posed by warrants. It is the right of security itself that is a prerequisite to peoplehood. The arbitrary use of state violence can suppress dissent, as has likely happened in the war on terrorism; can insult less-powerful citizens as being unworthy of equal membership in the polity, as "broken-windows policing" has done to the poor and to racial minorities in several major cities; and can undermine the mutual trust necessary to sustaining governments and the communities that birthed them. These dangers to the polity stem from warrantless searches and seizures, such as the recent racial roundup of all young black males in Oneonta, New York; the racial profiling of minority drivers in communities throughout the nation; and police video-camera surveillance of public spaces, for which no warrant is required. In such cases, the harm to the individual, who lacks the assurance offered by visible signs of an independent judge's deliberation and who may face the fear of police violence, is ample.[31]

Judicial invalidation of legislation authorizing invasive warrantless searches with little cause, or exclusion of evidence seized in disregard of personal privacy, can educate legislators, police, and the public alike in republican morality. Judicial action can deter majoritarian domination, promote sound public deliberation by media coverage of the *reasons* for decision, which only judges must articulate, and heighten public awareness of the dangers posed by an overweening state. If the process is imperfect, it is better than one in which the judiciary has no power with which to engage the other branches' attention. The exclusionary rule is a great attention-getter, and it is usually the only tool available to judges that enables them to act on their own initiative rather than awaiting a private civil suit that may never come. Criminal defendants usually have by far the greatest incentive to bring constitutional violations to light when the remedy may be exclusion of damning evidence. The word "remedy" may itself be misleading, for the Framers likely assumed that most searches in the new republic would be done pursuant to warrants and that judges simply would not issue bad warrants in the first place. Similarly, the text of the Fourth Amendment definitionally means that police who obey the Constitution's commands will never possess evidence that it would be "unreasonable" to obtain. The exclusionary rule empowers the judge not simply to give the defendant personally but to give the People as a whole the political benefit to which the Fourth Amendment's substance entitles them.[32]

These conclusions have been stated before, but none has justified the exclusionary rule's return of the parties to the status quo ante as primarily a benefit to the People because it regulates the state's use of *political* violence. The Cato Institute, perhaps the most respected of the nation's libertarian think tanks, although not drawing on the unique role of the Fourth Amendment in regulating political violence, has recognized on different grounds the role that the exclusionary rule plays in the American version of constitutional checks and balances, a role that matters both in unjustified warrantless searches and ones done beyond the restrictions laid down in a warrant.[33] Concerning the latter situation, Cato explained,

> The executive branch cannot be permitted to make a mockery of the search warrant. When law enforcement officers disregard the terms of a warrant, the Constitution's particularity requirement is undermined and a valid specific warrant is transformed into a general warrant. Since judicial officers are not on the scene when search warrants are flaunted, the most opportune time to sanction such lawlessness is when executive branch representatives (prosecutors) come into court seeking the judge's permission to introduce the illegally obtained evidence. The only way the judiciary can maintain the integrity of its warrant-issuing process is by withholding its approval. The judicial branch cannot—and should not—rely on the executive branch to discipline its own agents.
>
> The exclusionary rule fits neatly within the Constitution's separation-of-powers framework.[34]

Any lesser remedy, Cato suggested, would unduly weaken the judiciary's power to check abuses.[35] Thus, Cato reminds its readers that

> [t]he men who framed and ratified the Constitution recognized "the insufficiency of mere parchment delineation of the boundaries" [among] . . . the three branches of government. "The great security," wrote James Madison, against a gradual concentration of the several powers in the same department consists in giving those who administer each department the necessary constitutional means and personal motives to resist encroachments of the others. The provision for defense must, in this, as in all other cases, be made commensurate to the danger of attack.

The exclusionary rule is a "commensurate" judicial response to the executive branch's attack on the judiciary's warrant-issuing prerogative.[36]

These words and the Revolutionaries' experience caution not only against the judiciary's gutting the exclusionary rule but also against its creating doc-trine unduly deferential to the other branches. That need not mean that judges must always second-guess their executive brethren. They might, for example, offer roadmaps for Congress to create effective legislative safeguards or new institutions involving the citizens most affected to have a say in the crafting of search and seizure policy, all the while holding out the threat of evidentiary exclusion and judicial review if the roadmaps are ignored. Indeed, because, un-der the theory articulated here, the People should have a more direct role in deliberative governance concerning search and seizure policy, the Court should consider whether, in appropriate cases, its best course of action is to guide Congress and state legislatures toward creating mechanisms that involve the People. One example would be the creation of institutions, along the lines of those discussed earlier, like the American Bar Association's recommendation of citizen supervisory panels whenever the state uses video cameras to watch pedestrians in the war on terrorism. Other examples include one city's experi-mental crafting of a Collaborative Agreement involving representatives from numerous "stakeholder" groups—from black residents to white residents, from street officers to commanders, from young to old—and a host of reforms pro-posed under the rubric of "transparent policing."[37]

5 Modern Implications II

Precedent and Political Meaning

Interpretative Attitude

Courts may also use the expressive political understanding of the Fourth Amendment for guidance in crafting precedent on specific questions of constitutional doctrine. How to do so turns on an understanding of the proper role of history in constitutional interpretation.

Some light is shed on that role by recent historical work on the Founding generation's conception of language, especially political language. During the years surrounding the American Revolution, there were two predominant theories of political language. The one in ascendance at the time of the 1776 Declaration of Independence used language "as if it constituted a fixed and unvarying medium of expression existing apart from the changing contexts of history, a medium stable in its grammar and vocabulary, certain in its meanings, and unambiguous in its capacity to express universal truth." This view stemmed from fear of the sort of abuses of power to which the British had subjected the colonists and a belief that clear and exact language could control future abuses. It sounded, in language of the "rule of law, and not of men," an almost religious "confidence in the redemptive power of language precisely framed and deeply revered." The Anti-Federalists continued to embrace through the time of the Constitution's ratification this "profoundly conservative" view of language "guided by a concern to fend off historical change, preserve familiar values, and prescribe the limits of acceptable political behavior." Indeed, much of the Anti-Federalist objection to the Constitution charged that its language was too ambiguous to protect republican liberty, its words given too radical and new meanings by the Federalists, its content devoid of a clear Bill of Rights.[1]

By the time of ratification, however, this conservative vision of language had been eclipsed by its competitor, a more expansive vision grounded less in reason than in experience. This view was passionately embraced by the Federalists. They had come to see the "virtuous" republicanism of 1776 as naïve. State constitutions and bills of rights had thus far proven ineffective in preventing political turmoil, democratic license, majoritarian abuses, and dangerous violence like Shays' Rebellion. Virtue had, in Federalist eyes, proven a fragile basis for liberty, and governmental power was not entirely dangerous to liberty but sometimes necessary for its protection. Faction was inevitable and needed to be funneled to productive purposes. Moreover, Federalists came to recognize that they were involved in an experiment and that, just as past experience since 1776 had taught the new nation much about governance, so would future experience teach new lessons. Constitutional language had the capacity to embody general principles and to provide them with special authority. But that same language necessarily needed to be capacious enough to allow experience to reveal better ways to further those principles and to vest the language with still greater authority. For the Federalists, constitutional texts were seen "as a guide to innovative action, as blueprints encompassing the best judgments of the 'science of politics,' judgments inevitably imperfect and subject to change as the future unfolded." Furthermore, reaching agreement on the terms of a Constitution required political compromise, and that, in turn, required a certain level of generality in language, allowing disputes over meaning to be waged in political contest and debate.[2] The leading historian of American political language, John Howe, summarized the Federalist view thus:

> By contrast, other political writers [such as the Federalists] understood that language, far from constituting an autonomous realm of universal meaning separated from the flux of history, was inextricably embedded in human experience. As a consequence, not only its vocabulary and grammar but its very uses and signification changed over time. Given its evolving, adaptive nature, language was suited to serve not primarily as an agent of political preservation and control, but as an instrument of political exploration and creativity to be deployed in the construction of a continuously unfolding political future. Fluid rather than stable in its structure and meaning, language mirrored nature imperfectly and thus served as a medium through which nature's truths, in politics as elsewhere, were continuously contested.[3]

This fluidity did not render language meaningless. Nor is this vision of language inconsistent with an important role for history in meaning creation.

History leading up to a provision helps in understanding the content of the evolving principles therein embodied. Later history and earlier history can combine to teach new lessons about the best ways to serve those principles in the face of new challenges. History can reveal a people's commitments and exercise a restraining hand to slow commitmentarian evolution so that commitments are neither so ephemeral as to be meaningless nor so unchanging as to be pointless. For Howe, the Federalist victory in ratifying the Constitution was likewise a victory for the experience-informed Federalist concept of language. The Anti-Federalists did ultimately succeed in their quest for a Bill of Rights, but it was a Bill of Rights guided by James Madison's hand, and Madison was imbued with the Federalist vision of adaptive language and had written expressly about that vision's wisdom. The Federalist victory was never complete, however, for Anti-Federalist views continued to contend with Federalist ones throughout much of American history.[4]

Whether Howe is right that Federalist language concepts achieved a decisive victory, those concepts are most consistent with the soundest understandings of how lawyers should use history. The intellectual historian must document the thinking of a generation, including many multiple and contradictory views. But "[t]he task of constitutional interpreter is to determine which, if any, of those details are relevant to the modern construal of the constitution." Lawyers must "look for a story that best brings principled coherence to as much of the Constitution as possible, and . . . discard the rest." Lawyers must be careful to portray the historical record accurately and to acknowledge conflicting currents. But in choosing which currents to navigate and what lessons to fish from them, "lawyers must acknowledge that they are transforming the historical record into legal material and they must accept their responsibility for that creative process." Lawyers thus ultimately use history as a source of insight into how others answered similar questions in the past to illuminate how we should constitute our political community today.[5]

The Federalist vision of political language included an acceptance of the power of metaphor to structure thought and convey what "literalist" language cannot, and one metaphor has special resonance here: that of the People as a "body," perhaps a growing child's body. Under this metaphor, some constitutional choices breed "corruption" and "disease" in the "body politic," undermining the harmonious functioning of its varying parts, stunting its growth, perhaps leading it to wither and die. But other constitutional choices promote healthy maturation; strong, smooth, skilled operation; and a healthy mind and soul, essential links to a prospering body. The Federalists sought a healthy body politic, and all the Constitution's provisions should be understood as aimed toward that end. This aspiration is little more than an attitude toward words, empty in itself. But the experience embodied in history can teach lessons— admittedly ones informed by political value choices about of what "health" consists—about how to keep the American People, as the patient, prospering. It is foolish to believe that history can reveal simplistic solutions or incontestably determinate answers to complex modern problems. But history can inform, and it is in this light that I suggest that the history recounted here can support a small set of principles or, perhaps even better, "lessons" that can at least help to guide and structure Fourth Amendment interpretive construction in useful ways.[6] Here, in summary form, are these lessons:

1. State violence, in the form of searches and seizures, is also always a form of state expression, one that can stigmatize and insult individuals and groups, with real political consequences, altering the distribution of power in society and the perceived legitimacy of government.

2. Likewise, the state's power to search and seize is closely linked to First Amendment ideas of free expression and has historically too often been used to suppress dissent and difference.

3. The Fourth Amendment aims at taming these and other aspects of state violence. The amendment arose not merely from a cold, rational theory of governance but from an experience of struggle animated by emotions of indignation, retribution, and the thirst for liberation. The relevance of those emotions for individuals and communities should not be ignored in the process of constitutional interpretation.

4. The Fourth Amendment's reference to a right of "the People" is not linguistic window dressing. The amendment's protections are central to crafting a shared sense of peoplehood. Promoting involvement of an energized, monitorial People—a People with a real voice in how they are governed—in making the amendment's promise real is best understood as an essential aspect of the amendment's meaning.

5. The amendment binds all three branches of government, and each must play a role in checking and balancing the others to prevent abuses of Fourth Amendment rights. For the courts, the warrant-issuing authority and the suppression hearing are essential tools for their properly playing their constitutional role.

6. The probable-cause "requirement" embodies notions of individualized justice and the necessity for reliable proof as central tools for protecting the dignity and respect of individuals and groups and of the People and is not lightly to be trifled with.

7. But the dignity and respect of individuals and groups, and the very existence of the American People, require protection from private violence and a state powerful enough to do so. However, there is presumptively little tension between the demands of individualized justice and of public safety. To the contrary, the best working assumption is that creative thinking can render these goals entirely compatible.[7]

In only the briefest fashion, I offer here a taste of how these principles or lessons can alter the way in which the Court crafts Fourth Amendment precedent in a few selected areas. Sometimes these lessons bring coherence to seemingly inconsistent doctrine; other times they offer a principled basis for critiquing that doctrine.

Stigma and Voice

Stigma and Humiliation Considered

Social stigma and humiliation in being subjected to state violence have sometimes implicitly played a role in the Court's jurisprudence, while other times wrongly failing to play such a role. One example of an implicit role is the Court's treatment of "administrative searches and seizures"—those conducted for a purpose other than criminal-law enforcement. For an administrative search or seizure, the Court eliminates or modifies the warrant requirement, the probable-cause requirement, or both. Furthermore, warrantless, suspicionless searches are generally permitted only for administrative and not ordinary criminal-law-enforcement-related searches and seizures. Many administrative-search cases have involved the constitutional validity of drug-testing programs, such as urine testing of safety-sensitive railroad employees or drug testing of high-school athletes. Although not specifically so labeled, the Court also treats drunk-driving and other roadblocks as administrative seizures.[8]

Many searches and seizures have dual purposes, one goal being criminal investigation, the other goal being protecting roadway safety, promoting infant health, or fostering some similar civil purpose. In dual-purpose cases, the Court has held that the *"primary programmatic purpose"* must be one other than criminal investigation and prosecution, or the search will not be deemed administrative. This purpose inquiry is *not* a subjective one—the actual mental state of the police or other governmental actors is irrelevant. Rather, the inquiry is an objective one. How the inquiry is to proceed and how "programmatic purpose" is precisely defined the Court has not said. Critics are left looking for ways to reconcile seemingly inconsistent cases.[9]

Thus, the Court has said that a drunk-driving roadblock has a primarily administrative purpose—keeping the roads safe—even though the very evidence of a safety risk, specifically, the indicators of intoxication, necessarily leads to arrest and likely criminal prosecution. On the other hand, urine testing pregnant women for cocaine use, where a positive result meant coercion into drug treatment under threat of criminal prosecution for failure to comply with *all* mandates of the treatment program—a program designed and run jointly by both hospital personnel and the police—was *not* primarily administrative. In both types of cases there was a safety justification—road safety on the one hand, child safety from drug addiction and genetic malformation on the other. In both cases, there was extensive police involvement, though the drunk-driving case involved *only* the police, while the pregnant women's case involved far more patient interaction with health-care workers than with law enforcement. Moreover, a driver testing positive on a sobriety test would necessarily be arrested, while the women testing positive for cocaine would receive only psychological therapy and medical treatment, avoiding involvement in the criminal justice system entirely if they successfully complied with all treatment-program mandates. Yet the entirely *police-run* drunk-driving roadblocks were dubbed "administrative," while the hospital-personnel-focused pregnant women's urine-testing program—in which police played but a secondary role—was dubbed criminal investigation related in nature. This seemingly odd result can be explained by focusing on social stigma.[10]

Social science reveals the absence among most of the public of the sort of retributive indignation toward drunk drivers that we feel toward "true" criminals—so long as no one is hurt. The public does support drunk-driving criminalization to aid deterrence and promote public safety. But the public also overwhelmingly favors treatment programs for offenders over jail time and even over large fines or impoundment of the defendants' cars. Likewise, the public favors spending tax dollars on education programs and media campaigns. Furthermore, jury willingness to acquit drunk drivers has not changed, and it has in fact *increased* since 1958. Americans simply do not view drunk drivers who do not cause injuries as worthy recipients of the retributive punishment characteristic of our criminal justice system.[11]

Illicit-drug users such as cocaine addicts are, however, vilified. They are seen as transmitters of diseases like AIDS; accused of "bizarre and frightening behavior," from staring at the sun until blinded to running naked while throwing dog feces; and deemed unfit to waste therapeutic resources in coddling them. They are subhuman, in the words of former president Reagan, creatures whom "[a]ll Americans of good will are determined to stamp out . . . [as] parasites." They are the enemy on whom we must wage war.[12]

Child abusers are perhaps even worse, especially when it is the mother who is the abuser. In our culture, being a mother means obliging oneself to the obligations of "preservative love, nurturance, and training" of one's children as a substantial life responsibility. A mother who callously endangers her children's physical health and security is no real mother at all. When such endangerment is extreme, the mother becomes a "monster," a danger to the social sinews that hold society together, a threat, therefore, to the social survival of us all. Pregnant addicts are both drug users *and* abusive mothers. As political scientist Iris Marion Young explains, "The level of passion directed against pregnant addicts often seems higher than that felt by ordinary criminals. It is not just anyone who has harmed her baby as, for example, by shooting it up with cocaine. It is the child's *mother.*"[13]

Now we are in a position to harmonize the drunk-driving roadblock and pregnant drug addict cases. The former do not come close to suffering the social stigma and retributive rage that society will heap upon the latter. Society as the audience will therefore likely understand cocaine urine testing of pregnant women who are threatened with criminal prosecution if they continue to be untreated as being more consistent with the retributive purposes of the criminal justice system than is stopping drunk drivers.

The Court's most recent case on this question, *Illinois v. Lidster,* further clarifies this point. In *Lidster,* one week after a fatal hit-and-run accident, police set up a checkpoint to locate witnesses to the crime. As each car approached the checkpoint, an officer would stop the car for ten to fifteen seconds to ask whether its occupants had seen the crime and would hand the driver a flyer asking for assistance. When Robert Lidster approached the checkpoint in his minivan, his van swerved, nearly hitting one of the officers, who subsequently smelled alcohol on Lidster's breath, administered a sobriety test, and arrested Lidster. Lidster was convicted of driving under the influence of alcohol and appealed on the ground that much of the evidence against him should have been suppressed as the fruit of an illegal checkpoint seizure. Although the trial court rejected this claim, two Illinois appellate courts accepted it, and the U.S. Supreme Court accepted certiorari.[14]

At first blush, there was ample reason to support the Illinois appellate court decisions favoring suppression. Unlike in the drunk-driving cases, and many of the urine drug-testing cases, there was no imminent danger to public safety, indeed no "civil" purpose at all. The sole reason for the roadblock—one run by the police alone—was to investigate crime. Indeed, the Court had recently held in *Indianapolis v. Edmond*[15] that a roadblock to find those transporting illicit drugs served no immediate safety purpose and was, therefore, a traditional criminal search, thus requiring probable cause and a warrant or a recognized exception to the warrant requirement.

But in *Lidster* the Supreme Court held otherwise, upholding the conviction and the constitutionality of the search. Not all criminal-law-enforcement objectives, explained the Court, are the sort that demand presumptive unconstitutionality absent individualized suspicion. "The stop's primary law enforcement purpose," concluded the Court, was "*not* to determine whether a vehicle's occupants were committing a crime, but to ask vehicle occupants, as members of the public, for their help in providing information about a crime in all likelihood committed by others." The Court continued: "The police expected the information elicited to help them apprehend, not the vehicle's occupants, *but other individuals.*" Moreover, in such a situation, requiring individualized suspicion makes no sense, for no individual is stopped because he or she is suspected of, or even potentially sought for, involvement in any crime. "Like certain other forms of police activity, say, crime control or public safety, an information-seeking stop is not the kind of event that involves suspicion, or lack of suspicion, of the relevant individual."[16] Additionally, concluded the Court,

information-seeking highway stops are less likely to provoke anxiety or to prove intrusive. The stops are likely brief. The police are not likely to ask questions designed to elicit self-incriminating information. And citizens will often react positively when police simply ask for their help as "responsible citizen[s]" to "give whatever information they may have to aid in law enforcement."[17]

Furthermore, said the Court, the law ordinarily allows police to seek voluntary public cooperation in solving crime; the Fourth Amendment "does not treat a motorist's car as his castle"; the traffic delay was brief; and proliferation of similar checkpoints is unlikely given "limited police resources and community hostility to related traffic tie-ups." Therefore, the Court declared, a more flexible reasonableness balancing test like that in the drunk-driving roadblock cases was appropriate, indeed classifying those latter cases as another example of "special law enforcement concerns . . . justify[ing] highway stops without individualized suspicion."[18]

The suspicionless, informational roadblocks before the Court in *Lidster* survived this reasonableness balancing test. The stop was tailored to serve a grave public concern (finding a killer), for it was located where there was a good chance of finding drivers with knowledge about the crime; the delay (including time waiting in a line of cars) was brief—a few minutes at most; and the contact provided little reason for anxiety or alarm, given that all cars were systematically stopped, and there were no allegations of discriminatory or other unlawful police behavior during questioning.[19]

The Court never expressly explained *why* information-seeking stops are less likely to provoke anxiety than are many other roadblocks, nor did the Court address *why* the *Lidster* stop was more like a sobriety checkpoint, or even a pure public-safety measure (like crowd control), than like a drug-trafficker stop. Implicitly again, however, the level of stigma seems to be an important factor. A driver stopped to be questioned about witnessing a crime is treated like a respectable citizen rather than a potential criminal. Neither the driver nor knowing observers are likely to see the investigation as even potentially stigmatizing. To the contrary, the Court seems right in suggesting that the police show citizens a sign of respect when they assume that they will help in finding the killer of a seventy-year-old bicyclist (the hit-and-run driver's victim). To categorize the stop, therefore, as one whose primary purpose was other than the "general interest in crime control" seems right.[20]

Whether the more flexible resulting balancing test for administrative seizures was met on the *Lidster* facts may be more debatable, as Justice Stevens,
joined by Justices Souter and Ginsburg, argued in their opinion concurring in
part and dissenting in part. Justice Stevens agreed with the majority's primary-
purpose analysis but favored a remand for additional fact-finding on the application of the reasonableness balancing test. Justice Stevens questioned whether
there were less intrusive, equally effective or even more effective alternatives,
such as placing flyers on Post Office employees' cars, given the victim's having
finished working there just before the fatal accident. Stevens also questioned
whether the majority had underestimated the impact of the delay on drivers
at a location where many of them were likely tired, leaving a factory at the
end of their shift. The accompanying large surge of vehicles at the roadblock
could not easily be justified by an investigatory method so likely to be ineffective, Stevens maintained. Because the roadblock was unpublicized, he also
speculated that waiting drivers, who would not know the purpose of the search
until reaching the checkpoint, might be alarmed at being ensnared in an un-
expected midnight roadblock—facts and possibilities entirely ignored by the
majority. Stevens's search for equally or, in his view, *more* effective, but less
intrusive, alternatives better reflects history's lesson, and that of the Framers'
social-contract theory, that individualized suspicion and public safety are presumptively compatible so that the former should not easily be sacrificed.[21]

The Court also missed an opportunity because of its ready presumption
that such roadblocks will not proliferate. The Court could have explained that,
should their presumption prove wrong, police might improve the chances of
roadblocks surviving constitutional review if they included in their program
some mechanisms of community input and review. The community need not
necessarily exercise a veto, but its input could discourage abuses, suggest alternatives, help to improve effectiveness, and reduce alarm and annoyance, perhaps by creating pressure for the police to first try some of the sorts of options suggested by Justice Stevens. Such a community-oversight suggestion
would admittedly be dicta, but it would be useful dicta along lines that the
Court has occasionally used before and in recognition of the importance of
giving the People, and not just individuals, a voice in setting search and seizure policy.[22]

Stigma and Humiliation Wrongly Minimized

Although the *Lidster* Court implicitly considered stigmatic concerns in its decision, other times the Court has wrongly *expressly* rejected any serious inquiry
into individual and group stigma, humiliation, and consequent righteous indignation. Famously, in *Terry v. Ohio*, the Court first held that police can engage in brief investigatory stops based upon just "reasonable suspicion" that

criminal activity is afoot rather than requiring full probable cause. Police can further frisk the person stopped for weapons if there is also reasonable suspicion that he is dangerous. In so holding, the Court recognized, citing a report of the President's Commission on Law Enforcement and Administration of Justice, that "[i]n many communities, field interrogations are a major source of friction between the police and minority groups."[23] The Court elaborated:

> While the frequency with which "frisking" forms a part of field interrogation practices varies tremendously with the locale, the objective of the interrogation, and the particular officer, it cannot help but be a severely exacerbating factor in police-community tensions. This is particularly true in situations where the "stop and frisk" of youths or minority group members is "motivated by the officers' perceived need to maintain the power image of the beat officer, an aim sometimes accomplished by humiliating anyone who attempts to undermine police control of the streets."[24]

Yet the Court minimized the value of these observations in deciding whether the exclusionary rule should be available as a remedy for admittedly insulting stops and frisks. Said the Court, "The wholesale harassment by certain elements of the police community, of which minority groups, particularly Negroes, frequently complain, will not be stopped by the exclusion of any evidence from any criminal trial." Correspondingly, noted the Court, "a rigid and unthinking application of the exclusionary rule" would be "in futile protest against practices which it can never be used effectively to control" and "may exact a high toll in human injury and frustration of efforts to prevent crime." Curiously, at the same time as it said that fear of abuses of the stop-and-frisk power "cannot properly dictate our decision with respect to the powers of the police in genuine [i.e., nonabusive] investigative and preventive situations," the Court conceded that "the degree of community resentment aroused by particular practices is clearly relevant to an assessment of the quality of the intrusion upon reasonable expectations of personal security caused by those practices." Moreover, said the Court, when the judiciary identifies overbearing or harassing police conduct or police conduct lacking adequate evidentiary justification, it must condemn the conduct and exclude its fruits, and "other remedies" (presumably lawsuits and administrative sanctions) may be pursued by the parties.[25]

What the Court seemed to be saying is that, if a court is confronted with evidence that a particular stop-and-frisk was "overbearing or harassing"— presumably meaning one "motivated by the perceived need to maintain the power image of the police officer"—then suppression of evidence might be appropriate. But absent such case-specific evidence of officer wrongdoing, the Court could not take into account the *risk* of such abuses' arising or their impact on the community in crafting the law governing stop-and-frisks. Ill-motivated officers will do wrong anyway, reasoned the Court, while more crimes would go undetected.[26]

Furthermore, and even more confusingly, the Court contradicted itself on the role of community *perceptions* in determining what is reasonable under the Fourth Amendment. On the one hand, the Court suggested that community perceptions hold great weight. On the other hand, the Court also suggested that it could do little to improve those perceptions via an exclusionary remedy and, therefore, apparently did not take those perceptions into account in crafting the relevant constitutional rule. In doing this, the Court wrongly conflated the choice of the appropriate *remedy* for violation of a constitutional rule with the choice of what the *substance* of that rule should be—a conflation later repeatedly condemned by the Court in other opinions.[27]

The Court's approach in *Terry* is also hard to square with its later case law declaring police officers' subjective intentions irrelevant under the Fourth Amendment. Moreover, if it is the officer's "image," the victim's "humiliation," and the community's "resentment" that matters in reasonableness balancing— and frisking *"cannot help but be* a severely exacerbating factor in police-community tensions"—then individual and community *perceptions* should hold great weight. Indeed, ignoring those perceptions, as later experience has shown, both undermines crime-control efforts because distrustful communities cease assisting the police *and* can spark community violence. The Court's later case law has complicated this state of affairs by rendering even an officer's racist discriminatory selection of whom to stop irrelevant under the Fourth Amendment, while making such discrimination almost impossible to prove under the Fourteenth. Additionally, if resentment arises from the widespread use of stop-and-frisks based on mere reasonable suspicion, then the Court's later-adopted position that such suspicion can be not only lower in *quantity* than probable cause but also based on evidence of lesser *quality* should further increase officer discretion over whom to stop, thus potentially further exacerbating community tension and indignation.[28]

The Court's vagueness, unwillingness adequately to consider community emotional impact, downplaying of stigma and humiliation, and throwing up of its hands about its ability to prevent abuses has led to a steady deterioration in the evidence needed to establish reasonable suspicion and in the trust between police and the communities they control. Again, if the Court had, for example, set up a regime in which the community would be directly involved in setting stop-and-frisk policy and in monitoring the police—much like an experimental such program now under way in Cincinnati—community resentment *and* police "abuses," however defined, could be reduced; the effectiveness of criminal investigation and prevention increased because of the resulting rise in community trust and police-community cooperation; and the message sent that the police must respect citizens while protecting their safety. The Court need not set out the precise contours of such a mechanism, but it could set out broad outlines, allow for wide jurisdictional variation to take account of local conditions and resources, and give notice of the likelihood of future exclusion of evidence obtained by departments not making adequate efforts to reach out to the community. At the very least, the Court could have asked to have been briefed on the viability of such an option.[29]

I am not suggesting that more direct citizen involvement is the answer to all difficult Fourth Amendment questions. But it is an option that should be considered. The working assumption of the social-contract philosophy of the Framing era is that the state is necessary to taming private violence that would fray the bonds of peoplehood, and, simultaneously, an energized People acting directly or through their branches of government is necessary to taming state violence. Creative use of judicial incentives can foster a range of mechanisms to tame the state without unleashing a bestial war of man against man. What sometimes seems like a stark choice—safety *or* civil rights—need not be one. If more-aggressive policing is necessary to public safety, then more-aggressive monitoring by citizens, governmental transparency, and multibranch checking and balancing of the state is necessary too. When the state comes closer to de-livering both safety *and* justice, the state's legitimacy is enhanced. That, in turn, social-science research suggests, will promote obedience to law and coopera-tion with law enforcement, still further enhancing safety while reducing state incentives to excess because other options for effective policing are available.[30]

In a complex modern world with limited resources, direct citizen involve-ment in new deliberative institutions may sometimes be impracticable. Where that is so, or where the resistance of state institutions to more direct action cannot initially be overcome, next-best alternatives should be considered, such as data collection and reporting requirements (as has been used to combat ra-cial profiling) or videotaping searches, options that better enable other branches to police the executive or the executive to police itself. Political pressure for such measures is certainly increasing, and some police departments have vol-untarily increased their transparency. Justice Breyer recently suggested that he sees the availability of at least adequate tools for internal executive monitoring of its street-level law enforcers as relevant in determining Fourth Amendment reasonableness. In *United States v. Flores Montano,* the Court held that a suspi-cionless disassembly and search of a driver's gas tank at the border was reason-able under the circumstances.[31] Justice Breyer's brief concurring opinion read, in its entirety, as follows:

> I join the Court's opinion in full. I also note that Customs keeps track of the border searches its agents conduct, including the reasons for the searches. Tr. Of Oral Arg. 53–54. This administrative process should help minimize con-cerns that gas tank searches might be undertaken in an abusive manner.[32]

As brief as this opinion is, Justice Breyer's choosing to write it for the sole purpose of highlighting the availability of mechanisms to aid internal monitoring
shows the salience of that point for him.

Citizen ignorance of the technologies and procedures involved and lagging
citizen motivation to act as an effective watchdog can also be obstacles to useful direct involvement in monitoring the state, even when state institutions are
willing to be accommodating. In such instances, a careful focus on that subgroup of citizens most directly affected by a state search and seizure practice
offers a potential solution. One example is workplace alcohol and drug testing.
Where such drug testing is done of government workers or of private-sector
employees pursuant to government safety regulations, there is state action; the
Fourth Amendment is, therefore, involved. The affected workers have an interest in ensuring the accuracy and fairness of any testing program. But, more
than this, such programs sometimes go beyond their stated purpose of ensuring worker and public safety, serving as a way to assert the employer's authority, to silence and humiliate dissenting workers who are surreptitiously (rather
than randomly) chosen as a focus of attention, and to mold workers' off-the-
job lifestyles in ways that may have little to do with their job (for example,
altering clothes and choice of friends that might engender suspicion of drug
use or of efforts to subvert testing). These sorts of abuses are not simply the
imaginings of paranoid employees but have been documented in a number of
studies. Sometimes a strong employee union might offer sufficient protection
against such abuses. But where unions are weak, nonexistent, or corrupt, ensuring adequate worker voice in the employer's creation and operation of the
testing program, and in the government's formulation of any relevant regulations and policies, should be relevant factors in determining the program's reasonableness.[33]

My focus in this book has significantly, though not entirely, been on the
public, political functions of the Fourth Amendment because they are so often
ignored. But the text and history of the amendment assumes that it protects
both the "People" and individual "persons" with no conflict between them.
The *Atwater* case, discussed briefly in chapter 1, is a reminder that individuals,
not merely communities, can be stigmatized. In *Atwater* the Court upheld an
arrest of a mother for violating seatbelt laws, a violation punishable only by
a fine. Gail Atwater was driving with her three-year-old son and five-year-old
daughter in the front seat.[34] Here is how Justice O'Connor, in a dissent joined
by Justices Stevens, Ginsburg, and Breyer, described the scene:

> There is no question that Officer Turek's actions severely infringed Atwa-
> ter's liberty and privacy. Turek was loud and accusatory from the moment he
> approached Atwater's car. Atwater's young children were terrified and hysteri-
> cal. Yet when Atwater asked Turek to lower his voice because he was scaring

the children, he responded by jabbing his finger in Atwater's face and saying, "You're going to jail." Having made the decision to arrest, Turek did not inform Atwater of her right to remain silent. . . .

Atwater asked if she could take her children to a friend's house down the street before going to the police station. But Turek . . . refused and said he would take the children into custody as well. Only the intervention of neighborhood children who had witnessed the scene and summoned one of Atwater's friends saved the children from being hauled to jail with their mother.[35]

Once the children were gone, Turek handcuffed Atwater and drove her to the police station without securing her seatbelt. At the station, she "was forced to remove her shoes, relinquish her possessions, and wait in a holding cell for about an hour." She then appeared before a judge, who finally informed her of her rights and allowed her to be released upon posting bond. She next "returned to the scene of the arrest, only to find that her car had been towed."[36]

The majority agreed that Atwater had been gratuitously humiliated "by a police officer who was (at best) exercising extremely poor judgment." Indeed, the majority admitted that the injury done to Atwater personally far outweighed the City's countervailing concerns. Nevertheless, in the same breath the Court belittled her experience as "no more 'harmful to . . . privacy or . . . physical interests than the normal custodial arrest,'" the arrest and booking being "inconvenient and embarrassing to Atwater, but not so extraordinary as to violate the Fourth Amendment." Moreover, stressed the Court, case-by-case reasonableness determinations for arrests based on probable cause would consume judicial resources, involve the judiciary in an inappropriate least restrictive alternatives test, and create disincentives to arrest when there was no empirical evidence before the Court of a nationwide plague of warrantless arrests for petty offenses. Therefore, the arrest was reasonable.[37]

Justice O'Connor's dissenting opinion rejected the state's two proffered justifications for the arrest: it would encourage Atwater to appear for trial and promote enforcement of child-safety laws. O'Connor dismissed these justifications, for Atwater was a local longtime resident who had been driving slowly on a street with no traffic and who had no more of a criminal record than a failure-to-signal-lane-change violation ten years earlier and who had promptly apologized for the seat-belt violation and accepted responsibility. Such a woman was neither a flight risk nor a danger to the community. O'Connor also considered the *costs* to Atwater, her children, and the community of upholding arrest as a law-enforcement tool for such a minor offense:

> With respect to the related goal of child welfare, the decision to arrest Atwater was nothing short of counterproductive. Atwater's children witnessed Officer Turek yell at their mother and threaten to take them all into custody.

Ultimately, they were forced to leave her behind with Turek, knowing that she was being taken to jail. Understandably, the 3-year-old boy was "very, very traumatized." After the incident, he had to see a child psychologist regularly, who reported that the boy "felt very guilty that he couldn't stop this horrible thing . . . he was powerless to help his mother or sister." Both of Atwater's children are now terrified at the sight of any police car. According to Atwater, the arrest "just never leaves us. It's a conversation we have every other day, once a week, and it's—it raises its head constantly in our lives."[38]

O'Connor, while not necessarily adopting a least restrictive alternatives analysis, seemed to embrace at least a *less restrictive* alternatives analysis. Issuing a citation, O'Connor explained, very likely would have resulted in Atwater buckling up in the future and improved the children's welfare by teaching them "an important lesson in accepting responsibility and obeying the law. Arresting Atwater, though, taught the children an entirely different lesson: That 'the bad person' could just as easily be the policeman as it could be the most horrible person they could imagine."[39]

O'Connor further placed the burden on the state of proving that the incentives created by the majority's arrest-for-petty-offenses rule would not be to expand nationwide use of this means of law enforcement. The mere *risk* created to the nation's civil liberties based on the incentives structure created by the law was a sufficiently weighty concern to justify seeking a better way.

Additionally, the majority's rule vested unbounded discretion in the street officer because an arrest carries with it the authority to search the arrestee's person and the entire passenger compartment of the car, including any purse or package inside, in addition to the impoundment of the car and the inventorying of all its contents. O'Connor worried about the impact of this discretion on less politically powerful groups: "as the recent debate over racial profiling demonstrates all too clearly," a "relatively minor traffic infraction may often serve as an excuse for stopping and harassing an individual." Precisely because the Court has eschewed inquiry into officers' motivations, O'Connor believed that the justices must "vigilantly ensure that officers' poststop actions . . . comport with the Fourth Amendment's guarantee of reasonableness." Indeed, the "Court neglects the Fourth Amendment's command in the name of administrative ease" and "cloaks the pointless indignity that Gail Atwater suffered with the mantle of reasonableness."[40]

O'Connor nevertheless recognized that there may be unusual cases in which an arrest for a fine-only offense was necessary. To provide for this possibility, O'Connor favored this rule: Where there is probable cause to believe that a fine-only offense has been committed, the officer should ordinarily issue only a citation; he may, however, proceed further, but only if he points to *specific and articulable facts that, taken together with rational inferences drawn from those facts, reasonably warrant the additional intrusion of a full custodial arrest.*

Justice O'Connor's dissent better reflects the lessons of history than does the majority's opinion. O'Connor recognizes that needless humiliation of an individual is an important factor in determining Fourth Amendment reasonableness. Correspondingly, however, humiliation of the individual often causes corresponding injuries to other persons, groups, and communities, as well as to the People as a whole. Atwater's humiliation psychologically scarred her children, fostering in them attitudes of fear of, rather than trust in, the police. Healing those scars will impose costs in time and effort on the medical establishment, teachers, schoolmates, friends, and family. Moreover, effectively sanctioning her humiliation creates incentives for abuses by other officers throughout the nation. The fate of the People and its individual members are inseparably linked.

A least restrictive alternatives rule, if that is what O'Connor's opinion implies, also embraces the assumption that safety and civil rights are consistent because it forces the state to look for ways equally effective at achieving its law-enforcement goals while better protecting fundamental Fourth Amendment values. This logic is embraced by the Court for most "fundamental rights," and there is no question that the Fourth Amendment is "fundamental." There is no logical reason to treat the Fourth Amendment differently.[41]

Finally, O'Connor resists the majority's easy willingness to sacrifice the dictates of individualized justice. She insists on requiring specific evidence that a particular person under a relevant set of circumstances must nevertheless be arrested for a petty offense. The importance of that insistence should extend throughout the constitutional law of search and seizure.

Lapsed Commitment to Individualized Justice

The Court's lapsed commitment to individualized justice, of which O'Connor complained in *Atwater,* is characteristic of much of its Fourth Amendment jurisprudence. For example, the Court once permitted informants' tips—often coming from "stoolies" or other shady characters with a motive to lie—to count toward probable cause *only* if there was reliable proof *both* that the tipster was a truthful person *and* that he had a solid basis for his claims. But, decades ago, the Court replaced that test with one that looks to the "totality of the circumstances," always permitting tips to be considered in the probable-cause calculus, even if there was serious doubt about the informant's truthfulness or, if he were truthful, about whether he had personal knowledge or an equivalently trustworthy evidentiary basis to support his statements.[42]

The Court has also apparently weakened the quantity of evidence needed to establish probable cause, defining it as a "substantial chance" that there will be evidence of criminality found at a particular time and place. Judges and commentators alike have generally read this as meaning less than a 50 percent chance of guilt, the average of judges in a survey on the question being about a 46 percent chance of guilt. Although the Court avoids this sort of numerical precision, it has suggested that the figure might vary with the situation and might sometimes be even lower.[43]

Maryland v. Pringle illustrates the point, especially when we compare the Court's opinion to that of the lower courts. In *Pringle*, an officer stopped a car for speeding at about 3:00 a.m. There were three occupants in the car: the driver and owner; the front-seat passenger, Joseph Jermaine Pringle; and a back-seat passenger. When the driver, in response to the officer's request to produce license and registration, opened the glove compartment, the officer saw inside it a large amount of rolled-up cash. Although a computer check revealed no outstanding violations, the officer asked the driver to get out and issued him an oral warning, and a second patrol car arrived. The driver, in answering the officer's question on the point, denied having weapons or narcotics in the car and next consented to a vehicle search. That search uncovered $763 from the glove compartment and five glassine plastic baggies containing cocaine from behind the back-seat armrest.[44] As the Court of Appeals of Maryland explained,

> The armrest in the back seat was the type that goes up and down. At the time of the stop, the armrest was in the upright position and flat against the seat. When Officer Snyder pulled down the armrest, he found the drugs, which had been placed between the armrest and the back seat of the car and, absent the pulling down of the armrest, *were not visible.*[45]

The officer questioned all three men, telling them that he would arrest them all unless someone admitted to ownership of the drugs. None of the men admitted ownership of either the drugs or the money, and all three were arrested and taken to the police station. Later that morning, Pringle waived his *Miranda* rights and gave oral and written confessions that the cocaine was his and that he meant to sell it, though he denied that the other occupants knew anything about the drugs, and they were therefore released.

The trial court denied Pringle's motion to suppress the confession as the fruit of an illegal arrest, concluding that the arrest was done with probable cause. After a jury convicted Pringle of possession of cocaine and possession with intent to distribute it, he appealed his sentence of ten years without the possibility of parole.

The Court of Appeals of Maryland reversed, finding insufficient evidence of probable cause. Central to that court's decision was that there was no evidence that the drugs, and, for that matter, the money, were visible to all occupants before the officer stopped the car. Probable cause for an arrest, explained that court, had to involve adequate proof that Pringle specifically committed the crimes of simple possession and possession with intent to sell. The substantive criminal law of Maryland concerning "possession" required proof that Pringle *knew* that the drugs were present and that the defendant, singly or jointly, exercised an actual or potential restraining or directing influence over the drugs, that is, that he had dominion and control. Although the court relied primarily on cases on the sufficiency of the evidence to take the possession question to the jury at trial, a standard turning on whether a reasonable jury could find guilt beyond a reasonable doubt, the court recognized that probable cause involved a significantly lower "quantum" of evidence. Nevertheless, concluded the Maryland Court, there was *no* evidence here available to the officer at the time of the arrest that Pringle was specifically aware of the cocaine's presence, much less of his influence over it. Pringle's mere presence in the car, in close proximity to the cocaine, was insufficiently individualized evidence of *his* wrongdoing. The Maryland Court explained:

> Under respondent's reasoning, if contraband was found in a twelve-passenger van, or perhaps a bus or other kind of vehicle, or even a place, i.e., a movie theater, the police would be permitted to place everyone in such a vehicle or place [them] under arrest until some person confessed to being in possession of the contraband. Simply stated, a policy of arresting everyone until somebody confesses is constitutionally unacceptable.[46]

The state court likewise rejected the relevance of the large wad of money in the glove compartment because the officer also lacked evidence of the money's visibility to Pringle at the time of his arrest. Thus, concluded the Maryland court,

> The money in the case at bar was not in the plain view of the police officer or petitioner; rather it was located in a closed glove compartment and was opened by the car's owner/driver in response to the officer's request for the car's registration. There are insufficient facts that would lead a reasonable person to believe that *petitioner*, at the time of his arrest, had prior knowledge of the money or had exercised dominion and control over it. We hold that a police officer's discovery of money in a closed glove compartment and cocaine concealed behind the rear armrest of a car is insufficient to establish probable cause for an arrest of a front seat passenger, who is not the owner or person in control of the vehicle, for possession of the cocaine.[47]

The U.S. Supreme Court reversed, thoroughly rejecting the logic of the Court of Appeals of Maryland. In doing so, the Court stressed that the "probable-cause standard is incapable of precise definition or quantification into percentages

because it deals with probabilities and depends on the totality of the circumstances." Moreover, " 'the *quanta* . . . of proof' appropriate in ordinary judicial
proceedings are inapplicable to the decision to issue a warrant. . . . Finely tuned
standards such as proof beyond a reasonable doubt or by a preponderance of
the evidence, useful in formal trials, have no place in the [probable-cause] decision." Rather, said the Court, the probable-cause standard looks at all the
events leading up to the arrest to decide whether, "viewed from the standpoint
of an objectively reasonable police officer, [they] amount to 'probable cause.' "
At the same time, the Court recognized that the "long-prevailing standard of
probable cause protects 'citizens from rash and unreasonable interferences with
privacy and from unfounded charges of crime,' while giving 'fair leeway for
enforcing the law in the community's protection.' " Moreover, although the
probable-cause concept is a "fluid," nontechnical one, "turning on the assessment of probabilities in particular factual contexts—not readily, or even use-
fully, reduced to a neat set of legal rules—the *belief of guilt must be particularized
with respect to the person to be searched or seized.*"[48]

Despite these statements about particularized evidence of guilt, the Court
focused not so much on evidence of the *visibility* of the drugs and money to
Pringle as on their *accessibility* to anyone in the car:

> In this case, Pringle was one of three men riding in a Nissan Maxima at
> 3:16 a.m. There was $763 of rolled-up cash in the glove compartment *directly
> in front of Pringle.* Five plastic glassine baggies of cocaine were behind the
> back-seat armrest and *accessible to all three men.* Upon questioning, the three
> men failed to offer any information with respect to the ownership of the
> cocaine or the money.[49]

The Court criticized the state appellate court's declaration that "[m]oney,
without more, is innocuous," complaining that the state court's "consideration
of the money in isolation, rather than as a factor in the totality of the circumstances, is mistaken in light of our precedents."[50] Accordingly, said the Court,

> We think it an entirely reasonable inference from these facts that any or all
> three of the occupants had knowledge of, and exercised dominion and con-
> trol over, the cocaine. Thus a reasonable officer could conclude that there was
> probable cause to believe Pringle committed the crime of possession of co-
> caine, either solely or jointly.[51]

Finally, the Court rejected Pringle's argument that this was a mere "guilt-by-
association case." Pringle relied for this argument in part on *Ybarra v. Illinois.* In
Ybarra, police executing a warrant to search a tavern and its bartender for evidence of possession of a controlled substance conducted pat-down searches of

all the customers present, including Ybarra, and seized six tin-foil packets containing heroin from a cigarette pack retrieved from Ybarra's pocket. The Court invalidated the search, stressing that it was based on insufficiently individualized suspicion as to Ybarra and noting that "a person's mere propinquity to others independently suspected of criminal activity does not, without more, give rise to probable cause to search that person."[52] The *Pringle* Court distinguished *Ybarra* this way:

> This case is quite different from *Ybarra*. Pringle and his two companions were in a relatively small automobile, not a public tavern. In *Wyoming v. Houghton* [citation omitted], we noted that "a car passenger—unlike the unwitting tavern patron in *Ybarra*—will often be engaged in a common enterprise with the driver, and have the same interest in concealing the fruits or the evidence of their wrongdoing." [citations omitted]. Here we think it was reasonable for the officer to infer a common enterprise among the three men. The quantity of drugs and cash in the car indicated the likelihood of drug dealing, an enterprise to which a dealer would be unlikely to admit an innocent person with the potential to furnish evidence against him.[53]

The Court also distinguished another case, *United States v. DiRe*,[54] in which it found insufficient evidence of probable cause:

> In *DiRe*, a federal investigator had been told by an informant, Reed, that he was to receive counterfeit gasoline ration coupons from a certain Buttitta at a particular place. The investigator went to the appointed place and saw Reed, the sole occupant of the rear seat of the car, holding gasoline ration coupons. There were two other occupants in the car: Buttitta in the driver's seat and DiRe in the front passenger seat. Reed informed the investigator that Buttitta had given him counterfeit coupons. Thereupon, all three men were arrested and searched. After noting that the officers had no information implicating DiRe and no information pointing to DiRe's possession of coupons, unless presence in the car warranted that inference, we concluded that the officer lacked probable cause to believe that DiRe was involved in the crime. [citations omitted]. We said "[a]ny inference that everyone on the scene of a crime is a party to it must disappear if the Government singles out the guilty person." [citations omitted]. No such singling out occurred in this case; none of the three men provided information with respect to the ownership of the cocaine or money.[55]

Several points about the Court's reasoning in *Pringle* are noteworthy. First, there was no particularized evidence whatsoever that Pringle knew that the drugs or the money were there. Of course, the drugs and the cash were *accessible* to any person in the car, but the Court apparently inferred Pringle's knowledge of the drugs' presence entirely from the fact of its accessibility. To do that, the Court relied primarily on a very broad generalization, namely that a passenger in a car will "often be engaged in a common enterprise with the driver." The Court refined this generalization by making the further generalization that a drug dealer would likely not let an "innocent person" into a car for fear that such a person could later testify against the dealer. This latter point is questionable—my own life experience in high school and as a prosecutor shows that the contrary may often be true, that is, that sober people, users, and dealers can all be friends and yet, in certain settings, the sober ones are thoroughly unaware of their friends' criminality. Although some degree of generalization is involved in all human reasoning, reliance almost entirely on generalizations seems a long way away from the *individualized* suspicions that are meant to define probable cause.[56]

Second, the *Pringle* Court relied on the refusal of any one of the three suspects to admit to owning the drugs. Considering such evidence in connection with the probable-cause determination seems to violate the Fifth Amendment privilege against self-incrimination—a point made by Pringle in his brief but thoroughly ignored in the Court's opinion. Pringle thus faced a variation on the "cruel trilemma" that the privilege seeks to prevent: admit to the crime, resulting in your arrest and likely conviction; deny the crime, thus committing the offense of obstructing justice and again facing arrest; or remain silent, your reticence itself counting as evidence of your guilt and thus, yet again, resulting in your arrest. Furthermore, silence—the *absence* of certain evidence—plus two contestable generalizations seems a thin reed on which to rest the conclusion that Pringle had dominion and control over the drugs.[57]

Third, the Court conceded that in fact the evidence was equally consistent with Pringle *or* one of the other vehicle occupants *or* all three of them knowing of the drugs' presence. This is but another way of saying that there was a one-in-three chance that Pringle had dominion over the drugs. But a one-third probability is widely considered by courts and commentators to be far more consistent with reasonable suspicion than probable cause, despite the Court's protestations that probable cause cannot be quantified.[58]

There clearly was probable cause to confiscate the cocaine. But the Court's finding probable cause *to arrest* Pringle cheapens the probable-cause concept in a way that is hard to square with the Framers' commitment to individualized justice. The Maryland courts by far had the better judgment.

This entire picture is one of a precedential landscape that hides from our vision the passion with which the Revolutionary and Founding generations sought the kind of trustworthy, individualized justice represented by the specific warrant. The landscape also keeps in the shade the close connection between the struggle for robust search and seizure protections and the struggle for political voice. A jurisprudence more skeptical of informants, less willing to dispense with warrants, more insistent on reliable evidence of *individualized* wrongdoing, and more sensitive to free-speech and political-voice concerns would come closer to embracing the "lessons" taught by the history of the original Fourth Amendment.[59]

Conclusion of Part 1

In my analysis of the current implications of the history of the original Fourth Amendment, I often raised concerns about racial equality. That may seem odd given the amendment's ratification at a time when the Constitution embraced racial slavery. The short response to this critique is that even the original Fourth Amendment must today be read in light of the concerns about racial equality embodied in the Fourteenth Amendment. The longer response will follow in just a few pages, as part 2 explores search and seizure concepts during slavery and Reconstruction. For those who remain skeptical of my position here, I hope that part 2 will further strengthen the lessons articulated here and modify them in several ways. In particular, the later history will elevate the importance of racial consciousness, strengthen the link between free speech and the Fourth Amendment, and redefine "the People" in a more inclusive manner —a redefinition with important consequences. Part 2 is also primarily organized by the three interests protected by the Fourth Amendment—privacy, property, and freedom of movement—to emphasize the error of current doctrine in elevating privacy above the other two interests.[60]

For now, however, I stand on this reinterpretation of the history of the original Fourth Amendment. It is a history that reminds us that search and seizure rights are not mere technicalities protecting criminals from their just deserts. The concerns underlying the Fourth Amendment were passionate political ones that went to the heart of what it meant to be part of the "American people." At a time in which we wage a war with terrorism and face technological devices that can eviscerate the remnants of privacy, remembering the centrality of the Fourth Amendment to the American experience seems the most important lesson of all. The 1791 ratification of the Bill of Rights only began that experience, however, because the Fourth Amendment—which originally applied only to the federal government—was later incorporated against the states by the 1868 addition to the Constitution of the Fourteenth Amendment. In the process, the Fourth Amendment's meaning was refined to embrace lessons that the nation painfully learned from its struggles with slavery and Reconstruction. Those struggles, like the ones leading up to the original Fourth Amendment, occurred in the context of expressive political violence, this time violence inseparably tied to, and originating in, the brutality of human bondage.[61]

PART II

The Reconstructed Fourth Amendment

If the connection between expressive violence and metaphorical political slav-ery defined the original Fourth Amendment, it was the link between such violence and chattel slavery that defined the reconstruction of that amend-ment. The Fourth Amendment protects interests in free movement, privacy, and property. Limiting slaves' free movement via slave patrols, a pass system, and fugitive-slave laws gave masters control over both bondsmen's labor and their families, for the fear of forced family separation loomed over every poten-tially disobedient slave. Disputes over the federal government's involvement in enforcing slave locomotive controls ignited Northern anger.

The nature of the North-South dispute cannot be fully appreciated without exploring the meaning that such controls held for Southern masters, their bondsmen, and Northern whites and blacks. For white Southerners, mobility control was commanded by God and by the nature of a necessarily exclusion-ary white republicanism as part of the obligation owed by superiors to their dependent inferiors. Moreover, social and economic advancement required white mobility to head West with their slaves. Any effort to expand black loco-motive freedom was thus viewed as a blow at the heart of Southern civiliza-tion. The infamous *Dred Scott* case would eventually nationalize this Southern vision. Slaves, however, assigned their own mobility a doppelganger meaning. Identifying with the ancient Hebrews in the biblical Exodus story, slaves saw physical movement as individuals and as a people to be definitional to politi-cal and spiritual liberation. Yet most slaves, and many (though far from all) black intellectuals, embraced a complex inclusionary republicanism in which blacks were a nation-within-a-nation, thus still members of the broader Ameri-can polity.

Increasingly for many Northerners, black locomotive restrictions were anti-thetical to free-labor ideals and true republicanism. If not a truly inclusionary philosophy, Northern thinking evolved toward recognizing blacks as human beings entitled to the same civil (though not necessarily the same political and social) rights as whites. Furthermore, blacks were, so long as they remained on American soil (and many Northern whites wished to encourage the slaves sim-ply to leave the country), members of the American polity, albeit second-class members. Northern whites resisted fugitive slaves' recapture by enacting anti-kidnapping laws and personal-liberty laws that required more muscular due process and through mob actions. Northerners linked free physical movement to economic movement, the "right to rise," making controls on black loco-motion an affront to free-labor economics. That same set of economic ideas required free Northern white mobility to seek new opportunities out West, opportunities that would be denied were the territories to become slavery bas-tions in which free labor would be degraded. Northern whites thus agreed with Southern whites that black mobility represented a threat to the long-term sur-vival of the Southern way of life. The difference was that many Northerners hoped such containment of the institution of Southern slavery would indeed kill it. The alternative was the death of the Northern free-labor system and its accompanying robust republicanism. Although the original Bill of Rights ap-plied only to the federal government, examination of too-often-forgotten legal briefs in high-profile cases reveal that these contests were nevertheless waged expressly in Fourth Amendment terms when they reached the courts. Even when this was not so, Fourth Amendment protections, for example against certain seizures of the person, were implicitly involved by the federal govern-ment's marshaling of state force to seize slaves and return them to their mas-ters against their will.

Slaves were also denied *legal* privacy protections, yet, while lacking much actual individual privacy, they eked out a form of group privacy, enabling them to develop a counterculture hidden from whites' prying eyes. Recognizing group privacy has important implications for the unduly individualistic mod-ern understanding of the scope of Fourth Amendment privacy protections. Abolitionists assailed masters' invasions of individual privacy (modernly un-derstood to include bodily integrity) by whippings, rapes, and invasions of the sanctity of the slave family. White Southerners responded by silencing aboli-tionists' speech via seizures of their mail and their persons. This assault on white civil liberties in turn heightened Northern white fears of an aristocratic Slave Power bent on crushing a republicanism of free inquiry. Search and sei-zure activities and invasion of free-speech protections thus became closely linked in the Northern mind.

Southern property law recognized a white right to own blacks as human property, treating them as fungible rather than each as a unique, distinct being to be judged for his or her own special character and actions. White property law also precluded slaves' legal ownership of property. Yet slaves in practice engaged in a sort of property ownership with the tolerance of their masters. Slaves also had a sophisticated understanding of the dehumanizing consequences of their status as fungible property and of the denial of their own right to property ownership. Northerners saw the Southern system of property law as entrenching the power of an aggressive monied aristocracy that was seeking to spread its diseased culture throughout the nation. Confining, and thus ultimately ending, that system and all that it represented was essential to preserving citizen virtue. Northern opposition to the Slave Power's property concepts is thus rightly understood as rejecting any system of laws that treats humans as fungible, an observation with important implications for maintaining the probable-cause concept as one rooted in *individualized* suspicion.

The outbreak of the Civil War did not initially resolve these conflicts. Some Northern officials indeed continued enthusiastic enforcement of the federal fugitive-slave laws in the early months of the war. It is also too little noticed that Southern secessionists rooted a large part of their argument in the belief that Lincoln would halt the federal government's seizure of abolitionist literature in the South. That seizure had proceeded for decades as executive policy after Congress, in a debate couched expressly in Fourth and First Amendment terms, refused more express legislative authority for such action. Southern secessionists fervently declared that the peculiar institution could not long survive such an unimpeded abolitionist verbal onslaught.

The war also spurred many slaves to take their locomotive freedom into their own hands, fleeing to Union lines. Though at first resisted by many in the Union military and administration, the usefulness of slaves as purveyors of information and the direct visibility of their plight to Union soldiers, combined with other forces, helped to sway Union policy. Debates over acts permitting Northern "confiscation" of slaves forced the Union to wrestle expressly with its own understandings of property. The pressing Union need for manpower and the growing fever for a war to punish the recalcitrant South further spurred this Northern rethinking, resulting in the Emancipation Proclamation and the Union's acceptance of 180,000 former slaves into the military. Meanwhile, an increasingly manpower-strapped Southern homefront sought to tighten its grip on slave mobility as slave resistance simultaneously grew. The Thirteenth Amendment ended forever the national legality of such locomotive limits.

But that amendment did not kill the Slave Power, as Southern counterrevolution via Black Codes and state and private violence sought to re-create slavery in fact, if not in law. The Fourteenth Amendment's guarantees of due process, equal protection, and protection of the privileges and immunities of all U.S. citizens, which now included native-born and naturalized blacks, sought to drive the final stake into the Slave Power's still-beating heart. Much of the history of, and debate over, that amendment focused on unreasonable searches and seizures, such as the infamous seizure and banishment from South Carolina of the Northern white leader Samuel Hoar. Hoar in turn had gone to South Carolina to challenge the state's seizure of black seamen on ships docking in its port. If the costs of incarceration were not promptly paid, such seamen were sold into slavery. Other search and seizure disputes of importance in understanding the amendment included searches of black homes followed by seizure of black firearms, unjustified arrests, mandated passes for blacks away from plantations, beatings by state officials, legally authorized whippings, and revived patrols. The Fourteenth Amendment, in applying most of the Bill of Rights, including the Fourth Amendment, to the states, meant to end such practices. In incorporating the Fourth Amendment against the states, the Fourteenth Amendment thus altered the Fourth Amendment's meaning in ways examined in this book's final chapter.

The rejection of Southern modes of expressive political violence in favor of revised Northern ones must begin, however, by exploring the nature and meaning of the messages inherent in Southern brutality. Those messages in turn are inseparable from the network of meanings that formed the Southern honor culture.

6 Expressive Violence and Southern Honor

The violence inherent in antebellum racial slavery was not only about labor discipline and economic efficiency. Slavery had become identified with the Southern way of life.[1] Whites' violence toward slaves reflected and bolstered the distinctive culture of the White South. Such violence sent at least four messages central to Southern white identity: (1) that men of honor were in no way like slaves, (2) that the supposedly "moderate" use of violence sanctified slavery as a Christian institution blessed by God, (3) that racial difference created a "natural" slave class, and (4) that black slaves were dependent, childlike, and subordinate beings needing their master's benevolent and firm rule. These messages came not only from whites as individuals but also from statutory and common law and through mob assaults on suspected insurrectionists and abolitionists, whether white or black. Understanding the communicative violence of slavery sets the stage for understanding the search and seizure practices that were at slavery's heart. Those practices in turn rested on the South's distinctive honor culture.

Slavery and Southern Honor

Southern whites defined slaves as persons without honor. Therefore, for whites, being "honorable" or a "gentleman" meant being wholly unlike a slave. White violence against slaves helped to delineate white honor by dishonoring black slaves. Only by first understanding the antebellum White South's code of honor can the meaning of masters' physical assaults on their human property become apparent.[2]

The Southern code of honor depended to an extraordinary degree on the world of appearances. Honor lay in what others saw and thought of you, not in any deeper truth separate from surface masks. Because appearance rather than reality brought honor, one's physical condition or appearance invited honor or dishonor. Historian Kenneth S. Greenberg explains the significance of this point for slavery: "For white southerners, the whip on the back of the slave was a sign of the slave's bad character and 'vicious temper.'" Southerners thus particularly bristled at the abolitionist suggestion that whipping in fact revealed the masters' evil nature. To the contrary, Southerners saw the scars of whipping as permanently marking the slaves as flawed and outside the community of equals. "The scar, in a sense, spoke for itself—or rather about the man whose body carried it—regardless of the process or the larger set of relations that brought it into existence."[3]

Physical appearance was not the only aspect of the world of public images that defined Southern honor. The power to choose whatever image of oneself one wished to project—to wear a public mask—without that image being challenged was the hallmark of a gentleman. "Giving the lie"—intimating that a person's public image belied his true nature—was thus among the most powerful of insults to honor. The only appropriate reaction to such an insult was again expressive violence, usually in the form of a duel. The duel was a complex ritual designed to reassert equality between the participants by confirming the offended party's power not to be unmasked.[4]

Slaves were, therefore, expected to treat a master's words as true simply because the master spoke them, even though masters frequently lied to their slaves. Slaves were never, however, entitled to duel. A slave who suggested that a master lied faced a beating rather than a duel. Correspondingly, slaves were not permitted to duel one another, for they had no honor to defend. Nevertheless, masters might prod slaves into pseudoduels designed to confirm the slaves' dishonored status. The master would decide when each slave was to feel insulted and when and how they would fight, rapping one slave or another with a cane when fights—and thus damage to the master's valuable property—threatened. Such empty rituals confirmed the master's fullness, highlighting his power to use violence to defend his own honor while denying that same power to the degraded slaves.[5]

In addition to the mock duel, a wide array of violent rituals were practiced to maintain the sense of honor as the power to control the appearance of truth. An especially illustrative case involved a slave who was approached by his master's brother-in-law, Lewis Morgan, to buy stolen wheat from another slave on a neighboring plantation. Morgan planned to arrange to have the wheat resold at a profit. When the slave was detected, both masters punished the thieving slaves, beating them with five- to six-foot willow sticks, while they were nude, over the course of five hours. The master "required the poor slave to confess the truth, and then to deny it, and then back again, and so on, beating him from truth to lie, and from a lie to the truth, over and over again." The whipping was, of course, not about getting the truth—the slave dared not mention Morgan's involvement for fear of a more severe beating—but about "the master . . . telling both the slave and himself that truth was a matter of assertion and force—and the master had it in his control."[6]

Violence against slaves sent the message of their subordinate status in yet another way: revealing their cowardice in choosing slavery over death. Southern gentlemen were not afraid to die; mastery over the fear of death was seen as a precondition of being a free man. Death in battle or in similar struggle was a masterful gesture of resistance to submission. Relatedly, dependence was shameful. A gentleman was independent and in control, a master over his own fear as well as over dependence on others around him.[7]

Whites believed that a distinguishing feature of slaves was their inability to confront death without fear. Their submission was a choice of a life of humiliation over an honorable death. Slave rebellions or other forms of overt resistance were thus often viewed as the result of outside agitation rather than of slaves' independent choices. Open slave resistance was viewed as a challenge to white honor that required swift retribution. But the very success of that retribution in crushing nascent rebellions and discouraging new ones was seen as a sign of slave weakness and thus dishonor. Given the great difficulty of rebellion, slave resistance was in fact more often covert, involving feigned illness, slow or careless work, temporary flight, or petty thievery. But the covert nature of this resistance further confirmed whites' beliefs in the slaves' cowardly, lying nature. Each time that a master beat or whipped a slave into submission, he signified his belief that the slave was deserving of his subordinate status.[8]

Slaves themselves painfully recognized the subordinating messages in their masters' violence. Frederick Douglass was one of the rare slaves who succeeded in asserting his honor through counterviolence. Douglass's master had leased him to Edward Covey, famed as a "Negro breaker"—someone who could transform resisting slaves into docile ones. Covey repeatedly called Douglass a liar and beat and flogged him severely, until one day Douglass fought back, restoring his "manhood."[9] He described his feeling this way:

> It was a glorious resurrection, from the tomb of slavery to the heaven of freedom. My long-crushed Spirit rose, cowardice departed, bold defiance took its place; and I now resolved that, however long I might remain a slave in form, the day had passed forever when I could be a slave in fact. I did not hesitate to let it be known of me, that the white man who expected to succeed in whipping, must also succeed in killing me.[10]

Douglass was lucky. Most slaves would not so challenge their masters or, if they did so, were beaten, sold, or killed. But Covey told no one, wishing to protect his own reputation as a slave breaker. Douglass's self-described emotions showed, however, a keen understanding of the code of honor.[11]

Sanctifying Slavery

One perhaps surprising function of Southern white violence against slaves was the sanctification of slavery as a Christian institution. Christianity, especially Southern Protestantism, was central to the culture and society of the antebellum South. Southern clerics viewed the manner in which masters treated their slaves as a religious matter, a question of Christian ethics and of a mission to the slaves. This ethic prohibited unjustified, cruel, or severe punishment but embraced moderate and proportionate "correction" as necessary to foster slaves' proper obedience and subservience. While clerics viewed the existence of slavery itself—rather than the means by which it was implemented—as a political, not a religious, question, they nevertheless articulated a religious defense of race-based slavery in response to abolitionist religious arguments.[12]

The religious defense of slavery was rooted in the Bible, and apologists found numerous references there to justify slavery. Mosaic law was said to authorize the buying, selling, holding, and bequeathing of slaves as property. Abraham and other prophets held slaves, and the New Testament failed to condemn slavery. The Apostles were said to have received slaveholders into the church. But the most important biblical reference Southerners pointed toward was Genesis 9:25, Noah's curse on Ham, father of Canaan, for Ham's indiscretion toward Noah, which clerics read as specifically authorizing African American slavery.[13]

In the Bible's words, Noah became drunk and lay "uncovered inside his tent." Ham "saw his father's nakedness and told his two brothers outside."[14] But the brothers, Shem and Japheth, walked into the tent backward and covered their father with a garment without ever looking at him. When Noah awoke and discovered what his youngest son had done, he said,

> Cursed be Canaan! The lowest of slaves will he be to his brothers. . . . Blessed be the LORD, the God of Shem! May Canaan be the slave of Shem. . . . May God extend the territory of Japheth; may Japheth live in the tents of Shem, and may Canaan Be his slave.[15]

A Georgian in 1844 summarized the masters' interpretation of this passage this way: "From Ham were descended the nations that occupied the land of Canaan, and those that now constitute the African or Negro race." J. B.

Thrasher of Mississippi added that blacks "are the lowest and most degraded of the descendants of Canaan." And South Carolinian Iveson L. Brookes explained that Ham deserved "decapitation" for his crime, but a merciful God chose to punish him "by flattening his head, kinking his hair, and blackening his skin, thereby making him black and subject to slavery."[16]

Religious proslavery writers thus saw the master-slave relationship as sanctified by the Bible. This racialized relationship was a mutual one, in which the white master cared for the naturally degraded and dependent black African slave, and the slave labored for the master. This view was buttressed both by the natural-law argument that hierarchy and some form of submission are inherent in nature and by the religious and cultural embrace of patriarchy, in which the master heads a household, including slaves. In this patriarchal ideal, the master's relationship to the slave was portrayed as much like that of a father to his children, including "correction," the use of physical force, to teach the slaves role-appropriate behavior and their own limitations. Under this view, the measured use of the whip—or its threatened but unnecessary use— served holy purposes: to improve the lot of the slaves, who on their own would die or fall into barbarism, to teach them to better play the role assigned to them by God, and to express the supposed "love" that masters had for their slaves. This "love" required both care for and subjugation of black-skinned Africans. The inherent violence in slavery could thus be portrayed as bringing God's language to the world in a struggle against sin and apostasy.[17]

Racial Violence

The Southern clerics' emphasis on the story of Ham revealed the central role of racism in proslavery ideology and practice. Numerous justifications were offered for race-based subjugation, ranging from religion, states'-rights republicanism, and natural patriarchal rule to scientific racism. Most often, slaveholders themselves offered no justification for subjugation, simply assuming black inferiority. "Black equality was simply inconceivable, a subject not even open to discussion." Racism was not the sole justification for slavery—many Northerners embraced racist beliefs while condemning slavery. But racism served to justify enslaving blacks as a group. While many masters' racism led them to a purely practical defense of the institution—the idea, for example, that the "white [man] cannot endure heat and labor so well as the Negro"—developing proslavery ideology was also justified on the basis that blacks were "uplifted" by slavery from the conditions they would otherwise face.[18]

But this paternalistic view, like its practical alternative, involved an increasingly emotionally intense form of racism. Proslavery writers also often fused ancient philosophy and Christianity with their racism. Thus, Alfred Taylor

Bledsoe chastised abolitionists for their failure to see that blacks were "unfit" for civil society. Thomas R. R. Cobb, after citing the Greek idea that "some men were slaves by nature, and that slavery was absolutely necessary to a perfect society," recounted evidence from science and history to conclude that for the Negro, "a state of bondage, so far from doing violence to the law of his nature, develops and perfects it; and . . . in that state, he enjoys the greatest amount of happiness, and arrives at the greatest degree of perfection of which his nature is capable." Southern slavery, to a far greater extent than slavery in Athenian or African society, thus portrayed slaves' behavior and condition as the product of their inherent nature. Accordingly, race marked blacks as flawed in character and dishonored. Moreover, slaves were considered outsiders because "racism made them naturally so" and permanently and definitionally excluded them from the imagined community that constitutes the nation.[19]

Racism and violence were closely linked. "Emotionally simple and intellectually underdeveloped, black slaves were deemed inherently more responsive than whites to the motivating force of physical coercion."[20] The slave-management literature thus stressed that "tangible punishments and rewards, which act at once on their senses, are the only sort most [slaves] can appreciate."[21] Moreover, absolutely central to this literature was the importance of obedience. The *Farmers' Register* counseled masters that slaves "must obey at all times, and under all circumstances. . . . Unconditional submission is the only footing upon which slavery should be placed."[22] One planter wrote, "The slave should know that his master is to govern absolutely [and must] . . . obey implicitly."[23] The requirement of unconditional obedience was closely linked to race, and, as another planter explained, "We believe the Negro to belong to an inferior race. . . . We teach them . . . that to the white face belongs control, and to the black obedience." Although free blacks were an unavoidable anomaly in this racial scheme, they were increasingly oppressed in law and practice, and their uncomfortable presence (when they were allowed to remain in a state) never upset the basic understanding that violence against slaves helped to teach them and their masters the principle of black racial subordination.[24]

Racial violence also helped slave masters to protect their peculiar institution against the sentiment of nonslaveholding Southern yeoman farmers, who "assailed the power and pretensions of the slaveholders" but who, in their radicalism, "almost never included a sympathetic view of the slaves' plight." T. R. R. Cobb best articulated the racial justification for slavery that so appealed to the yeoman, explaining, "The mass of laborers not being recognized among citizens, every citizen feels that he belongs to an elevated class. It matters not that he is no slaveholder."[25] Cobb continued:

> He is not of the inferior race; he is a freeborn citizen; he engages in no menial occupation. The poorest meets the richest as an equal; sits at his table with

him; salutes him as neighbor; meets him in every public assembly, and stands on the same social platform. Hence, there is no war of classes. There is truthfully republican equality in the ruling class.[26]

The yeomanry embraced this logic, engaging in an increasingly violent rhetoric of racial denunciation, and repeatedly argued that free-white equality was "imminently threatened by the prospect of abolition." It should be no surprise, therefore, that they used skin color as a sign of dishonor and racial violence as a way to affirm their status as free whites.[27]

Patriarchy and Mutual Obligation

The biblical Ham story's lesson of mutual obligation also fits within the Southern cultural embrace of patriarchy, deference, and hierarchy. The image of slaves as children was thus among the more benevolent-sounding justifications for racial violence. Less benevolent images viewed blacks as animals, dangerous and unpredictable inferiors who needed to be penned. Viewed as children, slaves needed to be continually reminded of their dependent status lest they get into trouble. During the antebellum years, whites became increasingly obsessed with limiting slave autonomy, with rules controlling every detail of slave life. Owners also worried that slaves, "like children," would quarrel over food supplies or eat too much at once. Consequently, masters commonly provided a plantation cook. Furthermore, masters often limited slaves' independent religious activities and contact with other slaves on neighboring plantations, and even controlled what names slave parents gave their children.[28]

An infraction of these rules by a slave could result in punishment. While lip service (and sometimes more) was given to the need to make punishment proportionate and predictable, in practice it was often neither. Although practical concerns limited the degree of punishment—too excessive and random punishment encouraged confusion, resentment, and flight—masters centrally sought to convey to slaves their absolute lack of autonomy. Southerners believed violence was necessary to teach slaves "to be humble and submissive." A recalcitrant or unruly slave often paid the price for disobedience, especially if the disobedience occurred in front of other whites, as this was seen as a challenge to the master's honor. Moreover, masters feared that without punishment, other slaves might follow suit. Thus, as masters or their overseers "meted out punishment, reasoned judgment often gave way to passion. What might have been a moderate flogging grew into brutal retribution."[29]

Punishments could include stocks, private jails, public humiliation, fines, or deprivation of privileges. But the most common and symbolically important punishment was whipping. Whipping was sometimes "a public, ritualized display in which a sentence was carried out before an assembled throng."[30] Other times, it was "a casual affair in which an owner, overseer, or hirer impulsively chastised" the disobedient slave. "Either way, the prevalence of whipping was such a stark reminder of slave dependence that to the bondspeople . . . the lash came to symbolize the essence of slavery." A public flogging might take place before watching fathers, children, and other relatives. In particular, children watching this ritualistic violence could not help but draw the appropriate lessons about their subjugation.[31]

Slaves were furthermore expected to learn deference to all whites, not only to masters, as was demonstrated by the crime of slave "insolence." Frederick Douglass explained that a slave committed this crime "in the tone of an answer; in answering at all; in not answering; in the expression of countenance; in the motion of the head; in the gait, manner and bearing of the slave." One example was the 1851 trial of the slave Sole, or Solomon, for insolence to white patrollers. One patroller testified that Sole used "some very improper or unbecoming language such as asserting his Equality with any man and that he would die before he would submit to being whipt [sic] . . . to death."[32] In another case, a slave hired out to an iron works had his whip wounds salted, his genitals cut, and was forced to lug around a 58- to 75-pound iron ring because he had been "insolent and resisted."[33] In a third case, an owner sued two white men who had exchanged words with his slave and had thereafter chased the slave a mile, causing the slave's later death from hiding in icy water. The jury found for the assailants, concluding "that if they did pursue and attempt to beat said Negroe . . . they were justified in doing so by reason of impudent and impertinent language used by said Negroe towards them."[34]

The Violence of the Law

The law purported to restrain the worst excesses of violence toward slaves, but in practice it largely protected the authority of the master and, to a lesser extent, the power of whites over black slaves. Most antebellum jurisdictions adopted laws that punished masters for "cruelty" or "inhumanity" toward slaves; these vague restrictions were violated by only the most extreme cases. Some states specified particular prohibited punishments, such as scalding, burning, removing the tongue, or putting out the eye. The law was somewhat more protective of slaves facing assaults from third parties because such assaults harmed the owners' economic investment in the slave. Despite the weak protections they provided to slaves, these laws were rarely enforced, partly because of the evidentiary rule that slaves could not testify to reveal the circumstances of their abuse. Furthermore, statutes often protected the right of the owner or other in charge of a slave to inflict such punishment as may be necessary for the "good government of the owner." The common law also sometimes addressed violence against slaves, but it, like statutory law, continued to give great deference to masters, partly because of the educative function of punishing slaves into accepting their subordinate status.[35]

Among the most infamous cases on this last point is *State v. Mann*. John Mann had leased the slave Lydia from her owner. She tried to run away when Mann chastised her for some small offense, so Mann shot and wounded her. The then-respected jurist Thomas Ruffin authored the appellate court's opinion unanimously reversing Mann's conviction for assault and battery.[36] Ruffin explained:

> The end [of slavery] is the profit of the master, his security and the public safety; the subject, one doomed in his person and his posterity, to live without the capacity to make anything his own, and to toil that another may reap the fruits. . . . Such services can only be expected from one who has no will of his own; who surrenders his will in implicit obedience to that of another. Such obedience is the consequence only of uncontrolled authority over the body. There is nothing else which can produce the effect. The power of the master must be absolute to render the submission of the slave perfect. . . . We cannot allow the right of the master to be brought into discussion in the courts of justice. The slave, to remain a slave, must be made sensible that there is no appeal from his master; that his power is in no instance usurped; but is conferred by the laws of man at least, if not by the law of God.[37]

The Florida Supreme Court explained in another case that whipping was necessary because "the degraded caste should be continually reminded of their inferior position, to keep them in a proper degree of subjection to the authority of free white citizens." Indeed, slave law relied primarily on the power of sentiment, good Christian values, community pressure, and the master's self-interest in protecting his investment to restrain his use of force. The law implicitly recognized a coherent purpose in punishment: to undermine the slave's humanity in a way that "distinguished him from human beings who are not property."[38]

Indeed, slave laws also served this function by decriminalizing the rape of slave women, whether by white or black men. Although laws that prohibited the rape of young slave girls by blacks or mulattoes did evolve late in the antebellum period, the laws remained silent about rape by whites. Masters sometimes used rape as yet another way to mark slaves as property. Harriet Jacobs's tale is perhaps the most infamous example. When Jacobs reached age fifteen, her owner began to whisper foul words in her ear. He told her that she was his property and "that [she] must be subject to his will in all things." She resisted at first, by indicating a willingness to die rather than submit to his advances. Ultimately, she evaded his embraces by having an affair with another white man who treated her more kindly. The result, she said, was to feel "as if I was forsaken by god and man; as if all my efforts must be frustrated; and I became reckless in my despair."[39]

Mob Violence

Mob violence also served expressive purposes. As with punishment imposed by individual whites, sometimes the function of mob violence was to reinforce messages of black subjugation. The ultimate fate of North Carolina slave Lunsford Lane is a good example. Lane was an unusual slave, having made powerful friends among the Southern elite, one of whom ultimately purchased Lane and brought him to New York, where he was manumitted. He told his story to Northern audiences to raise money to free his family members. When he returned to North Carolina to do so, he was arrested and charged with giving abolitionist lectures. Wealthy and influential whites came to his defense, and he was acquitted. After his acquittal, a mob of poorer whites seized him and demanded that he tell the truth about his abolitionist activities. They rejected his version of events and stripped him, coating him with tar and feathers. Part of their purpose was to reject the authority of the local aristocracy, whom they despised. They also sought to reject his pretensions to equality, demonstrated by his association with white men of power who validated his statements as truth.[40]

Mobs acted to silence the voices of abolitionists or suspected insurrectionists, white as well as black. The antiabolitionist mob offered a means of violently silencing dissent while expressing the sanctity of slave society. The law and mobs worked together. State legislatures imposed bans on incendiary publications, mail was censored, dragnet sweeps were made of suspected fugitive-slave harborers, and dissenters were banished.[41] Mobs throughout the nation assaulted abolitionists for whom the law provided no protection. To Southerners, the mob and the law worked hand-in-hand to suppress abolitionist speech. Such suppression was an essential public defense of the "true republicanism" of the Southern slave economy. Southern mob violence, like violence committed by white individuals against slaves, expressed white supremacy in the most powerful and meaningful ways possible.[42]

When the state became involved in that violence in the form of searches and seizures, the messages sent of racial subordination were particularly powerful. Of the various interests protected by the Fourth Amendment, interferences with slaves' freedom of locomotion, that is, seizures of their person, had such great symbolic significance for both the North and the South that it became a major source of conflict between them. Supposedly local Southern laws governing the searches and seizures of slaves, free blacks, and their supporters snowballed into matters of passionate national interest.

7 Slave Locomotion

Sir William Blackstone was the author of *Commentaries on the Laws of England,* the most influential treatment of Anglo-American law during the antebellum period. Blackstone considered the three most basic rights secured by English law to be the rights of private property, personal security, and personal liberty. "Personal liberty," said Blackstone, meant "removing one's person to whatso-ever place one's own inclination may direct without imprisonment or restraint of law." Denial of this right was, however, central to the definition of slavery. As proslavery apologist T. R. R. Cobb explained, "the right of personal liberty in the slave is utterly inconsistent with the idea of slavery, and whenever the slave acquires this right, his condition is *ipso facto* changed." A slave who could, unmolested, leave his master when dissatisfied, roam in search of friends or entertainment or family, or go on a quest for a better life was no slave at all.[1]

No other single activity was more sharply limited than locomotion. Limit-ing locomotion was the lifeblood of Southern society's theory of mastery, as embodied in its statutes, plantation journals, regulations, and religious ser-mons. Slave patrols, passes, forced sales, manumission restrictions, jailing, con-trols on hiring out or hunting, prohibitions on unlawful assembly, antiliteracy rules, forced separation of families, fugitive-slave laws, coffles, and humiliation rituals all served to control freedom of movement. These totalizing locomotive snares were described by former slave Charles Ball as "principles of restraint." "No slave dare leave the plantation," wrote Ball, not for a "single mile" or a "single hour, by night or by day" at the risk of "exposing himself to the danger of being taken up and flogged." The experience for the slave was to be "a pris-oner for life." As former slave Fountain Hughes noted, it was a "jail sentence, was jus' the same as we was in jail."[2]

The Masters' Tools

Slave Patrols and Their Analogues

If slaves were metaphorical jail inmates, the most infamous jailers were the slave patrols or "paddyrollers." The need for patrols arose from slaves' vestigial "quasi-personal liberty," the reality that at night, on holidays, or on the Sabbath they might at times be left to their cabins or "leisure" so that "it cannot be expected that the watchful eye of the master can follow them." Patrols attempted to fill this surveillance gap.[3]

The importance of patrols varied among jurisdictions and waxed and waned at different times in antebellum history. Nevertheless, the idea of patrols was long an essential part of the scheme for controlling slave autonomy.[4]

In the nineteenth century, patrols' membership in many regions increasingly included few slaveowners and more lower-status men. Plantation owners in some regions saw patrol work as unsuitable to their social station, preferring to leave the work to their overseers, to pay fines in place of service, or, at least in North Carolina, to serve instead on patrol committees charged with supervising the local patrols. Nevertheless, other communities continued to select patrollers "from the full spectrum of the white social hierarchy" because of the fear that the less-propertied and lower-status men either would too easily wreak excessive violence upon bondsmen, compromising the masters' investment in human capital, or, alternatively, would be so slipshod in their vigilance as to create the danger of slave revolt and bloodshed. In still other instances, this concern was instead addressed by hiring well-paid professionals to do the job. Slaves well understood that too many patrollers lacked any incentive to avoid undue cruelty, one former slave recalling, "Paddyrollers was mean ez dogs." Said another former slave, "If you wasn't in your proper place when the paddyrollers come they lash you 'til you was black and blue." He continued: "The women got 15 lashes and the men 30. That was for jes bein' out without a pass." For other offenses, sometimes that of simple insolence, punishment could be far worse.[5]

Although patrol organization and membership varied with time and place, white males of the right age were generally potentially subject to patrol duty unless they fit into certain categories of statutory exemption. A would-be patroller summoned for duty by written notice or by a patrol captain would next appear before a local official, such as a justice of the peace, to be "qualified" or sworn in. Once sworn in, a patroller usually retained his appointment slip endorsed by the qualifying official or, alternatively, "a justice of the peace could issue the patroller a special warrant to carry while on duty." The slip or warrant could be shown to whomever might challenge the patroller's authority. Such challenges might issue from personal animosity, such as a master's warning a former overseer never to set foot again on the master's plantation unless he showed his patrol warrant; or challenges might stem from some paternalist masters' blocking patrols from entering their land as an insult to their honor, for such entry suggested that they could not well manage their own slaves. Some such masters raised especially fierce opposition to patrollers entering a dwelling without a more specific warrant—something required of most county officials entering dwellings but not legally required of patrollers, for whom their more general slip or warrant was sufficient. Patrol appointment notices and warrants also "almost completely shielded patrollers from litigious masters who became angry if patrollers viciously punished local bondsmen."[6]

Perhaps most importantly, however, the slip or warrant symbolized the collective nature of the patrol as an agent of the state. That point was made most clearly in the seminal North Carolina case *State v. Hailey,* in which only three of the eight men then appointed as patrollers in Anson County were present on the night that they tried entering Isham and Lucy Hailey's slave quarters to discipline slaves. The *Hailey* court held that "a majority of an appointed control group must be present to conduct any searches or administer any kind of punishment."[7] This was so because

> [patrols] partake of a judicial or quasi-judicial and executive character. Judicial, so far as deciding upon each case of a slave taken up by them; whether the law has been violated by him or not, and adjudging the punishment to be inflicted. Is he off his master's plantation without a proper permit or pass? Of this the patrol must judge and decide. If punishment is to be inflicted, they must adjudge, decide, as to the question; five stripes may in some cases be sufficient, while others may demand the full penalty of the law. All these acts upon the part of the patrol, require consultation and agreement, and a less number than a majority of the whole cannot act. . . . it does require that number to constitute (if the expression may be allowed) a court or tribunal for the performance of these duties, and when so constituted a plurality of those present must agree, or no punishment can be legally inflicted. We do not mean that the law requires, on the part of the patrol, any formalities in the discharge of their duties, or that any formal judgment must be pronounced, but that a majority of the patrol, properly constituted, must sanction each sentence passed. If a minority can act, then each individual patroller may act by himself, and every man's property would be subject to the uncontrolled judgment or passion of a single individual. This can not have been the scope and meaning of the act [creating patrols].[8]

These principles of warrant authority and collective action thus served *in theory* to restrain arbitrary patroller action. The two principles were taken seriously by the courts, even though that alone was often insufficient to achieve the desired restraint. For example, in the 1817 North Carolina case *Richardson v. Saltar,* the defendant, an authorized patroller, took three unofficial patrollers with him on his rounds. When they discovered on Major Owen's farm a bondsman belonging to Owen's neighbor, the slave produced an invalid pass. Saltar and his three friends responded by whipping the slave so brutally that he could not work for days. When the slave's owner sued the men for damages, the trial court decided against the owner, but, on appeal, the state's supreme court remanded the case for retrial. The then-governing 1794 North Carolina patrol law required at least two active patrollers to be present at a slave's punishment. But three of the four men had no slip or warrant, thus no authority, and Saltar "could not act as a patrol by himself." Restraint was also sought to be imposed by legal limits on the maximum number of lashes allowed.[9]

In practice such restraint was often an elusive goal. Patrollers had wide-ranging duties. They were expected to, and did, search slave cabins, disperse slave gatherings (including religious services), safeguard areas around and within plantations and towns, interrogate and detain suspected violators, and examine slave passes or tickets. They examined the papers of purportedly free blacks, in urban areas sent captured runaways to the guardhouse until reclaimed by their masters, investigated suspected thefts by slaves or their inappropriate interaction with poor whites, and administered punishments to violators on the spot. In plantation areas, they rode on horseback, a noisy but intimidating way to travel when confronting slaves on foot. Patrollers carried guns, whips, and ropes, and if they killed a slave, the local government usually paid the owner for the loss. In urban areas, patrollers walked more than rode, needing greater mobility, and often watched the homes of free blacks and their businesses, a form of "stationary patrolling" much like the modern police stakeout. For all practical purposes, patrols had nearly unlimited authority to search, seize, and exercise violence; if runaways were declared outlaws, patrollers could shoot them on sight. A slave with an expired pass might face punishment, but so could a slave with a valid pass who inadvertently angered a patroller. Slaves thus did what they could to avoid the patrols, using songs to warn of their approach, learning to vault backyard fences while on the run, and consulting conjurers and folk doctors for roots and plants thought to ward off those on the hunt for wayward bondsmen. Slaves hid in trees and "rubbed turpentine or manure on their feet, masking their scent from dogs and thus throwing patrollers off their trail." If caught, some slaves sought to bribe patrols with food, liquor, stolen goods, or even a song and dance, but often patrollers took what they could, then reneged on the deal.[10]

In times of crisis, such as war and real or imagined rebellions, slaves had even more reason to fear patrols, for masters, fearing mass getaways, sometimes sought to set examples to intimidate other slaves, while more home searches —even of white dwellings—and interrogations for weapons were conducted;

some exemptions from patrol service might also be briefly removed, and patrols were in general expected to be more active. Special patrols might even be appointed by executive, rather than the usual legislative or judicial, authority, as happened in Virginia in 1808 in response to a rumored insurrection. Those patrols were instructed to search "the Negro cabins and take every thing which we found in them, which bore a hostile aspect, such as powder, shot, etc." and to "apprehend every Negro whom we found from his home; and if he made any resistance or ran away from us, to fire on him immediately, unless he could be stopped by other means."[11]

Slave patrols were, of course, not the only authorities charged with regulating slave mobility. The patrols' closest cousins were the constables. Constables, unlike patrollers, had many duties beyond slave catching and often made enough money to have no need of another vocation. But, like patrollers, constables were appointed by local governments and had slave catching as an important part of their job.[12] A Norfolk, Virginia, constable described his job in a way that made the similarity of his duties to those of patrollers stark:

> It was part of my business to arrest all slaves and free persons of color, who were collected in crowds at night, and lock them up. It was also part of my business to take them before the Mayor. I did this without any warrant, and at my own discretion. Next day they are examined and punished. The punishment is flogging. I am one of the men who flog them. They get not exceeding thirty-nine lashes. I am paid fifty cents for every Negro I flog. The price used to be sixty-two and half cents. I am paid fifty cents for every Negro I arrest, and fifty cents more if I flog him. I have flogged hundreds. I have been thus employed since 1838. I never refuse a good job of that type.[13]

Both constables and slave patrols "had duties that were policelike in nature," and in some cities both "eventually gave way to paid police forces," forces that would one day perform the many tasks of modern police but that, until the Civil War, served primarily to control slaves.[14]

Slave patrols usually tracked runaways who stayed in the patrols' locality. Where a slave was suspected of fleeing to distant places, however, planters who could not spare themselves or their overseers' absence for long periods frequently turned to slave catchers. Slave catchers were private persons, not appointed by or functioning as local officials, who were hired for a short-term specific task of locating fugitive slaves for a fee. Although not the sole province of slave catchers, they did often use highly trained so-called Negro dogs, though "owners usually required that the slaves retaken not be 'bruised and torn by the dogs.'" Rather than use professional slave catchers, masters might send relatives or friends or use trusted slaves as spies or even occasionally order overseers to engage in the hunt. Masters who on rare occasions chose them-

selves to do the job of tracking down the runaway did so with "fanatical resolve." They did so especially when "slaves they trusted ran away," becoming
incensed that one of their "family" should flee "without any unjust or injurious treatment." They might travel hundreds of miles over the course of weeks,
and when they caught their human quarry, "it is difficult to believe hat they
did not seek a harsh retribution for such 'disloyalty.'"[15]

Ordinary citizens often aided in slave recapture also. Financial rewards provided one strong incentive for private action. The state usually paid a flat fee
for the capture, and owners might advertise an additional reward. A common
nineteenth-century procedure was to deliver the taken fugitive to a justice of
the peace for jailing. The slave would remain there until the owner came to
claim him and pay the reward and fees, or, if the owner were unknown, an ad-
vertisement seeking to find him might be placed in the paper, with the slave
resold if no response came after a specified time. Some statutes permitted hiring out the slave until claimed. To discourage individual greed's overtaking
masters' property rights, many jurisdictions created offenses like "inveigling"
or "enticing" slaves to leave their masters, perhaps with (usually false) promises
of freedom or of better conditions working for another master. Slaves or free
persons also faced punishment for harboring any slave in an effort to prevent
his or her capture.[16]

Containing the Slave's Heart and Mind

Planters sought to control slave locomotion by controlling slaves' minds and
hearts, as well as their bodies. Indeed, antebellum Southern legal systems reflected an understanding of locomotion control as rooted in an interaction
between the embodied slave and the ensouled slave: controlling the body's
movement would restrain the autonomy that stemmed from slaves' schemings
and passions, and limiting the bondsmen's knowledge and manipulating their
sentiments would restrain their physical movements.

Antiliteracy laws were perhaps the clearest example of this strategy. Four
slave states flatly prohibited teaching bondsmen to read and write, while most
others barred only teaching slaves in assembly, trying to limit slaves' reading to
Bible passages that teach obedience. A number of slave states did not, however,
legislate the antiliteracy principle, and there were occasional counterarguments
that slaves needed to read to know the Bible. Whites' indifference to slave literacy, combined with slaves' exhaustion or resignation, also had much to do
with the bondsmen's being unlettered. Some slaves would also learn to read
from the white children with whom they played, or they would steal books to
study at night by firelight. Nevertheless, the dominant social and legal literacy
prohibition had important symbolic significance in controlling slaves' movement. Illiteracy also increased slaves' dependence on whites, for only whites

could then read the Bible to slaves, and slaves could not write themselves passes. The wife of Frederick Douglass's master, Hugh Auld, helped the young Douglass learn to read. The reaction of Mr. Auld upon learning of these events captured much of Southern thinking in this area. "Master Hugh was astounded beyond measure," Douglass recounted, "and probably for the first time, proceeded to unfold to his wife the true philosophy of the slave system, and the peculiar rules necessary in the . . . management of human chattels." Hugh Auld forbade further instruction, explaining, "If he learns to read the Bible it will forever unfit him to be a slave. He should know nothing but the will of his master, and learn to obey it. As to himself, learning will do him no good, but a great deal of harm, making him disconsolate and unhappy." Auld cautioned, "If you teach him how to read, he'll want to know how to write, and this accomplished, he'll be running away with himself."[17]

Auld's tirade reflected a problem that the planter class preferred not to acknowledge openly, even to themselves: that slaves were "thinking property." Slaves were often prohibited by law from performing certain tasks, "thinking" tasks for which Southern racial ideology deemed them unfit. Were slaves routinely to perform such tasks well, that would be a reality hard to square with their supposed natural inferiority.[18] Equally important,

> There were also security reasons for not allowing slaves to be involved in such professions. The master class feared that if slaves could read, write, and perform professional tasks, such as practicing medicine or pharmacy, they would be in a position to run away, poison their masters, or lead revolts. These fears, while common to all master classes, were more pronounced in the South because of the racial fears of white Southerners.[19]

Closely related to the antiliteracy laws were the prohibitions on unlawful slave assembly. Although the terms of the statutes varied, they generally required more than one person in an "assembly" for "unlawful" purposes. "Unlawful" purposes included teaching reading and writing and attending slaves-only religious meetings, though some states barred slave gatherings for any purpose whatsoever. Exceptions to antiassembly laws frequently were carved out for biracial religious worship, services conducted by white ministers, or those attended by two respectable white persons appointed for that reason. Whites who permitted slave assemblies might face fines and, if slaves were injured or killed, civil liability too. In the rare instances where masters permitted slave assemblies, usually for the purpose of a "frolic," patrollers might break it up, especially if there was drinking or fighting or if white tempers flared from the fear of uprising.[20]

The pass system was also central to controlling slaves' physical and emotional autonomy. The law generally required a slave to bear a pass or ticket from the master. Most passes were specific, stating the slave's name, destination, and amount of time allowed about and bearing the owner's signature. Thus, one typical pass read, "All persons are requested to permit the bearer Adam to go from my house to Mrs. Martha Robert's house and to Mr. Wm. Watkin's in the county of Charlotte and home again without interruption." Another read, "Edward is sent to Rich[mond] to remain there till Monday next." Patrollers complained when some owners wrote more-general passes, such as ones good for an entire month, a practice more likely near urban areas, where owners allowed skilled slaves to hire their own time, perhaps letting them keep some of the salary paid. Southern whites worried that slaves with such autonomy would be up to no good, for "no vigilance on the part of [the] Patrol, even tho' it should be prolonged throughout the entire night can effectually restrain the robberies of evil-disposed slaves; for, under the protection of their general tickets, they can parade our highways from dark till daylight, with the most perfect impunity." Despite these complaints, calls to prohibit general passes met with little success, though such passes received special scrutiny from patrols. Moreover, urban bondsmen had need to move about town so regularly that more-general passes were needed, with larger cities like Charleston permitting the purchase from the city of a badge, good for one year, to be worn at all times. Badges might be made of brass or tin and stamped with the date, the slave's occupation, and a number that recorded payment. Similar badges existed for free blacks, and any slave or free black caught without one might be jailed.[21]

If slave passes gave slaves varying small degrees of autonomy, they also taught slaves the lesson that even such small measures of freedom existed at the masters' whim. Masters' policies varied, some viewing passes as rewards for good behavior, to "be withheld if the owner desired." An increasingly more widely held view was that giving passes made slaves happier and less likely to flee, so they should readily be given when asked for by a slave who had behaved well. Passes also might be needed if an owner used a slave for some task, commonly serving as a messenger. Either way, slaves without passes faced the tender mercies of the patrols and knew that getting a pass required either being about the masters' business or "earning" his good will and asking his permission. Even masters who wrote passes occasionally used them as an opportunity to humiliate their bearers, composing the pass to include an erotic or silly rhyme. Consequently, "Passes . . . prevented most slaves from going to most places most of the time."[22] As one former slave put it,

> Now I couldn' go from here 'cross the street or I couldn' go through nobody's house 'out I have a note or something from my master. An' if I had that pass, that was what we call a pass, if I had that pass, I could go wherever he sent me. An' I'd have to be back, now, wherever he sent me to, they, they'd give

me another pass an' I'd bring that back so as to show how long I'd been gone. We couldn' go out an' stay an hour or two hours or something like. But they'd give me a note so [that] would nobody interfere with me, an' tell who I belong to. An' when I come back, why I carry it to my master and give that to him, that'd be alright. But I couldn' jus' walk away like the people does now, you know. It was what they call, we were slaves.[23]

Passes were especially important when slaves "married abroad." Of course, the slave was an "outsider—an outsider first in the sense that he originated from outside the society into which he was introduced as a slave, second in the sense that *he was denied the most elementary of social bonds, kinship.*" Accordingly, every slaveholding state rendered legally binding marriage between slaves an impossibility. Nevertheless, de facto slave marriages took place in great numbers, a practice often encouraged by planters to reduce slave dissatisfaction and increase slave births, each healthy child adding to the master's wealth. Slaves would engage in ceremonies to mark the marriage, a common one being, as one former slave remembered, when "they just jumped over a broom and that made 'em married. Sometimes one of the white folks read a little out of the Scriptures to 'em, and they felt more married." Marriage "abroad" occurred when two slaves living on different plantations married.[24]

All masters decried marriage abroad as creating too much opportunity for slaves' autonomy and freedom from owner surveillance, creating a "feeling of independence from being, of right [that is, by authority of a pass], out of the control of the master for a time." Some large planters therefore discouraged it, while others flatly prohibited it.[25] Thus, one representative planter urged,

> Marriage at home should be encouraged among them. The practice of taking wives abroad, should as much as possible be prevented. It engenders a habit of rambling, which is injurious to the constitution of the Negro, besides removing him frequently, and at important times from the influence of the domestic police, which should always be strict. "Give the Negro an inch, and he will surely take an ell."[26]

Smaller planters, however, often had little choice, for the availability of "at home" marriage partners was so slim that marriage abroad became unavoidable. Marriage to partners at nearby plantations deterred runaways, with most masters often permitting weekend visitation of slave husbands to their wives, "weekend" frequently meaning Saturday night to Sunday dawn. Moreover, either one of the slaveowners of the couple could readily deny visitation, requiring that abroad fathers "constantly renegotiate this fragile privilege." Visiting privileges would also routinely be withdrawn in times of nearby rebellion, escape, sales, or other unrest, or when masters needed extra labor time of the husbands, or upon either master's simple whim. Such limitations prodded some husbands to risk going abroad without a pass, knowing that if caught, they would likely face swift punishment and humiliation before family members. One North Carolina slave remembered his father's visiting "sometimes widout depass. Patrollers catch him way up de chimney hidin' one night; they stripped him right befo' mammy and gave him thirty-nine lashes, wid her cryin' and a hollerin' louder then he did." Jim Threat remembered his father running away for several days because he was denied weekly visitation passes, hiding out in the day, coming to his family at night, until he "give himself up and took his whipping." Said Threat, "When they whupped a slave they made him say 'Oh, pray master' " to demean him before his family, "to show that he had to be humble." The master of Callie Elder's grandfather made him "wear long old horns" to debase him for his frequent truancy.[27]

If family life was necessary to encourage slaves' docility and reproduction, masters' practices and the law made clear that slaves' primary allegiance was expected to be to their master rather than their family. Humiliation rituals were therefore needed to reinforce this message. Flight without a pass, even to reunite with one's family, or efforts to protect family members from the master's wrath, sent unacceptable messages of slave autonomy that needed to be met by stronger countermessages, there being no more powerful means of communication than expressive or ritual violence.[28] Former slave, later antislavery activist, Samuel Ward put this point well in his ironic commentary on his mother's complaint about her husband's being brutally flogged:

[My father] received a severe flogging, which left his back in . . . [a] wretched . . . state. . . . This sort of treatment of her husband not being relished by my mother, who felt about the maltreatment of her husband as any Christian woman ought to feel, she put forth her sentiments in pretty strong language. This was insolent. Insolence in a Negress could not be endured—it would breed more and greater mischief of a like kind; then what would become of wholesome discipline? Besides, if so trifling a thing as the *mere marriage relation* were to interfere with the supreme proprietor's right of a master over his slave, next we should hear that slavery must give way before marriage! Moreover, if a Negress may be allowed free speech, touching the flogging of a Negro, simply because that Negro happened to be her husband, how long would it be before some such claim would be urged in behalf of some other member of a Negro family in unpleasant circumstances? Would this be endurable in a republican civilized community, A.D. 1819? By no means. It would sap the very foundation of slavery—it would be like—"the letting out of water": for letting the principle be once established that the Negress Anne Ward may speak as she pleases about the flagellation of her husband, the Negro William Ward, as a matter of right, and like some alarming and death-dealing infection it would spread from plantation to plantation, until property in husbands and wives would not be worth the having. No, no: marriage must succumb to slavery, slavery must reign supreme over every right and every institution however venerable or sacred; *ergo,* this free-speaking Anne Ward must be made to feel the great rigor of the domestic institution. Should she be flogged? That was questionable. . . . Well, then, . . . they could sell her, and sell her they would.[29]

Denial of passes and ritual humiliation were, however, not the source of slave families' greatest fears; lengthy forced separation or, worst of all, permanent separation across long distances sent perhaps the most unsettling psychological message of the masters' absolute command over slaves' locomotion and thus over slaves' autonomy and intimate life. Paternalist ideology led many masters and proslavery legal theorists to deny that family separation was common or that they or their neighbors regularly engaged in it. Yet it was quite common. Moreover, masters simultaneously argued that blacks lacked whites' deep capacity for bonding, so their suffering would be brief and modest, easily assuaged, for example, by readily remarrying in a new location.[30]

Short-term dislocation might occur when a master needed to move a slave to another holding for economic reasons or when a nearby planter in need briefly "borrowed" a slave. Slaves might be dispersed upon a master's death when he left his inheritance to a number of children or to settle estate debts. Abroad husbands might be hired out for distant labor for long periods to enhance a master's income stream. Slaves might also be given as gifts at a child's marriage. Outright sales by living masters might be used as a source of profit or made for any number of other reasons. If the sales were local, marriages might still survive, as was true for many of the forms of temporary separation. But long-distance sales were usually devastating to family relationships.[31]

Girls reaching sexual maturity faced the threat of sale and the related increased risk of sexual abuse when separated from their families. Those deemed especially pretty might be sold as prostitutes or "fancies," fancies generally being "of lighter skin and sold at higher prices than other slave women." Male slaves, indeed slaves of both sexes, were particularly likely to be sold when adolescent or young adults, with sales peaking between ages fifteen and twenty-five, because of their enhanced physical stamina and mastery of adult work skills, though sales threatened even eight- and ten-year-olds when they were able to work the cotton crop. Occasionally, statutory prohibitions against permanent separation of slave children from their mothers succeeded, but these laws governed only the interstate slave trade and were seldom enforced. Slaves, ever conscious of the threat to family survival posed by sale, sought to prolong childhood (for example, by keeping girls ignorant about sexuality to make them seem younger than they were) as a means of delaying the prospect of sale, and they also sang songs and told stories to strengthen their offspring for coping should the feared migration to distant places come to pass.[32]

Parents, particularly mothers, would plead for their children, with occasional success, whereas fathers were more likely to bargain with their labor, fleeing but sending word through other slaves of a willingness to return if the owner called off a planned sale. Thus, one father hid in the woods for a year until the planter promised family reunification, another threatened to commit suicide rather than leave his family, and a third, a successful escapee, volunteered for enslavement to be near his son once the boy's mother had died. Planters sought to circumvent these forms of resistance, however, by making sales stealthfully, the deal being a fait accompli before the parents or spouses learned what had happened. The ultimate lesson slaves learned from these reminders of their inability to control their own mobility or that of their family members was that "[p]ower lay in the hands of the master." Husbands "did not support their wives, who worked at the will of their master." It was the white master, not the husband, who "provided slave women with food, lodging, clothing, and medical care, assigned them tasks, supervised their work, disciplined them, determined the destiny of their children, and could impose nonnegotiable sexual demands." Challenging the masters' power raised the risk of retribution not merely by physical punishment but by forced splitting asunder of family ties, thus reinforcing slaves' sense of dependence on their masters and forging emotional as well as physical restraints on their mobility.[33]

To discourage any vestiges of slave autonomy, masters regulated not only the bondsmen's movement from and between plantations but also *within* the plantation. By the antebellum period, planters sought as an ideal to have their slaves live by rules. "Rules told them when to rise in the morning, when to go to the fields, when to break for meals, how long and how much to work, and when to go to bed." Rules instructed slaves in detail how each job was to be done, going so far as to dictate how far apart rows should be planted and how quickly slave songs should be sung in the field. Some planters used blowing horns to signal to slaves where they were to be at particular times of the day, Mississippi planter William Ethelbert Ervin, for example, using just such a horn as "the signal for each to retire to his or her house and remain there until morning." William Brown used a bell to rouse workers awake at four a.m., the signal to work, a horn, being blown just thirty minutes later. "By 1860, the accumulated list of suggested rules published in the dozens of articles on plantation management could have filled volumes."[34]

Rules were most often enforced in practice by physical punishment, despite much plantation literature that argued for minimizing the lash and some writers who advocated that slaveowners first try simple persuasion, which usually meant indoctrination by compelled attendance at church services or modest material rewards to win slaves' loyalty. The point of such detailed management of slaves' time and mobility even within the plantation was to "impress upon the slaves an automatic sense of place and duty that could bypass the rational process of human thought." "Habit is every thing," recorded a Louisiana planter in his diary. Argued another slaveholder, the slave who is "subjected to constant employment without the labor of thought . . . , is by far happier than he would be if emancipated, and left to think, and act, and provide for himself."[35]

Masters sometimes had reasons, usually economic ones, however, for giving in to slaves' demands for modestly increased control over their own mobility. The most important situation where this occurred was in slave hiring, a practice so widespread that every slave faced a good chance of being hired out at least once in his or her lifetime. Planters had an economic incentive to hire out slaves not currently needed to work the plantation but whose labor might be wanted in the future, and children hired out now might be more valuable for sale later. Hirers benefited from the flexibility of hiring slaves, when needed, at far lower prices than purchase would require. But hiring also enabled poorer whites to reap the psychic rewards of enhanced self-worth stemming from joining the esteemed ranks of the slaveowner. Much hiring was done on "hiring day"—New Year's Day—when many slaves would be placed on the auction block, usually to be hired out for a period of one year. Hiring also might be arranged for sometimes shorter periods by private agreements between neighbors, acquaintances, or business associates, or as a result of newspaper advertisements or via "hiring brokerages that functioned like slave pens, where slaves were sent by rural owners to be hired out." As noted earlier, hiring was one among many forms of forced slave movement that could mean at least temporary separation of slave families. But unlike other forms of locomotion control, hiring meant "divided mastery" between owner and hirer, and it was this division that occasionally gave slaves some small measure of added power modestly to protect their families and their own autonomy.[36]

A slave on the hiring auction block might be questioned by potential hirers. Slaves who feared impending hiring by someone of seemingly unpleasant temperament or in an undesirable location might give bad answers, promising to run away if hired out to the unwanted bidder or refusing to accompany him. Bidders did not want recalcitrant slaves, so this sort of gambit sometimes worked. When it did not, slaves who still refused to leave with their temporary masters might be whipped and jailed until they promised not to run away. Alternatively, slaves might try to ingratiate themselves with masters living in good locations or who seemed to clothe and feed their slaves well. Former slave Harriet Jacobs explained that such bidders on hiring day would face crowds of slaves, with each one begging, "Please, massa, hire me this year. I will work *very* hard, massa." It was usually hard to rent entire families, hirers resisting taking on children too young to work and paying lower prices than for individual

slaves. But, "Their use of slaves limited to a year's time, hirers had little patience for slaves left torpid by anger or depression." Many owners and hirers
thus saw economic advantage in hiring families, or at least in keeping husbands and wives in close proximity. Some planters, like James McDowell of
Mississippi in the 1840s, let young men with wives scour the neighborhood in
search of potential hirers, thus promoting slaves' greater satisfaction with a
placement.[37]

Historian Jonathan D. Martin describes slavery as involving, for each slave,
three forms of property: the slave's body, work, and subordination. Slaves
would threaten harm to each form of property to gain bargaining power in hiring. Slaves would threaten to, or would actually, harm their bodies, even to the
point of threatening suicide, unless masters included contract terms guaranteeing that slaves could visit their families during periods of hire. Slaves might
also run away or threaten to do so, or, if hired, might be so disobedient, "impertinent," and "obstinate" as to deny hirers the psychic benefits of another's
complete submission. "Sly disobedience was manifest," says Martin, "in petu-
lant scowls, dragging feet, and botched tasks, but some slaves went further,
brazenly threatening to run away from their hirers if not released from the hiring contracts." Fearing the prospect of being hired out to unwanted places,
slaves also sometimes approached whites they knew and asked to be hired by
them. Some slaves wanted to be hired out to avoid unbearable current circumstances.[38]

Slaves were also able to exploit a natural tension between owners and hirers.
Owners wanted their property well cared for, whereas hirers wanted to get as
much economic return and to attain as much mastery as possible for the period of hire, caring little about the condition in which the owners' investment
was returned. Except for the opinion of North Carolina's Judge Ruffin in *State v.
Mann*, the courts largely sided with the owners in these disputes. The prevailing rule became that hirers had the power to inflict "reasonable corporal punishment" but "in a qualified sense and to a limited extent," the fuller right
more "properly belong[ing] only to the owner." Hirers, therefore, often sought
owners' permission before putting slaves to dangerous work or disciplining
them. Hirers also faced the burden of proving that a slave's escape did not
result from the hirer's abusive behavior. Slaves were aware of these limits on
hirers' authority and threatened to report abuses to their masters or to flee to
those masters if maltreated. Slaves might also appeal to owners' practices as a
way to limit hirers' behavior, saying, for example, that "his marster don't whip
him." These various gambits succeeded often enough to give slaves some minimal control over their locomotion. Gaining enough control to keep family
nearby or to avoid the clutches of a potentially even more abusive hirer meant
much in the restricted world of slave mobility.[39]

Perhaps the greatest challenge to the mobility controls that defined slavery was the practice of self-hiring. With self-hiring, an owner sent a slave out to hire himself, often for a variety of tasks, in exchange for the slave's remittance to the owner of a set minimum sum by the week or the month, with the owner sometimes allowing the slave to keep earnings above that amount. Self-hirers usually worked and lived in cities and towns, away from their owners, and decided for themselves where and for whom to work, at what tasks, for how long, and at what prices they could negotiate. Problems were posed for self-hirers by the absence of any *legal* ability of slaves to contract and by the existence, at one time or another, of legislation in every Southern state prohibiting the practice—legislation generally instigated by poor whites who feared slave competition. This legislation was rarely enforced, largely because it was lucrative for owners and because hirers who were looking for short-term workers in urban areas did not want the inconvenience of seeking out an owner before contracting for each individual job. "Slaves had to be able to act independently if they were going to work as porters, hucksters, laundresses, and draymen, or if they were going to meet the demand for skilled labor by working as coopers, cobblers, or blacksmiths." The temporary, intermittent work done by self-hirers meant that they lived on their own in room or house rentals rather than with their temporary employers. Self-hirers also at times had a limited ability to turn down undesirable work in search of better conditions. The dominant Southern image of self-hirers at the time was that they were granted "a species of *quasi* freedom" given their increased autonomy, and some historians have agreed, saying that these slaves "dwelt in a shadowland enjoying a status neither fully slave nor entirely free," taking a great "step toward freedom." But this was not how self-hired slaves understood their situation.[40]

It was true that some slaves asked permission to engage in self-hire, but more often they were ordered to do so. Self-hirers were under constant pressure to find work to make their regular payments to their owners and to cover their own room and board. Work was often scarce, and illness or injury could render it impossible. Slaves who missed making their payments could be whipped like any other slave. Moreover, at any moment an owner could end slaves' status as self-hirers, putting them on the auction block and sending them to distant lands, far from loved ones, at the owner's caprice. Poorer whites who feared competition, or slaveholders who viewed self-hirers as bad examples of independence to their own slaves, might periodically jail self-hirers or attack them, usually with impunity. Self-hirers also faced the sense of, and actual, social exclusion and degradation accorded to all slaves and the ever-present fear of family separation. Thomas Jones, a self-hirer on the docks of Wilmington, North Carolina, for a time lived with his family in a rental house, yet he could not forget "the agony of the terrible thought, 'I am a slave, my wife is a slave, my precious children are slaves,'" a thought that "grew bitter and insupportable." Later, his family was "carried off into returnless exile," leaving a "heart broke,

[a] lonely man," who, while still a self-hirer, found that his home was now "darker than the hold of ships in which I worked."[41] Peter Randolph, having worked as a self-hirer, still lamented,

> Slavery is *Slavery,* wherever it is found. Dress it up as you may, in the city or on the plantation, the human being must feel that which binds him to another's will. Be they fetters of silk, or hemp, or iron, all alike warp the mind and goad the soul.[42]

Frederick Douglass, who was beaten by angry white workers while on self-hire in Baltimore, likewise insisted that he still "endured all the evils of being a slave."[43]

Hiring of one sort or another thus touched the lives of many slaves, giving many some increased measure of control over their mobility for limited periods of time. The practice had its white defenders but also its white critics, who feared that it allowed slaves too much participation in the decision about where they would work and that it promoted white conflict, the avoidance of such intrawhite strife being among the purported justifications for slavery. To proslavery ideologist Frank Ruffin, hiring was an "evil, existing among us," so great as to make the hirer himself "feel—only in reverse—'the horrors of slavery'" by giving the slave some influence over the conditions under which he would work. Hiring also undermined the paternalist vision purportedly embraced by many planters by infusing the language of the market into the master-slave relationship in a way that seemed to expose slaves for the human commodities that they were rather than the "extended family members" that so many masters purported them to be, reinforcing "an impersonal view of slaves as capital assets whose interest-bearing capacity needed to be protected by whatever means available." Yet the minimal power hiring gave some slaves over their own mobility was still just that: minimal, a temporally limited affair, a trip between Scylla and Charybdis, in which the slave still faced physical abuse, family breakup, uncertainty, and humiliation, for the master retained the near absolute right, upon mere whim, to control slaves' locomotion and that of their loved ones. Hiring practices thus ultimately served yet again, backed up by the force of law, to remind slaves that their mobility was not, and never would be, within their own control.[44]

The Interstate Slave Trade

The interstate slave trade was a tremendous source of profit in the antebellum South. Estimates range up to 70 percent of the interregional movement of slaves being accounted for by the slave trade, with most of the remaining movement caused by planters moving all or most of their slaves to work western lands. This commerce motivated some traders to kidnap blacks for sale, including, especially after the Fugitive Slave Act of 1850, the kidnapping of free Northern blacks, who were falsely portrayed as runaways and brought down South to be enslaved.[45]

Sales ordinarily took place at a local auction block, usually the same one used to trade other sorts of commodities. These auctions were "ceremonies of degradation, symbolic re-enactments of the violence of original enslavement, potent reminders of the slave's powerlessness and dishonor." The dishonor began with the traders asking slaves to lie, perhaps by greasing their skin to give it a healthier shine or altering their voices and manner of speech to hide a rebellious spirit. Potential buyers would, in turn, poke, prod, and question to uncover such deceit and to make informed judgments about whether slaves were "likely," that is, worth buying, good judgments of likelihood being a sign of white masculinity. One buyer described the typical inspection process: "my inspection was made in the usual manner: their coats being taken off and the breast, arms, teeth, and general form and appearance looked at." Inspection might last from fifteen to thirty minutes, most of it done in public, with bargaining taking as long as several days. Prospective buyers watched one another's inspections and shared their views of, and joked about, the slaves in the slaves' presence. Muscles would be rubbed, joints fingered, flesh kneaded in an effort to find physical flaws. Lips were pulled back and gums and teeth routinely inspected in a search for evidence of disease and age.[46]

Examinations might be far more intimate still. Palpating women's breasts and abdomens to make judgments about "breeding" quality and illness was to be expected, as was the stripping of most slaves to the waist, largely in a search for whipping scars that might reveal the "deformed" character of the runaway and the rascal. Evidence of disciplinary problems was especially dangerous to the prospect of a sale because habitual insubordinates were spoken of as carriers of an infectious disease that might pollute otherwise healthy slaves. A request had to be made, and a reason given, for looking below a woman's skirt, but such requests were often granted; the woman might be taken to an inner room, though the examination remained quite public, as James Redpath described one such stripping: "She was taken into the inner room, after the bidding commenced, and there indecently '*examined*' in the presence of a dozen or fifteen brutal men." There was an undeniable eroticism for many of the white buyers, who probed the women more intimately than judgments about their health required. In the words of historian Walter Johnson, this was but one part of the elaborate auction rituals in which "the violation of black bodies emphasized the inviolability of white ones. Through shared communion in the rites of the slave market—the looking, stripping, touching, bantering, and evaluating—whites confirmed their commonality with the other men with whom they inspected the slaves."[47]

Sale, of course, might yet again mean family separation. Moses Grandy powerfully conveyed the emotional brutality involved when he approached the trader who was leading the coffle in which his wife marched:

> I asked leave to shake hands with her which he refused, but said I might stand at a distance and talk with her. My heart was so full that I could say very little. . . . I gave her the little money I had in my pocket, and bade her farewell. I have never seen or heard of her from that day to this. I loved her as I loved my life.[48]

Some slaves were so distraught that they would take desperate action to avert a sale. Among the most infamous examples was that of Anna, who, when purchased with two of her children but not the rest and not with their father, jumped from the third floor of George Miller's tavern in Washington, DC. Anna survived but with a broken back and two shattered arms, saying of her action only, "I did not want to go." Her desperation led to the "first direct denunciation of the interstate slave trade in Congress," by Representative John Randolph. Other slaves reacted to the loss of the connections that gave their lives meaning and the fear of transport to the "killing fields of the lower South" with more resignation, succumbing to the " 'soul murder'—that left many of the trade's victims with little will to resist." Henry Bibb's story of his conversations with his wife in darkness after her rape by a trader who threatened to part her from her children if she did not submit is but one of many tales that makes the metaphor of soul murder palpable.[49]

Slaves sold to traders would be transported generally in a "coffle," a long row of slaves chained together for their march. Coffles could involve as many as three hundred bondsmen traveling six to eight weeks over hundreds of miles. Coffles might spend part of a trip on a steamboat or, later, traveling by rail. Leg irons and handcuffs were needed to guard against slaves' flight or violent resistance.[50] Charles Ball vividly described the precautions taken by the whites leading his fifty-slave coffle from Maryland to South Carolina:

> The women were tied together with a rope, about the size of a bed cord, which was tied like a halter around the neck of each; but the men . . . were very differently caparisoned. A strong iron collar was closely fitted by means of a padlock round each of our necks. A chain of iron was passed through the hasp of each padlock, except at the two ends, where the hasps of the padlocks passed through a link in the chain. In addition to this we were handcuffed in pairs.[51]

A slave in the upper South had "a one-in-three chance of being sold before the age of forty." Slaves dreaded being "sold down the river" into the reputedly more brutal conditions of the lower South, with places like the Louisiana sugar plantations having "especially grim reputations." These fears, combined with the danger of family separation, made masters' threats of sale a particularly powerful form of social control. Thus, the Brown family told one of their insolent male slaves that "plainly he must quit it, and . . . if he did not conduct himself correctly . . . that [the master] would not be troubled with him; but sell him and [his] wife the very instant they cease[d] to conduct themselves properly." Mary Bell warned a pregnant slave and her husband that "if they d[id] not make [her] crib full of corn that [she] w[ould] sell them in the fall for enough to fit it." One of Thomas Jefferson's slaves so feared being labeled "unproductive" that for several years he hid and left untreated a serious hiatal hernia, which eventually caused his sudden death. Sometimes an actual sale, rather than the mere utterance of a threat, would be made of a discontented slave as a warning to other slaves to fall in line.[52] Historian Robert H. Gudmestad summarized well the impact of these efforts in maintaining white domination over the slave population:

> [T]he lash "was not the ultimate sanction of the master's authority." Sale or even the threat of sale "may have been the keystone of coercive slave control" because it relied on terror rather than torture. A master's ability to separate slaves irrevocably from their families and loved ones was a punishment that inflicted mental and spiritual anguish far in excess of the physical pain produced by the whip. The sale of disobedient slaves was the most powerful long-term technique of discipline because bondservants feared it more than anything else.[53]

The Fugitive-Slave Laws

General Charles Cotesworth Pinckney, South Carolina delegate to the federal Constitutional Convention, reported to his state House of Representatives his relative satisfaction with the protections that the new Constitution provided for slavery: "In short, considering the circumstances, we have made the best terms for the security of this species of property it was in our power to make. We would have made better if we could; but on the whole, I do not think them bad." The constitutional provisions providing for, or later having the effect of, protecting slavery were indeed many, but the one most relevant here, and a major source of Pinckney's elation, was the Fugitive Slave Clause. As Pinckney boasted about the clause, "We have obtained a right to recover our slaves in whatever part of America they may take refuge, which is a right we had not before." That clause declared, "No person held to Service or Labour in one State, under the Laws thereof, escaping into another, shall, in Consequence of any Law or Regulation therein, be discharged from such Service or Labour, but shall be delivered up on Claim of the Party to whom such Service or Labor may be due." The phrasing of the clause—especially within a framework of supposedly limited federal governmental powers—was such that it might have been read as merely imposing upon the states an obligation, perhaps through a state judge or county sheriff, to "deliver up" a fugitive rather than authorizing congressional action to aid in the interstate runaways' recapture. Nevertheless, both Congress and the Supreme Court would ultimately understand the clause as authorizing just such federal action.[54]

In 1791, Governor Thomas Mifflin of Pennsylvania had sought the extradition of three Virginians accused of kidnapping and enslaving a free black Pennsylvanian, John Davis. When Virginia's Governor Beverly Randolph refused the extradition request, Mifflin asked President George Washington to request that the federal legislature act to avoid similar problems in future cases. Washington indeed approached Congress, but the ultimate result—the Fugitive Slave Law of 1793—may not have been what Mifflin had in mind.[55]

Section 3 of the 1793 law assumed that a slaveowner or his agent would seize a runaway and then authorized the runaway's being brought before a federal or state court judge "or any magistrate of a county, city or town corporate" where the seizure occurred for rendition proceedings. The claimant would there have to offer proof to the judge or magistrate's satisfaction that the person seized was a fugitive slave owned by the claimant. Proof could be presented through either oral testimony or an affidavit taken before a magistrate in the state from which the alleged slave had fled. A judge or magistrate who found adequate proof would issue to the claimant a certificate of removal. Section 4 of the law imposed a $500 penalty on any person who interfered with the rendition process, to be paid to the owner upon his suit, and also permitted the owner to sue separately for injuries—including physical damages to the slave or the claimant—caused by such interference.[56]

The certification authorized by the act "amounted to the retroactive licensing of any slave hunter who could satisfy a magistrate" by the necessary proof, thus likely shielding the hunter from civil or criminal liability. Testimony at the hearing was ex parte—that is, only the claimant's side of the case was guaranteed to be heard. The statute did not confer upon the alleged fugitive the rights to speak or to representation by legal counsel or to a jury. The only recourse left to an accused fugitive contesting his status was to appeal to the courts "in the jurisdiction from which he had fled—that is, according to slave-state law, wherein all blacks were regarded as slaves unless they could prove otherwise."[57]

Some Southerners continued to exercise what they saw as the constitutionally guaranteed common-law right of "recaption," retaking alleged slaves without obtaining the judicial blessing mandated by the 1793 legislation. Honest mistakes were made even when the proper procedures were followed, but the deliberate kidnapping of free blacks from Northern states also occurred. Indeed, the Pennsylvania Abolition Society warned its members on the day that Washington signed the law that free blacks were endangered and that Northern judges might too readily rely on suspect affidavits sworn before Southern judges. Moreover, although the recapture process still began with self-help by masters, the authority of the national government now stood behind a rendition process that had previously seemed to be a matter of interstate comity rather than federal power. Despite the summary nature of these processes, the act survived various constitutional challenges, including two failed assaults in federal court, one arguing that Congress lacked the power to enact the legislation, the other maintaining that it violated the Seventh Amendment's jury-trial guarantee. Interestingly, the statute also survived an attack on its constitutionality for violating the Fourth Amendment's guarantee against unreasonable searches and seizures. Chief Justice Isaac Parker of the Supreme Court of Massachusetts held in 1823 in *Commonwealth v. Griffith* that none of the protections of the Bill of Rights, including those in the Fourth Amendment, extended to slaves, for they had not been parties to the Constitution. Indeed, concluded Justice Parker, the Constitution was itself an agreement to treat slaves as simple property rather than as persons. Justice Parker's vision of the 1793 law was that it constituted congressional acceptance of the Southern doctrines that presumed that black fugitives were slaves and that slaves were mere things. Northern courts were indeed generally more amenable to this vision than were Northern legislatures, with the courts tending to overturn state statutory provisions for jury trial and upholding federal supremacy in this area.[58]

Nevertheless, the number of escaped slaves may have continued to rise, many fleeing to the free-black communities of the North or the haven of Canada. The slaveholding states tightened up their own fugitive-slave laws but believed their local and supporting federal efforts to be unduly stymied. The State of Virginia is a helpful case study. As early as 1798, the state prohibited abolitionist-society members from serving on juries and imposed fines for harboring slaves and the death penalty for encouraging slave rebellion. Free blacks were prohibited from transferring their freedom "register" to runaway slaves. By 1825, legislation created the danger that any master or skipper of a boat found to be carrying unauthorized slaves would pay heavy fines, restitution, and face a two-to-four-year prison sentence. Over time, Virginia extended the payment of statutory fees for apprehending runaways to those doing so in other specified Northern states, repeatedly raising the compensation provided. The growing numbers and assertiveness of Northern abolitionists in the 1830s and mounting Southern white fears for their safety in the wake of the Vesey Plot of 1822 in South Carolina, the Virginia insurrection scare of 1829, and especially

Nat Turner's Revolt of 1831 nevertheless led to growing insecurity among Virginia's and other Southern slaveholding elites.[59] In late 1832, responding to the escape of seventeen to eighteen slaves to New York City in a stolen whaleboat, proslavery activist and member of the Virginia General Court Abel Parker Upshur sent a heated letter of complaint to Virginia's Governor John B. Floyd:

> It is . . . of the utmost importance to all slave owners here, that the slaves should know that there is a power in the laws to render abortive, all future attempts of that kind. Indeed, the protection uniformly afforded by individuals and private societies in the North, to fugitive slaves from the South, is too notorious to be denied, and presents, as it seems to me, a fit occasion for the interference of the public authorities of the aggrieved states. It is perfectly certain that unless this abuse can in some mode or other, be speedily corrected, the Eastern Shore of Virginia, affording as it does and must continue to do, by its very position, every facility for the escape of slaves, will soon be wholly without that species of property. . . . It is obvious that the exertions of the original owners, can effect very little in reclaiming their slaves, from communities, organized against their rights. Hence, almost every attempt of that kind, has not only failed of success, but has subjected the party to insult, and personal danger.[60]

In response to concerns like Upshur's, the legislature in 1834 tightened the laws on enticing or aiding fugitive slaves. The following year, it chartered the Virginia Slave Insurance Company to insure against absconding slaves. The fires of fear were more heavily stoked, however, when in 1840 New York's Governor William Seward refused to extradite to Virginia three African Americans accused of stealing a slave. This time, Virginia's legislature reacted by increasing the rewards for apprehending fugitives near the borders with Ohio, Pennsylvania, and Maryland and created special penalties for anyone helping free black fugitives escape justice. Unregistered free blacks were prohibited from entering the state. Between 1845 and 1850, a significant number of persons languished in Virginia prisons for slave stealing and related crimes. Continued, perhaps modest, resistance to rendition by both Northern mobs and the law in some Northern states, and politicians exaggerating the real dangers of slave escape, combined with other social forces to lead Virginians and their Southern brethren to press for stronger federal action. Although the most active Southern agitators may not have gotten all that they sought, they unquestionably got stronger federal legislation in the form of the Fugitive Slave Act of 1850.[61]

The new act likely would not have passed but for its part in the grand Compromise of 1850 at a time of national crisis. Under the new law, a slaveowner or his agent could still seize a fugitive on his own but could also proceed by way of an arrest warrant issued by a federal officer. The act "created special federal commissioners who were not constrained by judicial traditions and so could act independently of state and local laws." The commissioner was to be appointed by a U.S. Circuit judge and given "concurrent jurisdiction" with federal judges in administering the law. Commissioners also had the authority to appoint "one or more suitable persons" to execute warrants, and this person or a subordinate was empowered to "summon the aid of bystanders as a *posse comitatus*. In addition, federal marshals and their deputies were drawn explicitly into the work of enforcement and made financially liable for nonexecution of warrants and the escape of fugitives from their custody." Once captured, an alleged fugitive appeared before a commissioner or federal judge for a summary hearing based on the claimant's ex parte evidence. The prisoner was prohibited from testifying and denied the rights to trial by jury and habeas corpus. If the prisoner was found to be an escapee owned by the claimant, a certificate of removal issued. That certificate was considered "conclusive," rendering "its holder immune to 'molestation' by court processes of any kind." The act also added criminal penalties and increased civil ones for interfering with its operation. Moreover, if there was good reason to fear forcible obstruction, "the claimant could have the fugitive delivered to him in his own state at government expense—the task to be performed by the marshal or other arresting officer and as many specially hired subordinates as the situation seemed to require." Finally, commissioners were paid a fee of ten dollars if they decided in the claimant's favor but only five dollars if they decided otherwise.[62]

The act seemed one-sided to many Northerners, as it ignored longstanding due-process protections and the "humanitarian sensibilities of many white Americans" and contained provocative language that referred to free-state legal procedures as "molestation." It also permitted the impressment of private citizens into service on behalf of the pursuing slaveholders.[63] Senator Charles Sumner railed against the act as a constitutional abomination:

> In denying the Trial by Jury [this act] is three times unconstitutional; first as the Constitution declares the "right of the people to be secure in their persons against unreasonable seizures"; secondly as it further declares, that "No person shall be deprived of life, liberty, or property without due process of law"; and thirdly, because it expressly declares that "in suits at common law . . . the right of jury trial shall be preserved." By this triple cord did the framers of the Constitution secure the Trial by Jury in every question of Human Freedom.[64]

Within days of the act's signing, blacks throughout the North organized protests and declared their intentions to defy the law. In Philadelphia, a black meeting pledged, "We owe ourselves, our wives, our children, and to our common nature, as well as to the panting fugitive from oppression, to resist this law at any cost and all hazards." An African Congregational Church in Syra-cuse similarly promised to take "the scalp of any government hound that dares follow on our tracks as we are resolved to be free, if it is not until after death." White abolitionists joined the chorus, with Boston's Lewis Hayden calling the act an "ungodly and anti-republican law" and a Philadelphia meeting con-demning the statute as "utterly at variance with the principles of the Constitu-tion . . . repugnant to the highest attributes of God, justice, and mercy . . . and horribly cruel in its expressed mode of operation."[65] New Bedford abolitionists vowed to trample the act

> under our feet, and our blood should flow freely from every vein and mingle with the blood of our revolutionary fathers, who fell on the field of battle defending the liberties of our country, before we should consent to be taken from the pure soil of Massachusetts as fugitive slaves.[66]

Frederick Douglass similarly declared, "Two or three dead slaveholders will make this law a dead letter."[67]

Many of the Southern drafters of the act were, despite their role in shaping its terms, skeptical from the start that it would succeed in adequately protect-ing Southern property rights in slaves. For these men, including militants like Andrew Butler and Jefferson Davis, the act nevertheless expressed a symbolic federal commitment to protecting slavery. Furthermore, if the act succeeded, the abolitionists would be in retreat, and if it failed, Southern unity would be enhanced. Likewise, many "grim warnings" were uttered throughout the South that continued union and national peace depended on the North's energetic commitment to the act's terms.[68]

Abolitionists' anger and defiance quickly put that commitment to the test. Growing acts of resistance eventually led Southerners to doubt the good faith of the law's Northern sponsors and the willingness of the Northern people to keep the promise made to their Southern brethren, embodied in the act's words. Yet "some 332 runaways were returned to their masters, and federal commissioners freed only eleven" during the 1850s. Moreover, although there is disagreement on the point, at least one historian has concluded that despite apparent Southern perceptions to the contrary, slave escapes to the North did not rise during that decade. Furthermore, in 1859 the U.S. Supreme Court up-held the constitutionality of the 1850 act, with no federal judge or attorney general or state supreme court (other than that of Wisconsin) ruling to the contrary, while state tribunals affirmatively upheld the law's constitutionality more than a dozen times. Additionally, the act for the first time required affir-mative Northern assistance in slave rendition. Actual or purported Southern perceptions that the federal government and the Northern state governments were ignoring Southern rendition demands were thus seriously distorted.[69]

The 1850 statute was accordingly one important quiver in the Southern bow aimed at autonomous black locomotion. The specifics of the reactions it would stir in the North would contribute much to the coming of the Civil War and the eventual constitutional death of restrictions on black free movement. But those reactions are best understood within the context of an analysis of the entire evolving Northern response to Southern law-imposed locomotive limitations, limits that were primarily, but not solely, placed on blacks. For the fuller Northern picture to make sense, more must first be said about the various forms of slave resistance and the meaning of mobility regulation for both the slaves and their masters.

8 Mobility's Meaning for the South

Mobility Control's Meaning for the Masters

To understand what it was that the Reconstruction amendments meant to end in dissolving the institution of slavery, it is not enough to examine the laws that defined a slave's status. Those laws both reflected and helped to create a white culture of mastery and a black counterculture of resistance. It was the master's culture itself, the culture of the "Slave Power," that Reconstruction sought to destroy.

Cultures are networks of myth and metaphor, systems of meaning that constitute the social world in which the culture's members live. These meanings assign social status, define in-group and out-group membership, even affect members' religious beliefs. A cluster of meaning-networks of special importance surrounded Southern legal and other limits on black free movement.

So central was the denial of free movement of black slaves to white self-definition that masters viewed runaways as defective or diseased. Those whites who challenged the wisdom or morality of black locomotive limits, particularly the abolitionists, were polluters, helping to spread the disease—polluters whose own movement into the body politic had to be barred to maintain its health. Locomotive controls indeed defined the boundaries of the body politic, and the skin on that body was white. Indeed, God Himself had blessed the white body politic as necessary to the righteous care of the dependent black race. A body that does not move for sustenance and does not grow for strength dies. White Southerners thus increasingly saw an entitlement to their own free movement, into the territories and throughout the nation, as essential to their survival. Simultaneously, they saw black free movement—for a slave who can go where he pleases is no slave at all—as an equal threat to white Southern society's very existence. This white Southern vision would briefly become *the nation's* legal vision with the Court's embrace of it in its entirety in *Dred Scott v. Sanford,* an embrace that would ultimately prove fatal to national unity.

The meanings assigned to locomotive limits by the black counterculture were in some ways a mirror image of those of the whites. If locomotive limits defined dependency, inferiority, and slavery, then bursting those limits—running away—rejected each of these definitions in favor of more liberating ones. Slaves' nascent political ideology and their religion accepted part of the message that blacks were a group distinct from whites. Yes, blacks were a nation, but they were a nation-within-a-nation, both separate from and yet part of the body politic that included whites. The Exodus story of the literal physical, and of the metaphorical spiritual and political, liberation of an entire people became a defining slave narrative. Many free black intellectuals, however, rejected the slaves' Christian universalism, buying into white exclusionary thinking turned on its head. For these thinkers, it was blacks who were superior, whites inferior, though other black intellectuals, particularly Frederick Douglass, saw blacks' chauvinism as the mere re-creation of whites' moral error. The struggle over the wisdom and meaning of the law's limits on blacks' locomotion was thus necessarily a contest over how Americans should define themselves as a people: inclusive or exclusive, dominating or liberating.

The Diseased Runaway

Runaways imposed significant economic costs on the master class and fostered fears of revolt, theft, and physical violence. But these instrumental concerns did not alone account for growing antebellum white Southern hysteria over slave flight. Running away touched at the heart of the Southern culture of racial honor.[1]

Masters professed to believe that slaves were better off than either free black or "free" Northern white labor. Planters thus became indignant at slaves' escapes, refusing to see them as rational moral choices bondsmen made to better their condition. Instead, flight was understood to be caused either by masters' mismanagement or slaves' bad character or disease. Accepting any other explanation challenged the very validity of the system. Slave flight accordingly had a disproportionate moral and psychological impact on masters, a challenge to their authority and worldview that simply could not go unmet.[2]

Antebellum white Southerners, drawing on Scottish moral philosophy, believed that all white men had an innate "moral sense," albeit one that could be enhanced by proper education. White Southern character ideals depended on an opposition between black and white. If whites had a moral sense, then blacks could not. Indeed, though not using the term "moral sense" in this connection, proslavery writers effectively embraced the vision of blacks as devoid of moral sense. "[T]he Negro was by nature a savage brute," according to Southern racial ideology, but "Under slavery, . . . he was 'domesticated' or, to a limited degree, 'civilized.' " Hence, "docility was not so much his natural character as an artificial creation of slavery." As one ideologue put it, "The negro must, from necessity, be the slave of man or the slave of Satan." Black character was, therefore, seen to be plastic, to be molded into pleasing or disagreeable shapes based on the artist's (the master's) skill. Black character was, however, only so malleable, for "innate racial traits limited his potential development to a more or less tenuous state of 'semi-civilization.' " Although blacks lacked an innate moral sense, they did have strong imitative abilities. A happy slave, it was said, wanted to be like his master and so would mimic the master's moral development as much as the slave was able. Good slaves, who were well governed, were thus much like children. Yet there were also bad slaves, those lacking the necessary plasticity, which left them immutably vicious, subhuman, more animal than man.[3]

This distinction between good and bad slaves infiltrated Southern thinking about slave flight. White Southerners distinguished between the act of running away and the character trait of being "a runaway." Any slave might occasionally run away for situational reasons, such as expecting a particularly harsh beating. A slave who ran away often, or perhaps for no reason fairly attributable to a master's mismanagement, was, however, a "runaway," a slave *defined by* a character or habit of running away, a vice made into an "immutable essence."[4]

The running away/runaway distinction made its appearance often in breach-of-warranty lawsuits in which a slave buyer complained of a slave's hidden "defect," specifically the slave's character as a runaway. In such suits, the seller argued that the slave ran from his new master because of bad governance, and the buyer argued that he unknowingly purchased a slave whose ill character was well-known to the original owner at the time of the sale. More than money was at stake in such cases because a verdict in favor of the seller generally implied character flaws in the buyer as a bad manager of his household. "[L]ike master, like man," the slave was but an extension of his master's will.[5] As one seller argued in a South Carolina case,

> no man could warrant the *future conduct* of a negro after a sale. . . . That a negro with proper treatment and good management, might behave very well to one man, while on the contrary he might behave very much amiss to another master. A difference of treatment, bad company, and the temptations of a village where drunkenness and intoxication prevail, and vicious habits are predominate, might seduce even the best of slaves to go astray.[6]

The appellate court in that case affirmed the eventual jury verdict for the seller. In another case, the seller was put in the odd position of arguing that his slave, Bill, had run from him before the sale but only because the seller himself had made "unnecessary threats," not because of any character defect in the slave. Several witnesses testified that they knew Bill by the nickname "Red Fox," earned both "because of his skill at evading the slave patrol *and* that he was an excellent worker." There was evidence from which it could be concluded that Bill had run from his original owner several times, and the buyer insisted that the seller had nevertheless falsely extolled Bill's character in every way. The trial and appellate courts found for the seller, allowing him to recover Bill's market value. This sort of debate about the quality of both slave and white character typified these breach-of-warranty cases.[7]

Ill slave character might also be viewed as a disease. Dr. Samuel Cartwright, author of a medical handbook for slaveowners, attributed blacks' inferiority to their alleged tendency to rebreathe their own air, covering their heads and faces as they slept so that largely impure air entered their lungs. White authority, said Cartwright, was needed by slaves to "vitalize and decarbonize their blood by the process of full and free respiration, that active exercise of some kind alone can effect." Cartwright attributed black-white differences to polygenesis, the idea that blacks and whites had thoroughly distinct origins rather than both descending from Adam and Eve. Black physiological inferiority, wrote Cartwright, rendered them subject to a variety of diseases, among those of special importance being "drapetomania," the "disease of running way." Because blacks were by nature "kneebenders," said Cartwright, "awe and reverence must be exacted," if they are not to "despise their masters, become rude and ungovernable, and run away." The only cure for drapetomania was to keep slaves firmly in "that submissive state which it was intended for them to occupy . . . and treat [them] like children, with care, kindness, attention, and humanity."[8]

Some historians have viewed Cartwright as a fringe proslavery thinker. In his polygenetic beliefs, this understanding is correct. But in his medicalization of slavery and his biological racism, he was well within the mainstream, and if common talk about runaways did not include such technical terms as "drapetomania," it did include terms describing slaves' "addictions" and "habits" in ways that embraced the same core concepts articulated by Cartwright in his medical manual.[9]

Fugitive slaves were portrayed as ugly, having missing or rotted teeth, twisted limbs, hollow eyes, and "pock-pitted skin." Their cropped ears, whipping scars, and branded R's on cheek, forehead, or breast for previous offenses had burned into their skin the hideousness of their nature. They were barbaric aliens, particularly the African-born ones, who might bear ritual scarification or filed teeth. They had "bewitching and deceitful tongues" and were a financial drain, requiring money to be spent on their recapture and imposing the "psychic cost of living with the knowledge that a fugitive's expression of personal autonomy likely would encourage others to test their master's authority, thereby lowering both comfort levels and profit margins even further." "Above all, they were not alone," presumably having allies among the Indian nations, some poor whites, free blacks, and maroon communities of runaways living in swamps, the mountains, or the wilds; they were "monsters in human shape," luring field hands into their ranks to expand the "nest of miscreants" into the potential "nucleus of a death-dealing guerilla army."[10]

Satan's Underground Railroad

The idea of an organized effort by outsiders to pollute slaves' minds, then steal them up North—of an "underground railroad"—was spawned in the Southern mind. The *Charlottesville Jeffersonian* warned in 1853 of "emissaries in our midst" orchestrating runaway escapes to Canada. Similarly, the *Shepherdstown Register* in February 1856 cautioned locals of "*agents* hereabouts, concerned in the secret operation by which so many of our citizens are robbed of their property," and in 1851, Richmond's *Watchman and Observer* declared that an underground railroad was helping to create a "uniform spirit of . . . *lawlessness*" throughout Southern society. Northern abolitionists' own talk of such a railroad confirmed these Southern suspicions.[11]

Northern abolitionists did, of course, aid significant numbers of slave escapes, and there was an underground railroad in the sense of a process by which escaped slaves made it to their freedom in the North, Canada, or "points south, west, and out to sea." Although this process was "sometimes organized in a network but more often not," white Southerners thoroughly exaggerated the degree of organization, imagining the railroad as a centrally managed network "doing the work of the spirit of darkness—producing distrust, and alienation, and hatred, and strife, where there should be confidence, and union, and friendship and love," a work of "unmixed and unmitigated evil—with not a solitary benefit to a solitary individual, either black or white, North or South." The psychic function of these imaginings was to relegate the runaways to minor roles, creatures with little agency who were at the mercy of unscrupulous outside agitators. The help that was provided by maroons, free blacks, and whites was viewed through this conspiratorial lens, leading especially to hysteria at the mere whiff of Northern interference. Few measures to combat these enemies, real or imagined, were too extreme. Virginia, for example, adopted legislation in March 1856 barring any water-going vessel owned by a nonresident from leaving Virginia without submitting to inspection and payment of a five-dollar fee. Licensed pilots, acting as paid inspectors, were obligated to search all vessels for slaves. When a search of one schooner, the *Keziah*, piloted by William Baylis, a Delaware captain, uncovered five slaves on board, Baylis was readily convicted by a jury of aiding slave escape and sentenced to forty years imprisonment. This case led the *Williamsburg Weekly Gazette* to describe Baylis's crime as "one of the highest and most heinous known to the law," warning its readers, "While there are traitors in our midst it behooves us to be upon our guard; not only vigilant but it is a duty imperative on all good citizens to seek out these traitors and to bring them to justice." Likewise, when the captain and crew of the schooner *Frances French* faced a kidnapping trial upon the discovery of a runaway on board, a protesting group of Norfolk citizens demanded that another Northern ship captain and one of his commercial associates leave Norfolk quickly or be, they warned, "*tarred and feathered and ridden on a rail* and shipped North to his *abolition friends.*"[12]

Southern white clerics shared this disgust for abolitionism. Although many clerics saw slavery as sanctified by the Bible, many also considered a society's choice whether to embrace slavery or not a political one. Once slavery was chosen, however, the proper behavior of the parties to the master-slave relationship was a religious one. Each had obligations to the other, the slave to labor for his master, the master to feed and clothe the slave and to bring him the word of God. Abolitionism offended these clerics both because it distorted God's word—the biblical embrace of slavery—and because it brought religion into what should be the purely civil question of whether slavery should exist. Perhaps paradoxically, opposition to abolitionist heresy brought Southern clerics into battle over the very issue that they deemed outside the religious sphere. South Carolina's Bethel Presbytery assailed "the efforts of Northern fanatics to identify abolitionism with the cause of religion." Beaufort, South Carolina, citizens declared their "unutterable disgust and loathing" of abolitionists for rendering the "names of Religion and Philanthropy prostituted to the purposes of the INCENDIARY." For Southern church leaders, abolitionism was un-Christian, a hypocritical use of religion to mask their true political aspirations.[13]

Ministers' flocks agreed. Thus, an Athens, Georgia, religious assembly urged legislators to pass laws barring the distribution of abolitionist literature in the South, and religious bodies organized anti-abolitionist protests. The South Alabama Presbytery deplored "the inculcation of Incendiary Papers and Pamphlets" as deserving the "reprobation of this community as destructive to the comfort of the Slave population, the interest of the church, and the Stability of established Institutions." The Baptist state convention in North Carolina labeled abolitionism "uncalled for, intrusive and pernicious," while Alabama's Tuscaloosa Presbytery described it as "wicked and fanatical" and Virginia's East Hanover Presbytery expressed that it "unequivocally & entirely disapprove[d] of & condemn[ed] the principles, plans, and efforts of the Abolitionists, as impolitic, unscriptural, & cruel." The abolitionists were seen as encouraging and

assisting slaves' escape and rebellion, which was necessarily linked to the ultimate extinction of the institution. In a real sense, then, it was the perceived
abolitionist assault on controls over slave locomotion that was ultimately being condemned as impious, insulting, and dangerous.[14]

The stronger scriptural defense of slavery, significantly sparked by the abolitionist postal campaign to spread the movement's word in the 1830s, was
linked to a related natural-law argument. The essence of this argument was
that inequality and submission by some to others were but aspects of the naturally hierarchical structure of all societies. Rights were not universal but vari-
able based on one's condition: "The rights of a father are natural, but they
belong only to fathers. Rights of property are natural, but only to those who
have property." Hierarchy was not oppressive, for, as it manifested itself in slavery, the master was but the head of a household in which his slaves were
among his children. "Both Christianity and Slavery are from Heaven; both are
blessings to humanity; both are to be perpetuated to the end of time."[15]

By the 1850s, the dominant evangelical position sought to characterize slavery as equivalent to Northern free labor in important respects. James Henley
Thornwell was the leading clerical exponent of this view, insisting that slavery
was "not involuntary servitude." Thornwell elaborated:

> If by voluntary be meant, however, that which results from hearty consent,
> and is accordingly rendered with cheerfulness, it is precisely the service
> which the law of God enjoins. Servants are exhorted to obey from considera-
> tions of duty. . . . Whether in point of fact, their service in this sense shall be
> voluntary, will depend upon their moral character. But the same may be said
> of free labor.[16]

Preacher Fred Ross similarly saw slavery as "belonging to the same category
as master and hireling. . . . slavery as a system of labor, is *only one form* . . . [God
uses] *to elevate* man." To attack slavery, argued religious spokesmen of a similar
ilk, was to assault the sacred obligation to work and its inherent moral dignity.
Some proslavery advocates even came to relabel slavery "liberty labor" and
"regulated liberty." The bottom line for most of these thinkers was that slaves
had a biblical obligation to consent to their condition, so obedience to God
can in no sense be condemned as rendering a man "unfree." Others argued
that slaves, by their own ignorance and vices, rendered themselves unfit for
any alternative condition, their choice of vice in this sense being a voluntary
entrance into servitude, or, more technically, "African slaves are made so by
their own *implied consent*." The condition of slavery therefore served as a training ground for moral uplift. Under this vision, the limitations on bondsmen's
free movement that partly defined their condition were in some sense voluntarily chosen and served the slaves' spiritual health while fulfilling God's will.[17]

The White Body Politic

If slaves were described as "free" in these religious and economic senses, they were never so described in the political sense, for all the major proslavery political theories of the time excluded them from the body politic.

There were two primary theories for this exclusion, both rooted in positions on the wisdom and meaning of the Declaration of Independence. The first view was that the Declaration's insistence that "all men are created equal" was, as Roanoke's John Randolph put it, "a most pernicious falsehood." Other men sneered at the document's "fine sounding and sentimental language" and declared its doctrine of equality dangerous. George Fitzhugh most forcefully stated that "men are not born physically, morally or intellectually equal," these inequalities of nature begetting inequalities of rights. Because blacks were born "weak in mind or body," said Fitzhugh, "Nature has made them slaves." History belied the Declaration's notion of inalienable rights, for " 'Life and liberty' are not 'inalienable'; they have been sold in all countries, and in all ages, and must be sold so long as human nature lasts." Slavery was indeed fundamental to the functioning of a sound society. Accordingly, the Declaration was "exuberantly false, and arborescently fallacious."[18]

The second view was that the Declaration was correct but was never intended to extend its clarion call for equality to blacks. As early as the drafting of the Declaration of Rights for Virginia's first constitution—which actually briefly predated the federal Declaration of Independence—arguments of a similar nature had great force in the South. Virginia's Declaration also had a free-and-equal clause. The first draft, by George Mason, stated that all men were "born equally free." When Robert Carter Nicholas protested that this statement was "the forerunner of civil convulsion," the delegates changed the language to "are by nature equally free," and significantly the legislature added "when they enter into a state of society," seemingly implying that slaves were outsiders to "society" and thus not declared "free."[19] When, in *Hudgins v. Wrights*, Chancellor George Wythe of the Richmond District Court of Chancery instead interpreted the free-and-equal clause as rendering slavery illegal in Virginia, the state's highest court, through the pen of Judge St. George Tucker, soundly rejected the chancellor's abolitionist reading:

> I do not concur with the Chancellor in his reasoning on the operation of the first clause of the Bill of Rights, which was notoriously framed with a cautious eye to this subject, and was meant to embrace the case of free citizens, or aliens only; and not by a side wind to overturn the rights of property, and give freedom to those very people whom we have been compelled from imperious circumstances to retain, generally, in the same state of bondage that they were in at the revolution, in which they had no *concern, agency or interest.*[20]

This belief—that blacks had "no concern, agency, or interest" in the nation's founding—underlay the view of many Southerners that, just as slaves were outside the protection of Virginia's Declaration, so were they outside the protection of the new political entity proclaimed in the Declaration of Independence. One Virginia congressman thus stated that "no ingenuity" could "torture the Declaration of Independence into having the remotest allusion to the institution of domestic slavery." The Confederacy's future vice president, Alexander Stephens, insisted that the Framers established "the first great principles of self-government by the governing race." Dr. Samuel Cartwright even noted in a medical journal that "Our Declaration of Independence . . . was drawn up at a time when negros were scarcely considered as human beings, *'That all men are by nature free and equal,'* . . . [was] only intended to apply to white men" and cannot, therefore, be quoted "in support of the false dogma that all mankind possess the same mental, physiological and anatomical organization, and that the liberty, free institutions, and whatever else would be a blessing to one portion, would, under the same external circumstance, be to all."[21]

Sometimes explicitly, sometimes implicitly, a commonality underlay many articulations of both theories: that white, or at least white Southern, political and economic health depended on black exclusion from the political nation. In some variants of this idea, class warfare was identified as the quintessential threat to democracy. Eliminating the lowest classes—"the mudsill"—from the political process prevented them (the slaves) from undermining democracy. It was, therefore, "slavery [that] ultimately made democracy work," the rights proclaimed in the Declaration of Independence being "universally applied to white Americans precisely because they were not applied to blacks."[22]

White Mobility

This general principle played out in dramatic fashion on the question of mobility. Southern whites saw their own freedom of movement as dependent on limiting black locomotion. Many of the major national political struggles of the antebellum era can be understood as rooted in this black/white locomotive tension. Southern planters saw the westward expansion of slavery as an economic necessity. A planter who had several children could bequeath only a portion of his land to each child, giving each relatively small estates. Over several generations, this shrinking of individual assets would multiply. Westward expansion would help to cure this problem by permitting planters' children to reproduce fortunes similar to those of their forebears. George Allen thus credited his "large supply of children" for his move from Alabama to Texas in 1850 "to provide a few acres of land . . . for the benefit of the rising generation." A Georgia planter, Charles Lyell, reportedly with a large family, was also eager to sell his plantation to "purchase a wider extent of land in Texas, and so be better able to provide for them."[23]

But it was more than just inheritance concerns that drove planters west. Material improvements brought status in antebellum Southern white culture, so one way for the young to meet parental pressures to succeed was to head west. Parents too, however, gave in to the material allure of the imagined frontier. Land required slaves to work it, so the urge to acquire real property necessarily meant, to white Southerners, the continued acquisition and relocation of human property. For this and similar reasons, it was said that, "For a young man, just commencing life, the best stock, in which he can invest Capital, is, I think, negro Stock . . . ; negroes will yield a much larger income than any Bank dividend." Letters from those already living in the West grossly exaggerated the benefits of doing so, while family members otherwise inclined to stay put would move to join relatives who had already emigrated. Some moved also because of complaints about exhausted soil and poor returns from their work back east. Small slaveholders' and planters' sons alike were caught up in this quest for upward mobility via migration. As historian James Oakes encapsulates the migration psychology of the era, "Massive demographic dislocation was inevitable in a slaveholding culture that glorified movement, viewed westward migration as inextricably linked to upward mobility, and made material success the nearly universal pursuit." Limiting slavery's westward expansion would thus necessarily limit the white mobility that Southerners so closely linked to social status and the accumulation of wealth.[24]

There were also political implications from Southern whites' perceived tie between their own mobility and controlling that of their slaves. If, for example, slaves could become free by traveling with their master into, or living in, a free state—something that might be necessary in the process of migrating west or because of temporary professional or personal demands—that would, in Southern eyes, amount to a confiscation of their property and so penalize them for exercising their own freedom to move about. Some free states indeed freed any slave who touched their soil. But many states required more, holding that brief transit through their territory with a slave did not bring the *system of slavery* onto their soil and therefore did not change the slave's status. But all antebellum Northern supreme courts agreed that a slave's working or being hired out in a free state did bring the undesired *institution* onto free soil, an impermissible outcome voided by the slave's thereby becoming free. Even many Southern judges, following early precedent, would have agreed, though the growing North-South tension over slavery put pressure on those judges to change their position, and, absent the aid of pro bono (unpaid) counsel, slaves would have had little practical recourse under these precedents anyway, such counsel being far less likely to be available in a slave state than a free state. Northern efforts to obstruct fugitive slaves' recapture would more unequivocally have been viewed by Southern masters as theft of their property and a clear breach of Northern responsibilities under the Constitution's Fugitive Slave Clause. Again, such obstruction, like the freeing of slaves who touched on Northern soil, interfered with *the masters'* free movement by denying them access to their human property.[25]

Moreover, Southerners came to see slavery's territorial expansion as critical to the institution's survival. Every free state newly admitted to the Union meant more senatorial representation for the free North. The more rapidly growing Northern population was already leading that section to greater representation than the South in the House of Representatives by the late antebellum period. Southerners feared that they would one day be outvoted by representatives in the national legislature who had no direct interest in slavery and might even be ideologically opposed to it. Gaining more slave territory therefore became a political imperative, and that meant moving yet more white masters and their slaves west. The national struggle over the expansion of a system in which some humans held property rights in other persons was thus inevitably also a conflict over white rights to mobility.[26]

In 1787, the old Congress under the Articles of Confederation passed the Northwest Ordinance, which prohibited slavery in the American territories north and west of the Ohio River, the area that now consists of the states of Ohio, Indiana, Illinois, Michigan, Wisconsin, and the eastern part of Minnesota. The Congress under the new Constitution reaffirmed the Northwest Ordinance in 1788. It is likely that those slaveholders who voted for the Ordinance saw it as protecting slavery's expansion. The Northwest Ordinance replaced an earlier Ordinance of 1784. When Congress passed that earlier legislation, it deleted a proposal that prohibited slavery from *all* western territories after 1800. By the Northwest Ordinance's limiting this idea to the *northern* territories, Congress seemed to be implying that slavery south of the Ohio River—in what is now the states of Kentucky, Tennessee, Alabama, and Mississippi—would be legal. Nor did the Ordinance immediately free a single slave. Nevertheless, in the long run, "By discouraging slaveowners from moving into the region, the Ordinance helped create a white majority in the Northwest that was hostile to slavery. Six free states would also eventually emerge in that region.[27]

Debate soon flared, sparked by the vast Louisiana Purchase in 1803. When, in 1819, Missouri, consisting of land that was part of the Purchase, sought admission as a new state, Northerners argued that the state should be free. Southerners insisted both that the Northwest Ordinance did not apply to the Louisiana Purchase but only to territories owned by the United States in 1787 and that the Ordinance was limited to land *east* of the Mississippi, thereby excluding Missouri. The result of this debate was the 1820 Missouri Compromise, in which the North and South agreed to limit the admission of new slave states from the Louisiana Purchase territory. Territories in the Louisiana Purchase above the 36° 30' line would enter the Union as free states, and those below the line would enter as slave states. This left the possibility of one or two new slave states. At the time of the Compromise, Southerners were not overly skeptical, as they viewed the northern portion of the Louisiana Purchase as a wasteland and assumed that the United States would continue expanding south and west, where new states would likely join as slave states. Over time, however, many Southerners came to believe that the Compromise was both unconstitutional and a bad bargain, while many Northerners "saw it as an almost sacred pledge to keep slavery out of the western territories." Nevertheless, the Compromise worked for over two decades, with only two new states, one slave (Arkansas) and one free (Michigan), entering the Union.[28]

This period of relative stability ended with the 1845 entry of Texas into the Union and with the Mexican Cession, the huge land area acquired by the July 1848 peace treaty with Mexico, which created the possibility of additional slave states. Congressional deadlock broke with the Compromise of 1850, under which California entered the Union as a free state but with no slavery restrictions in the territories of Utah and New Mexico. The Compromise also, of course, strengthened the Fugitive Slave Law.[29]

Only four years later, in 1854, the Kansas-Nebraska Act repealed the Missouri Compromise, opening what was formerly seen as Northern free territory to slavery, provided that the people in the territories, exercising their "popular sovereignty," so chose. "Popular sovereignty" permitted settlers who owned slaves to bring them into a territory, letting the settlers decide for themselves whether to become a slave state or a free state. Popular sovereignty had been championed by Lincoln's ultimately successful opponent for the 1858 U.S. Senate race in Illinois, Stephen A. Douglas. For Lincoln, however, popular sovereignty signaled both the geographic and the ideological spread of slavery, as it undermined the conditions for its eventual demise. Moreover, if slavery spread to the West, the area would become a Democratic stronghold, limiting the possibility of economic mobility for Northern free wage workers, who would no longer be able to find opportunity in the West. Furthermore, "popular sovereignty" was capable of supporting the new argument that even free states could turn to slavery. Lincoln warned, "This thing is spreading like wild fire over the country. . . . In a few years we will be ready to accept the institution in Illinois, and the whole country will adopt it." Suddenly, the slavocracy threatened to spread north and corrupt the virtues of free white labor. Many of Lincoln's fellow Northerners agreed.[30]

Meanwhile, the incentives for free- and slave-state settlers to flood territories to gain the majority needed to sway "popular sovereignty" to one side or the other played out in what became known as "Bleeding Kansas." The struggle in Kansas became brutally violent when massive electoral fraud led to proslavery settlers from Missouri claiming to have won power over the territorial government via the ballot box, and Northern settlers, denying the election's legitimacy, set up their own, arguably extralegal, government. The battle over Kansas thus came to symbolize a struggle over white mobility—Northern versus Southern free movement—that ultimately demanded some resolution.[31]

That battle was also at least implicitly tied to the role of blacks as members of the polity. Most Northerners of the time shared the racism of their Southern counterparts and would, at best, have relegated blacks to an inferior sort of membership in the political community. Many "Free-Soilers" opposed slavery precisely in the hope of keeping free territories free of any significant black presence. Yet if blacks were in some sense part of the political community, constitutional arguments for their freedom would seem stronger. Correspondingly, if, as white Southerners saw things, blacks were not and could not be members of the political community, at least in the sense of being protected by the federal Constitution and being within the ambit of the Declaration of Independence's commitment to equality, then slavery as an institution would be better poised to spread.[32] One version of the Southern vision of white slaveholders' mobility rights would indeed become the law of the land when the U.S. Supreme Court decided *Dred Scott v. Sanford*,[33] a case that definitively excluded blacks from the American "people," resting its logic primarily on the need to safeguard white mobility by controlling black locomotion.

Dred Scott: Mobility and Peoplehood

Born into slavery in Virginia, Dred Scott spent his life in the South until being purchased by U.S. Army surgeon Dr. John Emerson in 1833. For over two years, Scott lived in the free state of Illinois, where Emerson had been stationed. In 1836, Scott moved with Emerson upon his relocation by the army to the area that is now Minnesota, a region for which the Missouri Compromise had "forever prohibited" slavery. This region was part of what was then called the Wisconsin Territory, to which the recently enacted Wisconsin Enabling Act applied. That act reinforced the slavery ban of the Missouri Compromise in two ways: first, by declaring all settlers entitled to the rights and privileges secured by the Northwest Ordinance of 1787, which prohibited slavery; second, by declaring that the laws of Michigan, which also prohibited slavery, should govern in the territory until repealed or modified. No one, however, apparently objected to Dred Scott's status as a slave, for he remained in that condition during his nearly two-year sojourn in the Wisconsin Territory, marrying another slave during that period in a civil ceremony before a justice of the peace, even though slaves in the United States could not marry. Dred Scott remained in the Wisconsin Territory during this time, even though Emerson was transferred to St. Louis in October 1837. Emerson left Dred and his wife, Harriet, behind, but hired them out to other people in this purportedly slavery-free location.[34]

Emerson later married Eliza Irene Sanford and shortly thereafter brought Dred and Harriet back down South to live with the newlyweds in Louisiana. Only a few months later, however, the two slaves returned with their master to Fort Snelling in the Wisconsin Territory, where Emerson had again been relocated. There they remained until May 1840, when Emerson left his slaves in St. Louis while he went off to serve in the Seminole War. Although Emerson later moved to free territory in Iowa, he left his slaves in St. Louis, hiring them out. After his death in 1843, his wife, Irene, continued renting out Dred and Harriet, including time spent in the new state of Texas. When Dred finally tried to purchase his freedom and that of his family, including his two daughters, one born in free, the other in slave, territory, Mrs. Emerson refused to sell. In response, Scott sued for his and his family's freedom in the Missouri courts.[35]

Missouri's courts, like those in Kentucky, Louisiana, and Mississippi, had long granted freedom to slaves who had lived or worked in a free jurisdiction "long enough to be considered a resident." These courts relied on a 1772 English precedent, *Somerset v. Stewart,* under which a slave brought by his master into a free jurisdiction became forever free.[36] When *Scott v. Emerson* ultimately made its way up to the Missouri Supreme Court, however, that court decided that the old precedents no longer made sense, so that Scott remained a slave:

> Times now are not as they were when the former decisions on this subject were made. Since then not only individuals, but States, have been possessed with a dark and fell spirit in relation to slavery, whose gratification is sought in the pursuit of measures, whose inevitable consequence must be the overthrow and destruction of our government. Under such circumstances it does not behoove the State of Missouri to show the least countenance to any measure which might gratify this spirit. She is willing to assume her full responsibility for the existence of slavery within her limits, nor does she seek to share or divide it with others.[37]

Given growing Southern fears of the destruction of their "peculiar institution," Missouri's high court apparently now concluded that *any* exception to the master's power over his slave, even one rooted in longstanding precedent and in the idea that sojourning with one's master to a land of the free itself set one free, was now too dangerous to be tolerated.[38]

Scott did not, however, simply bow to the state court's will. In 1854, he filed a new suit, but this time in the federal courts, for battery and wrongful imprisonment. The suit was against John Sanford, Irene Emerson's brother, either as Scott's owner or as Irene's legal representative. The asserted basis for the federal courts' power to hear the case was "diversity jurisdiction," which can be extended to a suit between the citizens of different states, in this instance Scott claiming that he was a citizen of Missouri and that Sanford was a citizen of

New York. The various technicalities and subsequent history of the case do not matter here other than to note that it eventually made its way to the U.S. Supreme Court. The high Court ultimately chose to frame the case as essentially involving three broad issues: first, whether Scott, as a black person, could sue in federal court as a state citizen and as a citizen of the United States; second, whether the Missouri Compromise was constitutional in that it involved Congress's exercise of a purported power to prohibit slavery in the territories; and, third, whether Missouri was obligated to recognize Scott as free because he had lived *either* in Illinois *or* in the Wisconsin Territory.[39]

The Court could have framed the issues in very different, less expansive and controversial, ways, and there was a plausible technical argument that the citizenship question had never been properly brought before the Court. Moreover, the Court's own recent precedent, *Strader v. Graham*, decided in 1850, could have provided a way to hold against Scott without disturbing the Missouri Compromise. The principle for which *Strader* arguably stood was that each state is free to determine the status of persons (other than fugitive slaves) while domiciled in their territory, and the same was true for the federal government, its decisions on such questions having force only within a particular territory's limits. As applied to Scott's case, this rule would mean that Illinois and, as to the Wisconsin Territory, Congress could have declared Scott free, but once he returned to Missouri, Missouri's law rendering him a slave would restore him to that status.[40]

But the Court chose instead to try to settle some of the most contentious issues of the day and to do so in a way decidedly favorable to the South. Specifically, the Court would exclude all blacks, free or slave, from the political community of the United States, a move that, when combined with also invalidating the Missouri Compromise, would dramatically enhance white Southern freedom of movement by rendering the possibility of black mobility independent of white locomotion a legal nullity. It is likely that the composition of the Court had much to do with this outcome. Five of the justices were Southerners from slaveholding families. All were "universally supportive of slavery." Two of the four Northerners were "doughfaces"—Northern men with Southern principles. Seven of the justices were appointed by slaveholding Southern presidents, eight by Democratic presidents. Indeed, the Court "was a democratic stronghold at a time when that party was dominated by its southern, proslavery wing." The chief justice, Taney, was from a Maryland family that had made its wealth in slaves and tobacco. He had also served as President Andrew Jackson's attorney general, arguing in that capacity that blacks could be denied any political or constitutional rights. By the time that *Dred Scott* came before the Court, "Taney was a seething, angry, uncompromising supporter of the South and slavery and an implacable foe of racial equality, the Republican Party, and the antislavery movement." Taney's opinion for the Court is thus fairly read as a major statement of Southern ideology on the racial nature of the American polity and on the white Southern entitlement to untrammeled freedom of movement without interference with property rights in their slaves.[41]

From near the start of his opinion, Taney used the language of property when referring to slaves and the language of citizenship only when referring to whites. Thus, he phrased the initial question as, Does a "negro, whose ancestors were *imported* into this country, and *sold* as slaves, become a member of the political community formed and brought into existence by the Constitution of the United States," therefore having all the rights of such a citizen, including the right to sue in federal courts? Taney answered no. He considered the phrases "people of the United States" and "citizens" synonymous. Although each state had the power to decide the status of persons *within its own borders,* it could not do so when such persons entered the boundaries of other states. Nor would one state's granting someone *state citizenship* necessarily determine the question of *federal* citizenship, for "no State can, by any act or law of its own . . . introduce a new member into the political community created by the Constitution of the United States."[42] But the Framers of both the Declaration of Independence and the Constitution, said Taney, unquestionably meant to exclude *all* blacks, slave or free, from federal citizenship because

> [t]hey had for more than a century before been regarded as beings of an inferior order, and altogether unfit to associate with the white race, either in social or political relations; and so far inferior, that they had no rights which the white man was bound to respect; and that the negro might justly and lawfully be reduced to slavery. . . . He was bought and sold, and treated as an ordinary article of merchandise and traffic, whenever a profit could be made by it.[43]

Taney looked to, among other sources, colonial legislation that prohibited intermarriage and provided for the whipping of any black person who struck "any person of the English or other Christian nation," intending to erect an "impossible barrier" between the white race and those it "governed as subjects with absolute and despotic power." Such legislation, he believed, demonstrated a vision of blacks as "so far below [whites] . . . in the scale of created beings" that black-white intermarriage was unthinkable, regardless of whether blacks were enslaved or free. Taney conceded that the language of the Declaration of Independence "would seem to embrace the whole human family" but denied that its Framers so intended, for if they had such an intention, "instead of the sympathy of mankind, to which they so confidently appealed, they would have deserved and received universal rebuke and reprobation." This would have been so because blacks were "never thought of or spoken of except as property," so that treating them as anything else would have been "flagrantly inconsistent" with the Declaration's own principles.[44]

Taney further understood the bargain among the states embodied in the federal Constitution in terms that closely linked limits on black mobility with the safety of white Southern life, liberty, and property:

> it cannot be believed that the large slaveholding States regarded . . . [the African race] as included in the word citizens, or would have consented to a Constitution which might compel them to receive them in that character from another State. For if they were so received, and entitled to the privileges and immunities of citizens, it would exempt them from the operation of the special laws and from the police regulations [for example, bans on intermarriage and on black membership in the militia] which . . . [whites] considered to be necessary for their own safety. It would give to persons of the negro race, who were recognized as citizens in any one State of the Union, the right to enter every other State whenever they pleased, singly or in companies, without pass or passport, and without obstruction, to sojourn there as long as they pleased, to go where they pleased at every hour of the day or night without molestation, unless they committed some violation of law for which a white man would be punished; and it would give them the full liberty of speech in public and in private upon all subjects upon which its own citizens might speak; to hold public meetings upon political affairs, and to keep and carry arms wherever they went. And all of this would be done in the face of the subject race of the same color, both free and slaves, and inevitably producing discontent and subordination among them, and endangering the peace and safety of the State.[45]

In other words, national citizenship for *any* blacks meant black freedom of movement in the slave states, in turn implying black freedom of speech and freedom to use firearms wherever they went. But roaming, armed blacks freely speaking their minds meant rebellion against white rule, something to which the compacting states simply could never have agreed. Dred Scott therefore being neither a citizen of the United States nor, under Missouri law, a citizen of that state could not be heard in the federal courts. Though Taney could have stopped there, he went on to consider further the impact of Scott's having lived for a time in the Wisconsin Territory and in the State of Illinois. The Illinois question was easy, for under its earlier precedent in *Strader v. Graham,* Missouri law controlled whether, once Scott returned to Missouri, he was free or not. The answer, of course, was "not." The more complex question was the significance of Scott's time in a federal territory in which slavery had been prohibited.[46]

Taney engaged in some odd legalistic legerdemain concerning the Territories Clause of the Constitution, which empowered Congress to "dispose of and make all needful rules and regulations respecting the territory or other property belonging to the United States." Taney concluded that this clause extended only to U.S. territories owned at the time of the Constitution's drafting. In the Article IV language declaring that "[n]ew States may be admitted by the Congress to this Union," Taney did find an authority to govern the territories but only in such a way as to prepare them for statehood. But Taney's core argument concerning congressional power over the territories rested on his conclusion that the Bill of Rights applied in the territories. The gist of his analysis was this: if blacks are not and cannot be U.S. citizens, then they can be and have been made into white's property. But under the Fifth Amendment to the Constitution, no person may by federal action "be deprived of life, liberty, or property, without due process of law"; nor shall private property be taken for public use without just compensation. Taney declared, however, that "an act of Congress which deprives a citizen of the United States of his liberty or property, merely because he came himself or brought his property into a particular Territory of the United States, and who had committed no offence against the laws, could hardly be dignified with the name of due process of law." Nothing in the Constitution required treating human property as entitled to less protection than other kinds of property, nor could anything to the contrary in the "law of nations" be relevant to interpreting our own federal Constitution. If anything, suggested Taney, white property in slaves was entitled to *greater protection* than inanimate property, for the right to traffic in slaves, "like . . . ordinary article[s] of merchandise and property, was guaranteed to the citizens of the United States, in every State that might desire it, for twenty years." Furthermore, "the Government in express terms is pledged to protect it in all future time, if the slave escapes from his owner." Taney continued, "The only power conferred" on Congress over slavery is "the power coupled with the duty of guarding and protecting the owner in his rights." The Missouri Compromise, because it prohibited citizens from holding and owning slaves as property in certain territories, was thus constitutionally void and therefore of no help to Scott.[47]

Taney's opinion in *Dred Scott* further ignited Republican fears of a conspiracy to nationalize slavery that began with the Compromise of 1850. Lincoln warned in an 1859 speech of a future "second *Dred Scott*" decision that would make "slavery lawful in all the States." In the view of some Northerners, *Lemmon v. People,* then working its way through the courts, was likely to be such a case. The intervention of the Civil War prevented that from happening, so the case's history and precedential value are of no moment here.[48] But the fears that the case raised in some Northern hearts do matter, and they were well captured in 1859 by then-senator Salmon P. Chase of Ohio:

> What will the decision be? . . . It will be just as they claim, that they can take their slaves into New York over the railroads of New Jersey, through Pennsyl-

vania and through Ohio, Indiana, Illinois . . . to any state of the North, and that they can hold them there during all the time that it is convenient for them to be passing through. In other words, it is a decision in favor, not of the African slave trade, but of the American slave trade, to be carried out on the free states.[49]

Chase here seems to envision hordes of rapidly mobile slaveholders swarming over the North like viruses, infecting free states with their disease—slavery— fatal to Northern freedoms. Whatever were Northern worries about a future *Dred Scott*, however, the one that the Court actually decided had opened up federal territories to slavery by law, even prohibiting (via the principle of "popular sovereignty") a majority in any territory from voting otherwise. The Southern states were jubilant about this prospect, and Southern Democratic papers crowed about the outcome. *Dred Scott* stood as a cogent and powerful statement by the Southern master class of its position linking its mobility and corollary freedoms directly to its absolute control over the locomotion of the humans it held as property. The case is thus a stunning revelation of the deepest passions of the Southern heart about the guarantee of white mobility and black subjugation as conjoined twins whose separation would sound the death knell of the white vision of liberty.[50] Blacks, particularly black slaves, agreed with this assessment and therefore invested their own quest for freedom to move about with politically liberating and spiritually elevating meanings. They created a counterculture of resistance in which autonomous locomotion was the apotheosis of both liberty and spiritual enlightenment.

Mobility's Meaning for Slaves and Free Blacks

Flight, Real and Imagined, as Resistance

Slaves engaged in a wide variety of daily acts of resistance. Slaves stole food and drink, both for their own use and for barter. They malingered or feigned disabilities. Female slaves were suspected of "playing the lady" when they sought reduced workloads on the basis of the "liability of women . . . to disorders and irregularities which cannot be detected by exterior symptoms." Field hands might "misplace" tools, wound livestock, or falsify weights as a way to meet daily quotas. In urban factories, slaves smuggled contraband in their clothing, and in mines they concealed gold dust in their hair. Knowing that there would be a severe price to pay, they sometimes physically challenged masters, overseers, and other whites. Some refused whippings, others "feigned ignorance of how to do a particular chore" or "pretended to be ill rather than work to the limits that the master and mistress wanted."[51] Each act of resistance held powerful meaning for the slave in challenging white oppression:

> Slaves who risked their lives in their struggle not to be whipped were, in fact, making a personal statement about their sense of self-esteem and individual honor. Women who kicked and clawed their sexual abusers fought for their personal dignity. Those who burned gin houses, barns, corncribs, or smokehouses, even as acts of anger, served notice that they could be pushed only so far. Some slaves used poison or outright physical force to kill their masters. Capture always meant certain death, but they did it nevertheless. Whatever the individual act of resistance, it signified an attempt to retain or take back some control over a life that was by law assigned to someone else.[52]

Short of revolts, however—which were few given greater white numbers, slaves' isolation on plantations miles apart, and white control over weaponry and the law—the ultimate act of slave resistance was flight. "No single act of self-assertion was more significant among slaves," says historian Peter Wood, "than that of running away." Most flight was temporary, what today's historians call "truancy," though the number of truancy incidents (many by repeat offenders) has been estimated to be as large as fifty thousand per year by the Civil War's outbreak, far more than the about one thousand fugitives per year by then making it to the free states or to Canada. Truancy was one way for bondsmen, and especially bondswomen—who were charged with the primary responsibility for their children—to reconcile the impetus to leave slavery behind with the desire to stay near friends and family. Truants faced danger, for dogs hunted them down, they were often driven to hide in woods and swamps, and sure punishment awaited them upon their return. But truancy helped slaves to maintain family ties, supplement poor diets, and gain bargaining power with masters (some refusing to return without receiving some small amelioration of their condition). Truancy also allowed slaves literally to get the lay of the land and to develop networks of contacts should they risk "running away"—a more permanent flight, via a long journey over land or by water, into free territory. It was this sort of flight that held the greatest emotional power. Some slaves who were caught ran again and again, despite dogs, hunger, cold, and, upon capture, whipping, branding, and humiliation. Some of the recaptured suffered enormous brutality, notably "[s]evere whippings of three hundred lashes—followed by rubs of salt, vinegar and hot pepper," leaving many permanently injured. Generally, only the most self-confident, self-reliant individuals succeeded on this path.[53]

Where running away and revolt were not possible, slaves used rumors of flight to gain some small measure of power over their masters or to strengthen their courage and foster their hope. Rumors that ignited whites' panic about insurrection were thus sometimes started by slaves rather than merely reflecting white paranoia. One white politician was thus moved to note in the aftermath of Nat Turner's rebellion "that the blacks themselves have in some instances, had the address to put reports into circulation in order to enjoy the spectacle resulting from the unaccountable panic of the whites." Although whites understood that some rumored revolts may have had their source in slave fabrication, self-preservation still led whites to investigate even the most bizarre stories and to be set on edge, to the utter delight of some slaves. As one Virginian involved in the insurrection scare of 1831–32 admitted, "Our nights are sometimes spent in listening to noises. A corn song, or a hog call, has often been a subject of nervous terror, and a cat, in the dining room, will banish sleep for the night."[54]

Rumors might also have been aimed at other slaves for political purposes. Black preachers in Edgecombe County, North Carolina, convinced their congregations that "the national government had set them free . . . and that they were being unjustly held in servitude." Before President Van Buren's election in 1836, one fugitive slave recalled, rumors circulated that if elected, he would set the slaves free. Similar rumors spread through a Georgia plantation upon the election of William Henry Harrison. By imagining such powerful political allies in their struggle, slaves were aided in shaping a "fledgling political community, founded on shared perceptions, understandings and expectations" that would later "inspire them to act when those imagined allies tried to crush a rebellion launched by their owners."[55]

Exodus: Mobility and a Nation within a Nation

Slave imaginings of freedom played out in other important ways, for slaves' visions of mobility held a spiritual and political role in their emotional lives more important than the actual escape attained by so few. The biblical Exodus story held particular meaning for slaves, fugitives, and free blacks. The front page of the *Colored American* of October 20, 1838, retold the Exodus story via a dialogue between Moses and Pharaoh in which Pharaoh worries that freed Hebrews would be unable to care for themselves, would "amalgamate" (breed with) Egyptians, and destroy all honor and happiness. Moses responds by invoking liberty, rights, the Hebrews' nature as a chosen people, and by quoting a passage from Acts 17: "Hath not God '*made of one blood* all nations'?" When these entreaties fail, the column ends with God's command, "Go tell Pharaoh to let my people go!" Sojourner Truth later said of post-Reconstruction efforts to relocate African Americans to Kansas that "it is a good move for them. I believe as much in that move as I do in the moving of the children of . . . [Israel] going . . . [into] Canaan—just as much." Truth's sentiment reveals the emotional endurance of the slaves' commitment to biblical imagery of liberation.

Harriet Tubman was described as the slaves' Moses, and fugitives' journeys were described "as escapes to the Promised Land." Songs like "Go Down Moses" and "Now Let Me Fly" used images of the Promised Land and of crossing the River Jordan, and it was the plight of the Jews on their journey out of Egypt that framed black understanding of the Underground Railroad.[56]

What the slaves heard and what white preachers taught of Christianity were two entirely different things. Whites preached obedience to masters, a message blacks heard as hypocrisy. But blacks saw in the Exodus tale not simply freedom but retribution against their oppressors, with God sending "Moses to tell ol' Pharaoh to let my people go. Once again the mighty wind of God parted the Red Sea so the Hebrew children could cross over dry shod. Once again Pharaoh's army 'got drowned.'" David Walker in his *Appeal* called on whites to live up to their nation's promise or suffer the wages of sin, and he entreated blacks, "Though our cruel oppressors and murderers may (if possible) treat us as more cruel than Pharaoh did the Children of Israel, yet the God of the Ethiopians, has been pleased to hear our moans in consequence of oppression, and the day of our redemption from abject wretchedness draweth near."[57]

Yet, if the tale was partly used as a caution to white America, it was also a story that required slaves' suffering in the wilderness, a painful journey by which they would not simply move in space but be transformed in soul. The story was one of a pilgrimage in which the slave died, and a new individual in the image of God stepped freely into the world. But the pilgrimage did more than transform the individual. It also "linked the individual to a particular community of shared experience." Collective identity and group struggle in God's name thus gave birth, as did the migration of the Hebrews, to a nation, a people. If retribution on many whites was expected, however, they were not to be wiped from the earth, as were the biblical Canaanites. Rather, African Americans were God's chosen people, engaged in a prophetic migration to be a light unto the nations, for "the coming of the new millennium in the bounty of America required that African-Americans be free." The slaves thus heard Christianity's universal message of salvation. As God's chosen, the African American nation needed to be joined as a separate entity by its recurrent remembrance of oppression and liberation, its sense of self as distinct from other nations, and its commitment to a covenant of moral right. But this shared sense of peoplehood was not meant to be a form of "cultural or racial chauvinism," for that would "compromise the covenant."[58] Rather, they were to become a nation within a nation, for, as Eugene Genovese put it, black-American Christianity

> made possible a universal statement because it made possible a national statement. [This] national statement expressed a duality as something both black and American, not in the mechanical sense of being an ethnic component in a pluralistic society, but in the dialectical sense of simultaneously being itself

and the other, both separately and together, and of developing as a religion within a religion in a nation within a nation.[59]

The dominant strands in an Exodus-dominated slave religion thus inseparably linked mobility to peoplehood, black identity, and membership in the American political community.

Alternatives to Exodus's Biblical Universalism

Antebellum black intellectuals often did not share as fully in Christian universalism as did many of the slaves. Perhaps somewhat inconsistently, "black thinkers invariably conceded that blacks and whites were not quite the same, while simultaneously insisting that they were equal." This stance would seem inconsistent with Christianity-inspired "nation-within-a-nation" thinking. But while nearly all black intellectuals sought to prove that blacks were actually or potentially as worthy human beings as were whites, many black writers sought to invert the current hierarchy, marking blacks as not simply different but better. Whatever their views, all the thinkers explicitly or implicitly rooted their ideas in conceptions of manhood.[60]

Black males, free or slave, "were forbidden to exercise manhood rights—to vote, hold electoral office, serve on juries, or join the military." Blacks were viewed as too emotional, childlike, and irrational to exercise "men's" rights. Black men felt the sting of this judgment and aspired to prove their manhood. Some embraced white masculine ideals, as did David Walker when he wrote, "Are we MEN!!—I ask you, O my Brethren! are we MEN?" He continued: "How can we be so *submissive* to a gang of men, whom we cannot tell whether they are *as good* as ourselves or not, I never could conceive." His question resonated with other black writers of the age, including women, like Maria Stewart, who said to her male counterparts, "It is upon you that woman depends; she can do but little besides using her influence." Martin Delaney, in an 1852 pamphlet, boasted that blacks were "physically superior to either the European or American [Indian] races—in fact physically superior to any living race of men." Furthermore, said Delaney, blacks could endure changes in "habits, manners, and customs, with infinitely less injury to their physical systems than any other people of God's earth."[61]

Other thinkers simply rejected white masculinity standards, writing of blacks as a more feminine "redeemer race," far more moral, pious, and gentle than whites, and, therefore, the former and future world leaders. These writers usually focused not so much on physical distinctions between the races as on differences of morality and character. Whites descended "from a savage race of men," surviving by "traversing the woods and wilds, inhabiting rocks and caverns, a wretched prey to wild beasts and to one another," "drawn from their homes by a thirst for blood and plunder." Even those writers prone to more moderate sentiments might celebrate blacks' supposed greater ability to endure adversity and suffering or more noble history than that of the whites. Nevertheless, for the vast majority of antebellum black writers, black difference, even as superiority, uneasily coexisted with far more racially egalitarian sensibilities.[62]

Frederick Douglass, on the other hand, was hostile toward black chauvinism, worrying that black race pride could lapse into moral errors akin to those made by white supremacists and that, as he put it late in his life, "every pretension we set up in favor of race pride is giving the enemy a stick to break our own heads." He accepted, even heralded, nation-within-a-nation thinking, yet he counseled against separate black social and political organizations and favored a more thoroughgoing notion of the unity of man. Indeed, Douglass seemed to view blacks, because of their ill-treatment in poor climate, as suffering from a currently degraded physical and intellectual character, while fervently insisting that blacks would "one day be as illustrious" as whites and savagely attacking white theories of innate black inferiority, though arguably not entirely immune to them himself. Douglass's views on the desirable relationship *between* blacks and whites and his notions of union were, however, far closer to the likely views of most slaves, fugitives, and free blacks of the time.[63]

Although Douglass spent his early years of freedom deploring the Union, he came around to a strong interracial Unionist philosophy. Douglass embraced what historian Rogan Kersh has called a "moral unionism" consisting of three ideas: first, "ethical commonality," blacks' ethical vision being identical to "the true meaning of the [American] creed"; second, "unadulterated equality," the Constitution's language of a "more perfect union" expressing an aspiration toward racial inclusiveness and recognition of equal worth; and third, "mutual relationship," "as citizens, as brothers, as dwellers in a common country," blacks no longer being "forever doomed to be a stranger and a sojourner in this country." Douglass thus derided colonizationists, insisting that continued interchange with whites benefited blacks' future more than would separation. Douglass's Union was a Union of principle, the oppression in society stemming not from Union so much as the weak virtue of those in power: "The forms of the Union are good enough. If [only] the people were as good as those forms and appliances which form and characterize Union." He implored whites to add to blacks' love of government and to strengthen the country by bringing blacks closer into the fold of the institutions of Union. He warned each slaveholder to expect his deep-down conscience to plague him for his guilt "concerning thy *brother*."[64] In bold language, he described the Constitution as a document of racial unity and blessing:

> Its language is "we the people"; not we the white people, not even we the citizens, not we the privileged class, not we the high, not we the low, but we the

people, not we the horses, the sheep, the swine, and wheel barrows, we the people, we the human inhabitants; and, if negroes are people, they are included in the benefits for which the constitution of America was established and ordained.[65]

Some free black thinkers had reservations about the wisdom and practicality of achieving interracial Union, though these same thinkers might themselves be of two minds, denouncing "the unfriendly whites" with one breath and appealing to them as my "white brethren" with the next. Some went further, speaking of blacks as a "union apart," with Martin Delaney perhaps being the most well-known separatist. But most black writers and speakers held a positive vision of a union of *all* Americans. Positive references by black writers to such union per page of newspaper continued "at a steady clip" throughout the antebellum period. Even the "emigration-minded" Henry Highland Garnett said, "It is too late to make a successful attempt to separate the black and white people in the New World. America is my home, my country, and I have no other." Philadelphia's blacks in 1838 pronounced, "We love our native country, much as it has wronged us; and in the peaceable exercise of our inalienable rights, we cling to it." Similar sentiments were widely shared, most free blacks favoring a path toward interracial union but without sacrificing black unity and memory.[66]

What evidence exists suggests that most slaves held similar views. Former slaves' most vivid memories included the sense that their white masters treated them much like animals. Their insistent response was well captured by one of their number: "us ain't hogs or horses—us is human flesh." Like animals, they could be bred, whipped, or sold. Like animals, they were treated as if they had neither soul nor heart. These bestial images contradicted slaves' religious beliefs and self-understanding. Once again, they found hope for the ultimate recognition of their humanity in the stories of the "twin deliverers" of Moses and Christ and in the Christian message of human brotherhood.[67]

Perhaps curiously, however, slaves did not share many black intellectuals' attribution of white power to the "rapacious, acquisitive character of the Anglo-Saxon race." White Southern speech and writing was filled with racial stereotypes, such as the docile "Sambo," the rebellious "Nat," the devoted "mammy," and the lascivious "Jezebel." Yet neither black folklore nor the early-twentieth-century Work Projects Administration (WPA) interviews with former slaves revealed them to be holding similar stereotypes about whites. Indeed, such slave reduction of whites to simple categories, if it happened, has largely escaped the historical record. Of course, slaves did share in the theme of African American superiority, for example, singing work songs celebrating black diligence compared with white indolence and expressing pride in slaves' ability to outwit white folks, but rarely did this take the form of a claim of blacks' natural

physical or intellectual superiority to whites. Instead, "WPA informants stressed
. . . that the personalities of individual white people defied simple generalizations." Whites were not all alike; some were good, some were bad. Many former
slaves told stories about individual traits and actions of individual whites. "I
say I don't put all white folks in one sack," explained former slave Steve Douglas, for "God made lots of good white men, same as the nigger. He made lots of
good niggers—but you can't put all of them in one sack."[68]

Not all agreed. Some bemoaned whites as all alike or were willing to recall
only white brutality, but most saw whites as individuals, neither better nor
worse than blacks as a group, rejecting stereotypes of whites, perhaps because
they did not "have the cultural power to impose stereotypical images on white
people." Many slaves did expect retribution, but for most slaves this was primarily expected to come in the afterlife. Views on the racial character of the afterlife differed, some believing they would still serve whites there, but most believing that heaven meant freedom. Some slaves expected few whites to make
it through the pearly gates, with many of those who did enter occupying a
lesser rank than blacks or even serving as black slaves. One former slave said
that when white folks died, blacks shed false tears, while in their hearts they
believed the whites were "all going to hell like a damn barrel full of nails."
Some former slaves wished damnation on particular whites, while others expected it for many masters, especially the most cruel, or even expected that all
whites would have to account to heaven for the sins of their race. For most former slaves, however, divine justice meant that "in heaven people will be received according to the judgment of their souls rather than their skins, white
or black." Damnation or salvation turned on your actions and intentions, not
your race. It could not be otherwise, for "God created us all free and equal,"
in most of the bondsmen's views. As former slave Anthony Dawson put it,
"There's a difference in the color of the skin, but the souls is all white, or all
black, 'pending on man's life and not on his skin." The journey to the promised land was thus, for most blacks of the time, to be one of a black nation
within a broader interracial nation, of difference and commonality, of equal
respect, and of a heaven and a hell in which the righteous would rejoice and
the evil would burn.[69]

9 Mobility's Meaning for the North

Northern Reaction

Northern reactions to Southern visions of white versus black mobility were complex. Slavery headed toward extinction in the North early in the nation's history, generally through gradual emancipation schemes. Still, a few slaves were legally owned in some places in the North even as late as the start of the Civil War. Most antebellum Northerners increasingly came to oppose the spread of slavery beyond Southern borders, but few favored immediate emancipation everywhere. Some Northerners had strong commercial ties with the South, especially with the Southern cotton market, and did not want to anger their Southern brethren, on whom rested these Northern fortunes. Others understood the price of Union to be a slave South, a price they were willing to pay.[1]

Nor did opposition to slavery's expansion, or even to slavery itself, imply equal respect for slaves, for antiblack racism thoroughly infected most of the Northern white antebellum population. Among the Free-Soilers, therefore, were those who opposed slavery's expansion because it meant more unwanted exposure to African Americans. As one intellectual predecessor to this subset of Free-Soilers put it, "the great evil of slavery was introducing a race of people of different colour from the mass of the people." Colonizationists saw the end of slavery as lying in mass relocation of blacks to colonies in Africa. Among the growing number of Northerners who had moral compunctions about slavery, only the abolitionists preached the institution's immediate end, though many sought to do so by peaceful moral suasion, while others, like the infamous John Brown, saw violent resistance to evil as not only justified but morally compelled.[2]

Yet, if the bulk of the Northern population during the early antebellum period was largely indifferent to the plight of the slaves themselves, a variety of forces increasingly pushed the North toward more militant opposition to the institution. Southern assaults on abolitionists led ever-more Northerners to worry that the "Slave Power" was coming to crush *white* civil liberties. The continuing rise of a dominant Northern ideology that exalted productive "free labor" over degraded slave labor enhanced fears of Southern political power. Conflicts over whether new territories should be admitted as slave or free raised Northern worries about a potential imbalance of political power at the federal level. Meanwhile, enforcement of the fugitive-slave laws, especially that of 1850, confronted the North with its own complicity in slavery and its sense of being subjected to the Southern will. Fugitive-slave resistance and slave-catcher violence also helped to personalize the bondsmen's suffering, and abolitionists proved somewhat effective in the long run in expanding the numbers of Northerners able to empathize with the slaves' pain. Southern anger and militance over the slave question stiffened some Northern spines, and the majority of the North eventually came to see white slaveowners' society as violent, undisciplined, and unvirtuous. Moderates like Lincoln hoped that geographic containment of slavery would bring about its slow but eventual demise, a position increasingly hard to accept after *Dred Scott.* For these reasons, among others, growing numbers of Northerners rejected both the various ideologies supporting the Southern vision of white mobility and the Southern actions done to pursue that vision. Northern reaction was at its most virulent when the Slave Power's arm reached into Northern space, as it did in recapturing fugitive slaves. The two forms of Northern response to the runaway problem that best set the stage for understanding the North's own ideology of mobility were legal actions, either statutory or judicial, and mob actions, though both responses were often tightly linked.[3]

Legal Response

New Jersey offers an interesting example of Northern legal responses. As early as 1798, New Jersey became the then only slave state to permit free black immigration. Yet that state was also the last in the North to abolish slavery, which it did by an 1804 gradual-emancipation statute. Even while still a slave state, however, New Jersey had prohibited, by 1788, the removal of slaves from the state without their consent, and the state required masters to teach reading and writing to their young slaves, "a step in preparing them for freedom." After slavery's abolition in the state, in an 1821 code revision, New Jersey similarly imposed severe punishments on anyone who unlawfully removed blacks from the state. This provision was prompted by petitions from Middlesex County that asked for legislation "to prevent kidnapping and carrying from the State blacks and other people of color." Slaves owned by New Jersey residents (remember that this was *gradual* abolition) could not be sold beyond that state's borders and could accompany their owners who permanently left the state only under specified circumstances. Moreover, "Officials were empowered to search ships for blacks who were being forced out of the state, and anyone resisting faced the same penalties as [illegal slave] exporters," ranging from a $500 to a $1,000 fine, a potential prison sentence of one to two years at hard labor, or both. This provision apparently did not apply to Southern masters recovering their fugitive slaves, but even in that circumstance, this law made rendition harder because the master or his agent had to produce adequate documentation before the slave could be taken. These laws reflected "the almost universal belief in the North that slave catching was a dirty business, to be avoided by decent people," a sentiment shared even by abolitionists' opponents and those favoring "Union at all costs."[4]

By 1826, New Jersey adopted a "personal-liberty law" that required claimants to seek a judicial warrant ordering the county sheriff to arrest the purported fugitive. Only if the court was persuaded after a hearing that the person arrested was indeed a fugitive slave would his removal be judicially authorized. This law was meant to be "more humane and better calculated to prevent frauds and oppression" than did the federal 1793 fugitive-slave law, though it may have failed in achieving that goal. New Jersey's personal-liberty law, like those of some other states, such as New York and Pennsylvania, "represent[ed] a voluntary effort to find a workable balance between a duty to protect free blacks and the obligation to uphold the legitimate claims of slave owners." The constitutionality of New Jersey's version of personal-liberty laws was famously challenged in the state's courts in the 1836 case *State v. The Sheriff of Burlington,* later designated by historians "the *Hornblower Decision*."[5]

Nathan Mead, a Maryland slave who escaped to New Jersey in 1820, adopted the name Alexander Helmsley, marrying a woman purportedly freed in Maryland but lacking papers to prove it. The Helmsleys raised a family there until, in 1835, two Maryland attorneys—one claiming Nathan, on behalf of the executor of the deceased master, and the other claiming Nathan's wife and children —had the entire Helmsley family arrested via a warrant issued pursuant to New Jersey's laws governing the recapture of escaped slaves. Mrs. Helmsley and the children were apparently released after a habeas corpus hearing. Mr. Helmsley, represented by abolitionist attorneys, was tried before Burlington County Judge George Haywood, who thereupon declared Helmsley to be the claimants' slave, ordering him held in jail until returned to his owners. Helmsley's attorneys appealed the case to the New Jersey Supreme Court. On the appeal, Helmsley was represented by "more prominent counsel," a former reporter for the New Jersey

Supreme Court, William Halsted, and "a leader of the American Colonization Society, and a politician not disposed to abolition," William Halsted, a man whose involvement in the case demonstrated "the potency of claims to freedom by Blacks living in the North."[6]

Chief Justice Hornblower issued an opinion that came down squarely in Helmsley's favor. The chief justice found New Jersey's law unconstitutional and, though he denied doing so, unambiguously expressed the opinion that the federal 1793 fugitive-slave law was likewise unconstitutional. Concerning the federal law, Hornblower relied on a contrast between the Full Faith and Credit Clause of the federal Constitution, which expressly granted Congress the power to "prescribe the manner in which acts, records, and proceedings of one state could be proved in another," and the Fugitive Slave Clause, which contained no such language. Therefore, Hornblower concluded, no such power was intended to be given to the national government to legislate on the *manner* by which "persons residing in the free states, shall be arrested, imprisoned, delivered up, and transferred from one state to another, simply because they are claimed as slaves." Federal legislation, said Hornblower, would "bring the general government in conflict with the state authorities, and the prejudices of local communities," something to which the "American people would not long submit."[7]

Hornblower assailed the New Jersey law as authorizing "the seizure, and transportation out of this state, of persons residing here, under the protection of our laws." Yet those seized might be "free-born native inhabitants, the owners of property, and the fathers of families." To permit the removal of those who might be such persons "upon a summary hearing before a single judge, without the intervention of a jury, and without appeal," could not, he concluded, be constitutional. Any other position would, he warned, permit the seizure of free backs upon false or mistaken accusations, factual questions that New Jersey's constitution *required* to be determined by a jury.[8]

Turning to the relationship between state legislation and the federal Constitution, Hornblower agreed that states were obligated fully and fairly to execute their rendition obligations under the Fugitive Slave Clause. But that clause only required returning those *who actually owed service* to their masters, not those merely claimed to be burdened by such an obligation. Only a jury could decide whether someone claimed as a slave was indeed in that condition.[9]

Hornblower further distinguished between the Fugitive from Justice Clause and the Fugitive Slave Clause of the federal Constitution. The former did require surrender of a merely *alleged* criminal to the state seeking his presence, but there he would be sent not "to be delivered up, not to be punished, not to be detained for life, but to be *tried,* and if acquitted to be set at liberty."[10] Fugitive slaves summarily returned to another state would, however, never be tried before a jury, so the issue became

[w]hether he is to be separated forcibly, and for ever, from his wife and children, or be permitted to enjoy with them the liberty he inherited, and the property he has earned. Whether he is to be dragged in chains to a distant land, and doomed to perpetual slavery, or continue to breathe the air and enjoy the blessings of freedom.[11]

Although not bound in his decision by the law of any state other than New Jersey, Hornblower further felt compelled to address the contrary decision by the prestigious Chief Justice William Tilghman of the neighboring state of Pennsylvania in 1819, in *Wright, otherwise called Hall v. Deacon, Keeper of the Prison.* The *Wright* case, one of the few fugitive-slave cases considered by American courts in the early antebellum period, rejected the plea of an incarcerated alleged fugitive slave to a right to trial by jury before rendition under the Pennsylvania and federal constitutions. Chief Justice Tilghman rejected this plea, wrongly concluding that the whole tenor of the Constitution and the unwillingness of "our southern brethren" to consent to the federal Constitution absent strong security for their property in slaves contemplated a summary rendition proceeding. Once returned to the claimant's state, anyone claiming a "right to freedom" could "prosecute his right in the state to which he belonged."[12]

Hornblower resoundingly rejected what he saw as Tilghman's fictional claim that an alleged fugitive slave would receive a "fair trial" in the claimant's state. "So long as I sit upon this bench," Hornblower wrote, "I never can, no, I never will, yield to such a doctrine."[13] Outraged, Hornblower railed at the absurdity of Tilghman's assertion:

What, first transport a man out of the state, on a charge of his being a slave, and try the truth of the allegation afterwards—separate him from the place, it may be, of his nativity—the abode of his relatives, his friends, and his witnesses—transport him in chains to Missouri or Arkansas, with the cold comfort that if a freeman he may there assert and establish his freedom! No, if a person comes into this state, and *here* claims the servitude of a human being, whether white or black, *here* he must prove his case, and here prove it according to law.[14]

Accordingly, Hornblower established in New Jersey a right to a jury trial for any alleged fugitive slave and rejected any presumption of slave status on the basis of skin color. Furthermore, "although New Jersey was the Northern state with the largest number of slaves, its supreme court had staked out the most progressive position on the rights of blacks claimed as fugitive slaves."[15]

Hornblower's opinion was radical for its time. A number of Northern states by then had laws on the books meant to protect the rights of free blacks. New

York in 1808 prescribed severe penalties, later somewhat moderated, for kidnapping "free people of color." Ohio too had an antikidnapping law, though one less muscular than New York's. In 1820, Pennsylvania adopted strong antikidnapping legislation, which absolved justices of the peace and aldermen from participating in the administration of the 1793 federal Fugitive Slave Act. In response to pressure from Maryland, six years later Pennsylvania did authorize its judges, sheriffs, and magistrates to participate in the federal recovery process but made doing so more complex than the federal law required and effectively outlawed private capture-and-removal efforts. Indiana in 1816 and 1824 provided for a jury trial for alleged fugitives, though such a trial was not obligatory. New York in 1828 passed legislation entitling alleged fugitives to apply for a writ *de homine replegiando,* bringing their case before a jury, but its constitutionality was unclear under subsequent New York precedent—a clear right to jury trial in New York awaited the passage of legislation to that effect in 1840. Although Massachusetts had long permitted accused fugitives to take advantage of the *replegiando* writ and its accompanying jury trial, Massachusetts eliminated that writ in 1835.[16]

This seemingly overall favorable legislative stream was, however, countered by the judiciary. A New York court in 1825 had declared use of the *replegiando* writ to grant alleged fugitives jury trials unconstitutional, and a similar 1819 Pennsylvania decision quashed (rendered legally void) such a writ on constitutional grounds. A federal court in Indiana in 1816 rejected an attack on the 1793 law that had been made on the ground that it was beyond congressional power, and another federal court in New York in the mid-1830s concluded that the federal statute did not contravene the Seventh Amendment's right to a jury trial. Meanwhile, the Supreme Court of Massachusetts in 1823 was unpersuaded that the federal statute violated the Fourth Amendment's prohibition against unreasonable searches and seizures. In that case, *Commonwealth v. Griffith,* the court concluded that none of the Bill of Rights protections extended to slaves, for they were not "parties to the Constitution." Chief Justice Isaac Parker, the author of the opinion, went further, declaring that the Constitution constituted an *affirmative agreement to treat slaves as property.*[17]

Decisions like these commonly paired formalist judicial obligations with the judge's expression of personal regret. As a Pittsburgh recorder said in 1835, upon returning a fugitive to his master, "Whilst, as a man, all my prejudices are strong against the curse of slavery, and all its concomitant evils, I am bound by my oath of office to support the constitution of the United States and the constitution of Pennsylvania, not to let my feelings as a man interfere with my duties as a judge." Historian Don Fehrenbacher described such decisions as the judiciary's efforts to counteract more-progressive Northern legislatures because of rising anxieties about the fate of the Union given sectional tensions over the Missouri crisis, the Nat Turner rebellion, the rise of radical abolitionism and accompanying antiabolitionist riots, and the struggle in Congress over gagging debate about antislavery petitions.[18]

Because it was unreported, the *Hornblower Decision* initially had little impact on reversing this judicial tide. There was discussion of the opinion in a few newspapers, all of which distorted the opinion's content, and some of which lauded it, while others condemned it. But such coverage was never widespread and quickly died down. In New Jersey itself, the decision had a perhaps short-term unintended consequence. Because, technically, Justice Hornblower had invalidated only the New Jersey law, with no other law yet passed to take its place, while denying—contrary to much of his opinion's own language—that he had struck down the federal law, there was room to argue that the lax evidentiary standards and summary procedures of the federal statute survived. When Severn Martin was arrested in August 1836 as a suspected fugitive slave living in Burlington, New Jersey, several hundred people "attempted to rescue" Martin, a riot being forestalled only by the "energy and judgment of the Mayor." With calm restored, a county magistrate summarily remanded Martin under the 1793 law's procedures, and the claimant hurriedly removed Martin. At its next session, the New Jersey legislature cured the problem, passing a new law that gave alleged fugitives the right to demand a jury trial. The one proven citation to the *Hornblower Decision* by an antislavery lawyer of the time was Samuel P. Chase's reliance on a newspaper account of the case while he was trying to free the slave Matilda in 1837, though William Lloyd Garrison had also urged a prominent abolitionist attorney in Boston to use the opinion. The minimal short-term impact of the case would, as we will soon see, be dramatically changed when Hornblower's opinion was resurrected during the decade of the 1850s.[19]

Meanwhile, the U.S. Supreme Court struck its own blow against Northern personal-liberty laws and related legislation in two cases, *Prigg v. Pennsylvania* and *Jones v. Van Zandt*. In the first of these cases, Edward Prigg, as a Maryland claimant's agent, tried to recover Margaret Moran, who had been living in Pennsylvania for five years. Although Prigg first followed Pennsylvania's statutory procedures, upon meeting some resistance from the local justice of the peace, he simply carried off Moran and her children to Maryland. Prigg was extradited on kidnapping charges back to Pennsylvania, where he was tried and convicted, a verdict upheld by that state's supreme court and appealed to the U.S. Supreme Court. That Court came down in Prigg's favor.[20]

Justice Story, though he harbored antislavery sentiments, authored an opinion for the Court that reflected a conservative interpretive philosophy and a flawed understanding of history. Story agreed that the Fugitive Slave Clause was a "fundamental article, without the adoption of which the Union could never have been formed." He read the clause as ensuring masters the right to recapture their slaves by their own private effort in any state of the Union "without interference or restraint of any kind, provided that no breach of the peace were committed." That was what Prigg had done, so Story overturned his conviction, declaring Pennsylvania's 1826 law unconstitutional because it punished "the very act of seizing and removing a slave, by his master, which the constitution of the United States was designed to justify and uphold."[21]

Story also rejected the argument that the Fugitive Slave Clause left enforcement entirely to the states. To the contrary, he read the clause as conferring the power and responsibility of enforcement on Congress exclusively, declaring that no state laws could "in any way qualify, regulate, control, or restrain" congressional legislation on the matter. He thus held the 1793 federal act constitutional but denied that in the absence of federal legislation, the states had power to fill that gap. Concerning the 1793 act's provision authorizing local magistrates to administer the law, Story said that they could *choose* to do so absent contrary state legislation but left undecided the question whether they were *bound* to participate. "Thus he plainly implied that state governments had the option of barring state and local officials from participation in the recovery process."[22]

Story kept his majority on invalidating the Pennsylvania law while upholding the federal one, but he lost that degree of support on his claim of exclusive federal power and his intimation of the limited responsibilities of state officials. Chief Justice Roger B. Taney in particular dissented on these points, concluding that state officials not only could not interfere with rendition but had the duty to assist. Said Story, slaves were but a "species of property," with rendition a "right of property" to be protected by *all* the nation's governments. He further concluded that claimants pursuing fugitives took with them into the free state the home state's presumption that blacks were slaves until proven otherwise. What both Taney and Story "coolly ignored," however, "was the argument of counsel for Pennsylvania that the law of 1793, in certain of its provisions, violated personal rights guaranteed by the privileges-and-immunities clause, by the Fourth Amendment, and by the due-process clause of the Fifth Amendment."[23] Concerning the Fourth Amendment in particular, counsel had argued that

> in a free state every man is prima facie a free man who is at large. If so, he comes under that class called "people"; and the right of "the people" to be secure in their persons against unreasonable seizures is guarantied by the Constitution. Ay! but he is a slave, say the opponents of this doctrine. But that is not admitted. The very question at issue is, slave or free. Now, so long as he is not proved a slave, he is presumed free; and, therefore, if you seize him, it is a violation of this constitutional privilege.[24]

Counsel for Pennsylvania agreed that slaves were "no parties to the Constitution" and that " 'we, the people,' does not embrace them." But the whole question in a rendition case is whether the person claimed is slave or free, and free men are protected by the Constitution. The risk of carrying away a free man required fair procedures for determining a claimed person's true status. Explained counsel, "If one can arrest and carry away a free man 'without due process of law'; if their persons are not inviolate; your Constitution is a waxen tablet, a writing in the sand; and instead of being, as is supposed, the freest country on earth, this is the vilest despotism which can be imagined!"[25] Counsel continued, relying on an argument of the likely intentions of the Framers:

> Is it possible this [Fugitive Slave] clause can have such a meaning? Can it be, that a power so potent of mischief as this, could find no one of all those who had laid it in the indictment against the king of Great Britain, as one of the very chiefest of his crimes, "that he had transported our citizens beyond seas for trial," whose jealousy would not be aroused—whose fears would not be excited at a grasp of power so mighty as is claimed for this clause? Think you not that some of those ardent, untiring, vigilant guardians of liberty, would have raised a warning voice against this danger? And that, too, when only eighteen months after the formation of this charter, although they had already in the body of the instrument carefully guarded the writ of habeas corpus, and provided for the trial of all crimes by jury and in the state where committed, yet, as if their jealousy had been excited to fourfold vigilance, in their amendments provided for the personal security of the subject from "unreasonable seizure," and that no one should be "deprived of liberty without due process of law."[26]

Taney and Story remained unmoved, providing no serious response, or even attention to, these Fourth Amendment and related arguments.

Story's largely proslavery opinion nevertheless cast doubt on state-law provisions that permitted use of local police offices and other local officials to aid in rendition. *Prigg* also provoked resistance, "including a more determined opposition to the fugitive slave law itself." New York's Governor William H. Seward thus informed his state's legislature, "The authority of the decision cannot be extended to cases presenting facts materially varying from those which marked the case thus adjudicated. It is, therefore, believed that the privilege of habeas corpus and the right of trial by jury [for alleged fugitives] as yet remain unimpaired in this state." Massachusetts in 1843, and subsequently four other New England states, withdrew local assistance to rendition entirely, forbidding judges and magistrates from exercising jurisdiction and prohibiting any state officer from arresting or detaining suspected fugitives.[27] Pennsylvania amended its personal-liberty law belatedly in 1847 as the slavery question intensified during the conflict with Mexico. The new Pennsylvania statute barred state officials from participating in rendition, imposed punishment on any claimant effecting recapture by violence, and granted state judges authority "to issue the writ of habeas corpus, and to inquire into the causes and legality of the arrest or imprisonment of any human being within this commonwealth." Southern outrage was typified by a July 15, 1847, letter by Charles J. Faulkner to John C. Calhoun, which described the Pennsylvania statute as "the most deliberate and perfidious violation of all the guaranties of the Constitution which the fanaticism and wickedness of the abolitionists have resorted to, and the most serious and dangerous attack yet made on the institution of slavery," causing slaves to flee Maryland and Virginia "in gangs of tens and twenties."[28]

The Northern state governments' opposition to *Prigg* "reflected a widespread mood of resistance that also manifested itself in increasing private aid to runaways and in occasional outbursts of mass protest." But *Prigg* and events surrounding it also led Garrisonian abolitionists to curse the Constitution and the Union, splitting them further from mainstream antislavery, and many moderates still found it hard to reconcile the traditions of resistance to unjust laws with the duty of reverence for, and obedience to, all law. As one moderate antislavery justice from Ohio repeatedly declared from the bench, he must apply even unjust law as written, for substituting his personal conscience for the rule of law would "overturn the basis of society." Moral arguments for resistance, despite their widespread emotion and appeal, "carried more weight in mass meetings than . . . in courtroom proceedings."[29]

In *Jones v. Van Zandt,* the high Court's second opportunity to address Northern rendition legislation, lawyer Salmon P. Chase sought to reconcile moral appeals with legal ones. Van Zandt, originally a slaveholder on a Kentucky plantation, later became a rabid abolitionist, convinced by his growing understanding of biblical principles and those in the Declaration of Independence that slaveholding was a sin. He moved to Ohio, making his farm there into a stop on the Underground Railroad. He had the ill luck, however, while assisting nine slaves in escaping from Kentucky, to be caught by two men who were hoping to receive a reward for their efforts. Van Zandt was jailed, but two slaves escaped before the rest of the group were caught. The slaves' owner, Wharton Jones, sued Van Zandt in federal court to recover the costs of one of the lost slaves, Andrew, and of the reward money that he paid for most of his slaves being recaptured, as well as for amounts owed to him pursuant to the federal Fugitive Slave Law.[30]

Both in the federal trial court and once the case reached the U.S. Supreme Court, Van Zandt's counsel, Salmon P. Chase, the "attorney general of fugitive slaves," relied partly on natural-law arguments. Chase's brief in the high Court appealed to the "law of creation" and the Declaration of Independence as rendering the 1793 Fugitive Slave Law unconstitutional. He relied in part on *Somerset's Case,* which ended slavery in England. Chase's co-counsel, William

Henry Seward, likewise wrote, "We appeal to the Court to restore that revered instrument [the Constitution], its simplicity, its truthfulness, its harmony with the Declaration of Independence—its studied denial of a Right of Property in Man, and its jealous regard for the Security of the People."[31] Seward elaborated:

We humbly supplicate, that Slavery, with its odious form and revolting features, and its dreadful pretensions for the Present and for the Future, may not receive in this great Tribunal, now, sanction and countenance, denied to it by a Convention of the American States more than half a century ago. Let the spirit which prevailed in that august assembly, only find utterance here, and the time will come somewhat more speedily, when throughout this great empire, erected on the foundation of the Rights of Man, no Court of Justice will be required to enforce INVOLUNTARILY obligations of LABOR, and uphold the indefensible LAW OF PHYSICAL FORCE.[32]

For Chase and Seward, the specific provisions of the Constitution each embraced natural law. The 1793 act was thus unconstitutional both because Congress lacked authority to pass it and because it violated the Fourth Amendment's prohibition against unreasonable searches and seizures, as well as the Due Process Clause of the Fifth Amendment and the Seventh Amendment's guarantee of a jury trial. For Chase, these and all Bill of Rights provisions affirmed principles created by "the very nature of society and of government." "No court," he announced, "is bound to enforce unjust law."[33] The core of Chase's due-process argument was that Virginia originally proposed at the Constitutional Convention that "no free man shall be deprived of life, liberty, property, but by the law of the land." This proposal was replaced by the ultimate language in the Fifth Amendment: "No *person* shall be deprived of life, liberty, or property, without due process of law." Even fugitives are persons, Chase argued, thus entitled to the amendment's protections, and "unless it can be shown that no process of law at all, is the same thing as due process of law, it must be admitted that the act which authorizes seizure without process, is repugnant to a constitution which expressly forbids it."[34] Chase continued, this time focusing on the Fourth Amendment:

But the amendment, prohibiting imprisonment or other privation of liberty, without process, is not the only clause of the constitution infringed by this act. It is equally repugnant to that provision, which declares that "the right of the people to be secure in their persons . . . against unreasonable searches and seizures shall not be violated." I ask, how can the people be subjected to seizures more unreasonable, than under this act of Congress? Even upon the unwarrantable assumption that the escaping servant has no rights, the act still violates this provision of the constitution. The claimant must necessarily select the object of seizure. He is not confined, by the act, to Negroes, nor to slaves. He may seize any one, whom he chooses to claim as an escaping servant, and take him before a judge, or a magistrate, without authority except as the claimant's agent. He may be mistaken. He may intend to kidnap. No matter, he may seize, confine, transport; being responsible only in an action for a wrongful taking, if his victim shall ever be fortunate enough to find an opportunity to bring one. Surely, an act which authorizes seizure by private force, upon mere claim, violates that security from unreasonable seizure, which the constitution guaranties to the people.[35]

Chase concluded his Fourth Amendment argument with a further appeal, this time to the ultimate popular sovereignty, the rule of the People: "The American People, speaking through the constitution," said Chase, "have forbidden Congress to enact, and this Court to enforce any law which authorizes unreasonable seizures, or privation of liberty without due process of law. This prohibition, in my humble judgment, nullifies the act of 1793."[36]

Relatedly, Chase argued that seizure of a person for trial without a jury violated the Seventh Amendment's mandate that, "In suits at common law, where the value of the matter in controversy shall exceed twenty dollars, the right of trial by jury shall be preserved." Queried Chase, "Will it be said, that the value of a man or of his liberty is not measurable by a pecuniary standard, and, therefore, that the constitutional guaranty does not apply? I answer, that if Congress cannot authorize the less, surely it cannot authorize the greater aggression upon individual right." To the argument that rendition proceedings authorized by the 1793 Fugitive Slave Act did not involve a suit at "common law," Chase found no express grant of authority in the Constitution for processes contravening common law in this area, and in fact the Constitution expressly prohibited "imprisonment without process" as a means of enforcing such a claim.[37] Chase warned that implying a congressional power to create new procedures not expressly authorized by some concrete constitutional provision had dangerously broad implications:

> I insist, therefore, that Congress has no power to authorize the seizure and trial of any person without a jury. If Congress has such power in this case, then, in every other, where the constitution confers or guaranties a right, Congress may, without regard to constitutional restriction or limitation, adopt its own mode of enforcing that right, and the people must submit. If this be so, the constitution is waste paper, and we live under a despotism.[38]

Justice Levi Woodbury, writing for a unanimous Court, implicitly or explicitly rejected all Chase's arguments. The 1793 act was constitutional because it merely implemented the fundamental constitutional compromise over slavery. That compromise, not natural law, was the law of the land:

> it may be expected by the defendant that some notice should be taken of the argument, urging on us a disregard of the constitution and the act of Congress in respect to this subject, on account of the supposed inexpediency and invalidity of all laws recognizing slavery or any rights of property in man. But this is a political question, settled by each State for itself; and the federal power over it is limited and regulated by the people of the States in the constitution itself, as one of its sacred compromises, and which we possess no authority as a judicial body to modify or overrule. Whatever may be the theoretical opinions of any as to the expediency of some of these compromises, or of the right of property in persons which they recognize, this court has no alternative, while they exist, but to stand by the constitution and laws with fidelity to their duties and oaths. Their path is a straight and narrow one, to go where the constitution and the laws lead, and not to break both, by traveling without or beyond them.[39]

Rejecting a natural-law reading of the Constitution is one thing, but ignoring the text, history, and principles of specific provisions is another. No embrace of natural law is necessary to give meaning to the words of the Fourth Amendment. Perhaps Justice Woodbury could have crafted an argument that reconciled the seemingly inconsistent words of the Fugitive Slave Clause (as they were read by the Court) and the Fourth Amendment's protection against unreasonable searches and seizures. But he did not even try, *treating the compromise over slavery as the central defining feature of the founding document* so that no possible inconsistency between that purported bargain and specific Bill of Rights provisions need even be entertained.[40]

Van Zandt did not clarify *Prigg*'s meaning in any way that created new legal obstacles for Northern efforts to complicate fugitive-slave rendition. Political passions were inflamed, not doused. Southerners remained convinced that abolitionists induced and aided slave flight. Unfriendly Northern-state legislation and uncooperative local officials, combined with the threat of popular violence, made slave recapture difficult and expensive. Antislavery advocates' willingness to use legal technicalities to slow or obstruct rendition further increased recovery costs. Northern juries were unsympathetic to Southern damages claims, and claimants might face arrest for kidnapping. As late as 1849, two years after *Van Zandt* was decided, the Virginia legislature adopted a resolution that detailed these grievances. Southern political pressure in a Congress weak in antislavery opposition built on such complaints, resulting in passage of the infamous Fugitive Slave Act of 1850. That act, with its commandeering

of the entire Northern populace in the service of the Southern will, further galvanized Northern popular and legal opposition.[41]

Between 1854 and 1858, Michigan, Wisconsin, and all six New England
states enacted personal-liberty laws. Though purportedly designed to protect
free blacks' freedom, these laws were in fact meant to obstruct slave rendition,
particularly where there were guarantees of habeas corpus and a jury trial. In
1854, just on the heels of congressional passage of the Kansas-Nebraska Act, a
mass meeting in Wisconsin adopted this resolution: "Inasmuch as the Senate
of the United States has repealed all compromises heretofore adopted by the
Congress of the United States, we as citizens of Wisconsin, are justified in declaring and do hereby declare the slave-catching law of 1850 disgraceful and
also repealed." A conservative Whig, commenting on the provocation added to
the fugitive-slave controversy by the Kansas-Nebraska Act, pronounced that it
would mean "the complete nullification of the Fugitive Slave Law." The Massachusetts legislature in 1855 overrode the governor's veto to adopt an "Act to
protect the Rights and Liberties of the People," which "in several ways encroached on federal authority." In that same year, the Massachusetts legislature
adopted a resolution calling for repeal of the 1850 Fugitive Slave Act on the
ground that it violated the Tenth Amendment's reservation to the states and to
the people of "all powers not delegated to the United States by the Constitution, nor prohibited by it to the States."[42]

The courts entered the fray as well. In October 1852, the Lemmon family,
while emigrating from Virginia to Texas, made a stop in New York City. In
November of that year, a free person of color sought a writ of habeas corpus
from Judge Elijah Paine to free the slaves who had accompanied the Lemmons
to New York. Judge Paine granted the writ, concluding that once the slaves
entered New York territory, they were free. Virginia's newspapers immediately
expressed outrage, asking, must slaveholders go "dodging around the corners
of free states—and skulking and hiding from the watchdogs of abolitionism?"
Paine's "unrighteous decision," they declared, had evoked "just indignation"
throughout the South by endangering masters' free travel with their bondsmen, "one of the great objects of this Union." The Lemmons lost on appeal,
however, first to New York's intermediate appellate court, then to its highest
court, the New York Court of Appeals. That latter court found that New York's
1817 emancipation law prohibited importing any slave into the state "on any
pretence whatsoever except in the cases hereinafter specified." But the sole
exception had been repealed in 1841, said the court, leaving the statewide prohibition on slavery "absolute and unqualified."[43]

In October 1855, Virginian James Parsons caught his absconding slave, Jake
Green, as he fled from a train bound for Pittsburgh. A "considerable force" of
free blacks attempted to free Green and, in the ensuing confusion, succeeded.
Parsons, meanwhile, was arrested for kidnapping. Heated debate arose over the

case in the Virginia legislature, but the lawmakers could not agree on a course of action other than recommending to the governor that a commission attend the trial. Although prosecutors eventually dropped the charges against Parsons, Virginians drew the lesson that Northern mobs would "tear from [a master] . . . his property and the means of proving his innocence" while Northern state governments might "go through all the regular judicial forms to convict him by presumption of law, backed by a fanatical public sentiment."[44]

Other state-court decisions put state authorities in direct conflict with federal ones. Margaret Garner was an escaped Kentucky slave who had started cutting her children's throats rather than see them recaptured near Cincinnati in the mid-1850s. A state probate judge in the case ordered a federal marshal jailed for contempt when he refused to respond to a habeas corpus writ issued on behalf of Garner and other fugitives caught with her. The basis for the writ was the state court's conclusion that the Fugitive Slave Act was unconstitutional. But the marshal was himself freed by a habeas writ issued by a federal judge who rejected the state court's reasoning. In Mechanicsburg, Ohio, in 1857, when a crowd of armed men prevented a fugitive's arrest, a sheriff was struck in a fight with deputy marshals, who were then jailed for assault and battery but later freed by a federal judge. State officials correspondingly faced federal trials for obstructing federal officers from performing their duty. Salmon P. Chase ultimately arranged a compromise by which the claimant was reimbursed and all prosecutions discontinued. The next year, cross-indictments resulted from the famed "Oberlin-Wellington rescue." A federal grand jury indicted thirty-seven persons for violating the Fugitive Slave Act. But a county grand jury indicted a deputy marshal and three other persons involved for kidnapping. Again, a compromise eventually led to all prosecutions being dismissed, but only after two of the rescuers had been convicted. In a 3–3 vote, the Ohio Supreme Court dismissed the charges against these two men.[45]

The most infamous of these cases of direct state-federal conflict was *Ableman v. Booth*. That case began in March 1854 when a U.S. Marshal, accompanied by claimant Benjamin Garland, seized alleged fugitive slave Joshua Glover in Racine, Wisconsin, and jailed him pending issuance of a certificate of rendition. The next day, however, a mob organized by abolitionist Sherman M. Booth freed Glover, who escaped to Canada. When state authorities arrested Garland for assaulting the slave, a federal district court released Garland on a petition for habeas corpus. When Booth was next arrested on a federal warrant for violating the Fugitive Slave Act, he was in turn released by a habeas writ issued by the Wisconsin Supreme Court. He was, however, rearrested, tried, and convicted in federal court, so he again successfully sought a habeas writ from the Wisconsin Supreme Court. That court held for the second time that the federal Fugitive Slave Act was unconstitutional. Garland brought and won a separate suit against Booth pursuant to the federal act, while U.S. Attorney

General Jeremiah S. Black sought from the U.S. Supreme Court a writ of error directed to the Wisconsin Supreme Court. The clerk of the latter court refused to enter the writ on the court's record when the U.S. attorney served the writ. The chief judge of the state court had instructed the clerk to do just what he did. All this happened against a backdrop of resolutions by a two-day-long Wisconsin convention that revived "the doctrine of state interposition as a shield against undue expansion of federal power," a position, previously articulated by Southern states confronting a very different sort of issue, that allowed states to "nullify" certain federal acts as unconstitutional.[46]

Chief Justice Taney, writing for a unanimous Court on appeal, wrote an opinion that was a striking assertion of national power. The Union could not be preserved, wrote Taney, if the national government lacked authority to enforce its own laws through its own courts without state obstruction. Moreover, Taney saw federal supremacy as necessarily limiting state sovereignty: "[A]lthough the State of Wisconsin is a sovereign within its territorial limits to a certain extent, yet that sovereignty is limited and restricted by the Constitution of the United States." Taney explained that "the powers of the general government, and of the State, although both exist and are exercised within the same territorial limit, are yet separate and distinct sovereignties, acting separately and independently of each other, within their respective spheres." The very existence of the national government, however, Taney concluded, depended on its having "the power of establishing courts of justice, altogether independent of State power, to carry into effect its own laws." When Booth thereafter again sought a writ from the Wisconsin courts for release from federal court, the new chief judge of the Wisconsin Supreme Court denied the writ, describing its earlier actions as "a breach of that comity, or good behavior, which should be maintained between the courts of the two governments toward each other." *Ableman v. Booth* has had lasting authority as a statement of federal supremacy, but in its time it also extended "the power of federal courts as the guardians of slavery and its aggressive outreach."[47]

Despite these high-profile acts of resistance by Northern-state legal systems, the major pattern in free-state courts of the 1850s was one of "dutiful enforcement with intervals of violent resistance." To note that the state courts frequently either participated in or did not obstruct slave rendition, as was required by federal law, does not mean, however, that either the state court judges or the Northern populace more generally accepted the philosophical underpinnings of the Fugitive Slave Law. To the contrary, assertions of federal judicial power to protect slavery in *Dred Scott* and *Ableman,* limitations on rights to a jury trial and to habeas corpus in the 1850 federal act, and the violence over popular sovereignty in Kansas, among numerous other social forces, were pushing Northern legal ideology toward a strong antislavery position, or at least one of sectional restrictionism and containment. As the threat of disunion grew, state legislatures repeatedly turned back efforts to repeal or modify local personal-liberty laws, the South grew ever more discontented with enforcement of the 1850 act, and Congress proved unable to achieve further legislative reconciliation on the question, making the fugitive-slave issue still "one of the irreducible elements in the crisis of the Union" on the eve of the Civil War. Perhaps most emblematic of the ideological winds blowing through the 1850s free North was the political, if not the precedential, resurrection of the *Hornblower Decision*.[48]

In April 1851, then-senator Salmon P. Chase wrote Hornblower, mentioned that he had cited the *Hornblower Decision* in his brief in the *Van Zandt* case, and asked Hornblower for a copy of his original opinion. Hornblower responded with a lengthy letter praising Chase's stand "in behalf of right; in behalf of law; of justice; humanity, of the Constitution, of patriotism, of philanthropy, of universal emancipation of the human race in body & mind, and of all that is calculated to elevate our fellow men, to the dignity of manhood." Hornblower further bemoaned that the "sacred . . . soil of New Jersey, consecrated by the blood of our fathers, in their struggles for human liberty, is now desecrated by the feet of bloodhounds pursuing their victims."[49]

That summer, Hornblower's opinion was read aloud at, and ordered published by, an antislavery convention in Ohio. Newspapers meanwhile printed portions of Hornblower's letter to Chase. On July 30, 1851, Hornblower's opinion itself was printed on the front page of the *New York Evening Post*. Abolitionist attorney William Jay also arranged for publication and distribution of a pamphlet containing the opinion, a commentary on it, an excerpt of a letter from Hornblower to Jay attacking Daniel Webster for his support of the 1850 Fugitive Slave Law, and other materials.[50]

A second flurry of activity concerning Hornblower's opinion emerged during the 1854 Kansas-Nebraska Act crisis. The *Trenton State Gazette* reprinted the opinion with a front-page story describing its arguments as relevant to the 1850 federal law and to all other congressional actions on fugitive-slave rendition and agreeing with Hornblower on the necessity of a jury trial in all such proceedings. Horace Greeley's *New York Tribune* cited the opinion in urging judicial opposition to the federal act because it violated "reason and the vital principles of the Constitution." In March 1860, Senator Benjamin F. Wade of Ohio disputed the claim that courts had been unanimous in recognizing congressional power over slave rendition, again citing the *Hornblower Decision*. As historian Paul Finkelman put it, "By 1860 the Hornblower opinion had become part of the growing crisis of the Union." In that same year, Hornblower himself seemed happily to agree. In a letter to Senator Ten Eyck, Hornblower urged the introduction of a bill in Congress "to secure to citizens of this or any other state the same 'immunities,' they enjoy here, or every other state, or in other words, to carry into effect the provision of that section." Hornblower's point was that if Congress could enforce the Fugitive Slave Clause, which said nothing about a congressional power to legislate over slave rendition, then Congress must have the parallel power to legislate enforcement of the constitutional provision declaring that "The Citizens of each State shall be entitled to all Privileges and Immunities of Citizens in the several States," a provision that also lacked language empowering congressional action. The mere introduction of such a bill, thought Hornblower, would "add fuel to the fire already burning in the South" so that "what is now a comparatively small combustion will become a volcano." Mob action, not merely legislative debates and judicial opinions, had also already been adding "fuel to the fire" as popular action in the North increasingly expressed disdain for the Southern visions of white and black mobility.[51]

Mob Action

Free blacks, white abolitionists, and white Northern juries joined forces in popular, often violent, resistance to the 1850 Fugitive Slave Act's extension of the slavocracy very visibly into the North. Free-black communities had long created Masonic lodges, Odd Fellows lodges, Women's Good Samaritan Councils, Baptist and Presbyterian churches, and other organizations to meet community needs. These entities expanded in number and reactivated where dormant to resist the law. Vigilance committees to protect fugitive slaves from recapture and to meet their basic needs for food and clothing formed in Boston, Syracuse, New York, Harrisburg, and Detroit, among other locations. Although African Americans initially took the lead in almost all these instances, whites often joined later, leading to reorganization of these committees to take advantage of white members' legal skills.[52]

Those blacks who did not flee to Canada mobilized to defend their families and institutions, some even declaring "their immediate communities and surrounding cities free zones that slave catchers entered at risk to their own lives." Defense of the home became a metaphor for defense of the black community.[53] As Martin Delaney told attendees at a Pittsburgh meeting,

> If a slave pursuer enter my dwelling, one of us must perish. I have treasures there: there are a wife and children to protect; I will give the tyrant timely warning: but if the sanctuary of my home is violated, if I do not defend it, may the grave be to my body no resting place, and the vaunted heavens refuse my spirit.[54]

In Syracuse, the Reverend Jermain Loguen struck a similar chord, urging all blacks and freedom-loving people "to meet this tyranny and crush it by force or be crushed by it." Communities also created networks of safe houses, "temples of refuge" for fugitives in barbershops, homes, and churches. Church bells were used in towns to warn of the arrival of slave catchers. Free blacks working as porters, waiters, and chambermaids served as the eyes and ears of the community to spread the word of a recapture in progress or of a master traveling with a slave who needed to be freed. Threats of the invasion of any African American home were seen as threats to all black homes. When a warrant was issued in Boston to arrest Georgia fugitive slaves William and Ellen Craft, blacks on Belnap and Cambridge streets "became roused in this matter . . . making their houses like barracks" and arming their homes and themselves with guns, swords, and knives. William Craft, initially intending to stand against his recapture at his shop, was persuaded to go to the home of Lewis Hayden, where Hayden barricaded the windows and barred the doors. Hayden covered a table in his home with loaded weapons, while "his young son and a band of brave colored men [sat] armed to the teeth and ready for the impending death struggle with the U.S. Marshall and his armed posse." Hayden even threatened to explode gunpowder on his front steps, killing all within and nearby, rather than surrender the Crafts to the slave catchers. The Boston abolitionist community kept a constant watch on the slave catchers and had them repeatedly arrested for slandering William and conspiring to kidnap him. The slave catchers withdrew, and when President Fillmore threatened to send in the military, abolitionists had the Crafts spirited away to England.[55]

James Hamlet, a fugitive slave working as a porter in New York, inspired multiracial mass-protest meetings when arrested under the new 1850 law. In a meeting held in Boston just over a week after Hamlet's arrest, African American abolitionists vowed to use violence to protect fugitives and community members. At that meeting, Joshua Smith urged every fugitive to arm himself and illustrated "for the gathering how to run a slave catcher through." White merchants, abolitionists, and the black community saved Hamlet, this time by purchasing his freedom. Thousands of black and white New Yorkers gathered near city hall to celebrate his return. When six new fugitives arrived in New York the next day, the police refused to aid the slave catchers.[56]

In the case of Shadrach Minkins, resistance flared in the courtroom itself. Within half an hour of his being taken into custody by U.S. marshals acting under a fugitive-slave warrant, two hundred people converged on the courthouse to protest Minkins's treatment. Lewis Hayden led a large group that stormed its way into the courtroom, carrying Minkins off and on his way to Canada.[57]

One of the most well-known instances of violent resistance became known as the Christiana Riot. Escaped slave William Parker had organized the black community in Christiana, Pennsylvania, to thwart the Gap Gang of kidnappers. When, in early September 1851, Maryland slaveholder Edward Gorusch, his relatives, and a federal marshal confronted Parker and others at his home, where he was then sheltering two other fugitives, the two sides exchanged shots. Upon Mrs. Parker's sounding an alarm, "a large group of black defenders armed with guns and farm implements emerged from the surrounding houses and fields." White neighbors who showed up refused to comply with the marshal's command that they aid in recovery. Between 75 and 150 blacks joined the struggle, in which Gorusch was killed. Parker and the two other fugitives fled to Canada.[58]

Juries played an important role in the "Jerry Rescue" case. William McHenry, known as Jerry, was arrested as a fugitive in Syracuse as the city was hosting a Liberty Party convention. He fought back, with notice of the struggle quickly reaching the convention. A crowd of four to five thousand people threw stones at the hearing-room windows, while a smaller group broke in and carried off Jerry, who was recaptured by the police. Forty or fifty blacks and whites, the whites disguised in black face, broke into the back room of the police office and pried away the bolts and bars that confined Jerry, and this time they successfully whisked him off to Canada. Twelve blacks and fourteen whites were indicted for their role in the rescue, though all but three of the blacks fled to Canada. A grand jury also indicted a U.S. deputy marshal for attempting to kidnap Jerry. At the deputy's trial, attorney Gerrit Smith railed for seven hours against the Fugitive Slave Act's constitutionality. The jury promptly acquitted the deputy. Only one of the other indictees, a black man named Enoch Reed, was convicted of any of the charges made in connection with the rescue.[59]

Failed rescue efforts proved as important, however, as the successful ones. Thomas Sims, a seventeen-year-old fugitive, was captured in Boston only a few months after Shadrach Minkins's rescue. Police and federal marshals, determined to avoid a repeat of the Minkins incident, barred the windows to Sims's room, guarded him heavily, and randomly searched the crowds gathering outside the courthouse during the nine days of his imprisonment and trial. One hundred fifty armed guards ultimately escorted Sims to the wharf for his return to Georgia, followed by one hundred unhappy abolitionists. Although initial press coverage praised the relative decorum of the Sims rescue, highly publicized cases of successful recapture like his resulted in the "general public in Boston and elsewhere in the North express[ing] increasing sympathy for the slave." This effect was magnified by the serialization of Harriet Beecher Stowe's novel *Uncle Tom's Cabin* in the antislavery newspaper the *National Era* just months after Sims's return to bondage. "Stowe's novel created a sensation, selling 300,000 copies in just the first year of its publication" and converting "many to the antislavery cause both in America and abroad."[60]

Other successful rescues and failed attempts continued during the 1850s. Notably, in May 1854, fugitive Anthony Burns was arrested in Boston, where a bungled rescue attempt caused a guard's being fatally shot. With President

Pierce's approval, the marshal summoned the marines and the army. When the commissioner issued a certificate of removal, "it took the efforts of a large volunteer militia, an artillery company, a city militia of at least fifteen hundred men, and a company of Marines to assure the return of Anthony Burns to slavery in Virginia" in the face of a crowd of many thousands of angry onlookers. In the fall of 1858, an armed crowd threatened the police and freed Kentucky fugitive John Price from the hotel in which he was being held in Wellington, Ohio, where he had been moved after his arrest in nearby Oberlin. Although thirty-seven of the rescuers were indicted and twenty jailed, all were freed within one year, receiving a hero's welcome-home parade and a ceremony of "defiant speeches and triumphant songs." In New York, Harriet Tubman, of Underground Railroad fame, helped to free fugitive Charles Nalle after his arrest. Nalle was, however, rearrested. When a crowd of hundreds discovered the rearrest, "they stormed the judge's office to which . . . [Nalle] had been taken" and "armed with brickbats and clubs, faced defenders wielding pistols." In the ensuing confusion, Tubman and others freed Nalle.[61]

There were over eighty well-publicized rescues or attempts during the 1850s, each infuriating slaveholders and increasing Northern antislavery sentiment. The vast majority of fugitives who were arrested were likely returned to slavery, though that calculation ignores the numbers of escaped slaves who forever eluded arrest. The few convictions of resisters and the occasional complicity of Northern authorities and juries further angered the South. Northern mob actions and lawsuits used to harass slave catchers and to save fleeing bondsmen had powerful political and symbolic value. Although many abolitionists opposed violence and even opposed open defiance of the law, the bravery of the mobs, their obvious determination, and the suffering inflicted on them and the fugitives whom they sought to defend helped expand the range and zeal of Northern sympathizers with the antislavery cause. For the African American community, these actions offered them a voice in the public realm at a time when they had none. As historian R. J. M. Blackett put it, "At a time when most blacks could not vote and when the economic, social, and legal systems were arrayed against them, these actions expressed the political will of the people and their determination to defend their communities." Political expression through organized violence to build black solidarity and gain greater white respect for blacks' humanity would continue to be a crucial tool throughout the struggle against slavery, especially in the Civil War and Reconstruction, a dynamic to be discussed shortly. But full appreciation of the significance for the North of legislative, judicial, and mob action to foster both black and white mobility requires that these phenomena first be placed in a broader framework. Northern free-labor ideology and the growing influence of related ideas of moral unionism and peoplehood gave an emotional resonance for Northerners to the fugitives' plight that cannot otherwise be fully understood.[62]

Frenetic Free Labor

From the late eighteenth century through the nineteenth century, free-labor ideology increasingly dominated Northern conceptions of the good life. Although the ideology took various forms, the version that became most influential in shaping the law was that espoused by the Republican Party. The ideology had implications for social conceptions of privacy and especially property, but at its heart it was an obsession with both metaphorical and physical locomotion.[63]

Metaphorical locomotion was embodied in the "right to rise," to move from youth as a hired laborer to maturity as an owner of the means of production and as an employer of the rising young.[64] Abraham Lincoln concisely summed up this spiraling process of advancement:

[A] penniless beginner in the world, labors for wages awhile, saves a surplus with which to buy tools or land, for himself; then labors on his own account [a]while, and at length hires another new beginner to help him. This, say its advocates, is *free* labor—the just and generous, and prosperous system, which opens the way for all—gives hope to all, and energy, and progress, and improvement of condition to all.[65]

Free labor was good for all because widespread social mobility for individuals aided economic development overall, which in turn aided further social mobility. But the goal of all this movement was not wealth accumulation but independence. Independence for the many might indeed be endangered by the bigness of the few. The hero of antebellum free-labor legend was therefore the small producer and small-to-moderate landholder, the artisan, the craftsman, and the yeoman farmer, not the captain of industry. Enough wealth to free one from economic dependence on others also meant independent citizenship— free thoughts and free action as a member of the polity. The society valorized by free labor was one of a large middling class with high wages that reflected the high dignity and value of labor. Education would also improve skills and thus productivity, further raising the demand for, and thus market worth of, labor. In the reigning Republican variant of this ideology, there was, therefore, no conflict between labor and capital, for today's laborer was tomorrow's small capitalist, receiving his reward for a lifetime of hard work and savings. Some, like Lincoln, however, recognized a right to strike, at least in the sense of a right to withhold labor, as part of the right to rise, though in this, and in his tentative embrace of the formation of unions, he did not speak for his party.[66]

In addition to social mobility and the intense movement of daily labor, the ideology was intimately linked to physical mobility—to the settling of the

West. The territories were a place "for poor people to go and better their condition," Lincoln explained. Ample land was needed to ensure ample opportunity, and if the land could not be found in the East, it awaited the intrepid adventurer in the West. This westward migration benefited the East by avoiding the evils of overcrowding and the West by peopling its vast land. "Popular sovereignty," letting the people of a territory decide whether it would be slave or free, was thus no solution to the problem of slavery because each territory's choices had a social and economic impact far beyond its own borders. Moreover, slaveholders' domination of territories that would eventually become states would render the Northern free population a permanent political minority in the federal government, placing them at the relative mercy of the planter class.[67]

There was a strong moral and spiritual component to this obsession with locomotion. "Success," Lincoln would later say during the Civil War, "does not *as much* depend on external help as on self reliance." Anyone could become the self-made man by hard work, diligence, and intelligence. Hired laborers need not be fixed in that condition for life, the ideology preached, with Lincoln himself denying that there was in fact any permanent class of such laborers in the North. These values were rooted in the Protestant work ethic, according to which the successful exercise of the right to rise constituted a display of personal virtue. A person who lost in the "race of life" did so primarily because of his own shortcomings. "It is not the fault of the system," Lincoln again explained, but "because of either a dependent nature which prefers it, or improvidence, folly, or singular misfortune" that one becomes a wage laborer for life. Insisted another Republican in 1854, "every man holds his fortune in his own right arm; and his position in society, in life, is to be tested by his own individual character." Said Horace Greeley, "chance or luck" had "little to do with men's prosperous or adverse fortune," for most failures stemmed from persons' "own extravagance and needless ostentation," or, in the words of the *Springfield Republican*, "no oppression of the laborer [is] here which it is not in his power to remedy, or which does not come from his own inefficiency and lack of enterprise." In the view of prosperous or upwardly mobile Northerners, therefore, the bad worker blamed class conflict for his troubles and followed Democratic labor leaders when his own condition actually stemmed from his unreliability, indolence, viciousness, and unproductivity, his filthy and disorderly nature. The good worker was frugal, labored hard, saved, developed skills, planned ahead, strove for education, and used the ballot to protect the virtuous free-labor system.[68]

That system likewise defined the virtuous society and thus the advantages of the Northern over the Southern way of life. The North was a vibrant economy and culture, forward-looking, always changing. It was a dynamic place where equal opportunity, social mobility, and economic independence came to life.[69] Carl Schurz, a leading Republican orator of the day, painted this representative image:

> Cast your eyes over that great beehive called the free States. See by the railroad and telegraph wire every village, almost every backwoods cottage, drawn within the immediate reach of progressive civilization. . . . look upon our society, where by popular education and continual change of condition the dividing lines between the ranks and classes are at last obliterated; look upon our system of public instruction, which places even the lowliest child of the people upon the high road of progressive advancement.[70]

The same high praise was heaped on the free states of the West, where, said Ohio congressman Philemon Bliss, "the farmer works his own farm; the mechanic labors in his own shop, and the merchant sells his own goods," and although labor is sold there, it is "mainly as a temporary expedient to enable the laborer to acquire a small capital." Senator James Doolittle of Wisconsin went so far as to claim that four-fifths of Wisconsin's population was economically independent.[71]

By contrast, Northerners envisioned the South as a stagnant, aristocratic world, a fixed social hierarchy locked into romanticized understandings of a more backward past. As William Seward saw it when visiting the South, it was a place without enterprise or movement, a vision shared by Republican newspaper reporters traveling through the region. Southern civilization was decadent, its association between labor and slavery degrading the former in all its citizens' eyes, rendering Southern nonslaveholding white workers "poor, shiftless, lazy, uninstructed, cowed." George Weston saw most Southern whites as "retir[ing] to the outskirts of civilization, where they live a semi-savage life, sinking deeper and more hopelessly into barbarism with every succeeding generation." The South was a place of the very rich and very poor, with no real middle class of the intelligent farmers, mechanics, and artisans who were the real source of wealth. Southern immigrants to Northern states and their descendants were seen as ignorant, shiftless, illiterate or at least averse to reading, too content with their station in life. Residents of the Southern portions of free states were contaminated by their close commercial relations with the South, and these portions became "proverbial for the intellectual, moral, and political darkness which covers the land." The South was populated by whites who had become lazy, unkempt, denizens of a "dead society." Planters' wealth was unearned, thus undeserved, and they ruled over an impoverished population. They had rendered the South, as one Wisconsin voter put it, "a set of cowards, full of gasconade, and bad liquor, brought up to abuse negroes and despise the north, too lazy to work; they are not above living on the unrewarded labor of others."[72] The South was a diseased place, endangering the North with contamination:

It is unquestionable that the immigration from the South has brought into the free states more ignorance, poverty, and thriftlessness, than an equal amount of the immigration from Europe. Where it forms a marked feature of the population, as in Southern Illinois, a long-time must elapse before it is brought up to the general standard of intelligence and enterprise in the free states.[73]

Although most Northerners were content to prevent the spread of slavery's ills beyond Southern confines, many Republicans urged mass Northern migration to the South as a way to reconstruct it. Some were convinced that rather than await abolition for this migration, they could do it immediately and establish free-labor settlements in the border states to serve as a model of the superior way and to arouse poor Southern whites toward slavery's overthrow. The goal was to remake the inanimate South into the mirror image of the vibrant North.[74]

Relations between the races, of course, had to be taken into account in free labor's vision of a progressive North and its critique of a regressive South. Free blacks were poorly treated in the antebellum North. In only five Northern states, all in New England, were black men given equal suffrage, and four Western states barred blacks from even entering the state's borders. Blacks worked largely in menial jobs, facing near-universal racial prejudice and, especially in the West, facing constant discrimination, often being excluded from public education. Northerners, including Republicans, often used racist rhetoric. Colonizationists operated under the assumption that the United States was a white man's nation. Many Free-Soilers wanted not only to have land be distributed freely to white settlers in a place devoid of slavery but also to be free from physical contact with blacks. "Free soil" and free labor were not identical ideas—some Free-Soilers, for example, rejected the antiunionism of free labor —but the two ideas shared much in common. Still, both Republicans and Free-Soilers held a wide range of racial views, from Negrophobia to the minority that supported true racial equality. More important, they shared dominant racial themes inconsistent with slavery's survival.[75]

Indeed, by the eve of the Civil War, Lincoln articulated views that reflected a shaky but real Republican consensus on race relations, in a party that included many former Free-Soilers. This consensus relied on a distinction among four types of rights: natural (held by all men), civil (created by law to protect the natural ones), political (which could be regulated by the majority), and social (such as whom to marry). Most Republicans believed that blacks possessed natural rights and were entitled to civil ones but not to political or social ones. Accordingly, they did not believe in African American suffrage and favored voluntary colonization, and although they consistently affirmed blacks' basic humanity, they would pander to racial prejudice in a way that denied that humanity. In the free-labor vision, the right to keep the fruits of one's labor and to try to rise were natural. As Lincoln phrased it in his Senate campaign debates with Stephen Douglas, although the Negro is "perhaps" not equal to whites "in moral or intellectual endowment" and was not likely to succeed in competition with free whites, nevertheless the Negro is in his "right to eat the bread, without the leave of anybody else, which his own hand earns, . . . *my equal and the equal* of Judge Douglas and the equal of every living man." Moreover, even if Lincoln expressed doubts about the likelihood of black success, he believed that every man is entitled to try, "to have the chance."[76] Thus, he said,

> I believe a black man is entitled to it [to a chance]—in which he *can* better his condition—when he may look forward and hope to be a hired laborer this year and the next, work for himself afterward, and finally hire men to work for him! That is the true system.[77]

For similar reasons, most Republicans opposed laws that excluded free blacks from states, for doing so violated a man's natural right to live where he was born or to move freely where better times may await. By recognizing blacks as men entitled to the mobility and equality of opportunity shared by whites, Republicans in effect recognized blacks as members of the polity, inferior members to be sure, who could be denied political and social rights and encouraged to leave the country, but members of a sort nonetheless entitled to the equal civil rights offered by the law. Thus, for Lincoln and most Republicans, the thorough Southern exclusion of blacks as members of the nation, the denial of their natural rights to attempt physical and social (material) locomotion and to keep the fruits of their labor, and the corresponding degradation of white and black labor alike made Southern society immoral. As Lincoln historian Gabor S. Boritt summarized Lincoln's position, "In his estimate the man who robbed the black man of the fruit of his labor was on a par with, and in a sense was worse than, the man who robbed the white man thus."[78]

This last point is underscored by an examination of Lincoln's views on nation and peoplehood. These views were inseparable from his understanding of free-labor ideology and of his reading of the Bible. Political scientist Joseph R. Fornieri summed up Lincoln's vision of the American experience as one analogous to the biblical Exodus story. For Lincoln, the Founders collectively played Moses delivering his people from slavery and giving them "the law." "The law," however, was not the Ten Commandments but the American Decalogue, the

Declaration of Independence. Lincoln himself played the role of prophet, calling the People back to their ancient ways. The central command of the Declaration was that of equality, not of condition but of opportunity. Men were not equal in "color, size, intellect, moral development or social capacity" but in "certain inalienable rights, among which are life, liberty, and the pursuit of happiness." Because the Declaration created the political nation, the Union by definition included a commitment to the equality principle. A "nation" consisted of its territory, its people, and its laws, and the laws defining the American Union were those designed to protect human equality. In a reworking of the biblical proverb, the Union and the Constitution were a "picture of silver" framing equal liberty as the "apple of gold." "The picture," said Lincoln, "was made for the apple, not the apple for the picture."[79] Slavery was the opposite of equality and, unlike men of the Founding generation, Lincoln saw no distinction between political slavery and chattel slavery:

> When we were the political slaves of King George, and wanted to be free, we called the maxim that "all men are created equal" a self-evident truth; but now when we have grown fat, and have lost all dread of becoming slaves ourselves, we have become so greedy to be *masters* that we call the same maxim "a self-evident lie." The Fourth of July has not quite dwindled away; it is still a great day—*for burning firecrackers!!!*[80]

But of what did this equality consist, and from whence did it come? Here Lincoln again relied on biblical imagery, fused with free-labor ideals. When God expelled Adam and Eve from the Garden of Eden, God declared, "In the sweat of thy face shalt thou eat bread." This phrase, to Lincoln's ears, was a command that no good thing can be enjoyed "without having first cost labour." Because good things come from labor, it is to the laborer that the fruits belong. To steal another's fruit without expending one's own labor is to violate the biblical injunction *incumbent upon all*.[81] Yet again, Lincoln appealed to the Almighty as the source of authority for his constitutional interpretation:

> I say that whereas God Almighty has given every man one mouth to be fed, and one pair of hands adapted to furnish food for that mouth, if anything can be proved to be the will of Heaven, it is proved by this fact, that that mouth is to be fed by those hands, without being interfered with by any other man who has also his mouth to feed and his hands to labor with. I hold if the Almighty had ever made a set of men that should do all the eating and none of the work, he would have made them with mouths only and no hands, and if he had made another class that he intended should do all the work and none of the eating, he would have made them without mouths and with all hands. But inasmuch as he has not chosen to make man in that way,

if anything is proved, it is that those hands and mouth are to be cooperative through life and not to be interfered with. That they are to go forth and improve their condition as I have been trying to illustrate, is the inherent right given to mankind directly by the Maker.[82]

The equal right to the fruits of one's labor thus implied an equal right to be free from others' interference with the laborer's own efforts. The Declaration of Independence recited the equality principle as a guide for the future, to place a "stumbling block" in the way of those who would forget the principle and thus lead the people into despotism. The Constitution, in Lincoln's vision, equally embraced this principle but, to preserve territorial Union, included compromises with slavery. Yet those compromises were to be temporary ones, dictated by necessity, the Founders expecting later generations to complete their work of moving toward a "more perfect Union." That goal would be achieved in time by confining slavery to the South, for its confinement meant its eventual death. Lincoln made some statements that could be interpreted as putting territorial integrity over moral principle. But placing all his statements into context, and recognizing his appreciation of the practical limits to the speed of change, makes clear, as several leading scholars have noted, that he embraced a concept of Union as evolving toward a place where people of all backgrounds were united on a common territory by a shared commitment to equality, a Union in which, he eventually came to understand, African Americans could belong.[83]

Lincoln rejected the argument that some men are too vicious or ignorant to share in government, for he believed that the very experience of participation in collective self-government would help "the weak to grow stronger, the ignorant wiser; and all better, and happier *together.*" Among the highest purposes of civilization was, indeed, said Lincoln, to break the equation between "stranger" and "enemy," to "correct the evils, great and small, which spring from want of sympathy and from positive enmity among strangers," and to replace them with the stronger and more durable "bond of social and political union among us." "[L]et us discard all this quibbling about this man and the other man— this race and that race and the other race as being inferior," said Lincoln, and "unite as one people throughout the land, until we shall stand up once more declaring that all men are created equal." The Union meant movement of individuals, of groups, of the nation toward a better place in which aspirations for equality became realized.[84]

Lincoln left little doubt that race and ethnicity did not exclude anyone from membership in the polity. He recognized that the many immigrants to this land could not be united by actual blood but could claim to be "blood of blood and flesh of flesh of the men who wrote that Declaration" embracing its self-evident truth that "all men are created equal." In his Senate electoral debate with Stephen Douglas, he thus declared, "If Judge Douglas and his friends are not willing to stand by [the Declaration], let them come up and amend it. Let them make it read that all men are created equal, except Negroes."[85] He went further, linking the ideas of white-immigrant and black equality in the process of denouncing the nativist Know-Nothing Party:

> Our progress in degeneracy appears to me to be pretty rapid. As a nation, we began declaring that *"all men are created equal."* We now practically read it "all men are created equal *except negroes."* When the Know-Nothings get control, it will read "all men are created equal except negroes, *and foreigners, and Catholics."* When it comes to this I should prefer emigrating to some country where they make no pretense of loving liberty—to Russia, for instance, where despotism can be taken pure, and without the base alloy of hypocrisy.[86]

The Declaration in significant part defined the nation. Blacks, whether slave or free, and whites, immigrant or not, were all entitled to the founding document's blessings. Those blessings meant legal protection of natural rights, especially the right to reap the fruit of one's labors. If blacks were not, therefore, necessarily entitled to suffrage (though by the end of the war Lincoln would move toward hinting that they were) or to social equality, they were nevertheless entitled to recognition as part of the nation that the Declaration defined. The nation as a whole and its many individual members would, at least in this sense, move forward together.[87]

From a modern perspective, it is easy to find numerous statements by Lincoln that ring of racism to twenty-first-century ears. Furthermore, Lincoln's publicly stated views evolved (for example, by 1863 he had apparently rejected colonization), though I have made little effort to parse that evolution here, seeking to judge him on the whole of his life's contribution. When so judged, he was committed, at least on the level of principle, to an inclusive vision of multiracial and multiethnic equality of natural and civil rights, whatever might have been his personal preferences at one time or another that African Americans would *choose* to exercise those rights elsewhere than in America. If they stayed here, they stayed as part of the nation. That vision was informed by the spiritual journeys recounted in Exodus, which had also so inspired slaves who sought their freedom, and by free-labor ideals of individual social mobility and of national mobility toward a better way. Lincoln's vision cannot fairly be claimed to be the sole one, as it competed with other ideas of Union such as ethnocultural similarity and ties of affection (and he did on a very few occasions use the language of affection). But his views matter more than the competing ones, for a Union *defined by* the commitment to equality was the one that would ultimately prevail in the Thirteenth, Fourteenth, and Fifteenth Amendments. Indeed, for a brief time, the nation would do Lincoln one better, seeking in the last of these amendments to ensure political equality for all. It may fairly be argued that all the Reconstruction amendments owed more of an intellectual debt to abolitionists than to Lincoln. Under this interpretation, Lincoln's views on Union set a baseline below what the revised Constitution would come to embody, yet even that baseline is one that included African Americans within the polity created by the Declaration. In any event, before the Civil War, abolitionist thinking was thoroughly unpopular, with Lincoln's free-labor vision holding far more credibility. Frenetic free labor, particularly as embodied in Lincoln, thus gave a meaning to Northern understandings of real and metaphorical locomotion that intimately tied the North's battle—first against slavery's expansion, then against slavery's survival—to the very meaning of what it was to be an American.[88]

10 Privacy and Property

If I have less to say about the two remaining interests protected by the Fourth Amendment—privacy and property—than I have had to say about locomotion, it is in part because I have already said much about all three interests while discussing personal mobility. The three interests are so interrelated that one cannot be discussed without some attention to the others. For example, masters' control over slaves' mobility enabled them to break up slave families by sale or hire. But who is in a family and what happens in the family home are today ordinarily thought of as subsumed within the right to privacy. Furthermore, it was the slaves' status as property that enabled masters to control slaves' movement in the first place. The three interests are different but interdependent, the nature of each informing that of the others.[1]

Additionally, I have sought to emphasize those Fourth Amendment interests that are too often modernly devalued, and freedom of movement is, in my view, especially slighted by modern constitutional law. Aspects of privacy and property are also unduly minimized but not to the degree that this is so for mobility. In any event, mobility's story under slavery seems to me to offer the clearest perspective for understanding the other interests and for distinguishing antebellum conceptions of all three interests from those conceptions that held sway for the Framers' generation without my ignoring continuities in the two eras' understanding of these ideas. The slave experience highlights what should be understood as an increased national appreciation of mobility's value, a value that was always of importance but arguably relatively less central to the Revolutionary experience than were invasions of privacy (such as searches of homes, warehouses, and ships) as prerequisites to seizures of property (such as uncustomed goods). The primary lesson to be learned from antebellum slave privacy conflicts is that privacy can inhere as much in the group as in the individual. The primary teaching to be gleaned from that era's property-rights disputes surrounding slavery is that humans are not fungible things to be owned but unique, thinking and feeling individuals to be respected as such. Both these observations will have implications for the scope of modern Fourth Amendment privacy protections and the meaning of probable cause as a form of individualized suspicion, as I will explore in this book's concluding chapter. I also treat privacy and property together in a single chapter because their meaning enlivens an understanding of the importance of the Slave Power idea and how it links search and seizure practices to free-speech protections in a way that I have only hinted at so far.[2]

Slaves, of course, had no "rights" to privacy or property. But they did in practice experience a kind of privacy. They also sometimes at least had possession and significant control over some tangible property, and they keenly understood their position as human property and its unfortunate implications for their lives. It is not, however, the slave experience alone that matters. Slavery forced Northerners and Southerners to contend with the meaning of privacy and property concepts and with their role in the constitutional order, evolving concepts that were ultimately redefined in the Reconstruction amendments to the Constitution in the mid- to late 1860s.

"Property" was a word and a concept that was long important to Americans' self-definition. "Privacy" was important too, but it was not the word commonly used during antebellum times. State officials who invaded someone's home were clearly seen as intruding on some significant interest in a way that rendered the action a "search." That interest was not always given a single clear label, certainly not the label "privacy" in the sense that we mean it today. My use of the term might therefore seem anachronistic. I use it anyway because I believe it brings a clarity to events that would otherwise be missing.

Interestingly, abolitionist assaults on the brutality of denying slaves *legal* protection for their privacy led to Southern invasions of *white* abolitionists' property (seizing their mail) and freedom of locomotion (for example, by banishment) in an effort to suppress the abolitionist message. Southern efforts to suppress white civil liberties caused a backlash, fanning Northern fears of an aristocratic Slave Power bent on destroying true republicanism. These fears helped to advance a Northern critique of the Southern property system as a corrosive one likely to destroy Northern free labor. These intellectual and political struggles over the intertwined nature of locomotion, property, and privacy led the North haltingly toward a more inclusive political theory that recognized blacks' entitlement to protection of their rights in each of these three areas, while white Southerners' exclusionary thinking became further entrenched.

Privacy

Privacy Defined

Modernly, the meaning of the term "privacy" is disputed. Little will be gained here from entering that debate. All definitions recognize, however, as antebellum Americans implicitly did without using the term, that privacy at least includes a zone of protection for the body and for the home. Fondling someone's buttocks without their consent, crossing the threshold of another's home without permission, and peeping through a mostly closed window all impinge on privacy. The excessive use of force by the police or by other agents acting with the state's blessing likewise invades bodily privacy. Privacy also implies some measure of secrecy about one's affairs. Additionally, privacy is strongly linked to, though not entirely limited by, property. To enter one's car trunk or handbag is to invade privacy. Yet, argue some writers, privacy can also include "the private"—things that may not be secret but about which "the public," meaning any other persons, have no right to know or to intervene. If a man is talking about the intimate details of his love life to a friend while they are walking down the street, custom suggests that we should pretend not to, and even try not to, hear, lest we commit the sin of eavesdropping. The law might not protect the man who shares confidences with his friend, but common understandings will.[3]

Of the available definitions, the one that best expresses privacy's core is this: privacy is the creation of both real and metaphorical boundaries that protect us against the risk of being misdefined and judged out of context. Humans are complex, yet we tend to judge one another, often harshly, on the basis of a small sampling of one another's behavior. To be so judged wounds a person as unfair, for it takes time truly to learn each individual's nature. Moreover, we may want to present only certain aspects of our selves in certain circumstances, such as portraying strength and confidence to our employer and leaving revelations of weakness and worry to our spouse. Privacy gives us this ability to control when and how we reveal how much of ourselves to others.[4]

The control over self-revelation implied by privacy means that we build intimate relationships, such as with spouses, children, and friends, by revealing to them more of who we are. Privacy allows us to build a sense of individuality by expressing thoughts and feelings that we would fear articulating in a more public setting. Privacy builds self-esteem by allowing us to be judged by those who know us best, our good qualities as well as our bad, at least creating the possibility of being loved or chastised, fairly and in our entirety. Privacy is thus at the root of family and other intimate relationships, central to individual identity and autonomy, and a prerequisite to the formation and expression of diverse views, attitudes, and experiences that is at the heart of the idea of free speech and thought.[5]

Yet, though too often ignored, privacy inheres in groups as well as individuals. Indeed, the opportunity for groups to gather in homes, civic centers, schools, and churches—all the time substantially insulated from outsiders' eyes —may be necessary to promote the free exchange of ideas that define a democracy. Such an exchange can also encourage group solidarity, enhancing part of each individual's sense of self while emboldening group members eventually to express their views in a broader public forum. Apart from its role of promoting citizen involvement in political movements, privacy also encourages the diversity and autonomy purportedly valued by liberal states, because privacy frees citizens from the "tyranny of the prevailing opinion and feeling."[6] One commentator made the point this way:

> We all desire to live in separate communities, or among or within separate normative spaces. Privacy, or the ability to control data about yourself, supports this desire. It enables these multiple communities and disables the power of one dominant community to norm the others into oblivion. Think, for example, about a gay man in an intolerant small town.[7]

It is primarily this sense of "group privacy" that slaves managed to eke out, at least in a fashion, though they had some smaller measure of individual privacy as well. Masters fought to extinguish both sorts of privacy, for to do so is to deny the infinite worth and uniqueness of the individual that gives life its meaning and gives the group the solidarity that breeds resistance.[8] Any discussion of privacy must begin with the home, here meaning the slave's quarters.

Slaves' Individual and Family Privacy

The slave quarters were separated from the master's house (the "big house"), sometimes located a few hundred yards away and other times in scattered settlements around the plantation. Wooden shacks or cabins provided shelter for slave families. One of the cabins, though often set off from the others, might sometimes be occupied by a driver or black foreman and his family or even a white overseer or manager.[9]

Close living in tight quarters with ample face-to-face interaction made individual privacy hard to come by. The cabins themselves were designed to minimize such privacy, the earth floor being the only sound-absorbing material. Windows were usually just openings to let light in and sound out, with doors having large cracks in them, which allowed further sound seepage.[10] Richard Cordley vividly described his western Kansas cabin of the late 1850s:

The cabin was about fifteen feet square and of very simple construction. There was no chinking between the logs and I could almost roll through the openings into the yard. I could look out and see the ponies and the pigs and the cattle, and could hear the chickens talking in their sleep. Now and then I could hear the bark of a prairie wolf, or the screech of an owl in the woods, or the yell of an Indian who was late getting home. All around the cabin the family lay on their shelves, and were snoring in that peculiar piping key which none but an Indian larynx can produce. The music of the night was made all the more impressive by the deep base snoring of my Negro driver.[11]

Cabins might also be made of hewn post oak covered with cypress, sporting plank floors elevated a few feet off the ground. This did little to add to individual privacy and might even have reduced it further by "curtailing slave appropriation of goods commonly hidden in the root cellars of cabins built directly on the ground," so-called hidey holes.[12]

Plantation-management literature encouraged planters to keep their slaves from cross-cabin nighttime visiting. The 1861 *Plantation and Farm Regulation, Record, Inventory, and Account Book* recommended that every slave be required to remain in his quarters upon the blowing of a horn at nine o'clock. The book further urged managers or overseers to make frequent random surprise visits to the quarters at varying times of the night to ensure that all were present. More was at stake in masters' or overseers' visits to the quarters, however, than simple confinement of the slaves. The growing grip of paternalist managerial philosophy led the authors of both slave medical and management literature to imply that *any* slave activities divorced from white supervision threatened the health of the entire plantation. The successful masters' absolute rule was no longer "confined to the field or the workshop" but "followed their slaves to their cabins where they intervened in the most intimate aspects of slave life, regulating sanitation, health, religion, marital relations, and child rearing." Slaves now found themselves "fending off their owners' attempts to name their children, sanitize their cabin, and regulate their diet." Where masters fell down in their obligations to police life in the cabins, patrollers might step in to fill the supervisory gap.[13]

Nor were the cabins a sanctuary from white violence, especially sexual violence. Few slave families could protect their teenage daughters from rape by masters, overseers, or other white men. Though a maturing girl might receive a trinket for compliance, she also risked a flogging for refusal or resistance. Yet, under the right circumstances and with some luck, resistance might succeed. Gus Feaster, for example, described his white overseer, Wash Evans, as "a wicked man. He take 'vantage of all de slaves when he git half chance." Feaster recounted an incident that occurred when he was picking berries with his mother, his friend John, and John's mother, Lucy. Wash Evans rode up to the two women, who "kept telling him dat de missus want her berries and dat dey was 'ligious wimmins anyhow and didn't practice no life o' sin and vile wickedness. Finally he got down off'n his hoss and pull out his whip and low if dey didn't submit to him he gwine to beat dem half to death." The two children hid, and Fester heard Lucy and his mother plead with Evans until they finally "act like dey gwine to indulge in de wickedness wid dat ole man. But when he tuck off his whip and some other garments, my mammy and ole lady Lucy grab him by his goatee and further down and hist him over in de middle of dem blackberry bushes." Fester's mother reported the incident to her mistress, who fired the overseer. Not all slave women were so lucky. Many slave men indeed preferred to marry women on other plantations in the hope of being spared the sight of their wives being beaten, insulted, and raped while the husbands looked on helpless to halt the pain.[14]

Still, the cabins did manage to provide some minimal measure of privacy to slave families. These families taught their children both values that were different from the master's and sources of self-esteem that were rooted in black family and community life. Naming practices are one example. Slaves did not simply passively accept the names assigned to them by owners. They would choose names that were meaningful to them, perhaps naming a child after grandparents or other kin and trying to maintain connections and links to the African past through name selection. Mothers worked to keep their daughters sexually innocent, and despite the crowding of large families in small cabins, parents occasionally found sufficient privacy to be intimate with each other. In what were perhaps rare instances, slave cabins also became the site of overt expressive acts of resistance, including the display of abolitionist propaganda. Among the most notable of examples was a slave named California, owned by James McDowell but hired out to George H. Young and his wife. In the summer of 1847, Young penned a letter to McDowell complaining of the difficulties of managing slaves other than his own:[15]

> Your California especially has an idea that she is free. Goes & comes & does as she pleases, infuses a good deal of these feelings & notions in her children's heads, has Amalgamation prints stuck up in her cabin. Which I constantly fear will be observed by the Patrol & unpleasant difficulties ensue & the example of all this is against my own slaves.[16]

"Amalgamation prints" were outlawed antislavery literature. Although California was probably not literate, the mere presence of the prints was probably both a cause and a reflection of unrest in the cabins, or so Young believed. California was a laundress who was permitted to hire herself out, while her husband Isaac hired himself out to a local ferry, thus creating the conditions for California's gaining access to the prints. Furthermore, Mrs. Young was an "uncommon potential advocate," displaying unusual sympathy for the slaves under her control. She probably pressured Mr. Young, who apparently fancied himself a benevolent man, to adopt his policy of never punishing "my own if I can avoid it—& others not at all." Although these were unusual circumstances, they were not unheard of, and bondspeople proved more willing to possess, and made less effort to hide, illicit material during the Civil War. The mother of the slave Mattie Jackson, for example, posted a picture of Abraham Lincoln in her room, which her owner, William Lewis, discovered when he decided to search the premises. Lewis was so outraged that his slave had not even made an effort to hide the picture in a drawer or under a mattress that he "knocked her down three times, and sent her to the trader's yard for a month as punishment."[17] One historian described the bravery of these rare and noteworthy slaves, who used

> their homes—a slave cabin and a room in a slaveholding house—as places where they could encourage opposition to slavery and teach their children that others, outside the South, agreed. Slaves' culture of opposition . . . was at least sometimes nurtured at home under the careful attention of enslaved women. Some skilled women were able to procure materials with which to contest slavery's legitimacy, making their homes key locations in the rival geography.[18]

Some measure of family and individual privacy could also be found outside the cabins. Fathers taught sons skills like trapping wild turkeys, catching raccoons, and building canoes. Young children played games, often among themselves, but also in "promiscuous equality" with white children to whom they might be assigned as playmates. Games included hunting, fishing, picking berries, and raiding potato and watermelon patches. More important, slave children played among themselves games like Hoodoo Doctor and Conjure Man that were meant to give them some pretend measure of magical control over whites. They also engaged in petty theft to aid their play, taking corn kernels to use as playing cards or pilfering fruit from an orchard or eggs from a henhouse. They would challenge their creativity, making balls out of yarn with a sock covering it or making marbles out of bits of clay. Competitive games helped them to develop physical skills like riding and fishing. They roamed the woods and the fields, catching small game, fishing, skimming on ice in winter, playing hopscotch and ball and ring games, role-playing cooking or caring for babies, all of which formed a sense of solidarity and a "semi-autonomous realm, beyond the control of their masters." Though barred from formal education, they learned counting via hide-and-seek, the alphabet in other games, and riddle-solving in ring games accompanied by songs. A surprising number taught themselves to read, perhaps by scavenging old nails to make enough money to buy a spelling book, pretending to buy a book for a white child, or trading marbles to a white child in exchange for learning a letter or two. All these things would have been done beyond the prying eyes of the white adult masters.[19]

Slaves' Group Privacy

Most of the privacy in slaves' lives, however, was of the group more than of the individual. A separate secret world was made possible for the slave community because many plantations were too big to permit continual close supervision, it was often costly to do so, and most planters recognized a need for slaves to have some minimal world of their own. "Leisure" time consisted of evenings, late days on Saturdays (though many used Saturdays to do personal chores like cleaning cabins or, where permitted, tending garden plots), and the near-universal day of rest, Sunday. This separate world depended on group identification and solidarity. Though the community might be riven by divisions of status, gender, and personal conflict, its members still understood themselves "as a common people, a contradictory, unequal we." Work in the fields might even sometimes have been preferred to work in the big house, where slaves would be under the constant and close surveillance of whites and would face swift retribution for error, thus lacking even the chance to carve out some modest sense of shared group experience during the working day. In these slices of labor time and bits of respite from its rigors, the slaves formed a community.[20]

The community's survival depended on a code of silence and secrecy as a way to reduce the unpredictability of whites' interference with blacks' lives. Children were taught the value of silence from an early age, often through stories, such as that of the talkative slave and the frog. In this tale, a slave discovers a frog that can speak. When he reveals this miracle to his master, however, the master is skeptical and threatens to punish the slave if he is lying. The frog, of course, refuses to talk, so the master severely beats the slave. Only after the master leaves does the frog speak out. "A tol' yuh he othah day," said the frog, "yuh talk too much."[21] The point of the story was to teach that silence and secrecy meant survival, for

> [s]ilence kept masters ignorant of things going on behind their backs: the food slaves stole, the religious services held in secret, the escapes made by the boldest of slaves, the anger and hatred that blacks felt toward whites. Silence protected the slave quarters. It kept the slave's family and religious life removed from white invasion. In other words, the story taught the slave child how to protect African-American plantation communities, its families, its religious life and its sacred world.[22]

Similarly, children were cautioned not to repeat to whites anything heard in the slave quarters. Recalled Elijah P. Morris, born in Shelby County, Kentucky, in 1840, "Mothers were necessarily compelled to be severe on their children to keep them from talking too much. Many a poor mother had been whipped nearly to death on account of their children telling white children things." Similarly, black children were taught not to stare at whites in conversation lest the young slaves be accused of listening—in effect, of violating whites' privacy. Such deception helped black slaves not only to conceal information but to glean it from whites for use by the slaves' own community. Indeed, both younger and older slaves understood the survival value of the collection and dissemination of information without whites' awareness of what was happening. Thus, children might serve as lookouts to shield older slaves' activities. Richard Carruthers had played such a role in Texas, explaining, "If I see the overseer comin' from the Big House, I sing a song to warn 'em so they no get whipped." Adults too might use songs to notify other slaves of a dance or prayer meeting or to warn of the master's or overseer's approach. Slave women might gain access to food and clandestinely feed runaways. One slave might aid another to feign illness as a way of avoiding work, a tactic that worked best for women, whose masters did not want to work them into such ill health that they could not bear more slave children.[23] As one antebellum Virginia planter complained,

> They don't come to the field and you go to the quarters and ask the old nurse what's the matter and she says, "oh, she's not . . . fit to work sir"; and . . . you have to take her word for it that something or the other is the matter with her, and you dare not set her to work; and so she will lay up till she feels like taking the air again, and plays the lady at your expense.[24]

Information control was also found in the broader slave grapevine. The "grapevine telegraph" lay primarily in those mobile bondspeople, the "personal servants, plantation men performing transportation work, black river-workers, and temporary port crews" who had access to the wider world. They would carry messages, news, rumors, even items for trade, reaching into the plantations so that information and goods could be exchanged under whites' noses.[25]

Among the most important "private" group activities that solidified the bondsmen into a community were the secret religious services. Whites saw religion as a means of social control because it taught black slaves the virtues of orderliness and obedience. The law often required white supervision of any separate slave services, though enforcement of the law was haphazard. Even when the law did not intervene, however, planters generally insisted on the right to supervise separate services. Policing that purported right was again often haphazard because it took energy away from the main business of the plantation.[26]

The slaves, however, had a very different understanding of Christianity, one that emphasized the blessedness of the meek, the sinfulness of the oppressor, and the church as a place to formulate collective aspirations. The church enabled slaves to marshal the spiritual resources to withstand and resist the masters' seemingly total power.[27]

The opportunity for slaves to engage in their own communal counterworship was so important to them that even when they were forbidden to hold their own services, they would set off into brush arbors or other secret places to praise God. Such worship might take place after the mandatory white service, and at other times slaves might sneak out midweek.[28] As former slave Beck Ilsey remembered,

> When we'd have meetin' at night, wuz mos' always 'way in de woods or de bushes some whar so de white folks couldn't hear, an' when dey'd sing a spiritual an' de spirit 'gin to shout some de elders would go 'mongst de folks an' put dey han' over dey mouf an' some times put a clof in dey mouf an' say: Spirit don talk so loud or de patterol break us up.[29]

The God worshiped by the slaves was seen as offering deliverance and liberation *in this world*. "You got a right, I got a right. We all got a right to de tree ob life," they sang. As Frederick Douglass explained, when he and his fellow slaves rejoiced, "O Canaan, Sweet Canaan, I am bound for the land of Canaan," their "Canaan" was both the heaven of the afterlife and the North of their day. "Run to Jesus, shun the danger, I don't expect to stay much longer here" was also a call to flee North. "O my Lord delivered Daniel," they pleaded, "O why not deliver me too?" In services like these, led by preachers of their own choosing, the slaves forged a sense of group autonomy and a countermorality to that of their masters.[30]

Recreational activities were another way to form cohesive social bonds in a world independent from whites. The slaves shared secular and sarcastic songs of love, work, flogging, fleeing, hope, patrollers, rebellion, and defiance. Much of what little leisure time the slaves had was filled with fishing, dancing, fiddling, racing, telling tales, playing marbles, and strumming banjos. Outlaw parties were, when they happened, especially effective opportunities to build group cohesion and autonomy, a form of resistance to the masters' power.[31]

Outlaw parties took place deep in the woods, miles from the plantation. In some ways, they were similar to the occasional master-approved frolics held in the presence of whites, involving some of the same music, songs, and dance. But there were important differences. Some dance tunes at an outlaw party held political meaning, celebrating flight and resistance. Slave women challenged the androgynous appearance imposed on some bondswomen by work and dress, outfitting themselves in finer clothes. By exchanging homespun goods and produce from gardens, they could obtain pelts or decorative cloth from itinerant traders or exchange items among themselves to gather the raw material for their new clothing. They might cook for the fete by hiding in swamps or valleys. Theft was the main way to gather the goods needed for a party, slaves often reasoning that it was not theft at all, for they simply re-arranged things, moving some of the master's property (tangible goods) to aid his other property (the slaves themselves). Young people would gather in unoc-cupied cabins or the open air to court, engage in competitive amusements, and drink alcohol. The mere fact that the slaves as a group acted to control their own pleasure was an act of defiance, and patrollers, usually few in number, were reluctant to break up such large parties.[32]

Medicine and magic also helped slaves to create their own separate world. The belief that dreams could foretell the future brought some measure of pre-dictability to life. Conjurers were also believed capable of using spells, charms, and herbs to make mean masters kind or fend off misfortunes like whippings, forced separations, illness, or death. Magic thus created a sense of occasional power over white masters; the Reverend Charles Jones, a slaveholder, be-moaned in 1842 that slaves "have . . . been made to believe that they were under a protection that rendered them invincible. That they might go any-where and do anything they pleased, and it would be impossible for them to be discovered or known." Recounted a former slave, "Dey couldn't whip her. Dey used to say she was a conjer' and dey was all scared of her." Conjurers did indeed at times have a sort of power over whites, for the tales told by black nurses to the planters' children for whom they cared convinced many whites of the truth of the conjurers' claims. On one plantation, the conjurer, one-eyed Dinkie, who "wore a snakes skin around his neck, carried a petrified frog in one pocket and a dried lizard in the other," terrified the neighborhood. He was nei-ther flogged nor stopped by patrollers, even though he never worked. White ladies sought out his cabin for fortune-telling and for love potions, leaving the slaves in "mortal fear" of Dinkie's power.[33]

Slaves also insisted on using their own midwives, herb doctors, and nurses to tend to their ills, for they did not trust white healers. Slave healers used broths made from leaves, tree bark, and other substances to treat ills ranging from toothaches to fevers to whooping cough and diarrhea. They treated men-strual cramps with tea made from gum-tree bark, and colic with syrup made from a boiled rat's veins. By looking to their own to tend their health, they "strengthened their own community and gave men and women in their own group a chance to gain status and be important," thereby mediating the effects of white power.[34]

What privacy existed among slaves did not always benefit every individual.

As with most modern cultures, privacy could shelter spousal abuse, individual squabbles, and other violence. Yet, on the whole, it was group privacy that fostered the solidarity, counterculture, and self-esteem necessary for slaves' survival, and slaves eked out enough individual and family privacy to make the slave cabin a reasonably effective training ground for incorporation into the broader slave community.[35]

Northern Response

The North still often linked privacy to protected zones of property and the person. Free-labor ideology, of course, exalted acquisition of property and personal autonomy as ways to carve out a virtuous life. That slaves neither owned property nor their own persons, therefore, necessarily implied their loss of any real individual privacy. The North was halting and ambivalent in its growing understanding that slaves were sufficiently human to deserve the opportunity to seek their own property and personal freedom in a way that would enable blacks to have independent family lives. Northerners certainly exalted the institution of the family, and the abolitionists' appeals to invasions of family privacy and bodily integrity, and to the slaves' resulting physical and emotional pain, became their greatest weapons for affecting Northern public opinion. Abolitionists portrayed the pain of whippings, rapes, and forcible intrusions on family life as not just that of individual slaves but also of the enslaved as a group. Southern repression of the abolitionists would, however, do more to alter Northern perceptions of the slaves' plight than the images of shared black suffering ever did, leading Northerners to equate the Slave Power with the suppression of whites' freedom of speech and other civil liberties— repression accomplished via brutal governmental searches and seizures paired with violent mob action. The Northern response to the denial of slaves' privacy rights, therefore, cannot be understood without first more closely examining the philosophy and experience of that ultimately influential antebellum Northern minority: the abolitionists.[36]

THE ABOLITIONISTS

Moral Suasion. During the 1830s, the abolitionist movement arose as a coherent social force. Abolitionists then believed in pacifist agitation to achieve the immediate emancipation of the slaves. They believed that slavery spread because whites were indifferent to the slaves' suffering. The abolitionists' solution was "moral suasion"—the use of preaching from pulpits, press, speeches, and all other avenues of expression to overcome the ignorance that blocked white empathy. These abolitionists linked racism to persistent indifference. Northerners initially had little reason to feel empathy for subjugated black slaves because they believed that blacks were inferior and dangerous. That same racism blinded whites to the absurd abuse of free blacks in Northern and Southern states alike. Moreover, colonization schemes, and the gradualism espoused by organizations like the American Colonization Society, incurred abolitionist ire. Abolitionist James Birney explained that these schemes acted as "an opiate to the consciences" of those who would otherwise "feel deeply and keenly the sin of slavery." Furthermore, the abolitionists believed that the indifference of free whites to slavery's evils enabled slavery to thrive and made them accomplices in slaveholder oppression. It is far better to die "as the Negro's blighted friend," declared Amos A. Phillips in 1835, than to "sit in silken security, the consenter to and abettor of the manstealers' sin."[37]

Abolitionists' repulsion by slavery stemmed both from religious zeal and from a political belief that it was inconsistent with the Declaration of Independence. Slavery was but a form of tyranny—one far more extreme than that which the Founders faced under King George—and was at war with God's law. Abolitionists were revolted by the economic exploitation, sexual license, physical abuse, gambling, drinking, dueling, and disregard for family ties that they associated with slaveholding. They embraced a Christian egalitarianism that saw slavery and racism as the fundamental evils facing the country. They sought moral revolution, rooted in Christian empathy and love, as the way out of chaos. Without that revolution first, antislavery would degenerate into gradualism and the colonizationists' racism. Violence involving whites and blacks alike was unavoidable without moral revolution. This was confirmed by the Caribbean slave revolt, Nat Turner's attacks, and Walker's *Appeal*'s call to slave arms.[38]

William Lloyd Garrison, perhaps the leading nineteenth-century abolitionist, often used the technique of "imaginative substitution" to pierce whites' indifference.[39] He used this technique especially well before the Park Street Church congregation in Boston in 1829:

> Suppose that . . . the slaves should suddenly become white. Would you shut your eyes upon their sufferings, and calmly talk of constitutional limitations? No—your voice would peal in the ears of the task-masters like deep thunder. . . . The argument that these white slaves are degraded, would not then obtain.[40]

Garrison's thought experiment here could not compare in emotional power, however, to first-hand accounts of atrocities. These accounts would be offered by white observers, by reformed slaveowners, and, most movingly, by escaped or freed slaves.[41]

John Rankin, a white observer, attempted to use the same technique of imaginative substitution in a letter intended to transform his slaveholding brother and an audience of readers. He also added the details of individual instances of slaves' pain that he had observed. He offered "shocking accounts of whipping, rape, mutilation, and suicide" to "assault the barriers of indifference."[42] Then he imaginatively extended these experiences from the slaves to himself:

> My flighty imagination added much to the tumult of passion by persuading me, for the moment, that I myself was a slave, and with my wife and children placed under the reign of terror. I began in reality to feel for myself, my wife, and my children—the thoughts of being whipped at the pleasure of a morose and capricious master, aroused the strongest feelings of resentment; but when I fancied the cruel lash was approaching my wife and children, and my imagination depicted in lively colors, their tears, their shrieks, and bloody stripes, every indignant principle of my bloody nature was excited to the highest degree.[43]

Similar accounts by former slaveholders added the appeal of white guilt and repentance. But whites' accounts were still one step removed from blacks' own terrors. Henry Bibb, for example, could "move audiences to weeping as he recounted how his wife, naked and bound, had been whipped by her brutal master." White audiences responded even more deeply to Ellen Craft, a "light-skinned fugitive," who recounted graphic physical and emotional abuse. "That so fair-complected and, to whites, attractive a black person was "subject to be traded off to the highest bidder . . . touched even the most prejudiced souls," abolitionist Samuel May Jr. averred. Talks by especially literate fugitive slaves like Frederick Douglass not only added greater immediacy but by their "superior intellectual skills and public demeanor . . . belied the myth of inferiority." Published accounts of former slaves' experiences reached a still wider audience. Abolitionists sought to instill further respect for slaves by appealing to great historical figures, like Hannibal and the Pharaohs, who were believed to be dark-skinned, and by stressing the Bible's lesson that all men are made in God's image.[44]

Whites' accounts necessarily suppressed the reality of the black slave's experience, of which the whites knew little. Racist preconceptions and ignorance made it equally hard for whites fully to connect with blacks' own accounts. It should, therefore, be unsurprising that the most successful effort to build some measure of empathy came from a white woman who had little personal observation of slavery and did not entirely embrace all of the abolitionist agenda. Harriet Beecher Stowe's *Uncle Tom's Cabin* was published in 1852, about thirty years after abolitionist agitation had begun in earnest. The book experienced great success and had an enormous impact on the North. The literate North read the work, which sold three hundred thousand copies by the end of 1852. The characters and plot appealed to a wide audience: the ever-Christian Uncle Tom for pacifists, images of violent black masculinity for those attracted to militancy, support of colonization and rich racial stereotypes for Free-Soilers (those who often opposed slavery largely to keep the North free of blacks), Eliza Harris for activist women, and the effeminate and enervated owner of Tom for free-labor ideologues, who hated the planter class. Throughout the North, entrepreneurs invented dances, composed songs, and orchestrated dramatic readings based on the book.[45]

Although the Garrisonian abolitionists used moral suasion, they purported to eschew politics because politics that preceded moral change led to compromise and degeneracy. But the Garrisonians in fact carried a highly political message. They believed that Northern indifference not only was rooted in culture and in religious infidelity but was also inherent to the structure of the Constitution itself. According to Garrison, James Madison's notes on the Constitutional Convention demonstrated that the Framers deliberately placated slaveholders and subordinated slave interests to white necessity. "The very design of the [Framers'] alliance," said Garrison, was "union at the expense of the colored population of the country." Although the Framers occasionally professed universal brotherhood, according to Garrison, "in practice they continually denied it." "No union with slaveholders" became his eventual cry. Furthermore, he argued that disunion would eventually end Southern slavery as slaves fled to a free North that was no longer obligated by a tainted Constitution to return the fugitives to their purported owners.[46]

Garrisonian moral suasion ultimately disappointed many abolitionists, who later embraced politics and jettisoned their pacifism. Political abolitionists rejected disunionism as destructive, emphasizing compromise as essential to change. They also interpreted the Constitution as an antislavery document and thus a call to action against those slaveholders and apostates to our political religion, who had forgotten the Constitution's true mandates. But the real value of moral suasion ultimately lay in Southern and Northern reaction to abolitionist preaching, an explosion of expressive violence that helped to clarify Northern thinking about free speech and that helped to spark a central idea in resolving any perceived tension between open debate and equality: the idea of the Slave Power. That idea was understandable only in the context of repression and mobocracy as the initial nationwide reaction to abolitionist moral suasion.[47]

Repression and Mobocracy. Abolitionists experienced a series of successes in the early 1830s: the formation of the Northeast Anti-Slavery Society, the establishment of forty-seven local abolitionist societies in ten states, the influx of funding from black sympathizers and from the wealth of New Yorker Arthur Tappan, and the start of campaigns to aid free blacks and discredit the Anti-Colonization Society. These efforts culminated in the "great postal campaign," in which mass mailings of abolitionist literature began in May 1835 to "sow the good seed of abolition throughout the whole country."[48]

The North and South reacted violently to these efforts, and the violence was especially swift and severe after the start of the great postal campaign. In Charleston, South Carolina, a mob broke into the federal post office, seized mailbags containing Anti-Slavery Society pamphlets and threw them into a bonfire, and hanged Garrison and Arthur Tappan in effigy. In Nashville, Tennessee, gospel messenger Amos Dress received twenty lashes in a public market for the possession of abolitionist literature. In Washington, D.C., Reuben Crandall was jailed when he received botanical samples wrapped in an abolitionist newspaper. Local committees to censor mail sprang up throughout the South, heeding Virginia senator John Tyler's warning that abolitionists were a powerful combination organized to "despoil Southern property." Other Southern leaders demanded Northern support for a federal ban on the mailing of "all papers suspected of a tendency to produce an insubordinate and insurrectionary spirit among the slaves of the South." President Andrew Jackson urged Congress to enact the ban. Meanwhile, several Southern state legislatures passed resolutions urging Northern states to pass laws silencing abolitionism. Connecticut responded in 1836 with a "gag law" that banned roving abolitionist speakers, and other Northern legislatures denounced the abolitionists. Congress passed its own gag law in 1836, prohibiting floor discussion of abolitionist petitions to end slavery.[49]

In numerous Northern cities, antiabolitionist meetings sponsored by party politicians and conservative merchants endorsed the Southern view. Mobs besieged free blacks as well as abolitionists: mobs in New York seized black churches, burned homes, and attacked blacks on the street; mobs in Philadelphia damaged forty black homes during three nights of riots. In Philadelphia, and later in Boston, mob assaults against racially and gender-integrated gatherings most clearly revealed "the motives of the rioters in defending both male and white supremacy." In Cincinnati, abolitionist leader James Birney braved a mob assault. A wave of terror swept the nation, and, to abolitionists, the mobs seemed all pervasive.[50]

In fact, Jacksonian society embraced the mobs as a tool of popular democracy. Many whites believed that unscrupulous people manipulated the established legal procedures for their own ends. They argued that mobs preserved popular rule by stopping insidious groups that the duly appointed authorities were "powerless to restrain" because authorities were "hamstrung by legal formalities." The mobs were thus diverse groups, including working-class whites but also the white elite, such as lawyers, judges, congressmen, and local businessmen, "local squires," who often instigated, organized, and led the mobs.[51]

Abolitionists inspired such ire for many reasons. Some Northerners depended on the Southern cotton market and had other commercial ties with the South that might be threatened by the end of slavery. These ties might also be severed by angry Southerners. For example, in Alton, Illinois, a significant number of residents attacked and killed the well-known abolitionist Elijah Lovejoy. The residents of Alton, Illinois, were in competition with St. Louis for the business of the Deep South, depending on the favor of New Orleans customers. Racism played an important role. The white working class feared competition from floods of free black immigrants, and whites of all classes instinctively cringed at the abolitionist challenge to white supremacy. Abolitionists appealed to all persons for support and community, ignoring local hierarchies and traditional male prerogatives. This egalitarianism outraged local "gentlemen of property and standing," who sought to maintain their social position in the face of the changing economy and other challenges to their authority. Colonizationists, who watched their funding dwindle and their cause come under siege, warned of "amalgamation" and played to popular fears of radical changes in the social order. Abolitionists were portrayed as a "dangerous association," disloyal agitators inciting blacks to violence, threatening internal national peace and Union, and enticing women from their sewing parties. The wave of violence and threatened violence against abolitionists was expressive of fundamental social values. The antiabolition violence was meant to silence abolitionists, but it also affirmed and supported an existing order of racial, gender, and class hierarchy, a productive cotton-producing slave South, and a system of popular government in which the mob ensured that elite rule did not subvert the will of the white racist majority.[52]

The abolitionists responded to this violence by defending the right to free inquiry and debate. Historian Henry Mayer summarized one of Garrison's most stirring editorials on this subject:

> Tradition, fashion, and authority all combined to chill independent thought and encourage hypocrisy, he argued, yet a moral revolution could take place only if people freely exercised their right to challenge authority, to vindicate the supremacy of reason, and to reach their own conscientious judgment. "We have too little, instead of too much, dissent among us," he said bluntly.[53]

At the same time, Garrison understood that expressive violence endangers free inquiry the most because it silences dissent and affirms a rigid orthodoxy. The wave of violence against abolitionists, and their pleas for a right to speak, significantly benefited the movement in the short run. Discussion of its goals spread, ringing debates occurred in newspapers and legislatures, and the number of converts grew. Most important, a broad constituency began to form of antislavery sympathizers who blamed violence-prone "Southern influences" in the North for jeopardizing civil liberties. For Garrison, the Compromise of 1850 seemed a setback, however, both because it symbolized a new and enduring agreement to ignore the slaves' plight and because it sparked renewed violence against abolitionists. Garrison saw a link among the new political policies, the implied threats of expressive violence in proslavery agitation, the real violence, and the suppression of abolitionist speech. He urged opposition to the Compromise to secure free expression against the "intimidation of the national parties and religious denominations."[54] Henry Mayer again concisely summarized Garrison's position:

> He took the growing number of Democratic-organized pro-Union meetings—filled as they were with racist and anti-abolitionist vituperation—as a harbinger of the 1835-style "mobocracy," and he warned that the compromise propositions contained implicit corollaries that would stifle further discussion. "Remember," Garrison declared, "we do not want the right to talk tonight only, but tomorrow also, in accordance with our convictions.[55]

As Garrison had warned, violence again erupted against abolitionists. However, unlike in the 1830s, Northern newspapers from Philadelphia to Chicago rushed to the defense of the abolitionists' right to speak and assemble. Moreover, events surrounding the Compromise of 1850 proved merely to be the lull before the storm, as a powerful antislavery, albeit not abolitionist, spirit began to sweep the North. That spirit was inspired indirectly by the abolitionists' struggles for free expression. On March 7, 1850, Daniel Webster made a three-hour address on the floor of the U.S. Senate "truckling shamelessly" to the South's defense of the then-current regime. Garrison declared that Webster had "bent his knees anew to the Slave Power." It was through this sort of appeal, more than any other, that abolitionist thinking had its greatest influence on Northern antislavery action.[56]

THE SLAVE POWER

Ordinary citizens who reviled the antiabolitionist mobs began to accept the idea that slaveholders had contempt for other Americans' freedoms of peaceful assembly and expression. The mob violence suggested that the planter class "exercised a relentless dominance over political life in the North." These rumblings marked the start of what became known as the Slave Power conspiracy. Indeed, the idea gained momentum throughout the North, and partly because of this idea, certain areas of the Midwest became hotbeds of anti-Southern activity. The power of the idea lay partly in the contrast between the Northern free-labor ideology and the Southern slave aristocracy.[57]

Free-labor ideology expressed the belief that by dint of hard work and mobility a wage laborer could achieve independence as a self-employed farmer, artisan, or entrepreneur. The dignity of labor promoted a self-disciplined, independent, hard-working, and productive character. This elevated the free society of the North over the slave society of the South.[58]

Northern free-labor supporters considered the planter class to be "parasitic exploiters" of slaves, a class that viewed labor as degrading effort, to be confined to a subordinate class. Planters were the "corrupt custodians" of their own "perverted interests." The idleness of the planters encouraged immorality. Moreover, the planter-class minority kept nonslaveholding Southern whites impoverished and ignorant, rendering them "listless, mute, and helpless" in the face of this new aristocracy. The planter class conspired not only to defend their rule but to spread it North, expanding slavery's territorial dominance and crushing Northern liberties in an effort to nationalize slavery and dominate the federal government.[59]

Salmon P. Chase offered the most influential articulation of the Slave Power idea. Chase rooted his concept in the Constitution. He insisted that the Founders deplored slavery and hoped to see it die in the fullness of time. Although they could not immediately abolish slavery, they made certain that the federal government would not support it.[60] Chase concisely articulated his interpretation of the Constitution in his first Liberty Party address in December 1841. The Liberty Party had been formed in significant part by abolitionists who rejected Garrison's purported apoliticism. In that address, Chase declared that the Constitution left slavery wholly a creature of state law. According to Chase, the Fifth Amendment's protection against deprivations of "life, liberty, and property" without due process of law barred the federal government from sanctioning slavery within its territorial jurisdiction. When a slave entered federal territory, the slave became instantly free because the federal government could not recognize the master-slave relationship. The Fugitive Slave Clause was really a compact between Northern and Southern states, giving the federal government no authority to return slaves.[61]

Chase was a practical politician and sought to cleanse the Liberty Party of extremism and propel it to a platform of widespread appeal. He distinguished between abolitionism and antislavery. Abolitionism sought to abolish slavery everywhere, but antislavery aimed at the separation of the federal government from slavery and the Slave Power. While the eastern wing of the Liberty Party continued to use the moral appeals of abolitionism, the western Liberty Party embraced Chase's approach. Although no federal court adopted his constitutional interpretation in the antebellum years, Chase's briefs for fugitive slaves and his platforms and addresses for the Liberty and Free-Soil parties publicized his constitutional interpretation throughout the North. The Republican Party platforms of 1856 and 1860 also endorsed Chase's position that Congress lacked constitutional authority to recognize or create slavery anywhere under federal jurisdiction. Even though Republicans rejected some of Chase's legal interpretations, most Republicans endorsed his position that slavery was a local institution to be divorced from the federal government and that the Founders meant to restrict slavery.[62]

This constitutional interpretation vilified the South by portraying Northern free states as faithful to the Founders and Southern efforts to expand slavery's territory as subversive of the Founders' intended regime. A conspiracy of slaveholders had subverted this regime long before and captured the national government to foster slavery's growth. This group of planters and slaveholders barred nonslaveholders in the South from political office and deprived them of the civil liberties taken for granted in the North. Slaveholders also held a disproportionate share of federal offices. The absence of a Northern consensus on slavery, and fear of Southern threats of disunion, assisted the spread of the Slave Power conspiracy. The planters, as the *New York Times* put it, were "held together like the feudal barons of the middle ages by a community of interest and of sentiment and [act] together always for the promotion of their common ends." Chase even listed federal policies that demonstrated the existence of the Power, and other Republicans had their own lists.[63]

The Slave Power idea had always been linked to the crushing of Northern civil liberties. Participants in the Albany convention that launched the Liberty Party worried that "the Slave Power is now waging a deliberate and determined war against the liberties of the free states." Senator Thomas Morris of Ohio electrified the Senate in 1839 by declaring the reality of a new power bent on destroying the liberties of the nation, a Slave Power, the "goliath of all monopolies." Liberty Party leaders recognized the rhetorical appeal of the Slave Power as a destroyer of Northern liberties. But the Kansas-Nebraska Act and the *Dred Scott* decision widely convinced Republicans that a newly aggressive Slave Power was at work to nationalize slavery, taint Northern free labor, and crush Northern liberty. Like Lincoln, many Republicans now agreed that slavery and liberty were incompatible.[64]

The Slave Power threatened the cherished principle of majority rule. One Connecticut congressman told the House that the South sought "the complete overthrow of democratic institutions, and the establishment of an aristocratic, or even monarchical, government." Other Republican leaders revealed similar fears in their private correspondence.[65]

The Civil War confirmed Republican and wider Northern thinking on the Slave Power. Republicans and many Northerners believed that the Slave Power bred a selfish, ignorant, undisciplined, and violent Southern character inconsistent with republican government. The North sought to vanquish the Slave Power and spread the benefits of Northern civilization throughout the South. The Republican Party had, like Lincoln, embraced the idea that African Americans were "men" within the meaning of the Declaration of Independence, thus entitled to rights to life, liberty, and the pursuit of happiness. Moreover, abolitionists now had enormous popularity and were in high demand as speakers and "noble prophets." Abolitionist Wendell Phillips spoke for much of the North when he condemned the old South as an "aristocracy of the skin,"

PRIVACY AND PROPERTY   207

an anachronism recalling "the days of Queen Mary and the Inquisition." The South was "intolerant of free inquiry, hostile to self-rule, wedded to 'violence,' blighted by ignorance, mired in 'idleness.'" The goal of the war was to uproot what the Slave Power had wrought, "to absorb six millions of ignorant, embittered, bedeviled Southerners (black and white) and transmute them into honest, decent, educated Christian mechanics, worthy to be brothers of New England Yankees."[66]

The Slave Power was always linked with expressive violence. Violence against slaves, against Southern dissenters and Northern abolitionists, against antislavery Northern politicians, and ultimately against all of Northern civilization in a brutal and barbaric war defined Southern civilization. This violence was not simply about labor discipline but also about messages of racial aristocracy, of the violent subordination of one group to serve the "superior group's" selfish needs. This expressive racial violence made true freedom of speech impossible, crushing dissent and corrupting souls. The Slave Power was the essence of this violence, and that Power, like the illegitimate Confederacy, was to be forever swept away.[67]

What began as an abolitionist campaign for what we would today describe as slaves' privacy rights had thus blossomed into an assault on a Southern repressive regime that challenged all Fourth Amendment interests—privacy, property, and freedom of movement—for whites as well as blacks. From mail seizures to searches for abolitionist literature to dragnet sweeps of fugitive-slave harborers, Southern governments, allied with mobs partly consisting of government officials, used the power of search and seizure to squelch dissent and silence resistance. Southerners even went so far as to exclude outside agitators from their territory and banish the unwanted. Northern mobs had, of course, joined in the repression, but by the 1850s such popular violence was viewed by much of the North as evidence of the Southern Slave Power's growing ill effects on white Northern civil liberties, in effect, an extension of the Southern hand of repression into free territory. If the sectional struggle over privacy rights thus powerfully altered Northern thinking about search and seizure rights, so too would this be true of competing conceptions of property.[68]

Property

The Social Function of Property in Persons

In Mark Twain's novel *Huckleberry Finn*, Aunt Sally asks Huck whether anyone was hurt in a steamboat explosion. Huck responds, "No'm: killed a nigger." Aunt Sally expresses relief: "Well it's lucky," she declares, "because people do get hurt." Huck and Aunt Sally's relegation of African Americans to the category of nonpersons is not, however, argues Judge John T. Noonan Jr., in his path-breaking book, *Persons and Masks of the Law,* a simple expression of racial preju-dice. Rather, the law has played a central role in suppressing African Americans' humanity. The central plot line revolves around Huck's travels with Jim, a purported fugitive slave. Jim, it turns out, is fleeing from nothing, for, unbe-knownst to him, he has been emancipated by a will. When Jim discovers this fact, "he is changed from an enchained felon to a free man." "Could Mark Twain have satirized the magic of legal rule more sharply?" queries Noonan rhetorically. This magic is worked, argues Noonan, by removing the "mask of the law" from Jim's face.[69]

"Masks of the law" are "ways of classifying individual human beings so that their humanity is hidden and disavowed." Law thus engages in a special sort of categorization process that reduces the unique complexity of each individual person to the simpler contours of the category. The person in effect becomes his or her category, nothing more. There are advantages to this simplifying and generalizing process, for rule drafters cannot foresee an infinite number of concrete situations, and judicial bias may be reduced because judges are some-what constrained by rule. But there are disadvantages too, for rules, especially legal rules, affect the attitudes and conduct of the persons to whom they are addressed. Their force exists in the minds of their audience. If rules do too good a job in displacing their subject's humanity, they can work grave injus-tice. "Where monsters have appeared in American government," Noonan cau-tions, "they have appeared to issue from the sleep of rule."[70]

The masks created by the law are more than roles. A role is a part you play, but you are not identified solely and entirely with your role. Each of us plays many roles in life—teacher, parent, child, friend—but society does not reduce us completely to any one role or even to the sum of our life's roles. A mask, on the other hand, hides the human face, the source of emotion, affection, and connection, replacing it with the mask alone.[71]

In American culture, property-law rules are the most effective instruments of dehumanization. American lawmakers have lavished particular care on all forms of property, "proclaim[ing] to the dullest intellect that ownership was desirable." Property protection has been understood throughout American his-tory as among the most central principles for social organization. Influential thinkers like John Locke, on whom the Revolutionary generation often drew for inspiration, could be read as justifying the very existence of government by the need to protect property. To label something "property" has, therefore, often meant both to subject it to the near-totalizing control of another and to exalt that other's resulting power as worthy of near-sacred protection. The reality of property law is, of course, more complex because property is often subject to a variety of restrictions and its nature and hold on the American imagination varies with time, place, locale, and political and economic circumstances. But one powerful strand of the American *ideology* of property, and one that had particular force for much of the country during the antebellum period, is that of sacred dominion. To declare that a human was "property" thus "obliterated every anthropoid feature of the slave." The law that governed disposition of slaves, for example, sent a clear cultural message: "individuals do not have to be looked at when a conveyance is made. Whoever they were, those conveyed would be distributed in accordance with the general property rules appropriate to the sale or lease of a gift or mortgage or pledge or devise made." Thus does a person become a thing.[72]

This description of the law's function in rendering persons property itself overstates the case. The law as applied to slaves did reflect at least implicitly a conflict between the slaveowner's total dominion over his two-legged property and a concern for some measure of the slaves' humanity, a flawed attempt to reconcile the competing pressures of what law professor Mark Tushnet called "humanity" or "sentiment" and "interest." Proslavery ideologues likewise often recognized and defended the special nature of slave property in some contexts, and insisted that it be treated the same as tangible personal property in other settings. Nevertheless, the humanity-suppressing function of property law, if imperfectly achieved and subjected to conflicting social forces, still had an enormous impact on the life of the slave and on the life of the institution of slavery in national politics. Slaves, as property, lacked dominion over themselves and over the hallmarks of such dominion, primarily meaning that they lacked *legal* control over property of their own. For the country, resolution of the question of the degree to which slave property was unique and whether its concomitant masking of the human face made either moral or economic sense would come about only as a consequence of war and its aftermath.[73]

Historical causation is a hard thing to puzzle out, but it is likely fair to say that law often affects social attitudes and that attitudes influence law. The stereotyping effects of property law on slaves were therefore complemented by cultural stereotypes. Among the major white Southern stereotypes of slaves were "Jack," "Nat," and "Sambo." Jack, most common in Southern antebellum literature, was an often faithful worker, so long as he was well treated, but he insisted on his own work pace and maintained emotional distance from his master, sometimes unsuccessfully repressing his anger and being subject to outbursts of theft, flight, and emotional manipulation of overseers to escape work. Nat was "[r]evengeful, bloodthirsty, cunning, treacherous and savage, . . . the incorrigible runaway, the poisoner of white men, the ravager of white women." Nat hid his true hateful feelings until the opportunity arose to wreak violence. Sambo, on the other hand, was deeply loyal to his master, finding joy in service to his better, but "[i]ndolent, . . . humorous, . . . dishonest, superstitious, improvident, and musical, Sambo was inevitably a clown and congenitally docile." Again, planters and overseers were in practice probably at some level aware of the wide variety of slave personalities and were often counseled to "study their dispositions well," as different personalities benefited most from different sorts of treatment. But it was primarily through the lens of stereotyping slaves into a limited number of categories, of gross generalizations about slaves' inherent nature, and of the suppression of slaves' humanity, of their individual differences in heart, head, and action, that the planters viewed the world. Property law helped to create and perpetuate the planters' perspective.[74]

The Planters' Perspective on Property

Southern proslavery apologists recognized and accepted the commodified aspect of human property, that is, its nature as a means of obtaining wealth, with its value measured by the price it fetched in the marketplace. But these theorists preferred to celebrate the "proprietarian" aspects of animate property, that is, its largely noneconomic function in creating a just social order. The dominant vision of such an order was an organic racial hierarchy in which the market played a role but did not dominate, in which obligations to others—especially one's inferiors—mattered more than self-interest, and in which harmony reigned between labor and capital. Southern civilization epitomized this vision at its best, while Northern "free" society was the antithesis of the just life, a world that denied natural social hierarchy and concomitant obligations of paternalist care, aggravated labor's alienation from capital, and glorified monetary self-interest above all else.[75]

The root distinction between the admirable Southern society and the reprehensible Northern one lay, these theorists argued, in the very different rules about the holding of African Americans as slaves. Although some Southern thinkers rejected the idea of equality as simply an empirically incorrect description of human nature, and others sought to assign equality a narrow, seemingly technical definition, the dominant approach embraced a more capacious idea of equality *but only among citizens*. Not all persons deserve citizenship, however, because effective republican citizenship requires wisdom, and property ownership best helps to ensure the exercise of such wisdom by those with the capacity to do so. Only whites had the natural capacity for such wisdom, and although slaveholding (slaves being the highest form of property) was not mandated for citizenship, the paradigmatic citizen in Southern legal culture was the slaveholder. Slavery was the "cornerstone" of the "republican edifice," granting the slaveholder the leisure to become informed on current questions of politics.[76] Even nonslaveholders recognized the fundamental role of slavery in maintaining a just society. Accordingly,

> [The slaveholder's] interest being identical with his neighbors, in preserving existing institutions, the Southern politician addresses always a body of men

having a common sentiment, and not to be influenced to so great an extent by the "humbugs" of demagogues. This is an influential element informing public opinion, and acts thus *conservatively* upon the public men of the South.[77]

Slavery avoids class warfare, because each citizen, poor or rich, feels that he "belongs to an elevated class," and citizens thus salute one another as neighbors. Slavery strengthened the sense of yeoman independence of the small Southern property owner, even of the nonslaveholder, for "[w]hatever other differences existed between the large plantation owner and the subsistence farmer, they shared the crucial fact that they *were* property owners, categorically distinguishing them from slaves."[78]

At the same time, these proprietarian theorists argued, class differences would arise from the forces of competition, but these resulting informal hierarchies would be forever unstable, based on individual acquisitiveness and self-interest rather than social obligation. George Fitzhugh, one of the more extreme theorists, captured this sentiment well, insisting that all societies promote some form of slavery but that the North's form, "slavery to capital," was much worse than Southern chattel slavery. In the North, the universal spirit of trade and commerce made it "as much the business of trade to devour the poor, as of the whales to swallow herrings," with no practical method available to "prevent those evils that are starving and maddening the masses in Western Europe." By contrast, wrote T. R. R. Cobb, in the South, property rights in inferiors—and blacks were a naturally inferior race—fostered paternalist protection, freeing the slave from his own weaknesses and poverty. Said Cobb, "The Negroes . . . introduced into America were gross and stupid, lazy and superstitious."[79] But, immediately upon reaching America's shores,

> The Negroes thus imported were generally contented and happy. The lamentations placed in their mouths by sentimental poets, were for the most part without foundation in fact. In truth their situation when properly treated was improved by the change. Careless and mirthful by nature, they were eager to find a master when they reached the shore, and the cruel separations to which they were sometimes exposed, and which for the moment gave them excruciating agony, were forgotten at the sound of their rude musical instruments and in the midst of their noisy dances. The great Architect had framed them both physically and mentally to fill the sphere in which they were thrown, and His wisdom and mercy combined in constituting them suited to the degraded position they were destined to occupy. Hence, their submissiveness, their obedience, and their contentment.[80]

Slaves were thus freed from the tyranny of the market and the burden of choice, and their labor assured whites the independence required for true republican equality. Without white governance, the African American would become a "[s]lave of His Lust" and indolence, as the barbarism in emancipated Haiti and Jamaica, and the experience of Liberia, had shown. Incidents of physical abuse by masters were dismissed by protectionist thinkers as rare and extreme. More generally, the "slave is incorporated into and becomes part of the family. . . . Interest joins with affection in promoting this unity of feeling. To the negro, it insures food, fuel, and clothing, medical attention, and in most cases religious instruction. . . . It provides him with a protector."[81]

Slavery also dissolved the conflict between capital and labor, argued the pro-slavery ideologues. There were two major variants on this argument. One was the "alchemical" one, again best articulated by Cobb, who maintained that the slave's status as property necessarily converted his being from that of labor into capital. Because he was owned by and governed by capital, he had no separate existence from which to become a source of social conflict. "By making the laborer himself capital," wrote Cobb, "the conflict ceases, and the interests become identical."[82]

The second variant, best represented by William Henry Trescot, more plausibly argued that slaves' dependency on the benefits of sound white mastery eliminated the need for strife and the power to instigate it. The apparent *equality* between labor and capital encouraged and enabled conflict. By contrast, "At the South, labour is dependent on capital, and having ceased to be rivals, they have ceased to be enemies. Can a more violent contrast be imagined."[83]

These various threads of proprietarian apologies for slavery—promoting republican equality among white citizens, protecting black material and emotional needs, and ending class warfare—included an acceptance of the coexisting understanding of slaves as valuable commodities. Yet it was the proprietarian aspect of human property that justified slavery as a system *superior to* Northern "free" labor and that responded to Northern claims of the inhumanity of chattel labor. Some of the ideologues therefore well understood that the justifying force of their theories would dissolve if mere commercial market impulses were not prevented from overwhelming paternalistic ones. Cobb himself worried that viewing slaves, rather than land, as the primary form of personal wealth would lead planters to invest far more heavily in human rather than real property. Lacking the surplus income and the incentive properly to fertilize old lands, upon their exhaustion, the planter and his children would seek new lands, easily removing their truly valuable property, their slaves, to the new locale. But families that lack strong local attachments also lack the civic communal ties necessary for republican government. Such rootless individuals are likely to care more for their self-interest than their social obligations to others, undermining the attitudes necessary to a proprietarian vision of slavery. Cobb railed against this eventuality but offered no convincing bulwark against it.[84]

Cobb woefully underestimated the dangers of commodified thinking about slaves, for the amount of Southern wealth held in the form of slaves was vast. "[T]he worth of the slaves owned by the planters alone was almost equal to northern investments in railroads and manufacturing combined." By 1860, planter families, those possessing twenty or more slaves, were about 3 percent of the Southern population but owned at least $1.5 billion in slaves, representing more than half the total number of slaves. Only 25 percent of white Southern families owned slaves, but the slave population of just the eleven states of the Confederacy was approximately one-third of the total populace. Slavery was, therefore, a huge economic institution that represented the most productive form of wealth in the South, with slaves producing an income stream for their owners or heirs. It would take a virtuous soul indeed to avoid valuing such enormous wealth primarily by its market price.[85]

Slaveholders could not help but recognize another distinction between human and other forms of property: human property had a mind with which to think that controlled a body with which to move. Maintaining such property therefore required a degree of physical force and emotional control unnecessary with inanimate objects. Owners correspondingly feared any appeals to the slave mind that might induce the human property to protest its condition or simply to leave. During the first year of the Civil War, Kentuckian Joshua Speed wrote a letter to Treasury Secretary Salmon P. Chase urging the silencing of any talk of emancipation by federal officials. Such talk, said Speed, endangered border-state loyalty because "[s]lave property is unlike any other—It is the only property in the world that has locomotion with a mind to control it—All men know this—and hince the jealousy of any people where it exists with any outside interference with it." Likewise, a Georgia editor worried: "Slaves are human beings, and as such, are endowed with volition and reason—This fact makes the tenure of property in slaves more delicate and precarious than that of any other species of property." This particular Southern anxiety was especially well expressed in a public letter written by South Carolina politician Armistead Burr during the dispute surrounding the Compromise of 1850. Wrote Burr, "the great function of government, in modern times, is the protection of property. Property in slaves, of all other property, can least endure aggression, and most needs the arm of government."[86]

Yet Southerners simultaneously feared the arm of government—more specifically, that of the federal government—and argued that, in important respects, slave property was no different from other forms of property, meriting at least the same, and perhaps more, protection. A range of political doctrines on the nature of the Union arose to protect white Southerners' interests in their human property. These doctrines were rooted in the ideas that society exists to protect property rights and that, since the wealthy will be relatively few in number, minority rights in property must be secured against the will of a potentially tyrannous majority. An 1849 report of a state convention in Mississippi energetically affirmed property's paramount status over all competing concerns and denied Congress any power over slavery because the "right to property preceded the constitution—it is coeval with the history of man; it exists by a paramount law of nature; it is the subject of control by State sovereignty only." In that same year, the Kentucky legislature, upon reaffirming its slavery legislation, celebrated the "right of property [a]s before and higher than any constitutional sanction." The right of property *in man* was also natural, once again justified by the duty of the strong to rule the weak. "It is asked upon what principle slavery can be justified," queried George Sawyer in an 1859 book; he answered, "upon the principle of the superiority of mind over matter, of intellect and intelligence over instinct and brute force." Although proslavery extremists rejected the natural-rights arguments of antislavery advocates, it was this appeal to natural rights in property that was most widespread among Southern politicians, editors, and others and that best resonated among the South's poor and middle classes. Protecting *all* property rights thus elicited a religious fervor, with sharp opposition to agrarianism (land redistribution), socialism (which was equated with abolitionism), and any other doctrine challenging the absolute supremacy of individual rights in property.[87]

A strong national government, many proslavery writers and politicians feared, could threaten the sanctity of Southern white rights in human property *if* that government fell under the antislavery spell. The federal government could, at least in theory, assault slavery on many fronts; it could impose tariffs to render slavery unprofitable, use diplomacy to define what was "property" on the oceans, and rule against masters' interests in lawsuits in federal courts concerning the property rights of citizens in different states. The federal commerce power might be exercised to shut down the interstate slave trade, and federal power in the territories could be used to affect the status of blacks through instructions to territorial marshals, courts, and governors.[88]

To prevent such action, many thinkers embraced a vigorous states'-rights doctrine, justifying it in numerous ways. Local control made citizens better able to guard against demagoguery and corruption among government officials than could be attained by monitoring a more distant federal presence. A government removed from the people also tended toward centralization and consolidation. Moreover, these proslavery apologists maintained, variations in local geography and other conditions would make any uniform national rule irrational. Furthermore, the Constitution was to be strictly construed as limiting federal powers to those specifically enumerated in the document. The Union was a compact among the individual states rather than with the people, with the federal government the states' agent. Consequently, individual states could "nullify" federal actions that exceeded the scope of that agency under certain circumstances. Two further ideas arose between 1828 and 1833, during the struggle over the "tariff of abominations": first, that the federal government must equally burden all states because no state would have joined the Union knowing that the consequence would be that state's impoverishment; second, that the idea of safeguarding minority rights included protecting the life, liberty, and property of citizens of smaller states from the predations of national majorities.[89]

On property rights in slaves, the South generally considered the Constitution an immutable sectional agreement that safeguarded the local institution, with some Southerners fearing that *even debate* over slavery's extension into the territories would lower property values, destroy credit, and thereby eventually bring about the death of the peculiar institution. Even compensated emancipation was seen by some as a wild idea, financially unaffordable because anything less than compensation for the *full* value of each slave would be "subversive of the rights of property and the order and tranquility of society."[90]

In sum, the Southern white conception of property in persons erased the individuality of blacks' character and behavior, justifying white rule as a paternalistic obligation of the strong to the weak while fostering true republican equality. The sacrosanct status of property rights in persons generated a correspondingly locality-obsessed theory of Union hostile to any hint of "outside" interference. But the property, it turns out, had much to say about its own status as either person or thing.

Slave Understandings of Property

Slaves probably well understood their status as property and its dehumanizing implications. The slave narratives, at least, are filled with references that suggest such an understanding. Harriet Jacobs's narrative, written as "Linda Brent," *Incidents in the Life of a Slave Girl,* is an example. *Incidents* is replete with comments on rights of resale, inheritance laws, and self-descriptions as "merchandise," among numerous other references to slaves' legal status as property. Jacobs describes slaves as "God-breathing machines [that] are no more, in the sight of their masters, than the cotton they plant, or the horses they tend." She wails at having to spend a "day gathering flowers and weaving them into festoons, while the dead body of my father was lying within a mile of me. What cared my owners for that? He was merely a piece of property." As property, she knew that her master's threats to sell her child were credible. As property, she was subject to her master's sexual overtures and his insistence to her "that I was made for his use, made to obey his command in *every* thing." She asked her readers' pity, reminding them that they never knew what it was "to have the laws reduce you to the condition of a chattel, entirely subject to the will of another."[91] Even when her friend, Mrs. Bruce, buys Jacobs's freedom, Jacobs feels degraded by being treated as but a thing:

"The bill of sale!" Those words struck me like a blow. So I was *sold* at last! A human being *sold* in the free city of New York! The bill of sale is on record, and future generations will learn from it that women were articles of traffic in New York, late in the nineteenth century of the Christian religion. . . . I well know the value of that bit of paper; but much as I love freedom, I do not like to look upon it. I am deeply grateful to the generous friend who procured it, but I despise the miscreant who demanded payment for what never rightfully belonged to him or his.[92]

Frederick Douglass's narrative is another illustration of slaves' recognition of the importance of property concepts in defining the slave. "By far the larger part of the slaves knew," Douglass wrote, "as little of their ages as horses know of theirs and it is the wish of most masters within my knowledge to keep slaves thus ignorant." White wives sometimes grew unhappy, Douglass noted, with the presence of mulatto slave children likely sired by their white masters, which contributed to the sale of those offspring. "[C]ruel as the deed may strike any one to be, for a man to sell his own children to human flesh mongers," said Douglass, "it is often the dictate of humanity for him to do so; for, unless he does this, he must not only whip them himself but must stand by and see one white son tie up his brother, of but a few shades darker complexion than himself, and apply the gory lash to his naked back." Douglass writes of being hired out and denied sleep, of slave murder being treated as anything but a crime, of money being earned but its use denied, of life being a mere dehumanized tool of those who owned or rented him. His most vivid descriptions of his own status, however, are made in connection with the death of his master, Anthony, who left his estate to be shared between his relatively benign (from Douglass's perspective) daughter, Lucretia, and his cruel, drunken son, Andrew. Douglass "was immediately sent for, to be valued with the other property."[93] He described the experience:

We were all ranked together at the valuation. Men and women, old and young, married and single, were ranked with horses, sheep, and swine. There were horses and men, cattle and women, pigs and children, all holding the same rank in the scale of being, and were all subjected to the same narrow examination. Silvery-headed age and sprightly youth, maids and matrons, had to undergo the same indelicate inspection. At this moment, I saw more clearly than ever the brutalizing effects of slavery upon both slave and slaveholder.[94]

As Harriett Jacobs recognized, one of the disabilities of slaves' *being* property was that they could not legally *own* property. In a culture in which property ownership was sanctified, this was a great disability indeed. Yet slaves were allowed to acquire and hold personal property as a favor bestowed by the master, though any property so accumulated again legally belonged to the master, as did the slave. Nevertheless, by the 1800s, an informal, if not legal, economy of pseudo-ownership and trade among the enslaved thrived, with consequences for bondspeople and masters alike. Southern-state supreme courts generally recognized that slaves could hold property at their masters' sufferance, though the Louisiana court considered slaves "entitled" to their Sunday earnings.[95]

Both task and gang systems for assigning work gave slaves some small opportunity to earn their "own" property. In the task system, each slave was expected to perform certain tasks each day, such as hoeing a quarter of an acre or splitting one hundred wooden rails. Once the assigned daily tasks were done, portions of the remaining part of the day could be used by slaves for their own benefit. In the gang system, slaves worked a specified amount of time each day rather than to perform a preassigned set of tasks. The workday often ran from sunup to sundown. During the antebellum period, however, most slaves in gang-labor areas were usually not required to work for their masters on Sunday and might not be required to do so for at least part of Saturday, though such "leisure" time could be reduced or even eliminated during the harvest season.[96]

The challenge for slaves was finding enough time to work for themselves. During harvest season, the workday might be sixteen hours long. Much of what time remained in the day or week might need to be devoted to personal chores like fetching firewood, washing clothes, fixing cabins, or walking evenings and mornings to see children or spouses abroad. Accumulating property therefore meant laboring "by the light of a torch at night" or, in one former slave's words, "till the fowls crow for day, by moonlight & firelight." Some masters might ease the burden by providing a small stipend during harvest time, as did Charles Ball's overseer, who paid one cent for every pound of cotton harvested over the daily fifty-pound quota for adult men. Nevertheless, it remained a heavy burden.[97]

Having land to work was usually less of a problem. Masters generally at least let slaves work a garden patch adjacent to their cabins. Often, slaves would also be allotted larger plots of land away from the slave quarters. Ansy Jeffries of Marshall County, Mississippi, reported slaves having approximately two-acre "patches of land . . . to work as their own." Jerry Smithson of Yazoo County "always had an acre or two of ground" for his family and sometimes "as high as 3 or 4 acres." Low-country slaves "were allowed all the land they could tend without rent," an amount that probably averaged between four and five acres. One Louisiana plantation set aside fully 10 percent of its acreage for "the negroes for their own use" in addition to cabin gardens and chicken yards. Masters might, however, limit what could be grown on these plots; for example, some did not permit cash crops like cotton, tobacco, and rice for fear of stolen crops being passed off as the slaves' own.[98]

Slaves with special skills might earn money in ways other than farming.

Carpentry, blacksmithing, hat making, breaking wild horses, and unloading steamboats were among the sorts of tasks in which slaves might engage. Hiring out, when permitted by a master, was another way to earn money, though so much was due to be returned to the master that profits for the hired slave might be meager.[99]

Slaves might market goods in nearby cities, selling a wide array of items. In the Sunday markets of many Southern towns, slaves might regularly be seen hawking brooms, doormats, chairs, tables, chickens, eggs, fruit, pails, and tubs. Even on the plantation, some slaves did such a brisk business with visitors from outside the plantation to the slave's cabin that he or she was known as having "customers." Slaves also exchanged goods, money, and labor with one another and with masters and overseers.[100]

Some slaves earned enough to buy themselves out of slavery, though some masters might refuse to sell or would cheat the bondspeople, or circumstances might achieve the same result. For example, one slave found himself close to buying his freedom when his master died. Having no receipts to prove his finances, the slave was put on the auction block and sold. Other slaves saw "freedom" as not worth having in a South that imposed rigid restrictions on free blacks, perhaps requiring whites to stand in for blacks in business transactions or having a white guardian who, as one slave put it, "would stand in the relation of master to me," in which case "I preferred to remain with my old master and keep my money."[101]

Apart from occasionally enabling slaves to buy their freedom, and more often modestly improving their material well-being, "independent" slave economic activity also helped to strengthen family and community ties. A slave ripped from his family and placed in strange surroundings would feel lost. Working together to achieve economic goals was one way to "make kin," to build the solidarity and affection necessary to joining fictive family. Charles Ball, when wrenched from his wife and children in Maryland to live in a cabin with strangers, agreed to put all his earnings into a common stock if he were treated as one of the family, thus enabling him to share in a portion of garden proceeds. His cabinmates agreed and indeed thereafter treated him as family. Family and other obligations could also be strengthened by inheritance practices, and property concerns might enter into marriage decisions.[102]

Slaves might identify property as their own by branding livestock, crudely fencing cabin gardens, and publicly displaying their possessions. They dealt with alleged intracommunal theft by divination ceremonies to identify the thieves, with churches often also serving as the forum to settle property disputes. The gravest dangers to slaves' property might come, however, from masters capriciously changing rules or "asking" to be given some of the slave's property (and who would dare refuse?), though most masters seem not to have taken advantage of their legal rights.[103]

Another way for slaves to accumulate property was by hunting. The most valued of slaves would be chosen by masters to accompany them on the hunt. Although these huntsmen often did tasks auxiliary to the hunt, they might also be allowed to join in the hunting itself. Whites established a hierarchy of game, and slaves were often only allowed to seek out "inferior" animals. Whatever was caught had to be returned to the master, who then decided to whom to apportion what meat. Frequently, whites kept the partridges and ricebirds for their own table, leaving the owls, rabbits, raccoons, and opossums for the slaves. This was a great benefit for the slave, who could bring kill back to the quarters to share with family and friends or to exchange with whites, including nearby storekeepers for cash, household goods, or treats like liquor and candy. Huntsmen gained prestige and respect of many in the slave community by bringing sorely needed meat to the quarters, and they gained an enhanced sense of autonomy both from the kill and its fruits.[104]

With the indulgences of their masters, huntsmen might even take the field without direct white supervision, so long as they brought home meat. The huntsmen usually carried passes to protect them from the slave patrols and other whites. Said one Alabama slave, "at night if any ob de men wanted to break a night's rest, he cud go 'possum an' rabbit huntin', so long as he got a pass from his boss, an' wuz in de fiel' de nex' mawning on time." Explained another Alabaman, "slaves could hunt and fish on the plantation all they wanted," but "if they slipped off and the 'patrolers' caught them, they sure were in for a good beating." The benefits of hunting were so great, however, that slaves might take the field even without their owners' explicit sanction, though hunting, of course, could be done only when daily work for the masters was over, a relatively small amount of time.[105]

Because of the legal bar on slaves' ownership of property and of whites' fear of slaves with weapons, huntsmen generally lacked guns, having to rely on traps, dogs, or sticks. "Only the most trusted slaves," however, "carried guns with their owners' consent," despite legal restrictions designed to limit the use of guns to white males. Those who did carry also monopolized and guarded use of the weapon. Some slaveholders, partly from caprice and partly from fear of arming slaves and enhancing their autonomy, banned hunting entirely. Others, on the other hand, loaned guns to huntsmen, expecting their prompt return, but in some instances, "they apparently owned the guns outright."[106] More often, masters who allowed slaves to use weapons arranged affairs to limit slaves' perceptions of increased independence:

Slaveholders made certain that armed slaves never outnumbered whites on any given outing. On the occasions when whites hunted alone, they rarely took the field with more than one armed slave companion. Even the largest outings, which could include a score of slaves, usually only included a single armed huntsmen. Slaveholders also maintained the distance between slave huntsmen and white women. Slaveholders never overtly recognized the masculinity of their huntsmen, but as a drama of masculinity, hunting made this distance especially important. Slaveholders ensured that huntsmen never interacted with white women outside the presence of a white man—and then only rarely. Slaveholders also circumscribed the movements of their huntsmen when they shot for the pot. When slaveholders sent them into the field, the huntsmen customarily carried written passes, which any white person might demand for inspection. Particularly suspicious slaveholders monitored the amount of powder and shot carried by their huntsmen by comparing the amount of ammunition they dispensed with the number of kills their huntsmen brought back home.[107]

Whites permitted slaves' involvement in hunting because of the prize of meat and the opportunity to display white mastery. But why did whites more generally allow black slaves to accumulate and trade property? There were two reasons: first, masters would shift part of the cost of maintaining the slaves to the slaves themselves, expecting them to supplement their diets, clothes, and other needs with their own efforts; second, the informal slave economy was believed to enhance white control, for slaves could be threatened with suspension of their economic privileges should they fail adequately to comply with white demands. Yet slaves often did not view these opportunities as a gift. As one former slave, who had paid his master fifteen dollars per month from working as a wagon driver, responded when asked whether he owed his master a debt, "I do not owe him anything now. I think by rights, *he owes me*, for all the money *I paid him.*"[108]

Despite the benefits for masters, there were sporadic attempts to limit or halt slaves' trading, including Anti–Slave Traffic Associations and newspaper complaints about illegal trading. These associations might advertise laws against slave self-hiring, trading in liquor, and gathering in large groups and laws that required masters to feed slaves enough so that they did not need to go to market. But all this noise likely had little impact on the informal economy itself. Growing hostility toward blacks and the heightening of national tensions over slavery as an institution eventually led, however, to the replacement of protest associations with "rifle corps" and "vigilance committees" meant to root out abolitionists but also used to make slave marketing more difficult. Rising worldwide cotton demand also made masters more jealous of slaves' time so that slaves' independent economic activity may have been curtailed by the very late antebellum period. As one witness put it, the trend was "to take away the capacity of the negroes to take care of themselves."[109]

Slaves thus had direct experience with property ownership and its advantages, and many may have seen it as a reward for the fruits of their labor, while recognizing that this link was an insecure one, for they held these fruits at their masters' sufferance. Slaves also probably understood that their status as human property was what denied them a *legal* right to property ownership and thus denied their full humanity.

Northern Perceptions of Property

The Revolutionary generation of antislavery advocates coalesced around several core ideas. Notably, they believed that slavery violated the labor theory of value—the concept that only those who labor are entitled to its fruits. Relatedly, a number of Americans believed that English law, as articulated by Blackstone and as recited by Lord Mansfield in the *Somerset* decision, established a natural right to self-ownership. Slavery was therefore a form of theft, first of the person by force, then of the fruits of his labor, and finally of his progeny. Moreover, slavery set up an aristocracy, a group of people living in splendor off the fruits of others' labor. Aristocracies were antithetical to freedom and to majority rule. Civilization's very existence indeed required the maintenance of property rights, but for this generation, those rights were violated by slavery itself.[110]

"Modern" abolitionism began in the early 1830s. Although the new abolitionists reflected less of the Enlightenment spirit of reason that animated the early antislavery generation and more evangelical emotion, they shared much with their forebears, while adding to the intellectual mix. Antebellum abolitionists believed in immediatism, the necessity for ending slavery *now*, regardless of any other costs or concerns. Most of them embraced a significant racial egalitarianism. Yet property rights remained at the heart of their thinking.[111]

The antebellum abolitionists of course embraced the labor theory of value. But they also objected to slavery because it used law to turn people into property, a sin that offended against the image of God, in which human beings were made. As Theodore Weld declared, "ENSLAVING MEN IS REDUCING THEM TO ARTICLES OF PROPERTY," making, in Martha Ball's words, "merchandise of the image of God." To do so was to treat men as "brutes and things," to be "bought and sold like cattle in the market," rather than as but "little lower than the angels," as God intended them to be. Because owning *another* insulted God, these abolitionists further concluded, each human being owned only himself. As Joshua Giddings put it in the U.S. House of Representatives, because God gave man dominion over all other earthly creatures, "This is the title by which we claim property in the brute creation; but man can claim no such title to his fellow man."[112]

Antislavery extremists objected to slavery as building up an aristocracy of money, an "aristocracy" because of the command the slaveholders gained over both people and vast amounts of property. These aristocrats endangered democracy and forgot that free labor was the foundation of community. "What is the Slave Power?" Wendell Phillips thundered in 1860. "It is," he continued, "two thousand millions of dollars invested in one kind of property. You know the power of money." Another abolitionist captured a similar sentiment during the Civil War, reminding his readers that the slaveholders were a "haughty and intolerant aristocracy" and that the "disposition on the part of the rich is to trample the poor, and of the strong to crush the weak."[113]

The abolitionists held a variety of views on the function and degree of malleability of property rights. What they shared in all this diversity, however, was a general understanding that property rights should be judged by their usefulness in contributing to the general welfare. "[T]hey were only absolute in the sense of reward to individual laborers but were otherwise to be shaped and reshaped by circumstances."[114]

Antislavery Northerners outside the abolitionist community rejected the abolitionists' immediatism, commitment to racial equality, and evangelical emotionalism. Yet across the political spectrum, and increasingly in the North generally, they shared an analysis of property rights strikingly similar to that of the abolitionists. In practice, this meant that they did not see immediately ending slavery as more important than other goals like preserving the Union. Furthermore, however much they might object to property rights of man in man, they recognized that such rights had been enshrined in the Constitution. But they saw that constitutional compromise was based on fundamental misconceptions of the appropriate nature of property—the same critique embraced by the abolitionists, namely, that slavery violated the principles of just reward embodied in the labor theory of value, sinned against God's image, and risked the rise of an aristocracy. The free-labor aspect of this understanding of property, as conceived by Republicans, was especially well captured in a resolution at an 1851 Wisconsin mass meeting, which declared "that in our political system all property . . . is a right which society creates for the recompense of Labor; that with us all property is simply industry rewarded with its just fruits." This quotation also embodies the widening Northern understanding, within the limits of the labor theory of value, that legislative redefinition of property rights to serve the interests of the community was appropriate.[115]

Two Republican leaders who spoke about property rights often, William Seward and Abraham Lincoln, helped to move Republican thinking toward an acceptance of the malleability of property rights. Both men, implicitly or explicitly, saw a distinction between property and liberty, a distinction generally not previously adequately recognized. They further believed that where the two were in conflict, liberty should prevail. Seward, New York's senator during the 1850s and former Whig governor, explained that property was "jealous of liberty" and had "a bias toward oppression," property holders tending to flock together to attack others. The ideal society existed when "the rights and duties of the property classes are defined and regulated" while liberty is sufficiently "bounded as to secure property rights against social or individual aggression." Adjusting the proper balance between the two was thus the "great problem of government."[116]

Lincoln similarly recognized that the sectional conflict's resolution was stymied by the South's seeing the slaves as some $2 billion worth of property. Explained Lincoln, "Public opinion is formed relative to a property basis. Therefore, the slaveholders battle any policy which depreciates their slaves as property, what increases the value of this property they favor." But, said Lincoln, property in man was immoral, for "God gave man a mouth to receive bread, hands to feed it, and his hand has a right to carry bread to the mouth without controversy." The problem with the Democratic Party ("the democracy") of his time, said Lincoln, was that it held "the *liberty* of one man to be absolutely nothing, when in conflict with another man's right of *property*. Republicans, on the contrary are for both the *man* and the *dollar,* but in cases of conflict the Man *before* the dollar." Many Republicans shared Lincoln's sentiment.[117]

The North's theory of the just system of property law does not alone explain the intensity of Northern opposition to slavery's territorial expansion. That intensity stemmed from Northern fears that an aggressive South threatened the long-term survival of the North's superior free-labor society. The diseases of the Southern slave system—its control by a haughty and aristocratic Slave Power, its impoverishment of Southern society by robbing slaves of incentives to work, and its driving down and degrading the dignity and price of free white labor—did not ensure that the North would prevail in a contest between the two systems. This risk was especially fearful because the large farms of the South, reminiscent of ancient civilizations built on force, were a frightening contrast to the virtuous middling society of equal citizens, midsized lands, and independent farmers of the North. The Southern aristocracy's intolerance of opposition or dissent to their leeching away the fruits of free labor made them more frightening still. Yet, because the Constitution protected the Southern system of property ownership, the North saw itself as able to do little other than confine slavery to its Southern home, to cabin the backward, aristocratic, serflike society that was the very antithesis of freedom.[118]

The problem for the North was that it feared that the slave system's very weaknesses, combined with the new technology of the transportation revolution, would be precisely what would undermine Northern free society. Steamboats, railroads, and the growing demand for textiles were increasingly creating a national economy, reducing local price variation and enabling Southern slave labor to compete directly with Northern free labor. Slave labor was necessarily cheap, as masters sought to maximize profits. To compete, free labor's wages had to fall, which would erode or end the savings that enabled social mobility. This same transportation revolution also enabled more Northerners personally to visit the South, and they did not like what they saw.[119] William Seward, among others of the time, well articulated the nature of the threat:

> Hitherto, the two systems have existed in different states, but side by side within the American Union. This has happened because the Union is a confederation of states. But in another aspect the United States constitute only one nation. Increase of population, which is filling the states out to their very borders, together with a new and extended network of railroads and other avenues, and an internal commerce which daily becomes more intimate, is rapidly bringing the states into a higher and more perfect social unity or consolidation. Thus, these antagonistic systems are continually coming into closer contact, and collision results.
>
> Shall I tell you what this collision means? . . . It is an irrepressible conflict between opposing and enduring forces, and it means that the United States must and will, sooner or later, become entirely a slaveholding nation, or entirely a free-labor nation.[120]

Northern middle and lower classes would compete most directly with slave labor. The Republican appeal to the dangers posed by slavery to Northern workers was thus an effective one. Agitated by Democratic speakers, workers feared the competition to whites that might result from emancipation's "releas[ing] hordes of ex-slaves out of the South to clog up northern labor markets and drive down wages." Antimarket critiques of "free" labor itself being treated by capital as a mere commodity also struck a chord with the working classes. Nevertheless, the theory behind Seward's irrepressible-conflict speech— that black workers did not have to move North to compete with free labor— was one that the workingman could not ignore. Moreover, competitive forces were no guarantee that the best system would win the contest. Republican George Weston admitted that "[i]t is certainly true that wealth is more rapidly augmented under free, than under slave systems, and that, in a large sense, free labor is cheaper [due to productivity] than slave labor." Nevertheless, "although exhausting and impoverishing in all its results and all its influences, it [slavery] is irresistibly and unmistakably cheaper, when applied to the ruder processes of agriculture, than free labor, which it overpowers and reduces to its own level." Although many writers have argued that slave labor could not profitably have been used in industrial manufacturing, they are wrong. After 1880, the "obvious trends were mass production in large hierarchical business units; machinery to replace skilled labor; unskilled, virtually brute, labor to tend the machines; a bureaucracy to oversee the system; and an internal police to keep laborers from organizing." Had slavery as an institution not been destroyed before 1880, the direct conflict between slave and free labor in a national market may indeed have come about. Whether these fears were rational or not, they contributed to the widespread Northern belief that the Southern system of property law that rendered black persons property posed a real economic and moral danger to white Northern society.[121]

The stridency of some Northern rhetoric must be understood in this context. A corrupt Southern civilization's thieving the fruits of slave labor and blaspheming God's image was poised to make its local aristocracy a nationwide one. Were that to happen, the American Revolution for freedom, and thus by definition against aristocracy, would have failed, effectively meaning the death of the nation itself, at least as many Northerners had come to define it. If perhaps not always so starkly phrased, this summary lays bare the core fears of many Northerners. Yet this same unholy system of property law was embraced by the Constitution, which thus created a conundrum: how to save the Union from its aristocratic enemies without sacrificing that very Union's fabric as sewn together by the founding constitutional document itself? Northerners seemed to believe that they could somehow live with, perhaps must live with, this contradiction. The Civil War would soon prove them wrong.[122]

11 Civil War and Reconstruction

Civil War

The South Secedes

Upon Abraham Lincoln's election as president of the United States, a number of Southern states quickly seceded. Southerners feared the Republican Party was not simply a political opposition but a hostile force bent on destroying the slaveholding system. Secession's proponents feared that Lincoln would repeal fugitive laws, prohibit the interstate slave trade, reverse *Dred Scott* by reorganizing the Supreme Court, and abolish slavery in federal territories, forts, arsenals, and the District of Columbia. Said Senator Clement C. Clay of Alabama, the Republican Party platform was "as strong an incitement and invocation to servile insurrection, to murder, arson, and other crimes, as any to be found in abolitionist literature." A North Carolina editor feared that Republicans would "put the torch to our dwellings and the knife to our throats."[1]

There were many reasons for Southern secession, but two reasons that are given insufficient emphasis are the South's worries about the power of Northern ideas—of untrammeled free speech infecting the South—combined with virulent Southern racism and an associated perceived challenge to white supremacy. Southern leaders believed that the survival of their peculiar institution turned on tight internal unity that could be undermined by class or other divisions. Controlling the dissemination of antislavery ideas was central to the preservation of this unity.[2]

One early effort to ensure unity stemmed from Congress's 1836 adoption of a law requiring that all mail be delivered to its destination. Amos Kendall, President Andrew Jackson's postmaster general, led local postmasters to interpret this law to mean that the mail had reached its destination when it arrived at local post offices. In states worried about abolitionist sentiment, local postal authorities thus seized subversive literature and never sent it to its intended recipients. The law had criminalized a postmaster's "unlawfully" detaining the mail. But, as Attorney General Caleb Cushing concluded in his 1858 opinion about delivering the *Cincinnati Gazette*, "it cannot be unlawful to detain that which it is unlawful to deliver." By this statement Cushing recognized that states could make delivery of subversive antislavery literature from the local post office to the intended recipients a crime, and many states did just that.[3]

These understandings prevailed up until Lincoln's election, but Southerners feared that Lincoln might change this practice and appoint Republican postmasters who would flood the South with radical mail. Kendall originally justified his interpretation of the 1836 law on the basis of an obligation "recognized and guaranteed by the Constitution itself" to do nothing that would undermine the institution of slavery. Since Lincoln did not hold this view, Southerners could not believe that he would adhere to past practice, and Southerners more generally feared that Lincoln would use his power of federal patronage to produce an antislavery force within the slave states.[4]

Had Lincoln wanted to revise executive interpretations of the 1836 law, there certainly was some legislative history to support his doing so. Indeed, the 1836 statute was adopted after the defeat of a bill proposed by Senator John C. Calhoun that would have prohibited any deputy postmaster from knowingly receiving and mailing or delivering "any pamphlet, newspaper, handbill or other printed, written, or pictorial representation touching the subject of slavery, directed to any person or post office where, by the laws thereof [that is, by the laws of that state], their circulation is prohibited." Items deposited in the post office were to be burned if not withdrawn by their senders within one month. The bill's ultimate defeat was on constitutional grounds, including primarily the First Amendment's limitation on the federal government's abridging the freedom of the press and, according to at least one senator, Thomas Morris of Ohio, the Fourth Amendment's guarantee of the people's security in their "persons, houses, papers, and effects against unreasonable searches and seizures." Morris conceded that states could punish persons who read or distributed publications prohibited by state law but denied that postmasters were subject to such laws.[5] Morris recognized a close connection between Fourth and First Amendment rights in the proposed legislation:

[W]e, the free states . . . are called on to put the gag into the mouths of our citizens, to declare that they have no right to talk, to preach, or to pray, on the subject of slavery; that we must put down societies who meet for such purposes; that we shall not be permitted to send abroad our thoughts or our opinions upon the abstract question of slavery; that the very liberty of thought, of speech, and of the press shall be so embarrassed as to be in many instances denied to us.[6]

Morris's statement was also apparently a response to Southern calls for the North to suppress abolitionists. Calhoun indeed proposed his legislation because he believed that the circulation of antislavery literature in the South would toll the death knell for the peculiar institution. Calhoun's bill had been a response to President Jackson's call for congressional legislation to "prohibit, under severe penalties, the circulation in the Southern states, through the mail, of incendiary publications intended to instigate the slaves to insurrection." Calhoun had opposed such legislation because it assumed a congressional power to control postal circulation based on the content of the mail. But if Congress had such power and now used it to aid slavery, it would also in the future have "power to abolish slavery, by giving it the means of breaking down all the barriers which the slaveholding states have erected for the protection of their lives and property." The "means" for destroying slavery would be free distribution of abolitionist literature. Calhoun felt he was on safer ground to recognize the power over local mail distribution as residing in the states, with the postal authorities obligated to obey state law.[7]

Although Calhoun's bill was defeated, executive interpretation of the general 1836 act regulating the post office apparently gave him the victory he desired. Moreover, by the time of Lincoln's election, the presidential power to use the patronage power to further the governing party's agenda seemed well established. Lincoln had promised not to do so, but, given the history of the 1836 act, the growing sectional tensions over slavery in the ensuing decades, and the slaveowners' vision of the Republican Party as one of wild-eyed antislavery fanatics, Southerners simply did not believe Lincoln's assurances.[8]

Race prejudice loomed large in the secession debates as well. By February 4, 1865, one month before Lincoln's inauguration, seven Deep South states—South Carolina, Mississippi, Florida, Alabama, Georgia, Louisiana, and Texas—had enacted secession ordinances, representatives from those states meeting that very day in Montgomery, Alabama, to create a new government and a pro-slavery constitution. To bolster the new Confederacy, commissioners were sent from the already-seceded states to the conventions of the remaining Southern states considering secession. The apocalyptic picture they painted to their Upper South brethren was one of "the looming specter of racial equality," "the prospect of race war," and "racial amalgamation," three interrelated ideas that captured Southern white fears.[9]

Virginia's secession-convention debates exemplified Southern fears of unfettered free speech and rampant racial equality. Convention attendees worried that slavery in the Upper South states of Missouri, Kentucky, Delaware, Maryland, and even Virginia was too weak to survive the rise of a Southern Republican Party that appealed to nonslaveholding whites and was supported by federal patronage. Slaveowners worried that free speech would spark a debate like that concerning abolition of the institution in Virginia in the early 1830s, in the immediate aftermath of Nat Turner's rebellion. George Randolph warned the Virginia convention delegates of 1861 that proslavery ideology was too little appreciated by the masses to survive such renewed debate and that the fear generated by mere discussion of the prospect of abolition would encourage planters to flee further South with their valuable human property, thus surrendering the Upper South to free soil. Lincoln's vow not to oppose a constitutional amendment guaranteeing federal noninterference with slavery where it already existed did not calm these fears. Senator Thomas L. Clingman of North Carolina likewise worried that without secession, Lincoln would strip Southern armories of all weapons and that step-by-step abolition would create a "large free negro population," which meant the "destruction of society." Similarly, several months earlier, Henry I. Benning, associate justice of the Georgia Supreme Court, had predicted that Lincoln would end slavery, and "a war between the races would inevitably erupt, followed by Northern intervention on behalf of the blacks and a furied exile of the whites." The appeals to racial and related fears worked, and a number of Upper South states joined the new Confederacy.[10]

The Confederate constitution was designed to address these very fears. Any action by an individual Confederate state that abolished slavery was null and void, with slaveholders guaranteed rights to travel with their slaves anywhere in the Confederacy and slavery protected in the territories as well as the states. The euphemisms of the U.S. Constitution ("persons held to labor") were replaced with the unequivocal racialized term "negro slavery."[11] The new Confederate vice president, Alexander Stephens, summed up the philosophy underlying the new nation:

> Our new government is founded upon exactly the opposite idea [of equality recited in the Declaration of Independence]; its foundations are laid, its cornerstone rests, upon the great truth, that the negro is not equal to the white man; that slavery—subordination to the superior race—is his natural and normal condition.[12]

Slaves on the Move

The initial Northern response to the Confederate states' secession was a cautious one, as the North still embraced the faint hope that war could be averted. Lincoln in particular feared alienating the border states, especially believing that losing strategically important Kentucky would be a brutal blow to the Union cause. The efforts of the Peace Convention of Northern and Southern representatives meeting in Washington, DC, to seek a compromise had collapsed over Northern refusal to agree to remove barriers to the expansion of slavery into the territories. Nevertheless, Northerners at first proceeded in the hope of placating the Confederates. The Northern public was initially more concerned with restoring Union than ending slavery, a position publicly declared in the congressional Crittenden-Johnson Resolutions of 1861.[13]

But the tide of Northern home-front opinion began to take an angry, vengeful turn as the Confederacy seized U.S. forts, customs houses, arsenals, and post offices. Fort Sumter, the location of the first battle of the war, was only the initial significant Confederate seizure effort, with many others to follow. Southern planters also owed millions of dollars of debt to Northern merchants and bankers. Jefferson Davis officially authorized privateering against Northern ships, and Georgia's Governor Joseph Brown repudiated debt owed to the North and ordered funds to be deposited in the Georgia state treasury, a move that was soon imitated by other Confederate states. President Davis finally sought, and the Confederate Congress passed, legislation repudiating all Northern debts and requiring them to be paid into the Confederate treasury. Northerners were concerned not only with the military value of the seized coastal forts but also with their lost role in collecting customs revenue, and secession also endangered trade with Northern and Midwestern states as the Confederacy sought control over important waterways. Some Midwestern states like Iowa and Illinois had stayed neutral early on, but in January 1861 the Confederate capture of customs houses at New Orleans and placements of artillery along the banks of the Mississippi near Vicksburg roused the sleeping Midwesterners, who feared a lessening of trade on the mighty river.[14]

The seizures were a blow to national pride. Moreover, the assault on Northern private property and on federal property paid for with Northern tax revenues galvanized Northern unity in a way that secession alone had not. The Northern home front and politicians began calling for direct assaults on Southern property to undercut the South's economy as a way of winning the war. The defeat of Union troops at Manassas Junction, the first major battle of the war, on July 21, 1861, further heightened Northern calls for vengeance, for rumors spread of Confederate atrocities, including Southern soldiers cutting Union boys' throats and ghoulishly desecrating or mutilating their dead bodies. Meanwhile, Union soldiers returning from the battle told Congressman James Blaine that slaves "by the thousands" had been cooking, building earthworks, driving teams, "adding four millions," in Blaine's words, "to the population from which Confederates could draw their quotas of men for military service." Rumors of slaves building entrenchments and carrying arms led to a slowly dawning Northern realization that slaves were a resource that could hurt or help the Union cause.[15]

Simultaneously, slaves began to take matters into their own hands. In late May 1861, three Virginia fugitives asked General Benjamin Butler, Union commander at Fort Monroe, Yorktown, for sanctuary. Butler was a Massachusetts Democrat, and no abolitionist, but he nevertheless saw the tactical value in seizing slaves that might otherwise be used in the Confederate cause. That recognition dawned on him when the fugitives told him that they had labored in artillery earthworks. He declared a policy of treating runaways as "contraband." News of his decision raced through the slave grapevine so that nine hundred fugitives were at "Freedom Fort" by July 1861. In that same month, the House adopted a resolution declaring that it was no part of the duty of the soldiers to return fugitives. Other army commanders, however, viewed the growing number of fugitives behind Northern lines or on the march with Northern troops as distracting the military from its main duties, and some commanders were more sympathetic than others to the rights of slaveholders, especially loyal ones, under the fugitive-slave laws. A number of army officers therefore elected to return fugitives to their owners, effectively acting as federal marshals. Early in the war, soldiers followed these return orders. But personal experience with fugitives' suffering and with the invaluable information and services they provided to the Union troops led some soldiers increasingly to ignore commands to return fugitives to their masters.[16]

By March 1862, Congress, outraged about some commanders' countermeasures against the refugees, had approved an addition to the articles of war that prohibited the return of fugitives by members of the armed forces. This action had followed the first Confiscation Act of the emergency congressional session of the summer of 1861, which declared all slaves used in aid of the Confederate war effort to be forfeit and discharged them from any service owed to their rebellious owners. The vague act lacked any statement of who was to enforce its terms and required case-by-case determinations of which slaves had been used in aid of rebellion, rendering the legislation of little practical value but of great symbolic value in seemingly striking at the resources with which the Confederacy could wage war.[17]

Lincoln was not yet ready, however, to enforce action against slave "property" in any broad fashion. Though a significant number of other officers followed Butler's lead in putting fugitive slaves to work for Union forces as contraband, rather than returning them to their owners, General Fremont had gone further, issuing a proclamation that emancipated slaves in Missouri in August 1861. In March 1862, General David Hunter, commander of the Union's Department of the South, declared emancipation in Georgia, South Carolina, and Florida. Lincoln countermanded both orders. Fremont's replacement, General Halleck, then decreed that no fugitive slaves would be allowed to enter Union camps under his command, and any doing so must be immediately excluded.[18]

The usefulness of Halleck's order was limited, however, because soldiers were not willing to forgo the aid of African Americans as informants and laborers.

As one Union private put it, "If *a culled man* will dig trenches and chop timber and even fight the enemy, he is just the fellow we want." Front-line soldiers also could not ignore the military intelligence communicated by the slaves, with some slaves going back even hundreds of miles into Confederate territory to liberate family and friends, often bringing Union troops with them. Complained one South Carolina Confederate, "A negro brought the Yankees from Pinesville and piloted them to where our men were camped, taking them completely by surprise, capturing Bright and killing two of his men." Georgia planter Charles Colcock Jones Sr. cautioned his family about the fugitives: "They are traitors who may pilot an enemy into your *bedchamber!* They know every road and swamp and creek and plantation in the county, and are the worst of spies."[19]

Slaves who fled to Union lines faced major obstacles. They left family and friends behind, not knowing whether they would ever see them again or whether those remaining would face the masters' wrath. They had to evade masters, overseers, slave patrols, and Southern troops. Moreover, recapture or moving fronts might and did operate to return many fugitives to slavery, where they sometimes faced torture or execution upon their return. Nevertheless, they continued to come, and the war ultimately liberated hundreds of thousands of former slaves.[20]

Moreover, the Fugitive Slave Act of 1850 had not been repealed. In the summer of 1861, Attorney General Edward Bates stated the administration's policy when he instructed a federal marshal that all laws must be faithfully executed and that any failure to do so with respect to fugitive slaves would be a misdemeanor—an action again meant to placate loyal border states. Furthermore, there was some initial enforcement activity at the war's start in Chicago, where the Democratic marshal started arresting known fugitives, causing a panic in the African American community. The greatest furor surrounded the vigorous enforcement of the 1850 act by Washington, DC's Virginia-born federal marshal, Ward H. Lamon, who aided both kidnappers and legal owners and even entered army camps to arrest fugitives. In the spring of 1862, the district's military commander, General James S. Wadsworth, responded, sending soldiers to seize the city jail, arrest the jailer, and release all fugitives confined there. Lamon, his deputies, and local police recaptured the jail, but the incident ended peacefully with an exchange of prisoners, though additional conflicts arose in the ensuing months. Still, the rise in "hard war" fever, the increase in congressional action against slavery, and the changing executive policy made further enforcement of the act fitful, though Northern Democrats, conservative Republicans, and border-state congressmen managed to block the act's repeal until June 1864.[21]

Most Northern commentators had approved Lincoln's countermanding of Fremont's emancipation declaration, not necessarily because they disagreed with the policy but because they thought that the civil authorities, not the military, must control how the war should be waged. But the necessity for Fremont to act as he did seemed to underscore the failure of the First Confiscation Act to strike a punitive and debilitating blow—indeed to strike much of any blow at all—at the Confederate economy. Additionally, slaves' initiative in escaping to Union lines proved them more enterprising and independent than Northerners had first believed, leading many to doubt that the slaves would remain submissive much longer. Ulysses S. Grant's major victories, the capture of Fort Donelson on the Cumberland and Nashville in early February 1862, also virtually assured that the border states would not leave the Union, making it easier for Congress to contemplate stronger action against slavery. Congress indeed moved more decisively, abolishing slavery in the District of Columbia in April 1862 and in current or future territories in June of that year, and finally, in July 1862, passing the Second Confiscation Act, which declared the slaves of supporters of the rebellion who came under Union control forever free, without any longer requiring proof that individual slaves had been used to aid the Confederate war effort. That July, Congress also passed the Militia Act, which opened service in the federal militia to black men.[22]

In early March 1862, at Lincoln's request, Congress adopted a bill that gave financial assistance to any state that adopted a gradual emancipation scheme. Lincoln pressed the border states to take the deal, warning that they may not get another chance because "the institution [of slavery] in your States will be extinguished by mere friction and abrasion—by the mere incidents of war." When the states declined, Lincoln apparently recognized that his conciliatory approach would no longer suffice. Only five days after the Second Confiscation Act passed, Lincoln told his cabinet that he planned to emancipate slaves in rebellious states in his capacity as wartime commander in chief. He accepted their advice, however, that such an action would make him look desperate given how poorly the war had been going for the Union. Accordingly, he postponed any action and in the interim publicly refused to reconsider his decision not to allow blacks into the army, met with an African American faction to suggest voluntary colonization—an idea that he repeated publicly for the last time in his annual address to Congress in 1861—and replied to a *New York Tribune* editorial with his famous statement that he would save the Union even if doing so meant not freeing a single slave. All of these actions, in the view of at least one leading historian, were meant to lay the political groundwork for the Emancipation Proclamation by distancing himself from abolitionists.[23]

With the success of the Battle of Antietam, in September 1862, which stopped Robert E. Lee's attempted raid into Union-held Maryland, Lincoln had the victory he thought he needed. On September 22, 1862, he issued his Preliminary Emancipation Proclamation, which announced that on January 1, 1863, he would declare slaves in any still-rebellious areas "forever free." Although this Preliminary Proclamation was not well received at first by many in the North,

Lincoln moved to address race- and class-based concerns directly, acknowledging in his December 1862 annual message to Congress, "It is dreaded that the freed people will swarm forth and cover the whole land." But, he suggested, freed slaves could be housed on the plantations abandoned by fleeing Confederates. Once so housed, none would feel the need to move North. This statement contributed to a sharp improvement in Union morale, leading one Northern soldier from Indiana to quip in a letter to his hometown newspaper, "I want some of you smart, educated Knights of the Golden Circle to let me know when you see the first squad of negroes coming from the south to become citizens in Owen County. . . . The majority of the union soldiers are in favor of restoring the Union and the Constitution if it frees every slave in the South."[24]

Again, no state took up Lincoln's offer. Accordingly, on January 1, 1863, he signed the Final Emancipation Proclamation and declared, "We know how to save the Union. . . . In *giving* freedom to the *slave,* we *assure* freedom to the free." Union forces were given thousands of copies of the Proclamation to distribute as they fought their way deeper into the Confederacy. The Proclamation also called for the active recruitment of African Americans into the armed services, an action authorized by Congress since July 17, 1862, but delayed by Lincoln. After the Proclamation, black recruitment for military service vastly expanded, with Lincoln placing great emphasis on it as a way to fill the army's manpower needs and to build greater white acceptance for his emancipation policy.[25]

The Final Proclamation, coming from the commander in chief, had more weight with the soldiers than did the Second Confiscation Act, which helped to overcome resistance among conservative commanders, strengthened European pro-Union support, and encouraged still more slaves to flee as the grapevine again spread the word. As Confederate prisoners of war said at the time, the Proclamation "played hell with the South." As Union forces continued conquering the Mississippi Valley and pushed from southeast Tennessee through Georgia to the Atlantic coast, fugitives cascaded to the Union troops so that by the war's end some 15 to 20 percent of the Confederacy's slave population had taken advantage of the Proclamation. One refugee compared the new circumstances to the Underground Railroad: "It used to be five hundred miles to get to Canada from Lexington, but now its eighteen miles! *Camp Nelson* is *our* Canada!"[26]

The North had long resisted calling up black troops because Northern whites doubted that blacks had either the courage or the intelligence to be Union soldiers. Lincoln had worried that black troops would send border states scurrying to the Confederacy and had therefore balked at Secretary of War Simon Cameron's suggestion as early as December 1861 that former slaves take up arms against the rebels. Nevertheless Union commanders in South Carolina and Kansas organized units of former slaves, which Lincoln ordered to stand down. But the growing hard-war sentiment—the desire not just to win but to punish the rebels for their transgressions—combined with recognition of the increasing usefulness of African Americans to the war effort and a heightened need for troops led to new policies. The Second Confiscation Act had authorized the president to "employ as many persons of African descent as he may deem necessary and proper for the suppression of this rebellion, and . . . in such manner as he may judge best." The Militia Act had provided for the employment of blacks in "any military . . . service for which they may be found competent," granting freedom to all so employed. In August 1862, the War Department authorized formation of the First South Carolina Volunteers, the first official black Union regiment. The Final Emancipation Proclamation reiterated Lincoln's decision to see "such persons of suitable condition . . . received into the armed forces of the United States."[27] Lincoln explained his bottom-line rationale:

> Any different policy in regard to the colored man deprives us of his help, and this is more than we can bear. We can not spare the hundred and forty or fifty thousand now serving us as soldiers, seamen, and laborers. This is not a question of sentiment or taste, but of physical force which may be measured and estimated as horse-power and steam-power are measured and estimated. Keep it and you can save the Union. Throw it away, and the Union goes with it.[28]

Over 180,000 African Americans, 80 percent of whom were recruited in the South, wore Union blue by the war's end. In the last year of the war, 120,000 served, about the same number as the total number of remaining active Confederate troops. Although black troops did much support work, they proved themselves distinguished combatants, being involved in 40 major battles and 450 total military engagements. They constituted 120 infantry regiments, 10 batteries of light artillery, 7 cavalry regiments, and 12 heavy-artillery regiments. Commander Thomas Wentworth Higginson of the First South Carolina volunteers noted of black soldiers under his command, "They know the country, which white troops do not."[29] More important,

> Instead of leaving their homes and families, they are fighting for their homes and families, and they show the resolution and sagacity which a personal purpose gives. . . . It would have been madness to attempt with the bravest white troops what I have successfully accomplished with black troops.[30]

General David Hunter said of the black troops, in a letter to the secretary of war, that they were "hardy, generous, temperate, strictly obedient, possessing remarkable aptitude for military training, and deeply imbued with that religious sentiment (call it fanaticism, such as like) which made the soldiers of

Oliver Cromwell invincible." A report to the Union War Department soon noted that "sentiment in regard to the employment of Negro troops has been revolutionized by the bravery of the blacks. . . . Prominent officers, who used in private to sneer at the idea are now heartily in favor of it." As a Confederate newspaper editor admitted, the black soldier "fights willingly and fiendishly for his own freedom." Former slaves who took up the uniform and the rifle thus impressed many whites and fostered black racial pride and an altered demeanor among the former bondsmen. As one white soldier said of his black comrades, "Put a United States uniform on his back and the *chattel* is a *man*. You can see it in his look. Between the toiling slave and the soldier is a gulf that nothing but a god could lift him over. He feels it, his look shows it."[31]

Refugees' mass flight and word of events reaching the remaining slaves through the grapevine had powerful repercussions in the Confederacy. Early in the conflict, several Confederate states tightened their patrol and related laws for regulating slave movement. Texas in particular authorized calling out patrols "as often as the peace and quiet of the community may require." Texas "ordered every county to mount a regular slave watch; patrol captains were granted broader powers to compel local men to serve on the patrols, and patrols were permitted to inflict up to twenty-five lashes as deemed necessary." Mobs and local vigilance committees were organized, retaliating against whites or blacks rumored to be inciting slaves to revolt. In one Southern town, the doorkeeper of a tavern was ridden out of town on a rail for merely talking to a slave. White paranoia made local defense a primary concern. Slaveholder J. B. Mannary illustratively wrote to General John Pettus of Mississippi to warn that reports of slave unrest "have shown the necessity of organizing ourselves into Home Guards."[32] One slaveholder offered this explanation for why he joined such a guard:

> You have no idea of the danger we are apprehending from the blacks. We know that the moment Lincoln sends his abolitionists among our niggers, they will break out and murder all before them. . . . We cannot sleep at night for fear of the niggers. . . . We are compelled to mount guards at night ourselves for mutual protection and though there has been no outbreaks as yet, I believe this is the only thing that keeps them in check.[33]

Although calls for local volunteers waxed and waned over the course of the war, the frequent insistence on local defense added to a manpower competition between the national call for soldiers and local demands. Growing labor shortages from slave flight also created conflict between local and national Confederate authorities over where lay the greater need for the declining pool of slave labor. The remaining slaves—observing other slaves' flight, late in the war seeing their masters flee, hearing of broader events, and sensing white fear—became increasingly insubordinate. Bondspeople began openly to bargain with their masters and refused to work unless their conditions improved. Wrote one plantation mistress in her journal, "They have placed themselves in perfect antagonism to their owners and to all government and control. We dare not predict the end of all this, if the Lord in his mercy does not restrain the hearts and wills of this deluded people." Worried slaveowners increasingly denied slaves passes or canceled their "right" to be hired out, yet many masters perceived a sharp rise in slaves going abroad in the face of owners' denial of, or absence of, permission. As the wife of a Texan who had just recently left for Confederate service in the summer of 1863 complained about one slave, "Sam has been out. He started to see his wife last Saturday after dinner and returned late Monday evening. He is determined not to clear up trash and, no doubt expects to be a free man before another year." But it was not only Sam's behavior that troubled her: "The negroes [generally] are doing nothing," she said, "but ours are not doing that job alone; nearly all the negroes around here are at it. Some of them are getting so high on anticipation of their glorious freedom by the Yankees I suppose that they resist a whipping." These complaints were far from atypical.[34]

As slave resistance in the South and black sacrifices on the battlefield grew, so did sympathy for African Americans' plight. The antiblack draft riots in New York City generated a backlash among white employers, who fired Irish workers and replaced them with blacks. The *Atlantic Monthly* urged equal rights for blacks, comparing them favorably to New York's Irish population: "The emancipated Negro is at least as industrious and thrifty as the Celt, takes more pride in self-support, is far more eager for education, and has fewer vices. It is impossible to name any standard of requisites for the full rights of citizenship which would give a vote to the Celt and exclude the Negro." Field atrocities fostered still more sympathy. When the Union began fielding black soldiers, the Confederacy threatened to execute or enslave captured black soldiers. Despite Lincoln's responding threat to execute one rebel prisoner for every Union soldier killed by the rebels and to put one Confederate prisoner to labor for every black reenslaved, Nathan B. Forrest, on April 12, 1864, attacked a Union force at Fort Pillow that was more than half black, killing scores of black prisoners *after* they surrendered and giving others to masters as slaves. "News of this atrocity racked the North."[35]

By the war's end, there were over sixty-eight thousand black casualties, many from disease, but thousands dying in battle. These enormous sacrifices softened, though far from ended, Northern white racial prejudice and also did much to persuade Northern whites that blacks deserved to be part of "the transformed nation." Lincoln indeed thought the blood sacrifice of any soldier the highest sort of patriotism and began to suggest as early as August 1863 that the black blood spilled had earned them a place in the nation's future.[36] In a public letter to the president of the Springfield Union League, Lincoln wrote that, once peace came to the land,

> it will have been proved that, among free men, there can be no successful appeal from the ballot to the bullet; and that they who take such appeal are sure to lose their case, and pay the cost. And then, there will be some black men who can remember that, with silent tongue and clenched teeth, and steady eye, and well-poised bayonet, *they have helped mankind on to this great consummation*; while I fear there will be some white ones, unable to forget that, with malignant heart, and deceitful speech, they have strove to hinder it.[37]

By March 1864, Lincoln even wrote to Louisiana's Governor Michael Hahn and suggested that he consider allowing the vote for blacks who were "very intelligent, and especially those who have fought gallantly in our ranks," by April 1865 going further by publicly endorsing limited black suffrage. In his last annual message to Congress in December 1864, Lincoln threatened to resign if the people attempted reenslavement of African Americans, and in his second inaugural address, he gave an apocalyptic interpretation of the war as the necessary price for the sin of slavery.[38] Declared Lincoln, if God willed the war to continue until

> all the wealth piled up by the bond-man's two hundred and fifty years of unrequited toil shall be sunk, and until every drop of blood drawn with the lash, shall be paid with another drawn with the sword, as was said three thousand years ago, so still must it be said, " 'the judgments of the Lord are true and righteous altogether.' "[39]

The North apparently had come to agree with Lincoln, at least insofar as seeing slavery's end as necessary to end the conflict. On January 31, 1865, the Thirteenth Amendment to the U.S. Constitution, which ended slavery forever as an institution anywhere in the nation, was sent to the states for ratification. The sweeping Republican electoral victory in running on a platform urging the amendment's adoption had much to do with former congressional opponents of the measure now accepting its ultimate passage. Republican reports of the productivity of African Americans on abandoned Southern lands and of the enormous black contribution to the war effort also convinced many in the North that emancipated blacks would eventually make ideal free laborers who would enliven the South. Smart political maneuvering, even corruption, by congressional Republicans and fervent lobbying by Lincoln also contributed to the amendment's successful passage. Perhaps one of the ultimately most powerful contributors to the amendment's making its way to the states was that it would "bring peace by eliminating the Confederacy's reason for being." Republicans having made the amendment's ratification a condition for the readmission to the Union of any rebellious state, the amendment was ratified by the requisite number of states on December 18, 1865, only eight months after Lincoln's martyrdom on April 14, 1865, and after the war's effective end with the surrender of Robert E. Lee at Appomattox Courthouse, on April 9, 1865.[40]

From Persons to Property

The meaning of the Thirteenth Amendment and the social forces that made it possible—as well as the necessity for a Fourteenth Amendment to make up for the weaknesses of the Thirteenth—cannot be understood, however, without first examining changing Northern concepts during the Civil War about the meaning of "property," especially *human* property. As recent scholarship reveals, the most detailed discussions on these questions before the Emancipation Proclamation, and the ones most in the public eye, surrounded the debates over passage of the First and Second Confiscation Acts.

The problem for antislavery Northerners was that although they rejected the wisdom of some humans having property interests in others, they initially understood the Constitution as recognizing and protecting precisely those interests. As the war began, most Northerners understood slaves to be both persons *and* property, a status protected by the founding document. In the debates over the First Confiscation Act, conservatives warned that any wartime violation of the Constitution would have future tragic results. Federal interference with a local institution of property rights threatened to shred the fabric of federalism. Moreover, as one Maryland pamphleteer argued, the uncompensated seizure of slaves was forbidden by the Fifth Amendment's prohibition against taking "private property for public use without just compensation." Indeed, the First Confiscation Act would not seize slaves for public use at all, she maintained, because the act merely liberated slaves from the status of property rather than transferring their ownership to the government. Although Northerners opposed reenslavement, they generally had trouble at first accepting the idea that the former slaves, once freed, could make their own choices without some sort of white control, and the act made no provision for such control.[41]

Republicans responded that the act operated only on individuals who had used their property in aid of rebellion, not on the states, the law, or the institution of slavery itself, and the Constitution provided for forfeiture of property by a traitor. Conservative John Crittenden's rejoinder was that the act was nevertheless unconstitutional because the Constitution limited confiscation of a traitor's property only to the natural life of the traitor, a limitation that the act lacked. Radical Republicans, however, argued that the fugitive slaves were not criminals but "debtors" who owed labor, and they would not countenance criminal prosecution of the slave for "stealing himself." The final version of the act did indeed adopt the radical vision to some extent, describing masters as persons "claiming to be entitled to the service or labor of any other person," a description that separated the slave as a human being from the property that was his labor. A master who employed a labor-indebted person to aid in the insurrection would "forfeit all right to such service or labor, and the person whose labor or service is thus claimed shall be henceforth discharged therefrom, any law to the contrary notwithstanding." Accordingly, the act confiscated "only the labor of slaves, not their bodies and souls." Other radicals, like Thaddeus Stevens, simply did not understand all the handwringing over the slaveowners' property rights. Stevens roared, "If their whole country must be laid waste, and made a desert, in order to save this union from destruction, so let it be."[42]

By the time of the debates over the Second Confiscation Act, the North's punitive rage at the South, the independence shown in slave self-help, and growing frustration with Southern victories were prodding changes in Northern understandings of property under the Constitution. Pamphleteer Thomas Sizer, a moderate Republican, explained in the spring of 1862 that Northerners had been "assiduously educated in hatred of abolition" for generations, noting "how strong are the prejudices of a lifetime, even among educated and reasoning people." Northerners had simply come to accept slavery, and compromises with slaveowners, as a part of the American system. But now that slavery had struck at the heart of the republican system of constitutional government, Sizer concluded, the North was becoming "emancipated from the mental thraldom of slavery." Another pamphleteer, George Candee, bemoaned any vision of the Constitution as "Divine Revelation." The nation would be better served, indeed renewed and redeemed, suggested Virginian F. D. Parish, if the Constitution were purged of compromises with slavery, "sloughing off the old skin [of the Constitution] for a new one." Even the conservative border-state newspaper the *Frankfort (Kentucky) Daily Commonwealth* editorialized that slave property, though protected by the Constitution, should not have that protection "at the expense of all the other interests of man or of government itself."[43]

Emboldened by Union victories in February 1862, Republicans thereafter became yet more aggressive in their willingness publicly to attack the very concept of property in man. In noting that the Constitution never mentioned slavery but rather referred to "persons held to service," they amplified the very distinction between person and property implicit in the First Confiscation Act. Albert G. Riddle emphasized that this constitutional reference to slaves as "persons" meant that the founding document did not "erase from them the universal quality of subjects." The most ardent defenders of human bondage had by this time left Congress, and Democrats relied more on racial prejudice than on an explicit defense of property rights in human beings. The opponents of bondage further argued that property in persons should not be recognized precisely because it needed special protection to survive, a form of legal discrimination among categories of property that could not be justified. Furthermore, owning slave property had also conferred greater power and status than owning other sorts of property, an "aristocratic" distinction contrary to the most fundamental of American principles.[44]

Slave property was, of course, not the only property that would be subject to confiscation, though it was of particular importance in Northern eyes. Northerners believed that poor, nonslaveholding Southern whites hated the plantation elites and would readily return to the Union if given the right incentives, and land would provide just the motivation needed. Land might also be distributed to Union soldiers, both to reward them for their sacrifices and to bring sorely needed Northern influence into Southern territory. Radical Republicans like Indiana congressman George Julian and Pennsylvania congressman Thaddeus Stevens went so far as to suggest redistributing some of the land to the newly freed slaves after the war. Confiscation of property seemed a more practical alternative than trying to execute all the rebels.[45]

Perhaps most importantly, however, the wealthy slaveowners, the aristocratic "Slave Power," were widely seen as the "guilty authors of the rebellion." It was they who had long conspired to destroy free institutions, and it was their creation of "un-American" class differences and oppressively concentrated, abusive power that most threatened freedom. Confiscating their land and their slaves would consume the wealth that sustained them and break the back of their antirepublican rule. These themes were repeatedly struck in Northern pamphlets, letters, and newspaper editorials. The *New York Times* captured the prevailing sentiment when it described the war as one "of the aristocracy of the South, nominally against the working people of the North, but really against the whole people, and against Democracy itself." The Union thus had to "strike at the higher classes," a blow best struck both out of military necessity and to "depress the traitorous aristocracy who hated the Union and Democracy, and will always hate them." Only by emancipating the slaves and by confiscating the rebels' estates and dividing or cheaply selling their land among Union soldiers and poor Southern whites could the Slave Power be forever buried. For many Northerners, therefore, confiscation of planters' slaves and land would mean "bringing the North physically and morally into the South, thus creating a more truly unified and virtuous nation."[46]

If Lincoln shared many of these sentiments, he ultimately became an obstacle to their full fruition. When the Second Confiscation Act arrived on his desk, he threatened to veto it unless what he saw as a constitutional infirmity was corrected. The primary *legal* justification for the act, in Lincoln's mind, was as punishment of rebels for the act of treason. Yet, as conservative opponents of the Confiscation Acts had themselves previously noted, the Constitution limited confiscation of property to the lifetime of the traitor. The text of the act seemed permanently to deprive even traitors' descendants of their family's real estate after death. Although radicals vehemently objected to this stance, Congress ultimately sent Lincoln an explanatory addendum disclaiming any intent that the legislation result in confiscation beyond the traitor's natural life. Lincoln thereupon signed the bill. But as the *Massachusetts Daily Republican* explained, there is little incentive to confiscate property for the traitor's lifetime and then have to return it.[47]

The Second Confiscation Act made no provision for the slaves' postwar future (other than authorizing the president to make provision for the colonization of those *willing* to "migrate," though that was in a sense a strength because it arguably suggested that it was up to the slaves to try to make their own future). The act also did nothing affirmatively to protect slaves' civil liberties. Moreover, the mere fact that it spoke of "confiscation" expressed some ambivalence over the status of African Americans as property or persons. Nevertheless, the act itself and the debate surrounding it moved the North a long way toward accepting the idea that the Constitution needed change to prevent future rebellion, change that should begin by putting an end to the idea of man's owning property in man. In this way, the act laid the groundwork for the Thirteenth Amendment. As historian Silvana R. Siddali has so pointedly put it, "It would take a presidential proclamation to confirm the end of property status of slaves (at least in the mind of many white northerners) and the Reconstruction Amendments to enshrine their status as persons in the Constitution." It is important that Siddali speaks of the necessity of the Reconstruction *amendments*—in the plural—to ensure the constitutional personhood of former slaves. The Thirteenth Amendment certainly ended formal legal recognition of slaves as property. But it turns out that there is a netherworld between property and personhood, and the Thirteenth Amendment proved inadequate to the task of bringing the freedmen out of that netherworld. It would take the Fourteenth Amendment, and its incorporation of most of the federal Bill of Rights, including the Fourth Amendment, against the states to do that job.[48]

Reconstruction and the Mutated Fourth Amendment

Antebellum Roots of the Fourteenth Amendment

Section 1 of the Fourteenth Amendment begins by declaring that "[a]ll persons born or naturalized in the United States and subject to the jurisdiction thereof, are citizens of the United States and of the State wherein they reside." This Citizenship Clause is followed by three interrelated prohibitions against any state's doing the following: first, making or enforcing "any law which shall abridge the privileges or immunities of citizens of the United States"; second, depriving "any person of life, liberty, or property, without due process of law"; and third, denying any person within its jurisdiction "the equal protection of the laws." The Bill of Rights originally applied only against the federal government. The modern Court has held, however, that one major function of the Fourteenth Amendment's Due Process Clause was to apply (to "incorporate") most of the Bill of Rights against state-level action. But that function was instead probably meant by the framers of the 1860s to be served by the Privileges and Immunities Clause. That clause's meaning was significantly informed by the principles of the Equal Protection Clause. The Due Process Clause, although not irrelevant, merits the least attention in an exploration of the historical events that led up to the incorporation of the *Fourth Amendment* against the states.[49]

All three clauses of the Fourteenth Amendment were rooted in corresponding antebellum concepts of due process, equal protection, and privileges and immunities. Antebellum due-process theory had a procedural component that regulated *how* the state may deprive a person of his life, liberty, or property and a substantive component that regulated when and what may be taken. One dominant theme of the substantive strand of due-process doctrine was the prohibition against "class legislation," government action that affects one class's rights differently from another's. This prohibition was not absolute; it was limited to "vested" rights and noncurative legislation (terms whose complex definitions need not concern us here). Antislavery forces argued that African Americans in free states and in the territories had a natural vested right to freedom. To enslave them would, therefore, be to treat one class of free persons (African Americans) differently from another (whites) without good reason. This theory was not once accepted by the judiciary, though antislavery advocates like Salmon P. Chase embraced it with gusto.[50]

The theory was also occasionally resorted to in defense of the actions of antislavery whites, as in 1856, when Representative John Bingham of Ohio denounced a Kansas statute that made it illegal to utter any "sentiment calculated to induce slaves to escape from the services of their masters." Chase maintained that such a prohibition "abridges the freedom of speech and of the press and deprives persons of liberty without due process of law, or any process but that of brute force." Proslavery proponents, by contrast, argued that masters had vested property rights in slaves and that such rights were recognized by the Constitution. Therefore, freeing slaves in the territories or prohibiting their entry there would mean discriminating against human property relative to other forms of property.[51]

Equal-protection concepts relied on the social-contract theory that dominated nineteenth-century political thought—much the same theory in many respects as the one underlying the original Fourth Amendment of 1791. Under this theory, the sovereign's protection was the "quid pro quo" for inhabitants' giving up some of the rights that they held in the state of nature. The sovereign's protection included protection from others' physical aggression against one's person or property. But another strand of the doctrine extended to protection *from* the government as well as *by* the government. Although the state existed to protect fundamental rights, government might also pose a grave danger to those rights. The function of the law was to restrain such abuses. As Justice David Davis would later put it in *Ex Parte Milligan*, a case decided contemporaneously with the drafting of the Fourteenth Amendment, "By the protection of the law human rights are secured; withdraw that protection and they are at the mercy of wicked rulers, or the clamor of an excited people."[52]

The dominant view was that equal protection created no new rights but simply assured equal access to, and application of, existing rights structures. Even then, equal protection extended only to certain core rights, largely natural ones, leaving the state free to deny such protection for rights outside that limited center. Abolitionists argued that African Americans were entitled to equal protection, including formal legal guarantees of life, liberty, and property; equal access to the courts; and physical protection for their persons and property. Proslavery advocates instead viewed slaves as chattel and thus not entitled to equal protection. Moreover, although they often conceded in theory that free blacks were entitled to such protection, that was more lip service than reality. The concern of proslavery forces was with what they saw as the denial of equal protection for human property. Given the greater difficulty of safeguarding human property (it can flee), equal protection of *masters' rights* in such property required vigilant oversight by the law. The state *and* federal governments were obligated to provide such oversight for the protection of the laws truly to be equal.[53]

Although there were state-level variants on the concept, the federal Constitution's Comity Clause was the major ancestor of the Fourteenth Amendment's Privileges and Immunities Clause. The Comity Clause of Article IV declared that "[t]he Citizens of each State shall be entitled to all privileges and Immunities of Citizens in the several States." One major view of the Comity Clause was that it also served a particular sort of nondiscrimination function, restraining any individual state from providing lesser protection to sojourners from other states than it offers its own citizens. A New Yorker visiting North Carolina would thus not be entitled to rights received in his home state but would be entitled to whatever legal protections North Carolina afforded to its own residents, with one limitation: once again, only certain "fundamental rights" needed to be extended to the Northern sojourner.[54]

Some antebellum authorities, however, took a broader view, seeing the Comity Clause as guaranteeing sojourners a core set of rights that belonged to the citizen regardless of what rights were prescribed by the law of any individual state. The opinion authored by Justice Bushrod Washington in *Corfield v. Coryell* has often been cited as the best-known example of this limited absolute-rights theory of comity. Justice Washington catalogued a number of specific privileges and immunities, noting that these were but examples of a whole that would be "more tedious than difficult to enumerate"; his examples included "[p]rotection by the government," the "enjoyment of life and liberty," and the pursuit of "happiness and safety." Despite these sweeping phrases, Justice Washington saw Comity Clause privileges and immunities as limited to those that are, "in their nature, fundamental; which belong, of right, to the citizens of all free governments; and which have, at all times, been enjoyed by the citizens of the several states which compose this Union, from the time of their becoming free, independent, and sovereign."[55]

John Bingham of Ohio, though he agreed with this fundamental-rights limitation, went still further, concluding that the Comity Clause guaranteed such rights to its *own* citizens, not merely to sojourners. But he believed that the clause did not empower Congress to act when states failed to meet their comity obligations because the clause was silent on the existence of any congressional enforcement power—a gap that Bingham would later argue needed to be filled by the Fourteenth Amendment Privileges and Immunities and Enforcement Clauses. Bingham's view on limited congressional enforcement powers was consistent with the view of some antislavery advocates concerning the Fugitive Slave Clause, which also appears in Article IV, section 2; they argued that Congress lacked any power to enforce the Fugitive Slave Clause because of its silence about the extent of congressional power in the area of slave rendition.[56] Bingham, the principal draftsman of most of the Fourteenth Amendment's section 1 language, embraced a strongly egalitarian vision of comity, but he acknowledged its limits:

> [A]ll . . . classes [of] free inhabitants, irrespective of ages, sex or complexion, and their descendants were [made] citizens of the United States. No distinctions were made against the poor and in favor of the rich and against the free-born blacks and in favor of the whites. This Government rests upon the natural rights among men. There is *not*, and cannot be any equality in the enjoyment of political or conventional rights.[57]

Sectional disputes were sometimes framed in Comity Clause terms. However, because the Comity Clause governed a range of fundamental rights, the underlying right on which the dispute was based would vary with the circumstances, even though the rhetoric of comity rarely focused on what specific core rights were in question. One of the most prominent Comity Clause disputes of the era—the Negro Seamen's Acts—in fact involved underlying claims of search and seizure, as well as other related, rights. Ultimately this dispute was less about the general meaning of the Comity Clause than whether it reached African Americans and thus gave them protections equal to those given whites. Predictably, the Northern and Southern positions were, respectively, that it did and that it did not.[58]

Starting in 1822, several Southern states, most notably South Carolina, adopted legislation that required the arrest of any black crew members on ships coming into the state's port. These black seamen were to be jailed until their vessel departed, and they were to be sold into slavery if their ship's captain failed to pay for the state's providing room and board for its captives. Pro-black Northern politicians complained that the captured seamen were citizens of Northern states and thus entitled to Comity Clause protection against such seizures. The general Southern position on the Comity Clause, however, was that blacks were not citizens within the meaning of Article IV. Southerners relied on one of two different theories, either that national citizenship derived from state citizenship, and free blacks were often not treated as full and equal citizens even in their home states, or that Article IV citizenship was federally defined, and it excluded African Americans. In the words of Judge William L. Harris of Mississippi, writing in *Mitchell v. Wells,* Northern states were free to "confer citizenship on the chimpanzee orang-outange [sic]," but that did not "require of the States not thus demented, to forget their own policy . . . and lower their own citizens . . . to meet the necessities of the mongrel race thus attempted to be introduced into the family of sisters in this confederacy." The disputes over the Negro Seamen's Acts remained a near-constant source of sectional tension throughout the antebellum era.[59]

A related dispute became of increasingly powerful symbolic importance in the North: the banishment of Samuel Hoar. The Massachusetts legislature had sent Hoar, accompanied by his daughter, to Charleston, South Carolina, to mount a judicial challenge to that state's seamen's statutes. Hoar was denounced by the legislature as the "emissary of a foreign Government," meriting expulsion for his seditious plans. Ultimately, he was "ridden out of town on a rail by an enraged populace after the South Carolina legislature passed an act of attainder and banishment." It is hard to imagine a clearer example of a seizure of the person than a legislature's command that one be expelled. Furthermore, Hoar's expulsion was done to silence his voice and that of the Massachusetts legislature on the rights of free Northern blacks and to deny Hoar access to the courts, access presumably available to South Carolina's own citizens. The Hoar case, based on an underlying dispute about seizing black seamen, is thus best understood as fusing concerns about search and seizure, free speech, and judicial access.[60]

In the view of many Northerners, Hoar, a free Northern white man, had now himself been denied Comity Clause protection. Antislavery politicians repeatedly highlighted the case during the 1850s and 1860s. Moreover, the case "still burned bright in the memories of members of Congress, who repeatedly cited the incident." When John Bingham eventually introduced a precursor proposal to what became the Fourteenth Amendment, he gave a speech on the House floor on January 9, 1866, justifying his proposal. In that speech, he relied specifically on Hoar's plight and on the analogous suffering of other white, as well as black, men. His speech was prompted by Democratic discussion in response to a message from President Johnson declaring himself to favor "equal and exact justice to all men." Bingham accused the Democrats of favoring such justice only for *white men*.[61] Said Bingham,

> The spirit, the intent, the purpose of our Constitution is to secure equal and exact justice to all men. That has not been done. It has failed to be done in the past. It has failed in respect of white men as well as black men. . . . Time was within the memory of every man now within hearing of my voice, when it was entirely unsafe for a citizen of Massachusetts or Ohio who was known to be a friend of the human race, the avowed advocate of the foundation principle of our Constitution—the absolute equality of all men before the law—to be found anywhere in the streets of Charleston or in the streets of Richmond.[62]

Bingham continued, relying on his reading of the Comity Clause and how it had been offended by the Hoar case:

> To be sure, it was not because the Constitution of the United States sanctioned any infringement of his rights in that behalf, but because in defiance of the Constitution its varied guarantees were disregarded. . . .
>
> When you come to weigh these words, "equal and exact justice to all men," go read, if you please, the words of the Constitution itself: "the citizens of each State (being ipso facto citizens of the United States) shall be entitled to all the privileges and immunities of citizens (supplying the ellipsis 'of the United States') in the several states." [This guarantee] was utterly disregarded in the past by South Carolina when she drove with indignity and contempt and scorn from her limits the honored representative of Massachusetts, who went thither upon the peaceful mission of asserting in the tribunal of South Carolina the rights of American citizens.[63]

Bingham did not consider his proposed amendment to create any new state obligations but rather to enforce existing ones, primarily those embodied in the Comity Clause. His amendment would empower the federal government to enforce Comity Clause obligations when the state failed to do so. His reliance on the Hoar case, continuing the similar reliance by antebellum Northern politicians, suggests at least an implicit recognition that search and seizure protections were at the core of the "privileges and immunities" of U.S. citizens. Shortly after his speech, the Joint Committee on Reconstruction, of which Bingham was a member, reported a proposal similar to Bingham's, apparently recognizing the wisdom of his position. Although that proposal would eventually be replaced by very different language, the later versions of the proposed Fourteenth Amendment did not in any way involve rejection of its encompassing Fourth Amendment protections. Indeed, a wider examination of the Fourteenth Amendment's history and that of related legislation percolating through Congress at the same time underscores the importance of search and seizure rights to the Reconstruction Congress and sheds light on how those rights are best understood.[64]

Civil Rights Legislation, Search and Seizure, and the New Constitution

The history of the Fourteenth Amendment is in many ways inseparable from the history of the Freedmen's Bureau Acts, the Civil Rights Act of 1866, and similar actual and proposed legislation. Debates on these acts and on the Fourteenth Amendment itself implicitly or explicitly addressed questions of search and seizure, though the debates were often framed—especially concerning the Fourteenth Amendment—in general terms and grand principles rather than specifics. Still, the overwhelming weight of historians' opinions leaves little doubt that the framers, and probably the ratifiers, of the Fourteenth Amendment understood that it would apply the Fourth Amendment to the states, protection against unreasonable searches and seizures being among the "privileges and immunities" of U.S. citizens. Moreover, the vast majority of Black Code provisions and the many other acts of Southern counterrevolution involved searches and seizures. Everything from unjustified arrests, mandated passes to move about the countryside, beatings by state officials, legally authorized whippings, banishment, revived patrols, and invasions of homes encroached on fundamental rights to unimpeded locomotion, privacy, and possession and use of property, absent adequate justification, such as because of probable cause or involvement in a crime. Furthermore, search and seizure issues frequently arose in the context of state seizure of freed people's firearms, firearms partly needed by the former bondsmen to protect themselves from white violation. Just as First Amendment free-speech concerns were often inseparable from search and seizure questions during Reconstruction, so was the right to bear arms inseparable from the Fourth Amendment.[65]

The Southern turn to violence against African Americans and their white Republican supporters, including in the form of state-sanctioned searches and seizures, must also be understood in relation to the Southern honor culture. Antebellum Southern whites were enraged by what they saw as the insult of abolitionist and other Northern antislavery criticism of Southern culture. The Southern struggle to extend slavery into the territories was partly motivated by the implied insult of their system's being deemed unworthy for transport to new territory, thus their "resentment against any congressional measure that implied the moral inferiority of their region." Jefferson Davis well expressed similar rage at an 1858 Democratic rally in New York City, when he railed against "higher law" antislavery politicians like William Seward and demanded that they be tarred, feathered, and whipped. The Southern sense of insult stemmed from the belief that white honor was sustainable only with black slavery. The corollary, therefore, was that black freedom meant white disgrace. Indeed, as secession commissioners rode to urge additional states to join the Confederacy, they relied significantly on an appeal to Southern honor.[66]

Confederate soldiers were also particularly brutal in their treatment of black Union soldiers, both on the battlefield and when they were held (often not for long) as prisoners. White Southerners saw the Northern willingness to put blacks into the field as if they were worthy of a struggle with whites on equal terms as an affront to white Southern dignity. The shame of defeat, combined with the sight of some blacks carrying firearms, voting, and generally participating more fully in economic and political life, was more than most former rebels could bear. "With few exceptions the average white male Southerner could not imagine life without bondspeople fully under control—to give labor and deference to their owners and the prestige of the white skin to those without human property." Southern whites also resented the presence of "radical" Northern whites, seeing them both as culturally and morally inferior to Southerners and abhorring their advocacy of black civil and political rights. If slavery had to end, white Southerners' honor at least demanded that it take place under a system of continued racial dominance that reproduced the preexisting slave system as closely as possible. Because violence played such an important expressive role in communicating the master class's dominance over its human property, and because search and seizure laws and practices were fundamental to that regime, white Southerners returned, in barely disguised form, to such practices as the passes, humiliating violence, patrols, and other mechanisms of antebellum social control of blacks. Growing private violence, including race riots, supplemented that which was formally or informally sanctioned by the state. This violence also took place in a cultural context in which former Confederates maintained a strong sense of emotional connection to what would later become known as the Lost Cause and a belief that, although they were entitled to be treated as full and equal economic and political members of the American polity, they also "made up a distinct nation, a distinct population," in effect "becoming a quasi-ethnic minority" that would not bow to Northern tyranny, impiety, and lack of virtue.[67]

As word of Southern refusal to be reconstructed in the Northern free-labor image and of private and state-sanctioned Southern counterrevolution reached the North, the Congress turned with intense focus to legislative and constitutional changes to ensure that the Slave Power would not rise again.

The Freedmen's Bureau Bill was the first order of business. In March 1865, Congress had created, for an initial life of one year, the Bureau of Refugees, Freedmen, and Abandoned Lands to aid slaves in the transition to a life of freedom. The proposed new bill would have extended the bureau's life and enabled it to use military force in areas where ordinary judicial procedures had been interrupted, to protect the freedmen in, among other things, the "security of persons," a phrase that Kentucky representative L. H. Rousseau used during the debate about whether to include protection against unreasonable searches and seizures. Representative Lawrence Trimble, a Democrat, correspondingly objected that the bill would violate whites' Fourth, Fifth, and Sixth Amendment rights, the "inalienable rights of American freemen," to which supporters of the bill responded that the Black Codes' denial of such rights to the freedmen was just what made the Freedmen's Bureau necessary.[68]

Lyman Trumbull, the Chair of the House Judiciary Committee, reported the Freedmen's Bureau Bill to the full House and was the principal draftsman on that bill and on the Civil Rights Bill, and he used the same "security of persons" and similar language in both pieces of legislation. Trumbull justified the Freedmen's Bureau Bill under the then-pending Thirteenth Amendment prohibition against slavery and its empowering of Congress to enforce the end of involuntary servitude by appropriate legislation. In a debate over a related proposed joint resolution to disband the militias in most Southern states, Senator Wilson noted that former Confederates were going "up and down the country searching houses, disarming people, committing outrages of every kind and description." Members of Congress had also expressed concern about states' requiring freedmen to have passes to leave the plantations. President Andrew Johnson nevertheless vetoed the Freedmen's Bureau Bill on February 19, insisting that it improperly relied on military rule and denied the right to a jury trial. In subsequent debate over whether to override the veto, Trumbull expressed surprise at the veto of a bill meant to safeguard constitutional rights. He recounted a detailed history of the freedmen's oppression, in particular quoting a letter from Colonel Samuel Thomas in Vicksburg, Mississippi, who wrote that "nearly all the dissatisfaction that now exists among the freedmen is caused by the abusive conduct of this militia," which would "hang some freedmen or search negro houses for arms." The Senate nevertheless failed by two votes to override Johnson's veto, which made a vote on that question by the House unnecessary.[69]

Meanwhile, Congress had appointed a Joint Committee of Fifteen, also known as the Joint Committee on Reconstruction, including representatives from both houses, to make recommendations concerning how to respond to former Confederates' efforts effectively to reenslave the freedmen. The Joint Committee heard from Colonel H. S. Hall, a Texas Freedmen's Bureau official, who explained that Texas governor Jack Hamilton had authorized armed patrols, which were passing through black settlements, disarming freedmen, and robbing them of money and anything else that the former rebels could use, all purportedly done in the name of suppressing insurrection. An 1865 Mississippi Act that became the model for Black Codes in other states had analogously prohibited freedmen from possessing firearms, other weapons, or ammunition on pain of criminal prosecution, including being hired out by a sheriff or other officer "to any white person who will pay said fine and costs," if not quickly paid by the freedman.[70]

In House debates on the proposed Civil Rights Bill, which, like the Freedmen's Bureau Bill, would also protect the "security of persons," the Chair of the Judiciary Committee, Representative Henry Wilson, quoted Kent's *Commentaries* as saying that this right was among the "absolute rights of individuals." Wilson also relied on Blackstone's definitions of security and of the "right of personal liberty," which Wilson saw as within the scope of the rights protected by the bill. Thus, Wilson defined the right of personal security as "a person's legal and uninterrupted enjoyment of his life, his limbs, his body, his health, and his reputation" and the right of personal liberty as "the power of locomotion, of changing situation, or moving one's person to whatever place one's inclination may direct, without imprisonment or restraint, unless by due course of law."[71]

On March 6, 1866, President Johnson communicated to the Senate all the reports that Freedmen's Bureau assistant commissioners had made since December 1, 1865, on conditions in the South. These reports repeatedly raised issues of the rights to personal security and liberty and associated assaults on protections related to search and seizure. The report of Kentucky's Assistant Commissioner Fisk noted that a "town marshal takes all arms from returned colored soldiers, and is very prompt in shooting the blacks whenever an opportunity occurs." Accordingly, explained Fisk, throughout the state outlaws "make brutal attacks and raids upon the freedmen, who are defenseless, for the civil law-offices disarm the colored man and hand him over to armed marauders." Alabama's Assistant Commissioner Wager Swayne reported the use of state militias and special constables to compel blacks to enter into labor contracts and the ordering of military units to break into black homes to seize firearms and "whatever [else] their fancy or avarice desired."[72] In another report, Swayne recounted this incident:

Two men were arrested near here one day last week, who were robbing and disarming negroes upon the highway. The arrests were made by the provost marshal's forces. The men represented themselves as in the military and acting by my order. They afterwards stated, what was probably true, that they belonged to the Macon County militia.[73]

Swayne also testified before the Joint Committee on March 9, 1866. Swayne, upon being examined by Representative Boutwell, explained that white fears of black insurrection in Alabama had led to the organization of militias, which "were ordered to disarm the freedmen and undertook to search in their houses for this purpose." The next day, Captain J. H. Matthews, Freedmen's Bureau subcommissioner in Mississippi, described how militiamen patrolled the countryside, flogging freedmen and Union men and, upon rumors of an insurrection, carrying out the state governor's order to disarm the freedmen.[74]

In House debate over the Civil Rights Bill on March 24, 1866, Pennsylvania representative Leonard Myers also referred to the situation in Alabama, which he described as adopting "aristocratic and anti-republican laws, almost reenacting slavery." Representative Roswell Hart of New York insisted that the United States had a duty to secure for the people of the Southern states a republican form of government, as mandated by the Constitution's Guarantee Clause. Hart expressly described the right to keep and bear arms and those rights recited in the First, Fourth, and Fifth Amendments as necessary components of republican government. Representative John Bingham had earlier explained that the Civil Rights Bill would enforce "in its letter and its spirit the bill of rights"; he quoted section 1 of the Civil Rights Bill, reiterated his support for "amending the Constitution of the United States, expressly prohibiting the States from any such abuse of power in the future," and declared that the rights protected in the Civil Rights Bill were but those that had been enumerated in the Freedmen's Bureau Bill. Bingham's goal, he declared, was to "arm Congress with the power to punish all violations by State Officers of the Bill of Rights." Other members of the House had likewise recognized the Civil Rights Bill as protecting "the fundamental rights of the citizen," including the right to personal security, and had urged passage on the ground that such rights were meaningless without congressional power to enforce them. Once again, Johnson used his veto power, bringing it down on the Civil Rights Bill on March 27.[75]

This time, however, the bill's supporters garnered greater political strength. In the Senate override debate, Trumbull described the bill as protecting the "inherent, fundamental rights which belong to free citizens or free men in all countries," and he cited Kent's *Commentaries* for the proposition that these rights included personal security and personal liberty, rights that the Freedmen's Bureau Bill had also sought to protect. On April 6, the Senate voted to override Johnson's veto. While they were so voting, the Joint Committee was examining Brevet Lt. W. H. H. Beadle, Freedmen's Bureau superintendent in North Carolina, who described police brutality in Wilmington, including the repeated beating with baseball bats of a petite black woman and of a black man on a false weapons charge, the officials easily avoiding any punishment for their behavior.[76] Beadle continued:

> Some of the local police have been guilty of great abuses by pretending to have authority to disarm the colored people. They go in squads and search houses and seize arms. . . . Houses of colored men have been broken open, beds torn apart, and thrown about the floor, and even trunks opened and money taken. A great variety of such offenses have been committed by the local police.[77]

On April 9, 1866, both houses overrode Johnson's veto of the Civil Rights Bill. Section 1 of that bill redefined national citizenship as extending to any person born in any state or territory who was not an Indian or of foreign allegiance, regardless of color, granting them the "full and equal benefit of all [state, local, or territorial] laws and proceedings for the security of persons and property, as is enjoyed by white citizens." A revised Freedmen's Bureau Bill had already been working its way through the system, a bill described by Representative Eliot in the House as embodying the provisions of the Civil Rights Bill but giving the president the authority, through the secretary of war, to extend military protection to secure those rights until civil courts were properly in operation. This second Freedmen's Bureau Bill extended the bureau's life and included protection for the "full and equal benefit of all laws and proceedings concerning personal liberty, [and] personal security" without respect to race, color, or previous condition of slavery. Johnson once again vetoed this bill, but this time both houses quickly overrode the president's action, and the second Freedmen's Bureau Act became law. There is little doubt among scholars that the Civil Rights Act and Freedmen's Bureau Act were intended to provide freed people with protection for their fundamental rights, including especially much of the Bill of Rights and unquestionably extending to rights against unjustified searches and seizures.[78]

Throughout these legislative debates, language to be embodied in a proposed Fourteenth Amendment had been working its way through the Joint Committee and through both houses of Congress. Although not in the original amendment proposed by the Joint Committee, the final proposed amendment included a provision similar to, but going further than, the citizenship clause of the Civil Rights Bill. The final proposed language for what would become the Fourteenth Amendment declared that all persons born in the United States were citizens of the United States and of the state in which they reside, a provision adopted after long congressional debates in various contexts over the wisdom of making Indians, Chinese, and gypsies citizens. The final provision, however, permitted no exception to the principle of universal citizenship for the native born. This provision became part of section 1 of the Fourteenth Amendment, which also contained the Due Process, Equal Protection, and Privileges and Immunities Clauses.[79]

An earlier proposal by Thaddeus Stevens had been to prohibit discrimination against anyone in the exercise of his or her civil rights, but Bingham ultimately prevailed in replacing that language with the language of "equal *protection*," which arguably implied an affirmative duty to protect against deprivation of civil rights rather than permit an equal deprivation of them. Although debate was once again generally couched in grand terms of broad principle, a variety of comments by legislators also expressed an intention to incorporate at least significant portions of the Bill of Rights against the states. Furthermore, although the first proposed Fourteenth Amendment precursor (offered by John Bingham) preceded the initial proposal of the Civil Rights Bill, there was significant congressional discussion of an intention to protect the principles of that bill from constitutional challenge or repeal by a future legislature through the shield of the Fourteenth Amendment. When Howard introduced the proposed amendment in the Senate on behalf of the Joint Committee, he explained that it was influenced in its proposal by the desire to protect "the personal rights guaranteed and secured by the first eight amendments of the Constitution." He continued: "The great object of the first section of this amendment is, therefore, to restrain the power of the states and compel them at all times to respect these great fundamental guarantees." In the ensuing debates, no one questioned this premise, and Howard's explanation of an intention to protect the Bill of Rights against state infringement appeared on the front pages of the *New York Times* and the *New York Herald,* as well as being printed in the *National Intelligencer* and the *Philadelphia Inquirer.* Northern media coverage of his remarks was generally favorable.[80]

The citizenship provision, introduced by Senator Howard, seems intended in part to assure the result of at least partial or selective incorporation of the Bill of Rights against the states. This was so because the "privileges or immunities" protected by section 1—privileges including much of the Bill of Rights—were extended only to *citizens.* Senator John Henderson of Missouri, for example, expressly addressed *Dred Scott,* describing Taney's opinion as properly equating the American "people" with U.S. "citizens." Taney's error, said Henderson, was in ignoring the plain meaning of "the people" by excluding blacks. Taney had, said Henderson, recognized that citizens are entitled to Bill of Rights guarantees. The citizenship clause would correct Taney's flawed definitions of peoplehood and citizenship, bringing to African Americans the same protections that were extended to other citizens.[81]

Henderson's comments reflected evolving Republican understandings of citizenship, the first turning point having been an 1862 opinion by Lincoln's attorney general, Edwards Bates, on the meaning of a particular federal statute.

Bates had argued that native-born free African Americans were citizens within the meaning of the statute because under the Constitution citizenship signifies membership in the body politic, meaning that the individual is "bound to it by the reciprocal obligation of allegiance on one side and protection on the other." Bates considered contrary language in *Dred Scott* to be dictum and declared that federal law alone determined national citizenship, and all citizens of the nation were automatically citizens of their state of domicile. Although Bates expressly said that citizenship could be consistent with the denial of a range of rights (for example, white infants and women were citizens but could not vote), his opinion as a member of the Lincoln administration held powerful symbolic value.[82]

Debates over the Civil Rights Act of 1866 and related legislation further advanced this more inclusive Republican idea of citizenship. Indeed, strong evidence suggests that in light of the citizenship clause, Republicans generally expected that the Privileges and Immunities Clause, rather than the Equal Protection or Due Process Clauses, would prove the most important feature of section 1. The Fourteenth Amendment would allow for enforcement of rights contained in an expansive understanding of the Comity Clause. Thus, Senator Luke Poland of Vermont had expressed his view that the citizenship clause essentially declared what was already recognized in the Declaration of Independence and the Constitution. Nevertheless, he considered it desirable to remove any doubt about Congress's power "to enforce principles underlying the foundation of all republican government if they be denied or violated by the states." Importantly, Bingham had in debate "repeatedly condemned state law allowing banishment and confiscation," forms of state seizure of persons and property, again suggesting that the foundational principles of republican government of which Luke spoke included the Fourth Amendment. As one well-known historian has concluded, whatever aspects of the Bill of Rights were incorporated against the states by the Fourteenth Amendment, "the most important substantive [constitutional] rights, such as the right to keep and bear arms and freedom from unreasonable search and seizure, were very much on the minds of the Fourteenth Amendment's supporters."[83]

The Fourteenth Amendment passed the Senate by a 75 percent vote margin and the House by a 79 percent margin, sending it to the states for ratification. What evidence is available regarding ratification in the states has likewise been recognized as thoroughly consistent with incorporation of the most important provisions of the Bill of Rights. Although the former Confederate states had initially rejected the Fourteenth Amendment, the amendment was eventually ratified by a sufficient number of states, following new incentives created by the Military Bill, another bill passed over Johnson's veto. That bill divided the rebel states into five military districts, with military commanders having authority to use military tribunals to the exclusion of state courts to protect Bill of Rights guarantees. A Southern state could be admitted to representation in Congress only when it framed a state constitution that conformed in "all respects" to the federal Constitution and was based on a convention of delegates elected by universal male suffrage, excluding disenfranchised former Confederates. Southern states were also required to ratify the Fourteenth Amendment. Military rule would thus end only when a state accepted the amendment and rewrote its constitution to be consistent with the new regime. These requirements provided sufficient incentives to prod the Southern states into ultimate ratification of the amendment. Doing so also removed any serious cloud over the constitutionality of the Civil Rights Act of 1866, under which the Freedmen's Bureau had already begun bringing charges against "local officers for infringing the freedmen's right to keep and bear arms and the right against unreasonable search and seizure."[84]

Interestingly, some discussion of incorporation, specifically of the Fourth Amendment, arose again in Congress only a few years after the Fourteenth Amendment's ratification. The Civil Rights Act of 1871 provided for civil liability for any person who subjected another to deprivation of constitutional rights, privileges, and immunities under color of state law; it criminalized conspiracies to deny equal protection or equal privileges or immunities; and it empowered the president to suppress domestic violence when a state fails to protect the rights, privileges, or immunities of its citizens. In debates over the 1871 act, John Bingham again explained that section 1 of the Fourteenth Amendment protected the first eight amendments of the Bill of Rights against state infringement. Bingham urged adoption of the new bill as necessary to give meaning to the commitment of the Fourteenth Amendment's section 1 by passing all laws "for enforcing all the privileges and immunities of citizens of the United States," as guaranteed by the amended Constitution. Bingham recited the text of the incorporated amendments, including the search and seizure protections of the Fourth Amendment. Representative Horatio Burchard of Illinois, although he had no objection to the relevant section of the new bill, rejected Bingham's view that "privileges and immunities" included the first eight amendments. According to Burchard, those amendments largely contained only "rights." But, he said, the phrase "privileges and immunities" unquestionably included the provisions of the Fourth, Fifth, and Sixth Amendments to the Constitution. This comment adds to the already overwhelming evidence that the Fourth Amendment was so fundamental a guarantee that the Reconstruction Congress expected it to be protected against individual state infringement as a consequence of the Fourteenth Amendment's ratification.[85]

The search and seizure concerns of the drafters and ratifiers of the Reconstruction amendments were, of course, in some respects different from those of the drafters and ratifiers of the original Bill of Rights of 1791. Notably, the Slave Power—representing not only a powerful elite but also the hierarchical social system it had created, one dependent on the humiliation of one social group by another—was sustained in large part by abusive search and seizure practices. The Slave Power's sustenance derived from a racial bias so thorough as to deny the personhood of African Americans—even of "free" African Americans—enforcing that denial by suspicionless or low-suspicion seizures of persons (including brutal violence against them) and of their "property." The Civil War did not kill the Slave Power, as the pass systems, patrols, effective confinement to plantations, unjustified searches of homes, discriminatory arrests, and brutality of slavery were substantially re-created by the Black Codes and associated laws and practices. Searches of homes and persons were frequently undertaken to deprive the freedpersons of the means for protecting themselves from this effective reenslavement. The mere fact of group membership—of being black—created suspicion of crimes that were legislatively defined largely by such membership. This system of state-sanctioned violence was meant, in part, to silence the voices of African Americans as a group—to stop them from voting, parading, speaking, or otherwise agitating on behalf of group as well as individual interest. The laws themselves also sent unmistakable messages of white supremacy, messages reinforced by both private and state-sanctioned violence against the freedpeople. This was no longer a struggle against a foreign power—the British Empire—but against an internal enemy, the slavocracy that had poisoned the South's entire social, economic, and political system; that had threatened to infect the North; and that had cost the nation, and still continued to cost it, so much blood.[86]

Yet in other ways Reconstruction and Revolutionary concerns were similar. Both worried about aristocracy, denial of individualized justice, and restraint of governmental power. If anything, antebellum and Reconstruction experience strengthened some of the lessons of the Revolutionary and Constitution-framing eras. For example, the unremitting use by Southern states of the search and seizure power to suppress dissent tightened the link between Fourth Amendment and free-speech concerns. Whites, like Samuel Hoar, suffered from this repression too, which created a sense of shared interest, an understanding that silencing black voices inevitably meant gagging white speech as well. The concerns of individualized justice heightened and deepened as mere membership in a racial or political group became cause for suspicion. These brief illustrations from the history recounted here suggest a renewed, more sophisticated vigilance in making use of past lessons while considering them in light of new ones. The law on the street has evolved.[87]

12 Law on the Street

Introduction: Ten Lessons of History

My main task in this book has been to tell a story, a historical narrative that helps us to ask new questions about the Fourth Amendment's meaning or to see old questions in a new light. The story has now been told. Some specific issues may require still more detail, such as concerning the relative roles of the states and the federal government in enforcing Fourth Amendment guarantees or the precise division of specific enforcement responsibilities among each of the three branches of government. Moreover, constitutional theorists might seek a more extended defense of the way in which I use history here than the length of this book will permit—a defense that I have, in any event, already accomplished elsewhere.[1] My goal, however, is to start a new way of thinking, not to end it, to prompt future conversations rather than to halt past ones. The history told in the just-completed part of this book I hope has strengthened the arguments begun in part 1. In this last chapter, I want briefly to illustrate some further implications of the antebellum and Reconstruction history of search and seizure for the constitutional jurisprudence of the Fourth Amendment. Those implications include both new lessons and the reinforcement of old ones. The lessons recited in part 1 can thus be restated and expanded in this way:

1. *Individualized Justice.* Judging likely criminality on the basis of class membership, most notably one's race, runs counter to every concern of the Reconstruction Congress. The question is not simply one of equal protection but also of the way we understand the fundamental "privileges and immunities" guaranteed U.S. citizens. The Fourth Amendment is one of those guarantees, and it

requires adequate justification—presumptively in the form of probable cause—for the state's interfering with privacy, property, and freedom of movement. Any use of race to establish suspicion of crime should be judged skeptically and require strong justification. Indeed, any unduly group-based suspicions risk treating people like fungible property rather than as unique human beings, a form of treatment meant to die with slavery. On the other hand, the Reconstruction Congress was as concerned with whites' rights as blacks'. The black experience under slavery underscores the value of the individualized-justice principle to human dignity, but it is a principle that must be revitalized for all persons, regardless of race.

2. *Group Voices.* Search and seizure practices have long been used to suppress political expression and dissent. Although nineteenth-century popular and political thought embraced individualism, it is hard to read the relevant history and not be left with an impression of the importance of group membership, identification, interest, and expression to understanding the era. The Slave Power was feared in part because of its efforts to silence an unpopular, dissenting white minority, the abolitionists. Southern counterrevolution aimed both to silence black political expression and power on behalf of perceived black group interests and to silence the freedmen's defenders in the Republican Party. The tool used to silence black group voices and those of their defenders was expressive violence, frequently in the form of state searches and seizures. Even the Congress's concerns about searches and seizures to disarm the freedmen can be understood as stemming from the fear that they were done to put the freed bondsmen at the physical mercy of their former masters as a way of threatening them into silence. Any set of search and seizure practices that ignores group voices, or, worse yet, actively aids in silencing them, is suspect. Any search and seizure jurisprudence that is blind to the extraordinarily high political value of free speech risks a slide into tyranny.

3. *Freedom of Movement.* The radical denial of slaves' freedom of movement was central to their transformation into chattels rather than full legal persons. The elaborate system of slave passes, patrols, and fugitive-slave laws was designed to render slaves' locomotion subject to others' control via the ultimate power of the state. Any jurisprudential scheme that values privacy over free movement fails to recognize the central social importance of autonomous citizen locomotion.

4. *Property.* Perhaps to a somewhat lesser degree, something similar can be said about property. Residential property interests create privacy interests, and the relative absence of such privacy is typified by life in the slave cabins. Freedmen's possession of freely purchased firearms contributed to their safety and growing political independence. Too-easy seizure of property can deny persons physical comfort, moral autonomy, security, and the leisure time for fruitful family and community life, as the slaves' passion for their quasi property

demonstrated. Fourth Amendment doctrine cannot unduly slight property interests.

5. *Group Privacy.* Privacy's importance to the development of human personality, to the intellectual autonomy necessary to active citizenship, and to the fostering of bonds of family and friendship cannot be overstated. The importance of slaves' independent culture, built among the cabins—of group interaction hidden in many respects from the masters' ever-prying eyes—reveals the reality and crucial role of recognizing the privacy interests of groups, not only of individuals. Certain small groups hold a special status, particularly the family, as the havoc slavery caused to that institution starkly reveals. A purely individualistic conception of privacy that fails to honor separately the privacy of families and of community, of social and political groups, forgets the experience of slaves living under a system in which they struggled to preserve or achieve these things in the face of overwhelming onslaught.

6. *Humiliation.* Both the Revolutionaries and the slaves, later freedpeople, had experience with the insult involved in the expressive violence of state searches and seizures. A part, though only a part, of the Revolutionary experience of insult was class based—of "lowly" servants of the king searching the homes of their "betters." The direction of insult pointed the other way under slavery, however, with the socially dominant individuals and groups expressing through violence the subordinate status of a weaker, indeed nearly powerless, group. The post-Reconstruction Fourth Amendment must thus be seen as infused with more egalitarian values and as more concerned with group (rather than only individual) humiliation than the original Fourth Amendment of 1791.

7. *Shared Institutional Obligations.* All three branches of government, not only the judiciary, of course remain bound by the Fourth Amendment, a truth about which too little self-consciousness is now shown by our political institutions. However, antebellum and Reconstruction experiences highlight the importance of a Fourth Amendment federalism. Generalizations are hard here. Before the Civil War, Northern state governments often did a better job than did Southern state governments or the federal government in protecting against abusive searches and seizures, for example, through personal-liberty laws. But during Reconstruction, it was the federal government that led the charge against such abuses in the former Confederacy, and the Fourteenth Amendment clearly recognized a power of the federal government to step in when the states fail. The real lesson seems to be that a federalism-aware conversation must be fostered in many instances so that careful consideration is made of the respective roles of the state and national governments in setting constitutional search and seizure policy.[2]

8. *The Citizenry's Monitorial Role in Regulating the Police.* Nothing in antebellum and Reconstruction experience undercuts the importance of citizens

acting as watchdogs. The recognition of African Americans as part of the American people arguably suggests that they should have an energetic role in such monitoring, particularly where they remain disproportionately subject to abusive search and seizure practices. The experience of the too-frequent failure of all three branches of government at both the state and national levels to protect against such abuses further underscores the need for a further political check in the form of more direct citizen involvement in the crafting and monitoring of search and seizure policy. A sensitivity to the plight of the politically weakest groups further counsels the need for their participation in monitoring the police. Such monitoring also cannot ignore the flip side of the problem: any *failures* to execute searches and seizures, which result in the subjection of the less powerful to disproportionate violence and other criminality—in other words, inadequate protection of vulnerable communities—must likewise be guarded against.

9. *Ensuring a High Quantity and Quality of Evidence.* Nothing in antebellum and Reconstruction history lessens the central need for the state to justify intrusions on citizens' privacy, property, and free movement absent a high quantity and quality of evidence of criminal wrongdoing. Indeed, the willingness of slave masters to use such flawed indicators of criminality as skin color and to presume the untruthfulness of slave informants and the relative truthfulness of white ones reminds us of the importance of a quality evidentiary principle as a way of restraining government power.

10. *The Citizenry's Safety and the Least Restrictive Alternative.* This book began by emphasizing the dual nature of the Framers' social-contract philosophy: the obligation of the state to protect its citizens from private violence and of the people to protect itself from state violence. Reconstruction thinkers embraced a similar philosophy, and the challenge of protecting freedmen from violence without eviscerating everyone's civil rights preoccupied the Reconstruction Congress. This tension modernly seems heightened by the dangers of the war on terrorism. At the same time, the history of slavery emphasizes the extraordinary value of privacy, property, and free movement to a republican society. A least restrictive alternatives principle, properly understood, effectively safeguards these interests without unduly compromising public safety. Such a principle requires only that the state ensure a politically acceptable level of public safety in the ways that will do least damage to individuals' and groups' Fourth Amendment interests. An aggressive search and seizure policy can seem the easiest and highest visibility way to ensure safety. But it is not necessarily the best course of action. For example, some writers have suggested that less-invasive search technologies, like "target-hardening" to make assaults more difficult, and police-community trust-building efforts can do more to fight terrorism than simple roundups of Arab Americans. If this is so, such roundups

violate Fourth Amendment interests without improving safety at all, or at least not as much as would a less-intrusive policy. If an aggressive policing strategy is truly necessary, it should be adopted. But caution can be the better part of wisdom.[3]

Rather than undertake the task of illustrating all these lessons in greater depth, I will explore several selected ones through a small number of case examples, one concerning the relevance of flight to proving reasonable suspicion, a second concerning group privacy and privacy on-the-street for the "disorderly and the disreputable," and a third concerning technological surveillance. I will also make some brief comments about antiwar and other political protests and terrorism and about social-services searches and seizures based on reports of abused children. I will make little, if any, effort to offer a theoretical defense of my analyses. Nor do I claim them to be the final word on these subjects. Instead, I simply want to convey the flavor of an analysis informed by the ten historical lessons recounted here.

Much of this discussion will consider the role of racial, ethnic, and political minorities in the search and seizure policy-setting process. The discussion also illustrates the role of "respect." The meaning of this term is, of course, hotly contested, and much ink has been spilled over the years by academics struggling to give it definition. I do not plan to shed yet more intellectual blood over the matter, so I'll simply assert one definition that has been well expanded on elsewhere: "respect" means treating individuals and salient social groups "fittingly," that is, in accordance with their status concerning some specified attribute. Any lesser treatment is insulting. Theorists disagree over what attribute all humans share that requires treating each, in some sense, with the same status. It may be rationality, autonomy, the capacity to achieve moral goodness, or being made in God's image. Whichever the attribute, many theorists agree that showing equal respect for that attribute entails freedom of conscience, privacy, the right to own property earned by the sweat of one's brow, and freedom of movement.[4]

There is a second aspect to being treated fittingly, namely, its connection to a sense of belonging. To treat someone as a whole—as uniquely complete in him- or herself—enhances status. Simultaneously, treating a person as a part or member of a valued broader whole—as someone essential to making society what it is—also enhances status. The idea of "partnership" best expresses this ideal: each of us is a whole unto ourselves yet a valuable partner committed to, and essential for, the greater good.[5]

These explanations are, however, at a very high level of generality. Not every interference with freedom of movement or privacy or property can be deemed insulting. How and why individuals and groups may feel insulted can and should, however, inform the analysis. Yet one group might be hypersensitive—

insulted when there is no good reason to be—while another is hyposensitive, not insulted when they have every right to be. The ultimate decision about whether state conduct should fairly be understood as insulting is thus a normative one. But the recognition of rights to privacy, property, and locomotion in practice stems not from abstract philosophizing but from experience. The Fourth and Fourteenth Amendments grew from the *American* experience. Whether, therefore, state conduct is respectful or insulting depends on reading modern experience in the light of American history. The "lessons" of that history articulated in this chapter can thus be understood as guidelines for ensuring that the state treats the American people and the individuals and groups that compose it as free and equal human beings worthy of full membership in the American polity.[6] Unfortunately, these lessons have too often been forgotten by the high Court, a point well illustrated by the story of Judge Harold Baer.

Illustrating a Respectful Interpretive Method: Stops in "High-Crime" Areas

The Saga of Judge Baer

IF I SAW THE COPS, I'D RUN TOO

The Honorable Harold Baer, sitting in the U.S. District Court for the Southern District of New York, is a well-respected jurist with a distinguished career. In 1996, he was also the subject of angry calls for his impeachment by congressmen on both sides of the aisle and by then-president William Jefferson Clinton.[7]

Baer's sin had been to grant a motion to suppress evidence against a drug dealer. More precisely, his sin consisted of giving reasons for doing so that were culturally unacceptable, ready fodder for the politics of the 1996 presidential campaign.

Baer's first reason for granting the defendant's motion was that he found the officers' testimony at the suppression hearing simply unbelievable. The police claimed that they saw a woman named Carol Bayless double-park her car in a neighborhood center for the drug trade. Four men promptly crossed the street, leading Bayless simultaneously to pop open the trunk. One man opened the trunk, put two duffel bags in it, then closed it. When the men saw Officer Carroll and his partner stop their unmarked car, the men fled rapidly in different directions. The officers' suspicions now being aroused, they stopped Bayless's car, which sported Michigan license plates and which had been leaving the area at a legal speed. Bayless explained that the car was rented but produced an agreement in another person's name. She also denied that anyone put anything in her car. Officer Carroll accordingly arrested her, searched the trunk, and found drugs in the duffel bag.[8]

Bayless quickly confessed on videotape, admitting not only to this crime but also to twenty other drug buys. But Bayless told a very different story from Officer Carroll's about that day's events. Judge Baer summarized those differences:

> Officer Carroll testified that when he first observed defendant, she was driving a Red 1995 Chevrolet Caprice slowly along 176th Street. In contrast, defendant asserts that she did not drive to New York City from Detroit, rather she was . . . a passenger in the Caprice driven by Terry. Further, defendant did not get behind the wheel of the car until after it was stopped on 176th Street and Terry had exited the vehicle. Put another way, Officer Carroll apparently missed or overlooked the fact that the car had come to a halt, never saw the man exit the Caprice, and missed the million dollars [that her cohort Terry had earlier placed in the trunk] being taken out of the trunk. If we credit the defendant's statement, and I do, one cannot keep from finding Carroll's story incredible.[9]

Judge Baer believed Bayless because of the "candor and the breadth" of her confession, in which she freely implicated herself in numerous other crimes. Baer also disbelieved Officer Carroll because it made no sense that the four men who put items in the trunk fled from the police, yet the officers did nothing to stop those men or, at the very least, did not "call for backup assistance in locating the males." The most controversial part of his opinion, however, was his explanation for why he found the four men's flight irrelevant to whether Officer Carroll could reasonably suspect that criminal activity was afoot. Baer explained that such flight was perfectly understandable, even wise, behavior and "hard to characterize . . . as evasive conduct":[10]

> Police officers, even those traveling in unmarked vehicles, are easily recognized, particularly, in this area of Manhattan. In fact, the same United States Attorney's Office which brought this prosecution enjoyed more success in their prosecution of a corrupt police officer of an anti-crime unit operating in this very neighborhood. Even before this prosecution and the public hearing and final report of the Mollen Commission [on police corruption in New York City], residents in this neighborhood tended to regard police officers as corrupt, abusive and violent. After the attendant publicity surrounding the above events, had the men not run when the cops began to stare at them, it would have been unusual.[11]

Judge Baer went even further, suggesting that either conscious or subconscious racism infected the actions of New York's finest: "What I find shattering," said Baer, "is that in this day and age blacks in black neighborhoods and blacks in white neighborhoods can count on little security for their person."

Judge Baer saw this observation as contrary to the values embraced by our Constitution's Founding generation: "As Thomas Paine wrote just 220 years ago: 'here too is the design and end of government, viz., Freedom and security.'"[12]

BAER RECONSIDERS

Reaction to Judge Baer's opinion was swift and angry. Locally, former New York City police commissioner Raymond Kelly was outraged that Judge Baer had "impugned an honest officer." Nationally, presidential candidate and then-senator Bob Dole described Judge Baer's decision as "hardly an exception among President Clinton's judicial appointees . . . [an] example . . . from Bill Clinton's judicial hall of shame." Mike McCurry, President Clinton's press secretary, unwilling to allow Dole alone to adopt a law-and-order posture, reported that Clinton had encouraged the Justice Department to ask Baer to reconsider. McCurry suggested that the judge's action was on the list of the most "wrong-headed, stupid" judicial decisions. The press described McCurry as further declaring that Clinton regretted ever appointing Baer to the bench. A firestorm now erupted in the media as calls for Baer's impeachment mounted.[13]

Baer quickly relented, though he denied doing so. He granted the prosecution's motion to reconsider. At a new hearing, additional officers testified, allegedly confirming Officer Carroll's story. The defendant, Carol Bayless, also testified for the first time. Claiming that this new evidence placed the case into a wholly different light, Judge Baer declared that he now believed the police. He also used his new opinion as an opportunity to apologize for his original language: "Unfortunately the hyperbole . . . in my initial decision not only obscured the true focus of my analysis, but regretfully may have demeaned the law-abiding men and women who make Washington Heights their home and the vast majority of the dedicated men and women in blue who patrol . . . our great City." Despite the flip-flop, Judge Baer insisted that he had not given in to political pressure. He would, he said, "fearlessly" work against the "unfettered discretion of officers in the field." He cautioned that "[b]ecause the strongest advocates of Fourth Amendment rights are frequently criminals, it is easy to forget that our interpretations of such rights apply to the innocent and the guilty alike." Judge Baer's actions, however, seemed to belie his words, and judges and commentators stepped forward to defend against what they perceived had been a successful assault on judicial independence.[14]

A RADICAL THEORY

Why did Judge Baer's opinion inspire such ire that it became part of a presidential campaign and raised serious calls for the judge's impeachment? The answer: Judge Baer adopted a then novel perspective on the Fourth Amendment's meaning.

For Baer, Carol Bayless's fate was inextricably linked to that of her racial group, African Americans. Though Bayless herself was a confessed criminal, her fate in the courts and at the hands of the police had implications for the future of all African Americans. Baer thus openly worried about his "shattering" fear that blacks could "count on little security for their person." African Americans in certain inner-city communities had indeed too often suffered from police abuses. Baer saw his judicial role as imposing a duty to protect such communities because they are especially vulnerable to excessive state zeal in investigating crime.[15]

Baer was also unwilling to let the law in practice undermine the law on paper. He initially refused to be an accomplice in the officers' apparent "testilying" game. Baer had served on the Mollen Commission investigating police corruption in New York City, which had coined the term "testilying.". He was, therefore, especially sensitive to the possibility that officers might lie to evade Fourth Amendment strictures. Judge Baer was further reluctant to follow a "colorblind" jurisprudence that gave police the discretion in practice to use skin color as an indicator of suspicion.[16]

Perhaps because of Judge Baer's Mollen Commission work, he also understood that many in the lay African American community had a very different view than many whites and police did of what conduct justified "suspicion." Judge Baer gave that view voice: flight from the police, at least in this neighborhood, may be a wise way to avoid police harassment, not an acknowledgment of guilt.[17]

Baer also drew on American history as an important source of Fourth Amendment values. His treatment of history was cursory and limited to the Founding period. Yet he clearly recognized the need to turn to history to inform ourselves in resolving modern dilemmas. Additionally, he saw that history as reflecting a value of inclusion, of treating white and black alike to include all in the definition of an "American."[18]

Finally, Baer was unwilling to allow citizens' free movement to be infringed without a significant quantity of reliable evidence of individualized criminal wrongdoing. The police needed "reasonable suspicion" that Carol Bayless was involved in criminal activity before the officers could legitimately stop her car. If we ignore the flight of Bayless's alleged cohorts' as irrelevant, then the police were aware of only these facts: a Michigan resident was driving in an alleged high-crime area of New York City in the early morning hours, first loading her car with baggage before setting off. She drove at a normal speed and engaged neither in flight nor in furtive conduct. Such a visitor could easily have been leaving so early in order to arrive in her home state by nightfall. That totality of circumstances is thoroughly consistent with innocent behavior and could not alone create reasonable suspicion.[19]

Baer's original opinion was an excellent start toward a jurisprudence of respect. His second decision, which shied away from his original noble effort, was affirmed by the U.S. Court of Appeals for the Second Circuit. On April 3, 2000, the U.S. Supreme Court let that affirmance stand, refusing to hear Bayless's further appeal. Interestingly, the Supreme Court probably acted as it did because it decided a similar case that same term.[20]

The majority opinion in that case, *Illinois v. Wardlow*, reflects the high Court's current approach to the Fourth Amendment and highlights why Judge Baer's original position seemed so radical. Importantly, however, the dissenters in *Wardlow* moved in some ways even closer than Judge Baer originally did toward an alternative jurisprudence. Yet the dissenters' words drew no outrage, perhaps because their position lost or because their tone was more measured than Baer's, though the message was equally, if not more, radical.[21]

Illinois v. Wardlow

FLIGHT ISN'T RIGHT

William Wardlow fled upon seeing police officers patrolling an area known for heavy narcotics trafficking. Two officers chased him and ultimately stopped and frisked him. On his person, the officers found an illegally possessed .38 caliber handgun. Wardlow was convicted for illegally possessing that weapon. When his appeal made its way to the U.S. Supreme Court, a majority affirmed the conviction.[22]

The majority agreed that neither Wardlow's mere presence in a high-crime area nor his refusal to cooperate with the police could alone establish reasonable suspicion that he was involved in a crime. "But unprovoked flight," said the Court, "is simply not a mere refusal to cooperate." "Flight, by its very nature," the Court explained, "is not " 'going about one's business'; in fact, it is just the opposite." Indeed, "Headlong flight—wherever it occurs—is the consummate act of evasion: it is not necessarily indicative of wrongdoing, but it is certainly suggestive of such." That there might be innocent reasons for the flight was irrelevant, because, argued the majority, the Court "accepts the risk that officers may stop innocent people," especially given the "minimal intrusion" involved in stopping someone to investigate.[23]

The majority's approach differed sharply from Judge Baer's perspective. The majority was almost ostentatiously indifferent to African American views of the police and to the tension between individualized and group justice that was so central to Judge Baer's first opinion in *Bayless*.[24] The dissenters' perspective was the polar opposite of the majority's opinion.

VINDICATING JUDGE BAER

Justice Stevens dissented, joined by Justices Souter, Ginsburg, and Breyer. Stevens concisely summed up his position:

Compare, *e.g.*, Proverbs 28:1 ("The wicked flee when no man pursueth: but the righteous are as bold as a lion") with Proverbs 22:3 ("A shrewd man sees trouble coming and lies low; the simple walk into it and pay the penalty"). I have rejected reliance on the former proverb in the past, because its "ivory-towered analysis of the real world" fails to account for the experiences of the many citizens of this country, particularly those who are minorities.[25]

Justice Stevens, unlike Judge Baer, made no claim that he could understand minority perspectives by common sense or by drawing on his own life experiences. Instead, Justice Stevens looked to social-science research. There he found a wealth of material suggesting that large percentages of African Americans considered police brutality and harassment serious problems in their own communities. Indeed, one study found, in Justice Stevens's reading of the data, that African Americans in twelve cities were more than twice as likely as white residents in the same community to be dissatisfied with police practices.[26] Echoing Judge Baer, Justice Stevens saw these practices and minorities' reactions to them to be critical to Fourth Amendment analysis:

Among some citizens, particularly minorities and those residing in high crime areas, there is also the possibility that the fleeing person is entirely innocent, but, with or without justification, believes that contact with the police can itself be dangerous, apart from any criminal activity associated with the officer's sudden presence. For such a person, unprovoked flight is neither "aberrant" nor "abnormal." Moreover, these concerns and fears are known to the police officers themselves, and are validated by law enforcement investigations into their own practices. Accordingly, the evidence supporting the reasonableness of these beliefs is too pervasive to be dismissed as random or rare, and too persuasive to be disparaged as inconclusive or insufficient.[27]

Stevens concluded, therefore, that the characterization of a neighborhood as a high-crime area made an inference of guilt from unprovoked flight less appropriate than in a lower-crime area. This was so "because many factors providing innocent motivations for unprovoked flight are concentrated in high crime areas." In other words, ordinary, honest citizens living where crime is most widespread are also those who believe that they have the most to fear from the police.[28]

Stevens acknowledged, on the other hand, that flight can sometimes be a significant indicator of guilt. Given the concerns of minority communities, however, Stevens required highly reliable additional evidence before he would reach that conclusion. Consequently, Stevens closely examined the evidence in the *Wardlow* case in a way that the majority did not.[29]

The testifying officer in *Wardlow*, Officer Nolan, admitted that he did not have any credible information that specific criminal activity was then afoot when he saw Wardlow run. Officer Nolan did testify that Wardlow "looked in our direction and began fleeing." That interpretation of Wardlow's conduct seemed oddly incomplete to Justice Stevens. Four police cars drove through this area, yet "Presumably . . . [Wardlow] did not react to the first three cars, and we cannot even be sure that he recognized the occupants of the fourth as police officers." Absent more testimony, there was, therefore, little evidence to support Officer Nolan's conclusion that Wardlow ran from the police.[30]

Moreover, Stevens noted, Officer Nolan had further testified that he expected to find an enormous number of people, including drug customers and lookouts, in an area where drug sales take place. Yet Nolan never mentioned seeing anyone else nearby when Wardlow ran. That presumed absence of other people meant that there was no reason to believe that drug sales or other illegal activities were afoot.

Unlike the majority, therefore, Stevens sought more than the sort of evidence that is as consistent with guilt as with innocence. Unlike Judge Baer, however, Stevens never charged the police with a propensity to perjure themselves. Nevertheless, Stevens was unwilling to defer to police judgment unsupported by other evidence. Stevens's opinion thus added several features to the approach of Judge Baer. Both jurists considered minority perceptions and real-world evidence of police treatment of minority communities to be important. But Stevens crafted a more practical methodology than Baer's for gauging perceptions and practices by drawing on social science rather than on personal experience. Whereas Baer's independence from police judgment turned on credibility, Justice Stevens's independence turned on a willingness to carefully examine the quality of the evidence and the inferences that could fairly be drawn from it.

Stevens also required more evidence—a greater probability of guilt—than does current law, an issue Baer did not address. Because of the negative impact of certain actual or perceived police practices on individual minority members and on their communities, Stevens stepped cautiously. He asked for confident assurance of a justified belief in individual wrongdoing before he would permit the police to intervene in citizens' lives.

Stevens did not pay homage to history the way that Baer did, however fleeting and however limited to the original Fourth Amendment of 1791 was Baer's analysis. Nor did Stevens expose the problem of testilying to the light of day. Still, by looking to social science, carefully and critically examining the quality of evidence, giving voice to minority concerns in their own words (recorded in the social-science studies), and raising the bar necessary to establish reasonable suspicion Stevens at least implicitly outlined a more practical and potentially more radical way than Baer's to recraft the Fourth Amendment. Had Stevens looked to the history of search and seizure during slavery and Reconstruction and the lessons of that experience, he would have found far stronger support for his analysis. Nevertheless, his approach, then only one vote from garnering a majority of the Court, takes an excellent additional step toward a jurisprudence of respect.

The Judge Baer and *Wardlow* stories are largely about minority-community voices being suppressed in the judicial determination of Fourth Amendment "reasonableness." That disregard of dissenting perspectives stemmed from the judiciary's narrow vision of Fourth Amendment costs and benefits. Such silencing crushes the human senses of self-worth, uniqueness, and autonomy; our voices help to define who we are and how we plan to live. But in neither tale were minorities specifically targeted for searches of their cars, homes, and property. Were that to happen, it would constitute the phenomenon of "racial profiling." That phenomenon also silences minority voices, but it is nevertheless different from the sort of assault on a minority group's status that was involved in the cases of Bayless and Wardlow. Yet race still mattered in both instances. Race consciousness can thus have a place in the law beyond the most obvious of classic examples.[31]

Additionally, Justice Stevens and Judge Baer at least implicitly recognized the value of free movement and the seriousness of interference with it in a way that the *Wardlow* majority did not. Such movement, of course, definitionally happens on the street, not in a home or office. The high Court has similarly shown an even greater reluctance to recognize privacy interests on the street—finding not simply that they are small but that they are nonexistent, so that the Fourth Amendment does not even apply to such infringements on the street. The Court's conception of privacy is indeed a risk-based one: if you put yourself in a position where anyone might observe you, if you share information with another person—given that he may not keep it to himself—you assume the risk of revelation to anyone, and once you take on that risk as to anyone, you take it on as to everyone. In other words, for the Court, who is doing the observing (the state or private persons), how (by high technology or just unaided watching), and why (to enjoy the sight of passersby or to build a criminal case) are irrelevant. Additionally, privacy is something that only individuals, not groups, have, and property interests are often determinative of whether a privacy interest exists. These characteristics of the judicial notion of privacy combine to eviscerate any philosophical, sociological, or commonsense notion of privacy outside homes, offices, and related structures. Similarly, these characteristics also limit privacy protections against technological surveillance or against the limited and necessary sharing of certain types of information that occurs indoors.[32]

This notion of privacy seems starkly inconsistent with the lessons learned from the slaves' experience. Slave cabins were ramshackle affairs that made the risk of outsiders hearing or seeing intimate events inside the cabins significant. Cabins were so small and crowded that many intimate actions had to take place outside. Furthermore, the slaves did not own or lease or have any other legal property interest in the cabins, so a focus on property ownership as of significant weight likewise denied them privacy protection. Moreover, a sense of group privacy mattered to the slaves. They built a group culture and group ties of affection in joint activities that they often hoped would be unnoticed by, and that they often consciously sought to hide from, their masters. It was this small sense of group seclusion eked out by great effort that enabled them to live lives of meaning. The law's failure to recognize these privacy interests was part of what marked the slaves as outsiders to the polity. To be true to the lessons of their experience, privacy's meaning in the courts must be reconceptualized. The modern-day experience of a subset of the urban poor makes the point.

The Disorderly and the Disreputable. The "broken windows" theory and "order-maintenance policing" embrace an effort to use dominant cultural understandings to mark some groups as deserving of privacy and some not. The underlying idea of these policing theories is that there are dichotomies of persons, "orderly versus disorderly," "reputable versus disreputable," and "predictable versus unpredictable" people. The "disorderly, disreputable, and unpredictable" include the homeless, vagrants, public drunks, loiterers, and litterers. Once thought to be at most annoyances to others, advocates of order-maintenance policing now declare these persons collectively as the source of a message that the community cares little about enforcing cohesive social norms and that the law is, in effect, a paper tiger. In turn, say these theorists, others are encouraged to commit more-serious crimes, which leads to a cycle of violence, fear, and further disorder. The solution: mass stop-and-frisks, mass suspicionless searches of housing projects, prohibitions against "loitering" with known gang members, and aggressive, even repeated, arrests of minor misdemeanants. The "disreputable" become the "dangerous," and the known dangerous have little privacy protection.[33]

Social theorist Bernard Harcourt has documented the many flaws in order-maintenance theories. Harcourt maintains that there is little, if any, evidence that the assault on the disreputable reduces serious crime. To the extent that it may do so, the result probably stems from increased police surveillance rather than changing social norms created by "orderly" neighborhoods. Furthermore, the very idea of "disorder" is defined by the state and enormously enhances police discretion. In some neighborhoods, for example, sitting on building stoops to chat and "hang out" on the street are considered part of a vibrant social life, rather than loitering or creating the possibility of future criminality.

Moreover, the definition of some as disreputable turns them "into individuals to be watched, relocated, and excluded . . . to be controlled." Rather than condemning the act of loitering, we condemn the loiterer as an inferior and dangerous person who possesses unsavory attitudes and values. The very police policies crafted to control or banish the disreputable, however, shape the rest of us as well.[34] Harcourt explains:

> Mass building searches in the inner city are going to affect our conception of privacy, of authority, of political power, and of citizenship. Youth curfew laws are going to have an impact on the cultural and intellectual lives of our children. Anti-loitering ordinances will have an effect on street life. Curfews and anti-loitering ordinances will result in police records and contribute to legal or extralegal disenfranchisement. Policing techniques shape us. I am not thinking simply about the fact that the police may want to extend a practice such as mass building searches outside the inner city—which certainly may happen. I am thinking about the fact that the very occurrence of these police practices affects all of us.[35]

There are numerous alternatives to mass humiliation and privacy invasion, whether our goal is to lower crime or to strengthen order. For example, "target-hardening," such as designing subway turnstiles that cannot be jumped to prevent minor offenses such as fare-beating, may be tried. Public-works programs for the homeless, such as a successful, privately funded project now functioning on a small scale in New York City, can replace arrests. Even gun crackdowns can be less intrusive and costly if police request consent to search a person or home for guns on the condition that they will not prosecute if weapons are found, an approach being used with some success in St. Louis. These alternatives are especially important because current "quality-of-life initiatives" have disproportionately affected minorities while reinforcing the stereotype of black criminality. Heightened arrests of blacks reinforce these stereotypes and create a vicious circle. Technological advances, making the monitoring of the "disorderly" easier and more effective, may only worsen these trends.[36]

Professor David Harris illustrates this last point in the context of "electronic frisks" using concealed-weapons detectors. Such frisks would have many advantages, notably reducing the burden imposed on suspects (who would not know they had been frisked) and probably increasing the accuracy of finding weapons over that currently attained by traditional stop-and-frisks. Yet such detectors—precisely because they are less burdensome—may, under current Fourth Amendment precedent, be deemed "nonsearches," and thus entirely free from constitutional scrutiny.[37] Without such scrutiny, there is no reason to believe that these devices will be used in ways that escape the class and racial biases often evident in current police practices:

[W]hat reason is there to believe that these devices will be handled in a way that is any more racially and ethnically even handed than what the New York Attorney General's report shows us regarding traditional stops and frisks? As that report showed, African Americans and Latinos were much more likely to be stopped and frisked than whites, even controlling for racial composition and crime rate of precincts. And as is now well known, other high-discretion police tactics like the use of traffic stops show similar patterns of racial bias. In fact, would we not expect the same patterns to show up? Perhaps the biases would be worse, since the potential cost (in terms of risk taken by police) of an electronic frisk is actually lower for the officer than when an officer performs a traditional frisk. Thus using these devices would seem quite unlikely to get rid of racial profiling or similar tactics.[38]

A related relevant phenomenon is that the poor in urban areas, who are also disproportionately racial minorities, simply have less privacy than the rich. "People with more money are more likely to live in detached houses with yards; people with less money are more likely to live in apartment buildings with common hallways." "Because others can hear (sometimes smell) from the hallway what goes on inside apartments, the police can too. My neighbors cannot freely surround my house to hear what is happening inside; consequently, neither can the police." Also, because the urban poor live in less-comfortable places, they are more likely to spend less time in them than do the rich. "Other forms of entertainment are," however, "more costly than sitting on a front stoop or wandering the streets and talking to friends." There are more pedestrians on the street in poorer neighborhoods than in richer ones, which subjects the poor to observation by others. The poor are also more likely to work on assembly lines, shop floors, or hotel kitchens in which they share workspace with others, which renders them subject to surveillance if their employer permits it or if their workspace is open to the public. Current precedent, which rejects the idea that we have a privacy interest when there is a significant probability that other citizens can watch us, thus offers far less protection overall to the poor than to the rich. The expanded use by police of sensory-enhancement technology will often not invade any expectation of privacy that the law recognizes as reasonable. The social and individual costs of using these technologies will, therefore, once again fall disproportionately on the urban poor, a subset of whom constitute the "disorderly" persons whom order-maintenance policing seeks to control.[39]

There is little indication that the poor and disreputable are organizing effective political resistance; the courts also do not appear to offer much aid. The unsubstantiated claims of order-maintenance theorists are widely accepted, even among many members of poor, minority communities. Political support for order-maintenance policing is strong, and, in the process, groups and their members unnecessarily suffer increasing physical, status, and emotional harms while our wider notions of privacy and equality contract and erode. There seems to be little future prospect for enhancing the privacy rights of the disorderly absent newly vigorous judicial action.[40]

Technological Surveillance. The rich and powerful can also suffer under the Court's privacy theories, particularly in the area of technological surveillance. The greater political power of the rich may offer them redress in the long run if they are lucky, that is, if they know that they are being surveilled. But even then, they will face unjustifiable short-run invasions.

One important recent story helps to illustrate the point. In March 2001, the judges of the Ninth Circuit Court of Appeals learned that their computers had been secretly monitored by the Administrative Office of the United States Courts (AO). The AO's goal had been to discourage activities unrelated to the judiciary's work, like listening to music or surfing the Web for pornography. In May, the Ninth Circuit judges, outraged by this surveillance, blocked the system that allowed the monitoring of their computers. The judicial rebellion was led by conservative judge Alexander Kozinski, whose family escaped from then-Communist-controlled Romania when he was eleven years old. In computer monitoring, Judge Kozinski was reminded of his childhood in a totalitarian regime. "I know what it's like to always be on your guard," he explained in an interview. "Everything you say or do will be judged or reported, and you'll have to explain yourself for things that are really innocent." Though Judge Kozinski apparently maintains otherwise, there is strong reason to believe that the Ninth Circuit judges are not entitled to protection against this surveillance under the prevailing interpretation of the Fourth Amendment.[41]

Under current substantive law, employers can sometimes be held liable for damages caused by their employees' Internet usage. Sexually explicit e-mail messages at the workplace can create a "hostile environment," exposing the employer to liability under federal sexual-harassment laws. This liability creates an incentive for employers, including the federal government when acting as an employer, randomly to monitor employees' e-mails. A recognition of Fourth Amendment protection for e-mails between or among a small number of parties when the exchanges did not concern particular work tasks would help to preserve e-mails as "backstage areas." Such a recognition would require extending the exclusionary rule to civil sexual-harassment cases against governmental employers. A sensible constitutional rule would permit the government-as-employer to read or monitor a particular employee's e-mail only when there is individualized suspicion of wrongdoing. Thus, an employee might complain of receiving harassing electronic missives from a particular fellow employee, which would create the necessary suspicion. Such a rule would eliminate the government's incentive randomly to monitor all its employees' e-mail and Internet usage because the results of random searches would be suppressed. Yet the employer still could be expected to intercede when it had a particular suspicion of harassing behavior. A similar result might be achieved legislatively for private employers without the necessity of radical and politically difficult changes in substantive sexual-harassment law.[42]

The objection may still be made that employers, even government employers, own the computers and act in a "managerial" sphere in which efficiency, not public deliberation, autonomy, or personal growth, are the organizing principles.[43] However,

> surely this Taylorite vision of the modern workplace rooted in principles of industrial organization from the 1920s is hard to accept today. As e-mails, modems, and PCs break down the boundaries between work and home, there are progressively fewer private or public spaces for citizens to express themselves autonomously. The Internet has blurred the distinction between the home and the office, as Americans are spending more time at the office and are using company-owned computers and Internet servers to do their work from home. But as technology poses new challenges to geographic concepts of privacy, courts have not been encouraged to think creatively about how to reconstruct zones of individual privacy and free expression.[44]

Finally, information disclosure, like observation of our persons and activities, has implications for group self-definition. For example, the mere revelation of a person's sexual orientation without his or her consent is deeply invasive of the person's publicly chosen self, even if the person has not been observed engaging in a homosexual act. He or she faces particular dangers of being judged publicly on the basis of widespread stereotypes about gays, rather than on personalized, detailed knowledge about his or her complex individual nature. Correspondingly, if such acontextual disclosures feed stereotypes about gays, the gay community is also harmed. If such unchosen and acontextual disclosures abound, many gays may be forced either to make extraordinary, burdensome efforts to protect against revelation or to reveal their sexual orientation at times and places, and to audiences, that they otherwise would not choose. Unfair revelation of an e-mail written by Professor Lawrence Lessig, who was to be involved as an expert in the Microsoft trial, was, for example, incorrectly interpreted as revealing his sexual orientation to be gay. This troubled Lessig, both because he was heterosexual and because his supposed homosexuality had been offered as a way to impugn his motives in the Microsoft litigation. Would not the privacy invasion have been equally or more damaging if Lessig had in fact been a closeted homosexual? Observation and information disclosure are thus not two separate phenomena but merely two aspects of a single concept, "privacy invasion"—a ripping away of the masks by which we define our very natures.[45]

Note that my analysis of whether a privacy interest exists affects only whether the Fourth Amendment applies—whether the court, the legislature, or the executive must even bother to ask whether a police action was constitutionally reasonable or must simply automatically defer to that action. My analysis would significantly expand the scope of the Fourth Amendment's application. But the reasonableness of private acts in public places or of invasions of group privacy interests might turn on different concerns, and perhaps require different remedies, than would more traditional state invasions of individual privacy. In part 1, I discussed one such example: the ABA's recommendation of community oversight of urban police camera-surveillance programs. The existence of such a program, by providing oversight, might render the program reasonable rather than require the complete elimination of this form of surveillance. If safety concerns do indeed require the cameras, then their occasional use may be justified. But that does not mean that anything goes—limitations on police discretion, on the circumstances under which the cameras are used, on assuring accuracy, on how long the tapes are kept, and on ensuring continued monitoring by the People can lead to an effective, a "reasonable," balancing of safety against privacy and work to protect both. Under current constitutional law, there is no mandate for such limitations because the Fourth Amendment simply does not apply. The ABA's proposal is that and nothing more—an effort to persuade localities about what is wise policy. Under my approach to privacy, however, the Fourth Amendment would mandate reasonable procedures, empowering courts, if they saw fit, to insist on the creation of such procedures. Such insistence would not be a form of "judicial tyranny," for it would simply require the creation of mechanisms for giving the People, via those in the affected community, a way to have their voices heard, hardly a form of government by judiciary.[46]

The implications of recognizing group privacy and privacy in public (at least against state interference and observation) can be far more wide-reaching than these few examples illustrate. Just as the antebellum abolitionists were united by, and targeted for, their political views—which raised questions of individual and group free speech suffering from unjustified search and seizure practices—so can harsh police investigative tactics aimed at dissenting groups today, but in the name of safety in the war on terrorism, present a danger to civil liberties. Indeed, in several cases, some lower courts have already rejected mass bag searches or mass use of metal detectors on public streets at political demonstrations when there was no more specific information about terrorist danger at that locality than an "elevated" (second highest) national terror alert, a level that has prevailed for most of the past two years. The courts are justifiably worried about the dangers of terrorism, but the endless projected length of the terror war and a willingness to rely on the most vague and speculative information with which to wage it would mean forever deferring to police discretion in the name of safety. That would in turn mean a blank check for police surveillance and the practical death of the Fourth Amendment. Thus, these courts have wisely given special scrutiny to search and seizure practices and raised issues of free speech, free press, and free association.[47]

The lower courts have done less well in safeguarding families against unsubstantiated claims of child abuse. Child abuse is unquestionably a serious problem that requires state intervention. But the willingness of the state to permit departments of social services to search homes and to seize children from streets or schools for questioning with neither warrants, nor probable cause nor even reasonable suspicion—with little more than a hunch, or on the basis of simple rumor—has destroyed some family relationships and permanently psychically wounded both children and their parents, as Doriane Coleman has thoroughly and ably documented. To see such invasions as outside the scope of the Fourth Amendment's protection entirely—as many courts do—is a bit mysterious and ignores the special value of one form of group privacy, namely that of the family. Again, careful Fourth Amendment scrutiny would not mean that nothing can be done for abused children—Coleman surveys many viable options—but leaving the conduct of social-services agencies unregulated is itself a danger to children and families and ignores the lessons learned from the awesome pain that slaves experienced from the assault on their own families' privacy. A jurisprudence of respect, rooted in the experiences of expressive political violence that faced first the Revolutionaries and then the slaves, can do much to restore the Fourth Amendment as a means for strengthening the ties of peoplehood and the respect for human worth that too often lies sleeping in current truncated understandings of the People's Constitution.[48]

Notes

Notes to Chapter 1

1. For a summary of the plot of *The Matrix, see* Gerold J. Erion & Barry Smith, *Skepticism, Morality, and the Matrix, in* THE MATRIX AND PHILOSOPHY: WELCOME TO THE DESERT OF THE REAL 16, 16–17 (ed. William Irwin 2003) [hereinafter DESERT OF THE REAL] (also defining "the matrix").

2. *See generally* CHRIS SEAY & GREG GARRETT, THE GOSPEL RELOADED: EXPLORING SPIRITUALITY (2003).

3. Much of my recounting of these scenes comes from my own memory upon replaying the first two movies on DVD and having recently watched the third movie in my neighborhood theater. *See also* DESERT OF THE REAL, *supra* note 1, at 12, 27, 159, 169, 217, 41 (explaining the meaning and philosophical significance of the phrase "the desert of the real"). *See generally* SEAY & GARRETT, *supra* note 2 (summarizing the plots of the three *Matrix* movies).

4. *See generally* Andrew E. Taslitz, *Everyday Terrorism and the Social Contract: The Wisdom of a Least Restrictive Alternatives Analysis under the Fourth Amendment in an Age of Fear* (draft manuscript 2006) [hereinafter Taslitz, *Everyday Terrorism*]. Other scholars have addressed the role of the *Second Amendment* to the U.S. Constitution in taming political violence, the best work on this subject being DAVID C. WILLIAMS, THE MYTHIC MEANINGS OF THE SECOND AMENDMENT: TAMING POLITICAL VIOLENCE IN A CONSTITUTIONAL REPUBLIC (2003). But no one has yet explored the *Fourth Amendment's* role in taming political violence. Moreover, Williams distinguished between "ordinary private violence" and the "domestication of political violence," such as insurrection. *See id.* at 4. That distinction may make sense under the Second Amendment, with its concerns, in Williams's view, with governing both the people's resort to legitimate rebellion and the state's resistance to illegitimate insurrection. *See id.* But the distinction makes no sense under the Fourth Amendment, which reflects the insight that *all* violence by the state is political, as will be explained in more detail shortly. The Fourth and Second Amendments may thus play complementary roles in governing potentially regime-changing, or at least regime-threatening, periodic eruptions of great violence, and both amendments had their origins in such violence, namely that of the Revolutionary War. Of the two provisions, however, only the Fourth Amendment governs the "everyday violence" of the criminal justice system and of the intrusions of the state's civil justice system into daily private life. It is for this reason that I use "taming everyday political violence" as a better shorthand for describing the Fourth Amendment's function.

5. *See generally* Taslitz, *Everyday Terrorism, supra* note 4; PETER K. MANNING, POLICING CONTINGENCIES 16–21, 36, 46, 49 (2003). *See also* ANDREW E. TASLITZ & MARGARET L. PARIS, CONSTITUTIONAL CRIMINAL PROCEDURE 100–42, 284–309, 40–42, 420–22, 438–39 (2d ed. 2003). *See generally* CHRISTOPHER P. WILSON, COP KNOWLEDGE, POLICE POWER, AND CULTURAL NARRATIVE IN TWENTIETH-CENTURY AMERICA (2000).

6. *See* Atwater v. City of Lago Vista, 121 S. Ct. 1536, 1153 (2001).

7. *See generally* Taslitz, *Everyday Terrorism, supra* note 4.

8. *See id.* at 4–13; WILLIAMS, *supra* note 4, at 30–31, 38, 181–83, D. A. Lloyd THOMAS, LOCKE ON GOVERNMENT 23, 30 (1995).

9. JOHN LOCKE, THE SECOND TREATISE OF GOVERNMENT, *in* TWO TREATISES OF GOVERNMENT §3, 131–35 (ed. Peter Laslett 1960).

10. *See id.* at §§131, 135; THOMAS, *supra* note 8, at 63–64; *See* Taslitz, *Everyday Terrorism, supra* note 4, at 3–15.

11. *See, e.g.,* WILLIAMS, *supra* note 4, at 22–24, 49–50, 87–88; GORDON S. WOOD, THE AMERICAN REVOLUTION: A HISTORY 91–95, 123 (2002); *accord* Andrew E. Taslitz, *Slaves No More! The Implications of the Informed Citizen Idea for Discovery before Fourth Amendment Suppression Hearings,* 15 GA. ST. L. REV. 709, 719–26 (1999); Andrew E. Taslitz, *Condemning the Racist Personality: Why the Critics of Hate Crimes Legislation Are Wrong,* 40 B.C. L. REV. 739, 765–80 (1999) [hereinafter Taslitz, *Racist Personality*]. *See also* WILLIAMS, *supra* note 4,

at 14; Taslitz, *Everyday Terrorism, supra* note 4, at 11–14.

12. The Fourth Amendment speaks of the rights of the People to be "secure" in their persons, houses, papers, and effects. *See* U.S. CONST. amend. IV; J. S. MCCLELLAND, A HISTORY OF WESTERN POLITICAL THOUGHT 240 (1996); Thomas K. Clancy, *What Does the Fourth Amendment Protect? Property, Privacy, or Security?* 33 WAKE FOREST L. REV. 307 (1998) (invoking the term "security," often used as summarizing the heart of Locke's theory: to build a society in which men are "secure" from unreasonable exercises of both private and public violence); Taslitz, *Everyday Terrorism, supra* note 4, at 1–40; MANNING, *supra* note 5, at 36–37, 49; DONALD SCHON, THE REFLECTIVE PRACTITIONER 108 (1983) (source of "universe of one" quotation); Andrew E. Taslitz, *Stories of Fourth Amendment Disrespect: From Elian to the Internment,* 70 FORDHAM L. REV. 2357 (2002) [hereinafter Taslitz, *Stories*] (explaining modern infamous examples).

13. *See infra* part 1.

14. *See* Andrew E. Taslitz, *Hate Crimes, Free Speech, and the Contract of Mutual Indifference,* 80 B.U. L. Rev. 1283, 1312–16 (2000).

15. *See e.g., infra* chapter 2.

16. *See, e.g.,* Andrew E. Taslitz, *The Fourth Amendment in the Twenty-First Century: Privacy, Technology, and Human Emotion,* 65 LAW & CONTEMP. PROBS. 125, 158–89, 134–45 (2002) [hereinafter Taslitz, *Twenty-First Century*] (examining minority reactions to police invasions of privacy); Taslitz, *Stories, supra* note 12, at 2257, 2257–80 (discussing minority perceptions of, and reactions to, racial profiling and the high Court's views).

17. U.S. CONST. amend. IV.

18. *See* LEONARD W. LEVY, ORIGINS OF THE BILL OF RIGHTS 150–79 (1999); LEONARD W. LEVY, SEASONED JUDGMENTS: THE AMERICAN CONSTITUTION, RIGHTS, AND HISTORY 147–75 (1995); TELFORD TAYLOR, TWO STUDIES IN CONSTITUTIONAL INTERPRETATION 38 (1969); THE BILL OF RIGHTS: ORIGINAL MEANING AND CURRENT UNDERSTANDING 151–83 (ed. Eugene W. Hickok Jr. 1991); *see generally* NELSON B. LASSON, THE HISTORY AND DEVELOPMENT OF THE FOURTH AMENDMENT TO THE UNITED STATES CONSTITUTION (1937); William Cuddihy & B. Carmon Hardy, *A Man's House Was Not His Castle: Origins of the Fourth Amendment to the United States Constitution,* 37 WM. & MARY Q. 371, 378–91 nn. 38, 84, 91 (1980).

19. *See, e.g.,* County of Riverside v.

McLaughlin, 500 U.S. 44, 71 (1991) (Scalia, J., dissenting) ("One hears the complaint, nowadays, that the Fourth Amendment has become constitutional law for the guilty; that it benefits the career criminal (through the exclusionary rule) often and directly, but the ordinary citizen remotely if at all."); *see, e.g.,* Greg Wilson, *Convicted Killer May Walk Free, Technicality Is Key,* N.Y. DAILY NEWS, February 18, 2001, at A1; *see also* New Jack City (Warner Bros. 1991); The Sopranos: Funhouse (HBO Cable Television 1999). *See generally* JOEL BEST, RANDOM VIOLENCE: HOW WE TALK ABOUT NEW CRIMES AND NEW VICTIMS 28–47 (1999) (discussing how the news media brings new crime problems to the public's attention); Sarah Escholz, *The Media and Fear of Crime: A Survey of the Research,* 9 U. FLA. J.L. & PUB. POL'Y 37 (1997); Tracey L. McCain, *The Interplay of Editorial and Prosecutorial Discretion in the Perpetuation of Racism in the Criminal Justice System,* 25 COLUM. J.L. & SOC. PROBS. 601 (1992).

On the reasons offered by the media for the declining crime rate, *see* Vincent F. Sacco, *Media Constructions of Crime,* 539 ANNALS AM. ACAD. POL. & SOC. SCI. 141 (1995); Jeffrey Toobin, *Women in Black,* NEW YORKER, October 30, 2000, at 48 (discussing tough-on-crime Texas judges joining the bench during the tenure of then-governor George W. Bush); James Traub, *Giuliani's New York,* N.Y. TIMES MAGAZINE, February 11, 2001, at 62 (describing the crime-reducing stop-and-frisk tactics of the NYPD). For an example of a political assault on a judge for enforcing constitutional due process, see Clarence Page, *Ashcroft in Peril . . . or Due for a Grilling,* WASH. TIMES, January 12, 2001, at A15.

20. On the public's surprising support for the "suppression remedy," which excludes from the jury's hearing testimony about evidence illegally seized, *see* SHMUEL LOCK, CRIME, PUBLIC OPINION, AND CIVIL LIBERTIES: THE TOLERANT PUBLIC 45–47 (1999); *see generally* Arthur G. LeFrancois, *On Exorcising the Exclusionary Demons: An Essay on Rhetoric, Principle, and the Exclusionary Rule,* 53 U. CIN. L. REV. 49 (1984); Bill Renkin, *Abuse Evidence Reinstated: Justices Back Cops' Search in Terrell Case,* ATLANTA JOURNAL-CONSTITUTION, March 3, 2001, at A1; People v. Defore, 150 N.E. 585 (N.Y. 1926); *see also* United States v. Leon, 468 U.S. 897, 907 (1984). Current arguments against the suppression remedy and striking the "constable has blundered" theme are summarized in H.

RICHARD UVILLER, VIRTUAL JUSTICE: THE FLAWED PROSECUTION OF CRIME IN AMERICA 63–67 (1996). The leading academic stressing the primacy of truth-finding under the Fourth Amendment is Akhil Reed Amar. *See, e.g.,* AKHIL REED AMAR, THE CONSTITUTION AND CRIMINAL PROCEDURE: FIRST PRINCIPLES 20, 28 (1997) [hereinafter AMAR, FIRST PRINCIPLES]. *See also, e.g.,* HAROLD J. ROTHWAX, GUILTY: THE COLLAPSE OF THE CRIMINAL JUSTICE SYSTEM 32, 64 (1996); Michael J. Daponde, Comment, *Discretion and the Fourth Amendment Exclusionary Rule: A New Suppression Doctrine Based on Judicial Integrity,* 30 MCGEORGE L. REV. 1293, 1297, 1313 (1999); Sharon L. Davies, *The Penalty of Exclusion: A Price or a Sanction?* 73 S. CAL. L. REV. 1275, 1276 n. 6 (2000) (summarizing concisely the leading literature in the debate over the exclusionary rule); Richard A. Posner, *Excessive Sanctions for Governmental Misconduct in Criminal Cases,* 57 WASH. L. REV. 635, 638 (1982) (discussing excessive economic costs).

21. On "testilying" and judicial complicity in this phenomenon, *see* ALAN M. DERSHOWITZ, REASONABLE DOUBTS: THE O. J. SIMPSON CASE AND THE CRIMINAL JUSTICE SYSTEM 49–68 (1996) [hereinafter DERSHOWITZ, O. J.]; Christopher Slobogin, *Reform: The Police: Testilying: Police Perjury and What to Do about It,* 67 U. COLO. L. REV. 1037 (1996) [hereinafter Slobogin, *Testilying*].

22. *See* Alan M. Dershowitz, *Controlling the Cops: Accomplices to Perjury,* N.Y. TIMES, May 2, 1994, at A17; Gabriel J. Chin & Scott C. Wells, *The "Blue Wall of Silence" as Evidence of Bias and Motive to Lie: A New Approach to Police Perjury,* 59 U. PITT. L. REV. 233, 249 (1998) (discussing commonplace occurrence of dropsy testimony). For general background on the concept of abandonment, see TASLITZ & PARIS, *supra* note 5, at 136, 307.

23. People v. McMurty, 314 N.Y.S. 2d 196 (N.Y. Crim. Ct. 1970) (quoting Irving Younger, *The Perjury Routine,* THE NATION, May 1967, at 546); *see also* DERSHOWITZ, O. J., *supra* note 21, at 51 (interpreting then-judge Younger as effectively admitting that he accepted officers' dropsy testimony in many individual cases despite his awareness of the perjury problem). Though Younger's candid remarks were made three decades ago, the problem of testilying persists. *See generally id.* at 49–68; Slobogin, *Testilying, supra* note 21; MOLLEN COMM'N, THE CITY OF NEW YORK COMMISSION TO INVESTIGATE

ALLEGATIONS OF POLICE CORRUPTION AND THE ANTI-CORRUPTION PRACTICES OF THE POLICE DEPARTMENT 36 (July 7, 1994) (coining the term "testilying").

24. United States v. Payner, 447 U.S. 727, 734, 734–37 (1980); *see also* Pa. Bd. of Prob. and Parole v. Scott, 524 U.S. 357, 364 (1998); Smith v. Maryland, 442 U.S. 735 (1979); Rakas v. Illinois, 438 U.S. 128, 137–38 (1978); Stone v. Powell, 428 U.S. 465, 490 (1976); United States v. Calandra, 414 U.S. 338, 348 (1974). *See also* TASLITZ & PARIS, *supra* note 5, at 169–77 (discussing the balancing test); David A. Harris, *Addressing Racial Profiling in the States: A Case Study of the "New Federalism" in Constitutional Criminal Procedure,* 3 U. PA. J. CONST. L. 367, 367 (2001) ("[T]he new conservative majority['s] . . . direction . . . [is] unquestionably away from the protection of criminal defendants' rights and toward a more expansive view of police . . . power."). *See generally* United States v. Leon, 468 U.S. 897 (1984); Ohio v. Robinette, 519 U.S. 33 (1996); Florida v. Bostick, 501 U.S. 429 (1991); Illinois v. Krull, 480 U.S. 340 (1987).

25. *See generally* DAVID COLE, NO EQUAL JUSTICE: RACE AND CLASS IN THE AMERICAN CRIMINAL JUSTICE SYSTEM 16–62 (1999); Whren v. United States, 517 U.S. 806 (1996) (holding that police officer racial animus is relevant only under the Fourteenth, not the Fourth, Amendment); United States v. Armstrong, 517 U.S. 456 (1996) (setting high burden for even obtaining discovery to prove racial animus under the Fourteenth Amendment); *see also* David A. Harris, *"Driving While Black" and All Other Traffic Offenses: The Supreme Court and Pretextual Traffic Stops,* 87 J. CRIM. L. & CRIMINOLOGY 544 (1997); Omar Saleem, *The Age of Unreason: The Impact of Reasonableness, Increased Police Force, and Colorblindness on Terry "Stop and Frisk,"* 50 OKLA. L. REV. 451 (1997); David A. Sklansky, *Traffic Stops, Minority Motorists, and the Future of the Fourth Amendment,* 1997 SUP. CT. REV. 271. On the Court's colorblind jurisprudence and its harm to minorities, *see* Neil Gotanda, *A Critique of "Our Constitution Is Color-Blind,"* 44 STAN. L. REV. 1 (1991); Dwight L. Greene, *Justice Scalia and Tonto, Judicial Pluralistic Ignorance, and the Myth of Colorless Individualism in Bostick v. Florida,* 67 TUL. L. REV. 1979 (1993); Jerome McCristal Culp Jr., *Colorblind Remedies and the Intersectionality of Oppression: Policy Arguments Masquerading as Moral Claims,* 69 N.Y.U. L. REV. 162 (1994); *see generally*

COLE, *supra* (putting forth extended defense of the argument that the Court's colorblind criminal-procedure jurisprudence in a wide range of areas, including the Fourth Amendment, harms minority, especially African American, interests while protecting white interests); ANDREW KULL, THE COLOR-BLIND CONSTITUTION (1992) (tracing evolution of the colorblind ideal in constitutional law); TASLITZ & PARIS, *supra* note 5, at 396–418 (examining colorblind ideal in Fourth Amendment jurisprudence).

26. See Angela J. Davis, *Race, Cops, and Traffic Stops*, 51 U. MIAMI L. REV. 425, 427 (1997); Tracey Maclin, *Race and the Fourth Amendment*, 51 VAND. L. REV. 333, 337 n. 22 (1998) [hereinafter Maclin, *Fourth Amendment*]; David A. Harris, *Factors for Reasonable Suspicion: When Black and Poor Means Stopped and Frisked*, 69 IND. L. J. 659, 675 (1994); *see* TASLITZ & PARIS, *supra* note 5, at 421–25, 441–42, 443–45 (summarizing case law).

27. See Andrew E. Taslitz, *Racial Auditors and the Fourth Amendment: Data with the Power to Inspire Political Action*, 66 LAW & CONTEMP. PROBS. 221, 250 n. 235 (2003) [hereinafter Taslitz, *Racial Auditors*] (African Americans and Latinos generally); TOM R. TYLER & YUEN J. HUO, TRUST IN THE LAW: ENCOURAGING PUBLIC COOPERATION WITH THE POLICE AND THE COURTS 146–47 (2002) (discussing how African Americans, especially if young, are more dissatisfied with, and more unwilling to accept, police officer decisions than are whites). Some of the raw data might be interpreted to show little significant difference in racial attitudes toward the police. *See, e.g.,* David P. Leonard, *Different Worlds, Different Realities*, 34 LOY. OF L.A. L. REV. 863, 870 (2001) ("Attitudes toward the police might also be a measure of our different realities. . . . Several findings show little difference between African Americans and whites."). There is, however, much contrary data and interesting results when the intersection of race and other variables is examined. *See* Taslitz, *Racial Auditors, supra*, at 250 n. 235. Furthermore, minorities may sometimes be pleased with their local police yet have less trust than whites in the police in general. *See id.*; *see generally* JOHN L. BURRIS & CATHERINE WHITNEY, BLUE VS. BLACK: LET'S END THE CONFLICT BETWEEN COPS AND MINORITIES (1999); Taslitz, *Racial Auditors, supra*, at 239–58; TASLITZ & PARIS, *supra* note 22, at 438–39; RANDALL KENNEDY, RACE, CRIME, AND THE LAW 29–75 (1998); *see gen-*

erally Taslitz, *Racial Auditors, supra*, at 238–49 (offering examples of such agitation); Tracey L. Meares & Dan M. Kahan, *When Rights Are Wrong: The Paradox of Unwanted Rights, in* URGENT TIMES: POLICING AND RIGHTS IN INNER-CITY COMMUNITIES 3–30 (1999) [hereinafter URGENT TIMES] (critiquing "Rights, 1960s Style" as ignoring the modern need to protect inner-city communities of color from violent crime).

28. See generally Taslitz, *Racial Auditors, supra* note 27; Taslitz, *Twenty-First Century, supra* note 16; Taslitz, *Stories, supra* note 12; see TASLITZ & PARIS, *supra* note 5, at 94–102; Taslitz, *Racial Auditors, supra* note 27; *Twenty-First Century, supra* note 16 (reviewing scholarly literature on the privacy interests protected by the Fourth Amendment); Tracey Maclin, *The Decline of the Right of Locomotion: The Fourth Amendment on the Streets*, 75 CORNELL L. REV. 1258 (1990) [hereinafter Maclin, *Right to Locomotion*] (similar concerning freedom of movement); Daniel B. Yeager, *Search, Seizure, and the Positive Law: Expectations of Privacy outside the Fourth Amendment*, 84 J. CRIM. L. & CRIMINOLOGY (1993) (similar concerning property); see Taslitz, *Stories, supra* note 12, at 2293–94 (discussing the public uproar over initial trial-court suppression of evidence in a drug case); *see, e.g.,* KENNETH MEEKS, DRIVING WHILE BLACK: WHAT TO DO IF YOU ARE A VICTIM OF RACIAL PROFILING 11–15 (2000) (telling the tale of an innocent man on his way home from work detained by the police for apparently no reason); Jennifer R. Wyann, *Can Zero Tolerance Last? in* ZERO TOLERANCE: QUALITY OF LIFE AND THE NEW POLICE BRUTALITY IN NEW YORK CITY 107, 114 (ed. Andrea McArdle and Tanya Erzen 2001) (noting that of the 45,000 stops reported by the NYPD Street Crimes Unit in 1997 and 1998, only 9,500 resulted in arrests); *see, e.g.,* RICHARD LAWRENCE MILLER, DRUG WARRIORS AND THEIR PREY: FROM POLICE POWER TO POLICE STATE 55, 93, 96–97, 100, 106, 108–12, 117–19, 132–34, 138–39 (1996) (recounting numerous instances of, and data concerning, state seizure of property of the innocent); *see id.* at 49 (describing a "drug squad's surreptitious illegal search of a room when the occupant might return unannounced at any moment").

29. Bonnie Bucqueroux, *When Cops Become Combat Troops: The Controversial Use of Force to Seize Elian Gonzales Is Just Business as Usual in the War on Drugs*, SALON.COM,

May 2, 2000, at http://archive.salon.com/ news/feature/2000/05/02.swat/; *cf.* AMAR, FIRST PRINCIPLES, *supra* note 20, at 20–31 (emphasizing, albeit perhaps too exclusively, the role of the Fourth Amendment in protecting the innocent).

30. *See* COLE, *supra* note 25, at 5–13. *See generally* Margaret L. Paris, *Trust, Lies, and Interrogation,* 3 VA. J. SOC. POL'Y & L. 3 (1995) (discussing importance of state-citizen trust in the law of constitutional criminal procedure).

31. *See* Taslitz, *Racist Personality, supra* note 11, at 749–53, 757–63; Taslitz, *Racial Auditors, supra* note 27 (regarding stereotyping and disrespect under the Fourth Amendment), at 239–58 & nn. 235, 241 (minority-group perceptions of the importance of Fourth Amendment–like protections). There is countervailing data; *see* Andrew E. Taslitz, *Respect and the Fourth Amendment,* 94 J. CRIM. L. & CRIMINOLOGY 15, 25–26 & n. 62 (2003) [hereinafter Taslitz, *Respect and the Fourth Amendment*] (responding to the countervailing data and summarizing and analyzing both it and the supporting data).

32. *See, e.g.,* Taslitz, *Racist Personality, supra* note 11, at 756–66; ANDREW E. TASLITZ, RAPE AND THE CULTURE OF THE COURTROOM 134–51 (1999) [hereinafter TASLITZ, RAPE AND CULTURE]; *accord* RICHARD L. ABEL, SPEAKING RESPECT, RESPECTING SPEECH 18–80 (1998); KENNETH L. KARST, BELONGING TO AMERICA: EQUAL CITIZENSHIP AND THE CONSTITUTION 1–15 (1989).

33. *See* Taslitz, *Twenty-First Century, supra* note 16, at 158–65; Taslitz, *Racist Personality, supra* note 11; *see generally* Taslitz, *Stories, supra* note 12 (collecting historical examples); Ella J. Baker, *Bigger than a Hamburger, reprinted in* THE EYES ON THE PRIZE CIVIL RIGHTS READER: DOCUMENTS, SPEECHES, AND FIRSTHAND ACCOUNTS FROM THE BLACK FREEDOM STRUGGLE, 1954–1990 120, 120–21 (ed. Clayborne Carson et al. 1991). Professor Akhil Amar explains:

[A] great many government actions can be properly understood as searches or seizures, especially when we remember that a person's "effects" may be intangible. . . . Unlike the due process clause, in whose name so much has been done, the Fourth Amendment clearly speaks to substantive as well as procedural unfairness and openly proclaims a need to distinguish between reasonable and unreasonable government policy. For those who believe in a "substantive due

process" approach to the Constitution, the Fourth Amendment thus seems a far more plausible textual base than the due process clause itself.

AMAR, *supra* note 20, at 39–40. This book will try to illustrate some advantages of seeing certain issues as Fourth, rather than only Fourteenth, Amendment problems. The blindness of civil-rights activists in not seeing Fourth Amendment implications of Jim Crow may have stemmed from the flawed popular association between the Fourth Amendment and criminality. *See also* Lu-in Wang, *Suitable Target? Parallels and Connections between "Hate" Crimes and "Driving While Black,"* 6 MICH. J. RACE & L. 209 (2001) (demonstrating similar injuries and mechanisms for their infliction in both hate crimes and racial profiling).

34. *See* Taslitz, *Racist Personality, supra* note 11, at 746–59; Andrew E. Taslitz, *What Feminism Has to Offer Evidence Law,* 28 SW. U. L. REV. 171, 204–09 (1999); TOM R. TYLER ET AL., SOCIAL JUSTICE IN A DIVERSE SOCIETY 91–93 (1997) (arguing that decision accuracy and trustworthiness of evidence are aspects of procedural justice); Taslitz, *Stories, supra* note 12, at 2283 nn. 162–63, 2342–54 (similar point using history and political theory); TASLITZ, RAPE AND CULTURE, *supra* note 32, at 148–51 (discussing more-general constitutional obligations of legislatures); ROBIN WEST, PROGRESSIVE CONSTITUTIONALISM 41 (1994) (similar).

35. Erik G. Luna, *Sovereignty and Suspicion,* 48 DUKE L. J. 787, 787 (1999).

36. On the importance to judicial decision making of judge's attitudes, which are often embodied in the sorts of stories their opinions tell, *see* ANTHONY AMSTERDAM & JEROME BRUNER, MINDING THE LAW (2000).

37. *See* J. Thomas Greene, *Causes of Popular Dissatisfaction with the Administration of Justice,* 40 JUDGES J. 22, 22–24 (2001) (arguing that the public's perception that criminals go free on technicalities partly reflects court's failure to explain to laypersons the value of such rules).

38. No citations are offered for the historical summary constituting the remainder of this chapter because it is the burden of the entire remainder of this book to substantiate the accuracy of that summary.

39. *See* COLE, *supra* note 25 (documenting this disproportionate burden throughout many stages of the criminal justice system); Taslitz, *Stories, supra* note 12, at 2282–2354 (illustrating differing perceptions).

40. For a defense of the approach to constitutional interpretation used in this book, *see* Taslitz, *Respect and the Fourth Amendment, supra* note 31, at 15. For the sake of simplicity of expression, I sometimes use language that sounds like I am relying on the subjective intentions of the framers of the Fourth and Fourteenth Amendments, when I am instead looking at history as a conversation between ordinary people and elites that may limit and inform interpretation of constitutional language today. Similarly, just because I cite incorporationist theorists who sometimes speak of the various framers as "intending" that the Fourteenth Amendment apply most or all of the Bill of Rights to the states, it does not follow that I necessarily sign on to such intentionalist readings. I take the incorporation of the Bill of Rights against the states as a given because that is how the U.S. Supreme Court has seen the matter for decades, a position that is unlikely to change any time soon. I recognize, therefore, that some of the historical evidence I cite would be read differently by the small but well-respected group of anti-incorporationist thinkers. I make no detailed effort, however, to respond to each of their likely arguments. Instead, assuming the incorporationists are right, I canvass the history that explores the implications of incorporation for giving the modern Fourth Amendment meaning. Furthermore, as readers will soon see, there is historical evidence that can be read as suggesting that the Fourth Amendment was intended to be incorporated against the states even if most of the remaining Bill of Rights provisions were not.

But even if the incorporationists are wrong, my conclusions and reasoning would still stand. The leading anti-incorporationists do not generally argue that there would be no constitutional limitations on search and seizure in an anti-incorporationist world. To the contrary, the Fourteenth Amendment's various clauses would still regulate search and seizure but in a somewhat different fashion than follows from incorporation, the two most influential statements of variants of this view being George C. Thomas III, *When Constitutional Worlds Collide: Resurrecting the Framers' Bill of Rights and Criminal Procedure,* 100 MICH. L. REV. 145 (2001), and DONALD A. DRIPPS, ABOUT GUILT AND INNOCENCE: THE ORIGINS, DEVELOPMENT, AND FUTURE OF CONSTITUTIONAL CRIMINAL PROCEDURE (2003). I ultimately rest my argument on fundamental constitutional values revealed by the history of search and seizure through slavery and Reconstruction. Although I read those values through a Fourth Amendment lens, an anti-incorporationist might comfortably choose to use those values to inform the meaning of the Fourteenth Amendment standing alone as a regulator of search and seizure principles. The values revealed by the lived constitutional history of the American people thus support my conclusions apart from whatever any particular framer or group of framers may have subjectively intended. At the same time, however, if the fact of incorporation is granted, those fond of intentionalist thinking about incorporation's meaning should find much to whet their appetite in the pages that follow, even though the meal served may be still more satisfying for non-intentionalist readers.

Notes to Chapter 2

1. *The Declaration of Independence, in* THE CONSTITUTION OF THE UNITED STATES WITH THE DECLARATION OF INDEPENDENCE AND THE ARTICLES OF CONFEDERATION 81, 87 (Barnes & Noble ed. 2002). For a comparison between the original understanding of the Declaration of Independence and what later generations made of it through the time of Abraham Lincoln, *see* PAULINE MAIER, AMERICAN SCRIPTURE: MAKING THE DECLARATION OF INDEPENDENCE (1997). Although "unreasonable searches and seizures" were not specifically listed among the "repeated Injuries and Usurpations" by King George that were declared in the document, condemnation of general searches was implicit in its words, and, as we will see, they were an inseparable part of what led the "American mind" toward revolution. Later, and well before ratification of the Fourteenth Amendment, which applied most of the Bill of Rights to the states, the Declaration assumed a new and broader role, as Maier contends, becoming "a statement of values that more than any other expresses not why we separated from Britain, and not what we are or have been, but what we ought to be, an inscription of ideals that bind us as a people but have also been at the center of some of the most divisive controversies in our history." MAIER, *supra,* at xix.

2. *See* LEONARD LEVY, ORIGINS OF THE BILL OF RIGHTS 157–59 (1999) [hereinafter LEVY, ORIGINS] (on Otis's protest against the

NOTES TO CHAPTER 2

writs). John Adams's admiration for Otis and passionate belief that the dispute over the writs of assistance was at the heart of America's dispute with England was unmistakable: "Otis was a flame of Fire! Then and there was the first scene of the first Act of Opposition to the arbitrary Claims of Great Britain." 2 LEGAL PAPERS OF JOHN ADAMS 107 (ed. L. Kinvin Wroth and Hiller B. Zobel 1965) (also "Commencement of the Controversy" quotation); LEONARD LEVY, ORIGINAL INTENT AND THE FRAMERS' CONSTITUTION 227–28 (1988) [hereinafter LEVY, ORIGINAL INTENT] (more on Adams); *see generally* Tracey Maclin, *The Complexity of the Fourth Amendment: A Historical Review,* 77 B.U. L. REV. 925 (1997) (placing Fourth Amendment in the context of the dispute over the writs of assistance and other search and seizure controversies as among the major causes of the Revolution); SAMUEL DASH, THE INTRUDERS: UNREASONABLE SEARCHES AND SEIZURES FROM KING JOHN TO JOHN ASHCROFT 37, 41 (2004) (noting that the "writs of assistance were the yoke the colonists would not bear" and that "unreasonable searches and seizures were partly responsible for igniting the Revolution").

3. *See The Salt of the Earth, in* LYRICS OF THE ROLLING STONES (1998); *see generally* PAUL A. GILJE, RIOTING IN AMERICA 20–59 (1996) (summarizing rioting and mob action).

4. *See* LARRY D. ELDRIDGE, A DISTANT HERITAGE: THE GROWTH OF FREE SPEECH IN EARLY AMERICA 20–41 (1994) (describing British and colonial seditious-libel policy leading up to, but preceding, the Revolutionary era and explaining that "[c]olonial seditious speech fell into three broad categories: insulting or impugning government officials, criticizing government generally, and spreading false news.").

5. *See* NELSON B. LASSON, THE HISTORY AND DEVELOPMENT OF THE FOURTH AMENDMENT TO THE UNITED STATES CONSTITUTION 31 (1937) (on the prosecution against Coke); LEVY, ORIGINS, *supra* note 2, at 152 (similar); John V. Orth, *The Common Law, in* THE OXFORD COMPANION TO AMERICAN LAW 125, 125–26 (ed. Kermit L. Hall 2002) (on Coke's contribution to the development of the common law); SIR EDWARD COKE, INSTITUTES OF THE LAW OF ENGLAND (1648); LASSON, *supra,* at 31 (describing Coke as one "celebrated authority on the common law"); JAMES R. STONER JR., COMMON LAW LIBERTY: RETHINKING AMERICAN CONSTITUTIONALISM

23 (2003) (describing Sir Matthew Hale as "Coke's successor"); *see* LEVY, ORIGINS, *supra* note 2, at 152 (Hale as "legal luminary"); 1–2 SIR MATTHEW HALE, HISTORY OF THE PLEAS OF THE CROWN (ed. Solom Emlyn; listed 1736); LEONARD W. LEVY, SEASONED JUDGMENTS: THE AMERICAN CONSTITUTION, RIGHTS, AND HISTORY 149 (1995) (source of "rhetorical tradition" quotation and synthesis of the relevant works of Beale, Coke, and Hale) [hereinafter LEVY, SEASONED JUDGMENTS]. Sergeant William Hawkins and Sir William Blackstone continued the rhetorical tradition against general searches invented by Coke, Beale, and Hale. *See* 2 SERGEANT WILLIAM HAWKINS, A TREATISE OF THE PLEAS OF THE CROWN 81–82 (2d ed. 1724); 1 WILLIAM BLACKSTONE, COMMENTARIES ON THE LAWS OF ENGLAND 282–308 (1766–1769). Blackstone condemned hard-to-enforce substantive laws that might be used to justify promiscuous searches:

[T]he rigour and arbitrary proceedings of excise-laws seem hardly compatible with the temper of a free nation. For the frauds that might be committed in this branch of the revenue, unless a strict watch is kept, make it necessary, wherever it is established, to give the officers a power of entering and searching the houses of such as deal in excisable commodities, at any hour of the day, and, in many cases, of the night likewise.

1 BLACKSTONE, *supra,* at 308; *see id.* at 38. *See also* William J. Cuddihy & B. Carmon Hardy, *A Man's House Was Not His Castle: Origins of the Fourth Amendment to the United States Constitution,* 37 WM. & MARY Q. 371, 385 (1980); LEVY, SEASONED JUDGMENTS, *supra,* at 148–49 (Coke's impact on later American search and seizure law); Daniel J. Meador, *Court Procedure, in* THE OXFORD COMPANION TO AMERICAN LAW 647–48 (ed. Kermit L. Hall 2002) (Coke's impact on the common law generally and on American common law specifically); STONER, *supra,* at 11–12 (describing Coke as "perhaps the greatest of the English common-law judges"); LEVY, ORIGINS, *supra* note 2, at 152 ("foremost authority"); *see* LASSON, *supra,* at 31 (Coke as Crown's opponent).

6. *See* LASSON, *supra* note 5, at 31–32. These "insurrectionary speeches" denounced the levying of tonnage and poundage without Parliamentary consent. *See* 1 PAUL DE RAPIN-THOYRAS, HISTORY OF ENGLAND 665 (1747).

7. *See* LEVY, ORIGINS, *supra* note 2, at 155;

see Maclin, *supra* note 2, at 942–43 & nn. 97, 99.

8. *See* LEONARD W. LEVY, ORIGINS OF THE FIFTH AMENDMENT 386–87 (1968) [hereinafter LEVY, FIFTH AMENDMENT] (quoting Lovell); Paul S. Boyer, *Borrowed Rhetoric: The Massachusetts Excise Controversy of 1754,* 21 WM. & MARY Q. 328–51 (1964) (moredetailed background on the excise tax); LEVY, ORIGINS, *supra* note 2, at 155 (paraphrasing the Brattle Church minister); William J. Cuddihy, *The Fourth Amendment: Origins and Original Meaning* 723–24 (1990) (Ph.D. diss., Claremont Graduate School; available from UMI Dissertation Services, 300 North Zeeb Road, Ann Arbor, Michigan) (antitax tracts); *see id.* at 725 ("Apocalyptic rhetoric against the interrogation clause seemed out of all proportion to the degree of intrusion that the clause posed," threatening privacy less than did the searches long authorized by local excise laws).

9. *See* Cuddihy, *supra* note 8, at 721 (source of quotation and explanation of the significance of the Excise Act of 1754); Maclin, *supra* note 2, at 943; *see also* GILJE, *supra* note 3, at 24–34 (describing antiimpressment riots).

10. *See* LEVY, ORIGINS, *supra* note 2, at 155; LEVY, SEASONED JUDGMENTS, *supra* note 5, at 151 (quotation). *See also* M. H. SMITH, THE WRITS OF ASSISTANCE CASE 113–14 (1978); ROBERT W. T. MARTIN, THE FREE AND OPEN PRESS: THE FOUNDING OF AMERICAN DEMOCRATIC PRESS LIBERTY 1640–1800 63 (2001) (satirical attack).

11. MARTIN, *supra* note 10, at 63–64. For further accounts of Fowle's tribulations, *see* DANIEL FOWLE, A TOTAL ECLIPSE OF LIBERTY (1755); 1 ISAIAH THOMAS, THE HISTORY OF PRINTING IN AMERICA 129–34 (2d ed. 1874); CLYDE AUGUSTUS DUNIWAY, THE DEVELOPMENT OF FREEDOM OF THE PRESS IN MASSACHUSETTS 115–19 (1906); LEONARD LEVY, EMERGENCE OF A FREE PRESS 34–35 (1985).

12. *See* MARTIN, *supra* note 10, at 64–67; *see generally* FOWLE, *supra* note 11 (recounting Fowle's version of the affair).

13. *See* DASH, *supra* note 2, at 26–36 (summarizing the events surrounding the Wilkes prosecution); LEVY, SEASONED JUDGMENTS, *supra* note 5, at 155 (Wilkes a popular idol on both sides of the Atlantic); ROBERT R. REA, THE ENGLISH PRESS IN POLITICS, 1760–1774 40–85 (1963); RAYMOND POSTGATE, THAT DEVIL WILKES (1929); GEORGE NOBBE, THE NORTH BRITON: A STUDY IN POLITICAL PROPAGANDA ch. 16 (1939); GEORGE RUDE, WILKES AND LIBERTY (1962). For a brief discussion of Wilkes's impact on American constitutional-rights concepts more generally, *see* JOHN PHILLIP REID, THE AUTHORITY OF RIGHTS: A CONSTITUTIONAL HISTORY OF THE AMERICAN REVOLUTION 3, 25, 45, 57–58, 68–69, 99, 169–70, 186, 194 (1986); LASSON, *supra* note 5, at 43–44 (on *North Briton Number 45* and the king's speech); LEVY, ORIGINS, *supra* note 2, at 59, 159 (similar); TELFORD TAYLOR, TWO STUDIES IN CONSTITUTIONAL INTERPRETATION: SEARCH, SEIZURE, AND SURVEILLANCE AND FAIR TRIAL AND FREE PRESS 29 (1969) (content of the king's speech and of the cider excise-tax law).

14. *See* LASSON, *supra* note 5, at 44. Upon release, Wilkes remained publicly defiant, and "[p]andemonium broke loose in the streets of London" as hundreds of citizens celebrated his release. *See* DASH, *supra* note 2, at 29–30. *See also* LEVY, ORIGINS, *supra* note 2, at 159. Wilkes was sentenced to twenty-two months in prison. *See* DASH, *supra* note 2, at 35 (also describing the events surrounding Wilkes's sentencing).

15. *See* LEVY, ORIGINS, *supra* note 2, at 160–61; Huckle v. Money, 2 Wils. K.B. 206, 95 Eng. Rep. 768 (1763), *in* 5 THE FOUNDERS' CONSTITUTION 230 (ed. Philip B. Kurland and Ralph Lerner 1987) [hereinafter FOUNDERS' CONSTITUTION]; *see also* LASSON, *supra* note 5, at 44–45 (including "greatest consequences"); LEVY, ORIGINS, *supra* note 2, at 161. In another Wilkesite case, Money v. Leach, 97 Eng. Rep. 1075 (K.B. 1765), *in* 5 FOUNDERS' CONSTITUTION, *supra*, at 235, the government appealed its loss to the King's Bench, England's highest criminal court, only to lose again. The Chief Justice, Lord Mansfield, concluded that the Wilkes cases' warrants were illegal:

> Although the common law, he observed, authorized arrests without warrant and Parliament had often authorized searches and arrests on the basis of general warrants, in this case no circumstance existed justifying warrantless searches or arrests, and no act of Parliament was involved. Accordingly, a secretarial warrant, based on executive authority, leaving discretion to the endorsing officer, "is not fit." Mansfield thought that the "magistrate ought to judge; and should give certain directions to the officer"—a foundation for what later emerged as probable cause.

LEVY, SEASONED JUDGMENTS, *supra* note 5, at 156 (quoting Lord Mansfield).

16. 95 Eng. Rep. 807 (K.B. 1765) in 5 FOUNDERS' CONSTITUTION, *supra* note 15, at 233–35; Boyd v. United States, 116 U.S. 616, 626 (1886) (so describing *Entick*); LEVY, ORIGINS, *supra* note 2, at 162 (describing *Entick* as the "most important" of the Wilkesite cases); *see* LASSON, *supra* note 5, at 47; LEVY, ORIGINS, *supra* note 2, at 162.

17. EDWARD CARRINGTON, 19 STATE TRIALS OF THE UNITED STATES DURING THE ADMINISTRATION OF WASHINGTON AND ADAMS 122 (ed. Francis Wharton 1849); 5 FOUNDERS' CONSTITUTION, *supra* note 15, at 237.

18. *See* LEVY, ORIGINS, *supra* note 2, at 162. Dash contends that Lord Camden's rhetoric sounded like a blow against the king's power and that, for the colonists, *Entick* became the "benchmark for the rights of Englishmen." DASH, *supra* note 2, at 31. But, in Dash's view, the colonists were mistaken, for the holding of the case was a narrow one: "the secretary of state lacked jurisdiction to issue general warrants." *Id.* But what matters for the history leading up to the Fourth Amendment is what the colonists understood to be *Entick*'s meaning rather than the precise content of the case's holding.

19. CARRINGTON, 19 STATE TRIALS, *supra* note 17, at 122; FOUNDERS' CONSTITUTION, *supra* note 15, at 240.

20. LEVY, ORIGINS, *supra* note 2, at 160–61; *see* MARTIN, *supra* note 10, at 73; LEVY, SEASONED JUDGMENTS, *supra* note 5, at 155. For more on the Wilkes cases' effect on American preconstitutional politics, *see* PATRICIA BONOMI, A FACTIOUS PEOPLE: POLITICS AND SOCIETY IN COLONIAL NEW YORK 267–76 (1971); PAULINE MAIER, FROM RESISTANCE TO REVOLUTION: COLONIAL RADICALS AND THE DEVELOPMENT OF AMERICAN OPPOSITION TO BRITAIN: 1765–1776 162–77 (1972); Jack P. Green, *Bridge to Revolution: The Wilkes Fund Controversy in South Carolina 1769–1775*, 29 J. SOUTHERN HISTORY 19–52 (1963). Says historian Leonard Levy, "The Fourth Amendment, as well as the First and the Fifth, owes something to the Wilkes cases." LEVY, SEASONED JUDGMENTS, *supra* note 5, at 155. The Wilkes cases were covered by the colonywide press, unlike *Paxton's Case,* another seminal case in the history leading up to the Fourth Amendment (*see id.* at 155), for which media coverage was far more local to the area of Boston, Massachusetts. *See id.*

21. *See* LEVY, ORIGINS, *supra* note 2, at 162–63 (emphasis added).

22. *See* LEVY, SEASONED JUDGMENTS, *supra* note 5, at 157; LEVY, ORIGINS, *supra* note 2, at 160–61.

23. For a concise review of the British and American history of seditious libel, treasonous speech, and related efforts to squelch political dissent up to the ratification of the First Amendment, *see* MICHAEL KENT CURTIS, FREE SPEECH, "THE PEOPLE'S DARLING PRIVILEGE": STRUGGLES FOR FREEDOM OF EXPRESSION IN AMERICAN HISTORY 23–51 (2000) (rebellious colonists, in the exigency of war, suppressed Loyalist opinions, exiled their persons, arrested Quakers, and searched them based on a general warrant); *see also* MARTIN, *supra* note 10, at 88 ("Though these practices hardly bespeak an open press, we should bear in mind the context. Sedition was a very real threat."). Furthermore, it was after such acts of repression that Americans added state and federal constitutional provisions "that seem to have restricted some repressive revolutionary practices." CURTIS, *supra,* at 47. Nevertheless, there were a few American seditious-libel prosecutions after the Bill of Rights' adoption, "but there were also claims that such prosecution for seditious libel violated the guarantees of free speech and press." *Id.* at 48. Curtis suggests that there was nevertheless a strong popular free-speech tradition by 1791 that was far broader than that espoused by some common-law elites like Blackstone, and, though some defended the more restrictive views, the First Amendment was ratified in a context in which political libel prosecutions had almost disappeared. *See id.* at 50. Other thinkers have gone even further, flatly concluding that post-1791 seditious-libel prosecutions were squarely inconsistent with the original understanding of the First Amendment and were mere exercises of brute power. *See generally* Craig Smith, *The Hamiltonian Federalists, in* SILENCING THE OPPOSITION: GOVERNMENT STRATEGIES OF SUPPRESSION OF FREEDOM OF EXPRESSION 1–23 (ed. Craig R. Smith 1996). In any event, at least concerning the constitutionality of seditious-libel prosecutions, the more protective speech tradition had won out by the time that the ratification of the Fourteenth Amendment extended the protections of the First and Fourteenth Amendments to the states. *See* CURTIS, *supra,* at 46–51, 115–16, 433; MARTIN, *supra* note 10, at 154 (Jefferson's election in the

"Revolution of 1800" laid the modern concept of press liberty).

24. *See, e.g.,* DAVID LOWENTHAL, PRESENT DANGERS: REDISCOVERING THE FIRST AMENDMENT xxiv (2002) ("liberty/license" distinction); Andrew E. Taslitz, *Slaves No More! The Implications of the Informed Citizen Ideal for Discovery before Fourth Amendment Suppression Hearings,* 15 GA. ST. U. L. REV. 709 (1999) (First Amendment/Fourth Amendment relationship); Andrew E. Taslitz, *Hate Crimes, Free Speech, and the Contract of Mutual Indifference,* 80 B.U. L. REV. 1283 (2000) (defending similar point with emphasis on the First Amendment implications).

25. *See* GORDON S. WOOD, THE AMERICAN REVOLUTION 23–24 (2002); *see* MARTIN, *supra* note 10, at 75.

26. *See* MARTIN, *supra* note 10, at 75–76; WOOD, *supra* note 25, at 17–18 (noting huge costs to the British of the Seven Years' War), 23–24 (re-igniting standing-army controversy).

27. *See* WOOD, *supra* note 25, at 27–28; MARTIN, *supra* note 10, at 75.

28. MARTIN, *supra* note 10, at 24, 75–76. For eighteenth-century residents of the Empire, "the right to trial by jury was an essential element in their definition of restrained government." JOHN PHILLIP REID, THE AUTHORITY OF RIGHTS: A CONSTITUTIONAL HISTORY OF THE AMERICAN REVOLUTION 48 (1986). Juries offered disinterested decision makers independent of the Crown and "shared with the litigant a community interest in the security of his property." *Id.* at 49. Juries protected the citizenry from secret trials, "venal jurists, purchased testimony, dependent officials, and partial judgments." *Id.* The localism of juries was a safeguard against oppression by a distant power (*id.* at 51), and the jury itself was viewed as an instrument by which citizens and dissenting groups could preserve their liberty. *See id.* at 49. Maryland legislators therefore expressed the American sentiment well, describing the Stamp Act's turn to vice-admiralty courts as a move that "renders the Subject insecure in his Liberty and Property." *Maryland Resolves, 28 September 1765, in* PROLOGUE TO REVOLUTION: SOURCES AND DOCUMENTS ON THE STAMP ACT CRISIS, 1764–1766 53 (ed. Edmund S. Morgan 1959). Colonial juries had defeated imperial policy, nullified Parliamentary statutes, and protected local citizens while punishing royal officials who enforced "unconstitutional" laws. *See* REID, *supra,* at 53. Imperial

assaults on the jury by the Stamp Act and other legislation were thus perceived as assaults on colonial liberty and self-government. *See id.* at 53.

29. WOOD, *supra* note 25, at 28–29. The Stamp Act Congress resulted in fourteen resolutions condemning, among other things, British efforts to tax Americans who were not, and could not properly be, represented in Parliament or on British juries and the act's likely ill effects on the health of the American economy. *See* FRANCIS D. COGLIANO, REVOLUTIONARY AMERICA, 1763–1815: A POLITICAL HISTORY 33–34 (2000) (concisely summarizing the Stamp Act Congress resolutions).

30. *See* GILJE, *supra* note 3, at 38–40; WOOD, *supra* note 25, at 29. Oliver had reason to back down. The crowd had destroyed his "stable house and coach, symbols of upper-class affluence and the widening gap between the rich and the poor in Boston. Having finished with these the crowd then turned to his home, breaking windows, smashing furniture, tearing up the gardens, and emptying the wine cellar." COGLIANO, *supra* note 29, at 35. *See also* RAY RAPHAEL, A PEOPLE'S HISTORY OF THE AMERICAN REVOLUTION: HOW COMMON PEOPLE SHAPED THE FIGHT FOR INDEPENDENCE 12–13 (2001); WOOD, *supra* note 25, at 29.

31. *See* RAPHAEL, *supra* note 30, at 12–13; RICHARD WALSH, CHARLESTON'S SONS OF LIBERTY: A STUDY OF THE ARTISANS, 1763–1789 37 (1959); *see* GILJE, *supra* note 3, at 38–39; MAIER, *supra* note 20, at 3 (eighteenth-century Americans saw some riots as contributing to the public welfare). Internal events in Britain also contributed to the Stamp Act's repeal, for the American nonimportation effort heightened British fears about the economic impact of the act. *See* COGLIANO, *supra* note 29, at 35–36.

32. *See* TAYLOR, *supra* note 13, at 35–36; *see* LEVY, SEASONED JUDGMENTS, *supra* note 5, at 152 (defining the writs and explaining writ procedures); REID, *supra* note 28, at 196 (similar). A London writer of 1771 also railed against the British version of the writs as mere "general warrants" authorizing the "meanest custom-house officer" to enter any home, break any door, seize any prohibited goods. *See* "*Lucius,*" 126 POLITICAL REGISTER 9 (1771) (quoted in REID, *supra* note 28, at 196–97); LASSON, *supra* note 5, at 51, 56–57.

33. *See* LASSON, *supra* note 5, at 57, 60. Otis described the writs as "annihilating"

the status of a man's home as "his castle," "monsters in law" that "live forever, [yet] no one can be called to account." TAYLOR, *supra* note 13, at 37 (quoting Otis). This quote followed Otis's comparison to the common-law warrant for stolen goods, which lacked the defective unlimited geographic and temporal reach of the writs of assistance. *See id.*

34. LASSON, *supra* note 5, at 60.

35. TAYLOR, *supra* note 13, at 37–38 (again quoting Otis).

36. *Id.* at 38; RAPHAEL, *supra* note 30, at 13. Hutchinson had also insulted lower-class colonists by blaming the Knowles impressment riot—another important event in American search and seizure history, to be discussed shortly—on "Foreign Seamen, Servants, Negros, and Other Persons of Mean and Vile Condition." GORDON S. WOOD, THE RADICALISM OF THE AMERICAN REVOLUTION 34 (1991) (quoting Hutchinson); *see also* Gary B. Nash, *Social Change and the Growth of Pre-Revolutionary Urban Radicalism, in* The AMERICAN REVOLUTION: EXPLORATIONS IN THE HISTORY OF AMERICAN RADICALISM 20 (1976) (more on this point). It is likely that Hutchinson was correct about the prominent role played by seamen and African Americans; *see* Marcus Rediker, *A Motley Crew of Rebels: Sailors, Slaves, and the Coming of the American Revolution, in* THE TRANSFORMING HAND OF REVOLUTION: RECONSIDERING THE AMERICAN REVOLUTION AS A SOCIAL MOVEMENT 155–98 (ed. Ronald Hoffman and Peter J. Albert 1995). But that did not alter the likely intended insulting impact of Hutchinson's statements. *See* TAYLOR, *supra* note 13, at 38 (expressly linking the writs controversy to the assault on Hutchinson).

37. GARY B. NASH, THE URBAN CRUCIBLE: SOCIAL CHANGE, POLITICAL CONSCIOUSNESS, AND THE ORIGINS OF THE AMERICAN REVOLUTION 294–97 (1979). Pauline Maier has argued that the attack on Hutchinson's home had less to do with the Stamp Act than with its being "inspired by a group of merchants who feared they had been named in a set of recent depositions about smuggling." MAIER, *supra* note 20, at 58. Ray Raphael convincingly responds, "Even if the rioters had an interest in destroying some papers, however, the severity with which they destroyed everything else remains relevant to their feelings of underlying hostility [toward Hutchinson]." *See* RAPHAEL, *supra* note 30, at 320 n. 7.

38. *See* GILJE, *supra* note 3, at 3–31;

THOMAS BARROW, TRADE AND EMPIRE: THE BRITISH CUSTOMS SERVICE IN COLONIAL AMERICA, 1660–1775 91 (1967); John Lax & William Pencak, *The Knowles Riot and the Crisis of the 1740s in Massachusetts, in* PERSPECTIVES IN AMERICAN HISTORY 10 (1976); NASH, *supra* note 37, at 237–38.

39. GILJE, *supra* note 3, at 3, 31–33; RAPHAEL, *supra* note 30, at 11.

40. RAPHAEL, *supra* note 30, at 11.

41. *See id.* (estimates rioters in the thousands); GILJE, *supra* note 3, at 31 (estimating rioters as in the "[h]undreds, perhaps thousands"); RAPHAEL, *supra* note 30, at 11–12.

42. *See* GILJE, *supra* note 3, at 28, 38; RAPHAEL, *supra* note 30, at 14–16 (also describing the Whigs as "merchants, lawyers, and other colonists of comfortable means"). *See also* MAIER, *supra* note 20, at 86 ("The officers and committee members of the 'Sons of Liberty' were drawn almost entirely from the middle and upper ranks of colonial society."); WOOD, *supra* note 25, at 24 (quoting William Smith Jr.), 30.

43. *See* WOOD, *supra* note 25, at 31.

44. *See id.* at 32–34; JOHN DICKINSON, LETTERS FROM A FARMER IN PENNSYLVANIA (1768); *see generally* MILTON E. FLOWER, JOHN DICKINSON: CONSERVATIVE REVOLUTIONARY (1983); COGLIANO, *supra* note 29, at 41 (the circular letter "repeated the now familiar claim that Parliament had no right to tax the colonies for the purpose of raising revenue" and "urged the other colonies to resist the Townshend Acts"); TAYLOR, *supra* note 13, at 38. With the "unerring bad timing of an inept bureaucrat," customs collector Harrison chose to seize the *Liberty* just as an impressment gang had been forced by a waterfront crowd resisting the impressments to retreat to the warship *Romney*. ALAN AXELROD, THE COMPLETE IDIOT'S GUIDE TO THE AMERICAN REVOLUTION 80–81 (2000). The seizure of the *Liberty* and resistance to impressments were thus also importantly linked. *See also* COGLIANO, *supra* note 29, at 42 (describing the riot and its effects).

45. LEVY, SEASONED JUDGMENTS, *supra* note 5, at 303. John Phillip Reid is thus simply wrong in saying that search and seizure disputes, especially over the writs of assistance, were "not a cause of the American Revolution and . . . [were] mentioned as a grievance to strengthen the Whig case, not because it was of any practical significance." REID, *supra* note 28, at 198. Reid seems to be arguing that the writs had little practical impact in America because they were so

successfully resisted, rendering them "a grievance mainly because of American knowledge of the general warrants controversy in Great Britain." *Id.* What Reid fails fully to appreciate, and what I argue throughout this part of the book, is that search and seizure disputes were about more than just the writs of assistance and were intimately connected with both the theoretical disputes and the on-the-ground complaints and expressive violence of the everyday colonists that were at the heart of the Revolution. It might be correct that the writs alone, as one of but many grievances, "would not have led to separation from the mother country." *Id.* But the writs and other oppressive search and seizure practices never were alone, being part and parcel of the struggles over sovereignty, representation, and economic and political autonomy that sparked the dispute with the mother country.

In any event, whether search and seizure disputes "caused" the American Revolution is less important than the *meaning* that those disputes held for Americans by the time of the 1791 ratification of the Bill of Rights. Even Reid concedes that the dispute over the writs "may have contributed to the Bill of Rights." *Id.* at 198. If Reid eliminated the qualifying words "may have," he would have had it just right.

46. *See* LEVY, SEASONED JUDGMENTS, *supra* note 5, at 303.

47. *See* WOOD, *supra* note 25, at 39–40; LEVY, SEASONED JUDGMENTS, *supra* note 5, at 303.

48. *See* WOOD, *supra* note 25, at 42 (quoting William Knox), 43–44 (general background).

49. *See* WOOD, *supra* note 25, at 39, 41; LEVY, SEASONED JUDGMENTS, *supra* note 5, at 304.

50. *See* LEVY, SEASONED JUDGMENTS, *supra* note 5, at 304 (background, plus quoting Virginia's then governor); *see* WOOD, *supra* note 25, at 43–44.

51. WOOD, *supra* note 25, at 43–44 (quoting Massachusetts's governor Thomas Hutchinson); Thomas Paine, *Common Sense, in* THOMAS PAINE: COLLECTED WRITINGS 1–60 (1995); SCOTT LIELL, 46 PAGES: THOMAS PAINE, COMMON SENSE, AND THE TURNING POINT TO INDEPENDENCE (2003) (analyzing the history and impact of Paine's Revolutionary pamphlet *Common Sense*); JACK RAKOVE, ORIGINAL MEANINGS: POLITICS AND IDEAS IN THE MAKING OF THE CONSTITUTION

180, 186–202 (1996) (theory of sovereignty embodied in the U.S. Constitution and how federalism is consistent with unitary sovereignty in the People); FORREST MCDONALD, NOVUS ORDO SECLORUM: THE INTELLECTUAL ORIGINS OF THE CONSTITUTION 145–52, 228–29, 276–80 (1985) (similar); GARRY WILLS, EXPLAINING AMERICA: THE FEDERALIST 162–69 (rev. ed. 2001) (arguing that both James Madison and Alexander Hamilton, writing as "Publius" in *The Federalist Papers,* argued for a unitary sovereignty theory of the Constitution as consistent with the system of federalism and separated powers and responding to critics defending a contrary view). Indeed, James Madison defended the Supremacy Clause on the ground that the federal government had to have the final say or "it would have seen a monster, in which the head was under the direction of the members." ALEXANDER HAMILTON, THE FEDERALIST, *Number 44,* 231 (ed. Garry Wills 1982). Madison also traced the failure of confederacies to the "retention of sovereignty in their parts" (*see* WILLS, *supra*) and expressly condemned the idea of a "sovereign over sovereignty, a government over governments." *See* THE FEDERALIST, *Number 22, supra,* at 98.

52. *See* RAKOVE, *supra* note 51, at 203–43.

53. *See id.* at 203–05; John Adams, *Thoughts on Government, in* 1 AMERICAN POLITICAL WRITING DURING THE FOUNDING ERA, 1760–1805 403 (ed. Charles S. Hyneman and Donald S. Lutz 1983).

54. Theophilus Parsons, *Result of the Convention of Delegatee Holden at Ipswich in the County of Essex, in* POPULAR SOURCES OF POLITICAL AUTHORITY: DOCUMENTS ON THE MASSACHUSETTS CONSTITUTION OF 1780 341 (ed. Oscar Handlin and Mary Flug Handlin 1966).

55. 1 RECORDS OF THE FEDERAL CONVENTION OF 1787 132–34, 142 (ed. Max Farrand, rev. ed. 1937 [*reprinted* 1966]).

56. RAKOVE, *supra* note 51, at 209, 211–14, 233–34.

57. *See id.* at 236; *Federalist 10, in* 14 THE DOCUMENTARY HISTORY OF THE RATIFICATION OF THE CONSTITUTION 179 (ed. Merrill Jensen et al. 1976) [hereinafter DOCUMENTARY HISTORY]. Fisher Ames, at the Massachusetts convention, also rejected the idea that representatives were but fainter, more imperfect, copies of the people. To the contrary, argued Fisher in fine Federalist fashion, "The representation of the people is something more than the people." 2 THE

DEBATES IN THE SEVERAL STATE CONVEN-
TIONS ON THE ADOPTION OF THE FEDERAL
CONSTITUTION 8 (2d ed. 1836). *See also*
RAKOVE, *supra* note 51, at 236–39; *Federalist
55, in* 16 DOCUMENTARY HISTORY, *supra,*
at 112.

58. *See* RAKOVE, *supra* note 51, at 228–44.

59. *See* LEVY, ORIGINS, *supra* note 2, at
156; Crown Attorney Jeremiah Gridley, *in
Paxton's Case, reported in* 2 LEGAL PAPERS OF
JOHN ADAMS, *supra* note 2, at 131 (quoting
the authorizing legislation). For details
about the originating legislation, *see* SMITH,
supra note 10, at 17–50. For more on the
writs themselves, *see* APPENDIX I, REPORTS
OF CASES ARGUED AND ADJUDGED IN THE
SUPERIOR COURT OF JUDICATURE OF THE
MASSACHUSETTS BAY BETWEEN 1761 AND
1772 395–540 (1865).

60. *See* LEVY, ORIGINS, *supra* note 2, at
157.

61. *See* LEVY, SEASONED JUDGMENTS, *supra*
note 5, at 158 (on writs and the Townshend
Acts); COGLIANO, *supra* note 29, at 39–41
(details of the Townshend Acts, including
especially the customs duties); LEVY, ORI-
GINS, *supra* note 2, at 63–64; *see* GILJE, *supra*
note 3, at 47; RAPHAEL, *supra* note 30, at 32.

62. MAIER, *supra* note 20, at 126; George
Mason to Joseph Harrison, Boston, October
20, 1769, 3 SPARKS MANUSCRIPTS: PAPERS
RELATING TO NEW ENGLAND 40, 44 [here-
inafter NEW ENGLAND PAPERS]; Letter Extract
from Nathaniel Rogers, Boston, October 23,
1769, 3 NEW ENGLAND PAPERS, *supra,* at 40,
44; *see also* MAIER, *supra* note 20, at 127 n.
23 (discussing Rogers's letter extract).

63. GILJE, *supra* note 3, at 47.

64. RAPHAEL, *supra* note 30, at 33.

65. *See id.* at 33; WOOD, *supra* note 25, at
38; *see* RAPHAEL, *supra* note 30, at 33–34;
COLONIES TO NATION, 1763–1789: A DOCU-
MENTARY HISTORY OF THE AMERICAN REVO-
LUTION 249 (ed. Jack P. Greene 1975).

66. *See* RAPHAEL, *supra* note 30, at 34–36.
"Liberty poles" were tall poles erected "as a
symbol of defiance and rebellion" to colonial authorities, often serving as "the rallying points for anti-British protests and
riots." *See* AXELROD, *supra* note 44, at 78.

67. RICHARD MAXWELL BROWN, STRAINS
OF VIOLENCE: HISTORICAL STUDIES OF AMERI-
CAN VIOLENCE AND VIGILANTISM 56 (1975);
see also Richard M. Brown, *Violence and the
American Revolution, in* ESSAYS ON THE AMER-
ICAN REVOLUTION 103 (ed. Stephen G. Kurtz
and James H. Huston 1973).

68. LEVY, ORIGINS, *supra* note 2, at 166.

"William Henry Drayton," writes Levy,
"seems to have been the [one] exception," a
lone writer then urging special warrants in
place of warrantless searches and general
warrants. LEVY, SEASONED JUDGMENTS, *supra*
note 5, at 174 n. 54.

69. Cuddihy, *supra* note 8, at 1178–79
(source of quotation). "General searches
[thus] continued in the colonies" at this
time, writes Levy, "as the prevailing standard, not the specific warrants used in Massachusetts." LEVY, SEASONED JUDGMENTS,
supra note 5, at 160–61. "Nevertheless," he
continues, "some colonies became more
familiar with specific warrants and even
used them in various kinds of cases." Moreover, Otis's principled objection to the
breadth of the writs, from whatever source
their authority arose, while then bearing
"scarce fruit" in changed practices or calls
for change by colonial governments outside
Massachusetts, did catch fire before ratification of the Bill of Rights, though well after
the end of the Revolution. *See id.* at 161.

70. *See* Thomas Y. Davies, *Recovering the
Original Fourth Amendment,* 98 MICH. L. REV.
547, 655–68 & n. 302 (1999). I have noted
the availability and use of general searches
in many colonies before, during, and after
the Revolution, relying on Cuddihy's work.
Davies arguably reads the history very differently, offering a detailed critique of Cuddihy's analysis of general warrants. Cuddihy,
says Davies, argues "that the general warrant
was common in colonial practice and was
still widely used and approved of in some
states until the mid-1780s—virtually the eve
of the Fourth Amendment's adoption."
Davies, *supra,* at 655 n. 299. Davies instead
reads the history as showing that American
lawyers saw condemnation of general warrants as doctrine by the late 1760s, though
"some ignorant justices of the peace" continued to use general warrants for arrests or
searches of houses. *See id.* For Davies, the
favored status of specific warrants was well
settled prior to the first round of state search
and seizure provisions adopted in 1776 and
1777. *See id.* at 655 n. 299. The most accurate characterization, I believe, is that the
status of general versus specific warrants was
in flux, that there were conflicting and contradictory currents of views, and that common-law and elite theoretical critique and
perhaps popular perception and agitation
changed slowly and before widespread
change in actual practice. I see no need to
enter into the details of the Cuddihy-Davies

debate on this point, however, because it is clear that embrace of specific warrants became ever stronger as first ratification of the Constitution and then of the Bill of Rights approached, and by the time of the latter's ratification, rejection of general warrants was widely accepted as both a bedrock theoretical principle and an aspiration for practice. The sequence and pace of evolution of attitudes toward general warrants may be disputed, but the ultimate result by the time of the ratification of the Fourth Amendment cannot seriously be denied. Likewise, by that ratification date, concerns about general warrants unquestionably had stemmed *both* from the unrepresentative nature of their original roots in Parliament and from the entire flawed set of concepts that defined the general warrant's meaning. *See also* Speech by James Madison, June 8, 1789, *in* 2 THE BILL OF RIGHTS: A DOCUMENTARY HISTORY 1028 (ed. Bernard Schwartz 1971) [hereinafter SCHWARTZ, BILL OF RIGHTS]. The history of the evolution of the various state constitutional analogues having an influence on the Fourth Amendment is concisely summarized in LEVY, SEASONED JUDGMENTS, *supra* note 5, at 161–70. The text of the provisions themselves and of the relevant legislative history is collected in THE COMPLETE BILL OF RIGHTS: THE DRAFTS, DEBATES, SOURCES, AND ORIGINS 223–64 (ed. Neil Cogan 1997) [hereinafter COGAN, COMPLETE BILL OF RIGHTS]. For a more general history of the state bills of rights, *see* THE BILL OF RIGHTS AND THE STATES: THE COLONIAL AND REVOLUTIONARY ORIGINS OF AMERICAN LIBERTIES (ed. Patrick T. Conley and John P. Kaminski 1992) and WILLI PAUL ADAMS, THE FIRST AMERICAN CONSTITUTIONS: REPUBLICAN IDEOLOGY AND THE MAKING OF THE STATE CONSTITUTIONS IN THE REVOLUTIONARY ERA (exp. ed. 2001) (emphasizing early notions of popular sovereignty, dual sovereignty, representation, extralegal registers of the public will, equality, liberty, and the common good).

71. *See, e.g.,* Andrew E. Taslitz, *Respect and the Fourth Amendment*, 94 J. CRIM. L. & CRIMINOLOGY 15, 41–51 (2003); Cuddihy, *supra* note 8, at 345; LASSON, *supra* note 5, at 49–50.

72. 1 THOMAS H. COOLEY, A TREATISE ON CONSTITUTIONAL LIMITATIONS 611 (1927) (quoting Pitt). Similarly, Lord Camden, in purporting to condemn general warrants issued by the secretary of state, declared, "It is time to put an end to them." Entick v.

Carrington, 2 Wils. K.B. 274, 282 (1765). He continued, explaining that the secretary of state could not "lawfully break into a man's house and study to search for evidence against him; this would be worse than the Spanish Inquisition; for ransacking a man's secret drawers and Boxes to come at evidence against him, is like racking his body to come at his secret thoughts." *Id.* at 282–83.

73. *See* Davies, *supra* note 70, at 578; LEVY, ORIGINS, *supra* note 2, at 166, 173. Cuddihy, *supra* note 8, collects many such statements from the newspapers and other writings of the time, and Cuddihy's work on this point is summarized in LEVY, SEASONED JUDGMENTS, *supra* note 5, at 160. *See also* Huckle v. Money, 2 Wils. K.B. 206, 210, 95 Eng. Rep. 768, 772, 773 (1763); LASSON, *supra* note 5, at 44–45 n. 111 (discussing *Huckle*).

74. Dash summarized the nature of the writs of assistance this way:

A writ of assistance was the broadest and vaguest of all general warrants. The holder of such a writ had unlimited authority to enter any home, shop, ship, or warehouse, at his discretion, to search broadly for contraband or evidence of violation of the tax laws. Worse yet, the writ of assistance gave the holder the right to command the assistance of others to provide the manpower for sweeping dragnet searches.

DASH, *supra* note 2, at 36. *See also* Davies, *supra* note 70, at 578. When Charles I levied a tax on landholders and merchants without Parliament's approval, "the King's ministers ordered the arrest of persons who refused to pay it." *Id.* at 688 n. 397. During later debate in the House of Commons, "Coke denounced the illegality of the royal order for arrest that lacked a statement of cause (virtually a general, nonjudicial warrant)." Said Coke, "It is against reason to send a man to prison and not show the cause." STEPHEN D. WHITE, SIR EDWARD COKE AND "THE GRIEVANCES OF THE COMMONWEALTH," 1621–1628 231, 240 (1979) (citing 2 COMMONS DEBATES, 1628 100–14 (ed. Robert C. Johnson et al. 1977). For more on the significance of Coke's use of the phrase "against reason," *see* JAMES R. STONER JR., COMMON LAW AND LIBERAL THEORY: COKE, HOBBES, AND THE ORIGINS OF AMERICAN CONSTITUTIONALISM 13–26 (1992). Coke's distaste for arrest authority was so strong that he even challenged the authority of justices of the peace to issue arrest warrants before indict-

ment. *See* SIR EDWARD COKE, FOURTH PART
OF THE INSTITUTES OF THE LAWS OF ENGLAND
176–77 (1817, *reprinted by* Professional
Books Ltd. 1986) (originally published in
1644). *See also* 2 SERGEANT WILLIAM
HAWKINS, PLEAS OF THE CROWN 82 (1721).
"Hawkins' treatise was the most complete
and 'current' treatment of criminal procedure available to the Framers." *See* Davies,
supra note 70, at 578 n. 76, 579–80 (discussing Leach v. Money, 3 Burr. 1742, 1766,
19 Howell St. Tr. 1001, 1027, 97 Eng. Rep.
1075, 1088 (K.B. 1765) (emphasis added);
Leach, 3 Burr. 1766, 19 Howell St. Tr. 1027,
97 Eng. Rep. 1088. *See also* 4 WILLIAM
BLACKSTONE, COMMENTARIES ON THE LAWS
OF ENGLAND 288 (1769, *reprinted by* University of Chicago Press 1979).

75. *See* Davies, *supra* note 70, at 577–78
(background), 623–24 (quotations) ("Unlike
the constable, the justice of the peace was a
man of wealth and high status in the local
community. He did not personally make
arrests or searches; rather, he directed his
constable (who was regarded as an officer of
the judicial branch) to perform those
tasks."). The judicial warrant was the only
way for the justice of the peace to give the
constable binding instructions while indem-
nifying him against trespass claims. *See id.*

76. Bernard Schwartz, *The Rights of the
Colonists and a List of Infringements and Viola-
tions of Rights, 1772, in* 1 SCHWARTZ, BILL OF
RIGHTS, *supra* note 70, at 206 (quoting
Boston town meeting).

77. 1 BLACKSTONE, *supra* note 74, at 344;
Davies, *supra* note 70, at 577–78 n. 69
(quoting contemporaneous press accounts of
Chief Justice Pratt's jury instruction in
Leach); *See* Cuddihy, *supra* note 8, at 1126–
27 (quoting various contemporaneous
descriptions of officers); FATHER OF CANDOR,
AN ENQUIRY INTO THE DOCTRINE, LATELY
PROPAGATED, CONCERNING LIBELS, WAR-
RANTS, AND THE SEIZURE OF PAPERS 57 (1764,
reprinted 1970) (English pamphleteer condemning general warrants because they
allowed searches or arrests by common
fellows upon surmise); SMITH, *supra* note 10,
at 111 ("petty Officer" quotation).

78. 2 LEGAL PAPERS OF JOHN ADAMS 142
(ed. L. Kinvin Wroth and Hiller B. Zobel
1965). Otis's quotation about menial servants, of course, combines class-based
offense with a metaphor—that of Canaan's
curse—having far broader political significance. *See generally* STEPHEN R. HAYNES,
NOAH'S CURSE: THE BIBLICAL JUSTIFICATION

OF AMERICAN SLAVERY (2002). Haynes notes
that "the writings of abolitionists indicate
that by the 1670s the 'curse of Ham' was
being employed as a sanction for black
enslavement." *Id.* at 8. This was so because
the curse on Noah's son Ham was associated
with dishonor, perverse sexuality, and insult.
See id. at 9, 65–86; *See* LEVY, ORIGINS, *supra*
note 2, at 158 (quoting Otis).

79. 2 Cuddihy, *supra* note 8, at 1171
(emphasis added).

80. *See* LEVY, ORIGINAL INTENT, *supra* note
2, at 240–43 (1988).

81. *See* BERNARD BAILYN, THE IDEOLOGI-
CAL ORIGINS OF THE AMERICAN REVOLUTION
232 (1967) (" 'Slavery' . . . [a]s the absolute
political evil . . . appears in every statement
of political principle, in every discussion of
constitutionalism or legal rights, in every
exhortation of resistance [in eighteenth-
century political discourse]."); BARRY ALAN
SHAIN, THE MYTH OF AMERICAN INDIVIDUAL-
ISM: THE PROTESTANT ORIGINS OF AMERICAN
POLITICAL THOUGHT 200–05, 289–91, 295,
310–19 (1994). By "chattel slavery," I mean
the American variant of an institution in
which the slave is a nearly rightless "thing,"
the legal property of the master. *See, e.g.,*
ROBERT L. HAYMAN JR., THE SMART CULTURE:
SOCIETY, INTELLIGENCE, AND THE LAW 41–42
(defining chattel slavery); THOMAS D. MOR-
RIS, SOUTHERN SLAVERY AND THE LAW 1619–
1860 424–28 (1996) (defining slavery's
specifically American features); LIBERTY AND
COMMON-SENSE (1760) letter 2, 11.

82. SHAIN, *supra* note 81, at 297 (quoting
DUNCAN FORBES, HUME'S PHILOSOPHICAL
POLITICS 142 (1975)) (commenting on the
views of most of the British authors then
avidly read by Americans); FORBES, *supra*, at
142; *see* SHAIN, *supra* note 81, at 296;
Jonathan Mayhew, *The Snare Broken* (1766),
in POLITICAL SERMONS OF THE AMERICAN
FOUNDING ERA: 1730–1805 245 (1991).

83. THOMAS JEFFERSON, NOTES ON THE
STATE OF VIRGINIA 157 (1787, *reprinted by*
Harper and Row, 1964); *see also* WILLIAM B.
SCOTT, IN PURSUIT OF HAPPINESS: AMERICAN
CONCEPTIONS OF PROPERTY FROM THE SEV-
ENTEENTH TO THE TWENTIETH CENTURY 36
(1977); *Virtue,* NEW YORK EVENING POST,
November 16, 1747; *see also* SHAIN, *supra*
note 81, at 298–99 (discussing historical
context and significance of the quotation
from *Virtue*).

84. SHAIN, *supra* note 81, at 295, 306,
310–12; *see id.* at 295–301 (one major
aspect of "slavery" for eighteenth-century

Americans was the absence of corporate political liberty), 310 ("True liberty demanded that one live within a community of near equals capable of mutually restraining themselves."); George Washington, *Letter to Bryan Fairfax* (August 24, 1774), *in* GEORGE WASHINGTON: A COLLECTION 38 (ed. E. W. B. Allen 1988); BROOKE, LIBERTY AND COMMON-SENSE (1760), letter 2, 6 (Jonathan Maxcy, former president of Brown University, describing the effect of a socially unchecked tyrant).

85. *See* SHAIN, *supra* note 81, at 291–96, 299–300, 310, 312; *see also* William W. Freehling, *The Founding Fathers and Slavery,* 77 AM. HIST. REV. 81, 86 (1972) (John Jay recalled, "the great majority of Northerners accepted slavery as a matter of course."); *cf.* ORLANDO PATTERSON, SLAVERY AND SOCIAL DEATH: A COMPARATIVE STUDY 78 (1982) (slavery and dishonor); SHAIN, *supra* note 81, at 301 ("politically voiceless" characterization).

86. For more-detailed discussions of the meaning of "individualized justice" in the Fourth Amendment context, *see* Andrew E. Taslitz, *Stories of Fourth Amendment Disrespect: From Elian to the Internment,* 70 FORDHAM L. REV. 2257 (2002). *See generally* Taslitz, *Respect and the Fourth Amendment, supra* note 71 (why searches and seizures not based on sufficiently individualized judgments are insulting).

87. *See* LEVY, SEASONED JUDGMENTS, *supra* note 5, at 148, 150 (repudiation of colonial precedent). According to Levy, Americans regarded Coke as the "foremost authority on English law." *Id. See also* FRANCIS R. AUMANN, THE CHANGING AMERICAN LEGAL SYSTEM 46–47 (1940) (the Puritans studied Coke); CHARLES WARREN, A HISTORY OF THE AMERICAN BAR 174 (1911) (Thomas Jefferson said of Coke, "a sounder Whig never wrote."); *see also* LASSON, *supra* note 5, at 35–36 (Hale considered general warrants for stolen goods void, instead requiring particularity and "a showing, upon oath, of the suspicion and the 'probable cause' thereof, to the satisfaction of the magistrate."); LEVY, ORIGINS, *supra* note 2, at 179 (swift liberalization of colonial law); Cuddihy, *supra* note 8, at ch. 7 ("The ideas comprising the Fourth Amendment reversed rather than formalized colonial precedents. Reasonable search and seizure in colonial America closely approximated whatever the searcher thought reasonable.").

88. *See* LEVY, SEASONED JUDGMENTS, *supra*

note 5, at 151–53, 154, 160–61. Cuddihy maintains that "Massachusetts invented the statutory prototypes of the Fourth Amendment." *See* Cuddihy, *supra* note 8, at ch. 7. The royal governor, however, it should be noted, had vetoed the 1762 bill. *See id.*

89. *See* LEVY, SEASONED JUDGMENTS, *supra* note 5, at 161. Virginia adopted its Declaration of Rights on June 12, 1776, completing its constitution by the end of that month. *See id.* at 161. The Declaration's Article 10 read as follows:

> That general warrants, whereby any officer or messenger may be commanded to search suspected places without evidence of a fact committed, or to seize any person or persons not named, or whose offence is not particularly described and supported by evidence, are grievous and oppressive, and ought not be granted.

1 SCHWARTZ, BILL OF RIGHTS, *supra* note 70, at 235. *See also* LEVY, SEASONED JUDGMENTS, *supra* note 5, at 161–62 (analyzing Article 10). Levy apparently equates the phrase "supported by evidence" with "probable cause," though he observes that "[t]he concept of probable cause is stunted with respect to searches but considerably broader with respect to arrests." *Id.* at 161. Despite this provision's deficiencies, it demonstrated the growing concern of the drafting committee with specific warrants, Article 10 having been inserted despite the absence of any search or seizure provision in George Mason's original draft of the Declaration and in Thomas Jefferson's draft of a state constitution. *See id.* at 162. Edmund Randolph saw Article 10 as "dictated by the remembrance of the seizure of Wilkes's paper under a warrant from a Secretary of State." *See* SCHWARTZ, BILL OF RIGHTS, *supra* note 70, at 248. Yet, notes Levy, "Virginia went well beyond a condemnation of general warrants issued under executive authority." LEVY, SEASONED JUDGMENTS, *supra* note 5, at 162. *See also* COGAN, COMPLETE BILL OF RIGHTS, *supra* note 70, at 234–36. The Pennsylvania provision is particularly memorable, in one leading historian's words, because "it recognizes a right of the people in affirmative terms rather than merely declaring against general warrants or grievous searches." LEVY, SEASONED JUDGMENTS, *supra* note 5, at 162. Moreover, "It was also the first to require that the warrant be available only if the informant swore or affirmed that he had 'sufficient foundation' for specific information about the person, place, or

things described." *Id.* at 163. Accordingly, " 'Probable cause, attested to on oath, derives partly from Pennsylvania's contribution to the constitutional law of search and seizure." *Id.* at 163. *See* COGAN, COMPLETE BILL OF RIGHTS, *supra* note 70, at 234–36; *see* LEVY, SEASONED JUDGMENTS, *supra* note 5, at 163 (also concluding that the "Massachusetts provision on search and seizure was the most important of all the state models, because it was the one that the Fourth Amendment most resembles" and through which "Otis's influence at last bore triumphant fruits."). Article 14 of the Massachusetts Declaration of Rights read as follows:

> Every subject has a right to be secure from all unreasonable searches and seizures, of his person, his houses, his papers, and all his possessions. All warrants, therefore, are contrary to this right, if the cause or foundation of them be not previously supported by oath or affirmation; and if the order in the warrant to a civil officer, to make search in suspected places, or to arrest one or more suspected persons, or to seize their property, be not accompanied with a special designation of the persons or objects of search, arrest, or seizure: And no warrant ought to be issued, but in cases, and with the formalities, prescribed by the laws.

COGAN, COMPLETE BILL OF RIGHTS, *supra* note 70, at 234. There are two major distinctions between the Massachusetts provision and the Fourth Amendment: first, the Massachusetts provision omits any requirement that the search or seizure take place within specifically designated premises; second, and more important for my purposes, the Massachusetts provision uses only individualistic-sounding language ("Every *subject* has a right to be secure"), whereas the Fourth Amendment begins by stating a collective right ("The right *of the People* to be secure"). The Fourth Amendment thus seems to combine the substantive protections and concern for the individual expressed in the text of the Massachusetts provision with the Pennsylvania provision's focus on a collective right. Whatever may have been the specific intentions of the framers on these respective provisions, it seems odd to view the fusion of the collective and individual needs in the Fourth Amendment's text as merely random. The fusion is better understood as purposeful, rational, and significant.

90. *See* LEVY, SEASONED JUDGMENTS, *supra* note 5, at 164–65. The searches of Quakers and others

> were conducted cruelly and violently, and all sorts of books, papers, and records were confiscated. . . . Nothing that the British had done equaled the violation of privacy rights inflicted by Pennsylvania on its "Virginia exiles," in defiance of the state constitution and a writ of habeas corpus by the state chief justice, but with the support of Congress.

Id. at 164. *See also* Morgan Cloud, *Quakers, Slaves, and the Founders: Profiling to Save the Union,* 73 MISS. L. J. 369 (2003) (summarizing events surrounding detention of the Quakers). Of the three states then legislatively requiring specific warrants, one (Rhode Island) had no constitution, while another (New Jersey) had one but without a search and seizure provision. *See* LEVY, SEASONED JUDGMENTS, *supra* note 5, at 165. *See also* Frisbie v. Butler, Kirby 213 (Conn. 1787), *in* COGAN, COMPLETE BILL OF RIGHTS, *supra* note 70, at 262–63; LEVY, SEASONED JUDGMENTS, *supra* note 5, at 165 (analyzing *Frisbie*).

91. LEVY, ORIGINS, *supra* note 2, at 13–14 (on Lee's efforts to derail the Constitution); LEVY, SEASONED JUDGMENTS, *supra* note 5, at 165 (discussing Lee's proposed search and seizure provision, which read, "the Citizens shall not be exposed to unreasonable searches, seizures of their papers, houses, persons, or property."); *Federal Farmer, Observations . . . in a Number of Letters from a Federal Farmer* (New York 1787), *in* 2 THE COMPLETE ANTI-FEDERALIST 214–357 (ed. Herbert J. Storing 1981); 2 COMPLETE ANTI-FEDERALIST, *supra*, at 249, letter 4, October 12, 1787; COGAN, COMPLETE BILL OF RIGHTS, *supra* note 70, at 233, 238–42. The sense of insult at being subjected to another's mastery by arbitrary searches and seizures is stark in these demands. A Son of Liberty worried that general warrants would enable officers to search houses and seize the private papers of "[m]en of all ranks and conditions" whenever the officers' '*lordly masters* shall suggest, that . . . [the men subjected to these abuses] are plotting mischief against . . . [these lords'] arbitrary conduct." COGAN, COMPLETE BILL OF RIGHTS, *supra* note 70, at 240 (emphasis added). This Son of Liberty further worried that excise laws would mean that "our bed chambers will be subjected to be searched by brutal tools of power . . . and the most delicate part of our

families, liable to every species of rude or indecent treatment, without the least prospect, or shadow of redress, from those by whom they are commissioned." *Id.* A Columbian Patriot, in February 1788, likewise feared that we would "subject ourselves to the insolence of any petty revenue officer to enter our houses, search, insult, and seize at pleasure." *Id.* at 241. A Farmer and Planter, on April 1, 1788, made a particularly urgent protest against the proposed original Constitution's lack of search and seizure protections for exposing Americans to rummaging by the "very scurf and refuse of mankind." *Id.* at 241–42. The North Carolina and Rhode Island recommendations, however, were made *after* Congress had already recommended the Bill of Rights. *See* LEVY, SEASONED JUDGMENTS, *supra* note 5, at 174 n. 78. The Maryland Minority Report of April 26, 1788, also recommended a provision condemning general warrants, while the Massachusetts Minority Report (February 6, 1788) recommended a provision that would prevent "subject[ing] the people to unreasonable searches and seizures of their persons, papers, or possessions." COGAN, COMPLETE BILL OF RIGHTS, *supra* note 70, at 232–33. *See also* U.S. CONST. amend. IV. Samuel Dash expressed both dismay at, and an explanation for, the absence of a search and seizure provision in the original Constitution:

> A particular mystery in the Constitution that was ratified by the states is the failure of the delegates to include a provision against unreasonable searches and seizures in one of the articles of the Constitution. If, as we have seen, unreasonable searches and seizures were partly responsible for igniting the Revolution, it would be logical to assume that protection against such invasions of privacy would be given prominent attention in the new Constitution. For the same reasons the inclusion of a Bill of Rights was rejected, the majority of the delegates probably believed that a free democracy based on the will of the people had no reason to fear unreasonable searches and seizures by government officials.

DASH, *supra* note 2, at 41. The Anti-Federalists were equally dismayed by this omission, and their efforts, eventually backed by the efforts of James Madison, bore fruit in the current text of the Fourth Amendment.

92. *See* LEVY, SEASONED JUDGMENTS, *supra* note 5, at 169–70. Davies sees congressional action in the 1789 and 1791 acts as *mere policy choices* not indicative of the congressional understanding of the Fourth Amendment's meaning. *See* Davies, *supra* note 70, at 711–28 & nn. 467–70. This conclusion partly stems from his argument that the word "effects" in the Fourth Amendment (in place of the word "property" in Madison's draft) was meant to narrow the Amendment's scope so that the only types of real property protected were "houses." *See id.* at 710–14. Davies also argues that the Fourth Amendment embraced a common-law concept of "security" that excluded ships from its protection. *See id.* at 605–06, 711, 718 & n. 470. Tracey Maclin parses the provisions of the 1789 and 1791 acts to highlight instead that protection was provided at times for commercial premises. *See* Maclin, *supra* note 2, at 950–55. Both Davies and Maclin agree, however, that there is virtually no legislative history concerning congressional intentions and understandings for each of these two acts. *See* Davies, *supra* note 70, at 711–12 & nn. 470–71; Maclin, *supra* note 2, at 950. Davies thus relies for his interpretation of the acts on a series of contested inferences, many from silence, while conceding the plausibility (though, for him, ultimately not persuadabilty) of alternative interpretations. *See* Davies, *supra* note 70, at 711–18 & nn. 470–71.

Davies's reading of the word "effects" similarly relies on the Framers' expectation that customs collections would be a primary source of revenue for the new federal government, so they would not have wanted to extend Fourth Amendment protection in a way that would have frustrated such searches. *See id.* at 659, 711. Yet he concedes that the 1789 Collections Act did "require specific warrants for searches of *all* buildings rather than just houses," returning, without explanation, to his dismissive description of this provision as the result of mere "policy choice" rather than an interpretation of federal constitutional search and seizure power. *See id.* at 711–12 (emphasis added). He also notes that "sometimes" Congress later provided for warrantless search authority for commercial premises, choosing as his example 1791 provisions allowing revenue officers to search without warrants "buildings or rooms that had been registered as distilleries or liquor storerooms as part of the liquor licensing process." *Id.* at 712–14. But he concedes that these same provisions "generally required specific warrants for searches of houses *or other buildings*" and that the exemption of registered distilleries from the general warrant requirement plausibly could be justified as a waiver of rights implicitly imposed as a condition of registering to engage in the distillery business. *See id.* at 712–14 & n. 471 (emphasis added). As for the Fourth Amendment's embrace of an alleged common-law right to "security" that excluded ships, Davies here underestimates the extent to which the Fourth Amendment in some ways broke with pre-existing practices, as we will see shortly.

The 1789 and 1791 acts were indeed complex and debatably both internally inconsistent and inconsistent with each other in some respects. *See* Maclin, *supra* note 2, at 950–54 (making this point); Davies, *supra* note 70, at 711–12 & nn. 470–71 (summarizing the two acts' provisions). Cuddihy concludes, concerning the 1789 act when read in light of the 1791 act, that Congress's enactment of such legislation "while the Fourth Amendment was before it and [before] the ratifying legislatures facilitated incompatible interpretations of important segments of that amendment. Those who advocate adherence to the amendment's original understanding should consider that its authors expressed conflicting understandings of probable cause and of an enforcement mechanism." Cuddihy, *supra* note 8, at 1556. Maclin ultimately agreed with this assessment (*see* Maclin, *supra* note 2, at 954), though Levy has suggested the stronger inference be made that the adoption of the 1791 act—with far sharper teeth than the 1789 act by empowering magistrates to themselves independently assess probable cause rather than accepting the oath maker's sworn assertion of the cause of his suspicion—reflected the fact that the 1791 act was passed before formal ratification but *after* approval by the nine states necessary to the Fourth Amendment's effective ratification. *See* LEVY, ORIGINAL INTENT, *supra* note 80, at 245–46.

Ultimately, my dispute with Davies on the scope of the Fourth Amendment reflects a difference of emphasis in interpretive attitude. Davies relies more heavily than I do on official and elite statements about the law, though we both, of course, make use of such sources. For example, he relies on the "absence of *legal* complaints about general search authority regarding ships" and concedes that "Americans did express anger over customs officers using general writs to

search warehouses" but dismisses that observation because "the record does not indicate that those complaints ever became part of the *legal* grievance over general warrants." Davies, *supra* note 70, at 605, 608 (also noting that "the absence of complaints about warehouse searches is a pregnant silence in Otis's 1761 argument on behalf of the merchants of Boston; a similar silence exists in Dickinson's 1768 complaint and in Samuel Adams's 1772 complaint."). For me, however, history's role in the creation of constitutional meaning stems from a *conversation* between the legal and other elites and the People. *See* Taslitz, *Respect and the Fourth Amendment, supra* note 71, at 51–80, 90–98. That Americans during the Revolutionary period expressed anger over warehouse searches matters a great deal. Likewise, that Americans loudly protested the seizures of American ships like the *Active* and the *Liberty* by the British, discussed in more detail shortly, carries important weight. Indeed, according to Cuddihy, "In the last years before the American Revolution, Americans increasingly regarded not only houses but ships as castles." Cuddihy, *supra* note 8, at 1213. Partly this was so because of abusive, invasive ship searches by the British and partly because "[o]pinion against promiscuous searches afloat was an offshoot of deepening opposition to the same kind of searches on land by general warrant and writ of assistance." *Id.* at 1217–18. Perhaps equally important, however, "was that naval officers often stretched their power to search as auxiliary customs officers into an excuse for impressing merchants into the Royal Navy." *Id.* at 1218. Ship searches and the hated impressment of colonists thus became closely linked as colonial grievances. *See* Cuddihy, *supra* note 8, at 1218–19. Davies thus reads the history too narrowly when he declares that the colonial complaint about ship seizures "did not arise from ships being exposed to general [warrantless] search authority, but from 'customs racketeering' in the form of hypertechnical applications of customs rules or forfeiture proceedings based on perjured testimony from informers" (Davies, *supra* note 70, at 604), for that focus ignores, among other things, the ship-search/impressment link. Even the "customs racketeering" complaint, however, were it the sole relevant history (and it is not) would suggest only that a warrant preference rule may not have been understood to apply to ship searches. But the racketeering objection is still one to arbitrary, abusive searches and seizures by state actors, thus supporting, not undermining, the argument that the Fourth Amendment is best understood as including ships. Ships, warehouses, other commercial premises, homes, and free movement of the person are all sheltered by the Amendment's protection, though this does not necessarily mean that they are all sheltered in the same way or to the same degree.

93. Alexander Hamilton also noted that mere "parchment provisions" are inadequate in "a struggle with public necessity." LEVY, ORIGINS, *supra* note 2, at 21 (quoting Hamilton). Madison thus eventually came around to the view that a Bill of Rights "might educate the majority against acts to which they might be inclined," thus preventing "legislative as well as executive abuse, and above all preventing abuses of power by 'the body of the people, operating by the majority against the minority.' " *Id.* at 35. *See also* Taslitz, *Slaves No More! supra* note 24, at 426–34 (Founders' "informed citizen ideology" central to the Bill of Rights).

Notes to Chapter 3

1. *See* BARBARA J. SHAPIRO, BEYOND REASONABLE DOUBT AND PROBABLE CAUSE: HISTORICAL PERSPECTIVES ON THE ANGLO-AMERICAN LAW OF EVIDENCE 114 (1991).

2. *See id.* at 118–22; Richard M. Fraher, *Conviction according to Conscience: The Medieval Jurists' Debate concerning Judicial Discretion and the Law of Proof,* 7 LAW AND HISTORY REV. 32–40 (1989); ADHEAMAR ESMEIN, A HISTORY OF CONTINENTAL CRIMINAL PROCEDURE WITH SPECIFIC REFERENCE TO FRANCE (trans. J. Simpson 1913) (vol. 5 in *Continental Legal History Series*); C. L. VON BAR ET AL., A HISTORY OF CONTINENTAL CRIMINAL LAW (1916) (vol. 6 in *Continental Legal History* Series). The apparent purposes of the two-witness rule were to guard against forced confessions and those by the innocent but demented. *See* SHAPIRO, *supra* note 1, at 296 n. 9.

3. *See* SHAPIRO, *supra* note 1, at 122–23.

4. *See* Tracey Maclin, *The Complexity of the Fourth Amendment: A Historical Review,* 77 B.U. L. REV. 925, 926, 960–61 (1997); William Cuddihy, *The Fourth Amendment: Origins and Original Meaning* 853–54 (1990); *see also* SHAPIRO, *supra* note 1, at 127–29 (describing the 1275 English statute's requirement of "light suspicion").

5. *See* SHAPIRO, *supra* note 1, at 127–29.

6. *Id.* at 129.

7. *See id.* at 131–33; MICHAEL DALTON, THE COUNTREY JUSTICE 336–38 (1635); Maclin, *Complexity, supra* note 4, at 960–61; Cuddihy, *Fourth Amendment, supra* note 4, at 95; WILLIAM SHEPPARD, AN EPITOME OF ALL THE COMMON AND STATUTE LAW 649–50 (1659) (reformist repeating much of what earlier handbook writers had said).

8. *See* SHAPIRO, *supra* note 1, at 134; 4 SIR EDWARD COKE, INSTITUTES OF THE LAWS OF ENGLAND 177 (1628–1644). *But see* JULIUS GOEBEL & T. R. NAUGHTON, LAW ENFORCEMENT IN COLONIAL NEW YORK 419 (1944) (noting Coke's apparent confusion, as he contradicted himself elsewhere, saying in the *Twelfth Report* of his *Institutes of the Laws of England* that a justice of the peace can issue a warrant).

9. *See* SHAPIRO, *supra* note 1, at 134–35; 1 SIR MATTHEW HALE, HISTORY OF THE PLEAS OF THE CROWN 107–10, 579–80 (1736) (citing DALTON, *supra* note 7, at cap. 117b); SHAPIRO, *supra* note 1, at 135 (similar analysis of Hale). "Hale insisted," however, "that general warrants to apprehend all persons were void." SHAPIRO, *supra* note 1, at 302 n. 59.

10. *See* SHAPIRO, *supra* note 1, at 136.

11. *See id.* at 136–39; 2 WILLIAM HAWKINS, A TREATISE OF THE PLEAS OF THE CROWN 76–77, 84–85 (Savoy, 1724 ed.).

12. *See* SHAPIRO, *supra* note 1, at 138; RICHARD BURNS, THE JUSTICE OF THE PEACE AND THE PARISH OFFICER (1754). By 1780, Burns's handbook had reached its fourteenth edition. *See* SHAPIRO, *supra* note 1, at 303 n. 74. *See also* SHAPIRO, *supra* note 1, at 139 (analyzing Blackstone). *But see* Thomas Y. Davies, *The Fictional Character of Law-and-Order Originalism: A Case Study of the Distortions and Evasions of Framing-Era Arrest Doctrine in Atwater v. Lago-Vista,* 37 WAKE FOREST L. REV. 239, 321 n. 244 (2002) [hereinafter Davies, *Fictional Character*] (arguing Shapiro underemphasized the "crime-in-fact" requirement, a point that, if true, still does not alter the *definition* of probable cause).

13. *See* David Sklansky, *The Fourth Amendment and Common Law,* 100 COLUMB. L. REV. 1739, 1795–96 (2000); Craig S. Lerner, *The Reasonableness of Probable Cause,* 81 TEX. L. REV. 951, 973–76 (2003); Maclin, *supra* note 4, at 962–64. For more-detailed discussions of the Sugar Act, *see* RICHARD M. KETCHUM, DIVIDED LOYALTIES: HOW THE AMERICAN

REVOLUTION CAME TO NEW YORK 88–90 (2002); Cuddihy, *supra* note 4, at 1200–01; THE COMPLETE BILL OF RIGHTS: THE DRAFTS, DEBATES, SOURCES, AND ORIGINS V234 (ed. Neil H. Cogan 1997) [hereinafter COGAN, COMPLETE BILL OF RIGHTS]; Davies, *Fictional Character, supra* note 12, at 370–71 & nn. 446–51, 380 & n. 479. Davies argues strongly for the embrace of the "more probable than not" definition based on Framing-era dictionary definitions of the term "probable," such as those by Samuel Johnson and, especially, Noah Webster, who actively promoted the Constitution's ratification, and based on a post-Framing-era distinction between "belief" and "suspicion." See Thomas Y. Davies, *Recovering the Original Fourth Amendment*, 98 MICH. L. REV. 547, 706 n. 451 (1991) [hereinafter Davies, *Fourth Amendment*]; Davies, *Fictional Character, supra* note 12, at 380 & n. 480. But other scholars disagree, concluding that the quantitative meaning of probable cause was never clear. See Ronald J. Bacigal, *Making the Right Gamble: The Odds on Probable Cause*, 74 MISS. L. J. 279, 283–89 (2004).

14. See Davies, *Fourth Amendment, supra* note 13, at 650–54.

15. See id. at 650–54. However, "customs officers," as opposed to other sorts of officers, "did . . . sometimes enjoy a degree of statutory protection for wrongful seizures when they seized goods that had initially appeared to be untaxed but later were ruled not forfeit." *Id.* at 653–54. Specifically, late-colonial-period English statutes granted customs officers immunity from trespass suits if they seized goods or ships subsequently ruled not forfeit. See id. at 653–54 n. 295 (citing the Sugar Act, 4 Geo. 3, ch. 15, §46 (1764) (Eng.) as an example). Likewise, "American legislators also provided customs officers with a comparable protection in the event a ship or goods seized by customs officers was ruled not forfeit." Davies, *Fourth Amendment, supra* note 13, at 653–54 n. 295 (also noting similar protection granted by the 1789 Collections Act passed by the first Congress; see Act of July 31, 1789, ch. 5, §36, 1 Stat. 29, 47–48). It must be underscored that by the time of the Framing and ratification of the Fourth Amendment, immunity from trespass suits was granted *only* for searches and seizures done pursuant to *specific*, not general, warrants, contrary to Akhil Amar's suggestion that the law was otherwise. See Davies, *Fourth Amendment, supra* note 13, at 586–88 & n. 99. Tracey Maclin reminds his

readers, however, that even warrantless searches frequently would not result in liability because of a host of procedural obstacles. See Maclin, *supra* note 4, at 932–36. See also Davies, *Fourth Amendment, supra* note 13 (American understanding of Wilkesite-case lessons not limited to the content of seditious libel).

16. See Davies, *Fourth Amendment, supra* note 13, at 654.

17. See ANDREW E. TASLITZ & MARGARET L. PARIS, CONSTITUTIONAL CRIMINAL PROCEDURE 177–86 (2d ed. 2003) (modern concept).

18. See Davies, *Fictional Character, supra* note 12, at 369–72. Davies argues that pre–Fourth Amendment state constitutions also embraced the "in fact" standard, thus explaining why the Fourth Amendment's requirements of probable cause alone might have so troubled so many Anti-Federalists. See id. at 369–77.

19. See Davies, *Fourth Amendment, supra* note 13, at 607–08, 677–84, 723–24; Sklansky, *supra* note 13, at 1780–81.

20. See Davies, *Fictional Character, supra* note 12, at 337–38, 369–72, 392–94, 408–09.

21. See Davies, *Fourth Amendment, supra* note 13, at 557, 744–50; See Andrew E. Taslitz, *Condemning the Racist Personality: Why the Critics of Hate Crimes Legislation Are Wrong*, 40 B.C. REV. 739, 778–80 (1999); AKHIL AMAR, THE CONSTITUTION AND CRIMINAL PROCEDURE: FIRST PRINCIPLES 1–45 (1997); cf. Lawrence Lessig, *Fidelity and Constraint*, 65 FORDHAM L. REV. 1365 (1997) (courts must "translate" constitutional text and history to have meaning in the modern context); SAMUEL L. DASH, THE INTRUDERS: UNREASONABLE SEARCHES AND SEIZURES FROM KING JOHN TO JOHN ASHCROFT 44–45 (2004) (Framers' general intentions subsumed warrantless searches). See generally Maclin, *supra* note 4 (Framers and warrant preference rule).

22. See Maclin, *supra* note 4, at 962–63; Cuddihy, *supra*, note 4, at 1206–11 & n. 54 (*Active* seized in 1767 for departing from legal formalities, *Liberty* seized in 1768 on "shaky" suspicion of smuggling). The *Active* was not the only ship owned by Laurens that was involved in a seizure dispute. See Cuddihy, *supra* note 4, at 1207–12 (concerning the seizure of the *Ann* and two other vessels owned by Laurens: the schooner *Wambaugh* and the schooner *Broton Island Packet*). The seizures of the *Active* and of the

Ann—the latter also resulting in an after-the-fact probable-cause decree, this time upon the filing of an "oath of calumny" by the plaintiff swearing that he had not acted out of malice or revenge—were arguably instances of "customs racketeering"—hyper-technical or inconsistent enforcement of the customs laws to gouge selected colonists. *See id.* at 1209–10. For the best discussion of customs racketeering, *see* OLIVER M. DICKER-SON, THE NAVIGATION ACTS AND THE AMERI-CAN REVOLUTION 208–66 (1951). *See also* NELSON B. LASSON, THE HISTORY AND DEVEL-OPMENT OF THE FOURTH AMENDMENT TO THE UNITED STATES CONSTITUTION 172 (1937).

The Bostonians who protested the *Liberty's* seizure did so on the grounds of lack of probable cause. *See* Cuddihy, *supra* note 4, at 1210–12. When the *Liberty* first entered her cargo, the two observing customs officers noted no legal violations. *See id.* at 1211 n. 55. One month later, however, one of those customs officers, Thomas Kirk, declared that he and his colleague had been drunk and that "the ship's captain had asked him to look the other way while the vessel was being emptied clandestinely." *Id.* at 1211 n. 55. If believed, Kirk's testimony might have established particularized probable cause. *See* Davies, *Fourth Amendment, supra* note 13, at 604 n. 147. However, Kirk's testimony was likely perjurious. *See id.* at 604 n. 147. More important, "No evidence exists that the Bostonians had Kirk's testimony in mind in protesting the absence of probable cause for the *Liberty's* seizure, for that testimony was not published before 1769," well after the *Liberty's* seizure. Cuddihy, *supra* note 4, at 1211–12 n. 55.

Tracey Maclin has described the seizures of both the *Liberty* and *Active* as warrantless (see Maclin, *supra* note 4, at 962–64), though Lasson describes the former as hav-ing been done pursuant to a writ of assis-tance. See LASSON, *supra,* at 172. Whoever is right on this particular point, it is clear that no *specific* warrant existed for the seizure of either ship. In any event, most ship searches under both British and colonial law were overwhelmingly warrantless, and they were often linked in the public mind with the warrantless, arbitrary impressments of colo-nial seaman. *See* Cuddihy, *supra* note 4, at 1217–18. Concerning the latter point, for example, was the boarding of the *Pick Packet* of Marblehead by Lieutenant Panton of the HMS *Rose,* just as the controversy over the *Liberty's* seizure was concluding. *See id.* at

1218. Panton purported to be searching for smuggled cargo but "was looking for Jack-Tars instead. When a defiant crewman cut Panton's jugular open with a harpoon, the 'Journal of the Times' used the incident to illustrate the connection between ship searches and impressments as colonial griev-ance." *Id.* at 1218–19. This was but one example of the reality that "naval officers often stretched their power to search as aux-iliary customs officers into an excuse for impressing merchant mariners into the Royal Navy." *Id.* at 1218.

Additionally, Hancock had himself experi-enced a clearly warrantless abusive ship seizure two months before the better-publi-cized *Liberty* incident, as Cuddihy explains:

Hancock had two tidewaiters of the cus-toms service expelled from his sloop, the *Lydia,* which had just arrived at Boston, with a taxable cargo. To insure that nothing was smuggled ashore unseen, the law empowered tidewaiters to board entering vessels and observe their unloading. Since the pertinent statute did not define boarding to include searching below decks, Hancock ordered his captain and mate to keep the waiters out of the hold. When Hancock returned . . . the following day and found Owen Richards and another tidewaiter below, he ordered them to produce their authorization. Neither had a writ of assistance, and the commission of Richards, which presumably conferred the usual power to search all suspected ships without warrant, bore no date of authentication. At that point, Hancock had Richards hauled above deck, all the while ignoring Malcom's advice to administer a sound thrashing as well.

Id. at 1215. It is thus hard to believe that the intense publicity surrounding the seizures of the *Active* and the *Liberty,* especially when placed in the context of similar searches and seizures, did not focus on the absence of probable cause, *whether warrantless or not. See id.* at 1212–14. This conclusion is further supported by objections made about the "wretches" of the customs office and "pimp-ing tidewaiters" who "scoured every harbour and creek in the colonies with armed force, detained everything afloat from fishing smacks to wood boats, tumbled their cargos, and inspected even their ballast." *Id.* at 1216–17. Cuddihy indeed concluded that by the last years just before the Revolution, Americans had come to see both ships and homes alike as castles. *See id.* at 1215. There is thus ample support for reading the furor surrounding the seizures of the ships *Active* and *Liberty* as supporting an embrace of probable cause, as Maclin suggests. *See* Maclin, *supra* note 4, at 962–64. Likewise, the impact of these disputes on the Revolutionaries' worldview should not be underestimated. *See* THOMAS C. BARROW, TRADE AND EMPIRE 234 (1967) ("Indirectly, Hancock and his ship, the *Liberty,* had commenced a series of events leading to open revolution."); *id.* at 235 ("The publicity given to [the Laurens] affair served to crystallize public opinion and to furnish such propagandists as Sam Adams with effective arguments for a united front against the incursions of imperial authority."). *See also* Cuddihy, *supra* note 4, at 1210–12; LASSON, *supra,* at 72 & n. 71; *see also* Maclin, *supra* note 4, at 962–63 (quoting in part Cuddihy, *supra* note 4, at 1214).

Cuddihy's assessment of the probable-cause understanding as a "nebulous" one, but one shared by many colonists, and his view that Congress was itself confused (*see* Cuddihy, *supra* note 4, at 853–54, 1214–15), suggest both that preratification history cannot alone define the term and that there may be some room for its evolution and its variability with particular problems and circumstances. *See* Craig S. Lerner, *The Reasonableness of Probable Cause,* 81 TEX. L. REV. 951 (2003) (arguing for a flexible notion of probable cause). Nevertheless, the history does suggest that the probable-cause concept hovers somewhere around 50 percent likelihood of guilt, that it embraces a commitment to trustworthy evidentiary bases, and that it embodies commitments to individualized justice and adequate, persuasive justifications for searches and seizures that should not lightly be abandoned and that do not allow for nearly the level of flexibility in meaning that Lerner suggests.

23. 6 WRITINGS OF JAMES MADISON 375–76, 373, 380–81 (ed. Gaillard Hunt 1906) (source of quotations); JAMES R. STONER JR., COMMON LAW LIBERTY: RETHINKING AMERICAN CONSTITUTIONALISM 38–39 (2003).

24. *See* Sklansky, *supra* note 13, at 1785–87, 1791. *See also* GORDON S. WOOD, THE CREATION OF THE AMERICAN REPUBLIC 1776–1787 at 10, 13 (1969) (quoting John Adams, *Novanglus* (1774), *reprinted in* 4 WORKS OF JOHN ADAMS 3, 131 (Boston: Little, Brown, 1851)). *See also* 2 JOSEPH STORY, COMMENTARIES ON THE CONSTITUTION OF THE UNITED STATES §1902, at 679 (3d ed.,

Boston: Little, Brown, 1858). Several modern scholars seemingly agree with Story's understanding. *See, e.g.,* BRADFORD P. WILSON, ENFORCING THE FOURTH AMENDMENT: A JURISPRUDENTIAL HISTORY 16 (1986); Eric Schnapper, *Unreasonable Searches and Seizures of Papers,* 71 VA. L. REV. 869, 875–76 (1985). Moreover, Otis's argument against the writs of assistance "leaned heavily on the common law." William Cuddihy & B. Carmon Hardy, *A Man's House Was Not His Castle: Origins of the Fourth Amendment,* 38 WM. & MARY Q. 385, 392–98; Cuddihy, *supra* note 4, at 673–74, 392–98.

25. Joseph Story, *Codification of the Common Law, in* THE MISCELLANEOUS WRITINGS OF JOSEPH STORY 699, 702 (ed. William W. Story, Boston: Little, Brown, 1852). *See generally* RALPH V. WHITTEN, THE CONSTITUTION AND THE COMMON LAW 5–7 (1977) (summarizing Story's view of the common law); Sklansky, *supra* note 13, at 1786 (making similar argument).

26. STONER, *supra* note 23, at 25.

27. 2 STORY, COMMENTARIES, *supra* note 24, §1902, at 679–80 n. 2. General Wilkinson had, said Story, seized "two American citizens by military force, on account of supposed treasonable conspiracies against the United States, and transport[ed] them, without any warrant, or order of any civil authority, from New Orleans to Washington for trial." *Id.* For Story, this was a "very gross violation" of the Fourth Amendment. *Id. See also* Sklansky, *supra* note 13, at 1786–87; HARRY M. WARD, THE WAR FOR INDEPENDENCE AND THE TRANSFORMATION OF AMERICAN SOCIETY 49–64 (1999) (but also noting the pre–Fourth Amendment existence of, but "rarity and selectiveness in repression of civil liberty contrary to Revolutionary ideology").

28. Sklansky, *supra* note 13, at 1787–90 (quoting in part STORY, COMMENTARIES, *supra* note 24, §1902, at 679); Charles Wolfram, *The Constitutional History of the Seventh Amendment,* 57 MINN. L. REV. 639, 736 (1973); *see* STONER, *supra* note 23, at 4–5, 9–25, 165–67.

29. *See* U.S. CONST. amend. IV.

30. *See* Davies, *Fourth Amendment, supra* note 13, at 750.

Notes to Chapter 4

1. *See* Thomas Y. Davies, *Recovering the Original Fourth Amendment,* 98 MICH. L. REV. 547, at 679–81 (1999) [hereinafter Davies,

Fourth Amendment]; THE COMPLETE BILL OF RIGHTS: THE DRAFTS, DEBATES, SOURCES, AND ORIGINS 234–35 (ed. Neil H. Cogan 1997) [hereinafter COGAN, COMPLETE BILL OF RIGHTS].

2. *See* Davies, *Fourth Amendment, supra* note 1, at 679–80.

3. Curiously, Davies notes that nine of the sixteen provisions of the Pennsylvania Declaration of Rights used "peoplehood-like" language, which he attributes to the Pennsylvania constitution's being "the most radically democratic of the initial state constitutions." *Id.* at 679 n. 363. Additionally, he notes that the peoplehood formulation was "not unprecedented; Blackstone had described the right of personal security as one of 'the rights of the people of England.'" *Id.* (quoting in part 1 WILLIAM BLACKSTONE, COMMENTARIES ON THE LAWS OF ENGLAND 125 (1766–1769)) (cataloguing the "three principal or primary articles [of the rights of the people of England]: the right to personal security, the right of private property . . ."). Furthermore, declares Davies, "the collective tone of 'the people' is appropriate to a provision banning general warrants because such warrants, if allowed, would imperil the security of the entire community." Davies, *Fourth Amendment, supra* note 1, at 679 n. 363.

Davies also rather acidly dismisses Akhil Amar's theory (as Davies understands it) that the term "the People" demonstrates that the Framers' real concern was that search and arrest authority not be used to suppress free speech, thus making the Fourth Amendment primarily a device for protecting First Amendment concerns. *See id.* This book has in part sought to fill the gaps in Amar's evidence. Furthermore, Davies implicitly accepts a narrow, stunted definition of political expression. This book argues that the struggle over general warrants and writs of assistance upon which Davies relies was in fact a contest over political expression.

Equally important, Davies and Amar focus almost entirely on the history of the "original" Fourth Amendment of 1791, though Amar should know better, whereas part 2 of this book extends the analysis to the "reconstructed" Fourth Amendment of 1868, which unquestionably links the Fourth Amendment to free-speech concerns. *See* ANDREW E. TASLITZ & MARGARET L. PARIS, CONSTITUTIONAL CRIMINAL PROCEDURE 3, 427–37 (2d ed. 2003); Andrew E. Taslitz, *Slaves No More! The Implications of the*

Informed Citizen Ideal before Fourth Amendment Suppression Hearings, 15 GA. ST. U. L. REV. 709, 738–56 (1999).

4. COGAN, COMPLETE BILL OF RIGHTS, *supra* note 1, at 234–35; GARY ROSEN, AMERICAN COMPACT: JAMES MADISON AND THE PROBLEM OF THE FOUNDING 3–6 (1999) (making analogous point). *See also* Thomas Y. Davies, *The Fictional Character of Law-and-Order Originalism: A Case Study of the Distortions and Evasions of Framing-Era Arrest Doctrine in Atwater v. Lago Vista*, 37 WAKE FOREST L. REV. 239, 407–17 (2002) [hereinafter Davies, *Fictional Character*]; RICHARD K. MATTHEWS, IF MEN WERE ANGELS: JAMES MADISON AND THE HEARTLESS EMPIRE OF REASON 72 (1995) (noting Madison's fear of faction); *See* Davies, *Fourth Amendment, supra* note 1, at 698–99, 701–23 (noting that commentators have "almost uniformly" conceded that the text of Madison's original draft seems to prohibit only general warrants and arguing that the two-clause format was not "sneaked in" but was still a change in form rather than substance); *see* LEONARD LEVY, ORIGINS OF THE BILL OF RIGHTS 176–79 (1999) (tracing the Amendment's drafting history) [hereinafter LEVY, ORIGINS]. David Sklansky, *The Fourth Amendment and Common Law*, 100 COLUMB. L. REV. 1739, 1776–1811 (2000) (why Reasonableness Clause has important independent significance).

5. *See* Davies, *Fourth Amendment, supra* note 1, at 723–24; LEVY, ORIGINS, *supra* note 4, at 71–72. (summarizing Virginia, Pennsylvania, Delaware, New Hampshire, and Massachusetts provisions, all of which expressly or implicitly condemned general warrants). Importantly, the Massachusetts provision was written by John Adams, the great recorder of Otis's speech in Paxton's Case, a provision that most resembles the text of the Fourth Amendment. *See* COGAN, COMPLETE BILL OF RIGHTS, *supra* note 1, 234. The Massachusetts provision critically first protects by its terms a general right to be secure against "unreasonable searches, and seizures," described by Levy as "the first use of the phrase that would become *the prime principle of the Fourth Amendment*." LEVY, ORIGINS, *supra* note 4, at 171 (emphasis added). The ban on general warrants as one corollary of the "prime principle" followed second. Interestingly, Richard Henry Lee of Virginia had, ten days after the Constitutional Convention adjourned, both in an effort to wreck the ratification process and out of a sincere fear of a powerful national

government, framed his own bill of rights that included this search and seizure clause, modeled after the first clause in the Massachusetts provision: "[T]he citizens shall not be exposed to unreasonable searches, seizures of their papers, houses, persons, or property." *Id.* at 173. Levy describes the later congressional drafting history of the Fourth Amendment, which moved from an apparent ban on general warrants to the current broader two-clause formula rooted in the general reasonableness principle this way: "Thus, Otis and Adams finally had a belated but cardinal impact on the making of the Fourth Amendment." *Id.* at 177. *See generally* Sklansky, *supra* note 4.

6. *See also* Andrew E. Taslitz, *Peoplehood and the Fourth Amendment* (draft 2006) (elaborating on the concept of "Peoplehood").

7. *See* Andrew E. Taslitz, *The Inadequacies of Civil Society: Law's Complementary Role in Regulating Harmful Speech,* 1 U. MD. L. J. OF RACE, RELIGION, GENDER, & CLASS 305, 342–55 (2001) [hereinafter Taslitz, *Civil Society*].

8. THE FEDERALIST, *Number 83,* 563 (ed. J. Cooke 1961); *see also* Bradford Wilson, *The Fourth Amendment as More than a Form of Words: The View from the Founding, in* THE BILL OF RIGHTS: ORIGINAL MEANING AND CURRENT UNDERSTANDING 151, 158–59 (ed. Eugene W. Hickok Jr.) (similar interpretation of Hamilton's essay *Number 83* in *The Federalist*).

9. *See* Wilson, *supra* note 8, at 159; Taslitz, *Civil Society, supra* note 7, at 330–42, 355–73. Whether Hamilton was describing the preexisting state of the common law or his conception of the future state of the law under the new Constitution, he saw violation of search and seizure rights as at least partly violations of public protections—of a right of "the People." *See* Wilson, *supra* note 8, at 158–59.

10. *See, e.g.,* Cooper Industries, Inc. v. Leatherman Tool Group, Inc., 532 U.S. 424, 432 (2001) (nature of punitive damages); Wilson, *supra* note 8, at 159 (Founding generation's understanding of remedies for violations of search and seizure rights); *see also* Wilkes v. Wood, Lofft 1, 18–19, 98 Eng. Rep. 489, 498–99 (C.P. 1763) (Justice Pratt).

11. *See generally* Andrew E. Taslitz, *Stories of Fourth Amendment Disrespect: From Elian to the Internment,* 70 FORDHAM L. REV. 2257 (2002).

12. For a concise, accessible summary of the powers delegated to Congress by the Constitution, *see* LINDA R. MONK, THE

WORDS WE LIVE BY: YOUR ANNOTATED GUIDE TO THE CONSTITUTION 18–61 (2003). For an illustration of the power of congressional access to the media to shape policy, *see generally* TED GEST, CRIME AND POLITICS: BIG GOVERNMENT'S ERRATIC CAMPAIGN FOR LAW AND ORDER (2001). For a hard (as opposed to "soft") defense of a powerful role for legislatures generally in constitutional interpretation, *see generally* MARK TUSHNET, TAKING THE CONSTITUTION AWAY FROM THE COURTS (2000). *See also* TASLITZ & PARIS, *supra* note 3, at 468 (on news-media protections); *see generally* RANETA LAWSON MACK & MICHAEL J. KELLY, EQUAL JUSTICE IN THE BALANCE: AMERICA'S LEGAL RESPONSES TO THE EMERGING TERRORIST THREAT 114–15 (2004) (on congressional authorization of expansive executive search and seizure powers in the Patriot Act).

13. *See* JOHN J. DINAN, KEEPING THE PEOPLE'S LIBERTIES: LEGISLATORS, CITIZENS, AND JUDGES AS GUARDIANS OF RIGHTS 52–53 (1998) (state legislation); TASLITZ & PARIS, *supra* note 3, at 39–40 (incorporation); OREGON CODE OF CRIMINAL PROCEDURE 1864, c. 41, §§472–73 (1864).

14. Davies, *Fictional Character, supra* note 4, at 415–16. Although this quotation appears immediately following Davies's claim that warrantless arrests were governed by freestanding due process—a claim that I partly reject—he makes clear later that his comments also apply to the Fourth Amendment. *See id.* at 416–17.

15. *See* Miranda v. Arizona, 384 U.S. 436, 490 (1966) ("Congress and the States are free to develop their own safeguards for the privilege, so long as they are fully as effective as those described above in informing accused persons of their right to silence and in affording a continuous opportunity to exercise it."); County of Riverside v. McLauglin, 500 U.S. 44, 52–53 (1991) (states are expected to "experiment and adapt" ways "to integrate prompt probable cause determinations into their differing systems of pretrial procedures."). For an illustration of the complexity of the statutory law of electronic surveillance, *see* JAMES A. ADAMS & DANIEL D. BLINKA, ELECTRONIC SURVEILLANCE: COMMENTARIES AND STATUTES (2003). *See generally* Erik Luna, *Constitutional Road Maps,* 90 J. CRIM. L. & CRIMINOLOGY 1125 (2000) (roadmaps); *compare* Zurcher v. The Stanford Daily, 436 U.S. 547 (1978) (upholding search of newspaper office) *with* TASLITZ & PARIS, *supra* note 3, at 470–83,

488–90, 500–01, 507–10 (Congress reacted to *Zurcher* with legislation enhancing news media's search and seizure protections).

16. For a thorough summary and analysis of these standards, *see* Hon. Martin Marcus and Christopher Slobogin, *Challenges of the Technological Revolution: ABA Sets Standards for Electronic and Physical Surveillance*, 18 CRIM. J. 5 (2003); *cf.* Taslitz, *Slaves No More! supra* note 3, at 757–61 (1999) (commenting on the Fourth Amendment role of a "monitorial citizenry"). *See* AKHIL AMAR, BILL OF RIGHTS: CREATION AND RECONSTRUCTION at 64–66 (1998) (Fourth Amendment protects both individual and collective rights); *cf.* Lawrence Delbert Cress, *An Armed Community: The Origins and Meaning of the Right to Bear Arms*, 71 J. AM. HIST. 22, 31 (1984) (historian arguing that "in state after state, the phrases 'the people' or 'the militia' [were used to connote] the sovereign citizenry, described collectively," whereas "the expression, 'man' or 'person' [was typically] used to describe individual rights such as freedom of conscience.").

17. *See* Taslitz, *Slaves No More! supra* note 3, at 726–33, 750–51; *See* AMAR, BILL OF RIGHTS, *supra* note 16, at 62–67; AKHIL REED AMAR, THE CONSTITUTION AND CRIMINAL PROCEDURE 31–45 (1997). *See generally* Tracey Maclin, *The Complexity of the Fourth Amendment: A Historical Review*, 77 B.U. L. REV. 925 (1997); Christopher Slobogin, *Why Liberals Should Chuck the Exclusionary Rule*, 1999 U. ILL. L. REV. 363.

18. *See generally* Andrew E. Taslitz, *Racial Auditors and the Fourth Amendment: Data with the Power to Inspire Political Action*, 66 L. & CONTEMP. PROBS. 221, 244–48 (2003) (generally addressing the role of grass-roots political action under the Fourth Amendment); Morgan Cloud, *Quakers, Slaves, and the Founders: Profiling to Save the Union*, 73 MISS. L. J. 369, 421 (2003) (finding similar lesson in search and seizure history); ARIA GROUP, CINCINNATI POLICE–COMMUNITY RELATIONS COLLABORATIVE, *available at* http://www.ariagroup.com/FINAL_document.html (last visited March 18, 2004); Cloud, *supra*, at 374 (source of quotations).

19. *See* LEVY, ORIGINS, *supra* note 4, at 163–64; Oliver Dickerson, *Writs of Assistance as a Cause of the American Revolution, in* ERA OF THE AMERICAN REVOLUTION 52–67 (ed. Richard B. Morris 1939); William Cuddihy, *The Fourth Amendment: Origins and Original Meaning* (1990) (Ph.D. diss., Claremont Graduate School; available from UMI Disser-

tation Services, 300 North Zeeb Road, Ann Arbor, Michigan) (citing a manuscript letter); LEONARD LEVY, SEASONED JUDGMENTS: THE AMERICAN CONSTITUTION, RIGHTS, AND HISTORY 158–59 (1995) (discussing Trumbull's views); LEVY, ORIGINS, *supra* note 4, at 165 (source of quotation); Cuddihy, *supra*, at 19–20 (citing William Henry Drayton, *A Letter from Freeman of South Carolina* (Charles Town 1774)). For more details on resistance to the writs, such as in Virginia, Georgia, and South Carolina, *see* LEVY, SEASONED JUDGMENTS, *supra*, at 159; Dickerson, *supra*, at 68–71.

20. *See* LEVY, SEASONED JUDGMENTS, *supra* note 19, at 158–61 (source of quotation and summarizing judicial resistance to writs of assistance); Davies, *Fictional Character, supra* note 4, at 404–18 & nn. 558–94.

21. *See* Davies, *Fictional Character, supra* note 4, at 416 n. 589. Stanley N. Katz, *Introduction to Book I, in* 1 WILLIAM BLACKSTONE, COMMENTARIES ON THE LAWS OF ENGLAND vii–ix (published in four volumes, 1765–69; *reprinted by* University of Chicago Press 1979) (sources of quotations).

22. *See* PAUL O. CARRESE, THE CLOAKING OF POWER: MONTESQUIEU, BLACKSTONE, AND THE RISE OF JUDICIAL ACTIVISM 185–86, 197–98 (2003); ALEXANDER HAMILTON ET AL., THE FEDERALIST PAPERS, *Number 78*, 392–99 (ed. Garry Wills 1982) (source of quotations).

23. *See* CARRESE, *supra* note 22, at 190–93, 196, 199–207; HAMILTON, FEDERALIST PAPERS, *supra* note 22, at 395, 397.

24. *See, e.g.,* MICHAEL KAMMEN, SPHERES OF LIBERTY: CHANGING PERCEPTIONS OF LIBERTY IN AMERICAN CULTURE 73 (1986); BARRY ALAN SHAIN, THE MYTH OF AMERICAN INDIVIDUALISM: THE PROTESTANT ORIGINS OF AMERICAN POLITICAL THOUGHT 289–91 (1994); Andrew E. Taslitz, *Hate Crimes, Free Speech, and the Contract of Mutual Indifference*, 80 B.U. L. REV. 1283, 1312 (2000).

25. *See* CARRESE, *supra* note 22, at 200–03.

26. *Id.* at 201–02.

27. *See id.* at 202 (source of quotation); HARVEY C. MANSFIELD, AMERICA'S CONSTITUTIONAL SOUL 210 (1991) (similar argument from linking numbers 3, 49, and 78 of *The Federalist*); *see* CARRESE, *supra* note 22, at 197, 203 (Hamilton's defense of an independent judiciary); HAMILTON, FEDERALIST PAPERS, *supra* note 22, at 393, 397–99.

28. *See* CARRESE, *supra* note 22, at 204–05; Ralph Lerner, *The Supreme Court as Republican Schoolmaster*, SUP. CT. REV. 127, 127–80

(1967) (elaborating on the schoolmaster idea); HAMILTON, FEDERALIST PAPERS, *supra* note 22, at 395, 298 (discussing the moderating role of the courts), 398 (source of quotations); RICHARD K. MATTHEWS, IF MEN WERE ANGELS: JAMES MADISON AND THE HEARTLESS EMPIRE OF REASON 141–58 (1995) (discussing what Madison saw as the best justifications for a Bill of Rights).

I am not arguing, it is important to note, that antimajoritarianism was a primary purpose of the original Bill of Rights, though it is fairly understood as one, perhaps subordinate, purpose of the original Bill. With Amar, I agree that a greater emphasis on the Bill's function in checking majoritarian oppression came with the "Reconstructed Bill of Rights"—the Bill as modified by the process of incorporation against the states via the Due Process Clause of the Fourteenth Amendment. *See* Taslitz, *Slaves No More! supra* note 3, at 714; AMAR, BILL OF RIGHTS, *supra* note 16, at 215–46. Nor does my argument for a "special role" necessarily imply judicial supremacy. *See* LARRY D. KRAMER, THE PEOPLE THEMSELVES: POPULAR CONSTITUTIONALISM AND JUDICIAL REVIEW 78–80 (2004). Of greatest significance here is the consistency of the need to explore commitments and experience over time with the idea of a "customary Constitution" so familiar to the Founders, an evolving fundamental law blending arguments from natural law, morality, custom, and common and statutory law but consistent with, indeed essential to, the idea of the social contract and the People's consent. *See id.* at 9–18.

29. Virginia's governor, Edmund Randolph, arguing against the necessity for a Bill of Rights, expressed this sort of confidence in the judiciary, and in its unique role in a system of checks and balances, precisely in connection with constitutional protections against oppressive searches and seizures. *See* SAMUEL DASH, THE INTRUDERS: UNREASONABLE SEARCHES AND SEIZURES FROM KING JOHN TO JOHN ASHCROFT 42 (2004); 3 THE DEBATES ON THE FEDERAL CONSTITUTION 468 (ed. Jonathan Elliot 1836).

30. *See* TASLITZ & PARIS, *supra* note 3, at 8–10, 97–99, 169–70, 332–419 (cataloguing and analyzing various instances in which modern doctrine deems obtaining a warrant impracticable or unnecessary); Tracey Maclin, *The Central Meaning of the Fourth Amendment*, 35 WM. & MARY L. REV. 197

(1993) (extended argument for a warrant-preference rule); Davies, *Fourth Amendment, supra* note 1, at 550–56, 738–41 (although arguing that the Fourth Amendment does not govern warrantless searches at all, laying the case for the benefits of *specific* warrants and conceding that the "warrant preference construction comes closest to the original meaning."); MACK & KELLY, *supra* note 12, at 127–29 (expanding use of national security warrants); Tracey L. Meares & Dan M. Kahan, *When Rights Are Wrong: The Paradox of Unwanted Rights, in* URGENT TIMES: POLICING AND RIGHTS IN INNER-CITY COMMUNITIES 3, 3–30 (ed. Joshua Cohen and Joel Rogers 1999) (gangs); Howard Zinn, *Foreword, in* NANCY CHANG, SILENCING POLITICAL DISSENT: HOW POST–SEPTEMBER 11 ANTI-TERRORISM MEASURES THREATEN OUR CIVIL LIBERTIES 11 (2002).

31. *See generally* CHANG, *supra* note 30 (documenting such suppression); BERNARD HARCOURT, ILLUSION OF ORDER: THE FALSE PROMISE OF BROKEN WINDOWS POLICING (2001); TOM R. TYLER & YUEN J. HUO, TRUST IN THE LAW: COOPERATION WITH THE POLICE AND COURTS 131 (2002) (on the factors affecting trust between governments and the governed); Taslitz, *Stories, supra* note 11, at 2317–27 (on the Oneonta racial roundup); Andrew E. Taslitz, *The Fourth Amendment in the Twenty-First Century: Technology, Privacy, and Human Emotion*, 65 LAW & CONTEMP. PROBS. 125–28 (2002) (video surveillance); Taslitz, *Racial Auditors, supra* note 18, at 239–44 (racial profiling). On video surveillance, I recognize that the current Court would not even see the Fourth Amendment as implicated. They are wrong. *See generally* Taslitz, *Twenty-First Century, supra.*

32. *See* TASLITZ & PARIS, *supra* note 3, at 588–89 (discussing alternatives to the exclusionary rule); Taslitz, *Slaves No More! supra* note 3, at 759–61 (criminal accused as a monitor of police abuses); *cf.* Davies, *Fourth Amendment, supra* note 1, at 738–39; United States v. Leon, 468 U.S. 897, 921 (1984) (Stevens, J., dissenting).

33. *See, e.g.,* TASLITZ & PARIS, *supra* note 3, at 579–89; Timothy Lynch, *Policy Analysis No. 319: In Defense of the Exclusionary Rule*, CATO INSTITUTE 1, 11–14, 21–24 (October 1, 1998).

34. Lynch, *supra* note 33, at 11–12.

35. *See id.* at 12–13.

36. *Id.* at 21–22.

37. *See generally* Erik Luna, *Transparent Policing*, 85 IOWA L. REV. 1107 (2000).

Notes to Chapter 5

1. *See* JOHN HOWE, LANGUAGE AND POLITI-
CAL MEANING IN REVOLUTIONARY AMERICA
5–8, 204–09 (2004).
2. *See id.* at 204–17, 211 (faction in Federalist thinking generally); GARY ROSEN, AMER-
ICAN COMPACT: JAMES MADISON AND THE
PROBLEM OF THE FOUNDING 4, 12, 39–41,
61–63 (1999) (faction in Madison's thinking); GEORGE W. CAREY, THE FEDERALIST:
DESIGN FOR A CONSTITUTIONAL REPUBLIC
9–12, 15–20, 25–27, 31–32, 61–62, 81–82
(1989) (faction in the writings of Publius).
On the capaciousness of language to
embrace the lessons of experience, *see*
HOWE, *supra* note 1, at 213–16; *id.* at 213
(source of quotation). Madison himself
thought greater clarity impossible to achieve
his desired political ends. *See* ALEXANDER
HAMILTON ET AL., THE FEDERALIST, PAPERS,
Number 37, 179–80 (ed. Garry Wills 1982).
3. HOWE, *supra* note 1, at 5.
4. The point about evolving principles is
implied by Howe without his stating it so
directly. *See id.* at 5, 7 (connection between
history and language and flaws in originalism). *See* Andrew E. Taslitz, *Respect and the
Fourth Amendment*, 94 J. CRIM. L. & CRIMI-
NOLOGY 15, 51–80 (2003) (role of history in
interpreting the Fourth Amendment); *id.* at
70–80 (defining "peoplehood" and its significance); HOWE, *supra* note 1, at 12 ("Federalism's triumph in 1787–88 brought the
legitimation . . . of a newly inventive language of political discourse."). *See generally*
DAVID J. SIEMERS, RATIFYING THE REPUBLIC:
ANTIFEDERALISTS IN CONSTITUTIONAL TIME
219–25 (2002) (explaining how Anti-Feder-
alism played a continuing constitutional
role in the creation of a loyal opposition
tradition in America).
5. *See* DAVID C. WILLIAMS, THE MYTHIC
MEANING OF THE SECOND AMENDMENT:
TAMING POLITICAL VIOLENCE IN A CONSTITU-
TIONAL REPUBLIC 17–20 (2003) (quotations);
STEVEN L. WINTER, A CLEARING IN THE FOR-
EST: LAW, LIFE, AND MIND 351 (2001) (analo-
gous); Patricia J. Williams, *Alchemical Notes:
Reconstructing Ideals from Deconstructed
Rights*, 22 HARV. CIV. RTS.–CIV. LIB. L. REV.
401, 430 (1987) (illustration); *see* Andrew E.
Taslitz, *Condemning the Racist Personality:
Why the Critics of Hate Crimes Legislation Are
Wrong*, 40 B.C. L. REV. 739, 780 (1999) (also
citing additional sources).
6. *See* HOWE, *supra* note 1, at 98–127 (on
role of metaphors of the body, the family,

the theater, and their interaction in the
political thinking of the Founding generation); HOWE, *supra* note 1, at 105–10; Morgan Cloud, *Quakers, Slaves, and the Founders:
Profiling to Save the Union*, 73 MISS. L. J. 369,
418 (2003); Taslitz, *Respect and the Fourth
Amendment*, *supra* note 4.
7. Of course, subsequent history may
require altering or adding to these lessons,
as I have discussed elsewhere (*see, e.g.*,
Andrew E. Taslitz, *Stories of Fourth Amendment Disrespect: From Elian to the Internment*,
70 FORDHAM L. REV. 257, 282–84 (2002))
and will discuss in greater detail in forth-
coming works.
8. *See* ANDREW E. TASLITZ & MARGARET L.
PARIS, CONSTITUTIONAL CRIMINAL PROCE-
DURE, 361–402 (2d ed. 2003) (defining
administrative searches and reviewing the
doctrine). Until recently, defining administrative searches and seizures as those done
for purposes other than criminal investigation was completely accurate; the Court's
recent subtle change in definition would not
alter my reasoning but would unnecessarily
complicate my explanation. *See id.* at 361–
402; Andrew E. Taslitz, *A Feminist Fourth
Amendment? Consent, Care, Privacy, and Social
Meaning in Ferguson v. Charleston*, 9 DUKE J.
GENDER L. & POL'Y 1, 26–27 (2002) [here-
inafter Taslitz, *Feminist Fourth Amendment*].
9. *See* Taslitz, *Feminist Fourth Amendment*,
supra note 8, at 26–30.
10. *See id.* at 28 (discussing Michigan
Dept. of State Police v. Sitz, 496 U.S. 444
(1990), and its progeny), 1–10, 30–33,
62–77 (discussing Ferguson v. City of
Charleston, 532 U.S. 67 (2001)). I am over-
simplifying the facts a bit here because the
drug-testing policy in the *Ferguson* case
altered over time in ways not relevant here.
My textual summary of the case encapsulates the essence of the policy from and after
1990. *See id.* at 7–10.
11. *See id.* at 67–70 (summarizing the
research); *cf.* Brandon K. Applegate et al.,
*Public Support for Drunk-Driving Countermea-
sures: Social Policy for Saving Lives*, 41 CRIME
AND DELINQUENCY 171 (2001) (discussing
public's endorsement of legal deterrence and
rehabilitation, while also supporting socially
based interventions); *see* JAMES B. JACOBS,
DRUNK DRIVING: AN AMERICAN DILEMMA 4,
7, 9–10 (1989); *See* Rebecca Snyder Bromley,
*Jury Leniency in Drinking and Driving Cases,
Has It Changed? 1958 versus 1993*, 20 LAW &
PSYCH. REV. 27, 52–53 (1996).
12. *See* Taslitz, *Feminist Fourth Amendment*,

supra note 8, at 70–72 (summarizing data); RONALD REAGAN, PUBLIC PAPERS OF PRESIDENTS OF THE UNITED STATES: RONALD REAGAN (1991).

13. *See* SARA RUDDICK, MATERNAL THINKING 17–18 (1995) (what it means to be a mother and "preservative love"); EDWARD J. INGEBETSEN, AT STAKE: MONSTERS AND THE RHETORIC OF FEAR IN PUBLIC CULTURE 1–17, 99–23 (2001) (defining "monstrosity" and explaining its connection to motherhood); *see also* Joseph E. Kennedy, *Monstrous Offenders and the Search for Solidarity through Criminal Punishment,* 51 HASTINGS L.J. 829, 835–45, 858–68 (2000); IRIS MARION YOUNG, INTERSECTING VOICES: DILEMMAS OF GENDER, POLITICAL PHILOSOPHY, AND POLICY 77–78 (1997).

14. Illinois v. Lidster, 124 S. Ct. 885 (2004).

15. 531 U.S. 32 (2000).

16. 124 S. Ct. at 889 (emphasis added).

17. *Id.* at 889.

18. *See id.* at 889–90 (citing *Sitz,* 94 U.S. 444 ("sobriety checkpoint")).

19. *See Lidster,* 124 S. Ct. at 891.

20. *See id.* at 888–89.

21. *See id.* at 891–92 (Stevens, J., concurring in part, dissenting in part).

22. *See generally* Andrew E. Taslitz, *Racial Auditors and the Fourth Amendment: Data with the Power to Inspire Political Action,* 66 L. & CONTEMP. PROBS. 221 (2003); Erik Luna, *Constitutional Roadmaps,* 90 J. CRIM. L. CRIMINOLOGY 1125 (2000). *See also Hiibel v. Sixth Judicial District Court of Nevada, Humboldt County,* slip op. 2 (Breyer, J., dissenting) (on "strong dicta").

23. 392 U.S. 1, 14–15 nn. 2, 11 (1968).

24. *Id.* at 14–15 n. 11.

25. *Id.* at 14–15 & n. 14.

26. *See id.* at 14–15 & n. 11.

27. *See generally* United States v. Leon, 468 U.S. 897 (1984) (extended examination of this point in the process of crafting a "good faith exception" to the exclusionary rule).

28. *See* TASLITZ & PARIS, *supra* note 8, at 422–24, 443–45 (discussing case law); Whren v. United States, 607 U.S. 806 (1996) (officer pretext irrelevant under the Fourth Amendment); *Terry,* 392 U.S. at 14–15 n. 11, 17 & n. 14; Taslitz, *Racial Auditors, supra* note 22, at 244–45; DAVID A. HARRIS, PROFILES IN INJUSTICE: WHY RACIAL PROFILING CANNOT WORK 73–28 (2002) (exploring data showing that racial profiling is an ineffective crime-control tactic and can worsen matters by fostering community resentment);

United States v. Armstrong, 517 U.S. 456 (1996); Alabama v. White, 496 U.S. 325, 330 (1990).

29. On the deterioration in the evidence needed to establish reasonable suspicion, *see* David Harris, *Particularized Suspicion, Categorical Judgments: Supreme Court Rhetoric versus Lower Court Reality under Terry v. Ohio,* 72 ST. JOHN'S L. REV. 975 (1998). On the decline in police-citizen trust, *see* HARRIS, *supra* note 28, at 73–85.

30. *See* Taslitz, *Racial Auditors, supra* note 22, at 366; Andrew E. Taslitz, *Everyday Terrorism and the Social Contract: The Wisdom of a Least Restrictive Alternatives Analysis under the Fourth Amendment in an Age of Fear* at 1–40 (draft manuscript 2006). *See generally* MICHAEL IGNATIEFF, THE LESSER EVIL (2004).

31. *See* Taslitz, *Racial Auditors, supra* note 22, at 240–58 (on data collection and dissemination); TASLITZ & PARIS, *supra* note 8, at 59 (videotaping as a solution to criminal-procedure problems of police regulation); Erik Luna, *Transparent Policing,* 85 IOWA L. REV. 1107 (2000) (on videotaping and other ways to promote police transparency); 124 S. Ct. 1582 (2004).

32. *Id.* at 1587 (Breyer, J., dissenting).

33. *See* Taslitz, *Racial Auditors, supra* note 22, at 264–94; TASLITZ & PARIS, *supra* note 8, at 156–59 (explaining case law); Skinner v. Railway Labor Executives Ass'n, 489 U.S. 602 (1989) (state action); *see generally* KENNETH D. TUNNEL, PISSING ON DEMAND: WORKPLACE DRUG TESTING AND THE RISE OF THE DETOX INDUSTRY 98–114 (2004) (workplace drug testing as a "status degradation ceremony" that promotes a docile workforce); *id.* at 115–55 (on informal worker resistance); JOHN GILLIOM, SURVEILLANCE, PRIVACY, AND THE LAW (1994) (drug testing alters worker lifestyles, politics and the role of unions).

34. 532 U.S. 318 (2001); U.S. CONST. amend. IV.

35. 532 U.S. at 368–69 (O'Connor, J., dissenting).

36. *Id.* at 369.

37. *Id.* at 346–47 (quotation), 354–55 (quotation), 346–55 (core reasoning).

38. *Id.* at 370.

39. *Id.* at 370.

40. *Id.* at 372–73.

41. *See* MILTON R. KONVITZ, FUNDAMENTAL RIGHTS: HISTORY OF A CONSTITUTIONAL DOCTRINE 70, 84 (2001).

42. *See* TASLITZ & PARIS, *supra* note 8, at

183–86 (discussing the old *"Aguilar/Spinelli"* "two-pronged" test, arising from Aguilar v. Texas, 378 U.S. 108 (1964), and Spinelli v. United States, 393 U.S. 410 (1969)); see Illinois v. Gates, 462 U.S. 213 (1983) (replacing *Aguilar/Spinelli* with the new "totality of the circumstances" test).

43. See *Gates,* 462 U.S. at 218 n. 1; TASLITZ & PARIS, *supra* note 8, at 179–81 (describing the judges' survey and the scholarly commentary).

44. See Maryland v. Pringle, 124 S. Ct. 795 (2003).

45. Pringle v. State, 370 Md. 525, 531 n. 2 (2002) (emphasis added).

46. *Id.* at 545 n. 12.

47. *Id.* at 546.

48. 124 S. Ct. at 799–800 (emphasis added).

49. *Id.* at 800 (emphasis added).

50. *Id.* at 800 n. 2.

51. *Id.* at 800 n. 1.

52. *Id.* at 800 n. 1; Ybarra v. Illinois, 444 U.S. 85, 90 (1979).

53. *Pringle,* 124 S. Ct. at 801.

54. 332 U.S. 581 (1948).

55. *Pringle,* 124 S. Ct. at 801.

56. *Id.* at 801. See generally Andrew E. Taslitz, *Myself Alone: Individualizing Justice through Psychological Character Evidence,* 52 MD. L. REV. 1 (1993).

57. See *Pringle,* Brief of Respondent, 2003 WL 21953877; See TASLITZ & PARIS, *supra* note 8, at 617–18 (discussing the "cruel trilemma").

58. *Pringle,* 124 S. Ct. at 800 n. l; see TASLITZ & PARIS, *supra* note 8, at 177–83, 311–13 (comparing the quantum of proof necessary for "reasonable suspicion" versus "probable cause"). Outside the home, the Court has proven readily willing to dispense with the probable-cause requirement, often replacing it with the lower "reasonable suspicion" standard. See *id.* at 284–330. Here too, the Court has relied even more heavily on highly contestable generalizations, and it has openly accepted evidence *less reliable* than that used in determining probable cause. See *id.* at 314–15.

The Court has indeed, albeit in dicta, repeatedly suggested that, in some cases, search warrants can be issued on mere reasonable suspicion—contrary to the Fourth Amendment's literal command that no warrants issue but upon probable cause. See Kaupp v. Texas, 538 U.S. 626, 630–31 (2003). Taken together, there is a pattern of retreat from commitments to individualized

justice, to a robust quantitative standard for probable cause, and to an insistence on trustworthy evidence.

59. Given space constraints, I have not here offered a detailed analysis of the Court's weak understanding of the connection between First and Fourth Amendment concerns, though I have begun that task elsewhere. See, e.g., Andrew E. Taslitz, *Slaves No More! The Implications of the Informed Citizen Ideal before Fourth Amendment Suppression Hearings,* 15 GA. ST. L. REV. 709 (1999).

60. See generally Andrew E. Taslitz, *Hate Crimes, Free Speech, and the Contract of Mutual Indifference,* 80 B.U. L. REV. 1283 (2000) [hereinafter *Mutual Indifference*]; TASLITZ & PARIS, *supra* note 8, at 427–38.

61. See generally Taslitz, *Mutual Indifference, supra* note 60; Andrew E. Taslitz, *The Fourth Amendment in the Twenty-First Century: Technology, Privacy, and Human Emotions,* 65 L. & CONTEMP. PROBS. 125 (2002).

Notes to Chapter 6

1. See, e.g., PETER KOLCHIN, AMERICAN SLAVERY 1619–1877 92 (1993).

2. See KENNETH S. GREENBERG, HONOR AND SLAVERY xiii, 3–22 (1996); see generally BERTRAM WYATT-BROWN, SOUTHERN HONOR: ETHICS AND BEHAVIOR IN THE OLD SOUTH 46 (1982).

3. See GREENBERG, *supra* note 2, at 3–7; Andrew E. Taslitz, *Condemning the Racist Personality: Why the Critics of Hate Crimes Legislation Are Wrong,* 40 B.C. L. REV. 739, 773–78 (1999) [hereinafter Taslitz, *Racist Personality*]; JAMES OAKES, SLAVERY AND FREEDOM: AN INTERPRETATION OF THE OLD SOUTH 4, 6 (1990) [hereinafter OAKES, SLAVERY AND FREEDOM].

4. See GREENBERG, *supra* note 2 at 3, 8, 7–9, 11, 24–37, 62–64, 74–74; J. W. WILLIAMS, DUELING IN THE OLD SOUTH: VIGNETTES OF SOCIAL HISTORY 4 (1980) (arguing dueling in the South was commonplace before 1825 and "less than rare" through the Civil War). *But see* OAKES, SLAVERY AND FREEDOM, *supra* note 3, at 16 (declaring dueling to be uncommon).

5. See GREENBERG, *supra* note 2, at 11–12, 34–35; OAKES, SLAVERY AND FREEDOM, *supra* note 3, at 15–16.

6. *See* OAKES, SLAVERY AND FREEDOM, *supra* note 3, at 14–24; GREENBERG, *supra* note 2, at 41, 24–50; *Narrative of the Life of James Curry, in* SLAVE TESTIMONY: TWO CENTURIES

OF LETTERS, SPEECHES, INTERVIEWS, AND AUTOBIOGRAPHIES 137 (ed. John Blassingame 1977).

7. See GREENBERG, *supra* note 2, at 87–88, 93, 95–98, 107–10. For more general background, *see id.* at 87–114.

8. *See* OAKES, SLAVERY AND FREEDOM, *supra* note 3, at 18, 98, 102–03; 109; Andrew E. Taslitz, *Slaves No More! The Implications of the Informed Citizen Ideal for Discovery before Fourth Amendment Suppression Hearings,* 15 GA. ST. L. REV. 709, 440–41 (1999) [hereinafter Taslitz, *Slaves No More!*]; *cf.* JAMES OAKES, THE RULING RACE: A HISTORY OF AMERICAN SLAVEHOLDERS 160–69 (1998) [hereinafter OAKES, RULING RACE]. For general background, *see* GREENBERG, *supra* note 2, at 11–13, 15–16, 91–114; *see also* JOHN HOPE FRANKLIN & LOREN SCHWENINGER, RUNAWAY SLAVES: REBELS ON THE PLANTATION 2–7 (1999).

9. *See generally* BULLWHIP DAYS: THE SLAVES REMEMBER (ed. James Mellon 1988) (quoting slaves' narratives of being dishonored); GREENBERG, *supra* note 2, at 35–36; FREDERICK DOUGLASS: MY BONDAGE AND MY FREEDOM 128–53 (Johnson Publishing Company 1970) (1855); FREDERICK DOUGLASS, NARRATIVE OF THE LIFE OF FREDERICK DOUGLASS, AN AMERICAN SLAVE, WRITTEN BY HIMSELF (1860) (ed. Benjamin Quarles 1960) [hereinafter DOUGLASS, NARRATIVE OF THE LIFE] (recounting the story of the Covey incident).

10. DOUGLASS, NARRATIVE OF THE LIFE, *supra* note 9, at 74.

11. *See* GREENBERG, *supra* note 2, at 36–37.

12. *See generally* MITCHELL SNAY, GOSPEL OF DIVISION: RELIGION AND SEPARATISM IN THE ANTEBELLUM SOUTH 3, 41–42, 53–77, 81, 95–96 (1993). For more general background, *see id.* at 78–109; GREENBERG, *supra* note 2, at 110–12; OAKES, RULING RACE, *supra* note 8, at 105; KOLCHIN, *supra* note 1, at 192.

13. *See* SNAY, *supra* note 12, at 54–58; KOLCHIN, *supra* note 1, at 192–93.

14. Genesis 9:25.

15. *Id.*

16. SNAY, *supra* note 12, at 56 (citing PATRICK HUES MELL, SLAVERY: A TREATISE SHOWING THAT SLAVERY IS NEITHER A MORAL, POLITICAL, NOR SOCIAL EVIL 15 (1844)); J. B. Thrasher, *Slavery, a Divine Institution: A Speech Made before the Breckinridge and Lane Club, November 5th 1860* 8 (Port Gibson, Miss.: Southern Reveille Book and

Job Office, 1861); GREENBERG, *supra* note 2, at 111 (quoting IVESON BROOKES, A DEFENSE OF THE SOUTH 23 (1850)).

17. SNAY, *supra* note 12, at 68–73, 85–88. Although the Southern social order was diverse and religious teachings could sometimes act as a break on brutality, the logic of the religious defense of slavery nevertheless sanctified racial violence. *See* Andrew E. Taslitz, *Hate Crimes, Free Speech, and the Contract of Mutual Indifference,* 80 B.U. L. REV. 1283, 1322—25 (2000) [hereinafter Taslitz, *Mutual Indifference*] (debunking counterarguments).

18. *See* ROGERS M. SMITH, CIVIC IDEALS: COMPETING VISIONS OF CITIZENSHIP IN U.S. HISTORY (1997); *see* OAKES, RULING RACE, *supra* note 8, at 130–43; Taslitz, *Racist Personality, supra* note 3, at 774–75.

19. *See* KOLCHIN, *supra* note 1, at 181; OAKES, RULING RACE, *supra* note 8, at 132–33; OAKES, SLAVERY AND FREEDOM, *supra* note 3, at 30–31; Alfred Taylor Bledsoe, *Liberty and Slavery; or, Slavery in the Light of Moral and Political Philosophy, reprinted in* COTTON IS KING, AND PRO-SLAVERY ARGUMENTS 270, 300 (ed. E. N. Elliot 1860); THOMAS R. R. COBB, AN INQUIRY INTO THE LAW OF NEGRO SLAVERY IN THE UNITED STATES OF AMERICA 17, 51 (1858, *reprinted by* Univ. of Georgia Press 1999); OAKES, SLAVERY AND FREEDOM, *supra* note 3, at 31, 74 (quoting BENEDICT ANDERSON, IMAGINED COMMUNITIES: REFLECTIONS ON THE ORIGINS AND SPREAD OF NATIONALISM 135 (1983)); *see also* GREENBERG, *supra* note 2, at 15, 135.

20. OAKES, SLAVERY AND FREEDOM, *supra* note 3, at 130.

21. OAKES, RULING RACE, *supra* note 8, at 153–54 (quoting 1 *Cotton Planter and Soil of the South* 233 (1857)); *compare id.* at 164–69 with EARL J. HESS, LIBERTY, VIRTUE AND PROGRESS: NORTHERNERS AND THEIR WAR FOR THE UNION (2d ed. 1997) (analyzing the North's views of Southern "virtue").

22. OAKES, RULING RACE, *supra* note 8, at 154; 6 FARMERS' REGISTER 32 (1837).

23. 6 SOUTHERN AGRICULTURIST 281–82 (1833).

24. OAKES, RULING RACE, *supra* note 8, at 154; *see generally* IRA BERLIN, SLAVES WITHOUT MASTERS (1974).

25. OAKES, SLAVERY AND FREEDOM, *supra* note 3, at 31 (assailing slaveholders pretensions); COBB, *supra* note 19, at ccxiii.

26. COBB, *supra* note 19, at ccxiii.

27. *See* OAKES, SLAVERY AND FREEDOM,

supra note 3, at 131–32; GREENBERG, *supra* note 2, at 15.

28. *See* KOLCHIN, *supra* note 1, at 111–12, 118–19; State v. Mann, 13 N.C. (2 Dev.) 263, 266–67 (1829) (per curium); *see also* OAKES, RULING RACE, *supra* note 8, at 132.

29. *See* KOLCHIN, *supra* note 1, at 118–32; FRANKLIN & SCHWENINGER, *supra* note 8, at 42–44; *see also* OAKES, SLAVERY AND FREEDOM, *supra* note 3, at 144–45.

30. *See* FRANKLIN & SCHWENINGER, *supra* note 8, at 42–48; KOLCHIN, *supra* note 1, at 121 (quotation).

31. KOLCHIN, *supra* note 1, at 121, 142; OAKES, SLAVERY AND FREEDOM, *supra* note 3, at 19–21.

32. THOMAS D. MORRIS, SOUTHERN SLAVERY AND THE LAW 296–97 (1998); KENNETH M. STAMPP, THE PECULIAR INSTITUTION: SLAVERY IN THE ANTEBELLUM SOUTH 145 (1982) (quoting Frederick Douglass).

33. FRANKLIN & SCHWENINGER, *supra* note 8, at 45.

34. *See id.* at 44–45; Records of the Superior Court, Richmond County, Georgia, Charles Hall v. Richard Mooney and Gilbert NcNair, 13 December 1831, *in* Writs 1829–1831, 209–10, Records of the Court, Records Retention Center, Augusta, Georgia; FRANKLIN & SCHWENINGER, *supra* note 8, at 149–82.

35. There is a dispute among historians over whether slave law restrained or enhanced masters' power. *Compare* A DOCUMENTARY HISTORY OF SLAVERY IN NORTH AMERICA 23 (ed. Willie Lee Rose 1976) *with* Andrew Fede, *Legitimized Violent Slave Abuse in the American South, 1619–1865: A Case Study of Law and Social Change in Six Southern States*, 29 AM. J. LEGAL HIST. 93, 101, 132 (1985). Andrew Fede has more convincingly argued, however, that the law only "appeared to protect slaves from violent white abuse," thus serving a "legitimizing purpose." *Id.* at 93, 101, 132. Fede's argument that law enhanced masters' power is more convincing for the reasons noted in MORRIS, *supra* note 32, at 183–97 (quoting in part 2 JOHN CODMAN HURD, THE LAW OF FREEDOM AND BONDAGE IN THE UNITED STATES 100 (1858, *reprinted* 1968)) ("good government" quotation); RANDALL KENNEDY, RACE, CRIME, AND THE LAW 30 (1997); Taslitz, *Mutual Indifference, supra* note 17, at 1332—35.

36. 13 N.C. (2 Dev.) 263 (1829) (per curium); MORRIS, *supra* note 32, at 190–93; see KENNEDY, *supra* note 35, at 32–33.

37. State v. Mann, 13 N.C. (2 Dev.) 263, 266–67 (1829) (per curium). *See also* ROBERT COVER, JUSTICE ACCUSED: ANTISLAVERY AND THE JUDICIAL PROCESS 77 n. (1975); MARK TUSHNET, THE AMERICAN LAW OF SLAVERY 1810–1860: CONSIDERATIONS OF HUMANITY AND INTEREST 35–37, 62–65 (1981); KENNEDY, *supra* note 35, at 33–34; *but see* JENNY BOURNE WAHL, THE BONDSMAN'S BURDEN: AN ECONOMIC ANALYSIS OF THE COMMON LAW OF SOUTHERN SLAVERY 149–51 (1998) (some very modest efforts made by courts to limit owners' power in the three pre–Civil War decades).

38. Luke v. State, 5 Fla. 185, 187 (1853); *see also Mann,* 13 N.C. (2 Dev.) at 266; KENNEDY, *supra* note 35, at 33–34; TUSHNET, *supra* note 37, at 36; MORRIS, *supra* note 32, at 182.

39. *See* KENNEDY, *supra* note 35, at 34–35; MELTON McLAURIN, CELIA, A SLAVE 109 (1991); HARRIET A. JACOBS, INCIDENTS IN THE LIFE OF A SLAVE GIRL, WRITTEN BY HERSELF 27–42, 53–57 (ed. Jean Fagin Yellin 1987).

40. *See* HARRY V. JAFFA, CRISIS OF THE HOUSE DIVIDED: AN INTERPRETATION OF THE ISSUES IN THE LINCOLN-DOUGLAS DEBATES ch. 9 (1982); GREENBERG, *supra* note 2, at 43–46.

41. See Taslitz, *Slaves No More! supra* note 8, at 738–43; AKHIL REED AMAR, THE BILL OF RIGHTS: CREATION AND RECONSTRUCTION 236 (1998).

42. *See* MARY FRANCES BERRY, BLACK RESISTANCE, WHITE LAW: A HISTORY OF CONSTITUTIONAL RACISM IN AMERICA 54 (1994); Taslitz, *Racist Personality, supra* note 3, at 773–77; Taslitz, *Slaves No More! supra* note 8, at 743–46.

Notes to Chapter 7

1. OXFORD COMPANION TO AMERICAN LAW 67 (ed. Kermit Hall 2002) (on Blackstone's *Commentaries*); THOMAS D. MORRIS, SOUTHERN SLAVERY AND THE LAW, 1619–1860 337 (1996) (on Blackstone's three most basic rights); 1 WILLIAM BLACKSTONE, COMMENTARIES ON THE LAWS OF ENGLAND 125, 130 (1765–69) (quotations); THOMAS R. R. COBB, AN INQUIRY INTO THE LAW OF NEGRO SLAVERY IN THE UNITED STATES OF AMERICA, TO WHICH IS PREFIXED AN HISTORICAL SKETCH OF SLAVERY 105 (1858, *reprinted* 1968) (quotations).

2. STEPHANIE M. CAMP, CLOSER TO FREEDOM: ENSLAVED WOMEN AND EVERYDAY

RESISTANCE IN THE PLANTATION SOUTH 13, 15 (2004); CHARLES BALL, SLAVERY IN THE UNITED STATES: A NARRATIVE OF THE LIFE AND ADVENTURES OF CHARLES BALL, A BLACK MAN 125 (1859); REMEMBERING SLAVERY: AFRICAN AMERICANS TALK ABOUT THEIR PERSONAL EXPERIENCES OF SLAVERY AND EMANCIPATION 282 (ed. Ira Berlin 1998) [hereinafter BERLIN, REMEMBERING SLAVERY] (quoting Fountain Hughes).

3. PETER KOLCHIN, AMERICAN SLAVERY, 1619–1877 122 (1993); MORRIS, supra note 1, at 338; COBB, supra note 1, at 107, 109 ("watchful eye" quotation); CHRISTIAN PARENTI, THE SOFT CAGE: SURVEILLANCE IN AMERICA, FROM SLAVE PASSES TO THE WAR ON TERROR 14–20 (2003) (patrols and surveillance).

4. See JENNY BOURNE WAHL, THE BONDMEN'S BURDEN: AN ECONOMIC ANALYSIS OF THE COMMON LAW OF SOUTHERN SLAVERY 112–14 (1998).

5. SALLY E. HADDEN, SLAVE PATROLS: LAW AND VIOLENCE IN VIRGINIA AND THE CAROLINAS 99–104 (2001); JOHN HOPE FRANKLIN & LOREN SCHWENINGER, RUNAWAY SLAVES: REBELS ON THE PLANTATION 150–56 (1999); 14 (1) THE AMERICAN SLAVE: A COMPOSITE AUTOBIOGRAPHY 141, 144 (ed. George P. Rawick 1973–1976) ("black and blue" and "lashes" quotations from W. L. Bost, a former western North Carolina slave interviewed by WPA workers in 1937); MORRIS, supra note 1, at 298 (discussing the case of Sole, a slave who was sentenced to two hundred lashes for the crime of insolence to patrollers).

6. See HADDEN, supra note 5, at 71–78, 88–89, 129–32 (patrol duties and procedures and source of quotations); FRANKLIN & SCHWENINGER, supra note 5, at 150–56 (generally summarizing patrols' composition and authority).

7. State v. Hailey, 28 N.C. (6 Iredell) 11 (1845); HADDEN, supra note 5, at 89 (quotation summarizing Hailey opinion and commentary on collective nature of the patrol).

8. Hailey, 28 N.C. at 11.

9. Richardson v. Saltar, 4 N.C. (Taylor) 505 (1817); HADDEN, supra note 5, at 78–79, 105 (including as source of quotation); 1 EDWARD CANTWELL, THE PRACTICE OF LAW IN NORTH CAROLINA: LEGISLATIVE AND EXECUTIVE POWERS 377 (1860) (noting limits on the number of lashes permitted by patrols). County officials reacted to the Saltar case by "allowing a slave thought to be behaving oddly to be detained by a single patroller

until he could 'bring together a requisite number of Patrollers to act in the business.' " HADDEN, supra note 5, at 79 (quoting Clause 4, Patrol Regulations for the County of Rowan (Salisbury, N.C., 1825)).

10. See HADDEN, supra note 5, at 105–22; id. at 117 ("turpentine or manure" quotation), 121–29 ("stationary patrolling"); FRANKLIN & SCHWENINGER, supra note 5, at 155.

11. HADDEN, supra note 5, at 137–49 (why slaves had particular reason to fear patrols in times of crisis); FRANKLIN & SCHWENINGER, supra note 5, at 152–53 (patrol search authority and special appointment procedures in times of crisis); JOHN HOPE FRANKLIN, THE MILITANT SOUTH, 1800–1861 72–73 (1956); Legislative Petitions, Petition of Samuel Templeman to the Virginia General Assembly, 21 December 1809, Virginia State Archives, Richmond, Virginia.

12. See HADDEN, supra note 5, at 83–84.

13. GEORGE TEAMOH, GOD MADE MAN, MAN MADE THE SLAVE: THE AUTOBIOGRAPHY OF GEORGE TEAMOH 176–76 n. 20 (ed. Nash Boney, Rafia Zafar, and Richard Hume 1990).

14. HADDEN, supra note 5, at 84.

15. See id. at 80 (including quotation from JACOB STROYER, MY LIFE IN THE SOUTH 62 (1879, reprinted 1898) ("bruised and torn by the dogs")); FRANKLIN & SCHWENINGER, supra note 5, at 156–58 (function and methods of slave catchers), 169–70 (similar, plus "fanatical resolve," "slaves they trusted," and "harsh retribution" quotations); Howard County Register of Wills (Petitions), Petition of Robert H. Hare to the Howard County Court, 4 May 1852, reel M-11, 024, Schweninger Collection, Maryland State Archives, Annapolis, Maryland ("injurious treatment" quotation).

16. See HADDEN, supra note 5, at 81 (financial rewards, state fees, owner advertisements, and role of ordinary citizens); MORRIS, supra note 1, at 343–45 (common procedures upon a fugitive slave's capture and the crimes of inveigling and enticing); WAHL, supra note 4, at 110–11, 132–35 (jailing of escaped slaves and civil and criminal liability for kidnapping slaves or aiding their escape).

17. See PARENTI, supra note 3, at 20, 23–25 (state laws, forging passes, secret learning, Douglass), MORRIS, supra note 1, at 347–48 (counterarguments that slaves should read, firelight study, symbolism, typicality of Auld's views); KOLCHIN, supra note 3, at 116 (illiteracy and dependence on whites,

inability to write passes); FREDERICK DOUG-
LASS, LIFE AND TIMES OF FREDERICK DOUG-
LASS 70–72 (1881) (quotations).

18. *See* Paul Finkelman, *Introduction: The
Centrality of Slavery in American Legal Development, in* SLAVERY AND THE LAW 15–16 (ed.
Paul Finkelman 1997); Jacob I. Corre, *Thinking Property at Memphis: An Application of
Watson, in* SLAVERY AND THE LAW, *supra,* at
437, 437–48 (comparing the American system of racial slavery to other nonracial slave
societies less fearful of slaves' ability to
think).

19. Finkelman, *supra* note 18, at 16.

20. *See* MORRIS, *supra* note 1, at 346–47
(unlawful-assembly laws and their purposes
and enforcement); WAHL, *supra* note 4, at
137 (fines and civil liability).

21. HADDEN, *supra* note 5, at 110–14;
CAMP, *supra* note 2, at 19; PARENTI, *supra*
note 3, at 25; pass written by Thomas L.
Spragins, 4 August 18[??], Section 86, Spragins Family Papers, Virginia Historical Society, Richmond (concerning the slave Adam);
pass written by John Bassett, 25 February
1826, Bassett Family Papers, Virginia Historical Society, Richmond) (concerning the slave
Edward); petition, undated, S.C. General
Assembly papers, Index number 0010 003
ND00 02812 00, South Carolina Department
of Archives and History, Columbia ("robberies of evil-disposed slaves" quotation).

22. HADDEN, *supra* note 5, at 111–12;
CAMP, *supra* note 2, at 20, 30 (passes prevented slave movement quotation; passes
often given for specific tasks).

23. BERLIN, REMEMBERING SLAVERY, *supra*
note 2, at 282–83 (quoting Fountain
Hughes).

24. PEGGY COOPER DAVIS, NEGLECTED STO-
RIES: THE CONSTITUTION AND FAMILY VALUES
30 (1997) (slave marriages generally); MOSES
I. FINLEY, ANCIENT SLAVERY AND MODERN
IDEOLOGY 75 (1980) (emphasis added)
(slaves as outsiders); KOLCHIN, *supra* note 3,
at 32, 123 (why some planters encouraged
marriage; marriage ceremonies; definition of
marriage abroad); B. A. BOTKIN, LAY MY BUR-
DEN DOWN: A FOLK HISTORY OF SLAVERY 86
(1989) ("jumped over a broom" quotation);
HERBERT GUTMAN, THE BLACK FAMILY IN
SLAVERY AND FREEDOM, 1750–1925
273–81 (1976) (slave marriage rituals
detailed).

25. *See* KOLCHIN, *supra* note 3, at 122–24;
Bennet H. Barrow, *Rules of Highland Planta-
tion* (1838), *in* PLANTATION LIFE IN THE
FLORIDA PARISHES OF LOUISIANA, 1836–

1846, AS REFLECTED IN THE DIARY OF BENNET
H. BARROW 408–09 (ed. Edwin Adams Davis
1943) (quotation).

26. Rev. Dr. Henry James Thornwell, *The
Policy of the Southern Planter, in* 1 AMERICAN
COTTON PLANTER AND SOIL OF THE SOUTH
295 (October 1857).

27. *See* KOLCHIN, *supra* note 3, at 123
(smaller planters); MARIE JENKINS SCHWARTZ,
BORN IN BONDAGE: GROWING UP ENSLAVED
IN THE ANTEBELLUM SOUTH 176 (2000)
(similar); WILMA A. DUNAWAY, THE AFRICAN-
AMERICAN FAMILY IN SLAVERY AND EMANCI-
PATION 60–62, 64, 79–80 (2003) (back-
ground on marriage, passes, and visiting
privileges; renegotiation quotation); 2(a)
OPHELIA EGYPT, H. MASUOKA, & C. S. JOHN-
SON, UNWRITTEN HISTORY OF SLAVERY:
AUTOBIOGRAPHICAL ACCOUNT OF NEGRO
EX-SLAVES 4 (1945 Fisk University Archives)
(chimney hiding); 14(a) GEORGE P. RAWICK,
THE AMERICAN SLAVE: A COMPOSITE AUTOBI-
OGRAPHY 101 (1972); 16(b) RAWICK, AMERI-
CAN SLAVE, *supra,* at 13; 12 GEORGE P.
RAWICK, THE AMERICAN SLAVE: A COMPOSITE
AUTOBIOGRAPHY: SUPPLEMENT I 330 (1977)
[hereinafter RAWICK, SUPPLEMENT I]; 9 RAW-
ICK, SUPPLEMENT I 1524; 10(a) RAWICK,
AMERICAN SLAVE, *supra,* at 12:309–10; *see
also* GREAT SLAVE NARRATIVES 211 (ed. Arna
Bontemps 1969); ELIZABETH FOX-GENOVESE,
WITHIN THE PLANTATION HOUSEHOLD:
BLACK AND WHITE WOMEN OF THE OLD
SOUTH 49–50, 373–74 (1988) (on emascula-
tion of male slaves).

28. *See* DAVIS, *supra* note 24, at 31 (quoting T. R. R. Cobb on the dangers to the master from slave marriages); DUNAWAY, *supra*
note 27, at 53, 62–67 (the slave's "strongest
affection" was purported to be "love of his
master," not ties to black kin; also, examples
of humiliation); Andrew E. Taslitz, *Hate
Crimes, Free Speech, and the Contract of
Mutual Indifference,* 80 B.U. L. REV. 1283,
1316–37 (2000) (on expressive or ritual
violence).

29. SAMUEL WARD, AUTOBIOGRAPHY OF A
FUGITIVE NEGRO 15–17 (1855, *reprinted*
1968).

30. *See* KOLCHIN, *supra* note 3, at 125–26;
DUNAWAY, *supra* note 27, at 53; COBB, *supra*
note 1, at x (denying that family separation
was common); EMILY WEST, CHAINS OF
LOVE: SLAVE COUPLES IN ANTEBELLUM SOUTH
CAROLINA 145–54 (2004) (family separation
was in fact quite common).

31. SCHWARTZ, *supra* note 27, at 158–59,
162 (short-term versus long-term dislocation

and their effects); DUNAWAY, *supra* note 27, at 59, 66–67, 78–83 (effect of master's death or inheritance; reasons for hiring husbands for distant labor; effect of long-distance sale on family relationships); WEST, *supra* note 30, at 141–54 (impact of local or temporary separation versus distant or permanent separation and of slaves as marriage gifts).

32. *See* SCHWARTZ, *supra* note 27, at 155–56, 159, 162 ("fancies" quotation), 173.

33. *See id.* at 163–65; DUNAWAY, *supra* note 27, at 56–57, 81 (power in the hands of the masters); FOX-GENOVESE, *supra* note 27, at 297, 299 (quotation regarding masters, not husbands, supporting and controlling slave wives).

34. Taslitz, *Mutual Indifference, supra* note 28 (pervasiveness of rules); KOLCHIN, *supra* note 3, at 118 (quotation to similar effect); JAMES OAKES, THE RULING RACE: A HISTORY OF AMERICAN SLAVEHOLDERS 157 (1998) (content and volume of rules and quotation concerning the latter); CAMP, *supra* note 2, at 24 (blowing horns); WILLIAM ETHELBERT, ERVIN DIARY, 31 December 1846, Southern Historical Collection, University of North Carolina, Chapel Hill (quotation regarding the same); MARK M. SMITH, LISTENING TO NINETEENTH-CENTURY AMERICA 35–36 (2001) (William Brown's use of horns and bells).

35. *See* OAKES, *supra* note 34, at 157–58; PLANTATION LIFE IN THE FLORIDA PARISHES OF LOUISIANA, 1836–1846, AS REFLECTED IN THE DIARY OF BENNET H. BARROW 408 (ed. Edwin Adams Davis 1943, *reprinted* 1967) ("habit" quotation); 14 DEBOW'S REVIEW 177–78 (1853) ("without the labor of thought" quotation).

36. *See* JONATHAN MARTIN, DIVIDED MASTERY: SLAVE HIRING IN THE AMERICAN SOUTH 2–3, 11, 13, 45–48, 107–09 (2004). Martin emphasizes that slaves could be subjected to forced movement as well as to compelled immobility:

> Going and coming were certainties in slave life. Slaves were moved by their owners from plantation to plantation or from farm to city; they were sold away; they were forced to migrate westward with owners; and, not least of all, they were hired out—both near and far, in groups or alone, with family members and without.

Id. at 45.

37. *See id.* at 46–51; HARRIET A. JACOBS, INCIDENTS IN THE LIFE OF A SLAVE GIRL, WRITTEN BY HERSELF 15 (ed. Jean Fagan Yellin 1861, *reprinted* 1987) (emphasis in original).

38. *See* MARTIN, *supra* note 36, at 51–56, 64; John Walker Tomlin to Benjamin Brand, 6 January 1809, Benjamin Brand Papers, Virginia Historical Society, Richmond, Virginia (describing hired slave as "impertinent" and "obstinate").

39. *See* MARTIN, *supra* note 36, at 93–100, 120–25, 133–34; State v. Mann, 13 N.C. 263 (1829); James v. Carper, 4 Sneed (Tenn.) 397 (1857) ("reasonable corporal punishment" quotations); William Anderson to Farish Carter, 5 August 1853, Farish Carter Papers, #2230, folder 53, Southern Historical Collection, Wilson Library, University of North Carolina, Chapel Hill ("marster don't whip him" quotation).

40. *See* MARTIN, *supra* note 36, at 160–61, 164–66 (independent work ability quotation), 168, 170, 174–75; RICHARD C. WADE, SLAVERY IN THE CITIES: THE SOUTH, 1820–1860 48–49 (1964) ("*quasi* freedom" quotation of a New Orleans resident in 1859); 11(2) DEBOW'S REVIEW 196 (August 1851) (contributor bemoaning that self-hired slaves were "half free slaves").

41. *See* MARTIN, *supra* note 36, at 172, 175, 177, 179; THOMAS H. JONES, THE EXPERIENCE OF THOMAS H. JONES, WHO WAS A SLAVE FOR FORTY-THREE YEARS, WRITTEN BY A FRIEND, AS RELATED TO HIM BY BROTHER JONES 32–33 (1862).

42. PETER RANDOLPH, SKETCHES OF SLAVE LIFE; OR, ILLUSTRATIONS OF THE "PECULIAR INSTITUTION" 58 (1855).

43. FREDERICK DOUGLASS, MY BONDAGE AND MY FREEDOM 199 (ed. William L. Andrews 1987).

44. See MARTIN, *supra* note 36, at 1–5, 102–03; 12 SOUTHERN PLANTER 376–79 (December 1852) (Frank Ruffin's diatribe against slave hiring). My emphasis is on the life of slaves, but it is worth noting that free blacks were often viewed as an anomaly (given the ideology of black racial inferiority) and as a potentially dangerous example of black autonomy that might weaken slave subordination, a fear that often led to laws that discouraged manumission, even to the exile of free blacks, and to limitations on their "freedom."

45. *See* DUNAWAY, *supra* note 27, at 24–32 (profit source; kidnapping); HOWARD DODSON & SYLVIANE A. DIOUF, IN MOTION: THE AFRICAN-AMERICAN EXPERIENCE 46, 54 (2004) (interregional slave trade and kidnapping of free blacks); ROBERT H. GUDMESTAD,

A TROUBLESOME COMMERCE: THE TRANSFOR-
MATION OF THE INTERSTATE SLAVE TRADE 19
(2003) (but noting wide variation in estimates of the relative percentages of movement due to trade versus migration, though
westward slave migration as a percentage fell
after 1820).

46. DUNAWAY, *supra* note 27, at 37 (auc-
tion block); JAMES OAKES, SLAVERY AND
FREEDOM: AN INTERPRETATION OF THE OLD
SOUTH 22, 24 (1998) [hereinafter OAKES,
SLAVERY AND FREEDOM] (degradation cere-
monies); Finkelman, *supra* note 18, at 15
(more on degradation); KENNETH S. GREEN-
BERG, HONOR AND SLAVERY 38–39 (1996)
(greasing skin and other lies); WALTER JOHN-
SON, SOUL BY SOUL: LIFE INSIDE THE ANTE-
BELLUM SLAVE MARKET 137–42 (1999)
(details of the inspection and sale process).

47. *See* JOHNSON, *supra* note 46, at 143–48
(details of the sale process and its significance), 149–50 (quotation); JAMES REDPATH,
THE ROVING EDITOR; OR, TALKS WITH SLAVES
IN THE SOUTHERN STATES 246–52 (1859)
(antislavery journalist describing the stripping of female slaves).

48. MOSES GRANDY, NARRATIVE OF THE
LIFE OF MOSES GRANDY, LATE A SLAVE IN THE
UNITED STATES OF AMERICA 16 (1844).

49. GUDMESTAD, *supra* note 45, at 35
(Anna's story and its consequences); JOHN-
SON, *supra* note 46, at 64, 68 ("soul murder"
and Henry Bibb's story).

50. DODSON & DIOUF, *supra* note 45, at 48
(coffle nature and size; rail travel); GUDMES-
TAD, *supra* note 45, at 54, 46 (similar, plus
irons and cuffs); DUNAWAY, *supra* note 27, at
34 (steamboats).

51. DODSON & DIOUF, *supra* note 45, at 48
(quoting and discussing Charles Ball).

52. DUNAWAY, *supra* note 27, at 41–44
(chances of sale); DODSON & DIOUF, *supra*
note 45, at 53 ("sold down the river"); letter
dated 2 March 1835, Hamilton Brown
Papers, Southern Historical Collection,
University of North Carolina, Chapel Hill
(Brown letter); letter dated 11 March 1864,
Alfred W. Bell Papers, William L. Perkins
Library, Duke University, Manuscripts,
Durham, North Carolina (Mary Bell's warn-
ing); letter dated 10 June 1856, James Gwyn
Papers, Betts, Jefferson's Farm Book 31–32,
Southern Historical Collection, University of
North Carolina, Chapel Hill (hiatal hernia);
GUDMESTAD, *supra* note 45, at 44 (actual
versus threatened sales).

53. GUDMESTAD, *supra* note 45, at 44.

54. 4 DEBATES ON THE ADOPTION OF THE

FEDERAL CONSTITUTION 286 (ed. Jonathan
Elliot 1898; *reprinted in* New York, 1987)
(Pinckney "best terms" quotation); PAUL
FINKELMAN, SLAVERY AND THE FOUNDERS:
RACE AND LIBERTY IN THE AGE OF JEFFERSON
3–7, 8–33 (Pinckney's involvement in the
Fugitive Slave Clause), 87–99 (congressional
debates), 100–01 (alternative ways to read
the clause); 4 JONATHAN ELLIOT, THE
DEBATES IN THE SEVERAL STATE CONVEN-
TIONS ON THE ADOPTION OF THE FEDERAL
CONSTITUTION 286 (1896) (Pinckney quota-
tion on right to recover slaves as a right not
had before); U.S. CONST. art. IV, §2, ¶3 (Fugi-
tive Slave Clause); DON E. FEHRENBACHER,
THE SLAVEHOLDING REPUBLIC: AN ACCOUNT
OF THE UNITED STATES GOVERNMENT'S RELA-
TIONS TO SLAVERY 208–09, 219–25 (2001)
(summarizing arguments that the Fugitive
Slave Clause did not authorize congressional
enforcement action and the U.S. Supreme
Court's rejection of those arguments); A
HOUSE DIVIDED: THE ANTEBELLUM SLAVERY
DEBATES IN AMERICA 1776–1865 23–24
(ed. Mason I. Lowance Jr. 2003) [hereinafter
LOWANCE, HOUSE DIVIDED] (reproducing the
Fugitive Slave Law of 1793, reflecting Con-
gress's view that it did have authority to
enforce the Fugitive Slave Clause).

55. FINKELMAN, *supra* note 54, at 80–81
(Mifflin seeks extradition); FEHRENBACHER,
supra note 54, at 209–10 (Mifflin's request of
President Washington and Congress's
response); LOWANCE, HOUSE DIVIDED, *supra*
note 54, at 23–24 (content of first congressional statute on fugitive-slave recapture).

56. *See* FINKELMAN, *supra* note 54, at 98–
99; LOWANCE, HOUSE DIVIDED, *supra* note
54, at 23–24.

57. FEHRENBACHER, *supra* note 54, at 212.

58. *Id.* at 212–13, 217; In re Susan, 23 Fed.
Cases 444 (1818) (congressional power); In
re Martin, 16 Fed. Cases 881 (N.Y. 1834 or
1835) (No. 9154) (the law withstood assault
on jury-trial guarantee); Commonwealth v.
Griffith, 2 Pickering 11 (1823) (no Fourth
Amendment violation).

59. R. J. M. Blackett, *"Freemen to the Rescue!": Resistance to the Fugitive Slave Law of
1850, in* PASSAGES TO FREEDOM: THE UNDER-
GROUND RAILROAD IN HISTORY AND MEMORY
133–34 (ed. David W. Blight 2004) (rising
numbers of escaped slaves); PHILIP J.
SCHWARZ, SLAVE LAWS IN VIRGINIA 120–37
(1996) (Southern states' perception of the
ineffectiveness of the 1793 federal Fugitive
Slave Law and history of the Virginia
example).

60. Abel Parker Upshur to John B. Floyd, October 1832, Virginia Executive Papers, Letters Received, Library of Virginia; SCHWARZ, *supra* note 59, at 133–34 (discussing this letter and its consequences).

61. SCHWARZ, *supra* note 59, at 131–36; *see generally* MICHAEL F. HOLT, THE FATE OF THEIR COUNTRY: POLITICIANS, SLAVERY EXTENSION, AND THE COMING OF THE CIVIL WAR (2004) (arguing that partisan exaggerations and politicians' missteps and miscalculations played important roles in the various antebellum disputes over slavery and the eventual coming of the Civil War).

62. FEHRENBACHER, *supra* note 54, at 231–32 (details and quotations); Blackett, *supra* note 59, at 134 (brief summary of the provisions of the 1850 act). As Fehrenbacher explains, under the Fugitive Slave Act of 1850, "The writ of habeas corpus was technically still available but rendered useless by the mandated conclusiveness of the certificate of removal." FEHRENBACHER, *supra* note 54, at 415 n. 2. Furthermore, "Legal representation for alleged fugitives, which the law neither required nor forbade, was often volunteered by local antislavery lawyers." *Id.*

63. FEHRENBACHER, *supra* note 54, at 232–33; LOWANCE, HOUSE DIVIDED, *supra* note 54, at 26–30 (reproducing the text of the 1850 act).

64. AKHIL REED AMAR, THE BILL OF RIGHTS: CREATION AND RECONSTRUCTION 270 (quoting EMANCIPATOR AND REPUBLICAN, November 14, 1850). John Bingham, one day to be the primary draftsperson of section one of the Fourteenth Amendment, later expressed agreement that the 1850 act violated the rights to due process and to a jury trial. *See* CONG. GLOBE, 36th Cong., 2d Sess. 83 (1861). The U.S. Supreme Court, however, expressed the contrary view that the act was "in all its provisions, fully authorized by the Constitution of the United States." Ableman v. Booth, 62 U.S. (21 How.) 506, 526 (1858) (chastising state judges on jurisdictional grounds when a Wisconsin trial judge had held that the act violated the Seventh Amendment and the state's Supreme Court held that the act violated jury-trial rights affirmed by the Fifth Amendment Due Process Clause).

65. Blackett, *supra* note 59, at 135 (Northern blacks' organization of protests); *Pennsylvania Freeman*, October 31, 1850 ("panting fugitive"); CAROL M. HUNTER, TO SET THE CAPTIVES FREE: REVEREND JERMAIN WESLEY LOGUEN AND THE STRUGGLE FOR FREEDOM IN CENTRAL NEW YORK, 1835–1872 112 (1993) (Syracuse church statement); 3 WENDELL PHILLIPS GARRISON & FRANCES JACKSON GARRISON, WILLIAM LLOYD GARRISON 1805–1874 323 (1885–89, *reprinted* 1969); SAMUEL J. MAY, THE FUGITIVE SLAVE LAW AND ITS VICTIMS 22 (1861, *reprinted* 1970); BENJAMIN QUARLES, BLACK ABOLITIONISTS 199 (1969).

66. KATHRYN GROVER, THE FUGITIVE'S GIBRALTAR: ESCAPING SLAVES AND ABOLITIONISM IN NEW BEDFORD, MASSACHUSETTS 218 (2001).

67. 2 THE FREDERICK DOUGLASS PAPERS, 1847–1854 277 (ed. John Blassingame 1982).

68. *See* FEHRENBACHER, *supra* note 54, at 232–33.

69. *See* Stanley W. Campbell, *Fugitive Slave Act, in* THE OXFORD COMPANION TO UNITED STATES HISTORY 294 (ed. Paul S. Boyer 2001) (abolitionist anger, acts of resistance, and Southern doubts); FEHRENBACHER, *supra* note 54, at 240, 246 (arguing that slave escapes did not rise during the 1850s and that state and federal courts were generally supportive of enforcing the 1850 Fugitive Slave Act); WILLIAM A. LINK, ROOTS OF SECESSION: SLAVERY AND POLITICS IN ANTEBELLUM VIRGINIA 108 (2003) (numbers of slaves returned and freed under the new federal fugitive-rendition statute during the 1850s but noting that Southern perceptions of lax enforcement mattered more than the reality); Ableman v. Booth, 62 U.S. (21 How.) 506, 526 (1859) (declaring the 1850 act constitutional).

Notes to Chapter 8

1. *See generally* JOHN HOPE FRANKLIN & LOREN SCHWENINGER, RUNAWAY SLAVES: REBELS ON THE PLANTATION 1–42 (1999) (summarizing many of the costs to masters of slave flight and lesser forms of slave resistance); ARIELA J. GROSS, DOUBLE CHARACTER: SLAVERY AND MASTERY IN THE ANTEBELLUM SOUTHERN COURTROOM 47–71, 73 (2000) (role of honor and dishonor generally in antebellum Southern slave law) ("From the perspective of honor culture, slaves' agency was threatening in its capacity to throw masters' honor into question."); Andrew E. Taslitz, *Slaves No More! The Implications of the Informed Citizen Ideal for Discovery before Fourth Amendment Suppression Hearings*, 15 GA. ST. L. REV. 709, 740–41 (1999) (Southern fears of slave flight, revolt, theft, and physical violence and the

resulting cultural impact of these perceived challenges to white supremacy); WILLIAM A. LINK, ROOTS OF SECESSION: SLAVERY AND POLITICS IN ANTEBELLUM VIRGINIA 99 (2003) (similar).

2. See Andrew E. Taslitz, *Condemning the Racist Personality: Why the Critics of Hate Crimes Legislation Are Wrong*, 40 B.C. L. REV. 739, 767–68 & nn. 165–66 (1999) (summarizing the argument of some proslavery apologists that slavery was better for both whites and blacks than the selfish struggle between labor and capital promoted by "free" Northern labor); GROSS, *supra* note 1, at 83–87 (slaves' flight as evidence of disease); THOMAS D. MORRIS, SOUTHERN SLAVERY AND THE LAW, 1619–1860 340 (1996) ("One of the most frequent threats to the notion of the person as a thing, of course, was the slave runaway."); PETER H. WOOD, BLACK MAJORITY: NEGROES IN COLONIAL SOUTH CAROLINA FROM 1670 THROUGH THE STONO REBELLION 239 (1974) (flight as challenge to the white Southern worldview).

3. GROSS, *supra* note 1, at 79–80 (moral senses, plasticity of character, happy slaves, good versus bad slaves); GEORGE M. FREDERICKSON, THE BLACK IMAGE IN THE WHITE MIND: THE DEBATE ON AFRO-AMERICAN CHARACTER AND DESTINY, 1817–1914 52–54 (1971) ("savage brute" and "semi-civilization" quotations); Dr. Samuel Cartwright, *Negro Freedom an Impossibility under Nature's Laws*, 30 DEBOW'S REVIEW 651 (1860) ("slave of Satan" quotation); To the Editor of the Farmers' Register, *Remarks on Overseers and the Proper Treatment of Slaves*, 5 FARMERS' REGISTER 302 (1837) (plasticity); WILLIAM L. VAN DEBURG, HOODLUMS: BLACK VILLAINS AND SOCIAL BANDITS IN AMERICAN LIFE 64–67 (2004) (slave villains versus slaves who were loyal retainers).

4. GROSS, *supra* note 1, at 79–83.

5. *Id.* at 79–85.

6. Lowry v. M'Burney, 1 Mill Const. 237 (S.C. 1817).

7. See GROSS, *supra* note 1, at 83–85; Ward v. Reynolds, Docket No. 4181, Book 221, Perry Cty. Cir. Ct., January 1858, Ala. Sup. Ct. Records, Alabama Department of Archives and History, Montgomery, Alabama, *appeal reported in* 32 Ala. 384 (1858).

8. GROSS, *supra* note 1, at 87–88; Samuel A. Cartwright, *Diseases and Peculiarities in the Negro Race*, 11 DEBOW'S REVIEW 64–69, 184–89, 209–13, 331–37, 504–10, *reprinted in* 2 THE INDUSTRIAL RESOURCES, STATISTICS, ETC., OF THE UNITED STATES AND MORE PARTICULARLY OF THE SOUTHERN AND WESTERN STATES 315–27 (ed. J. D. B. DeBow 1854).

9. See GROSS, *supra* note 1, at 87–89; *see generally* Ariela Gross, *Pandora's Box: Slave Character on Trial in the Antebellum Deep South, in* SLAVERY AND THE LAW 291, 292–319 (ed. Paul Finkelman 1997) (on the medicalization of slave vice, especially running away).

10. VAN DEBURG, *supra* note 3, at 52–56; HERBERT APTHEKER, AMERICAN NEGRO SLAVE REVOLTS 346 (1943/1968) (quoting Richard A. Lewis et al. to Thomas Bragg, August 25, 1856); Herbert Aptheker, *Maroons within the Present Limits of the United States*, 24 JOURNAL OF NEGRO HISTORY 167, 176 (April 1939); LINK, *supra* note 1, at 99–100 (abolitionists as imagined allies).

11. LINK, *supra* note 1, at 99–100; CHARLOTTESVILLE JEFFERSONIAN (1853), quoted in *State Affairs*, RICHMOND WHIG, September 3, 1853 (emphasis added); *Underground Railroad*, SHEPHERDSTOWN REGISTER, February 16, 1856; *The Underground Railroad*, (RICHMOND) WATCHMAN AND OBSERVER, May 22, 1852 (emphasis added).

12. LINK, *supra* note 1, at 99–100, 103–04; David W. Blight, *Introduction: The Underground Railroad in History and Memory, in* PASSAGES TO FREEDOM: THE UNDERGROUND RAILROAD IN HISTORY AND MEMORY 1, 3 (ed. David W. Blight 2004) (sometimes organized in a network); LARRY GARA, THE LIBERTY LINE: THE LEGEND OF THE UNDERGROUND RAILROAD 3, 18 (1961) (no evidence of a centrally managed network); *The Underground Railroad*, WATCHMAN AND OBSERVER, May 22, 1851 (spirit of darkness); *An Abolitionist in Trouble*, WILLIAMSBURG WEEKLY GAZETTE, June 30, 1858 (Baylis and the *Keziah* affair); John T. Kneebone, *A Breakdown on the Underground Railroad: Captain B. and the Capture of the Keziah, 1858*, 48 VIRGINIA CAVALCADE 74–83 (Spring 1999) (more details on the *Keziah* affair); *Kidnapping at Norfolk*, RICHMOND ENQUIRER, June 1, 1858 ("tarred and feathered") (emphasis in original).

13. See MITCHELL SNAY, GOSPEL OF DISUNION: RELIGION AND SEPARATISM IN THE ANTEBELLUM SOUTH 9–11, 28–33 (1993); "Records of the Presbytery of Bethel, 1824–1849," Historical Foundation of the Reformed Presbyterian Church, Montreat, North Carolina [hereinafter Montreat]; RICHMOND ENQUIRER, October 16, 1835.

14. SNAY, *supra* note 13, at 30–32; 4 "Min-

utes of the South Alabama Presbytery, 1835–1840," Montreat; "Records of Concord Presbytery, 1825–1836," Montreat; *Proceedings of the Fifth Annual Meeting of the Baptist State Convention of North Carolina* (New Bern, NC: Recorder Office, 1835); WALTER B. POSEY, THE PRESBYTERIAN CHURCH IN THE OLD SOUTHWEST, 1778–1838 80 (1952); 2 "East Hanover Presbytery Minutes, 1835–1843," Montreat, 10.

15. See SNAY, *supra* note 13, at 67–77; SOUTHERN PRESBYTERY REVIEW 572–73 (March 1849); CHRISTIAN INDEX, February 13, 1861 (Rev. E. W. Warren of Georgia).

16. JAMES HENLEY THORNWELL, THE RIGHTS AND DUTIES OF MASTERS 27–28 (1850); JOHN PATRICK DALY, WHEN SLAVERY WAS CALLED FREEDOM: EVANGELICALISM, PROSLAVERY, AND THE CAUSES OF THE CIVIL WAR 112–35 (2002) (discussing Thornwell and related authors equating slavery to Northern free labor or defending the former's superiority over the latter).

17. See DALY, *supra* note 16, at 112–15; FREDERICK ROSS, SLAVERY ORDAINED OF GOD 94 (1857) (elevating man); WILLIAM C. BUCK, THE SLAVERY QUESTION 16 (1849) (emphasis added).

18. Paul Finkelman, *The Centrality of Slavery in American Legal Development, in* SLAVERY AND THE LAW 3, 11 (ed. Paul Finkelman 1997); WILLIAM S. JENKINS, PRO-SLAVERY THOUGHT IN THE OLD SOUTH 60 (1935) (quoting John Randolph); HARVEY WISH, GEORGE FITZHUGH: PROPAGANDIST OF THE OLD SOUTH 96–98 (1943) ("sentimental language" quotation from John Henry Hammond); GEORGE FITZHUGH, SOCIOLOGY FOR THE SOUTH, OR THE FAILURE OF FREE SOCIETY 177–82 (1854); *see also* EUGENE D. GENOVESE, THE WORLD THE SLAVEHOLDERS MADE (1969) (on the implications of Fitzhugh's thought).

19. Finkelman, *supra* note 18, at 10; 1 A. E. DICK HOWARD, COMMENTARIES ON THE CONSTITUTION OF VIRGINIA 58 n. 2 (1974) (Virginia legislature reached final agreement on its Declaration of Rights on June 12, 1776); 1 THE PAPERS OF GEORGE MASON, 1725–1792 275–77, 283–99 (ed. Robert A. Rutland 1970); VA. CONST. OF 1776, art. 1, *reprinted in* 10 SOURCES AND DOCUMENTS OF UNITED STATES CONSTITUTIONS 49 (ed. William F. Swindler 1979).

20. Hudgins v. Wrights, 11 Va. 134, 141 (Va. 1806) (emphasis added); Finkelman, *supra* note 18, at 10–11; ST. GEORGE TUCKER, A DISSERTATION ON SLAVERY WITH A PRO-

POSAL FOR THE GRADUAL ABOLITION OF IT, IN THE STATE OF VIRGINIA (1796) (Tucker wanted to change the law to abolish slavery but did not believe that slavery could be abolished on the basis of the law as it stood).

21. JAMES OAKES, THE RULING RACE: A HISTORY OF AMERICAN SLAVEHOLDERS 143 (1998); *Appendix*, CONG. GLOBE, April 10, 1848, at 524, 526 (Virginia congressman); 4 PROCEEDINGS OF THE VIRGINIA STATE CONVENTION OF 1861 385–87 (ed. George H. Reese 1965) (Alexander Stephens); Samuel A. Cartwright, *Report on the Diseases of and Physical Peculiarities of the Negro Race,* 7 NEW ORLEANS MEDICAL AND SURGICAL JOURNAL 691–715 (May 1851), *excerpts reprinted in* DEFENDING SLAVERY: PROSLAVERY THOUGHT IN THE OLD SOUTH, A BRIEF HISTORY WITH DOCUMENTS 157, 172–73 (ed. Paul Finkelman 2003) [hereinafter FINKELMAN, DEFENDING SLAVERY].

22. FINKELMAN, DEFENDING SLAVERY, *supra* note 21, at 37 (source of all quotations except the "mudsill" quotation); James Henry Hammond, *Speech on the Admission of Kansas, U.S. Senate,* CONG. GLOBE, 35th Cong., 2d Sess., March 4, 1858, at 961–62 ("mudsill" quotation).

23. OAKES, RULING RACE, *supra* note 21, at 80–81; George Allen to William Williams, September 12, 1850, Allen Papers, 2 CHARLES LYELL, A SECOND VISIT TO THE UNITED STATES 13 (1849).

24. OAKES, RULING RACE, *supra* note 21, at 69–73, 75–76, 80–81; LESLIE HOWARD OWENS, THIS SPECIES OF PROPERTY: SLAVE LIFE AND CULTURE IN THE OLD SOUTH 16 (1976) (slaves better than bank dividends, quoting Louisiana slaveholder James Steer).

25. PAUL FINKELMAN, DRED SCOTT V. SANDFORD: A BRIEF HISTORY WITH DOCUMENTS 2, 15–17 & n. 19, 22 (1997); Commonwealth v. Aves, 18 Pick. 193 (Mass. 1836) (slaves became free the moment they were brought within the jurisdiction). For a more detailed discussion of the case law on the effects of slaves entering or working in free territory, *see* PAUL FINKELMAN, AN IMPERFECT UNION: SLAVERY, FEDERALISM, AND COMITY 104–25 (1981).

26. *See* FINKELMAN, DEFENDING SLAVERY, *supra* note 21, at 43–44 (Southern fears of being outvoted in a future Northern-dominated national legislature); DON E. FEHRENBACHER, THE DRED SCOTT CASE: ITS SIGNIFICANCE IN AMERICAN LAW AND POLITICS 81 (1978) (comparing the confident

South of 1787 with a South worried about its political vulnerability in the Union); MICHAEL F. HOLT, THE FATE OF THEIR COUN-TRY: POLITICIANS, SLAVERY EXTENSION, AND THE COMING OF THE CIVIL WAR 28–29 (2004) (Southern imperative to expand slav-ery into the Western territories, both to avoid Northern domination and, for at least a few Southerners, to ensure that slavery remained prosperous).

27. *See* FINKELMAN, DRED SCOTT, *supra* note 25, at 8 (passage and contents of the Northwest Ordinance); PAUL FINKELMAN, SLAVERY AND THE FOUNDERS: RACE AND LIB-ERTY IN THE AGE OF JEFFERSON 31, 34–37 (1996) (politics leading up to, and impact of, the Northwest Ordinance).

28. *See* ALLEN C. GUELZO, ABRAHAM LIN-COLN: REDEEMER PRESIDENT 133 (1999) (Louisiana Purchase and Missouri Compro-mise); FINKELMAN, DRED SCOTT, *supra* note 25, at 9 (impact of, and respective Northern and Southern views on the meaning of, the Missouri Compromise).

29. FINKELMAN, DRED SCOTT, *supra* note 25, at 9 (Texas, Utah, New Mexico); GUELZO, *supra* note 28, at 139–40, 145–46 (Mexican Cession, California, Utah, Mexico, Fugitive Slave Law); CHARLES M. CHRISTIAN, BLACK SAGA: THE AFRICAN-AMERICAN EXPERIENCE: A CHRONOLOGY 49 (1999) (Fugitive Slave Law).

30. GUELZO, *supra* note 28, at 182–88; 4 THE COLLECTED WORKS OF ABRAHAM LIN-COLN 67 (ed. Roy P. Basler 1959) [hereinafter LINCOLN, COLLECTED WORKS] (Lincoln "wildfire" quotation); FINKELMAN, DRED SCOTT, *supra* note 25, at 10 (many Northern-ers' fear of the slavocracy and the impact of its spread).

31. FINKELMAN, DRED SCOTT, *supra* note 25, at 10 ("popular sovereignty"); NICOLE ETCHESON, BLEEDING KANSAS: CONTESTED LIBERTY IN THE CIVIL WAR ERA 2–8, 28–32 (2004).

32. *See, e.g.,* MICHAEL LIND, WHAT LIN-COLN BELIEVED: THE VALUES AND CONVIC-TIONS OF AMERICA'S GREATEST PRESIDENT 18–19, 32, 107, 110, 125, 150–51 (2005) (Free-Soilers and racism); ROGERS M. SMITH, CIVIC IDEALS: CONFLICTING VISIONS OF CITI-ZENSHIP IN U.S. HISTORY 165–242 (1997) (tracing the antebellum history of a white-supremacist United States bent on excluding African Americans from the polity); FRANCIS D. ADAMS & BARRY SANDERS, ALIENABLE RIGHTS: THE EXCLUSION OF AFRICAN-AMERI-CANS IN A WHITE MAN'S LAND, 1619–2000

131–66 (2003) (summary of the pre-*Dred Scott* antebellum-era struggle to continue the exclusion of African Americans from what the majority saw as a necessarily white nation); *cf.* ADAM ROTHMAN, SLAVE COUN-TRY: AMERICAN EXCEPTIONALISM AND THE ORIGINS OF THE DEEP SOUTH (2005) (extended effort to explain why slavery flourished and spread in the Deep South as the nation grew, including the massive forced migration of slaves, while the institu-tion gradually disappeared in the North, all in the face of the nation supposedly com-mitted to the principle of equality among free men).

33. 19 How. (60 U.S.) 393 (1857). For a concise summary of the *Dred Scott* case and its significance for American law, *see* John E. Semonche, *Scott v. Sandford, in* THE OXFORD GUIDE TO UNITED STATES SUPREME COURT DECISIONS 277, 277–79 (ed. Kermit L. Hall 1999).

34. FINKELMAN, DRED SCOTT, *supra* note 25, at 10–17.

35. *See id.* at 17–20.

36. *See id.* at 20–21; Somerset v. Stewart, 1 Lofft (G.B.) 1 (1772). *See generally* STEVEN M. WISE, THOUGH THE HEAVENS MAY FALL: THE LANDMARK TRIAL THAT LED TO THE END OF HUMAN SLAVERY (2005) (detailing the *Somer-set* case's history). The *Somerset* rule was modified by the *Slave Grace* case, 2 Hagg. Admir. (G.B.) 94 (1827), which held that, though a slave coming to reside in England became free while there and could not be forced to leave, he reverted to the status of a slave if he returned to a slave jurisdiction. *See* FINKELMAN, DRED SCOTT, *supra* note 25, at 21. "For the most part, southern states did not initially follow the *Slave Grace* prece-dent," so "Scott's lawyers no doubt expected him to win his freedom." *Id.*

37. Scott v. Emerson, 15 Mo. 576, 586 (1852).

38. *See* FINKELMAN, DRED SCOTT, *supra* note 25, at 22 ("The decision was frankly political. It was not made on the basis of legal precedent but because of popular prej-udice.").

39. *See id.* at 32–33.

40. *See id.* at 31–32 (reviewing both the arguments that the Court could have relied on *Strader* and the counterarguments); Strader v. Graham, 10 How. (U.S.) 82 (1850). My explanation of the *Strader* principle is an extension of Finkelman's analysis and goes a bit further, perhaps, than did Justice Nel-son's draft opinion relying on *Strader,* but

under any of these interpretations, a more
conservative route, concluding that Missouri
law controlled Scott's status while there and
that he was thus a slave, was available to,
but rejected by, the *Scott* Court. *See* FINKEL-
MAN, DRED SCOTT, *supra* note 25, at 31–32.
  41. *See* FINKELMAN, DRED SCOTT, *supra*
note 25, at 29–30; CARL BRENT SWISHER,
ROGER B. TANEY 154 (1935) (quoting unpublished opinion of Attorney General Taney).
  42. FINKELMAN, DRED SCOTT, *supra* note
25, at 57–59 (excerpting opinion); *Dred
Scott*, 60 U.S. at 403–06 (emphasis added).
  43. 60 U.S. at 407.
  44. *Id.* at 407–10.
  45. *Id.* at 416–17.
  46. *Id.* at 432–54; *see Strader*, 10 U.S. at 82.
  47. 60 U.S. at 432–52, 500.
  48. FINKELMAN, DRED SCOTT, *supra* note
25, at 47–49, 3 LINCOLN, COLLECTED
WORKS, *supra* note 30, at 404; FEHREN-
BACHER, *supra* note 26, at 60–61, 444–45;
Lemmon v. The People, 20 N.Y. REPORTS 562
(1857).
  49. NEW YORK EVENING POST, August 31,
1859; *see also* FINKELMAN, DRED SCOTT, *supra*
note 25, at 48.
  50. *See* FINKELMAN, DRED SCOTT, *supra*
note 25, at 49–52, 127–226.
  51. VAN DEBURG, *supra* note 3, at 50–51
(daily acts of resistance and urban slaves);
FREDERICK L. OLMSTED, THE COTTON KING-
DOM: A TRAVELLER'S OBSERVATIONS ON COT-
TON AND SLAVERY IN THE AMERICAN SLAVE
STATES 94 (1861) (ed. Arthur M. Schlesinger
1969) (quotations); Deborah Gray White,
*Simple Truths: Antebellum Slavery in Black and
White, in* PASSAGES TO FREEDOM: THE
UNDERGROUND RAILROAD IN HISTORY AND
MEMORY 33, 57–58 (ed. David W. Blight
2004) (challenging whites and quotations
on feigning ignorance and illness).
  52. White, *supra* note 51, at 57–58.
  53. *Id.* at 58, 60–61 (revolts, truancy,
repeated flight); WOOD, *supra* note 2, at 23;
VAN DEBURG, *supra* note 3, at 51 (numbers
of truants versus numbers of fugitives);
CHRISTIAN PARENTI, THE SOFT CAGE: SUR-
VEILLANCE IN AMERICA FROM SLAVERY TO
THE WAR ON TERROR 15–16 (2003) (motivations for, and advantages of, truancy and
other flight); HOWARD DODSON & SYLVIANE
A. DIOUF, IN MOTION: THE AFRICAN-AMERI-
CAN MIGRATION EXPERIENCE 31 (2004) (salt
rubs and self-reliant individuals).
  54. VAN DEBURG, *supra* note 3, at 58
(rumors igniting white panics); STEVEN
HAHN, A NATION UNDER OUR FEET: BLACK

POLITICAL STRUGGLES IN THE RURAL SOUTH
FROM SLAVERY TO THE GREAT MIGRATION
57–60 (2003) (panics detailed); *Evils of Slav-
ery,* THE LIBERATOR, January 28, 1832 (quot-
ing Virginian); MERTON DILLON, SLAVERY
ATTACKED: SOUTHERN SLAVES AND THEIR
ALLIES, 1619–1865 156 (1990).
  55. *See* HAHN, *supra* note 54, at 59–61;
DILLON, *supra* note 54, at 135, 187–88;
EUGENE D. GENOVESE, FROM REBELLION TO
REVOLUTION: AFRO-AMERICAN SLAVE
REVOLTS IN THE MAKING OF THE MODERN
WORLD 128–29 (1979).
  56. *Colored American,* October 20, 1838;
THEOSOPHUS SMITH, CONJURING CULTURE:
BIBLICAL FORMATIONS OF BLACK AMERICA 68
(1994) (Sojourner Truth); Eddie S. Glaude Jr.,
*A Sacred Drama: "Exodus" and the Under-
ground Railroad in African-American Life, in*
PASSAGES TO FREEDOM: THE UNDERGROUND
RAILROAD IN HISTORY AND MEMORY 291,
292 (ed. David W. Blight 2004) (Harriet Tub-
man, Exodus, and spirituals); ARTHUR H.
FAUSET, SOJOURNER TRUTH: GOD'S FAITHFUL
PILGRIM 175 (1938, *reprinted by* Russel Co.,
1971).
  57. White, *supra* note 51, at 46–47 (blacks
and whites heard two different things);
EDDIE S. GLAUDE JR., EXODUS! RELIGION,
RACE, AND NATION IN EARLY NINETEENTH-
CENTURY BLACK AMERICA 4–9, 95 (2000)
(hypocrisy, soul transformation, collective
identity, morally right nation within a
nation); Albert J. Robateau, *The Blood of the
Martyrs Is the Seed of Faith: Suffering in the
Christianity of American Slaves, in* THE
COURAGE TO HOPE: FROM BLACK SUFFERING
TO HUMAN REDEMPTION 33 (ed. Quinton
Hosford Dixie and Cornel West 1999)
(Moses to Pharaoh quotation); DAVID
WALKER'S APPEAL IN FOUR ARTICLES,
TOGETHER WITH A PREAMBLE, TO THE COL-
ORED CITIZENS OF THE WORLD, BUT IN PAR-
TICULAR, AND VERY EXPRESSLY, TO THOSE OF
THE UNITED STATES OF AMERICA xiv (1829,
reprinted by Hill and Wang 1965).
  58. Glaude, *supra* note 56, at 300 (pilgrim-
age and new millennium).
  59. EUGENE D. GENOVESE, ROLL, JORDAN,
ROLL: THE WORLD THE SLAVES MADE 280–81
(1976). Genovese thought that slave religion
blocked political identity, but other historians argue quite the opposite. *See* GLAUDE,
supra note 57, at 7.
  60. MIA BAY, THE WHITE IMAGE IN THE
BLACK MIND: AFRICAN-AMERICAN IDEAS
ABOUT WHITE PEOPLE, 1830–1925 41–54, 65
(2000).

61. GAIL BEDERMAN, MANLINESS AND CIVI-
LIZATION: A CULTURAL HISTORY OF GENDER
AND RACE IN THE UNITED STATES 1880–1917
20 (1995) (manhood rights forbidden); BAY,
supra note 60, at 40–41 (aspirations to prove
manhood); DAVID WALKER, "ONE CONTIN-
UAL CRY": DAVID WALKER'S "APPEAL TO THE
COLORED CITIZENS OF THE WORLD" (1829–
30): ITS SETTING AND ITS MEANING 79 (ed.
Herbert Aptheker 1965); MARIA W. STEWART,
AMERICA'S FIRST BLACK WOMAN POLITICAL
WRITER: ESSAYS AND SPEECHES 37, 46, 48, 57
(ed. Marilyn Richardson 1987); MARTIN
ROBINSON DELANEY, THE CONDITION, ELEVA-
TION, EMIGRATION, AND DESTINY OF THE
COLORED PEOPLE OF THE UNITED STATES 36
(1852, reprinted by Arno Press 1968).
62. BAY, supra note 60, at 42–48, 51–54;
HOSEA EASTON, A TREATISE ON THE INTELLEC-
TUAL CHARACTER, AND CIVIL AND POLITICAL
CONDITION OF THE COLORED PEOPLE OF THE
UNITED STATES, AND THE PREJUDICE EXER-
CISED TOWARD THEM: WITH A SERMON ON
THE DUTY OF THE CHURCH TO THEM 10–11
(1837) ("savage race" and related quota-
tions).
63. BAY, supra note 60, at 66–71 (Douglass
on moral errors); WALDO E. MARTIN JR., THE
MIND OF FREDERICK DOUGLASS 97 (1984)
("race pride" quotation); ROGAN KERSH,
DREAMS OF A MORE PERFECT UNION 160–61,
163–68 (2001) (nation within a nation;
Douglass's views closer to most slaves, fugi-
tives, and free blacks).
64. KERSH, supra note 63, at 160–61, 164–
67; Bernard R. Boxill, Douglass against the
Emigrationists, in FREDERICK DOUGLASS: A
CRITICAL READER 30 (ed. Bill E. Lawson and
Frank M. Kirkland 1999); Frederick Douglass,
Of Morals and Men, in 2 THE LIFE AND WRIT-
ING OF FREDERICK DOUGLASS 170–74 (ed.
Philip S. Foner 1950); COLORED AMERICAN,
April 1, 1837 ("forms of the Union" quotation); 2 THE FREDERICK DOUGLASS PAPERS
478 (ed. J. W. Blassingame 1979–94) [here-
inafter DOUGLASS PAPERS]; 3 id. at 93.
65. Frederick Douglass, The Constitution of
the United States: Is It Pro-Slavery or Antislavery? (T. Halifax and W. Birtwhistle 1860),
excerpted in THE ANTISLAVERY ARGUMENT 356
(ed. William H. Pease and Jane H. Pease
1965).
66. See KERSH, supra note 63, at 156, 158–
59, 162 & n. 25; THEODORE DRAPER, THE
REDISCOVERY OF BLACK NATIONALISM 42
(quoting Henry Highland Garnet); A DOCU-
MENTARY HISTORY OF THE UNITED STATES
178, 385 (ed. Herbert Aptheker 1962)

(Philadelphia blacks' pronouncement of love
for their native country). Even separatists
like Martin Delaney sometimes used nation-
within-a-nation language. See KERSH, supra
note 63, at 156. For a concise overview of
black thought at the time on moral unionism and its alternatives, see id. at 153–68.
67. See BAY, supra note 60, at 127–43; Tom
Windham, in 11 FEDERAL WRITERS' PROJECT,
THE AMERICAN SLAVE: A COMPOSITE AUTOBI-
OGRAPHY, pt. 7 at 211 (ed. George Rawick
1972–73) (collecting most of the former-
slave narratives) [hereinafter COMPOSITE
AUTOBIOGRAPHY] ("us ain't hogs" quotation); DAVID BRION DAVIS, THE PROBLEM OF
SLAVERY IN AN AGE OF REVOLUTION, 1770–
1823 556 (1975) ("twin deliverers"). There
are well-known dangers in relying too heavily on Work Projects Administration interviews with surviving former slaves, so I have
tried to do so throughout this book primarily where there is corroborating evidence.
See BAY, supra note 60, at 114–16 (discussing strengths and weaknesses of the WPA
narratives).
68. BAY, supra note 60, at 165, 167–68,
171, 173–77; Steve Douglas, 4 COMPOSITE
AUTOBIOGRAPHY, SERIES II, pt. 3, supra note
67, at 1228 ("all white folks in one sack").
69. BAY, supra note 60, at 169–77, 179–80,
182–83; 18 Unwritten History of Slavery, in
COMPOSITE AUTOBIOGRAPHY, supra note 67,
at 136 (Fisk University); Robert Burns, 12
COMPOSITE AUTOBIOGRAPHY, OKLAHOMA
NARRATIVES, SUPPLEMENT, SERIES I, supra
note 67, at 81; James Southall, in THE WPA
OKLAHOMA SLAVE NARRATIVE 409 (ed. T.
Lindsay Baker and Julie P. Baker 1996);
Anthony Dawson, id. at 124.

Notes to Chapter 9

1. See, e.g., EDGAR J. MCMANUS, BLACK
BONDAGE IN THE NORTH 160–88 (1973)
(summarizing gradual abolition laws in the
North and their impact, including replacing
bondage to individual masters with a kind
of bondage to the white community as a
whole via the ideology of white supremacy);
JOANNE POPE MELISH, DISOWNING SLAVERY:
GRADUAL EMANCIPATION AND "RACE" IN
NEW ENGLAND, 1780–1860 (1998) (linking
gradualism in New England to a regional
identity that marked blacks as dangerous
outsiders to the community); MICHAEL
LIND, WHAT LINCOLN BELIEVED: THE VALUES
AND CONVICTIONS OF AMERICA'S GREATEST
PRESIDENT 18, 107, 125–32, 150–51 (2005)

(Northern opposition to slavery's spread); Andrew E. Taslitz, *Hate Crimes, Free Speech, and the Contract of Mutual Indifference*, 80 B.U. L. REV. 1283, 1311, 1370–71 (2000) (arguments that slavery was at least the temporary price of union, plus Northern commercial ties to the South and other reasons for Northern opposition to the immediatism of the abolitionists); Paul Finkelman, *Chief Justice Hornblower of New Jersey and the Fugitive Slave Laws of 1793, in* SLAVERY AND THE LAW 113, 115 (ed. Paul Finkelman 1997) ("New Jersey was home to some blacks still in servitude when the Civil War began.").

2. See LIND, *supra* note 1, at 15, 18–19, 85–88, 107, 110, 125–32, 150–51, 195–205, 209, 213, 224–26, 270–71 (Free-Soilers, the goal of a white North and West, and the colonizationist movement); MELISH, *supra* note 1 (New England racism); ARTHUR ZILVERSMIT, THE FIRST EMANCIPATION: THE ABOLITION OF SLAVERY IN THE NORTH 225 (1967) (quoting Aaron Kitchell, a leader of New Jersey's Jeffersonians and a negrophobe likely to side with the proslavery South after 1801); Finkelman, *supra* note 1, at 116 (also discussing Kitchell); Taslitz, *Mutual Indifference, supra* note 1, at 1362–74 (abolitionists and their repression in the North); *see generally* MERRILL D. PETERSON, JOHN BROWN: THE LEGEND REVISITED (2002) (on Brown's violent tactics and their contribution to the coming of the Civil War and the end of slavery).

3. See Taslitz, *Mutual Indifference, supra* note 1, at 1336–37, 1351–56, 1362–79.

4. See Finkelman, *supra* note 1, at 114–19 (history of gradual abolition in New Jersey including ship searches and general Northern attitudes); ZILVERSMIT, *supra* note 2, at 159 (preparing for freedom); Act of November 25, 1788, 1788 N.J. ACTS 13, 486–88; Marion Thompson, *New Jersey Laws and the Negro*, 28 J. NEGRO HISTORY 156, 179 (1943); Act of February 24, 1820 §§ 11–21, 1820 N.J. LAWS 74–80; PAUL FINKELMAN, AN IMPERFECT UNION: SLAVERY, FEDERALISM, AND COMITY 71, 76–77, 83 (1981) (on slave transit in New Jersey).

5. See Finkelman, *supra* note 1, at 118, 120–21 (background to New Jersey's 1826 personal-liberty law and to the *Hornblower* case); *Opinion of Chief Justice Hornblower on the Fugitive Slave Law*, p. 14, NEW YORK EVENING POST, 1851, *reprinted in* 1 FUGITIVE SLAVES AND AMERICAN COURTS: THE PAMPHLET LITERATURE 97–104 (ed. Paul Finkelman 1988) (unreported opinion) [hereinafter

Hornblower Opinion, with page cites to the pages of the opinion itself]; THOMAS D. MORRIS, FREE MEN ALL: THE PERSONAL LIBERTY LAWS OF THE NORTH, 1790–1861 57 (1974) ("workable balance" quotation); State v. The Sheriff of Burlington, No. 36286 (N.J. 1836) (unreported decision, New Jersey State Archives, Helmsley Case File, under *Nathan, Alias Alex. Helmsley v. State*).

6. Finkelman, *supra* note 1, at 121–22 (case background summarized; quotations other than from *Hornblower Opinion*); BENJAMIN DREW, A NORTH-SIDE VIEW OF SLAVERY, THE REFUGEE; OR, THE NARRATIVES OF FUGITIVE SLAVES IN CANADA (1856) (on the Helmsleys); *Important Decision*, THE LIBERATOR, July 30, 1836, at 124 (reporting on the case); *Upholding Slavery*, 20 THE FRIEND 281–82 (June 11, 1836).

7. See Finkelman, *supra* note 1, at 122–23 (analyzing the opinion); U.S. CONST. art. IV, §1–2 (Full Faith and Credit Clause and Fugitive Slave Clause); *Hornblower Opinion, supra* note 5, at 4–5.

8. *Hornblower Opinion, supra* note 5, at 5–6.

9. See *id.* at 6.

10. *Id.* at 6.

11. *Id.* at 6–7.

12. 5 Sergeant & Rawle 62 (Pa. 1819) (Tilghman opinion); Finkelman, *supra* note 1, at 124, 138 n. 46 (challenging the historical analysis and intentionalist claims of Justice Tilghman); *see generally* Paul Finkelman, *The Constitution and the Intentions of the Framers: The Limits of Historical Analysis*, 50 PITT. L. REV. 349–98 (1989) (arguing that intentionalist interpreters of the Constitution often fail as historians).

13. *Hornblower Opinion, supra* note 5, at 6.

14. *Id.* at 6.

15. See Finkelman, *supra* note 1, at 125.

16. DON E. FEHRENBACHER, THE SLAVEHOLDING REPUBLIC: AN ACCOUNT OF THE UNITED STATES GOVERNMENT'S RELATIONS TO SLAVERY 215–16 (2001) [hereinafter FEHRENBACHER, SLAVEHOLDING REPUBLIC] (summary of Northern states' laws); Finkelman, *supra* note 1, at 125–27 (similar, plus *replegiando* writ); Ohio Session Laws (1818–19), 17th Sess., 56–58 (Chillicothe, state printer 1819); New York Session Laws, 31st Sess. (Albany: John Barber, 1808), 108–09; 2 Revised Laws of the State of New York, 36th Sess. (Albany: H. C. Southwick, 1813), 209–10; New York Session Laws, 40th Sess. (New York: William Gould, David Banks, and Stephen Gould, 1818), 143; Pennsylvania

Session Laws, 47th Sess. (Harrisburg: C. Gleim, 1820), 104–06; Pennsylvania Session Laws (1825–26), 50th Sess. (Harrisburg: Cameron B. Krause, 1826), 50–55; 2 Revised Statutes of the State of New York (Albany: Packard and Van Benthuysen, 1829) 464–65; 2 JOHN CODMAN HURD, THE LAW OF FREE-DOM AND BONDAGE IN THE UNITED STATES 30, 127–28, 129 (Boston: Little, Brown, 1858–62).

17. *See* FEHRENBACHER, SLAVEHOLDING REPUBLIC, *supra* note 16, at 217; Wright v. Deacon, 5 Sergeant and Rawle 62 (Pa. 1819); Jack v. Martin, 12 WENDELL 311, 324 (N.Y. Supreme Court 1834); MORRIS, *supra* note 5, at 5–69; *In re Susan*, 23 Fed. Cases 444 (1818); Commonwealth v. Griffith, 2 Pickering 11, 14, 15 (Mass. 1823). *See also* In re Martin, 16 Fed. Cases 881, 883 (N.Y. 1834 or 1835) (Seventh Amendment challenge).

18. FEHRENBACHER, SLAVEHOLDING REPUB-LIC, *supra* note 16, at 217–18; *Report of the Case of Charles Brown, a Fugitive Slave Owing Labour and Service to Wm. C. Drury of Wash-ington County, Maryland, Decided by the Recorder of Pittsburgh, February 7th, 1835* 55, *reprinted in* FUGITIVE SLAVES AND AMERICAN COURTS: THE PAMPHLET LITERATURE (ed. Paul Finkelman 1988). *See also* ROBERT M. COVER, JUSTICE ACCUSED: ANTISLAVERY AND THE JUDICIAL PROCESS 119–21 (1975) (addi-tional expressions of personal regret by the Northern judiciary).

19. *See* Finkelman, *supra* note 1, at 127–34 (also quoting local newspaper reports of the time).

20. *See* FEHRENBACHER, SLAVEHOLDING REPUBLIC, *supra* note 16, at 219–20; Prigg v. Pennsylvania, 16 Peters 539, 611, 613, 625–26 (1842).

21. *Prigg,* 16 Peters at 539, 611, 613, 625–26; FEHRENBACHER, SLAVEHOLDING REPUB-LIC, *supra* note 16, at 220. Fehrenbacher argues that Story relied on bad history in claiming that the Fugitive Slave Clause was at the time of its drafting the linchpin with-out which there would have been no Union. *See id.* at 218 ("The idea that the fugitive slave clause had been regarded as indispen-sable in 1787 and was therefore an espe-cially sacrosanct part of the Constitution did not have much basis in fact."). *But see* ALFRED W. BLUMROSEN & RUTH G. BLUM-ROSEN, SLAVE NATION: HOW SLAVERY UNITED THE COLONIES AND SPARKED THE AMERICAN REVOLUTION (2005) (arguing that the South saw Union as a better way to protect slavery than continued loyalty to Britain).

22. *See* FEHRENBACHER, SLAVEHOLDING REPUBLIC, *supra* note 16, at 221.

23. *See id.* at 220–21 (summarizing differ-ing justices' views); *Prigg,* 16 Peters at 618–22, 622–33; DON E. FEHRENBACHER, THE DRED SCOTT CASE: ITS SIGNIFICANCE IN AMERICAN LAW AND POLITICS 44 (1978) (Taney and Story "coolly ignoring" the Fourth Amendment, the Privileges and Immunities Clause, and the Due Process Clause arguments of counsel).

24. Prigg v. Pennsylvania, *Summary of Oral Argument, in* 2 LANDMARK BRIEFS AND ARGU-MENTS OF THE SUPREME COURT OF THE UNITED STATES: CONSTITUTIONAL LAW 497, 519 (ed. Philip B. Kurland and Gerhard Casper 1978).

25. *Id.* at 516–17.

26. *Id.* at 517. For counsel's privileges-and-immunities argument, *see id.* at 516.

27. *See* FEHRENBACHER, SLAVEHOLDING REPUBLIC, *supra* note 16, at 221–22, 412 n. 53–57 (doubt cast, state-law provisions, and more-determined opposition to federal law); *Governor William Seward's Message of August 16, 1842, in* 63 NILES' NATIONAL REGISTER 28 (September 10, 1842); Joseph Nogee, *The Prigg Case and Fugitive Slavery, 1842–1850,* 39 J. NEGRO HISTORY 200–02 (1954) (sum-marizing Northern state-law responses to *Prigg);* ACTS AND RESOLVES PASSED BY THE LEGISLATURE OF MASSACHUSETTS IN THE YEAR 1843 33 (Boston: Dutton and Went-worth, Printers to the State, 1843); MORRIS, *supra* note 5, at 117–19; Paul Finkelman, *Prigg v. Pennsylvania and Northern State Courts: Anti-Slavery Use of a Pro-Slavery Deci-sion, in* 25 CIVIL WAR HISTORY 6–8, 21 n. (1979) (citing laws passed in Vermont, 1843; Connecticut, 1844; New Hampshire, 1846; and Rhode Island, 1848).

28. Pennsylvania Session Laws, 71st Sess., at 206–08 (Harrisburg: J. M. C. Lescure, 1847); MORRIS, *supra* note 5, at 117–19; FEHRENBACHER, SLAVEHOLDING REPUBLIC, *supra* note 16, at 222 (Southern outrage); Chauncey S. Boucher & Robert P. Brooks et. al., *Correspondence Addressed to John C. Cal-houn, 1837–1849,* AMERICAN HISTORICAL ASSOCIATION ANNUAL REPORT, 1929 385–87 (Washington, DC: American Historical Asso-ciation, 1930).

29. *See* FEHRENBACHER, SLAVEHOLDING REPUBLIC, *supra* note 16, at 222–24 (mood of resistance and weight of moral argu-ments); Jones v. Van Zandt, 13 Fed. Cases 1047, 1048–49 (1843); Norris v. Newton, 18 Fed. Cases 322, 326–27 (1850); COVER, *supra*

note 18, at 260–61 (quoting and discussing the cases).

30. *See* FEHRENBACHER, SLAVEHOLDING REPUBLIC, *supra* note 16, at 224 (Chase's efforts to reconcile moral and legal appeals); MARK S. WIENER, BLACK TRIALS: CITIZENSHIP FROM THE BEGINNINGS OF SLAVERY TO THE END OF CASTE 134–36, 138–39 (2004) (Van Zandt case background).

31. *See* FEHRENBACHER, SLAVEHOLDING REPUBLIC, *supra* note 16, at 224 (Chase's representation); WIENER, *supra* note 30, at 144, 150–51 (attorney general for fugitive slaves, *Somerset* case, and summary of Chase's brief), 151–52 (quoting Seward).

32. WIENER, *supra* note 30, at 151–52 (quoting Seward).

33. *See* FEHRENBACHER, SLAVEHOLDING REPUBLIC, *supra* note 16, at 224.

34. *Van Zandt, An Argument by S. P. Chase, in* 1 FUGITIVE SLAVES AND AMERICAN COURTS: THE PAMPHLET LITERATURE 341, 428–31 (ed. Paul Finkelman 1988) [hereinafter FINKELMAN, SLAVES AND COURTS] (Series II of the sixteen-volume SLAVERY, RACE, AND THE AMERICAN LEGAL SYSTEM 1700–1872 (ed. Paul Finkelman 1988)).

35. *Id.* at 431.

36. *Id.* at 436.

37. *Id.* at 432–33.

38. *Id.* at 432–33.

39. *Van Zandt,* 5 How. at 231.

40. *See id.* at 231 (making no real effort to explore the Fourth Amendment in detail or to reconcile it with the Court's reading of the Fugitive Slave Clause).

41. *See* FEHRENBACHER, SLAVEHOLDING REPUBLIC, *supra* note 16, at 225–30, 414 n. 68; Resolution of February 7, 1849, Virginia Session Laws, 73rd and 74th Years of the Commonwealth 250–54 (Richmond: William R. Ritchie, 1850).

42. *See* FEHRENBACHER, SLAVEHOLDING REPUBLIC, *supra* note 16 at 236–38, 244 (overview); MORRIS, *supra* note 5, at 195–98 (personal-liberty laws); Norman L. Rosenberg, *Personal Liberty Laws and Sectional Crisis, 1850–8161, in* 1 CIVIL WAR HISTORY 30–44 (1971); Vroman Mason, *The Fugitive Slave Law in Wisconsin, with Reference to Nullification Sentiment,* Proceedings of the State Historical Society of Wisconsin . . . 1895, at 122–44 (Madison: State Historical Society of Wisconsin, 1895); Amos A. Lawrence to William Appleton, March 6, 1854 (quoted in JANE H. PEASE & WILLIAM H. PEASE, THE FUGITIVE SLAVE LAW AND ANTHONY BURNS: A PROBLEM IN LAW ENFORCEMENT 28 (1975));

House Documents, 34th Cong., 1st Sess., No. 81 (Serial 867); U.S. CONST. amend. X. Fehrenbacher adds, "Ohio's name is sometimes added to this list, but the mild [personal-liberty] legislation enacted by the state in 1857 was substantially repealed within a year." *See* FEHRENBACHER, SLAVEHOLDING REPUBLIC, *supra* note 16, at 418 n. 27.

43. *See The Lemmon Slave Case in New York,* LYNCHBURG VIRGINIAN, November 24, 1852; New York Superior Court, The People of the State of New York ex rel. of Louis Napoleon v. Jonathan Lemmon, Respondent, in House Document No. 35 11–18 (1852); New York Court of Appeals, Report of the Lemmon Slave Case 1–13; *The Slave Case in New York,* LYNCHBURG VIRGINIAN, November 30, 1852; *The New York Slave Case,* MARTINSBURG GAZETTE, December 1, 1852; *The Slave Case in New York,* VIRGINIAN FREE PRESS, November 18, 1852; *Report of the Special Committee Relative to the Slave Case,* House Document No. 60 (1852–53); N.Y. Court of Appeals, *Report of the Lemmon Slave Case,* 13–14, 16–43, 121–30, 139–45; *The Slavery Question: Arguments of the Lemmon Case before the Court of Appeals,* NEW YORK DAILY TIMES, January 25, 1860; *The Lemmon Slave Case,* RICHMOND INQUIRER, April 17, 1860; STAUNTON SPECTATOR, May 1, 1860; WILLIAM A. LINK, ROOTS OF SECESSION: SLAVERY AND POLITICS IN ANTEBELLUM VIRGINIA 108–10 (2003) (summarizing the above documents and the *Lemmon* case).

44. *See* LINK, *supra* note 43, at 111–18; *Report of J. R. Rucker, Esq. Relative to the Case of James Parsons, Jr.,* [Virginia] House Document No. 68 (1855–56); [Virginia] *Governor's Message Relative to the Case of James Parsons, Jr.,* [Virginia] House Document No. 68, February 19, 1856.

45. *See* FEHRENBACHER, SLAVEHOLDING REPUBLIC, *supra* note 16, at 238–39 (summarizing these state-federal conflicts); Julian Yanuck, *The Garner Fugitive Slave Case,* MISS. VALLEY HISTORICAL REV. 40, 47–66 (1953–54); STANLEY W. CAMPBELL, THE SLAVE CATCHERS: ENFORCEMENT OF THE FUGITIVE SLAVE LAW, 1850–1860 161–67 (1968); Benjamin F. Prince, *The Rescue Case of 1857,* 16 OHIO ARCHAEOLOGICAL AND HISTORICAL SOCIETY PUBLICATIONS 292–309 (1907); Ex Parte Bushnell, Ex Parte Langston, 9 OHIO REPORTS 78 (1859); NAT BRANDT, THE TOWN THAT STARTED THE CIVIL WAR 115–237 (1990) (Oberlin-Wellington).

46. Ableman v. Booth, 21 How. (62 U.S.) 506 (1859); HAROLD M. HYMAN & WILLIAM

WIECEK, EQUAL JUSTICE UNDER LAW: CONSTI-
TUTIONAL DEVELOPMENT 1835–1875 198–99
(1982) (*Ableman* background and analysis);
In re Booth and Rycraft, 3 Wis. 144 (1855);
See FEHRENBACHER, SLAVEHOLDING REPUB-
LIC, *supra* note 16, at 237 (Wisconsin resolu-
tions and nullification); *see generally*
WILLIAM J. WATKINS JR., RECLAIMING THE
AMERICAN REVOLUTION: THE KENTUCKY AND
VIRGINIA RESOLUTIONS AND THEIR LEGACY
(2004) (Southern reliance on nullification
doctrine).

47. *Ableman,* 21 How. (62 U.S.) at 506,
516, 518, 526; HYMAN & WIECEK, *supra* note
46, at 199–201; Ableman v. Booth, 11 Wis.
517 (1860); Booth v. Ableman, 18 Wis. 519
(1864).

48. *See* FEHRENBACHER, SLAVEHOLDING
REPUBLIC, *supra* note 16, at 231–48 (degree,
meaning, and evolution of Northern resistance); Finkelman, *Chief Justice Hornblower,
supra* note 1, at 129–34 (1850s resurrection
of the Hornblower opinion).

49. Hornblower to Salmon P. Chase, April
9, 1851, SALMON P. CHASE PAPERS, Manuscript Division, Library of Congress; Finkelman, *Chief Justice Hornblower, supra* note 1,
at 130.

50. *See* Finkelman, *Chief Justice Hornblower,
supra* note 1, at 130–32.

51. *See* Finkelman, *Chief Justice Hornblower,
supra* note 1, at 129–34; TRENTON STATE
GAZETTE, June 15, 1854, reprinting the
Hornblower Decision from the NEW YORK
EVENING POST, August 1, 1851; *The Fugitive
Law Beginning to Tumble,* NEW YORK TRI-
BUNE, July 12, 1854; CONG. GLOBE, 36th
Cong., 1st Sess., app. 52, Debate of March 7,
1860 (Wade).

52. R. J. M. Blackett, *"Freemen to the Rescue!": Resistance to the Fugitive Slave Law of
1850, in* PASSAGES TO FREEDOM: THE UNDER-
GROUND RAILROAD IN HISTORY AND MEMORY
133, 136–38 (ed. David W. Blight 2004).

53. *Id.* at 138.

54. FRANK A. ROLLING, LIFE AND SERVICES
OF MARTIN DELANEY 76 (1883, *reprinted* New
York: Arno Press, 1969). For a different ver-
sion of what Delaney said, *see* J. Ernest
Wright, *The Negro in Pittsburgh* 65–66 (1937)
(unpublished manuscript prepared for the
Works Progress Administration).

55. *See* ANONYMOUS, THE REV. JERMAIN
LOGUEN AS A SLAVE AND A FREEMAN: A NAR-
RATIVE OF REAL LIFE 392–93 (1859, *reprinted*
New York: Arno Press, 1968). Blackett, *supra*
note 52, at 139–41 (temples of refuge, com-
munity resistance, and the Crafts); JAMES

OLIVER HORTON & LOIS HORTON, BLACK
BOSTONIANS: FAMILY LIFE AND COMMUNITY
STRUGGLE IN THE ANTEBELLUM NORTH 101
(1979) (quoting Lewis Hayden); Lois Horton,
*Kidnapping and Resistance: Antislavery Direct
Action in the 1850s, in* PASSAGES TO FREE-
DOM: THE UNDERGROUND RAILROAD IN HIS-
TORY AND MEMORY 149, 160–61 (ed. David
W. Blight 2004) (warrant, gunpowder, explo-
sion threats, and spiriting away the Crafts to
England).

56. *See* Horton, *supra* note 55, at 159–61.

57. *Id.* at 162–64; FEHRENBACHER, SLAVE-
HOLDING REPUBLIC, *supra* note 16, at
233–34.

58. *See* Horton, *supra* note 55, at 162;
FEHRENBACHER, SLAVEHOLDING REPUBLIC,
supra note 16 at 234. *See generally* THOMAS P.
SLAUGHTER, BLOODY DAWN: THE CHRISTIANA
RIOT AND RACIAL VIOLENCE IN THE ANTEBEL-
LUM NORTH (1994).

59. *See* Horton, *supra* note 55, at 168–69;
FEHRENBACHER, SLAVEHOLDING REPUBLIC,
supra note 16, at 234–35.

60. *See* Horton, *supra* note 55, at 165
(including "sympathy for the slave" quotation), 166 (including two quotations concerning Stowe).

61. *See* Horton, *supra* note 55, at 171, 173
(including all quotations); FEHRENBACHER,
SLAVEHOLDING REPUBLIC, *supra* note 16, at
237.

62. *See* Horton, *supra* note 55, at 166, 169;
Blackett, *supra* note 52, at 143.

63. *See generally* MICHAEL S. GREEN, FREE-
DOM, UNION, AND POWER: LINCOLN AND HIS
PARTY DURING THE CIVIL WAR 34 (2004)
(free-labor ideology permeating Northern
life); JAMES L. HUSTON, CALCULATING THE
VALUE OF THE UNION: SLAVERY, PROPERTY
RIGHTS, AND THE ECONOMIC ORIGINS OF THE
CIVIL WAR (2003) (Northern property con-
ceptions).

64. *See* GABOR S. BORITT, LINCOLN AND
THE ECONOMICS OF THE AMERICAN DREAM
160–61, 180–81 (1994).

65. 3 THE COLLECTED WORKS OF ABRAHAM
LINCOLN (ed. Roy P. Basler 1953) [hereinafter
LINCOLN, COLLECTED WORKS].

66. *See* BORITT, *supra* note 64, at 9, 177–
78, 181; HUSTON, *supra* note 63, at 9, 69, 82,
90; GREEN, *supra* note 63, at 41.

67. *See* BORITT, *supra* note 64, at 164; 3
LINCOLN, COLLECTED WORKS, *supra* note 65,
at 268; ERIC FONER, FREE SOIL, FREE LABOR,
FREE MEN: THE IDEOLOGY OF THE REPUBLI-
CAN PARTY BEFORE THE CIVIL WAR 54–65
(rev. ed. 1995) [hereinafter FONER, FREE

SOIL]; LIND, *supra* note 1, at 129–30, 133 (popular sovereignty); HUSTON, *supra* note 63, at 170–73 (Free-Soiler fears of the negative consequences of popular sovereignty for the overall Northern free white population).

68. *See* BORITT, *supra* note 64, at 160 (virtue), 178 (Lincoln, self-made man); 3 LINCOLN, COLLECTED WORKS, *supra* note 65, at 479 (success versus self-reliance); HUSTON, *supra* note 63, at 69 (hard work, diligence, intelligence); GREEN, *supra* note 63, at 31–32 (no permanent laboring class; free labor as a path to financial, political, and intellectual freedom); FONER, FREE SOIL, *supra* note 67, at 11, 23–24, 27 (race of life, Lincoln on not system's fault, Protestant roots, Greeley); NEW YORK TRIBUNE, May 15, 1854 (another Republican and individual character); V LINCOLN, COLLECTED WORKS, *supra* note 65, at 374 (dependent nature of lifetime wage laborer); HORACE GREELEY, HINTS TOWARD REFORMS 326 (1850); SPRINGFIELD REPUBLICAN, October 20, 1858; HEATHER COX RICHARDSON, THE DEATH OF RECONSTRUCTION 7–8 (2001) (good versus bad free laborers).

69. *See* FONER, FREE SOIL, *supra* note 67, at 11–18, 27–31; Andrew E. Taslitz, *Condemning the Racist Personality: Why the Critics of Hate Crimes Legislation Are Wrong*, 40 B.C. L. REV. 739, 765–77 (1999) (free labor and virtue).

70. 1 SPEECHES, CORRESPONDENCE, AND POLITICAL PAPERS OF CARL SCHURZ 131 (ed. Frederic Bancroft 1913); FONER, FREE SOIL, *supra* note 67, at 11 (Schurz's background).

71. CONG. GLOBE, 35th Cong., 2d Sess., Appendix 241; 1st Sess. 982; FONER, FREE SOIL, *supra* note 67, at 30.

72. *See* FONER, FREE SOIL, *supra* note 67, at 26, 47–52, 55–56, 68–70; CONG. GLOBE, 30th Cong., 2d Sess., Appendix 315 (Republican John G. Palfrey, a former Maine Democrat); GEORGE WESTON, THE POOR WHITES OF THE SOUTH 5 (1856); *Egyptian Darkness*, unidentified newsclipping, Scrapbook, Logan Family Papers, Library of Congress (proverbial darkness); H. B. Evans to John F. Potter, March 8, 1858, John F. Potter Papers, State Historical Society of Wisconsin ("full of gasconade").

73. WESTON, *supra* note 72, at 7.

74. *See* FONER, FREE SOIL, *supra* note 67, at 52–53.

75. *See id.* at 261 (state law); JONATHAN H. EARLE, JACKSONIAN ANTI-SLAVERY AND THE POLITICS OF FREE SOIL 13–16 (2004) (over-

view); LIND, *supra* note 1, at 18, 107, 110, 125–32, 150–51 (Free-Soiler racism).

76. *See* FONER, FREE SOIL, *supra* note 67, at 89–90, 95–99; BORITT, *supra* note 64, at 172–73; EARLE, *supra* note 75, at 16; 4 *id.* at 24–25; ROBERT L. HAYMAN JR., THE SMART CULTURE 65–66 (1998) (defining the distinctions among "civil," "political," and "social" rights and their continuing force through Reconstruction).

77. 4 LINCOLN, COLLECTED WORKS, *supra* note 65, at 24–25.

78. *See* FONER, FREE SOIL, *supra* note 67, at 291 (Republicans and black exclusion); BORITT, *supra* note 64, at 172–73. Most recently, Michael Lind and, before that, Lerone Bennett Jr., have argued that Lincoln spoke at best of blacks' *theoretical* right to a narrow sort of equality but one that he believed could only be achieved by Blacks in their own geographically separate country, for blacks could not succeed in competition with whites, and whites would not long in practice tolerate black presence no matter what the theoretical commitment to civil equality. *See* LIND, *supra* note 1, at 100–14, 224–26, 229–30; *see generally* LERONE BENNETT JR., FORCED INTO GLORY: ABRAHAM LINCOLN'S WHITE DREAM (2000) (taking an even harsher view of Lincoln as a thoroughgoing white supremacist forced into actions contrary to his most fundamental antiblack feelings and beliefs). Lincoln was unquestionably a racist by modern standards and had long supported colonization. But by the time of his death, he had ceased public support for colonization and had even begun to hint privately, however modestly, of support for suffrage for at least some blacks. It is very likely that the sacrifices made by black soldiers in the Civil War, combined with a variety of other circumstances, had moved Lincoln toward a public position that was more willing to accept a continuing role for free African Americans in the American polity, whatever may have been his private misgivings. *See* Taslitz, *Mutual Indifference, supra* note 1, at 1343–60 (tracing evolution of Lincoln's views on race). Furthermore, the biblical allusions that informed Lincoln's thinking on race suggested a role for free blacks, again however limited, and at least a rhetorical commitment to principles of civil equality that recognized blacks as part of America. His eventual and tepid progress toward accepting more equal political rights, and his apparent resistance to social equality, are not incompatible with the

description of him as eventually accepting blacks as part of the polity. Neither free white children nor free white women had the vote at the time, nor did they have social equality, in any modern sense of the term, with adult white men. *See, e.g.,* ALEXANDER KEYSSAR, THE RIGHT TO VOTE: THE CONTESTED HISTORY OF DEMOCRACY IN THE UNITED STATES 53–104 (2000). Yet free white women and children born in America were nevertheless considered "citizens." *See id.*; STEVEN MINTZ, HUCK'S RAFT: A HISTORY OF AMERICAN CHILDHOOD (2004). Furthermore, Southern ideology entirely excluded African Americans from *all* rights of the citizen, including civil ones. Finally, many writers underestimate the impact that many aspects of abolitionist thinking had on Lincoln. *See generally* CARL F. WIECK, LINCOLN'S QUEST FOR EQUALITY: THE ROAD TO GETTYSBURG (2002). Whatever may have been in Lincoln's heart, the sum of his publicly and privately stated thinking on race is fairly understood as coming to recognize blacks as part of the polity, citizens of a sort, albeit second-class ones. That is not a laudable position, and it pales in moral splendor next to the thinking of many white and black abolitionists who more thoroughly embraced vibrant notions of true racial equality. Nevertheless, Lincoln's position represented an important advance in a so thoroughly racist antebellum society. Moreover, I use Lincoln's words here as a symbol of a broader evolution in free white Northern understandings of race. Even readers who cringe at the attribution of anything positive to Lincoln's position on race, and who therefore reject my characterizations of it, will be harder pressed, I maintain, to argue that the Reconstruction amendments did not later recognize full African American membership in the polity, at least concerning civil and political rights, even if that recognition was a halting, painful, and confusing one for many whites of the time.

79. *See* JOSEPH R. FORNIERI, ABRAHAM LINCOLN'S POLITICAL FAITH 133–34 (2003) (Lincoln and Exodus); 2 LINCOLN, COLLECTED WORKS, *supra* note 65, at 405–06 (inalienable rights); ROGAN KERSH, DREAMS OF A MORE PERFECT UNION 172–78 (2001) (Declaration, nation, apples of gold); ABRAHAM LINCOLN: HIS SPEECHES AND WRITINGS 513 (1946, *reprinted* ed. Roy P. Basler 1989) (picture of silver) [hereinafter LINCOLN, SPEECHES AND WRITINGS]; Proverbs 25:11.

80. 2 LINCOLN, COLLECTED WORKS, *supra* note 65, at 318.

81. *See* FORNIERI, *supra* note 79, at 20; 1 LINCOLN, COLLECTED WORKS, *supra* note 65, at 411–12.

82. 10 LINCOLN, COLLECTED WORKS, *supra* note 65, at 44–45; 4 *id.* at 3.

83. *See* FORNIERI, *supra* note 79, at 144–53; HARRY V. JAFFA, CRISIS OF THE HOUSE DIVIDED: AN INTERPRETATION OF THE ISSUES IN THE LINCOLN-DOUGLAS DEBATES 375–76 (1982); 2 LINCOLN, COLLECTED WORKS, *supra* note 65, at 406 (stumbling block); KERSH, *supra* note 79, at 168–97 (Lincoln on race and Union). Lincoln's original colonization adviser, James Mitchell, authored an 1862 report that recommended colonization partly because of his belief that, as a practical matter, whites would not accept true equality with blacks and that race war might result. Yet even Mitchell conceded that if blacks remain in America, they must be treated as equal citizens, going so far as to say that they must have equal *political* rights, for anything else would be "the overthrow of republicanism and the establishment of imperialism." *See* LIND, *supra* note 1, at 196–98; James Mitchell, *Letter on the Relation of the White and African Races of the United States, Showing the Necessity of the Colonization of the Latter: Addressed to the President of the U.S.* 4–28 (Government Printing Office, 1862).

84. *See* KERSH, *supra* note 79, at 184–87; LINCOLN, SPEECHES AND WRITINGS, *supra* note 79, at 279, 401–03, 444, 493, 688; 2 LINCOLN, COLLECTED WORKS, *supra* note 65, at 320. In Lincoln's speech urging unity as "one people," he spoke primarily of European immigrants, but, argues historian Rogan Kersh, when placed in the context of his other statements, he "evidently referred to African-Americans as well." KERSH, *supra* note 79, at 185. This is not to deny that Lincoln was a complex man, sometimes saying inconsistent things, including, argues Michael Lind, favoring exclusion of blacks from the North even postemancipation and never really personally abandoning the hope of even forced colonization. *See* LIND, *supra* note 1, at 204–32, 337. Lind's views are subject to significant challenge. What matters most here, however, is that Lincoln's publicly stated principles by the time of his death dictate an embrace of equality, peoplehood, and free movement and that, in any event, my more optimistic reading of Lincoln's vision certainly better captures the

vision ultimately embraced by the Fourteenth Amendment, as Lind apparently concedes. *See id.* at 245 (Fourteenth Amendment gave blacks the legal right to live and work anywhere in the United States).

85. FORNIERI, *supra* note 79, at 154–55; 3 LINCOLN, COLLECTED WORKS, *supra* note 65, at 499–500; LINCOLN, SPEECHES AND WRITINGS, *supra* note 79, at 422; KERSH, *supra* note 79, at 185 & n. 104.

86. 2 LINCOLN, COLLECTED WORKS, *supra* note 65, at 323; *see* FORNIERI, *supra* note 79, at 156–57. Also relevant is Lincoln's recognition that, as historian Joseph Fornieri has put it, "justifications for the mastery of one group over another (whether based on the accidental qualities of heredity, race, ethnicity, or intelligence) could be used to deprive not only blacks of their rights but other groups of people as well." FORNIERI, *supra* note 79, at 157. In Lincoln's own words,

Understanding the spirit of our institutions to aim at the *elevation* of men, I am opposed to whatever tends to *degrade* them. I have some little notoriety for commiserating the oppressed condition of the negro; and I should be strangely inconsistent if I could favor any project for curtailing the existing rights of *white men,* even though born in different lands, and speaking different languages from myself.

3 LINCOLN, COLLECTED WORKS, *supra* note 65, at 380.

87. *See* FORNIERI, *supra* note 79, at 153–64; KERSH, *supra* note 79, at 168–97; Taslitz, *Mutual Indifference, supra* note 1, at 1343–60.

88. *See* FORNIERI, *supra* note 79, at 153–64; KERSH, *supra* note 79, at 168–97; Taslitz, *Mutual Indifference, supra* note 1, at 1343–60.

Notes to Chapter 10

1. On family breakups, *see generally* WILMA A. DUNAWAY, THE AFRICAN-AMERICAN FAMILY IN SLAVERY AND EMANCIPATION 18–83 (2003). On modern concepts of relational and family privacy, *see* Mary I. Coombs, *Shared Privacy and the Fourth Amendment, or the Rights of Relationships,* 75 CAL. L. REV. 1593 (1987); Doriane Lambelet Coleman, *Storming the Castle to Save the Children: The Ironic Costs of a Child Welfare Exception to the Fourth Amendment,* 47 WM. & MARY L. REV. 413 (2005).

2. On the importance of group privacy—a concept too often ignored or minimized in Fourth Amendment commentary and

jurisprudence, *see* Andrew E. Taslitz, *The Fourth Amendment in the Twenty-First Century: Technology, Privacy, and Human Emotions,* 65 L. & CONTEMP. PROBS. 125, 158–69 (2002) [hereinafter Taslitz, *Privacy and Human Emotions*]. On inadequate emphasis given to freedom of movement, *see* Tracey Maclin, *The Decline of the Right of Locomotion: The Fourth Amendment on the Streets,* 75 CORNELL L. REV. 1258 (1990).

3. *See* Taslitz, *Privacy and Human Emotions, supra* note 2, at 169–80 ("privacy in public" and information disclosure); *cf.* Andrew E. Taslitz, *A Feminist Fourth Amendment? Consent, Care, Privacy, and Social Meaning in Ferguson v. City of Charleston,* 9 DUKE J. GENDER L. & POL'Y 11 (2002) [hereinafter Taslitz, *Feminist Fourth Amendment*] (autonomy-related values under the Fourth Amendment).

4. *See* Taslitz, *Privacy and Human Emotions, supra* note 2, at 153–58; *see generally* JEFFREY ROSEN, THE UNWANTED GAZE: THE DESTRUCTION OF PRIVACY IN AMERICA 8–25, 137–38 (2000).

5. *See* Taslitz, *Privacy and Human Emotions, supra* note 2, at 153–58; ANITA L. ALLEN, UNEASY ACCESS: PRIVACY FOR WOMEN IN A FREE SOCIETY 52 (1988) ("The exercise of privacy-promoting liberties enhance persons and personal relationships in ways that cannot be ignored by those who feel ethically constrained to treat persons as more than things."); ROSEN, *supra* note 4, at 8 (discussing how control over which masks we reveal promotes intimate relationships); PATRICIA ANN BOLING, PRIVACY AND THE POLITICS OF THE INTIMATE LIFE 79 (1996) (privacy promotes diversity); JUDITH WAGNER DECEW, IN PURSUIT OF PRIVACY: LAW, ETHICS, AND THE RISE OF TECHNOLOGY 66 (1997) (privacy marks a zone of interests beyond the legitimate concerns of others to protect against pressures to conform or to reveal one's vulnerabilities); FERDINAND DAVID SCHOEMAN, PRIVACY AND SOCIAL FREEDOM (1992) (freedom from scrutiny and judgment permits us to talk, think, and act in ways that express our unique individual identity).

6. *See* Taslitz, *Privacy and Emotions, supra* note 2, at 158–59; JOHN STUART MILL, ON LIBERTY 11 (1859, *reprinted by* Haldeman-Julius 1925) (tyranny of prevailing opinion).

7. LAWRENCE LESSIG, CODE AND OTHER LAWS OF CYBERSPACE 152–53 (1999).

8. *See* Taslitz, *Privacy and Emotions, supra* note 2, at 155–58.

9. *See* DAVID DELANEY, RACE, PLACE, AND THE LAW 1836–1948 34 (1998).

10. SHARLA M. FETT, WORKING CURES: HEALING, HEALTH, AND POWER ON SOUTHERN SLAVE PLANTATIONS 87 (2002) (tight quarters); MARK M. SMITH, LISTENING TO NINETEENTH-CENTURY AMERICA 82–83 (2001) (earth floors, windows, doors).

11. RICHARD CORDLEY, PIONEER DAYS IN KANSAS 52 (1903).

12. *See* A Mississippi Planter, *Management of Negroes upon Southern Estates*, DEBOW'S REVIEW 621–27 (June 1851) (oak and planks); FETT, *supra* note 10, at 173 (hidey holes).

13. *See* PLANTATION AND FARM INSTRUCTION, REGULATION, RECORD, INVENTORY, AND ACCOUNT BOOK, FOR THE USE OF THE MANAGER ON THE ESTATE OF PHILIP ST. GEORGE COCKE, AND FOR THE BETTER ORDER AND MANAGEMENT OF PLANTATION AND FARM BUSINESS IN MANY PARTICULARS 5, 13, 15 (2d ed., Richmond, VA: J. Randolph, 1861), Philip S. George Cocke Papers, 1854–71, Virginia Historical Society, Richmond, Virginia; SMITH, *supra* note 10, at 173 (slave medical and management literature).

14. JOHN W. BLASSINGAME, THE SLAVE COMMUNITY: PLANTATION LIFE IN THE ANTEBELLUM SOUTH 154, 164 (rev. and enlarged ed. 1979) (cabins no sanctuary from rape; trinkets; and preference for marrying abroad); 2 THE AMERICAN SLAVE: A COMPOSITE AUTOBIOGRAPHY: SOUTH CAROLINA NARRATIVES, pt. 2, 57, 65–66 (ed. George P. Rawick 1972) (quotations concerning Wash Evans) [hereinafter RAWICK, AMERICAN SLAVE]; EMILY WEST, CHAINS OF LOVE, SLAVE COUPLES IN ANTEBELLUM SOUTH CAROLINA 129 (2004) (summarizing Wash Evans account).

15. *See* BLASSINGAME, *supra* note 14, at 151 (slaves' independent family values); STEVEN MINTZ, HUCK'S RAFT: A HISTORY OF AMERICAN CHILDHOOD 98–100 (2004) (naming practices); JACQUELINE JONES, LABOR OF LOVE, LABOR OF SORROW: BLACK WOMEN, WORK, AND THE FAMILY FROM SLAVERY TO THE PRESENT 33 (1985) (sexual innocence); STEPHANIE M. H. CAMP, CLOSER TO FREEDOM: ENSLAVED WOMEN AND EVERYDAY RESISTANCE IN THE PLANTATION SOUTH 96–98 (2004) (California's story).

16. Young to McDowell, 24 July 1847, McDowell Papers, Special Collections Library, Perkins Library, Duke University, Durham, NC.

17. CAMP, *supra* note 15, at 97–99, 113,

115–16; Mattie J. Jackson, *The Story of Mattie Jackson, in* SIX WOMEN'S SLAVE NARRATIVES 14 (ed. Henry Louis Gates Jr. 1988).

18. CAMP, *supra* note 15, at 116.

19. Deborah Gray White, *Simple Truths: Antebellum Slavery in Black and White, in* PASSAGES TO FREEDOM: THE UNDERGROUND RAILROAD IN HISTORY AND MEMORY 33, 55 (ed. David W. Blight 2004) (fathers teaching sons); BLASSINGAME, *supra* note 14, at 183–84 (games with white children); MINTZ, *supra* note 15, at 107–10 (competitive games, informal education, learning to read).

20. BLASSINGAME, *supra* note 14, at 105–06, 153, 178–79 (separate secret world, games, and chores); CAMP, *supra* note 15, at 94 (understanding as a common people); JONES, *supra* note 15, at 27 (fieldwork versus the big house).

21. White, *supra* note 19, at 55; LAWRENCE W. LEVINE, BLACK CULTURE AND BLACK CONSCIOUSNESS: AFRO-AMERICAN FOLK THOUGHT FROM SLAVERY TO FREEDOM 99 (1977).

22. White, *supra* note 19, at 56.

23. MINTZ, *supra* note 15, at 105–08 (children taught silence, Elijah Morris, Richard Carruthers); SYLVIANE A. DIOUF, GROWING UP IN SLAVERY 65 (2001) (Elijah Morris); BLASSINGAME, *supra* note 14, at 137–39 (warning songs); JONES, *supra* note 15, at 31 (clandestine feeding); White, *supra* note 19, at 61–62 (feigning illness).

24. DEBORAH GRAY WHITE, AR'N'T I A WOMAN? FEMALE SLAVES IN THE PLANTATION SOUTH 80 (rev. ed. 1999) (quotation); White, *supra* note 19, at 61 (background).

25. DELANEY, *supra* note 9, at 37 (grapevine defined); CAMP, *supra* note 15, at 108–09 ("grapevine telegraph" described).

26. White, *supra* note 19, at 46–48 (religion as social control); IRA BERLIN, GENERATIONS OF CAPTIVITY: A HISTORY OF AFRICAN-AMERICAN SLAVES, 208–09 (2003) (white supervision).

27. *See* BERLIN, *supra* note 26, at 206, 209.

28. *See* White, *supra* note 19, at 46–48.

29. LEVINE, *supra* note 21, at 41; *see also* White, *supra* note 19, at 47.

30. LEVINE, *supra* note 21, at 39, 51 (songs quoted); White, *supra* note 19, at 48 (Douglass and the North as deliverance).

31. *See* BLASSINGAME, *supra* note 14, at 17–18, 105–06 (leisure activities generally); CAMP, *supra* note 15, at 60–92 (outlaw parties).

32. CAMP, *supra* note 15, at 60–61, 64–65,

69, 71, 75–77, 79 (overview); 14(1) GEORGE
P. RAWICK, FROM SUNDOWN TO SUNUP: THE
MAKING OF THE BLACK COMMUNITY 157
(1972) (on organized, master-supervised frol-
ics); EUGENE D. GENOVESE, ROLL, JORDAN,
ROLL: THE WORLD THE SLAVES MADE 3–7,
570, 577–80, 584 (1974) (similar); ROGER D.
ABRAHAMS, SINGING THE MASTER: THE EMER-
GENCE OF AFRICAN-AMERICAN CULTURE IN
THE PLANTATION SOUTH 83–106 (1992)
(arguing that bondspeople sometimes
remade approved frolics into rituals infused
with the slaves' own meanings); AUSTIN
STEWARD, TWENTY-TWO YEARS A SLAVE AND
FORTY YEARS A FREEMAN 20 (1847, *reprinted*
Reading, MA: Addison-Wesley, 1969) (slaves
not viewing party preparation as theft).

33. White, *supra* note 19, at 49–50 (magic
and conjurers overview); LEVINE, *supra* note
21, at 74 (Reverend Jones and the former
slave); BLASSINGAME, *supra* note 14, at 113
(power over whites; one-eyed Dinkie);
WILLIAM WELLS BROWN, MY SOUTHERN
HOME 71 (1880) (Dinkie's appearance).

34. *See* White, *supra* note 19, at 50
(overview and quotation); *see generally* FETT,
supra note 10 (background on healing,
health, and power); WHITE, *supra* note 24, at
124–25 (summarizing healing practices and
their significance).

35. *See* WEST, *supra* note 14, at 68–74
(black husbands beating wives; intracommunal black sexual abuse); CAMP, *supra* note
15, at 7 (violence at outlaw parties).

36. *See, e.g.,* Orin Kerr, *Technology, Privacy,
and the Courts: A Reply to Colb and Swire,* 102
MICH. L. REV. 933, 933–35 (2004) (courts
still rely heavily on property concepts in
determining what seem to be Fourth
Amendment privacy issues); Daniel Yeager,
*Search, Seizure, and the Positive Law: Expecta-
tions of Privacy outside the Fourth Amendment,*
84 J. CRIM. L. & CRIMINOLOGY 249 (1993)
(extended examination of case law supporting a similar proposition). Support concerning the way analogous ideas played out in
the antebellum era can be found in the
remainder of this chapter.

37. *See* JAMES BREWER STEWART, HOLY
WARRIORS: THE ABOLITIONISTS AND AMERI-
CAN SLAVERY 35–74 (1996) (tracing dramatic
rise and increasing coherence of the aboli-
tionist movement in the 1830s); *id.* at 43–44
(quoting Birney and Phillips); CHARLES
JOHNSON & PATRICIA SMITH, AFRICANS IN
AMERICA: AMERICA'S JOURNEY THROUGH
SLAVERY 343–47 (1998) (noting Garrison's
influence, but also noting that his embrace

of feminism and nonresistance eventually
led to a split in the American Antislavery
Society, which he had co-founded in 1833).
I am not suggesting that there were no abolitionist influences in American culture
before the 1830s; obviously, there were. *See*
STEWART, *supra,* at 11–35 (describing the
early abolitionist movement). But it was in
the 1830s that a coherent movement for
nationwide immediatism in the antebellum
era began. I focus on Northern abolitionists
because I am here particularly concerned
with Northern perceptions of events.
Though persecuted and few and far between
after the early 1830s, however, it should not
be forgotten that there were still active,
indigenous Southern abolitionists. *See* STAN-
LEY HARROLD, THE ABOLITIONISTS AND THE
SOUTH, 1831–1861 127–48 (1995).

38. *See* STEWART, *supra* note 37, at 32, 41,
44–48, 52 (source of abolitionist views,
Christian ideals, evangelistic attitudes, primacy of the cause); HENRY MAYER, ALL ON
FIRE: WILLIAM LLOYD GARRISON AND THE
ABOLITION OF SLAVERY 53, 72–73, 115, 263–
64, 445, 475 (1998) (Garrison on immediatism and on the necessity of moral change
to bring political change, plus describing
one abolitionist's preachings).

39. *See, e.g.,* JOHNSON & SMITH, *supra* note
37, at 343–46 (Garrison's background);
MAYER, *supra* note 38, at xiii–xxi, 65–66
(similar, plus discussing "imaginative substitution").

40. NAT. PHIL. 22, 29 July 1829, American
Antiquarian Society, Worcester, MA; *see also*
MAYER, *supra* note 38, at 66 (quoting Garrison). In his Park Street address, from which
the quotation is taken, Garrison had reluc-
tantly embraced gradualism, a position he
rejected as unduly cautious just a short time
later. *See id.* at 68.

41. *See, e.g.,* STEWART, *supra* note 37, at 60
(giving a former slaveowner's account of
Southern atrocities); THE CLASSIC SLAVE
NARRATIVES (ed. Henry Louis Gates Jr. 1987).

42. SAIDIYA A. HARTMAN, SCENES OF SUB-
JECTION: TERROR, SLAVERY, AND SELF-MAK-
ING IN NINETEENTH-CENTURY AMERICA 17–
18 (1997).

43. JOHN RANKIN, LETTERS ON AMERICAN
SLAVERY 56 (1837, *reprinted by* Negro Universities Press 1970).

44. *See* STEWART, *supra* note 37, at 60, 62,
137 (Bibb, Craft, May, Hannibal and the
Pharaohs, Douglass); Henry Louis Gates Jr.,
Introduction, in THE CLASSIC SLAVE NARRA-
TIVES ix—xvii (ed. Henry Louis Gates Jr.

1987) (summarizing the importance of the publishing of former slaves' experiences to the antislavery cause). For a superb analysis of the depth and breadth of Douglass's thought and of his power to persuade through stirring language, see WALDO E. MARTIN JR., THE MIND OF FREDERICK DOUGLASS (1984).

45. See HARTMAN, supra note 42, at 17–23 (barriers to white empathy); MAYER, supra note 38, at 419–20 (sentiment, Stowe's literary phenomenon, sales statistics for Uncle Tom's Cabin); STEWART, supra note 37, at 41–42, 160–62, 164–66 (Stowe's sole contact with slavery had been a few hours spent on a Kentucky plantation; also discussing time of abolitionism's emergence, Northern interest in the literary and dramatic versions of the novel, readership, dances, political significance of the characters). See generally HARRIETT BEECHER STOWE, UNCLE TOM'S CABIN (1852, reprinted by Macmillan 1994).

46. See MAYER, supra note 38, at 168–70, 263, 313, 326–28, 452 (including quoting Garrison); William Lloyd Garrison, Address to the Friends of Freedom and Emancipation in the United States, THE LIBERATOR, May 31, 1844, at 86 ("The American Union was effected through a guilty compromise between the free and slaveholding States, in other words, by immolating the colored population on the altar of slavery.").

47. See MAYER, supra note 38, at 98–99, 102–22, 274–77, 287, 297, 326, 362, 368–69, 381–83, 385, 392, 428–30, 451, 472–73, 502–04 (overview); STEWART, supra note 37, at 98–99, 150–59, 165–74 (discussing increasing abolitionist militancy during the 1850s and contrasting Garrisonian abolitionists' support for revolution with the Liberty Party's support for abolition by compromise and reform within the existing constitutional framework); James Brewer Stewart, Peaceful Hopes and Violent Experiences: The Evolution of Reforming and Radical Abolitionism, 1831–37, 17 CIVIL WAR HISTORY 293, 298, 303–04 (1971) (explaining the shift in the tactics of some abolitionists from moral suasion to revolutionary Garrisonianism and reformist majoritarianism and stating that abolitionists Birney, Smith, Stanton, Wright, and Whittier later insisted that political action by abolitionists was necessary); MARK E. BRANDON, FREE IN THE WORLD: AMERICAN SLAVERY AND CONSTITUTIONAL FAILURE 57–62, 74–77, 101–03 (1998) (summarizing theories of antislavery constitutionalists, including Alvan Stewart, Theodore Dwight

Weld, Lysander Spooner, Frederick Douglass, and Wendell Phillips).

48. STEWART, supra note 37, at 65–66, 70–71 (in part quoting Lewis Tappan on the "great postal campaign"); see generally Stewart, supra note 47, at 298.

49. See STEWART, supra note 37, at 70–72 (detailing the violent reaction to the great postal campaign in Charleston, New York City, Cincinnati, Boston, and Alton, Illinois, and discussing President Jackson's urging the ban of antislavery literature in his 1835 annual message to Congress, the Southern resolutions, and the limited Northern legislative response, with the exception of Connecticut); MAYER, supra note 38, at 70–71, 83–85, 196–97 (similar, plus quoting Senator John Tyler and noting that, though Jackson agreed that the federal government lacked the authority to censor the mail, he also agreed with his postmaster general's suggestion that mail did not have to be delivered in the face of community opposition). See generally LEONARD L. RICHARDS, GENTLEMEN OF PROPERTY AND STANDING: ANTI-ABOLITION MOBS IN JACKSONIAN AMERICA 55–57 (1970); WILLIAM LEE MILLER, ARGUING ABOUT SLAVERY: THE GREAT BATTLE IN THE UNITED STATES CONGRESS (1995) (discussing the history and significance of the gag rule).

50. See MAYER, supra note 38, at 189, 197 (antiabolitionist meetings and mob violence detailed); STEWART, supra note 37, at 72 (similar, plus discussion of a Utica mob breaking up an abolitionist convention and "rough[ing] up" several delegates; also, composition of the Cincinnati mobs that repeatedly attacked James Birney's press and composition of the mob as the "pillars of the community").

51. STEWART, supra note 37, at 64–66, 71.

52. See JOHNSON & SMITH, supra note 37, at 346 (commercial ties); HARRY V. JAFFA, CRISIS OF THE HOUSE DIVIDED: AN INTERPRETATION OF THE ISSUES IN THE LINCOLN-DOUGLAS DEBATES 196–97 (1959) (Lovejoy's killing and economic competition with St. Louis); MAYER, supra note 38, at 66–67 (gentlemen of property and standing; abolitionist supporters, including skilled laborers, men, women, and children, who ignored local statuses and leadership; New York mob fearing change in the social order; colonizationist leadership of New York mobs and dismay at Garrison's receiving financial support from English abolitionists and the wealthy Arthur Tappan, plus abolitionist values

undercutting patriarchy and traditional deference).

53. MAYER, *supra* note 38, at 344–45.

54. *See id.* at 208, 326, 345, 397–402, 407, 490, 506 (Garrison and expressive violence, the Compromise of 1850, and quotations from Garrison); Garrison, *supra* note 46 (expressions of concern about renewed mob violence and the Compromise of 1850); STEWART, *supra* note 37, at 73–74 (efforts to silence abolitionists and mob violence publicized abolitionist principles and created a broad constituency of antislavery sympathizers concerned with preserving civil liberties). For a more detailed explanation of the evidence that Garrison understood that *expressive* violence endangered free inquiry most of all, *see* Andrew E. Taslitz, *Hate Crimes, Free Speech, and the Contract of Mutual Indifference*, 80 B.U. L. REV. 1283, 1372 & n. 614 (2000) [hereinafter Taslitz, *Mutual Indifference*].

55. MAYER, *supra* note 38, at 397 (in part quoting Garrison).

56. *See id.* at 397–99 (including quoting Garrison); STEWART, *supra* note 37, at 152, 155–58, 160–62, 169 (Whigs and Democrats opposing the Slave Power after the Compromise of 1850; Northern protests recalled over the seizure of fugitive slaves; *Uncle Tom's Cabin* phenomenon in the North; Northern opposition to *Dred Scott* recalled); AKHIL REED AMAR, THE BILL OF RIGHTS: CREATION AND RECONSTRUCTION 231–46 (1998) (explaining the effect of suppression of abolitionist speech on the North's view of the Civil War and Reconstruction); William Lloyd Garrison, *Speech of the Hon. Daniel Webster on the Slavery Question*, THE LIBERATOR, March 15, 1850, at 42 (reprinting the first half of Webster's "indescribably base and wicked speech").

57. STEWART, *supra* note 37, at 76–77 (describing fear of many Northerners that slaveholders had contempt for the freedoms of all other Americans; "relentless dominance" quotation; and describing the Slave Power conspiracy); ERIC FONER, FREE SOIL, FREE LABOR, FREE MEN: THE IDEOLOGY OF THE REPUBLICAN PARTY BEFORE THE CIVIL WAR ix–xxxviii, 76–78, 79–80 (summarizing free-labor ideology and explaining that antiabolitionist violence sparked the spread of strong antislavery attitudes throughout the North); Andrew E. Taslitz, *Condemning the Racist Personality: Why the Critics of Hate Crimes Legislation Are Wrong*, 40 B.C. L. REV. 739, 739, 773–78 (1999) [hereinafter Taslitz,

Racist Personality] (explaining Northern disapproval of Southern "virtue"); Andrew E. Taslitz, *Slaves No More! The Implications of the Informed Citizen Ideal for Discovery before Fourth Amendment Suppression Hearings*, 15 GA. ST. L. REV. 709, 743–45 (1999) [hereinafter Taslitz, *Slave No More!*] (explaining the inconsistency between the Slave Power and civil liberties); Garrett Epps, *The Antebellum Background of the Fourteenth Amendment*, 67 L. & CONTEMP. PROBS. (2004) (Slave Power must be seen as a defining antebellum idea controlling Fourteenth Amendment interpretation).

58. *See* FONER, *supra* note 57, at 11–18, 39, 43 (origin and spread of free-labor ideology and Northern belief in free-labor society's superiority to Southern planter slavocracy); STEWART, *supra* note 37, at 78–79 (origins of Northern free-labor ideology).

59. *See* STEWART, *supra* note 37, at 80.

60. *See* FONER, *supra* note 57, at 73, 75–76.

61. *See id.* at 76, 78 (overview); U.S. CONST. amend. V; STEWART, *supra* note 37, at 97 (describing the Liberty Party as exemplifying "political antipolitics").

62. FONER, *supra* note 57, at 80–84.

63. *See id.* at 87–89 (overview); *cf.* Taslitz, *Slaves No More! supra* note 57, at 744 (Slave Power challenged the Lockean notion of toleration at the heart of the idea of equal inalienable rights); *see also* LEONARD L. RICHARDS, THE SLAVE POWER: THE FREE NORTH AND SOUTHERN DOMINATION (2000) (arguing that the Slave Power was real and not simply a matter of Republican ideology); *see* N.Y. TIMES, June 10, 1856, at 4; CONG. GLOBE, 31st Cong., 1st Sess., App. 473, 479 (1850) (printing the text of a speech by Representative Chase of Ohio entitled "Union and Freedom, Without Compromise").

64. *See* FONER, *supra* note 57, at 90–91, 93, 96–97 (overview and citing from B. F. MORRIS, THE LIFE OF THOMAS MORRIS 32–34, 119–20, 181, 217 (1856) (goliath)); RUSSELL B. NYE, FETTERED FREEDOM 225 (1949) (Slave Power waging war quotation) (citing PLUNKETT, LIBERTY PARTY 46); JULIAN P. BRETZ, THE ECONOMIC BACKGROUND OF THE LIBERTY PARTY, Alt R, xxxiv, 251 n. (January 1929)).

65. FONER, *supra* note 57, at 101; CONG. GLOBE, 36th Cong., 2d Sess. 551 (1864).

66. *See* Taslitz, *Slaves No More! supra* note 57, at 744–76 (the Slave Power, caste-based philosophy, and suppression of white liberties linked and feared by many in the North); STEWART, *supra* note 37, at 197–98 (peace depended on spreading Northern

civilization South), 185 ("noble prophets"), 197, 201 (quoting Wendell Phillips); FONER, *supra* note 57, at 290 (mainstream Republicans claimed that the Declaration of Independence's proclamation of human equality included the black man); EARL J. HESS, LIBERTY, VIRTUE, AND PROGRESS: NORTHERNERS AND THEIR WAR FOR THE UNION 103–07 (2d ed. 1997) (arguing that the end of the Civil War reinforced Northern liberty values and that veterans believed that material prosperity and political rejuvenation would accompany the South's adoption of Northern values).

67. *See generally* Taslitz, *Mutual Indifference, supra* note 54, at 1367–72.

68. *See generally* Taslitz, *Slaves No More! supra* note 57, at 738–46 (summarizing relevant history and its implications); Michael Kent Curtis, *The 1859 Crisis over Hinton Helper's Book, The Impending Crisis: Free Speech, Slavery, and Some Light on the Meaning of the First Section of the Fourteenth Amendment,* 68 CHI.-KENT L. REV. 1113, 1117, 1123–36 (1993) (discussing Southern suppression of free speech and noting that "Republicans invoked rights referred to in the . . . Fourth Amendment (involving unreasonable searches and seizures aimed at antislavery activists and publications) . . . to criticize state political repression that the 'slave power' aimed at opponents of slavery"); AMAR, *supra* note 56, at 234–35, 267 (publication bans, mail censorship, dragnet sweeps, banishment); MARY FRANCES BERRY, BLACK RESISTANCE, WHITE LAW: A HISTORY OF CONSTITUTIONAL RACISM IN AMERICA 53–57 (1994) (summarizing mob assaults on abolitionists during the antebellum period); JOHNSON & SMITH, *supra* note 37, at 346–47 (1998) (recounting mob assault and arson against National Anti-Slavery Convention of American Women in Philadelphia in 1838); *see generally* MICHAEL KENT CURTIS, FREE SPEECH, "THE PEOPLE'S DARLING PRIVILEGE": STRUGGLES FOR FREEDOM OF EXPRESSION IN AMERICAN HISTORY 117–300 (2000) (detailed historical examination of Southern efforts to suppress free speech).

69. *See* MARK TWAIN, ADVENTURES OF HUCKLEBERRY FINN 223–24 (1885, *reprinted by* Barnes & Noble Books 2003); JOHN T. NOONAN, PERSONS AND MASKS OF THE LAW: CARDOZO, HOLMES, JEFFERSON, AND WYTHE AS MAKERS OF THE MASKS 11–12 (1976, paperback 2002).

70. *See* NOONAN, *supra* note 69, at 4, 6, 14–19 (overview and quotations); Andrew E.

Taslitz, *Individualizing Justice through Psychological Character Evidence,* 52 MD. L. REV. 1, 14–21, 88–90, 110–13 (1993) (psychological categorization processes); Cass Sunstein, *On the Expressive Function of Law,* 144 U. PA. L. REV. 202 (1996).

71. *See* NOONAN, *supra* note 69, at 19–20.

72. *See id.* at 41–43 (including quotations); *see generally* D. A. LLOYD THOMAS, LOCKE ON GOVERNMENT 11–53, 89–123 (1995) (Locke's theories on the social contract and the social function of property); JENNIFER NEDELSKY, PRIVATE PROPERTY AND THE LIMITS OF AMERICAN CONSTITUTIONALISM: THE MADISONIAN FRAMEWORK AND ITS LEGACY (1990) (extended critique of Framers' ideology of property); STEVEN DEYLE, CARRY ME BACK: THE DOMESTIC SLAVE TRADE IN AMERICAN LIFE (2005) (vivid illustration of slaves' status as property).

73. *See* MARK V. TUSHNET, THE AMERICAN LAW OF SLAVERY, 1810–1860 44–121 (1981); MARK V. TUSHNET, SLAVE LAW IN THE AMERICAN SOUTH: STATE V. MANN IN HISTORY AND LITERATURE 48–50 (2003) ("sentiment" versus "economic maximization"); ARIELA J. GROSS, DOUBLE CHARACTER: SLAVERY AND MASTERY IN THE ANTEBELLUM SOUTHERN COURTROOM 3 (2000) (examining "the paradoxes that arose from slaves' double identity as human subjects and the objects of property relations *at one and the same time"*) (emphasis in original).

74. BLASSINGAME, *supra* note 14, at 224–25, 246–48 (overview and most of the quotations); 8 SOUTHERN AGRICULTURIST 368 (July 1834) (a Virginia planter's advice to "study their dispositions well"); WILLIAM L. VAN DEBURG, HOODLUMS: BLACK VILLAINS AND SOCIAL BANDITS IN AMERICAN LIFE 42–67 (2004) (white images of slaves); CLAYTON ROBERTS, THE LOGIC OF HISTORICAL EXPLANATION 27–30, 41–43, 50–51, 90, 98–99, 115–16, 123–24, 251–60 (1996) (the problem of historical causation); C. BEHAN MCCULLAGH, JUSTIFYING HISTORICAL DESCRIPTIONS 171–228 (1984) (similar).

75. *See* GREGORY S. ALEXANDER, COMMODITY AND PROPRIETY: COMPETING VISIONS OF PROPERTY IN AMERICAN LEGAL THOUGHT, 1776–1970 211, 214 (1997).

76. *See id.* at 216–20; James Henry Hammond, *Letter to an English Abolitionist, in* DREW GILPIN FAUST, IDEOLOGY OF SLAVERY: PROSLAVERY THOUGHT IN THE ANTEBELLUM SOUTH 177 (1981) (slavery is "truly the 'cornerstone' and foundation of every well-designed and durable 'republican edifice' ");

Frank I. Michelman, *Possession vs. Distribution in the Constitutional Idea of Property*, 72 IOWA L. REV. 1319, 1330 (1986) (describing undemocratically made decisions, like those about citizenship, as part of the "exclusionary response" to property's political significance); THOMAS R. R. COBB, AN INQUIRY INTO THE LAW OF NEGRO SLAVERY IN THE UNITED STATES, TO WHICH IS PREFIXED AN HISTORICAL SKETCH OF SLAVERY ccxiii (1858, *reprinted* 1968) (slaveholder leisure and informed citizenship); *see generally* Taslitz, *Racist Personality, supra* note 57, at 765–73.

77. COBB, *supra* note 76, at ccxiii (emphasis in original); *see also* ALEXANDER, *supra* note 75, at 219 ("The nonslaveholding white owner's perception of himself as the equal of his much wealthier neighbors facilitated the acceptance of the ideology of proslavery republicanism among lower classes of whites as well as the elite planter class.").

78. COBB, *supra* note 76, at ccxiii ("elevated class"); ALEXANDER, *supra* note 75, at 219 ("subsistence farmer") (emphasis in original).

79. *See* ALEXANDER, *supra* note 75, at 219–20, 222 (informal hierarchies, analysis of Cobb); FAUST, *supra* note 76, at 277, 282 (concerning Fitzhugh).

80. COBB, *supra* note 76, at cli–clii, clvi–clvii.

81. *Id.* at ccxvii–ccxviii; ALEXANDER, *supra* note 75, at 223–24.

82. *See* ALEXANDER, *supra* note 75, at 230; COBB, *supra* note 76, at ccxiv.

83. *See* ALEXANDER, *supra* note 75, at 230–31 (summarizing second variant); WILLIAM HENRY TRESCOT, THE POSITION AND COURSE OF THE SOUTH 10–11 (Charleston, S.C.: Walker and James, 1850).

84. *See* ALEXANDER, *supra* note 75, at 235–40 (overview); COBB, *supra* note 76, at ccxxi.

85. JAMES L. HUSTON, CALCULATING THE VALUE OF THE UNION: SLAVERY, PROPERTY RIGHTS, AND THE ECONOMIC ORIGINS OF THE CIVIL WAR 27–36 (2003) [hereinafter HUSTON, VALUE OF THE UNION].

86. HUSTON, VALUE OF THE UNION, *supra* note 85, at 43–45 (overview); Joshua Speed to Salmon P. Chase, September 2, 1861, in 3 THE SALMON P. CHASE PAPERS: CORRESPONDENCE 931 (ed. John Niven, James P. McClure, and Leigh Johnson 1996); (MACON) GEORGIA JOURNAL AND MESSENGER, October 24, 1849; Armistead Burr to Thomas Byrd et al., *in* COLUMBUS (GEORGIA) ENQUIRER, June 3, 1851.

87. *See* HUSTON, VALUE OF THE UNION, *supra* note 85, at 47–52 (overview); *Jackson, Mississippi, Meeting*, VICKSBURG (MISSISSIPPI) WHIG, October 9, 1949; VICTOR B. HOWARD, THE EVANGELICAL WAR AGAINST SLAVERY AND CASTE: THE LIFE AND TIMES OF JOHN G. FEE 46 (1996) (quoting the Kentucky law); GEORGE S. SAWYER, SOUTHERN INSTITUTES; OR, AN INQUIRY INTO THE ORIGINS AND EARLY PREVALENCE OF SLAVERY AND THE SLAVE TRADE 14 (1858).

88. *See* HUSTON, VALUE OF THE UNION, *supra* note 85, at 47–49.

89. *See id.* at 52–57. For a detailed and partially cautious approval of some of Calhoun's political ideas, *see* H. LEE CHEEK JR., CALHOUN AND POPULAR RULE: THE POLITICAL THEORY OF THE DISQUISITION AND DISCOURSE (2001).

90. *See id.* at 55–56, 62 (overview); Thomas Roderick Dew, *Abolition of Negro Slavery, in* FAUST, *supra* note 76, at 27 (quotation), 23–77 (more relevant material, especially the Virginia General Assembly's 1831–32 debate over emancipation); *see also* SECESSION DEBATED: GEORGIA'S SHOWDOWN IN 1860 149–50 (ed. William W. Freehling and Craig M. Simpson 1992) (remarks of Governor Joseph E. Brown of Georgia). The 1828 protective tariff on imported goods, the highest by that point in history, was called the "tariff of abomination" by Southerners, who wanted cheaper goods to purchase and thought that the tax operated primarily to enrich Northern coffers at Southern expense. *See* CHARLES ADAMS, THOSE DIRTY ROTTEN TAXES: THE TAX REVOLTS THAT BUILT AMERICA 81–82 (1998). The 1832 tariff, though it somewhat reduced taxes, "elicited a hostile reaction that produced the first serious constitutional crisis since Hamilton's taxes." *Id.* at 82. South Carolina nullified both taxes, though a compromise with the South was reached when President Jackson threatened military action. *See id.* at 82. On the theory of nullification, *see* WILLIAM J. WATKINS JR., RECLAIMING THE AMERICAN REVOLUTION: THE KENTUCKY AND VIRGINIA RESOLUTIONS AND THEIR LEGACY (2004).

91. *See* JON-CHRISTIAN SUGGS, WHISPERED CONSOLATIONS: LAW AND NARRATIVE IN AFRICAN-AMERICAN LIFE 27–29 (2000); HARRIET BRENT JACOBS (LINDA BRENT); INCIDENTS IN THE LIFE OF A SLAVE GIRL 6, 8, 78, 16, 56 (ed. L. Maria Child 1861, *reprinted* New York: Harcourt Brace Jovanovich, 1973).

92. JACOBS, *supra* note 91, at 206; *see also* SUGGS, *supra* note 91, at 29–30.

93. FREDERICK DOUGLASS, NARRATIVE OF THE LIFE OF FREDERICK DOUGLASS, AN AMERICAN SLAVE 17, 19, 49 (1845, *reprint* ed. Robert O'Meally 2003) (quotations); *id.* at 17, 19, 23, 24, 26, 28, 30, 34–35, 50–61, 67, 72, 75, 82, 86–87, 90 (key details of his life as human property).

94. *Id.* at 49.

95. *See* JACOBS, *supra* note 91, at 4 ("The reader probably knows that no promise or writing given to a slave is legally binding; for, according to Southern law, a slave, *being* property, can *hold* no property.") (emphasis in original); DYLAN C. PENNIGROTH, THE CLAIMS OF KINFOLK: AFRICAN-AMERICAN PROPERTY AND COMMUNITY IN THE NINETEENTH-CENTURY SOUTH 45–46, 208 n. 3 (2003) (legal versus informal ownership and Louisiana Sunday earnings); THOMAS D. MORRIS, SOUTHERN SLAVERY AND THE LAW, 1619–1850 350 (1996) (sanctification of property by slaves).

96. *See* PENNIGROTH, *supra* note 95, at 46–47; FREDERICK LAW OLMSTED, THE COTTON KINGDOM: A TRAVELLER'S OBSERVATIONS ON COTTON AND SLAVERY IN THE AMERICAN SLAVE STATES, 1853–1861 191–95 (1861, *reprinted* 1996) (describing the task system); Philip P. Morgan, *Work and Culture: The Task System and the World of Low-Country Blacks, 1700–1880*, WM. & MARY Q. 565–71 (October 1982).

97. *See* PENNIGROTH, *supra* note 95, at 50–52, 54; 17 FEDERAL WRITERS' PROJECT, THE AMERICAN SLAVE: A COMPOSITE AUTOBIOGRAPHY: FLORIDA NARRATIVES (ed. George Rawick 1972–73) [hereinafter RAWICK, AMERICAN SLAVE] (Duncan Gaines on torchlight); Claim of Joseph James, p. 2, Liberty County, Georgia, Case Files, Southern Claims Commission, Record of the Third Auditor, Allowed Case Files, Records of the U.S. General Accounting Office, Record Group 217, National Archives, Washington, DC [hereinafter SCC]; CHARLES BALL, SLAVERY IN THE UNITED STATES: A NARRATIVE OF THE LIFE AND ADVENTURES OF CHARLES BALL 217, 271–73 (1836).

98. PENNIGROTH, *supra* note 95, at 47–49; Claim of Miller Jeffries, n.p., Marshall County, Mississippi, SCC; Philip D. Morgan, *The Ownership of Property by Slaves in the Mid-Nineteenth Century*, 49 J. SOUTHERN HISTORY (No. 3) 415 (1983) (on low-country slaves).

99. *See* PENNIGROTH, *supra* note 95, at 51, 53–54.

100. *See id.* at 60–62, 66.

101. *See id.* at 54–55; Claim of Benjamin S. Turner, Supplemental Testimony, April 21, 1871, Dallas County, Alabama, reel 6, Alabama Allowed Case Files, Southern Claims Commission, Microfilm Publication 2062, Wallace State Community College (quotation).

102. *See* BALL, *supra* note 97, at 192–93; PENNIGROTH, *supra* note 95, at 86–91, 103–07.

103. *See* PENNIGROTH, *supra* note 95, at 91–92, 94, 98–100.

104. NICHOLAS W. PROCTOR, BATHED IN BLOOD: HUNTING AND MASTERY IN THE OLD SOUTH 123–29, 149–53 (2002).

105. *See id.* at 160, 162; 1 RAWICK, AMERICAN SLAVE, Supplement, Series 1, Alabama, Part I, *supra* note 97, at 308 (quoting first Alabama slave), 113 (quoting second Alabama slave).

106. *See* PROCTOR, *supra* note 104, at 162–64.

107. *Id.* at 141.

108. *See* PENNIGROTH, *supra* note 95, at 55–57; William Harris, p. 3, Chatham County, Georgia, SCC (emphasis in original).

109. PENNIGROTH, *supra* note 95, at 68–70; Testimony of Samuel B. Smith, Esq., November 19, 1863, pp. 3–4, File 7, Records of the American Freedman's Inquiry Commission, File 0-328 (1863), Entry 12, Letters Received 1805–89, Correspondence 1800–1947, General Records of the Adjutant General's Office, Record Group 44, Washington, DC.

110. *See* HUSTON, VALUE OF THE UNION, *supra* note 85, at 106–10. On the *Somerset* case, *see* STEVEN M. WISE, THOUGH THE HEAVENS MAY FALL: THE LANDMARK TRIAL THAT LED TO THE END OF HUMAN SLAVERY (2005).

111. *See* HUSTON, VALUE OF THE UNION, *supra* note 85, at 109–17; ROBIN WEST, PROGRESSIVE CONSTITUTIONALISM: RECONSTRUCTING THE FOURTEENTH AMENDMENT 9–44 (1994) (arguing that abolitionist egalitarianism informs the Fourteenth Amendment and prohibits the "dual sovereignty" of one individual's being subject to another's will).

112. *See* HUSTON, VALUE OF THE UNION, *supra* note 85, at 110–11; THEODORE WELD, THE BIBLE AGAINST SLAVERY (1838, *reprinted* 1970); Martha V. Ball to James G. Birney, May 10, 1848, Birney Papers, William L. Clements Library, University of Michigan;

Resolutions of New England Conference Methodist Episcopal Church, in PHILADELPHIA PENNSYLVANIA FREEMAN, July 16, 1846 ("brutes and things" and "angels"); AUGUSTA (MAINE) KENNEBEC JOURNAL, November 3, 1854 ("like cattle"); Joshua Giddings, February 13, 1847, CONG. GLOBE, 29th Cong., 2d Sess., Appendix, 457.

113. *See* HUSTON, VALUE OF THE UNION, *supra* note 85, at 111–12; Wendell Phillips, N.Y. TRIBUNE, March 21, 1860, p. 8; 1 JOHN S. C. ABBOTT, HISTORY OF THE CIVIL WAR IN AMERICA iii, iv (1863–66).

114. HUSTON, VALUE OF THE UNION, *supra* note 85, at 111–13.

115. *See id.* at 113–15; MILWAUKEE DAILY SENTINEL AND GAZETTE, February 17, 1851, *in* 87 A DOCUMENTARY HISTORY OF AMERICAN INDUSTRIAL SOCIETY 57 (ed. John R. Commons et al. 1910); *see also* JAMES L. HUSTON, SECURING THE FRUITS OF LABOR: THE AMERICAN CONCEPT OF WEALTH DISTRIBUTION, 1765–1900 324–28 (1998) (on labor/property connection among Republicans).

116. *See* HUSTON, VALUE OF THE UNION, *supra* note 85, at 115–18; William H. Seward, *The Dominant Class in the Republic, 1856, in* 4 THE WORKS OF WILLIAM H. SEWARD 254–55 (ed. George E. Baker, 2d ed. 1887).

117. *See* HUSTON, VALUE OF THE UNION, *supra* note 85, at 115–18; Abraham Lincoln, Speech at Hartford, Connecticut, March 5, 1860, *in* 4 THE COLLECTED WORKS OF ABRAHAM LINCOLN 3–4 (ed. Roy P. Basler et al. 1953–55) [hereinafter LINCOLN, COLLECTED WORKS]; Abraham Lincoln, Speech at New Haven, Connecticut, March 6, 1860, *in* 4 LINCOLN, COLLECTED WORKS, *supra,* at 15–16; Abraham Lincoln, Speech at Leavenworth, Kansas, December 3, 1859, *in* 3 LINCOLN, COLLECTED WORKS, *supra,* at 499; Abraham Lincoln, Speech at Janesville, Wisconsin, October 1, 1859, *in* 3 LINCOLN, COLLECTED WORKS, *supra,* at 485; Abraham Lincoln to Henry L. Pierce and Others, April 6, 1859, *in* 3 LINCOLN, COLLECTED WORKS, *supra,* at 375.

118. *See* HUSTON, VALUE OF THE UNION, *supra* note 85, at 67–103.

119. *See id.* at 70, 74, 94–96, 115–18.

120. WILLIAM H. SEWARD, *Irrepressible Conflict, 1858, in* 4 THE WORKS OF WILLIAM H. SEWARD, *supra* note 116, at 292.

121. *See* HUSTON, VALUE OF THE UNION, *supra* note 85, at 98–100; GEORGE W. WESTON, SOUTHERN SLAVERY REDUCES NORTHERN WAGES 5 (1856).

122. *See* HUSTON, VALUE OF THE UNION, *supra* note 85, at 67–103.

Notes to Chapter 11

1. DON E. FEHRENBACHER, THE SLAVEHOLDING REPUBLIC: AN ACCOUNT OF THE UNITED STATES GOVERNMENT'S RELATIONS TO SLAVERY 295–97 (2001); CONG. GLOBE, 36th Cong., 2d Sess. 486 (Clement Clay); JOSEPH CARLYLE SITTERSON, THE SECESSION MOVEMENT IN NORTH CAROLINA 135 (1939) (a North Carolina editor).

2. FEHRENBACHER, *supra* note 1, at 301–03; MICHAEL KENT CURTIS, FREE SPEECH, "THE PEOPLE'S DARLING PRIVILEGE": STRUGGLES FOR FREEDOM OF EXPRESSION IN AMERICAN HISTORY 131–300 (2000) (surveying the relevant history in detail).

3. *See* FEHRENBACHER, *supra* note 1, at 302; CURTIS, *supra* note 2, at 173–75; *Yazoo City Post Office Case,* 8, ATT'Y GEN. 489, 494 (1858) (Caleb Cushing).

4. *See* FEHRENBACHER, *supra* note 1, at 302–03; EDWARD MCPHERSON, THE POLITICAL HISTORY OF THE UNITED STATES DURING THE GREAT REBELLION 189 (4th ed. 1882) (Amos Kendall).

5. *See* CURTIS, *supra* note 2, at 158–75 (recounting history of the defeated bill); CONG. GLOBE, 24th Cong., 1st Sess. 165 (1836) (bill's content); 12 CONG. DEB. 1167 (1836) (Morris on Fourth Amendment).

6. 12 CONG. DEB. 1168.

7. *See* CURTIS, *supra* note 2, at 159, 164, 172 (summarizing Calhoun's and Morris's views); Andrew Jackson, *Seventh Annual Message to Congress, in* 3 A COMPILATION OF THE MESSAGES AND PAPERS OF THE PRESIDENTS, 1789–1897 175–76 (ed. James Richardson 1896); JOHN C. CALHOUN, SPEECHES OF JOHN C. CALHOUN DELIVERED IN THE CONGRESS OF THE UNITED STATES FROM 1811 TO THE PRESENT TIME 19–90 (1843).

8. *See* FEHRENBACHER, *supra* note 1, at 302–03.

9. *See* ANNE SARAH RUBIN, A SHATTERED NATION: THE RISE AND FALL OF THE CONFEDERACY, 1861–1868 100–02 (2005); CHARLES B. DEW, APOSTLES OF DISUNION: SOUTHERN SECESSION COMMISSIONERS AND THE CAUSES OF THE CIVIL WAR 77–80 (2001).

10. *See* FEHRENBACHER, *supra* note 1, at 303–06; Thomas L. Clingman, *Speech on the State of the Union, Delivered in the Senate of the United States, February 4, 1861, in* SOUTHERN PAMPHLETS ON SECESSION, NOVEMBER 1860–APRIL 1861 284, 287 (ed. Jon L.

Wakelyn 1996); SECESSION DEBATED: GEORGIA'S SHOWDOWN IN 1860 19–20 (ed. William W. Freehling and Craig M. Simpson 1992).

11. See FEHRENBACHER, supra note 1, at 306–07; see generally MARSHALL L. DEROSA, THE CONFEDERATE CONSTITUTION OF 1861: AN INQUIRY INTO AMERICAN CONSTITUTIONALISM (1991) (on the unique features and philosophy of the Confederate constitution); WILLIAM C. DAVIS, LOOK AWAY! A HISTORY OF THE CONFEDERATE STATES OF AMERICA 55–70, 93–124 (2002) (summarizing the history, adoption, and ratification of the Confederate constitution).

12. Alexander Hamilton Stephens, Corner-Stone Speech, March 21, 1861, reprinted in HENRY CLEVELAND, ALEXANDER STEPHENS IN PUBLIC AND PRIVATE: WITH LETTERS AND SPEECHES 721 (1866); see also FEHRENBACHER, supra note 1, at 307 (discussing Stephens's speech).

13. See FEHRENBACHER, supra note 1, at 311–14.

14. See SILVANA R. SIDDALI, FROM PROPERTY TO PERSON: SLAVERY AND THE CONFISCATION ACTS, 1861–1862 2–3, 27–43 (2005).

15. See id. at 32–34, 41–42, 62–68, 72–77; 1 JAMES G. BLAINE, TWENTY YEARS OF CONGRESS: FROM LINCOLN TO GARFIELD 342 (1886).

16. See Bruce Levine, Flight and Fight: The Wartime Destruction of Slavery, 1861–1865, in PASSAGES TO FREEDOM: THE UNDERGROUND RAILROAD IN HISTORY AND MEMORY 216–19, 249–50, 313 (ed. David W. Blight 2004); SIDDALI, supra note 14, at 50–53.

17. FEHRENBACHER, supra note 1, 218–19, 249–50; SIDDALI, supra note 14, 3–7.

18. FEHRENBACHER, supra note 1, at 216–19.

19. SIDDALI, supra note 14, at 175; WILLIAM H. FREEHLING, THE SOUTH VS. THE SOUTH: HOW ANTI-CONFEDERATE SOUTHERNERS SHAPED THE COURSE OF THE CIVIL WAR 102 (2001) (quoting Union private); Levine, supra note 16, at 222–24; CLARENCE L. MOHR, ON THE THRESHOLD OF FREEDOM: MASTERS AND SLAVES IN CIVIL WAR GEORGIA 78 (1986); LEON LITWACK, BEEN IN THE STORM SO LONG: THE AFTERMATH OF SLAVERY 53 (1979); THE CHILDREN OF PRIDE: A TRUE STORY OF GEORGIA IN THE CIVIL WAR 930 (ed. Robert Manson Myers 1972) [hereinafter MYERS, CHILDREN OF PRIDE].

20. See Levine, supra note 16, at 211–12, 219–20.

21. See FEHRENBACHER, supra note 1, at 248–50.

22. See SIDDALI, supra note 14, at 3–4, 12–29, 101–15, 112–29, 152, 154–55; Levine, supra note 16, at 219–20, 226–27.

23. See LEVINE, supra note 16, at 219–20; FEHRENBACHER, supra note 1, at 314–17; THE COLLECTED WORKS OF ABRAHAM LINCOLN 318 (ed. Roy P. Basler et al. 1953) [hereinafter LINCOLN, COLLECTED WORKS].

24. See LEVINE, supra note 16, at 220; ARMSTEAD L. ROBINSON, BITTER FRUITS OF BONDAGE: THE DEMISE OF SLAVERY AND THE COLLAPSE OF THE CONFEDERACY, 1861–1865 199–200 (2005); 5 LINCOLN, COLLECTED WORKS, supra note 23, at 434; Abraham Lincoln, Annual Message, December 1, 1862, in THE LANGUAGE OF LIBERTY: THE POLITICAL SPEECHES AND WRITINGS OF ABRAHAM LINCOLN 620, 637 (ed. Joseph Fornieri 2003) [hereinafter FORNIERI, LANGUAGE OF LIBERTY]; James K. Wells, April 16, 1863, An Indiana Volunteer Advises His Neighbor, in INDIANA MAGAZINE OF HISTORY 178–79 (ed. Charles G. Talbert 1957) (Union soldier's letter).

25. See LEVINE, supra note 16, at 220–21; FEHRENBACHER, supra note 1, at 320–23; 5 LINCOLN, COLLECTED WORKS, supra note 23, at 537; THE AFRICAN-AMERICAN ARCHIVE: THE HISTORY OF THE BLACK EXPERIENCE THROUGH DOCUMENTS 327–29 (ed. Kai Wright 2001) [hereinafter WRIGHT, AFRICAN-AMERICAN ARCHIVE (reproducing Proclamation).

26. See LEVINE, supra note 16, at 220–22; JAMES MCPHERSON, THE NEGRO'S CIVIL WAR: HOW AMERICAN NEGROES FELT AND ACTED DURING THE WAR FOR THE UNION 55, 65 (1965, reprinted 1982); LITWACK, supra note 19, at 21, 55.

27. See LEVINE, supra note 16, at 226–27; EDWARD MCPHERSON, THE POLITICAL HISTORY OF THE UNITED STATES DURING THE GREAT REBELLION 197, 274 (2d ed. 1865); LITWACK, supra note 19, at 73; 6 LINCOLN, COLLECTED WORKS, supra note 23, at 30.

28. 8 LINCOLN, COLLECTED WORKS, supra note 23, at 1–2; see also DUDLEY TAYLOR CORNISH, THE SABLE ARM: BLACK TROOPS IN THE UNION ARMY, 1861–1865 265, 288 (1987); JOSEPH T. GLATTHAAR, FORGED IN BATTLE: THE CIVIL WAR ALLIANCE OF BLACK SOLDIERS AND WHITE OFFICERS 167 (1990).

29. See LEVINE, supra note 16, at 227–28; MCPHERSON, supra note 26, at 168–69; GLATTHAAR, supra note 28, at 79, 122.

30. MCPHERSON, *supra* note 26, at 169 (quoting Union officer).

31. *See* LEVINE, *supra* note 16, at 228–29; MCPHERSON, *supra* note 26, at 170; GLATTHAAR, *supra* note 28, at 122, 135; LITWACK, *supra* note 19, at 75–100, 111; MACON TELEGRAPH AND CONFEDERATE, October 12, 1864; LITWACK, *supra* note 19, at 101 (quoting white soldier); HENRY T. JONES, LIFE WITH THE FORTY-NINTH MASSACHUSETTS VOLUNTEERS 169 (1890).

32. ROBINSON, *supra* note 24, at 39, 42, 45–47 (including quotation summarizing Texas law); Ninth Legislature of the State of Texas, 1862, *General and Special Laws of the State of Texas*; J. B. Mannary to Pettus, May 18, 1861, Official Archives, Mississippi Department of Archives and History, Jackson.

33. ALLEN PINKERTON, THE SPY OF THE REBELLION, BEING A TRUE HISTORY OF THE SPY SYSTEM OF THE UNITED STATES ARMY 187 (1885); *see also* ROBINSON, *supra* note 24, at 46.

34. *See* LEVINE, *supra* note 16, at 224–25; ROBINSON, *supra* note 24, at 45–47, 109–10, 138–45, 178–82; MYERS, CHILDREN OF PRIDE, *supra* note 19, at 1247 ("perfect antagonism" quotation); Lizzie Neblett to William H. Neblett, August 5, 1863, Neblett Papers, University of Texas Library (concerning Sam).

35. PHILLIP SHAW PALUDAN, A PEOPLE'S CONTEST: THE UNION AND CIVIL WAR, 1861–1865 213–14 (1996) (including "atrocity" quotation); 14 ATLANTIC MONTHLY 517 (October 1864).

36. PALUDAN, *supra* note 35, at 214; MELINDA LAWSON, PATRIOT FIRES: FORGING A NEW AMERICAN NATIONALISM IN THE CIVIL WAR NORTH 163 (2003).

37. LINCOLN, COLLECTED WORKS, *supra* note 23, at 410; LAWSON, *supra* note 36, at 169; Abraham Lincoln, Letter to James C. Conklin, August 26, 1863, *in* FORNIERI, LANGUAGE OF LIBERTY, *supra* note 24, at 666, 669–70.

38. *See* LAWSON, *supra* note 36, at 169, 171; ERIC FONER, RECONSTRUCTION: AMERICA'S UNFINISHED REVOLUTION, 1863–1867 49 (1988); 7 LINCOLN, COLLECTED WORKS, *supra* note 23, at 243; 8 LINCOLN, COLLECTED WORKS, *supra* note 23, at 399–403.

39. 8 LINCOLN, COLLECTED WORKS, *supra* note 23, at 332–33, 356.

40. *See* FEHRENBACHER, *supra* note 1, at 332–33, 356 (sending Thirteenth Amendment to the states); MICHAEL S. GREEN,

FREEDOM, UNION, AND POWER 162–69 (Republican Party's 1864 election platform, political maneuvering, quotation concerning the Confederacy's reason for being); HEATHER COX RICHARDSON, THE DEATH OF RECONSTRUCTION ix, 10–12 (2001) (Northerners becoming convinced that blacks would make ideal free laborers); CHARLES M. CHRISTIAN, BLACK SAGA: THE AFRICAN-AMERICAN EXPERIENCE: A CHRONOLOGY 210, 212 (1999) (dates of Lee's surrender and Thirteenth Amendment's ratification); BRUCE ACKERMAN, WE THE PEOPLE 132–59 (1998) (tracing the process of ratification of the Thirteenth Amendment and the electoral victory of 1864); HAROLD M. HYMAN & WILLIAM WIECEK, EQUAL JUSTICE UNDER LAW: CONSTITUTIONAL DEVELOPMENT 1835–1875 305 (1982) (presidential pressure for Southern ratification).

41. *See* SIDDALI, *supra* note 14, at 84–89; U.S. CONST. amend. V (Takings Clause).

42. SIDDALI, *supra* note 14, at 88–92, 253–61; CHICAGO TRIBUNE, April 8, 1861 ("debtor" "stealing himself" quotation); CONG. GLOBE, 37th Cong., 1st Sess. 412 (Thaddeus Stevens).

43. SIDDALI, *supra* note 14, at 147–50; Thomas J. Sizer, *The Crisis: Its Rationale, Part II—Restoration of Legitimate Authority, the End and Object of the War* (1862); George Candee, *Plan for Conquering Treason, Letter to President Lincoln, by a Citizen of Kentucky* 6 (1862); F. D. Parish to John Sherman, Sherman Papers, Library of Congress, April 18, 1862; FRANKFORT (KENTUCKY) DAILY COMMONWEALTH, December 13, 1861.

44. SIDDALI, *supra* note 14, at 152–62; PAUL FINKELMAN, SLAVERY AND THE FOUNDERS: RACE AND LIBERTY IN THE AGE OF JEFFERSON 3–7 (1996) (summarizing Constitution's provisions supporting "slavery" without using the word); Remarks of Albert G. Riddle, January 28, 1862, CONG. GLOBE, 37th Cong., 2d Sess. 498–99.

45. SIDDALI, *supra* note 14, at 192–200.

46. *See id.* at 201 ("guilty authors of the rebellion"), 202–11 (general), 212 (Northern virtue); N.Y. TIMES, July 25, 1862.

47. SIDDALI, *supra* note 14, at 241–43; SPRINGFIELD (MASSACHUSETTS) DAILY REPUBLICAN, July 19, 1862.

48. *See* SIDDALI, *supra* note 14, at 247–50 (general), 250 (quotation), 257–60 (reproducing Second Confiscation Act); *see also* HYMAN & WIECEK, *supra* note 40, at 251.

49. *See* U.S. CONST. amends. IV, XIV; ANDREW E. TASLITZ & MARGARET L. PARIS,

CONSTITUTIONAL CRIMINAL PROCEDURE 39–40 (2d ed. 2003) (incorporation doctrine); AKHIL REED AMAR, THE BILL OF RIGHTS: CREATION AND RECONSTRUCTION 163–214 (1998) (textual and historical analysis demonstrating an intention to incorporate the first eight amendments of the Bill of Rights via the Fourteenth Amendment's Privileges and Immunities Clause). *But see* George C. Thomas III, *When Constitutional Worlds Collide: Resurrecting the Framers' Bill of Rights and Criminal Procedure,* 100 MICH. L. REV. 145 (2001) (arguing against the dominant incorporationist position but recognizing a role for history that could still support a non-incorporationist variant of my position).

50. *See* EARL M. MALTZ, THE FOURTEENTH AMENDMENT AND THE LAW OF THE CONSTITUTION 3–9 (2003) [hereinafter MALTZ, FOURTEENTH AMENDMENT].

51. *See id.* at 7, 81–83; CONG. GLOBE, 34th Cong., 1st Sess., App. 124 (1856). This form of class-based reasoning at least seems implicit in their arguments, although Maltz is unclear about whether he is making precisely this point, which nevertheless logically follows directly from his other arguments.

52. *See* MALTZ, FOURTEENTH AMENDMENT, *supra* note 50, at 1–12; Ex Parte Milligan, 71 U.S. (4 Wall.) 295 (1866); *see also* 10 OPINIONS OF THE ATTORNEY GENERAL 382, 393–94 (1862).

53. *See* MALTZ, FOURTEENTH AMENDMENT, *supra* note 50, at 16–25.

54. *See id.* at 29–32; U.S. CONST. art. IV, §2.

55. *See id.* at 32–34, 37–50; Corfield v. Coryell, 6 F. Cas. 546, 551–52 (1823).

56. *See* MALTZ, FOURTEENTH AMENDMENT, *supra* note 50, at 32–34, 38–39, 40–50; CONG. GLOBE, 35th Cong., 2d Sess. 984–85 (1859).

57. CONG. GLOBE, 35th Cong., 2d Sess. 985 (1859); *see* MALTZ, FOURTEENTH AMENDMENT, *supra* note 50, at 32–34, 37–50.

58. MALTZ, FOURTEENTH AMENDMENT, *supra* note 50, at 35–52.

59. *Id.* at 34–37, 40; DON E. FEHRENBACHER, THE DRED SCOTT CASE: ITS SIGNIFICANCE IN AMERICAN LAW AND POLITICS 69–71 (1978); 1 HENRY WILSON, HISTORY OF THE RISE AND FALL OF THE SLAVE POWER IN AMERICA 576–86 (1872); CARL B. SWISHER, HISTORY OF THE SUPREME COURT OF THE UNITED STATES: THE TANEY PERIOD: 1836–1864 378–82, 392–93 (1974); H.R. Rep. 80, 27th Cong.,

3d Sess. 2 (1843); Mitchell v. Wells, 37 Miss. 264 (1859); *see also* CONG. GLOBE, 35th Cong., 2d Sess. 970 (1859) (remarks of Rep. Clark); 31st Cong., 1st Sess., App. 288 (1850) (remarks of Sen. Butler).

60. *See* MALTZ, FOURTEENTH AMENDMENT, *supra* note 50, at 35–37; GEORGE F. HOAR, AUTOBIOGRAPHY OF SEVENTY YEARS 24–27 (1903); WILSON, *supra* note 59, at 578–82; AMAR, *supra* note 49, at 236 ("ridden out of town on a rail" quotation).

61. *See* MALTZ, FOURTEENTH AMENDMENT, *supra* note 50, at 36 (antebellum antislavery politicians); CONG. GLOBE, 38th Cong., 1st Sess. 2983–84, 2984, 2990 (1864) (remarks of Reps. William Kelley and Eben Ingersoll); CONG. GLOBE, 38th Cong., 2d Sess. 193, 237 (1865) (remarks of Reps. John Kasson and Greer Smith); CONG. GLOBE, 39th Cong., 1st Sess. 41, 157–58, 474–75, 1263 (1865–66) (remarks of Sen. John Sherman, Rep. John Bingham, Sen. Lyman Trumbull, and Rep. John Broomall); *id.* at App. 142 (remarks of Sen. Henry Wilson); CONG. GLOBE, 31st Cong., 1st Sess., App. 1012–13 (1854); CONG. GLOBE, 41st Cong., 1st Sess., App. 1661–62 (1850) (remarks of Sen. Winthrop); AMAR, *supra* note 49, at 236 ("burned bright"); Charles Fairman, *Does the Fourteenth Amendment Incorporate the Bill of Rights?* 2 STAN. L. REV. 5, 22 (1949) (Hoar incident a "stock example" in the Reconstruction Congress); EARL M. MALTZ, CIVIL RIGHTS, THE CONSTITUTION, AND CONGRESS, 1863–1869 53–54 (1990) [hereinafter MALTZ, CIVIL RIGHTS] (discussing Bingham and Johnson).

62. CONG. GLOBE, 39th Cong., 1st Sess. 157–58 (1866).

63. *Id.*

64. *See* MALTZ, CIVIL RIGHTS, *supra* note 61, at 54–55.

65. *See* AMAR, *supra* note 49, at 267–68 (Fourth Amendment's incorporation against the states); STEPHEN P. HALBROOK, FREEDMEN, THE FOURTEENTH AMENDMENT, AND THE RIGHT TO BEAR ARMS, 1866–1876 14–15, 31, 129, 136–38, 187 (1998) (Fourth Amendment–Second Amendment connection). But see Thomas, *supra* note 49, at 145 (arguing against incorporation of any of the Bill of Rights against the states but finding Fourteenth Amendment values regulating state search and seizure practices).

66. *See* BERTRAM WYATT-BROWN, THE SHAPING OF SOUTHERN CULTURE: HONOR, GRACE, AND WAR, 1760s–1880s 198–201 (2001).

67. WYATT-BROWN, *supra* note 66, at 210 ("average white male Southerner" quotation), 218 (Confederate treatment of black Union soldiers), 230, 255–56 (shame of defeat); ANNE SARAH RUBIN, A SHATTERED NATION: THE RISE AND FALL OF THE CONFEDERACY, 1861–1868 141, 149, 157, 159–71, 211, 245–47 (white resentment and response), 246–47 ("distinct nation" and "quasi-ethnic minority"); Susan-Mary Grant, *"The Charter of Its Birthright": The Civil War and American Nationalism, in* LEGACY OF DISUNION: THE ENDURING SIGNIFICANCE OF THE AMERICAN CIVIL WAR 188, 196–97, 199 (ed. Susan-Mary Grant and Peter J. Parish 2003) (rise of cult of the Lost Cause).

68. *See* HALBROOK, *supra* note 65, at 13–15; CONG. GLOBE, 39th Cong., 1st Sess. 606–07 (February 17, 1866), App. at 69 (February 3, 1866) (Rep. Rousseau's remarks), 648 (February 5, 1866) (Rep. Trimble's remarks); *see generally* THE OXFORD COMPANION TO UNITED STATES HISTORY 291–92 (ed. Paul S. Boyer 2001); GEORGE R. BENTLEY, A HISTORY OF THE FREEDMEN'S BUREAU (1955); WILLIAM MCFEELY, YANKEE STEPFATHER: GENERAL O. O. HOWARD AND THE FREEDMEN (1888, *reprinted* 1994).

69. *See* HALBROOK, *supra* note 65, at 1–6, 9, 11, 14, 20–22; CONG. GLOBE, 39th Cong., 1st Sess. 915 (February 19, 1866) (Sen. Wilson's remarks), 941 (February 20, 1866) (Trumbull's remarks quoting Col. Thomas's letter); CONG. GLOBE, 39th Cong., 1st Sess. 512, 517 (January 29, 1866) (Chairman Eliot cites, as an example of Black Codes the Freedmen's Bureau Bill was designed to nullify, an Opelousas, Louisiana, statute that required freedmen to have a pass, prohibited their residence in town, and prohibited their religious and other meetings).

70. HALBROOK, *supra* note 65, at 1–4, 22–23; Report of the Joint Committee on Reconstruction, H.R. No. 30, 39th Cong., 1st Sess., pt. 5, at 49–50 (1866) (concerning Col. H. S. Hall); Laws of Miss., 1865, at 165 (November 29, 1865); Ex. Doc. No. 6, 39th Cong., 1st Sess. 195–96 (1867); J. BURGESS, RECONSTRUCTION AND THE CONSTITUTION, 1866–1876 47, 51–52 (1902) (saying of the Mississippi Act, "This is a fair sample of the legislation passed by all the 'States' reconstructed under President Johnson's plan. . . . The Northern Republicans professed to see in this new legislation at the South the virtual re-enslavement of the negroes.").

71. HALBROOK, *supra* note 65 at 24–25; CONG. GLOBE, 39th Cong., 1st Sess., 1117–

18 (March 1, 1866); 1 WILLIAM BLACKSTONE, COMMENTARIES ON THE LAWS OF ENGLAND 140–41 (ed. St. George Tucker 1803).

72. *See* HALBROOK, *supra* note 65, at 27–28; Ex. Doc. No. 70, House of Representatives, 39th Cong., 1st Sess. 238–39 (1866) (Fisk's report), 292 (Swayne's report).

73. Ex. Doc. No. 70, House of Representatives, 39th Cong., 1st Sess. 297 (1866).

74. HALBROOK, *supra* note 65, at 29–30; B. KENDRICK, THE JOURNAL OF THE JOINT COMMITTEE OF FIFTEEN ON RECONSTRUCTION, pt. 3, at 140, 244 (1914) (statements of Swayne and Matthews).

75. HALBROOK, *supra* note 65, at 28–31; CONG. GLOBE, 39th Cong., 1st Sess. 1621 (March 24, 1866) (Rep. Myers); *id.* at 1629 (Rep. Roswell Hart); CONG. GLOBE, 39th Cong., 1st Sess. 1291–92 (March 9, 1866) (Rep. Bingham); CONG. GLOBE, 39th Cong., 1st Sess., App. 157 (March 8, 1866) (Rep. Wilson on "fundamental rights"); CONG. GLOBE, 39th Cong., 1st Sess. 1270 (March 8, 1866) (Rep. Martin Thayer on the need to empower Congress to enforce the Bill of Rights).

76. HALBROOK, *supra* note 65, at 30–32; CONG. GLOBE, 39th Cong., 1st Sess. 1757 (April 4, 1866) (Trumbull's comments); Report of the Joint Committee, pt. 2, *supra* note 70, at 271–72.

77. Report of the Joint Committee, pt. 2, *supra* note 70, at 272.

78. *See* HYMAN & WIECEK, *supra* note 40, at 414–15; HALBROOK, *supra* note 65, at 31–32, 36, 39–44; 14 Stat. 27; CONG. GLOBE, 39th Cong., 1st Sess. 2773 (May 23, 1866) (remarks of Rep. Eliot); 14 Statutes at Large 173 (1866) (Freedmen's Bureau Bill); HYMAN & WIECEK, *supra* note 40, at 414–31; AMAR, *supra* note 49, at 196 n., 235, 260–61; *see generally* DAVID SKILLEN BOGEN, PRIVILEGES AND IMMUNITIES: A REFERENCE GUIDE TO THE UNITED STATES CONSTITUTION 12–58 (2003) (history of the concept of privileges and immunities and links among Reconstruction civil-rights legislation, the Fourteenth Amendment, and the incorporation concept).

79. *See* HALBROOK, *supra* note 65, at 17, 33–38, 42; CONG. GLOBE, 39th Cong., 1st Sess. 2890 (May 30, 1866) (proposed citizenship clause). The Civil Rights Act of 1866 extended citizenship to all persons in the United States, "excluding Indians not taxed," an exclusion absent from the Fourteenth Amendment. *See* WRIGHT, AFRICAN-AMERICAN ARCHIVE, *supra* note 25, at 385.

80. *See* HALBROOK, *supra* note 65, at 17, 33–38, 42; KENDRICK, *supra* note 74, at 83 (Thaddeus Stevens's original section 1 antidiscrimination proposal to the Joint Committee); MALTZ, CIVIL RIGHTS, *supra* note 61, at 82–92 (similar); KENDRICK, *supra* note 74, at 85, 87–88 (Bingham's equal-protection substitutes, the first of which failed but the second of which, along with additional language, was adopted by the Joint Committee, which one week later dropped Stevens's original language); CONG. GLOBE, 39th Cong., 1st Sess. 27, 65–66 (May 23, 1866) (remarks of Sen. Howard); I. BRANT, THE BILL OF RIGHTS 337 (1965) (no one in debate challenged Howard's premise); N.Y. TIMES, May 24, 1866, at 1, col. 3; NATIONAL INTELLIGENCER, May 24, 1866, at 3, col. 2; PHILADELPHIA INQUIRER, May 24, 1866, at 8, col. 2; *see also* CHICAGO TRIBUNE, May 29, 1866, at 23, col. 3 (Howard's speech was "very forcible and well put, and commanded the close attention of the Senate"); BALTIMORE GAZETTE, May 24, 1866, at 4, col. 2 (summarizing Howard's speech this way: "the section is a general prohibition upon all of the States of abridging the privileges and immunities of the citizens of the United States, and secures for all the equal advantages and protection of the law.").

81. *See* HALBROOK, *supra* note 65, at 37–38; CONG. GLOBE, 39th Cong., 1st Sess. 2890, 2897 (May 30, 1866) (Sen. Howard's proposed citizenship clause); *id.* (June 8, 1866) (remarks by Sen. Henderson); Scott v. Sanford, 60 U.S. 393 416–17 (1857).

82. *See* MALTZ, FOURTEENTH AMENDMENT, *supra* note 50, at 53–63; 10 OPINIONS OF THE ATTORNEY GENERAL 382, 388, 398–99, 407–08, 412 (November 29, 1862).

83. *See* MALTZ, FOURTEENTH AMENDMENT, *supra* note 50, at 53–63; HALBROOK, *supra* note 65, at 37–38; CONG. GLOBE, 39th Cong., 1st Sess. 2961 (June 5, 1866) (remarks of Sen. Luke Poland); MALTZ, CIVIL RIGHTS, *supra* note 61, at 58 (banishment quotation), 58–59 (overview); CONG. GLOBE, 39th Cong., 1st Sess. 1089–90 (1866) (Bingham's remarks); HALBROOK, *supra* note 65, at 100–01 (quotation concerning incorporation of the most important rights, such as search and seizure).

84. *See* HALBROOK, *supra* note 65, at 59, 70–71; ROBERT J. KACZOROWSKI, THE POLITICS OF JUDICIAL INTERPRETATION: THE FEDERAL COURTS, THE DEPARTMENT OF JUSTICE, AND CIVIL RIGHTS, 1866–1876 38 (1985) (citing Freedmen's Bureau Archives).

85. *See* HALBROOK, *supra* note 65, at 119–31; CONG. GLOBE, 42d Cong., 1st Sess., App. 83 (March 31, 1871) (Bingham's remarks); *id.* at App. 314–15 (April 6, 1871) (Burchard's remarks).

86. In addition to the preceding discussion in this chapter, *see* Andrew E. Taslitz, *Hate Crimes, Free Speech, and the Contract of Mutual Indifference,* 80 B.U. L. REV. 1283, 1343–47, 1368–90 (2000) (Slave Power, suppression of free speech, Black Codes); Andrew E. Taslitz, *Slaves No More! The Implications of Informed Citizen Ideology for Discovery before Fourth Amendment Suppression Hearings,* 15 GA. ST. U. L. REV. 709, 738–56 (1999) (search and seizure and racial dominance); Andrew E. Taslitz, *Condemning the Racist Personality: Why the Critics of Hate Crimes Legislation Are Wrong,* 40 B.C. L. REV. 739, 765–77 (1999) (legal and extralegal violence).

87. *See* Andrew E. Taslitz, *Racial Profiling, Terrorism, and Time,* 109 PENN. ST. L. REV. 1181 (2005) (illustrating the applications of a Reconstruction-informed Fourth Amendment to the modern problem of racial profiling).

Notes to Chapter 12

1. Andrew E. Taslitz, *Respect and the Fourth Amendment,* 94 J. CRIM. L. & CRIMINOLOGY 15 (2003) [hereinafter Taslitz, *Respect*].

2. *See, e.g.,* George Dix, *Fourth Amendment Federalism: The Potential Requirement of State Law Authorization for Law Enforcement Activity,* 14 AM. J. CRIM. L. 1 (1987).

3. *See* Tracey Maclin, *The Central Meaning of the Fourth Amendment,* 35 WM. & MARY L. REV. 197, 237, 239 (1993); Tracey Maclin, *The Complexity of the Fourth Amendment: A Historical Review,* 77 B.U. L. REV. 925 (1997); Nadine Strossen, *Michigan Department of State Police v. Sitz: A Roadblock to Meaningful Judicial Enforcement of Constitutional Rights,* 42 HASTINGS L. REV. 285, 288 (1991).

4. *See* Taslitz, *Respect, supra* note 1, at 45–51.

5. *See id.* at 50–51.

6. *See id.* at 51–80.

7. *See* James D. Zirin, *Judges Who Dip into Politics,* N.Y. TIMES, July 16, 1996, at A1; Senator Robert Dole, *Luncheon Address at American Society of Newspaper Editors* (March 21, 1997), http://www.asne.org/kiosk/archive/convention/conv96/dole.htm; The White House, Office of the Press Secretary, *Press Briefing by Mike McCurry* (March 21,

1996), http://clinton6.nara.gov/1996/03/
1996-03-21-press-briefing-by-mike-
mccurry.html; National Drug Strategy Network, *NewsBriefs, Judge Cites Police Abuse and
Corruption, Throws Out Seized Drug Evidence
and Confession, Incites Controversy about the
Exclusionary Rule* (March 1996), http://
www.ndsn.org/march96/baer.html; National
Drug Strategy Network, *NewsBriefs: New York
Federal Judge Reverses Decision in Controversial
Drug Case; Clinton, Dole Had Threatened to
Ask for Resignation, Impeachment* (April 1996)
[hereinafter *New York Federal Judge Reverses
Decision*], http://www.ndsn.org/april96/bay-
less.html; Bruce Fein, *Not for the Thin-
Skinned: Scathing Criticism of Federal Judges Is
Constructive*, LEGAL TIMES, May 13, 1996 at
22; *Liberal Judgments*, Transcript, Online
Newshour (April 2, 1996), http://www.pbs
.org/newshour/bb/law/baer1_4-02.html.

8. United States v. Bayless, 913 F. Supp.
232, 234 (S.D.N.Y. 1996).

9. *Id. at 239–40* (citation omitted).

10. *Id.* at 236, 242 & n. 17.

11. *Id.*

12. *Id.* at 240; *see generally* DAVID COLE,
NO EQUAL JUSTICE: RACE AND CLASS IN THE
AMERICAN CRIMINAL JUSTICE SYSTEM 158
(1999).

13. See Raymond W. Kelly, *Handcuffing the
Police*, N.Y. TIMES, February 1, 1996, at A21;
Dole, *supra* note 7; *New York Federal Judge
Reverses Decision, supra* note 7; United States
v. Bayless 201 F.3d 116, 119, 123, 125 (2d
Cir. 2000).

14. *See* United States v. Bayless, 921 F.
Supp. 211, 217–18 (S.D.N.Y. 1996); United
States v. Buenaventura-Ariza, 615 F.2d 29, 31
(2d Cir. 1980); United States v. Sokolow, 490
U.S. 1, 11 (1989) (Marshall, J., dissenting);
see David Cole, *Civil Rights and Civil Liberties
in 1996: Hope in the Face of Adversity*, LEGAL
TIMES, December 23, 1996, at 33; *Judges:
Attacks on Baer Go Too Far*, LEGAL TIMES,
April 1, 1996, at 12; *cf. The Vindication of
Judge Baer?* N.Y. POST, April 3, 1999, at 16.

15. *Bayless*, 913 F. Supp. at 240. *Cf. The
Vindication of Judge Baer? supra* note 14.

16. See David Cole, *When Running Is Reasonable; Police Brutality in High-Crime Neighborhoods*, LEGAL TIMES, March 4, 1996, at 20
(summarizing Judge Baer's background).

17. *See Bayless*, 913 F. Supp. at 242; *cf.*
COLE, *supra* note 12, at 16–62 (how colorblind Fourth Amendment jurisprudence dis-
criminates against minorities).

18. *See Bayless*, 913 F. Supp. at 240.

19. *See* ANDREW E. TASLITZ & MARGARET L.

PARIS, CONSTITUTIONAL CRIMINAL PROCE-
DURE 340–42 (2d ed. 2003); *Bayless*, 913 F.
Supp. at 240.

20. *See* United States v. Bayless, 201 F.3d
116, 120 (2d Cir. 2000), *cert. denied*, 529 U.S.
1061 (2000).

21. 528 U.S. 119 (2000).

22. *Id.* at 121–22.

23. *Id.* at 124–26.

24. On the tension between group and
individualized justice, see Andrew E. Taslitz,
*Condemning the Racist Personality: Why the
Critics of Hate Crimes Legislation Are Wrong*,
40 B.C. L. REV. 739, 746–65 (1999) [here-
inafter Taslitz, *Racist Personality*]; *see also*
Omar Saleem, *The Age of Unreason: The
Impact of Reasonableness, Increased Police
Force, and Colorblindness on Terry "Stop and
Frisk*," 50 OKLA. L. REV. 451, 453 (1997).

25. *Wardlow*, 528 U.S. at 126, 129 & n. 3
(Stevens, J., dissenting).

26. *See id.* at 132 & n. 7 (Stevens, J., dissenting). There are subtleties in the reading
of the data that can, however, result in different, if less persuasive, interpretations of
the data. *See* Taslitz, *Respect, supra* note 1, at
62 n. 56.

27. *Wardlow*, 528 U.S. at 132–34 (Stevens,
J., dissenting).

28. *Id.* at 139 (Stevens, J., dissenting).

29. *Compare id.* at 124–26 (majority's
analysis) *with id.* at 132–39 (dissent's
analysis).

30. *Id.* at 137–38 (Stevens, J., dissenting)
(quoting Officer Nolan's testimony).

31. On racial profiling, *see generally* David
A. Harris, *"Driving While Black" and All
Other Traffic Offenses: The Supreme Court and
Pretextual Traffic Stops*, 87 J. CRIM. L. & CRIM-
INOLOGY 544 (1997); Katheryn K. Russell,
*"Driving While Black": Corollary Phenomena
and Collateral Consequences*, 40 B.C. L. REV.
717 (1999). On the emotional and political
impact of silencing dissenting perspectives,
see ANDREW E. TASLITZ, RAPE AND THE CUL-
TURE OF THE COURTROOM 134–48 (1999).

32. *See generally* Andrew E. Taslitz, *The
Fourth Amendment in the Twenty-First Century:
Technology, Privacy, and Human Emotions*, 65
L. & CONTEMP. PROBS. 125, 125–50 (2002).

33. *See* BERNARD E. HARCOURT, ILLUSION
OF ORDER: THE FALSE PROMISE OF BROKEN
WINDOWS POLICING 23–55, 127–59, 163
(2001) (defining, illustrating, and critiquing
the "broken windows" and related "order-
maintenance" approaches to policing). For a
critique of these sorts of policing techniques
as a pretense for controlling the poorest,

weakest members of our society, *see* ZERO
TOLERANCE: QUALITY OF LIFE AND THE NEW
POLICE BRUTALITY IN NEW YORK CITY (ed.
Andrea McArdle and Tanya Erzen 2001)
[hereinafter MCARDLE & ERZEN, ZERO TOLER-
ANCE]. *See also* William J. Stuntz, *The Distrib-
ution of Fourth Amendment Privacy,* 67 GEO.
WASH. L. REV. 1265, 1266–67 (1999).
34. HARCOURT, *supra* note 33, at 130, 150,
163.
35. *Id.* at 163.
36. *Id.* at 171, 213, 221–24; *see generally*
SUSAN L. MILLER, GENDER AND COMMUNITY
POLICING: WALKING THE TALK (1999);
Alexander Tsesis, *Eliminating the Destitution
of America's Homeless: A Fair, Federal
Approach,* 10 TEMP. POL. & CIV. RTS. L. REV.
103 (2000); *see generally* GLENN C. LOURY,
THE ANATOMY OF RACIAL INEQUALITY 29–43,
60–73 (2002) (explaining the roles of stigma
and self-fulfilling prophecies, based on cog-
nitive preconceptions, in perpetuating racial
subordination).
37. David A. Harris, *Back to the Future: Are
Technologically Assisted Searches a Way to
Achieve Better Police/Minority Relations?* 4–9
(describing the technology), 12 (nonsearches) (unpublished manuscript).
38. Harris, *supra* note 37, at 10; *see also*
ELIOT SPITZER, THE NEW YORK POLICE
DEPARTMENT'S "STOP & FRISK" PRACTICES: A
REPORT TO THE PEOPLE OF THE STATE OF NEW
YORK FROM THE OFFICE OF THE ATTORNEY
GENERAL (December 1, 1999).
39. Stuntz, *supra* note 33, at 1270–71.
40. *See, e.g.,* Andrea McArdle, *Introduction,*
in MCARDLE & ERZEN, ZERO TOLERANCE,
supra note 33, at 5–12; Tracey L. Meares &
Dan M. Kahan, *When Rights Are Wrong: The
Paradox of Unwanted Rights,* in URGENT
TIMES: POLICING AND RIGHTS IN INNER-CITY
COMMUNITIES 3, 18–19 (1999) (arguing that
a majority of poor, minority, inner-city residents favor order-maintenance policing as a
way of attaining neighborhood safety); Harris, *supra* note 37, at 109 (worrying that legislative protections against police uses of the
new surveillance technologies are unlikely).
41. *See* Matt Richtel, *To One Judge, Cyber-
monitors Bring Uneasy Memories,* N.Y. TIMES,
August 18, 2001, at A7.
42. *See* JEFFREY ROSEN, THE UNWANTED
GAZE: THE DESTRUCTION OF PRIVACY IN
AMERICA 79–90, 127 (2000); Andrew E.
Taslitz, *The Inadequacies of Civil Society: Law's
Complementary Role in Regulating Harmful
Speech,* 1 MARGINS 305, 350–54 (2001) (sum-

marizing the law and justifying the theory
of hostile-environment sexual harassment).
The exclusionary rule generally applies only
in criminal, not civil, litigation. *See* TASLITZ
& PARIS, *supra* note 19, at 479–80. *See also*
Neil A. Lewis, *Plan for Web Monitoring in
Courts Dropped,* N.Y. TIMES, September 9,
2001, at A20.
43. *Cf.* ROBERT POST, CONSTITUTIONAL
DOMAINS: DEMOCRACY, COMMUNITY, MAN-
AGEMENT 236 (1995) (arguing for greater
governmental authority to limit speech
when the state acts in the "managerial
sphere"); Andrew E. Taslitz & Sharon Styles-
Anderson, *Still Officers of the Court: Why the
First Amendment Is No Bar to Challenging
Racism, Sexism and Ethnic Bias in the Legal
Profession,* 9 GEO. J. LEGAL ETHICS 781, 811–
812 (1996) (illustrating the application of
the "managerial sphere" to the regulation of
lawyers' speech in professional contexts).
44. ROSEN, *supra* note 42, at 83–84.
45. *See* WILLIAM ESKRIDGE JR., GAY LAW:
CHALLENGING THE APARTHEID OF THE
CLOSET 174–95, 181, 236 (1999). *Cf.* DAVID
A. J. RICHARDS, IDENTITY AND THE CASE FOR
GAY RIGHTS: RACE, GENDER, RELIGION AS
ANALOGUES 193 (1999) ("Abridgement of
. . . intimate life play[s] the role . . . [it does]
in inflicting . . . evil because . . . [it is] so
intimately tied up with the sense of ourselves as embedded in and shaped by networks of relationships to other persons with
the moral powers of rational choice and reasonable deliberation over the convictions
and attachments that give shape and meaning to our personal and ethical lives.").
46. AMERICAN BAR ASSOCIATION TASK
FORCE ON TECHNOLOGY AND LAW ENFORCE-
MENT, TENTATIVE DRAFT STANDARDS CON-
CERNING TECHNOLOGICALLY ASSISTED
PHYSICAL SURVEILLANCE (tentative draft
1997).
47. *See, e.g.,* Bourgeois v. Peters, No. 02-
16886, slip op. (11th Cir. 2004) (mass mag-
netometer searches); Stauber v. City of New
York, No. 03 Civ. 9162, slip op. (S.D.N.Y.
2004) (mass bag searches at Republican
National Convention).
48. *See generally* Doriane Lambelet Coleman, *Storming the Castle to Save the Children:
The Ironic Costs of a Child Welfare Exception
to the Fourth Amendment,* 47 WM. & MARY L.
REV. 413 (2005); Mary I. Coombs, *Shared
Privacy and the Fourth Amendment, or the
Rights of Relationships,* 75 CAL. L. REV. 1593
(1987).

Index

Ableman v. Booth (1859), 171–172

Abolitionism: "Amalgamation prints," 192; antislavery movement compared to, 205; display of abolitionist propaganda by slaves, 192–193; distribution of abolitionist literature in the South, 136, 228; disunionism, 201; federal government's seizure of abolitionist literature, 93; Garrison and, 329n40; gradualism, 199, 329n40; immediatism, 221; Liberty Party, 205; mob violence opposing, 104, 202–203; "modern" abolitionism, 221; popularity in North, 12, 186, 206; pre-1830s, 329n37; property rights, 221; racial equality, 221; searches and seizures, 12–13; seizures of abolitionist mail in the South, 188, 226–228; socialism, 214; suppression of, 12, 104, 188, 198; as un-Christian, 136; white supremacy, 203

Abolitionists, 198–204; African American, 175; Christian egalitarianism, 199; colonization of slaves, 199, 203; Declaration of Independence, 199; ending slavery, 157; first-hand accounts of atrocities, 199–200; freedom of speech, 22, 203–204; gag laws against, 202; Garrisonians, 201; labor theory of value, 221; mass mailings/postal campaign, 201–203; mobocracy, 201–204; moral suasion, 198–201; Nat Turner's Revolt (1831), 199; Northern, 329n37; prohibition from serving on juries, 126; racism, 199; Reconstruction Amendments, 186; Slave Power, 204–207; slavery, 199; Southern assaults of, 158; Southern view of, 131, 136–137; successes, 201; underground railroad, 135

Abraham, 98

Accessibility, 86, 87–88, 246

Active (sloop), 51, 296n92, 299n22

Actual representation, 29–31

Adams, John: Fourth Amendment, 302n5; Massachusetts Declaration of Rights, 42; mirror theory, 31; Otis and, 42, 284n2, 302n5; sovereignty of colonial legislatures, 30; writs of assistance, 17, 284n2

Adams, Sam, 299n22

Administrative searches and seizures, 72–76, 306n8

African Americans: African American abolitionists, 175; attitudes toward police,

282n27; flight from police, 264–270; as "men," 206; police abuses, 268; stop-and-frisks, 273. See also Blacks

Agrarianism (land distribution), 214

Alabama, secession debates in, 228

Alien and Sedition Acts (1798), 22

Allen, George, 139

Allen, William, 35, 61

Amar, Akhil: Bill of Rights, 304n28; immunity from trespass suits, 299n15; majoritarian oppression, 304n28; on searches and seizures, 283n33; "the People," 302n3; tort remedies, 60

American Bar Association Standards on Technologically-Assisted Surveillance, 59–60

American Civil Liberties Union, 60

American Colonization Society, 199

American Revolution: evidence, 13; general searches, 4–5; general warrants, 56; individualized justice, 13; ineluctability of independence, 30; political dissent, 13, 18; potential failure of, 225; probable cause, 13; Reconstruction, 257; searches and seizures, 22, 42, 284n1, 284n2, 289n45; state force, 18; taxation without representation, 28–29; writs of assistance, 18, 34, 56, 289n45

Ames, Fisher, 290n57

Ann (ship), 299n22

Anna (a slave), 123

Anti-Colonization Society, 201

Anti-Federalists: Bill of Rights, 70; language, view of, 68–69, 70; loyal opposition tradition in America, 306n4; probable cause, 49, 299n18; representatives' responsiveness and accountability, 30; searches and seizures, 295n91; size of Congress, 31

Anti-kidnapping laws, 92, 162

Anti-loitering ordinances, 272

Anti-Slave Traffic Associations, 220

Antimajoritarianism, 304n28

Antislavery movement: abolitionism compared to, 205; antislavery literature, 226–228, 330n49; antislavery spirit in North, 204; aristocracy of money, 221–222

Antiunionism, free labor and, 181

Apostles, the, 98

Appeal (Walker), 152, 199

Arrest warrants, 37

198; physical mobility, 178–179; popular sovereignty, 179; Republican Party, 178; Slave Power compared to, 204; social mobility, 178; tenets, 178, 198, 204; virtuous life/society, 179–180, 198
Free Soilers, 143, 157, 181
Freedmen, searches and seizures of, 248–253
Freedmen's Bureau, 248, 250–253, 256
Freedom of conscience, respect and, 262
Freedom of movement, 131–186; anti-kidnapping laws, 92; blacks, 147; Fourth Amendment, 89; free-labor ideals, 92; interference with, 262–263; meaning in the North, 157–186; meaning in the South, 131–156; modern constitutional law, 187; natural rights, 182; personal-liberty laws, 92; privacy, 259; searches and seizures, 2; slaves (*see* Slave locomotion); social mobility, 178; Southern whites, 139–143; Thirteenth Amendment, 93; upward mobility via migration, 140; to white Southerners, 91–92
Freedom of speech: abolitionists, 22, 203–204; blacks, 147; contest between slavers and abolitionists, 22; Fourth Amendment, 89, 257, 302n3; Hoar case, 246; mail delivery, 227–228; the People, 302n3; privacy, 190; racial violence, 207; searches and seizures, 23, 71, 302n3; the South, 226, 228–229; tradition of, 287n23
Fremont, John, 231, 232–233
Frisbie v. Butler (1787), 42
Frisking, 77
Fruits of one's labor: blacks, 185, 221; free-labor ideology, 183–184; labor theory of value, 221; Lincoln, 183–184, 185; slavery, 221, 225
Fugitive from Justice Clause, 160
Fugitive Slave Act (1793): administration of, 162; common law, 168–169; constitutionality of, 164, 166–167; Declaration of Independence, 166; "*Hornblower Decision*," 160; personal-liberty laws, 159; Seventh Amendment, 162; slave locomotion, 125–126
Fugitive Slave Act (1850): Civil War, 130, 232; Compromise of 1850, 142; constitutionality, 170, 171, 176; Douglass on, 129; due process, 128; enforcement, 173, 232; habeas corpus, 128, 315n62; kidnapping of free Northern blacks, 122; Massachusetts, 170; Northern response, 128, 130, 158; passage, 169–170; repeal, 232; slave locomotion, 127–130; Tenth Amendment, 170; Webster (Daniel) and, 173
Fugitive Slave Clause: Chase on, 205; federal government's authority to return slaves, 205; Fourth Amendment, 169; "*Horn-*

blower Decision," 160; Northern responsibilities, 141; slave locomotion, 124–125; slave rendition, 245; Story and, 163–164, 322n21
Fugitive Slave Law (1793). *See* Fugitive Slave Act (1793)
Fugitive Slave Law (1850). *See* Fugitive Slave Act (1850)
Fugitive-slave laws: Lincoln and, 226; the North, 126; slave locomotion, 91, 124–130, 259; Virginia, 126–127
Fugitive slaves: "attorney general of fugitive slaves," 166; Civil War, 173, 231–232; due process, 167; Fifth Amendment, 167; free-labor ideology, 177; portrayal of, 134–135; trial by jury, 161, 162. *See also* Slave rendition
Full Faith and Credit Clause, 160

Gage, Thomas, 34
Garland, Benjamin, 171
Garner, Margaret, 171
Garnett, Henry Highland, 155
Garrison, William Lloyd: abolitionism, 329n40; apoliticism, 205; Compromise of 1850, 142–143; effigy of, 202; on Framers, 201; free expression, 203–204; gradualism, 329n40; "*Hornblower Decision*," 163; imaginative substitution, 199
General searches: American Revolution, 4–5; class prejudice, 37–39; Coke and, 18; colonial era (1607-1775), 4–5; common law, 35; Fourth Amendment, 18; Hale and, 18; individualized justice, 41; insult, 41; political degradation, 5; process by which decisions were made, 32; typical searches, 34–35
General warrants: American Revolution, 56; antebellum version, 12; Bill of Rights, 291n70; Camden and, 292n72; Coke and, 41; colonial era (1607-1775), 42–43; Davies and, 291n70; definition, 17; Delaware, 302n5; Drayton and, 291n68; *Entick v. Carrington*, 287n18; Fourth Amendment, 56; Framers, 56; Hale on, 298n9; House of Commons debates, 22; immunity from trespass suits, 299n15; Madison and, 302n4; Maryland, 295n91; Massachusetts, 302n5; New Hampshire, 302n5; objections to, 36; Parliamentary authorizations, 286n15; Pennsylvania, 294n89, 302n5; political expression, 302n3; Privy Council warrants, 18; seditious libel prosecutions, 21; slave patrols, 12; Sons of Liberty, 295n91; taxation without representation, 23; Virginia, 302n5; virtual representation, 32; Wilkes cases, 22; writs of assistance, 288n32, 292n74

About the Author

Andrew E. Taslitz is Professor of Law at the Howard University School of Law, where he teaches Criminal Law, Criminal Procedure, and Evidence. He is the author of nearly fifty articles in the area of criminal justice, most of which have recently focused on search and seizure issues, and of five books, including *Constitutional Criminal Procedure* (2d ed. 2004) and *Rape and the Culture of the Courtroom* (1999).